The Texas Frontier and the Butterfield Overland Mail, 1858–1861

The Texas Frontier

AND THE

Butterfield Overland Mail

1858–1861

GLEN SAMPLE ELY

University of Oklahoma Press : Norman

This book is published with the generous assistance of the Summerfield G. Roberts Foundation, Dallas, Texas.

LIBRARY OF CONGRESS CATALOGING-IN-PUBLICATION DATA

Ely, Glen Sample.
The Texas frontier and the Butterfield Overland Mail, 1858–1861 / Glen Sample Ely.
    pages cm
Includes bibliographical references and index.
ISBN 978-0-8061-5221-9 (hardcover : alkaline paper)
  1. Frontier and pioneer life—Texas, West. 2. Butterfield Overland Stage Line—History. 3. Roads—Texas, West—History—19th century. 4. Texas, West—History, Local. 5. Texas, West—History—19th century. I. Title.
  F391.E48 2016
  976.4'05—dc23

2015036823

The paper in this book meets the guidelines for permanence and durability of the Committee on Production Guidelines for Book Longevity of the Council on Library Resources, Inc. ∞

1 2 3 4 5 6 7 8 9 10

To Margaret Badenoch Conkling and Roscoe Platt Conkling,
frontier explorers and Butterfield sleuths extraordinaire

Margaret B. Year
and
Roscoe P. Conkling

Extend to you Happy Christmas Greetings.

and
All good wishes for the New Year
December 1929

Margaret and Roscoe's 1929 engagement Christmas card,
photograph taken on the Butterfield Road in what is now
Guadalupe Mountains National Park, Texas. Conkling Papers,
courtesy of Seaver Center for Western History Research, Los
Angeles County Museum of Natural History.

Contents

Preface

The pioneering studies of the Butterfield Overland Mail by Margaret and Roscoe Conkling and Jesse Wallace Williams inspired this history of Texas's antebellum frontier. I started this project in 1989 while filming a historical documentary on Guadalupe Mountains National Park. In 1998, Joe Reid Allen of Comanche, Texas, started participating in many of my research trips across Texas. Allen is a retired school superintendent who has long been active in preserving local history. Previously a member of the Crane County Historical Commission, he currently serves on the Comanche County Historical Commission.[1]

Over the years, Allen has selflessly contributed countless hours to this work. His considerable expertise in the field proved pivotal in locating and interpreting historic sites. Allen possesses an intuitive sense of West Texas's geography. He has an innate feel for the lay of the land and for a trail's direction, even when not visible to the eye. In addition, I am indebted to Allen and his gracious wife, Doniece, for fine lodging and hospitality on numerous occasions.

In 1998, Patrick March Dearen of Midland, Texas, also started participating in these field trips, schedule permitting. I became close friends with Dearen in 1989 after interviewing him for the Guadalupe Mountains documentary. Dearen, a noted West Texas author, gave much of his time to this project, providing invaluable assistance and generously contributing his considerable knowledge of regional history. As might be imagined, I, Allen, and Dearen have shared many memorable experiences across Texas.

Over the past quarter century, I have conducted extensive research in city, county, state, and national archives. This in-depth archival research enabled me to identify the approximate location of many historic sites. Field research using metal detectors confirmed these locations. Sample ground surveys were conducted at each site, and the position of artifacts was recorded on 1:24,000 scale topographic maps. Joe Allen found most of the artifacts pictured in this book.

I conducted this study with the full cooperation of Texas landowners from the Red River to the New Mexico line. On many occasions, landowners and their families participated in the field research. Many of these landowners have since become close friends. I will be forever grateful to them for their trust and hospitality. Because of increasing privacy concerns, in this volume I have deliberately avoided all mention of landowners' names, as well as detailed directions to and archival information concerning the exact location of some historic sites.

The endnotes contain considerable information about sites, settlements, and persons along Texas's vast frontier. Those interested in local history will discover much new and useful information. Equally important, the endnotes also serve to correct numerous inaccuracies published in the historical record over the past 150 years. As a result, some endnotes are lengthy. Despite their length, many readers will find them worth perusing.

I would offer a cautionary note regarding period Texas maps: many of these are inaccurate and should not be referenced. Over the past quarter century, I have carefully studied hundreds of county, state, and national maps. In addition, I have personally visited many of the places that appear on these maps. The maps cited in this book are the most accurate.

In the antebellum period, the modern-day city of El Paso had an alternative name: Franklin. For the sake of clarity, in this volume I use only the name "El Paso." In addition, to avoid repetition, I use the terms "Hispanic," "Mexican American," and where appropriate, "Tejano," interchangeably throughout this study. The same applies to the terms "Native Americans" and "Indians."

This study is a distinct western/Texas history hybrid. My major professors at Texas Christian University, Todd M. Kerstetter and Gregg Cantrell, offered perceptive insights and constructive criticism that greatly improved this work. Kerstetter provided a solid grounding in western, Native American, and environmental history, while Cantrell shared his considerable knowledge of Texas history. I was fortunate to have had the opportunity to work with these gifted scholars. Longtime mentors Harwood Perry Hinton, Jr., and Diana Davids Hinton served as unofficial postgraduate advisors. I am indebted to Jerry Thompson, Rick McCaslin, and Howard R. Lamar, who kindly reviewed the manuscript and provided constructive suggestions.

John Cahoon, director of the Seaver Center for Western History Research at the Natural History Museum of Los Angeles County, California, permitted me several lengthy visits to peruse the Conkling Papers. This collection furnished much of the research material included in this study. I thank Mr. Cahoon for his kindness and patience.

Joan Kilpatrick, Doug Howard, Joni Scoggins, Virginia Allen, Bobby Santiesteban, Susan Dorsey, and the staff of the Texas General Land Office Archives always extended a warm welcome. Kit Goodwin, Brenda McClurkin, Cathy Spitzenberger, and Ben Huseman at the University of Texas at Arlington's Special Collections Library were consistently gracious and generous. Suzanne Campbell and Shannon Sturm at Angelo State University's West Texas Collection have been exceedingly kind and helpful to me throughout the years. Mary Williams, Fort Davis National Historic Site's gifted historian and walking encyclopedia of western frontier history, contributed immeasurably to this project.

Additional thanks are due to B. Byron Price, Charles E. Rankin, J. Kent Calder, and Stephanie Attia Evans at the University of Oklahoma Press; J. P. "Pat" McDaniel and Jim Bradshaw at the Nita Haley Memorial Library in Midland, Texas; Claudia Rivers and Laura Hollingsed at UTEP Special Collections Library; Pat Worthington at the El Paso County Historical Society Archives; Garland Richards, Lana Richards, and Ann Pate at the Fort Chadbourne Foundation; John Anderson and Donaly Brice at the Texas State Library and Archives Commission; Gary Zaboly for his excellent maps; all of the county clerks along the Butterfield route in Texas; Alice Specht and Ellen Simmons at Hardin-Simmons University Library; Dave Kuhne and Cynthia Shearer at the TCU Writing Center; Kay Edmonson and Jill Kendle at TCU Library's Interlibrary Loan Department; Beth Callahan at TCU Library's Government Documents Department; Barb Angus at the El Paso Museum of History; Randolph "Mike" Campbell, Ryan Schumacher, and reviewers at the *Southwestern Historical Quarterly;* Tai Kreidler, Janet Neugebauer, Monte Monroe, Randy Vance, and Lynn Whitfield at the Southwest Collection, Special Collections Library, Texas Tech University; Lambshead Ranch, Texas Scottish Rite Hospital, Tarrant Regional Water District, Fort Concho National Historic Landmark, Fort Davis National Historic Site, and Guadalupe Mountains National Park; book designer David Timmons; copyeditor Sally Bennett Boyington; Mary Belle Jones, Mitchell Davenport, Cecil McMorris, John Crain, Steve Christian, Donna Smith, Bob Bluthardt, William Preston Krebs, Patricia Anne Newman, Richard Easter, Gary Williams, Margaret Lindley, Bernie Sargent, Walter Shepard, Robert Wooster, Earl Baker, Thomas "Ty" Smith, Win Graham, Elizabeth Heath, Bethel Eiland, Peck Edwards, Mildred Nored, Travis Roberts, Sr., Stan and Pat Turner, Jerry Yarbrough, Hal Joyce, Mr. and Mrs. Hugh Stone, Tom and Val Beard, Bobby and Linda McKnight, T. Lindsay Baker, Leslie Bergloff, Magoffin Home State Historic Site, Texas Historical Commission, Chris Lacy, Annie Riggs Memorial Museum, Historic Fort Stockton, Fort Stockton Historical Society, Betty Hargus, Bill Hargus, Martha King, Lee Alford, Ike Roberts, Sue Roberts, James Irby, Bill Phillips, Cumbie Ivey, Travis Roberts, Jr., Harvey and Wallie Hicks, Bobby and Pat Jones, Heraclio, Dora, and George Parada, Joe Allen Neill, Farris Neill,

Rusty Culp, James Weatherby, Jack Graham, Hugh and Patsy King, Jack Holden, Ann White, Stewart Caffey, Jim and Sally Bucherie, Rosalie Gregg, Jim Kollman, Richard Koehn, Jim Tinkler, Paul Patterson, Nona Kiser, Lolo Lopez, Jessie Whitlow, Eugene Vinson, Bobby Mathiews, Len Jackson, Claud Elsom, Lee Harris, Mart Adams, Tom and Betty Alex, the Blackstock Family, Janice Wobbenhorst, Julia Ellison Jenkins, Alan Sparks, Steve King, Roger Turner, Greg Brown, the Cowden Family, Dan Meeks, Richard Munson, Johnny Lowrance, Larry Henderson, Conoly Brooks, Wayne McCabe, Ronnie and Amanda Krejci, Jim Hurst, Burr Agnew, Donna Hunt, Caroll Martin, J. R. and Jay Roberts, Davis Holdman, Dan Penner, Dennis Webb, John Williams, Henry and Ted Paup, Davey Griggs, Mike and Sandy Orton, Skeet Lee Jones, Robert Bachman, Martha Doty Freeman, Jennifer Sproul Whitesell, Carleton White, June and D. D. Barker, Cal Sugg, Mark Hursh, Jim Ed Miller, Doug Fernandes, Marie Turner, the Charles Armstrong family, Katherine and Suzanne Sullivan, Norman Stovall, Jock March, Len Bennett, Mr. and Mrs. Dan Spencer, Harlan Hopper, Mark Owen Rosacker, Brad Wells, John Moses, Neil Mangum, John Berry, Jr., Brent Wauer, Barry Scott, John Burns, Quendrid and Ralph Veatch, Clinton Newbold Ely, Joseph Scanlon Sample, Helen Scanlon Sample, John Glen Sample, and the Reverend Melinda Ann Veatch.

I give special thanks to Judge David D. Jackson and the officers of the Summerfield G. Roberts Foundation for their belief in and support of this project. A publishing subvention from the Summerfield G. Roberts Foundation made possible this work's important visual record of Texas's antebellum frontier, over one hundred pages of images and illustrations (a considerable number of them in color, and many published here for the first time). Without this generous funding, the reader would not have been able to see photographs of the historic sites referenced in the text, most of which are on private property.

Finally, the field trips across Texas and the wonderful people and history encountered along the way, from the Red River to the Rio Grande, remain the highlights of a lifetime. I am very grateful to have had this extraordinary opportunity.

The Texas Frontier and the Butterfield Overland Mail, 1858–1861

Chapter 1

The Texas Frontier and the
Butterfield Overland Mail

The Forty-Niners, Oscar E. Berninghaus. Oil on canvas, before 1942. Courtesy of Sid Richardson Museum, Fort Worth, Texas.

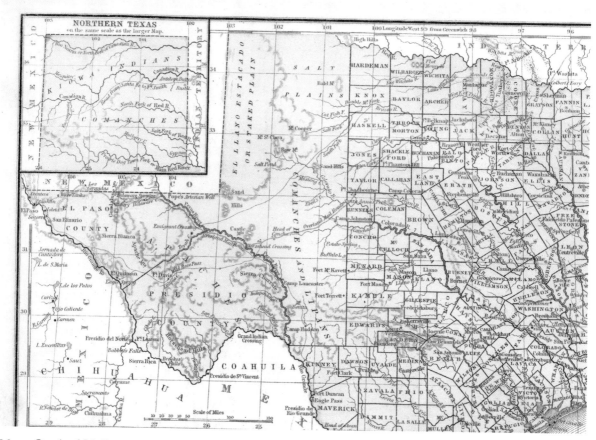

Map 1. Overland Mail route, 1858–59. Detail from *S. A. Mitchell's 1859 No. 12 Map of the State of Texas*, courtesy of Virginia Garrett Cartographic History Library, Special Collections Library, University of Texas at Arlington. The map incorrectly shows the mail road on the west side of the Pecos River. It ran along the east side.

This is the story of the antebellum Texas frontier, from the Red River to El Paso. It is also the tale of the people who lived and worked along that frontier and the communities in which they lived. Because Texas's western frontier was so vast and varied, a convenient way to access it was to travel across it. The Butterfield Overland Mail, which passed through the Lone Star State on its way from St. Louis to San Francisco, provided the perfect vehicle in which to take such a journey. From 1858 to 1861, this transcontinental mail line, 2,795 miles in length, linked America's East and West. A trip aboard an overland stagecoach afforded an excellent opportunity to observe the frontier firsthand.[1]

Many of the people living and working on the Texas frontier during this period had connections to the mail line. Some worked as agents, overseers, station managers, stage drivers, conductors, clerks, cooks, and livestock handlers for the company. Others provided cattle, horses, mules, merchandise, corn, flour, and forage to mail stations. Indeed, one cannot talk about Texas's antebellum frontier without also discussing Butterfield and its significant economic imprint upon the region; the two are inextricably intertwined.

Far more than some faded, romantic relic of the Old West, the Butterfield Overland Mail provides the ideal window through which to view the land and those who inhabited it. Traveling along the antebellum frontier via the Butterfield itinerary affords one a personal opportunity to learn about the regional and national strands that shaped the western part of the state and to see how these threads played out and interacted across this vast expanse. During the Texas portion of their journey (740 miles), overland travelers encountered a multitude of people, places, and perspectives.[2]

Watching the Texas countryside roll by through their stagecoach windows, passengers frequently commented on the state's diverse geography, from the Upper or Western Cross Timbers' post oak forests near Gainesville to El Paso's parched Chihuahuan Desert. The Lone Star State features a major environmental transition zone where the humid American South gradually yields to the arid West. At Gainesville near the Red River, the annual rainfall is forty-two inches a year, whereas El Paso receives only ten inches. This metamorphosis from South to West is discernable from Gainesville, near the ninety-seventh meridian, west to Fort Chadbourne, Texas, at the one-hundredth meridian. Along this 220-mile stretch, the natural surroundings are both southern and western. From Fort Chadbourne to El Paso, however, the topography is more typical of the American West.[3]

During the nineteenth century, the Texas frontier was also a sectional transition zone, where different populations and lifeways intersected and sometimes clashed. For example, the Western Cross Timbers served as a dividing line between various Native American tribes. On the eastern side of these woods lived the Caddos and the Wichitas. On the western side, tribes more typical of the Great Plains and American West held sway, namely, the Apaches, the Comanches, and the Kiowas. In the mid-nineteenth century, Indian lifeways in West Texas centered on the horse culture, buffalo hunting, raiding, and trading.[4]

By the time Butterfield started its mail service in 1858, Native Americans living in this transition zone could no longer effectively challenge European American expansion onto their lands. West of the one-hundredth meridian, however, the Comanches and Apaches enjoyed relative parity with the U.S. Army. The diminutive garrisons the U.S. Army stationed at federal outposts in western Texas were never an intimidating deterrent for raiding warriors. In western Texas, neither the Indians nor the army could dominate the other. Out on this contested frontier, a stalemate existed. Military historian Robert Wooster says that the antebellum U.S. Army "never possessed the men, horses, or equipment it believed necessary to defeat the Indians." Compounding the problem was the federal government, which "failed to establish a clear, effective Indian policy, an oversight that the army's lack of strategic planning only exacerbated." The State of Texas never factored into this equation, as it lacked the funds to field an effective military force. Texas Rangers were largely absent beyond Fort Chadbourne.[5]

At any time, the Comanches and Apaches could have obliterated Butterfield operations west of the one-hundredth meridian, but they chose not to. While the stage stops challenged Indian access to important natural resources in the region, they also offered attractive assets. The stations provided a steady supply of livestock for warriors seeking to enhance their personal wealth. Additionally, attacks on stage stops gave the raiders an opportunity to prove their bravery in battle, thus enhancing their status within the tribe. It remained in the Comanches' and Apaches' best interests to periodically raid the stations' corrals, let the mail company restock them, and then empty them again. Overland stage stops, local settlements, and military outposts all offered considerable inducements for Native Americans. Following their depredations, Indians exchanged stolen livestock for guns, ammunition, and other trade goods with comancheros from New Mexico and with merchants on the Arkansas River.

In 1838, Republic of Texas Indian commissioner George W. Bonnell described the Comanches as "a nation of robbers." Bonnell believed that any agreements with the tribe were worthless, recalling the phrase "As faithless as a Camanche [*sic*] treaty." One could say much the same regarding Texans. The Comanches held no illusions as to Anglo intentions in West Texas. Incessant encroachment onto tribal lands left little doubt that Texas was not honoring its agreements either.[6]

W. W. Newcomb points out that ultimately neither the Texans nor the Comanches put much stock in the treaties they signed: "They knew whatever promises they made would likely be broken." Compounding the situation were the terms of Texas's annexation to the United States. When Texas became a state in December 1845, it retained title to all its lands. After annexation, the Lone Star State repudiated Native American rights, despite federal insistence to the contrary. As David La Vere notes, "This refusal conflicted with United States policy which recognized Indian land claims by right of occupancy and believed these could only be extinguished by treaties."[7]

During conversations with several Texas tribes in 1848, federal Indian agent Robert Neighbors reported that "great doubt exists in the minds of all principal Indian chiefs . . . [and] they are suspicious of the promises made." The Indians' fears proved well-founded, for Texas did not intend to recognize Native American claims to tribal lands. Commissioner Bonnell insisted that the state should not grant Native Americans rights to the lands they lived on. Instead, the tribes should instead be legally classed as "tenants at will."[8]

Comanches understood the nature of this contested frontier and were not deceived by European American speeches, treaties, and gifts. Penateka Comanche chief Buffalo Hump remarked, "For a long time a great many people have been passing through my country; they kill all the game and burn the country, and trouble me very much." Buffalo Hump did not believe what white men promised, "[b]ecause," as he said, "they wish to settle in this country. I object to any more settlements. I want this country to hunt in." Another Penateka Comanche chief, Ketumse, complained, "Over this vast country, where for centuries our ancestor roamed in undisputed possession, free and happy, what have we left?" Ketumse noted that the tribe relied on native game to survive, most of which the settlers killed or ran off. Whites were forcing the Indians "into the most barren and sterile portions" and leaving them "to starve."[9]

Native Americans faced a difficult decision regarding encroachment on their traditional lands. The Five Civilized Tribes attempted to peacefully integrate into nineteenth-century American society by adopting the customs and attire of whites. In their efforts to emulate Southern planters, some even acquired slaves. Their strategy ultimately failed in the 1830s when President Andrew Jackson forcibly removed them from their Southern lands and relocated them to Indian Territory. Fighting back feelings of betrayal, Chickasaws and Cherokees persisted in their efforts to assimilate in their new homes, only to experience the sting of racism and rejection once again.[10]

Other tribes accommodated European American westward expansion by agreeing to live on reservations. In 1854, the State of Texas allocated lands for two federal reservations in Young and Throckmorton Counties. In 1855, Ketumse settled on the Comanche Clear Fork reservation in Throckmorton County and urged his followers to follow the white man's path. The lawless and unsettled condition of Texas's antebellum frontier, however, was not the best-suited laboratory in which to conduct a reservation experiment or to change Anglo attitudes toward Native Americans.

Raids by nonreservation Comanches and white outlaws kept the region in a state of constant agitation and residents on edge. While some settlers accepted the Native Americans, others worked to sabotage the reservations. One lawless group, consisting of opportunistic demagogues, vigilantes, and horse thieves, agitated area settlements by fanning the flames of fear and hatred. This mob continually terrorized the reservation Indians until they finally abandoned the Clear Fork in the summer of 1859 and moved to a new home north of the Red River. Richard Maxwell Brown says that in frontier regions like Texas, "law and order was often a tenuous thing . . . [and] law enforcement was frequently inadequate." Many settlements lacked secure jails. The application of justice in the courts was "uneven," and "outlaw gangs took full advantage of the social disorganization."[11]

The federal government and the State of Texas, with their muddled and often contradictory policies, never provided the security, stability, and resources necessary for these Indian reservations to take root and flourish. The Penateka chiefs Ketumse and Buffalo Hump chose different strategies to deal with the Anglos' westward expansion. In contrast to Ketumse's assimilation efforts, Buffalo Hump refused to live on a reservation and continued to hunt and raid. Ultimately, neither strategy—accommodation and resistance—succeeded. By 1875, the U.S. Army had forcibly relocated the remaining Comanches from Texas to Indian Territory. For nineteenth-century European Americans, only one outcome was possible: Native Americans must yield to the inevitable; Manifest Destiny was the supreme law of the land.

One recent study says that following the removal of the Penatekas from their Clear Fork reservation in 1859, the "Comanches had all but vanished from Texas." Another book states that after 1859, "the only Indians remaining in Texas were the few hundred Alabama and Coushatta Indians" who lived in East Texas. A third publication claims, "By 1860 Texas found itself virtually denuded of Indian peoples." Such blanket statements invariably prove hard to substantiate. Period reports from the U.S. Army's Departments of New Mexico and Texas, from the U.S. Bureau of Indian Affairs, and from newspapers show otherwise. During the antebellum period, various bands of Comanches maintained a presence in West

Texas. These groups lived in the Llano Estacado and in camps along the Canadian River and its tributaries in the Texas Panhandle. Other Comanches roamed traditional tribal ranges west of the one-hundredth meridian throughout the year, raiding Butterfield stations and settlements along the frontier. Also during this time, Mescalero Apaches were living in the Trans-Pecos's Guadalupe, Davis, Chisos, Quitman, Sierra Diablo, and Eagle Mountain ranges. These three studies highlight a problem that occurs when writers take something that may be true for a localized area and extrapolate it as being accurate for an entire region.[12]

In addition to the Western Cross Timbers, another informal demarcation line between Native American tribes in Texas was the Pecos River, in this case, between Comanches and Apaches. The Pecos River boundary was fluid, however, and the two tribes occasionally ranged on both sides of the river. Although Comanches sometimes traveled through the Trans-Pecos to Mexico, typically much of the region west of the Pecos was Mescalero Apache territory. Some Lipan Apaches also ranged west of the Pecos; however, much of their traditional lands were in central and South Texas.[13]

The Texas frontier also served as a sectional transition zone for Anglo-American identity, a place where southern ideology clashed with western perspectives. In East Texas, the majority of residents were from the Upper and Lower South. As one traveled west across the state, this percentage plummeted. Beyond the one-hundredth meridian, most people were of Mexican ancestry. The majority of these Hispanics were not concerned with southern culture, and none of them owned slaves.

Despite the influx of Anglos to the region, Mexican Americans succeeded in keeping their values and identity intact. Before the Civil War, this part of Texas was more culturally akin to the American West than to the South. Southerners averaged only 3 percent of the population. In neighboring New Mexico Territory (which included Arizona), the number was less than 1 percent. Regarding slavery, in western Texas the peculiar institution was almost nonexistent. West of the one-hundredth meridian, less than 1 percent of all residents were African American. Next door, in New Mexico Territory, these percentages were even lower.[14]

The cultural transition zone in Texas between South and West possessed a mixed identity. In 1861, some counties in the region wanted to secede from the Union, while others did not, preferring to keep the status quo. Many of those opposed to secession depended on the federal government and its related agencies. Prior to the Civil War, Washington played a far greater role in shaping West Texas than did the state legislature. During this period, the U.S. Army and the U.S. Postmaster General quickly became West Texas's major benefactors. Soldiers and civilians built roads, forts, and sub-posts and guarded passenger, mail, and freight traffic. Federal payrolls and contracts provided an enormous boost to the local economy. Many of the region's earliest settlements owe their existence and survival to this federal presence.

LeRoy Hafen says, "The postal service became an important political agency binding the western pioneer to his government and his home in the East." The federal government, through its mail service and military, was a "pioneering agency, leading the emigration, encouraging settlement, and making safe the routes of travel." Echoing Hafen, Richard White says that the American West, which includes West Texas, "more than any other section of the United States, is a creation not so much of the individual or local efforts, but of federal efforts"; indeed, White contends, "the federal government shaped the West."[15]

Studies by William Ransom Hogan, Sam Haynes, Thomas "Ty" Smith, and Robert Wooster show that both the Republic of Texas and the Lone Star State lacked sufficient resources to make internal improvements and protect its citizens. For example, without the U.S. Army to deter them, raiding Comanches, Kiowas, and Apaches depopulated much of Texas's western frontier during the Civil War. Throughout this period, Texas Ranger regiments proved uneven and ineffective. Ultimately, it was the federal government and not Texas that facilitated Anglo, Hispanic, and African American settlement in the region. Economically and militarily, the State of Texas was largely absent west of the one-hundredth meridian.[16]

The U.S. Army, in conjunction with the postmaster general's overland mail service, spurred economic development of the region and its infrastructure. Some of the oldest European American buildings in western Texas are overland mail stations and frontier forts. In 1846, the value of all property in Texas was $34 million. In the second half of the nineteenth century, the U.S. Army spent twice that figure, or more than $70 million, in the Lone Star State, much of it in West Texas. Robert Wooster aptly describes the area as "a child of federal subsidy."[17]

Frontier settlers worried that if Texas seceded, the U.S. Army and the Butterfield Overland Mail would leave. Residents would lose lucrative government contracts and markets for their agricultural products. Payrolls would disappear, severely impacting local stores, hotels, and saloons. In addition, citizens were anxious about losing military protection against depredating Indians. It is no surprise, then, that Forts Davis, Stockton, Duncan, Inge, Mason, and Martin Scott were all located within counties voting against secession.

In western Texas, residents were more isolated and removed from the South and its slave economy. The federal government and its agencies exerted far more influence over the region than did the South. It is important to note that as southern ideology and the cotton agriculture that accompanied it migrated westward, it encountered an increasingly resistant cultural and environmental barrier. In arid West Texas, widespread cotton farming held little promise. El Paso County received only ten inches of rain annually.

During the 1850s, the U.S. government tried to surmount the region's natural limitations with a four-year $100,000 effort to "reclaim" West Texas for agricultural purposes. Attempts by U.S. secretary of war Jefferson Davis and his subordinate, Captain John Pope, to drill artesian wells near the Pecos River ultimately proved an expensive boondoggle that many ridiculed as "Pope's Folly." Pope's artesian well experiment in the Pecos Valley marked the first of several attempts by the federal government to stimulate settlement and the development of irrigation agriculture in the area.

Pope and his fellow boosters believed that American ingenuity and scientific expertise could overcome a myriad of challenges, including environmental limits imposed by Mother Nature. Scientifically based irrigated agriculture would make the western desert bloom like a rose, creating a manmade Garden of Eden. Large-scale agriculture beyond the one-hundredth meridian, however, would remain an elusive mirage until after World War I with the construction of federal water projects and advancements in agricultural techniques, including affordable irrigation technology.[18]

Over the past 150 years, Pope's Folly and subsequent reclamation endeavors promoting the same bankrupt ideology have caused immeasurable damage to West Texas. The environmental toll that irrigated agriculture has exacted from the region has been steep. Because of excessive pumping of underground aquifers, many of the area's historic springs are now dry.

This issue highlights the incompatible worldviews among those living in western Texas, conflicting concepts regarding property, ownership, and use of the region's natural resources. Contrasting Anglos and Native Americans, C. L. Sonnichsen says, "The gulf between the two races was widened and deepened because they were so completely opposite in their system of values." Many whites were more interested in individual enrichment rather than the needs or greater good of the community. Anglo traditions regarding land ownership, title, and private property were foreign to Comanches and Apaches. "The Comanches had no concept of land value," note Ernest Wallace and E. Adamson Hoebel. "As herding hunters, land was a matter of unconcern for them. . . . [O]ne may speak of their country as being merely communally occupied."[19]

William Cronon reinforces this point, arguing that Native Americans conceived of their acreage as a "collective sovereignty," while whites regarded land in terms of "individual ownership." Because of their nomadic lifestyle, Indians did not live in a fixed place. Instead, they seasonally ranged over their territories throughout the year. To whites, however, the land appeared empty. Seasonal ranging did not equate to homesteading acreage and making improvements to it. If the Indians were not living on a parcel, Anglos considered it vacant and theirs for the taking.[20]

Richard White observes, "The American view of nature . . . revolved chiefly . . . around judgments of its economic usefulness." In his research, Ted Steinberg discusses America's "transformation of nature—land, water, pine trees . . . into a commodity (a thing that can be traded for profit)." Steinberg argues that Americans' historical propensity of "[p]utting a price on the natural world and drawing it into the web of commerce led to sweeping changes in ecosystems throughout the nation." Viewing Texas's antebellum frontier through this lens, one can already see the impact of Anglo commodification of natural resources playing out along the Butterfield route.[21]

While Anglo environmental worldviews created conflict with Native Americans, they also sparked tensions with Mexican Americans in West Texas. Many Hispanics living in the nineteenth-century American West held concepts regarding land and natural resources that fell somewhere between those of whites and those of Native Americans. Most Tejanos living west of the one-hundredth meridian, in towns such as San Elizario, Socorro, and Ysleta, shared regional natural resources. Water, salt, and grass belonged not to one individual but to the greater community. The Tejano lifestyle in the Trans-Pecos resembled that of communal villages in northern New Mexico. Sarah Deutsch's study of New Mexico villages found that in most cases, "each settler owned a small agricultural lot, a house, and the land immediately surrounding his house. The rest of the [land] grant, the pasturage and water, was held and managed communally."[22]

Along the Rio Grande in El Paso County, Texas, Mexican Americans living on the San Elizario, Socorro, and Ysleta Land Grants shared their resources, including their acreage and their labor in a cooperative effort, creating a "mutual dependency." Residents relied on their local acequia system for their drinking water and to irrigate crops. Tejanos grazed their cattle together on the communal grants. Throughout the year, the men would form wagon trains and head out on well-worn trails to harvest salt at the Guadalupe Mountains Salt Lakes or Juan Cordona Lake on the Pecos River. Richard White notes that "unlike Anglo Americans, many Hispanics saw these resources as the possessions of the communities as well as [of] individuals." Anglo worldviews regarding land and natural resources, therefore, "posed a dual threat, [both] economic and cultural," to Hispanics and Native Americans alike in the American West.[23]

Whites on the western frontier saw these natural resources as their private path to prosperity. Early on, they moved swiftly to lock up local assets such as water, grass, timber, and minerals. Anglos would share natural resources with others, but for a price. In the case of area salt deposits, whites filed land claims on various salt lakes, sparking confrontations with Hispanics who had used these communal deposits for generations. In 1854, James Wiley Magoffin, one of the richest residents of El Paso County, Texas, attempted to seize control of the San Andres Salt Lake in neighboring New Mexico. After an armed confrontation, Magoffin backed down. In 1877, the issue resurfaced when another Anglo salt ring tried to charge Tejanos for harvesting the Guadalupe Mountains Salt Lakes, sparking the larger and more violent Salt War in San Elizario, Texas.[24]

These, then, were the primary concerns of the day that Butterfield passengers encountered as they rode along the Texas frontier. From clashing worldviews on regional resources to divisive sectional and national issues to diverse ecosystems, races, and cultures, the nature of Texas's antebellum frontier was complex and multilayered. Riding an overland stagecoach with travelers of the period affords the reader a front-seat window from which to experience these issues firsthand, from the banks of the Red River to El Paso.

Before we commence our journey across the Lone Star State, however, some history of this transcontinental mail line is in order. On September 16, 1857, Postmaster General Aaron Brown signed an agreement with John Butterfield of Utica, New York, and his associates of the Overland Mail Company, to provide mail service from St. Louis and Memphis to San Francisco. The six-year contract, at $600,000 per year, stipulated that the service be semiweekly (twice a week) in four-horse coaches or spring wagons and that each trip be made within twenty-five days. Muriel Wright points out that Congress "left the responsibility and the actual selection of the route to . . . President Buchanan's administration." According to the *San Francisco Bulletin,* John Butterfield was "an old friend and chum of President Buchanan." Buchanan's postmaster general was Aaron Brown, an ardent southerner from Tennessee. Brown had received numerous bids for the mail contract but rejected them all. Instead, he selected his own route, one of a southern orientation, running through Missouri, Arkansas, Oklahoma, Texas, New Mexico, Arizona, and California.[25]

Brown argued that the optimal year-round climate of the southern route would ensure timely and reliable overland service. While aspects of his argument had merit, many in Congress correctly perceived that regional bias had strongly influenced his decision. Northern lawmakers were rightly concerned that a southern overland mail route would set a precedent for the nation's first transcontinental railroad and that the tracks of the railroad would follow the ruts of the overland mail line. Postmaster General Brown certainly hoped this would be the case, describing his selection "as the pioneer route for the first great railroad that may be constructed to the Pacific." Northerners were not about to let this happen. A California newspaper called the postmaster general's decision a "foul wrong" and "an outrage," while a Chicago paper blasted it as "one of the greatest swindles perpetrated upon the country by the slave-holders." Ultimately, Congress deadlocked on the route of the Pacific railroad. As Ray Billington and Martin Ridge note, "So long as sectionalism plagued the nation, no road could be built."[26]

Postmaster General Brown awarded Butterfield and his associates the overland contract for several reasons. Besides his friendship with President Buchanan, John Butterfield had many years of experience operating mail and express services. As Muriel Wright points out, "The greatest stager of the time, if not for all time, was John Butterfield. . . . [H]is ability and character and that of his associates were unquestioned at Washington." One of Butterfield's associates in the venture was William G. Fargo of Wells, Fargo and Company, founded in 1852. Butterfield and Fargo, along with Henry Wells, were the three principal founders of American Express Company in 1850. W. Turrentine Jackson says that both Wells and Fargo stood to make a considerable sum from their ancillary express and financial operations in the West that connected to the great transcontinental mail line. "It seems quite natural that Wells, Fargo & Co., the only one of the four express companies operating in the trans-Missouri West, would have the greatest continuing concern for the success of the Overland Mail Company."[27]

The Overland Mail Company established its offices at 82 Broadway in New York City. Financially, the business was a joint stock company, with $2 million in capital, consisting of 20,000 shares of $100 each. As of August 1858, the company had sold almost 20 percent of these shares. Stockholders were liable for all debts incurred. Company officers included John Butterfield as president, Alexander Holland as treasurer, and John Livingston as secretary. Confidential credit reports for 1860 noted that the firm was "in prosperous condition and making money fast" and that the "owners are all . . . wealthy."[28]

The postmaster general's establishment of a transcontinental mail service between St. Louis and San Francisco, along with U.S. Army outposts in the region, offered the real prospect of making money from the federal government and related agencies on the Texas frontier. Many among the first wave of settlers moving westward after 1848 sensed a golden opportunity to capitalize on Washington's increased presence in the region. Some of these frontier entrepreneurs got rich, some went broke, and others lost their lives.

Overland mail stations and military forts required regular supplies and services. Butterfield stage stops and frontier outposts needed corn and hay for livestock, as well as beef and produce for soldiers and employees. They depended on merchants to serve their local communities and freighters to haul supplies. They also needed civilian personnel to perform specific services. While there are few surviving corporate records documenting Overland Mail Company operations in Texas, military quartermaster records and interviews with former employees reveal much detail about Butterfield's economic impact on the Lone Star frontier. In many cases, the mail company hired the same forage, livestock, and freighting contractors that supplied military outposts in West Texas.[29]

Some frontier residents, in an effort to maximize their income, worked several jobs at once. Butterfield stage driver Henry Skillman also supplied beef to Fort Bliss in El Paso County. George Lyles, manager of Smith's Ranch Butterfield Station, held the hay contracts for Fort Bliss and Fort Quitman (also in El Paso County). When not helping manage Butterfield's Clear Fork Station in Throckmorton County, J. G. Irwin worked as a beef contractor for nearby Camp Cooper. Adam Rankin Johnson managed a string of Overland Mail Company stations from the Middle Concho to the Pecos while working simultaneously as a Texas Ranger, state surveyor, and water freighter.[30]

During the antebellum period, Texas's primitive transportation network hampered its economic development. The state boasted few well-developed thoroughfares that permitted the timely movement of goods to market. Throughout the 1850s, the U.S. Army and Butterfield built and maintained much of West Texas's road system, which was used by countless soldiers, emigrants, freighters, and stagecoaches. The Overland Mail Road was the nineteenth-century equivalent of the modern interstate highway system, stimulating greater passenger traffic, commercial freighting, and economic development on the western frontier. Regional use of these antebellum transportation networks continued long after the Civil War into the twentieth century, demonstrating the enduring historical significance of Butterfield and the army in Texas.[31]

Along various sections of the Lone Star frontier, the U.S. Army was almost invisible, leaving isolated Overland Mail employees to defend their stage stops against raiding Comanches and Apaches. As a defensive deterrent, Butterfield constructed stout rock stations that resembled minifortresses. The mail company staffed these stations with its own private army, typically four to five persons per station, each armed with a Sharps rifle and a Colt Navy revolver.[32]

The stagecoaches used by the Overland Mail Company in West Texas were not the heavy wooden Concord coaches seen in such popular Western movies as *Stagecoach*. Along the arid frontier, it was too taxing on livestock to pull a cumbersome Concord through deep sand roads in dry weather or through boggy stretches after heavy rains and flooding. In Texas, the typical passenger vehicle was the lighter, canvas-topped Celerity wagon, also known as a mud wagon. On average, Celerity wagons cost $700 each.[33]

Much of the time, four-mule teams were hitched to Butterfield's mud wagons, although horses were used on some sections of the route. The livestock varied in cost: the lead mules at the front of the team ran $35 to $40 each, whereas higher-grade mules (known as "wheelers") costing $70 to $80 each were used at the back of the team, closer to the coach. The Overland Mail Company kept ten to twenty mules on hand at each station. Butterfield's larger regional depots kept fifty to sixty animals in reserve for needed adjustments along the line.[34]

Travel on a Celerity wagon during this time was far from luxurious. Customers grumbled about chronic overcrowding of the coaches, citing instances when the mail company tried to cram six or seven people into a space designed to accommodate only four. One traveler lamented, "Ordinary sized men have not the slightest chance of being at ease on their seats." Other passengers groused about the coaches' interminably slow rate of travel across Texas, typically three to five miles per hour. The special overland correspondent for the *San Francisco Daily Evening Bulletin* denounced the company's practice of using "miserable little worn-out mules" on the Texas portion of the route.[35]

The Overland Mail Company built most of its stage stops during the summer of 1858. Within a year, it had erected more than fifty in Texas alone. Typically, Butterfield placed the stations near water sources but far enough away to allow Native Americans access. Workers constructed the stage stops out of wood, adobe, rock, or a combination thereof. Building a station took about fifteen days with a three-man crew, who earned 75 cents to $1 a day. The more elaborate rock structures cost about $1,500 in labor and materials, while adobe and lumber buildings ran about $150 to $200 each. Freighters hauled finished wood for the doors, roofs, window frames, and floors to West Texas from San Antonio. Each stage stop usually had two to three rooms, measuring fifteen by fifteen feet, with an attached corral. Corrals were seven to eight feet high, built of adobe and/or wood, although some featured stacked rock walls.[36]

Some of the larger stations had floor plans that were more elaborate and spacious. Stage conductor Parker Burnham recalled several that were sixteen by thirty feet on one side and sixteen by thirty feet on the other side, with a gateway between leading to the station entrance. At the back was a sixteen-foot-square courtyard. In these larger buildings, some of the rooms might have finished wood flooring. Leon Holes Station, situated in Pecos County nine miles west of Fort Stockton, featured five rooms, including a dining room, a kitchen, two bedrooms, and a storeroom. The storeroom contained grain, commissary supplies, tools, and ammunition. Many of the stage stops also included portholes in the walls for employees to shoot at attacking Indians. As El Paso County district judge Josiah Crosby said, none of the structures were "Fifth Avenue hotels. They were rude buildings, improvised . . . from the materials at hand." Crosby never recalled seeing shingled roofs on the buildings or glass in their windows.[37]

Employees constructed furniture for the station on-site. Workers made tables out of unfinished pine boards, and chairs, more often benches, from split logs. Beds were rough-hewn and simple in design. Stocking the overland mail stations created a sizeable demand for frontier goods, which was welcome news for regional merchants. The following list illustrates the average cost for station supplies in West Texas: flour was $8 a barrel, bacon 25–30 cents a pound, coffee 40 cents a pound, tea 50–60 cents a pound, sugar 20–25 cents a pound, salt 30–35 cents a pound, and dried fruits 25–30 cents a pound. Station employees seldom ate canned meats. Butterfield preferred to keep fresh beeves and hogs at its stage stops.[38]

The Overland Mail Company kept a large supply of corn and hay on hand for the livestock, as the local terrain was usually too sparse to support a station's requirements year-round. Local grasses were most prevalent from spring to early fall, during the so-called rainy season. Leaving the stage stop to go out and cut hay was often a deadly task. Raiding Comanches and Apaches targeted employees out on forage detail. Parker Burnham recalled, "At times you couldn't put value on hay, for it was impossible to get a man to go out and cut it. . . . [T]hey wouldn't cut it for $50 an hour." Burnham remembered "three instances" of men being "killed by the Indians while cutting hay." As a result, the mail companies increasingly resorted to hiring contractors to freight in the necessary forage by wagon train. To avoid any possible shortfalls, the mail contractors laid in an eight- to nine-month supply, ten to twelve tons of hay at $20 per ton, and 300 to 400 bushels of corn, at $3 per bushel.[39]

Seeking federal contracts and employment with the Overland Mail Company, some people left their Hill Country homes in Burnet, Mason, Fredericksburg, and San Saba and moved to West Texas. Some of these were German Texans. One prominent German businessman operating on this section of the frontier was Louis Martin, who lived in Mason County at Hedwig's Hill on the Llano River. During 1857 and 1858, Martin secured federal hay and beef contracts for several army outposts, including Fort Chadbourne on the Butterfield Road.[40]

Perhaps no person in West Texas understood the dynamics of the federal frontier economy better than forty-one-year-old J. D. Holliday, a native of Kentucky. Holliday owned Comanche Springs in Pecos County. The springs, located at Fort Stockton, were among the most important water sources in West Texas. This astute entrepreneur also worked as the station manager for the Overland Mail Company and division manager for George Giddings's San Antonio–San Diego Mail Line, a smaller operation competing with Butterfield. In 1859, the U.S. Army established Fort Stockton on Holliday's land near the stage stop. Shortly thereafter, Holliday became the post's sutler, commodities contractor, and postmaster. Through his shrewd real estate deals and lucrative government contracts, the Kentuckian repeatedly demonstrated a keen acumen in maximizing business opportunities in this remote region.[41]

Finally, I offer one last consideration before we start our Butterfield journey across the Lone Star frontier. It is instructive to look at how Texas communities along the old overland road today are utilizing their nineteenth-century history. Some cities are promoting their heritage in an effort to attract more visitors while others are ignoring it. Commemorating history is sometimes like opening Pandora's box. There is still much in the past that remains unknown. The Texas frontier story contains many skeletons, some previously exhumed and others that still lie buried.

With the background of the antebellum frontier and the Overland Mail Company now in place, we start our tour of Texas at Colbert's Ferry on the Red River, Butterfield's gateway to the Lone Star State.

John Butterfield, president of the Overland Mail Company. Conkling Papers, courtesy of Seaver Center for Western History Research, Los Angeles County Museum of Natural History.

Aaron V. Brown, U.S. postmaster general, 1857–59. *Harper's Weekly*, March 19, 1859.

The first eastbound stage leaving San Francisco. *Harper's Weekly*, December 11, 1858.

THE OVERLAND MAIL STARTING FROM SAN FRANCISCO FOR THE EAST.—[FROM A PHOTOGRAPH]

Celerity mud wagon typically used by the Overland Mail Company in Texas. From *Frank Leslie's Illustrated Newspaper*, October 23, 1858, courtesy of University of North Texas Libraries, Archives and Rare Books, Denton.

CHAPTER 2

From the Red River to Young County

THE OVERLAND MAIL.—THE START FROM FORT SMITH, ARKANSAS, FOR THE PACIFIC COAST.—FIRST COACH DRIVEN BY JOHN BUTTERFIELD, JR.,"—THIS ILLUSTRATION APPEARED IN VOL. VI., OCT. 23D, 1858

The Overland Mail—The Start from Fort Smith, Arkansas, for the Pacific Coast—First Coach Driven by John Butterfield, Jr., from *Frank Leslie's Illustrated Newspaper*, October 23, 1858. Print on paper: engraving, hand colored. Courtesy of the Bancroft Library, University of California, Berkeley (BANC PIC 1963.002:0474-A).

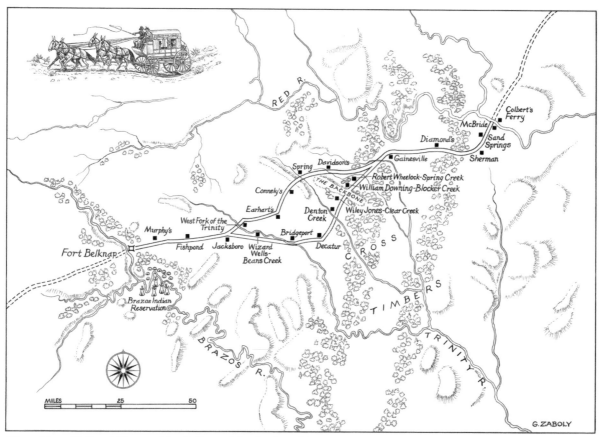

Map 2. From Colbert's Ferry to Fort Belknap. Map by Gary Zaboly.

L ooking across the Red River into Texas from Indian Territory in 1858, one would have seen a tranquil, idyllic setting that belied the sectional divisions simmering throughout the region. North Texas was a tinderbox waiting for a match. When the Overland Mail Company commenced operations in the Lone Star State that year, several factors were already combining that would, within thirty months, force it to relocate its route northward. Grayson County, on the south bank of the Red River, and Cooke County, its neighboring county to the west, encompassed a chaotic mix of disparate elements. This region was the point in Texas where the Deep South, Upper South, and western frontier converged. Fire-eater secessionist slaveholders encountered farmers and ranchers who owned few, if any, slaves and wanted Texas to stay in the union. Strong and divergent opinions mixed and interacted, and not always peacefully. In 1858, much of the area was in a raw, frontier state, largely undeveloped and with few cities. Chronic raiding of the outlying communities by Native Americans kept residents on edge, never knowing when or where the next depredation would strike.

Settlers' anxieties reached a feverish pitch after October 16, 1859, when the radical abolitionist John Brown attacked the federal arsenal at Harpers Ferry, Virginia, intent on fomenting a violent slave insurrection. Proslavery residents of North Texas's Red River region were convinced that John Brown types would soon infiltrate their communities and incite dissension. Setting a match to the tinder was not long in coming. North Texas succumbed to a full-scale panic after a series of fires broke out in Dallas, Denton, and Pilot Point nine months later in the summer of 1860. Convinced that persons of a John Brown mindset had set the fires to spark a slave revolt, local vigilance committees killed between thirty and one hundred people, both black and white. Law enforcement officials looked the other way as lawless brigands carried out their bloody work. Evidence later revealed that the conflagrations were accidental, caused by the "exceedingly hot summer" and the stocking by local merchants of "new and volatile phosphorous matches."[1]

The facts mattered little to those obsessed with insurrectionist conspiracies. Vigilantes in Fort Worth hung alleged abolitionist William Crawford in July 1860 and a few months later, on September 13, 1860, strung up Methodist minister Anthony Bewley from the same tree. Left dangling from the limb, Bewley's corpse was finally cut down the following day by locals, who buried the reverend "in a shallow grave. Three weeks later his bones were unearthed, stripped of their remaining flesh, and placed on top of Ephraim Daggett's storehouse, where children made a habit of playing with them." Bewley's murder left his wife and eight children destitute. The incendiary frontier newspaper the *White Man* offered its grisly congratulations to the minister's assailants, saying, "Good *lick*."[2]

Subsequent studies of the Texas Troubles of 1860 found no evidence of wrongdoing by those lynched. "But the damage had been done," Donald Reynolds notes. "Southern-rights extremists in Texas and throughout the South made skillful use of the Texas Troubles in fire-breathing speeches and editorials to whip up secessionist sentiments." While many Texans had previously supported Governor Sam Houston's moderate unionist policy, the slave insurrection panic of 1860 pushed a significant number of the state's moderates into the secessionist camp.[3]

Such is the situation that the Overland Mail Company faced in Texas as it sent its first coach westward in the fall of 1858. The particulars of Butterfield's contract with the U.S. Postmaster General called for stagecoaches to cross into Texas at or near Preston, in far northern Grayson County. In June 1858, Abel Rathbone Corbin wrote to U.S. secretary of war John Floyd on behalf of the Overland Mail Company informing Floyd of the route through Texas. Corbin said, "From Fort Smith [Arkansas] the route passes to Preston on the Red River, to Fort Belknap, to Camp Cooper; thence along [Captain R. B.] Marcy's trail of 1849 to the Big Springs of the Colorado." From Big Spring, Texas, the overland road was to follow Lieutenant Nathaniel Michler's 1849 trail "to Mustang Springs, to the springs of the White Sand Hills, and to the Rio Pecos." From Emigrant Crossing on the Pecos, the Butterfield route would traverse the Upper Road to El Paso through the Guadalupe Mountains and Hueco Tanks. Corbin profusely thanked Secretary Floyd for "his kind expressions in regard to [the army] furnishing through protection to the Overland Mail from St. Louis & Memphis to San Francisco."[4]

Secretary Floyd, however, had no intention of providing a personal armed escort for the Overland Mail Company. Floyd wrote to Corbin, "You will perceive the impracticability of complying with your request. Instructions, however, will be given to the Commanders of the Departments of Texas and New Mexico . . . to afford such protection to the stages as the military service of their commands will permit." Considering the commanders' slender resources and the diminutive garrisons at their disposal, the U.S. Army could render only slight assistance. One can read between the lines of Floyd's letter to see that Butterfield was on its own.[5]

Without military escort, overland mail service along Marcy's and Michler's California Emigrant Road faced the prospect of disruptive and deadly Comanche raids. A shortage of dependable water also plagued the remote route. In places, the primitive road was little more than a faint trace. During the summer, the searing and brutal heat along the sandy trail made travel most unpleasant. In sum, the California Emigrant Road was isolated, infrequently used, and dangerous. After receiving Floyd's discouraging reply, the Overland Mail Company scrambled to adjust its route through Texas. With only two months remaining before the start of its overland operation, Butterfield was in a bind.

During the summer of 1858, intense lobbying by residents of Sherman and McKinney succeeded in moving the entry point from Preston to Colbert's Ferry and rerouting the road through Sherman, Texas. Albert Deane Richardson, a journalist and author traveling westward on the Butterfield route in September 1859, said he crossed into Texas at Preston, but he was mistaken. Early Butterfield timetables also listed Preston, but the mail company's first westward coach crossed at Colbert's Ferry on September 20, 1858.[6]

Preston was a major Red River crossing from 1846 to 1850. At its peak, traffic totaled almost one thousand wagons a year. Silas Colville and Holland Coffee's trading post formed the nucleus of the settlement. Preston enjoyed the reputation of "a ribald, boisterous, and profane frontier town and a frequent destination of Indians seeking liquor." An armed fracas in Preston in October 1846 led to Coffee's murder. In 1853, the U.S. Army supply depot closed after only eighteen months of use. The growth of Sherman and McKinney gradually siphoned commerce and traffic away from Preston, and by the end of the 1850s, the village's heyday had passed. Today the townsite lies under Lake Texoma, constructed in 1944.[7]

Seven miles downstream from Preston is Colbert's Ferry, Oklahoma (formerly Indian Territory). For several decades, this crossing served as the nation's northern gateway into Texas. To the period observer reclining on the rust-colored beach, the diverse parade of personalities, races, and cultures making their way up and down the muddy riverbank was assuredly a singular sight to behold. Joseph G. Mitchell built the first ferry here in 1842 but died just five years later. When Benjamin Franklin Colbert, a Chickasaw Indian, purchased Mitchell's farm and ferry "sometime prior to 1852," he hired Pennsylvania native Joseph Bonaparte Earhart to make improvements on Mitchell's ferry operations. Earhart subsequently managed a Butterfield station to the west at Hog-Eye Prairie, on the Jack-Wise County line. Colbert's Ferry was a stage stand on the Overland Mail line from 1858 to 1861. After the Civil War, carriages, wagons, and livestock continued to utilize the crossing. Noted travelers making use of the ferry included Frederick Grant, son of Ulysses S. Grant, as well as Frank James, Jesse James, and the Younger brothers.[8]

William Tallack, a twenty-nine-year-old English Quaker riding a Butterfield coach eastward in the summer of 1860, arrived at the Red River crossing at sunset. "We entered the dark and tangled jungle which for many hundred miles skirts the Red River," he noted. "[T]he trees hereabouts were densely festooned with wild vines, bright convolvuli, and crimson trumpet-flowers. The scene was a mixture of forest, garden, swamp, vineyard, hopyard, and jungle all in one." Tallack described the trail to the ferry landing as primitive, with old tree stumps protruding throughout. A log corduroy road kept the coach from miring in the muck but jostled the passengers. Tallack mentioned eating dinner at Colbert's in a large log house.[9]

Waterman Ormsby, Jr., a correspondent for the *New York Herald* and the only through passenger on Butterfield's maiden westward run, arrived at Colbert's on September 20, 1858, just before ten in the morning. The station's larder featured sugar, butter, and pastry, items rarely seen on more remote sections of the route. After a good meal, Ormsby wrote, "Mr. Colbert, the owner of the station and of the ferry, is a half-breed Indian of great sagacity and business tact. He is a young man—not quite thirty, I should judge—and has a white wife—his third." The *Herald* reporter continued, "He is nearly white, very jovial and pleasant, and, altogether, a very good specimen of the half-breed Indian." Orsmby noted that the ferry keeper had some of his slaves working on lowering the steepness of the riverbank. Other slaves ferried stage passengers across to the Texas shore on a raft, using poles to move the vessel. The fare for a four-horse coach was $1.25.[10]

By 1858, Colbert was clearing $1,000 a year on his ferry operations, no small sum for the period. One of his slaves, Kiziah Love, lived at Colbert's when it was a Butterfield station. "Master Colbert run a stage stand and a ferry on Red River and he didn't have much time to look after his farm and his niggers," Love recalled. "[H]e had lots of land and lots of slaves. His house was a big log house, three rooms on one side and three on the other, and there was a big open hall between them. There was a big gallery clean across the front of the house. Behind the house was the kitchen and the smokehouse. The smokehouse was always filled with plenty of good meat and lard."[11]

After the Civil War, the Chickasaw ferry keeper erected a larger, more refined home named Riverside on the site, representative of his increased material success and prominence in the community. Colbert operated the ferry here for more than forty years, from 1849 until his death in 1893. Former employee John Malcolm fondly recalled, "B. F. Colbert was one of the best men I ever worked for. He was strictly honest and a perfect gentleman in every sense of the word, and expected every one else to be the same."[12]

Colbert's family came to Indian Territory from the South as part of President Andrew Jackson's Indian removal program in the 1830s. Many Chickasaws, Cherokees, and other members of the Five Civilized Tribes believed that by assimilating into the white man's culture they would finally gain acceptance and respect in nineteenth-century America. Some industrious and prosperous Indians, such as Colbert, sported fine clothing and built large, elaborate homes. In their attempt to cultivate the wealthy southern planter image, these Native Americans even acquired slaves. In 1860, Benjamin Franklin Colbert owned twenty-six slaves. His former slave, Kiziah Love, recalled, "That was a sorry time for some poor black folks but I guess Master Frank Colbert's niggers was about as well off as the best of 'em. . . . My Mistress' name was Julie Colbert. She and Master Frank was de best folks that ever lived. All the niggers loved Master Frank." Love said, "[The Colberts] let us do a lot like we pleased jest so we got our work done and didn't run off." Comparing her masters to white slave owners, she said, "I don't 'spect we could of done that way iffen we hadn't of had Indian masters."[13]

One notable exception to Love's statement was Colbert's brother, Henry Clay "Buck" Colbert, born in 1832, who became the constable for Panola County, Chickasaw Nation. Love recalled, "Master Frank had a half brother that was as mean as he was good. I believe he was the meanest man the sun ever shined on. His name was Buck Colbert." Love said, "He was sho' bad to whup niggers. . . . [H]e'd beat 'em most to death." She remembered, "Master Buck kept on being bad till one day he got mad at one of his own brothers and killed him. This made another of his brothers mad and he went to his house and killed him. Everybody was glad that Buck was dead." Love's account of Buck Colbert's death conflicts with a July 1858 *Dallas Herald* article noting that a man named Fiera Train killed Panola County sheriff H. C. Colbert with a shotgun blast at Preston, Texas, when the two fell to quarrelling after sampling Train's whiskey.[14]

Even though southern whites forced Chickasaws such as Colbert to relocate to Indian Territory, some of these Native Americans still emulated the planter lifestyle. Ironically, despite all their efforts at assimilation, these Indians never gained the acceptance and respect they so greatly desired. Anglos such as Ormsby still viewed them as "nearly white, a good specimen for a half breed." Worse, they in turn oppressed African Americans, using them as slaves on their farms and ranches. Native Americans found their efforts to conform, first in the South and later on the frontier, frequently frustrated.

One Chickasaw skeptical of assimilation was Holmes Colbert, B. F. Colbert's son, who was born at Colbert's Ferry in September 1890. During a visit to the Red River region in 1930, Butterfield historians Margaret and Roscoe Conkling found him to be "one of the most gracious, hospitable and altogether charming characters of our trip" and stated, "He upholds the fine reputation of his father for kindest [*sic*] and helpfulness to all." During this same visit, a former classmate of Holmes told the Conklings, "He was the most charming young man and very promising scholastically. He was educated for the law, but claims 'that he could not learn to lie like a white man.'" Holmes Colbert's remarks about lying Anglos no doubt reflected his anger from watching his father spend a lifetime trying to emulate the white man and never gaining full equality or respect. No matter how hard the Chickasaws tried to fit into nineteenth- and twentieth-century American society, many Anglos still considered them inferior.[15]

At Colbert's Ferry, the river landing was a third of a mile below the stage stop. The Overland Mail Road ran southwest from the station's log cabin, down a gradually sloping hill to the water's edge. From the ferry in Indian Territory, it was 720 feet across the river into Texas. In October 1858, the Chickasaw Legislature's House of Representatives gave Colbert a toll ferry license, but the measure did not become law until a year later, on October 8, 1859, when the Chickasaw Senate and Governor Dougherty W. Colbert approved the legislation.[16]

The one-year delay caused B. F. Colbert considerable frustration. By late 1858, the Butterfield station keeper was having problems with his neighbors across the river, the McBrides, who owned the ferry landing in Texas. A contentious dispute erupted after county commissioners in Grayson County, Texas, granted both Colbert and the McBrides permission to operate a ferry on Red River. These competing interests were anxious to capitalize on the considerable traffic generated by the Overland Mail line. Forty-year-old Michael A. McBride, a feisty Irishman, and his thirty-five-year-old wife, Martha, a South Carolina native, had built a home and general store near their river landing. The McBrides had purchased the site and the surrounding acreage from Clinton and Almarine Alexander in 1855. Over the years, the McBrides had a long business relationship with the Alexanders, who were among the largest merchants and wholesalers in North Texas and likely furnished supplies to the McBrides' general store. The establishment did an extensive trade with overland travelers, especially in liquor sales, since Indian Territory was dry.[17]

In an effort to resolve the Red River standoff, Colbert in early December 1858 appealed to the federal government. He wrote to the Department of the Interior asking for clarification on the legal boundaries of the Red River. Colbert argued that according to federal treaties, the Chickasaws' jurisdiction over the Red River extended to the south bank. The tribe's exclusive control over the watershed, Colbert reasoned, thus granted him exclusive ferry rights. After receiving Colbert's letter in mid-December, James W. Denver, commissioner of Indian affairs (part of the Department of the Interior), referred the matter to Douglas Cooper, U.S. Indian agent for the Chickasaws at Fort Washita, Indian Territory. Cooper then inexplicably took twenty months to file his findings in the case.[18]

In the meantime, violence broke out on the Texas side of the river. On October 15, 1859, a group of Chickasaws paid a visit to the store at the Grayson County ferry landing. The Indians demanded that the clerk there sell them some liquor, but he refused their request. The Chickasaws "then went off, got drunk, came back while the clerk was at supper, set fire to his establishment, and burned it down," causing $20,000 in damages. Such incidents occurred with regularity into the 1870s. John Malcolm, who worked at Colbert's Ferry after the Civil War, recalled that the Texas store, known as "First and Last Chance," was two hundred yards from the ferry landing. The business sold groceries, dry goods, and whiskey. It was the first chance for travelers coming into Texas to purchase spirituous liquors, and the last chance for those heading north to Indian Territory. Malcolm said, "Nearly every week or two, Indians would come four or more in a bunch, go across to the store [in Texas] and stay a few hours, come back loaded down with whiskey and feeling good. Then I had to keep my eyes open for they would shoot and we would have trouble."[19]

In the end, the federal government took no concrete action in resolving the Red River ferry dispute. In August 1860, Agent Cooper referred the matter to the commissioner of Indian affairs, imploring both Colbert and McBride in the interim "to take no steps which will be likely to produce ill feeling, or lead to a breach of the peace." The following month, the acting commissioner of Indian affairs, Charles E. Mix, wrote to his superior, Jacob Thompson, the secretary of the interior, recommending that the issue be resolved as soon as possible. Mix noted, "There is a good deal of angry feeling existing in this quarter, . . . which threatens the peace of the border." Thompson in turn kicked the controversy up the federal chain to Attorney General Jeremiah S. Black, asking him to issue a ruling. The attorney general demurred, claiming that he lacked copies of the pertinent documents, including ferry licenses and federal treaties. "For the want of these," Black said, "I am unable to answer your question."[20]

Twenty-one months after Colbert's first appeal, the Red River controversy remained unresolved thanks to the muddled and bungled federal response, so typical of the antebellum period. On a myriad of pressing issues, whether Indian policy, frontier defense, or questions of federal-state jurisdiction, the U.S. government repeatedly proved unable to take coherent, effective action to address the needs of its citizens. The ferry controversy continued to fester into 1871, when Benjamin Colbert was finally able to acquire title to the Texas side of the river. Colbert purchased the land from the McBrides through a third party. Ultimately, the McBrides did well with their riverfront acreage, more than doubling their original investment.[21]

From Colbert's Ferry, it was fourteen miles to the next stop westward, at Sherman, Texas, the county seat of Grayson County. In 1860, the county's population numbered 5,711. Two years earlier, county commissioners had authorized construction of a new overland road and the requisite bridges from Red River to Sherman and then westward to Whitesboro, Texas, and the Cooke County line. The first section of this stage road led southwest from McBride's ferry landing, passing just west of Duck Creek, north of present-day Denison.[22]

From here, the road continued southwest to Sand Springs, once an important watering stop on Denison's west side. Visitors to the springs noted "strong currents of water boiling up at the foot of the rocky bluff." Travelers who paused to water their animals at the springs sometimes carved their initials into the soft sandstone. Two of the earliest inscriptions date from 1840 and 1858. Today, young couples inscribe their professions of love into the same cliff that California forty-niners and Butterfield passengers used 150 years ago. Sand Springs now lies submerged beneath Denison's Waterloo Lake, constructed in the late nineteenth century.[23]

A mile and a half southwest of Sand Springs, the Butterfield Road crossed Iron Ore Creek, one of Grayson County's principal drainages. From Iron Ore Creek, the trail led another six miles to the downtown square of Sherman, founded in 1847. Upon his arrival on September 20, 1858, Waterman L. Ormsby, the *New York Herald* reporter, remarked that Sherman was "a pleasant little village of about 600 inhabitants, and is known for its enterprising citizens." Another Butterfield passenger, H. D. Barrows of Los Angeles, passed through in late December 1860 on his wedding trip to St. Louis; he described Sherman as a "bright thriving town." Like many other communities across Texas, Sherman had exerted substantial energy lobbying the Overland Mail Company to make the town a station on its transcontinental route. Apparently, city fathers went so far "as to secure champagne for the entertainment of stagecoach officials" when they were considering locations in Grayson County. The Butterfield stage stop in Sherman was at the town's livery stable on Lamar Street, situated on the south side of the downtown square. The Overland Mail Company's sizeable station and stable was "the most imposing looking public institution in Sherman; not, of course, the handsomest building, but large, with its wide doors always open, and having a look of night and day work unceasing." Today, Knight's Furniture Store occupies the site.[24]

The finest lodging in Sherman was at the Anderson House, a two-story tavern with its own stable, located on the north side of the town square. The proprietor, N. B. "Byrd" Anderson, promised "to accommodate the traveling public in the best style," with a table "at all times . . . furnished with as good as this upper country will afford." Anderson charged $1.50 per night. William Tallack, traveling eastward on the Butterfield in 1860, observed that a better class of people operated this portion of the stage line in North Texas: "With the uninhabited solitudes of the desert and prairie we have left behind us the rough and often villainous station-keepers and their coarse fare. The stations hereabouts and henceforward are kept by persons . . . whose accommodations and manners are a decided improvement on what we have hitherto met with."[25]

Exhibiting the utmost in customer service, Henry Bates, Butterfield's Division Six superintendent (from Red River to Fort Chadbourne, Texas), personally met Ormsby's coach upon arrival. The forty-two-year-old Bates and his four children, all from New York, shared living quarters in Sherman with David Babcock, another Overland Mail Company agent, along with stage driver Ira Meicenhaner and I. B. Archer, the hostler in charge of the company's livestock. One regional newspaper joked that residents of Sherman were so starved for entertainment that they "all put on clean shirts when they hear the overland mail stage coming." The Anderson House soon became the regular gathering place to celebrate the stagecoach's arrival. With movie theaters and television far off in the future, in antebellum Texas watching the Butterfield stage roll into town was the next best thing for entertainment—maybe even better.[26]

In April 1859, a Texas correspondent visiting Sherman witnessed the arrival of the overland coach. The vehicle, carrying three passengers, had made the trip from San Francisco to Grayson County in fifteen days. Within ten minutes of the stage's arrival, the local Butterfield crew had outfitted a new coach with a fresh team that "started off at a seven miles an hour trot, which, we are told, is the gait they keep up *all* the time." The station turnaround time in Sherman was indeed quick; six months earlier, Ormsby noted that he had but a few minutes to mail a letter at the post office before reboarding his ride. While the reporter was off posting his letter, Superintendent Bates ordered Ormsby's vehicle swapped out for a new one, deciding that its heavy load of ammunition (destined for Butterfield stations along the line) was "too much of an incumbrance [*sic*] for the mail." Shortly thereafter, the new coach and its solitary passenger were rolling out of town, first on Washington Street and then back onto the county's new overland road, which paralleled present-day Highway 56.[27]

From Sherman, it was nineteen miles to Diamond's Station, located just west of Whitesboro, Texas. The road "lay across a fine rolling prairie, covered with fine grass, but with no trees and scarcely a shrub." Ormsby's driver made the trip in three hours, averaging five miles per hour. By the time his coach reached the stage stop, the sun had set and "the beautiful moonlight lit up the vast prairie, making its sameness appear like the boundless sea and its hills like the rolling waves." Ambrose B. White founded Whitesboro in 1848, and ten years later, he built the Westview Inn to capitalize on traffic from the Overland Mail Company. In its formative period, the town had its share of saloons along with a rowdy reputation. "Women folks were forbidden to get out on Saturday nights because there was so much shooting. Men were often shot in the streets."[28]

The Butterfield station keepers in Whitesboro were the Diamond family, namely, John Roberson Diamond, his spouse, Emeline Rebecca, and their ten children. In 1850, the Georgia natives started a farm and horse ranch one mile west of town, close to the Grayson-Cooke County line. Ormsby's coach paused at Diamond's Station in September 1858 to swap out mules for a fresh team. The New York reporter found the spectacle of the livestock handlers trying to harness the station's unbroken and rebellious mules amusing.

When not dealing with feisty mules, employees had to contend with volatile customers. In 1859, some months after Ormsby passed through, a Butterfield coach carrying Dr. J. C. Tucker pulled up to Diamond's at sunset, and the passengers disembarked for dinner. Trouble had been brewing in Tucker's stagecoach for some hours before the meal stop in North Texas; during the trip through Arkansas, several of the passengers had gotten into a nasty argument and exchanged insults.[29]

One of these, "Dutchy," a rotund German, had refused to refrain from smoking his pipe in the tightly enclosed space. A fellow traveler, "Texas," who hailed from the Lone Star State, grabbed Dutchy's pipe from his mouth and tossed it out the coach window. The German's loud snoring also proved intolerable. Texas said, "We'll have to get shut of this porker," and he proceeded to unlatch the carriage door. "The next jolt the stage made, the door gave way, and out went Dutchy, heels over head, into the road."[30]

Texas had issues not only with Dutchy but also with a young Frenchman in the coach, who did not appreciate Texas's attention to his attractive female companion. Shortly after crossing the Red River into Texas, the Frenchman admonished Texas, "Damn you, don't you address this lady!" Texas replied, "Well[,] Frenchy, you *do* speak English well enough to apologize at the next station." A half hour later the overland coach pulled up to Diamond's, and after dismounting, Texas and Frenchy decided to settle their differences with a duel in the station's corral. After promising Dr. Tucker that he would "fix the . . . frog eater," Texas entered the corral and faced his opponent before a crowd of half a dozen Butterfield employees. In the exchange of shots that followed, Texas killed Frenchy. By that time, the stage driver had finished his dinner and fresh livestock were in harness. Tucker and Texas "could only seize some food and jump into the coach as the . . . wild mustangs started off on a fierce gallop." There was no discussion about presenting the matter to local authorities. Tucker and Texas rode on together until New Mexico, when Texas got off at Deming. Such were the rough-and-tumble aspects of overland travel during the antebellum period.[31]

By the fall of 1860, Diamond's Station had augmented its workforce, with James Jackson Diamond joining his brother John at the stage stop. During this period, several other Diamond brothers also moved to Texas from Georgia, including William Winfield Diamond, a lawyer in Sherman, and George Washington Diamond, who initially lived in East Texas before settling in Whitesboro.[32]

The Diamonds, fervent fire-eaters, hosted several large secession rallies at the Overland Mail Company's stage stop. Despite an obvious conflict of interest, the brothers appeared quite comfortable advocating separation from the federal government, the same government that employed them through its Butterfield mail contract. Station keeper J. R. Diamond chaired one meeting on November 23, 1860. Also present was brother J. J. Diamond. At a second secession rally, on December

15, 1860, J. J. Diamond and prominent Cooke County planter James G. Bourland were on the committee that issued the following resolution: "The Black Republicans . . . have set on foot an organization throughout the Northern frontier . . . for the purpose of extinguishing negro slavery in the Southern States." The resolution further stated that this organization employed whatever "hellish . . . means necessary" to achieve its goals, "whether by John Brown raids or by inciting the negroes to rebellion and destruction of our lives and property as in the late demonstration in Texas," that is, the Texas Troubles during the summer of 1860. J. J. Diamond subsequently served as a Cooke County delegate to the Texas Secession Convention in 1861. Brother W. W. Diamond also went as a convention delegate, but for neighboring Grayson County. Both brothers signed the convention's resolution advocating secession.[33]

In the Texas secession referendum held on February 23, 1861, the Red River counties of Grayson, Cooke, and Montague all voted against disunion, three of twenty Texas counties to do so. Several counties along the Red River and the western frontier strongly agreed with Governor Sam Houston (1859–61) that secession would spell disaster for Texas, a prediction that proved all too true. Many local dissenters opposed Confederate military conscription and wanted to stay clear of the war. Along the Overland Mail Road in North Texas, there was a violent collision of sectional ideologies as the prevailing North/Midwest/Upper South majority clashed with a radical fire-eater Lower South minority.[34]

For example, in Cooke County, 90 percent of the population did not own slaves, and many did not grow cotton. Despite the planters' minority status, they controlled 50 percent of the local economy. These slave owners, wielding their considerable wealth and political power along with a good measure of fear, intimidation, and violence, succeeded in suppressing the will of the majority. Foremost among these North Texas fire-eaters was James G. Bourland, a wealthy Red River planter and captain in the Texas Rangers. Bourland and the Diamond brothers would soon play prominent roles in the Civil War history of Gainesville, Texas, the next Butterfield station, fifteen miles to the west.[35]

In 1854, one traveler joked that Gainesville, the Cooke County seat, was "a collection of five or six log cabins dignified with the name of a town." The community's prospects had improved by 1857, when a member of a federal wagon train passing through described Gainesville as "a flourishing village & the center of a considerable trade." The following year, Butterfield passenger Waterman Ormsby called it a prosperous "little town . . . [where] after hastily swallowing supper and changing horses, we were off again." In 1858, Cooke County's population was 2,530, and by 1860, it had grown to 3,760. W. R. Strong, who moved to the county in June 1846, recalled that the Butterfield stage stop in Gainesville was at the northeast corner of the intersection of Rusk and California Streets. California Street derived its name as the thoroughfare used by emigrants and Butterfield coaches en route to the Golden State. In 1860, the postmaster for Gainesville was Jeremiah E. Hughes, a forty-four-year-old New Jersey native.[36]

The first westward Butterfield coach arrived here far ahead of schedule on the evening of September 20, 1858. Company superintendent Henry Bates, wanting to minimize any disruption caused by the early arrival, had sent an express rider ahead notifying stations to be at the ready when the coach came through. The Overland Mail Road through this section of North Texas, recently completed, was unfamiliar to the express rider, who subsequently lost his bearings in the nocturnal woods. Thus, the early arrival of Ormsby's coach at Gainesville and the next several stations westward caught Butterfield employees off guard, leading to some frantic scrambling by station keepers to get the meals and livestock changes ready. The initial confusion along the North Texas line obliged Superintendent Bates to accompany Orsmby for some distance to help facilitate smooth transitions at each stage stop. Despite the logistics mix-up and resultant inconvenience, the *Herald* reporter commented favorably on the new thoroughfare: "Though only opened one month before I passed over it, it was already pretty well marked with wagon tracks." Ormsby noted that "there were very few heavy grades" and judged that "with the combined efforts of the counties and the mail company," the Butterfield route would soon become "an excellent road."[37]

Although a flourishing law-abiding town during the Butterfield years, by the fall of 1862, Gainesville had succumbed to a pervasive paranoia, lawlessness, and wholesale lynching. George Washington Diamond, brother of the Whitesboro station keeper, in an account written after the war, vigorously defended the hangings, spuriously claiming that the problems had started with Butterfield. "Early in the year 1858, after the organization and establishment of the 'Overland Mail' through Texas, people of every shade of opinion and men guilty of every species of crime began to pour into the state from all quarters of the globe." Diamond argued that this influx of people substantially transformed the character of the region. "This sudden and rushing tide caused alarm" among some area residents, he said, "because the actions and conduct of so many strangers in their midst created suspicions and fears." One can read between the lines to discern his underlying point: many Overland Mail Company employees in Texas were from the North, which in the minds of the slaveholders immediately made them suspect as real or potential abolitionists.[38]

Part of Diamond's argument was no doubt rooted in the case of George Humphreys, a New Yorker working for Butterfield in Grayson County. In its 1859 spring term, the Grayson County Court indicted and convicted Humphreys for gambling with a negro slave. The *Dallas Herald* described the Butterfield employee as "an avowed abolitionist" and noted that shortly after his conviction, Humphreys left Texas for California. Upon his departure, Humphreys allegedly neglected to collect some letters left for safekeeping in Gainesville. One of these communications, purportedly written to Humphreys by E. C. Palmer, was quite inflammatory in nature.[39]

In a November 1858 letter, Palmer, a former resident of Marshall, Texas, who had recently moved to Gainesville, wrote, "We will have a general war soon between the North and South I hope. And the Northern people had . . . [better] begin to practice killing *the dam* [*sic*] *Southern sons of bitches.*" When confronted with the document, Palmer acknowledged writing it to the Overland Mail employee but then failed to provide the local Gainesville citizens committee with an "explanation satisfactory" for doing so. The committee's chairman, slaveholder Samuel C. Doss, was a son-in-law of prominent planter James Bourland. Palmer subsequently fled Cooke County and recanted his confession, claiming that Doss's group had coerced him into admitting authorship of a forged letter. The truth concerning the letter mattered little, as some Gainesville residents were already firmly convinced that "there exists in our midst a well organized element harboring a deep-rooted hostility to Southern institutions, . . . the ultimate design of which is, thro' secret organizations, . . . to strike a decisive blow at that peculiar institution of the South—slavery." In a resolution passed on October 14, 1859, two days before John Brown's raid on Harpers Ferry, the Cooke County committee vowed to keep a vigilant eye on local residents and proclaimed a zero tolerance policy for persons expressing antislavery views.[40]

Expanding on his theories concerning the Overland Mail and associated population growth, George Washington Diamond said that some of the region's recent arrivals "seemed to be restless and adventurous in their dispositions, manifesting an unfriendly spirit toward the older settlers. This produced its natural result," according to Diamond, "and in a short time mutual distrust and dislike, criminations and recriminations characterized the intercourse between the two parties." Temperatures along the Red River went from a simmer to a boil after citizens of Grayson, Cooke, and Montague Counties voted against secession in the February 23, 1861, statewide referendum, an action that incensed the minority planter class and their followers. Diamond, ignoring the fact that many original, well-respected pioneers cast their ballots against disunion, claimed that the "bold denunciation of the act of secession . . . was the foundation upon which unscrupulous men bent on ruin and plunder based their criminal conduct."[41]

The area's antisecession vote of 1861, in combination with the Texas Troubles of 1860 and John Brown's Raid in 1859, created a dangerous and violent paranoia among the slaveholding elites and their coterie. This faction was now certain that slave-insurrection plots and abolitionist traitors were lurking around every corner. By 1862, the group had consolidated their political power and control over local military units. The South was at war, there were rumors of a pending Union invasion of North Texas, and anyone who espoused sentiments against the Confederacy did so at his own peril.

Matters came to a head in April 1862. On April 16, the Confederate Congress passed the Conscription Act, compelling mandatory military service in the Confederate Army. The announcement sparked widespread resentment and grumbling among citizens living in the Red River country and along the western frontier. Many of these residents had voted against secession and, like Sam Houston, had wanted Texas to stay in the Union. They held scant affection for the Confederacy and had no interest in serving in the rebel army. They also had little use for rabble-rousing abolitionists. They wanted to be left alone on their farms where they could look after their families.[42]

Some of these disaffected citizens joined the Union League or Peace Party, a clandestine group of locals determined to escape service in the Confederate Army. While the majority of Peace Party members did not advocate violent unrest against rebel authorities, "a few" did. Within several months, the actions of this minority had sparked a lethal chain reaction, later known as the Great Hanging at Gainesville. During October 1862, Cooke County authorities, under District Provost Marshal James Bourland's direction, conducted a Peace Party witch hunt, arresting over 150 suspected unionists and eventually hanging 40. Two others died attempting to escape.[43]

The great-grandson of one hanging victim characterized the district provost marshal as a "ruthless Confederate partisan" and noted that as "one of the largest slaveholders of the county, Bourland had much to fear [from the rumored Union invasion], . . . and the massacre that followed was all the bloodier for Bourland's exercise of pure self-interest." Bourland and his allies kept tight control over the citizens court (more a kangaroo court) issuing the death sentences. William W. Bourland, Bourland's eldest son, served as court constable. The majority of court jurors, which included Bourland's son-in-law Samuel C. Doss, were slaveholders. Another member of the court was Wiley Jones, a Cooke County commissioner who lived on the Overland Mail Road at Clear Creek near the Wise County line.[44]

After a suspect's "trial" and conviction by the citizens court, a slave named Bob Scott would convey the condemned man by wagon to a giant elm tree at the southeast corner of California Street and Pecan Creek. Under the supervision of Captain Alexander Boutwell, the hangmen attached a rope to the tree limb. The prisoner then stood up in the wagon and the executioner fixed the noose round his neck. George W. Diamond witnessed one of the hangings, that of Henry Childs. "The carriage was then driven from beneath the limb, and in a moment more the body of Henry Childs dangled in the air," Diamond recalled, "while the branches of the obstinate and unyielding elm trembled like an aspen under the weight and shuddering motion of the dying man."[45]

After the hangings, family members buried some of the victims, while others went unclaimed. Authorities made another slave, Frank Foreman, wrap the unclaimed bodies in blankets, inter each in a shallow hole along Pecan Creek, and throw some dirt on top. A short time later, wild pigs began rooting around the creek-side graves and disturbed the corpses. Mrs. Diston recalled seeing these hogs dragging her stepfather's arm through Gainesville. Today, the hanging site on Pecan Creek is largely forgotten, identified only by a pink granite marker set back some distance from California Street. A few miles to the east in a cemetery outside of town, the headstone of one hanging victim, Nathaniel M. Clark, succinctly sums up events: "Murdered by a mob, October 13, 1862."[46]

The Great Hanging at Gainesville graphically illustrates the consequences of what happens when mob hysteria takes hold of a community and residents go temporarily insane, when law-and-order and due process crumble beneath the onslaught of lawless vigilantism. During the fall of 1862, Gainesville citizens descended into a dark pit of paranoia, witnessing numerous extralegal actions against their neighbors by local authorities, yet taking no action to stop it. One member of the Great Hanging jury, Thomas Barrett, said that "a good many innocent men were arrested" by Bourland's men. A reign of terror gripped the region. "Reason had left its throne. The mind of almost every man I saw seemed to be unhinged," Barrett recalled, "and wild excitement reigned supreme."[47]

James J. Diamond played a prominent role in the notorious Great Hanging at Gainesville. He served on the local vigilance committee investigating the Peace Party and as adjutant for the Twenty-First Texas Brigade, which assisted in rounding up suspect citizens. In 1863, James Bourland appointed his brother John R. Diamond to lead a local frontier battalion. Diamond's command was active in helping Bourland arrest deserters. Throughout the remainder of the war, Bourland continued to employ the same ruthless tactics previously utilized against Peace Party suspects. Deserters captured by Bourland often "disappeared" while in his custody, never making it to trial.[48]

By the waning months of the Civil War, staunch Bourland supporters J. J. Diamond and J. R. Diamond had become disillusioned and turned against him. After the war, J. J. Diamond ran a newspaper in Houston, where he died of yellow fever in 1867. J. R. Diamond, former station keeper for the Overland Mail Company, returned to his farm and ranch in Whitesboro. He ran into financial difficulties and went bankrupt in 1868, when the District Court of the United States for the Western District of Texas seized most of his assets. Credit reports advised that Diamond was "not noted for business capacity," that there was "too much whiskey," and that "creditors should look to the collection of their claims at once." J. R. Diamond died in 1880 and is buried in the family cemetery near the stage station. After the war, brother George Washington Diamond joined his brother in Whitesboro, where he practiced law and worked at the local newspaper. He also authored a spirited defense of Bourland and the vigilante court, seeking to justify their actions.[49]

More than 150 years later, the Great Hanging at Gainesville still generates considerable controversy. For several decades, local residents have been at odds over whether to publicize the hangings as a heritage tourism attraction or to ignore them. The historic parallels between Salem, Massachusetts, and Gainesville, Texas, are intriguing, as are the modern contrasts in how each city markets its history, image, and public memory. Salem has had great success in attracting tourist revenue by promoting their witch trials of 1692, when a court sentenced fourteen women and five men to hang. Salem currently boasts fifteen witch trial–related attractions and museums, including Salem Witch Hunt, Salem Witch Village, Salem Witch Museum, Haunted Witch Village, and Gallows Hill Museum. The city also features a statue of the famous fictional witch, Samantha from the television show *Bewitched*, in its Lappin Park.[50]

In marked contrast, Gainesville, with its Civil War metaphorical witch hunt, seems wary of following Salem's example. Gainesville proudly commemorates the Butterfield Overland Mail with two prominent markers: one on the north side of the courthouse on California Street, the other on Grand Avenue/FM 372 at Star Street. In addition, the name of the local community theater is the Butterfield Stage Players. However, Butterfield is not what Gainesville is best known for. As the witch trials are for Salem, the Great Hanging remains Gainesville's most significant event, yet its chamber of commerce focuses instead on the city's patriotism and its selection by Rand McNally/*USA Today* as "The Most Patriotic Small Town in America." Gainesville is not "running away from the horrible event," says Mayor Jim Goldsworthy, but prefers instead to "hang our moniker on being the most patriotic town in America and drive our tourism that way."[51]

Conflicting agendas over public memory continue to roil the community. October 2012 marked the 150th anniversary of the Great Hanging at Gainesville. To commemorate the anniversary, the Cooke County Heritage Society, which runs the city's Morton Museum, planned an elaborate history symposium and historic site tour. As part of its event promotion, the society placed a billboard advertisement on Interstate 35. Mayor Pro Tem Ray Nichols disapproved of the "sensational" nature of the billboard, which he said "put the city in a bad light." Rick McCaslin, foremost authority on the Great Hanging, explains, "Having a [150th] celebration of a time when they hanged people [for] being loyal to the United States would not go well with the most patriotic town label." The heritage society's museum, which is dependent on city funding, took down the interstate advertisement and pulled out of the anniversary observance. Steve Gordon, symposium organizer and former president of the Cooke County Heritage Society, says that the society's executive board felt intimidated about holding the event: "We got scared because the city gives the museum money. I'm very bitter about it. Gainesville has been hiding from the Great Hanging since it happened."[52]

Along the historic Butterfield Trail in Texas today, it is fascinating to observe the choices that communities make in selectively packaging their heritage and identity to visitors, in promoting some aspects while ignoring others. For more than two decades, Gainesville has considered various proposals for a Great Hanging commemoration and visitor attraction, but none of these materialized. The community sits atop a prime tourist location. It is the gateway into Texas, the first stop south of Red River on Interstate 35. With its close proximity to the Winstar Mega Casino just north of the river that attracts considerable traffic, the city could be earning significant tourist revenue by coming to terms with its past and utilizing that past to good economic advantage.[53]

This is not to suggest that Gainesville should create Salem-type tourist attractions featuring Great Hanging themes. More appropriate is a spacious, attractive, and well-designed visitor center along Interstate 35, featuring a balanced historical interpretation and a wealth of visuals and multimedia exhibits. A natural complement to such a visitor center and an excellent way to draw visitor traffic downtown would be docent-guided Great Hanging tours of the city with interpretative stops at all significant sites. Perhaps one day, Gainesville will make peace with its history and pragmatically embrace it rather than avoiding it.

After Gainesville, the next Butterfield station was at Davidson's, seventeen miles distant in southwestern Cooke County. According to passenger Waterman Ormsby, the ride from Gainesville to Davidson's took two hours and ten minutes. Much of this section of the route ran through the Cross Timbers. Some nineteenth-century visitors found these woods to be both unsightly and a barrier to passage, but Ormsby found them enchanting. "The trees grow wide apart, and are mainly of post oak," he noted. "[A]s I rode through them, the open spaces, absence of underbrush, and clean looking grass gave the entire wood the appearance of a vast orchard, and I could not get rid of the impression that there was plenty of fruit at hand." The *Herald* reporter, obviously taken with his surroundings, noted, "The frequency of these beautiful spots was quite remarkable. . . . I was quite sorry when we had passed them."[54]

The Cross Timbers was a prominent natural feature on the Butterfield Road. Actually two narrow strips, the Lower and Upper Cross Timbers caught the attention of virtually every traveler who passed through them. Located between the ninety-sixth and ninety-eighth meridians, these forests consist mainly of post oak and blackjack oak, varieties often described as the stunted oaks of Texas, which pale in size when compared to other native trees, such as the live oak. In the summer of 1860, William Tallack described the Cross Timbers as a "specially densely-wooded tract of Northern Texas, stretching for two hundred and fifty miles, and with a breadth of about forty miles." The Cross Timbers did not impress Albert Richardson, who in 1859 described his ride "on a barren soil among thin groves of low scrubby oaks."[55]

Located in the Upper or Western Cross Timbers near present-day Rosston, Texas, Davidson's Station derived its name from the station keeper, Dr. John Franklin Davidson. Born in 1811 in Maury County, Tennessee, Davidson came to Texas in January 1836 and served at the Battle of San Jacinto as surgeon for the First Regiment of Texas Volunteers. In 1850, he was living in Rusk County, but by 1858, he and his wife, Mary Malinda, and their three children had relocated westward, near the Cooke-Montague County line. County officials designated Davidson's home a polling place for elections, and neighbor William Downing served as election judge. In June 1859, Davidson patented his claim to 320 acres on Williams Creek, which included the Butterfield station site. Within a short time after moving to Cooke County, Davidson's medical practice was prospering, as were his farm and ranch operations. By 1860, the doctor owned ten slaves and was, by local standards, a wealthy man.[56]

Davidson's Station, built of logs, sat on a foundation of cut limestone slabs. Twenty feet from the stage stop was an old rock well, now filled with dirt and stones. In 1871, the doctor sold his home and property, which had grown to 1,400 acres, to Whorton C. Inglish and moved the family to Florida, where Davidson died in 1891. Inglish's son, Bailey, told Butterfield historians Margaret and Roscoe Conkling that when he was a young man the old stage stop was still standing. At the western edge of the station site, there is a wide U-shaped notch in the bank of Williams Creek made by coaches and wagons over the years. After descending into the creek bottom, overland stagecoaches traveled down the streambed a short distance before exiting and turning west toward modern Rosston. Today, one can easily discern this trace near Williams Creek and FM 922, as it heads west to Clear Creek and the next stop, Spring Station, thirteen miles from Davidson's in neighboring Montague County.[57]

Butterfield employees built Spring Station on Braden Branch of Denton Creek in late 1858, when the Overland Mail Company was fine-tuning its Texas route and constructing additional stage stops. Two overland reporters, Waterman Ormsby in

September 1858 and J. M. Farwell in October 1858, made no mention of this Montague County station. In November 1858, however, a *San Francisco Daily Evening Bulletin* correspondent named Baer listed "Spring Station" as the next stop after Davidson's. Thomas and Ann Sales managed the station, and overland stage driver William Donoho bunked at their home.[58]

The "Spring" in "Spring Station" refers to a rock-lined well at the stage stop. This water source served emigrants, settlers, and the Overland Mail Company. Local historians believe the well dates from "around 1849, the time when people were headed west . . . to [the] gold rush of California. The well was a stopping place for many weary travelers on the Old Butterfield Trail." According to longtime area resident Cecil Foster, not far from the well was a "Butterfield . . . transfer station [where fresh] . . . horses that could be substituted for tired stage horses, were kept in pens at the station." Foster got his information from his father, who was born near the stage stop. Additionally, in 1938 Butterfield historian J. W. Williams interviewed Jack Freeman, another old-timer, who told him that "a stage depot was located on this land. . . . The old well and some of the rocks of the chimney are the present remains of the former landmark."[59]

The spring still flows today, thanks to local preservation efforts. Montague County citizens refurbished the housing for the old well, which is located just north of Braden Branch. A short distance away, quarried stone from the stage stop lies undisturbed among the tall grasslands. At the summit of Valentine Bluff overlooking the station, one can see an excellent trace of the Butterfield Road immediately south of the present county road. Here the Overland Mail Company constructed an elaborate rock-lined channel down the steep hillside. This stone passageway is still visible amid the thick brush and trash that choke the upper ravine.[60]

As the Overland Mail Road traversed this section of southeastern Montague County, the landscape became noticeably more rugged and remote. Here settled portions of North Texas gave way to a raw, largely unsettled antebellum frontier. During the same week that Waterman Ormsby rode through in September 1858, Native Americans carried out a series of deadly attacks near the Cooke-Montague County line. The *Dallas Herald* reported, "On the head of Denton and Clear Creeks several families have been murdered and most of the stock carried off." The newspaper said that "the people are alarmed and are rapidly forting up. . . . Those depredating will be likely to continue until the Indians receive a drubbing at the hands of the whites." Five months later, in February 1859, the manager of Spring Station sent news with the eastbound stage driver of the brutal slaughter of a thirteen-year-old boy. Indians "horribly" murdered the young teen, "with bows and arrows . . . shooting eighteen arrows into his body and head," and "they took off the whole of his scalp."[61]

From Spring Station, it was eleven miles to the next stop, at Connely's in Wise

County. Connely's Station, managed by Joel Jackson Connely, of Spice Valley, Indiana, and his wife, Arbery, sat atop a picturesque hill overlooking Brushy Creek. Waterman Ormsby presented a colorful description of Connely's and conditions along the Butterfield route upon his arrival here in September 1858: "Just on the edge of the . . . Cross Timbers we came to a station on the new road, where we had the first of a series of rough meals, which lasted for most of the remaining journey." Ormsby continued, "The house was built of rough logs laid together roughly, and the chinks filled in with mud. The house was about twenty feet square, forming one room, and was occupied by two men keeping bachelors' hall, as might well be judged from the condition of things, of which the reader may imagine."[62]

Butterfield employees served Ormsby breakfast on top of a box, with the reporter seated on a water pail. His fellow diners included several drivers and hostlers. Ormsby's breakfast, shortcake cooked over coals and slathered with butter, was "edible." He had little time to savor his meal, as the station attendants were soon telling him to "hurry up before the chickens eat it." Ormsby's westbound coach departed soon thereafter. Several months later, in early November, a *Daily Alta California* reporter ate dinner here, misspelling the station name as "Cowley's."[63]

At Connely's today, a distinct trace of the mail road passes close to the station site, running southwest through the post oaks and cutting across the adjacent prairie, down to the banks of Brushy Creek, where it crosses and ascends the other side. One can still observe a large cut in the west bank of Brushy Creek and a significant depression heading away from the watershed, across a pasture dotted with grazing cattle. Standing in the bottom of Brushy Creek, one is transported back to another time. The lush surrounding vegetation, the sandy creek bed cool to the touch, and the absolute stillness harken back to the time when the sound of an approaching Butterfield stagecoach unexpectedly punctuated the silence here, the four mules and coach lumbering into view, clanking and creaking down one stream bank and up the other, then heading quickly out of sight.[64]

After the Civil War, J. J. Connely moved six and a half miles north of Decatur, Texas, near the Cowen/Flat Rock community. His daughter, Clarinda, married Carlo B. Ball, whose family were early settlers in the Cowen area. Connely went into partnership with Ball, operating the county's first flour mill, located on the old Merill property one and a half miles northeast of Decatur, the Wise County seat. Business reports characterized Connely as a "solvent" and "straight-forward" man. In October 1868, a band of Indians terrorized the central part of the county, killing settlers and carrying off captive children. When the warriors reached J. J. Connely's house, the only defenders were Connely and several women and children. The situation rapidly deteriorated when Connely discovered only one round of ammunition for the defenders' lone gun. "On realizing the danger of the situation, Mr. Conelly [*sic*] ordered all the women on the place in men's apparel, and to indicate their preparedness by brandishing hoes, broom handles and sticks as if they were deadly weapons. The 200 Indians rode away, outwitted by the brain of one man."[65]

For settlers in the Cross Timbers, Native American depredations were an accepted hazard of daily life. Along the Wise-Jack County line, one of the more seasoned Indian fighters was Texas Ranger captain Joseph Bonaparte Earhart. In March 1860, Earhart wrote to Governor Sam Houston, reporting several deadly raids in Wise and Jack Counties. The captain observed that the country was full of Indians "stealing all the time" and making good use of their scalping knives. He noted, "Last Wednesday they stole all of our horses on the frontier and killed one of our best citizens while he was at his work. . . . What can we do, we must protect ourselves."[66]

When not out pursuing Indians, Earhart operated the Butterfield stage stop sixteen miles west of Connely's. Earhart's Station formed the nucleus of an important pioneer community situated on the Wise-Jack County line. The Ranger captain was the same Earhart who in 1849 helped B. F. Colbert establish his ferry on the Red River. From Grayson County westward to Jack County, Earhart was well-known among North Texas residents. Born in Pennsylvania in 1812, he moved numerous times, to Ohio, Virginia, Arkansas, and Indian Territory, before finally settling in Texas. Once in the Lone Star State, he was first an Indian trader at Preston in 1845. Then, from 1850 to 1852, he operated a steam-powered gristmill and sawmill on Iron Ore Creek, north of Sherman. In 1855, he swapped his mill operations for a farm and herd of cattle on the Wise-Jack County line at Hog-Eye Prairie, bordered by Martin's Creek. The stream got its name from Joe Henry Martin, Earhart's son-in-law and neighbor, who married Earhart's daughter, Eliza, in February 1861. Martin was a Wise County commissioner from 1858 to 1862.[67]

From 1858 to 1860, J. B. Earhart served on the neighboring Jack County Commissioners Court. In 1860, the forty-five-year-old Earhart and his thirty-eight-year-old wife, Mary, had six children. The couple owned two young female slaves. Also living at their log cabin stage stop were Butterfield conductor Isaac Knight and his wife, Ellen, of New Hampshire. Earhart's son Liff recalled that the Overland Mail Company established a "recuperating station" for its livestock near the stage stop on the east side of Martin's Creek. Employees built a large blacksmith shop, stables and corrals for up to two hundred mules, and quarters for the hostlers charged with resting and rehabilitating the animals. Butterfield officials were no doubt aware of the need for such a recuperating station, but perhaps they became even more so after reading a stinging commentary on their operations in the *San Francisco Daily Evening Bulletin*.[68]

The newspaper's reporter, traveling east on the Overland Mail line in late November 1858, remarked, "I have sometimes thought, . . . while sitting in the coach, dragged by four weak and puny mules across the plains, that I would be the first to censure most loudly the Company." The correspondent observed, "The trip would be pleasant, provided horses were substituted for the miserable little worn-out mules that are made to drag the coaches." His complaints turned to praise north of Red River, however, as he left behind the "wild and desolate regions" of Arizona, New Mexico, and Texas. Once in Indian Territory, teams of horses replaced the mules all the way to Fort Smith, Arkansas. "The horses are in as good condition as the mules are out of condition," the *Bulletin* reporter noted. "When the horses are attached to the stage, they dash along at the rate of eight miles an hour [as opposed to five miles per hour with mules], and the wearied passengers feel inspired with new life."[69]

Another correspondent, J. M. Farwell, writing for San Francisco's *Daily Alta California*, traveled eastward on the Butterfield in early November 1858. Arriving at Earhart's, Farwell noted that a hurricane had ravaged the surrounding countryside from Jack County to Parker County several days before his arrival, seriously injuring many people. When not dealing with nature's storms, the Earharts also contended with recurring Comanche raids. Earhart's son Liff said these Indian attacks were frequent during his childhood and his father suffered considerable livestock losses. As a defensive measure, the family constructed a special pass-through in the station's chimney to enable a man to move between the cabin and the corral "to surprise Indians when they came to steal."[70]

The depredations made a deep impression on the young boy and left him fearful. Liff recalled one event at age eleven when he and the family were away from the station for a few hours. In their absence, the stage arrived with Henry Bates, Butterfield's Division Six superintendent. Bates disembarked, and while waiting for the Earharts' return, the rotund superintendent took a nap on the front porch of the stage stop. Bates had a glass eye, which stayed open when he slept. When the Earhart family came home, Liff saw the portly man lying on the porch with his eye open and assumed that Indians had killed him. The young lad "ran away from the house as far and as fast as he could, [and for some time after, it was] difficult to quiet him and reassure him."[71]

At Earhart's Station today, bucolic solitude is the norm. The natural beauty encircling the site is outstanding. The high bluffs on which the stage stop is situated offer dramatic, sweeping views of the Cross Timbers countryside. Below the station is Martin Creek, which features flat tablelands that suddenly drop off into a beautiful stone canyon. This canyon boasts unusually shaped, fluted rocks and numerous life-sustaining tinajas, some of which serve as deep, cool swimming holes in the heat of summer. One source of Martin Creek's water comes from Ear-hart Springs, which seeps out through a break in the limestone channel.[72]

Nearby are the remnants of Hog-Eye, a settlement dating from the 1850s to the 1890s. Over the years, numerous writers have speculated as to the origins of the community's name. According to Albert Gallatin McClure, who moved here in the mid-1870s, "the story goes that in the first settling of the Prairie a fiddler was among the lot and the only tune he could play was 'Hog Eye' and at every dance every set called to the floor danced 'Hog Eye.'" Residents of Hog-Eye had a strong commitment to higher education. In 1860, this isolated community boasted its own schoolteacher, forty-eight-year-old W. W. Nash of Kentucky, who lived with the Earharts.[73]

From Earhart's it was seven miles to the next stop, at West Fork of the Trinity River. In September 1858, Jack County commissioners reviewed plans for a new road from Jacksboro "to the [West Fork of the Trinity River] crossing near Robert Bean's, known as Bean's Crossing," and then intersecting the existing Butterfield route to Gainesville near J. B. Earhart's on the eastern county line. A month later, in October 1858, commissioners (one of whom was Earhart) officially approved this new segment of the overland route through Jack County. None of the three newspaper correspondents riding the Butterfield in the fall of 1858 mentions West Fork Station. This is because the Overland Mail Company added the stage stop to its itinerary in late 1858 or early 1859.[74]

Albert Richardson, traveling westward on the Butterfield, arrived at West Fork Station at one in the morning on September 28, 1859. Because of recent heavy rains, the coach could not cross the swollen river. "The little station was full; so we slept refreshingly upon corn husks in the barn, or in the western vernacular, 'the stable,'" Richardson remarked, and "after breakfast we crossed the stream on foot by a slippery log, while drivers and [the] conductor brought over heavy mail bags and trunks on the same precarious bridge. On the west bank another waiting coach was soon rolling us forward among mesquite groves."[75]

Liff Earhart recalled that West Fork Station, located on the east side of the river, consisted of a residence, a blacksmith shop, a storehouse, and stables. Station manager Robert Bean was a farmer who also served as Jack County judge from 1860 to 1862. In 1860, the forty-year-old judge and his thirty-five-year-old wife, Nancy, had six children. Bean, originally from Arkansas, also worked on the Precinct One Overland Road crew responsible for maintaining the route and bridges in the northeastern section of the county. By law, all able-bodied male residents of a precinct helped maintain roads in their neighborhood on a rotational basis. The Beans owned six slaves, three male and three female, who lived in separate slave quarters at the stage stop. Although Robert Bean was Jack County's second-largest slaveholder, in February 1861 he voted with the majority of county residents, 76 to 14, against secession. In December 1862, Bean died unexpectedly during a commissioners court meeting. In honor of the judge, county commissioners passed a resolution of respect stating that the "[f]rontier of Texas has been deprived of an able friend, . . . He passed this life without a superior and few equals."[76]

Today, the ruins of Bean's Butterfield station lie in a field of long, flowing grass a short distance from the West Fork of the Trinity. The outline of the building reveals that the stage stop was diminutive in size, as Albert Richardson observed in 1859. Not far from the mail station are the rock foundations of five or six other buildings. There is also a small cemetery nearby, with numerous unmarked graves.[77]

To access the river crossing from the east side, Butterfield's stonemasons carved a sizeable channel, thirty yards long and eight feet wide, out of the steep limestone escarpment. A considerable amount of labor went into creating this section of the road. To help mark the upper portion of the channel for nighttime travel, overland employees stacked limestone retaining walls on both sides of the trail. Heading down to the Trinity, the limestone ledge transitions to a deep earthen gully, carved by stagecoach and wagon traffic over the years. At water's edge, a beautiful canopy of post oak, elm, and blackjack oak trees provides welcome shade in the broiling Texas summer.[78]

The riverbed at this point is solid gravel all the way across, which permitted easy passage for Butterfield coaches. On the west side of the ford, a distinct trace leads up to the top of the bank, where the old road crests and disappears from view. For the ten-mile trip from West Fork of the Trinity to the next station, in Jacksboro, coaches had an easy and uneventful passage. Upon arriving in Jacksboro, some visitors were none too impressed with their surroundings. One traveler described it as a "straggling village of frame and log houses, dreadfully dilapidated and propped up."[79]

Originally called Mesquiteville, by 1858 Jacksboro had approximately two hundred residents. During this period, Jacksboro was still so remote that the Overland Mail Company had to haul in wood for the log station's doorframes and floors from the nearest lumber mill, 150 miles distant. Butterfield built its stage stop on the southwest edge of Jacksboro, on the north bank of Lost Creek.[80]

Serving as the postmaster here must not have been a desirable position, as evidenced by the high turnover. William Nix, Jacksboro's first postmaster, lasted for only six months, from the post office's establishment on June 30, 1858, until January 15, 1859, when Dr. Ezra Cole replaced him. Cole held the position for a year, until February 23, 1860, when Dr. John B. Baird, the town's physician, took over.[81]

The turnover is understandable. In many respects, antebellum Jack County and its county seat of Jacksboro were still in a rough and undeveloped state. Arriving here in a Butterfield coach on September 28, 1859, Albert Richardson noted, "The Indians were so troublesome that the settlers dared not enter their fields to cut their wheat." Jacksboro's rowdier aspects became immediately apparent to Richardson when he disembarked from his coach.[82]

He found the Butterfield station manager nervously pacing the porch, "ravenously chewing tobacco, and casting uneasy glances at the navy revolver by his side. Three weeks before, he had killed an employee of the stage company in a sudden quarrel, upon the very spot we now conversed." Richardson said the manager "was under three thousand dollars bail to appear for trial; but in this lawless region men were seldom convicted of homicide, and never punished. Within a month there had been three other fatal shooting affrays nearby; and our driver enjoined us: 'If you want to obtain distinction in *this* country, kill somebody!'"[83]

The man that Richardson encountered at the Jacksboro overland station was Butterfield overseer Berry Lewis Ham, who was in charge of operations on this section of the route west to the county line. Jack County District Court records indicate that on August 30, 1859, four weeks before Richardson passed through, Berry Ham shot and killed William P. Lowe with a "Colt's Navy six shooter." The *San Francisco Bulletin* reported, "Ham, the station-house keeper, shot a stage driver named Lowe, who died in three hours after." Ham believed that Lowe was having an affair with his wife, Dorcas. The day after the shooting, Ham posted a $2,000 bail bond, with Jack County Clerk T. Jeff Reagan and James Speer acting as sureties.[84]

Berry Ham had previously served as Jack County commissioner in 1857. During 1860, he worked on the county's Precinct Two Overland Road crew. The Precinct Two section of the Butterfield Road started at Ham's Ranch west of Jacksboro at milepost five and ended at milepost ten. Besides running Jacksboro Station, Ham also managed Fishpond Station, the next stop west, near Fishpond Mountain (now Jermyn, Texas).[85]

In 1855, Ham and his wife, Dorcas, settled at Ham Spring, five miles from Jacksboro. In comparison to many of their neighbors in western Jack County, the Hams were prosperous. The couple had extensive landholdings, a large cattle herd, and several slaves. During their twenty-five-year marriage, the Hams had nine children. Their relationship was rocky, however, and the couple eventually split. In her 1862 divorce petition, Dorcas said that in September 1859, shortly after authorities charged Ham with killing Lowe, her husband cursed and abused her in "a very violent manner" and attempted to whip her. Throughout their marriage, Ham had frequently accused her of being unfaithful. On one occasion Berry had forcibly tried to take their children from her. Dorcas responded by discharging a shotgun at him. Ham dodged most of the blast, but some of the buckshot struck him in the side, "inflicting a most excruciating and painful wound which confined him to his bed for a long time." Under the final terms of the Hams' September 1863 divorce, Berry agreed to give Dorcas $3,000, twenty cows and calves, and 240 acres of land in Wise County. In return, he received sole custody of their six underage children.[86]

From Jacksboro Station westward, the Butterfield route approximates present-day Burwick Road. Several miles west of Jacksboro, the overland road passed through a scenic portion of the Western Cross Timbers known as Potato Valley. Near Ham Spring is an odd-looking potato-shaped mound called Tater Hill. Riding through this part of western Jack County, one traveler noted the "rolling beautiful land . . . [with] precipitous rocky bluffs of hills [that] jut into [the] valley and conical sandy hills . . . called 'Potato hills.'"[87]

This isolated section of the Cross Timbers was both beautiful and dangerous. In January 1859, Texas Ranger captain James Bourland reported, "Indians have been stealing on the Overland Mail route in the western portion of Jack County." In December 1860, the Dallas newspaper noted that Native American raiders killed five families in the outlying area around Jacksboro. Conditions proved so dangerous that "[t]he mail from Decatur, in Wise County, goes no further than Jacksboro, leaving Belknap unsupplied. It is no longer safe for the carrier to travel the road." The following week, a reporter for the same paper said that in the surrounding area he had "seen over one hundred houses and farms deserted by their owners, owing to the Indian disturbances."[88]

From Ham Spring, overland coaches passed over a series of long uphill climbs before reaching the far end of Potato Valley. Here the Butterfield Trail split off from modern Burwick Road and headed west. At this point, after pulling uphill for more than five miles, livestock often began to fade, necessitating construction of another relay station. In late 1858 or early 1859, the Overland Mail Company added Fishpond Station, situated southeast of Fishpond Mountain, to its itinerary. Traveling on the overland road in 1872, Miner K. Kellogg recorded in his journal that he camped at a derelict Butterfield station a few miles west of Potato Valley. Kellogg's impressions are the only known account of this remote Jack County station.[89]

"Encamp at Butterfield Ranch near good water hole in rocks . . . sketch abandoned Ranch of Butterfield from ledge of sandstone rocks over water hole." Kellogg said that the stage stop "lies in a bowl, surrounded by rugged oaks, the road running through [the] centre. . . . The ranch is an old stage tavern." Overland Mail Company employees built Fishpond Station's log cabin at the base of a hill, on the east bank of a creek. This winding, well-timbered stream contains deep water holes ideal for watering livestock. From the 1850s to the 1870s, numerous civilian and military parties camped at this site. Commenting on the station's locale, Kellogg noted, "Altogether the scenery this morning has been picturesque from the varied vistas . . . as much as any I have seen in Texas."[90]

From Fishpond Station, the Butterfield Road continued west-southwest, crossing present-day FM 1191 and then merging with Loving Ranch Road. Oliver Loving's son, J. C. Loving, and grandson, Oliver Loving II, established a family ranch in western Jack County in 1872. Just past the Jack-Young County line, the scenic wooded hills gradually fade away, transitioning into a broad expanse known as Salt Creek Prairie, which extends westward to Fort Belknap. M. K. Kellogg described this eighteen-mile section as an "open treeless prairie—noted for Indian massacres—the most dangerous place in this region." Kellogg was not exaggerating. Salt Creek Prairie "was long a favorite area for Comanche and Kiowa war parties . . . to waylay travelers and attack settlers." During Young County's frontier period, "some twenty-one graves were dug on the prairie for victims of Indian attacks." Before venturing farther on the overland road toward Fort Belknap, however, we must first make a detour to the Wise County communities of Decatur and Bridgeport.[91]

Waterman Lilly Ormsby, Jr., and daughter. Ormsby, a reporter for the *New York Herald*, was the sole through passenger on the first westbound Butterfield stagecoach. Conkling Papers, courtesy of Seaver Center for Western History Research, Los Angeles County Museum of Natural History.

Benjamin Franklin Colbert, owner of Colbert's Ferry, Indian Territory. Courtesy of Research Division of the Oklahoma Historical Society, Oklahoma City.

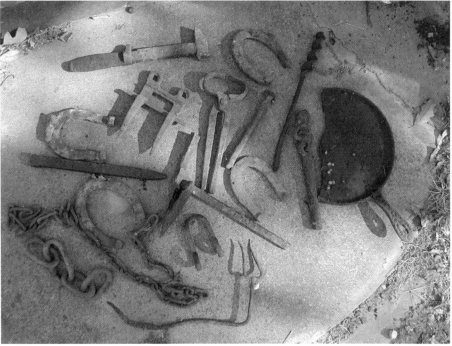

Colbert's Ferry Station artifacts. Photograph by the author.

Butterfield Road trace at McBride's Ferry landing on the Texas side of the Red River. Photograph by the author.

Inscription Rock at Sand Springs, Waterloo Lake, Denison, Texas. Photograph by the author.

Knight Furniture, Sherman, Texas, formerly the site of Sherman's Butterfield station. Photograph by the author.

J. C. Tucker, witness to the duel at Diamond's Station, Whitesboro, Texas, between "Texas" and "Frenchy." From J. C. Tucker, *To the Golden Goal and Other Sketches* (San Francisco: W. Doxey, 1895).

J. R. Diamond grave at Diamond family cemetery, Whitesboro, Texas. Photograph by the author.

Joe Allen at Diamond's Station ruins, Whitesboro, Texas. Photograph by the author.

Diamond's Station artifacts, Whitesboro, Texas. Photograph by the author.

James Bourland grave near Dexter, Texas. Bourland was a cosponsor of the secession rally at Diamond's Station with J. J. Diamond and was a leader of the Great Hanging at Gainesville. Photograph by the author.

"Murdered by a Mob." Grave of Nathaniel M. Clark in Clark family cemetery, Cooke County, Texas. Clark was one of Bourland's hanging victims. Photograph by the author.

Site of the Butterfield station in present-day Gainesville, Texas, at the northeast corner of Rusk and California Streets. Photograph by the author.

Butterfield crossing of Elm Creek on the west side of Gainesville, Texas, in the 1930s. Conkling Papers, courtesy of Seaver Center for Western History Research, Los Angeles County Museum of Natural History.

Davidson's Station ruins, Cooke County, Texas. Photograph by the author.

Butterfield Road trace leading to Williams Creek. Photograph by the author.

Davidson's Station artifacts. Photograph by the author.

Reconstructed well house at Spring Station, Montague County, Texas. Photograph by the author.

Well detail at Spring Station. Photograph by the author.

Spring Station ruins.
Photograph by the author.

Connely's Station
ruins, Wise
County, Texas.
Photograph by
the author.

Butterfield Road trace leading to Brushy Creek near Connely's Station. Photograph by the author.

Connely's Station artifacts. Photograph by the author.

Graves of Arbery Connely and Joel Jackson Connely, Ball Knob Cemetery, Wise County, Texas. Photograph by the author.

Joseph Bonaparte Earhart, manager of Earhart's Station, Jack County, Texas. From Cliff D. Cates, *Pioneer History of Wise County* (St. Louis: Nixon-Jones Printing, 1907).

Earhart's Station
ruins. Photograph by
the author.

Earhart's Station
artifacts. Photograph
by the author.

Martin's Creek near Earhart's Station. Named after Joe Henry Martin, Earhart's son-in-law. Photograph by the author.

Well at Hog-Eye settlement near Earhart's Station. Photograph by the author.

West Fork of the Trinity Station ruins, Jack County, Texas. Photograph by the author.

Landowners standing in Butterfield Road trace where it heads down to West Fork of the Trinity Crossing. Photograph by the author.

The Overland Mail Company constructed a retaining wall on the trace of the mail road leading down to West Fork of the Trinity Crossing. Photograph by the author.

West Fork of the Trinity Crossing. Photograph by the author.

Jacksboro Station site on the north bank of Lost Creek, Jacksboro, Texas. Photograph by the author.

SACRED TO THE MEMORY
OF
B. L. HAM.
BORN
OCT. 16, 1812,
DIED
NOV. 16, 1879,
AGD 67 YRS & 1 Mo

Grave of Berry Lewis Ham, Myrtle Cemetery, Ennis, Texas. Ham served as Jack County commissioner, Butterfield overseer, and manager of Jacksboro and Fishpond Stations. Photograph by the author.

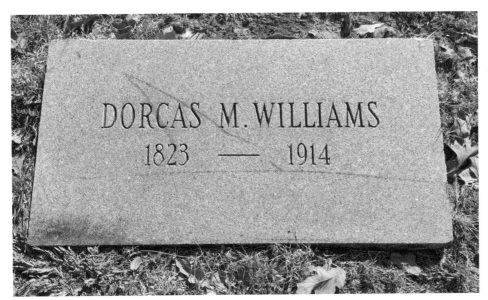

Grave of Dorcas M. [Ham] Williams, Oakwood Cemetery, Jacksboro, Texas. Dorcas married Berry Ham in 1838, and the Hams divorced in 1863 after a volatile marriage. She subsequently married Thomas W. Williams. Photograph by the author.

Joe Allen (*left*) and Patrick Dearen (*right*), on either side of the Butterfield Road trace leading to Fishpond Station, Jack County, Texas. Photograph by the author.

Patrick Dearen at Fishpond Station site. Photograph by the author.

Fishpond Station artifacts. Joe Allen photo.

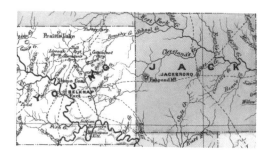

Detail of Jacksboro-Belknap segment of Butterfield Road, including Fishpond Mountain. From Map #76226, *Charles W. Pressler's 1867 Traveller's Map of the State of Texas,* courtesy of Texas General Land Office Archives, Austin.

CHAPTER 3

Detour to Decatur and Bridgeport

The Old Stage-Coach of the Plains, Frederic Remington. Oil on canvas, 1901. Courtesy of Amon Carter Museum of American Art, Fort Worth, Texas (1961.232).

It was the latter half of 1859 and residents of Wise County were feeling slighted. They were concerned that Sherman and Gainesville were reaping national publicity and economic benefits from the Butterfield Road while Wise County and its county seat of Decatur were missing out. A group of local citizens endeavored to correct this situation by persuading the Overland Mail Company to divert the Gainesville to Jacksboro section of the mail road through Wise County. In exchange for this rerouting, Wise County commissioners agreed to blaze a new road from the Cooke-Wise County line to Decatur and then west to the Jack County line. In addition, the group pledged to build a bridge across the West Fork of the Trinity, thus eliminating any high-water delays for the mail company in crossing the river.[1]

The main instigator behind this rerouting effort was Colonel William Hudson Hunt, an influential Wise County booster who settled in the Cactus Hill community in 1855. The colonel originally hailed from New York, as did John Butterfield. Hunt believed that Decatur and Wise County deserved to be on the overland road and to enjoy its commercial advantages. In addition, he viewed the proposed route change as an excellent opportunity to turn a tidy profit. Merchants in Decatur agreed. Increased overland traffic through their community would boost their business. By the end of 1859, Hunt had enlisted several like-minded speculators and investors looking to cash in on the Overland Mail line. The group named themselves the West Fork Bridge Company. The bridge they proposed to build would be for profit, a toll bridge constructed on the West Fork of the Trinity in western Wise County, near present-day Bridgeport, Texas. If accepted by Butterfield, the toll bridge would become the new overland crossing of the West Fork (and hopefully for the investors a major source of revenue).[2]

The directors of the West Fork Bridge Company constituted a veritable "Who's Who" of Wise County's leading citizens, namely, Colonel Hunt and Colonel Absalom Bishop, a Decatur merchant known as "the Father of Wise County," who served as the Wise County clerk and a Texas state representative. Others included George Isbell, Wise County judge in 1860; Pearce Woodward, Wise County justice of the peace and a county commissioner; Sylvanus Reed, a prominent stock raiser who lived at Hunt's home; Daniel Howell, a local merchant, Decatur postmaster, and future Wise County judge (1865); and Alfred Elmore Allen, Howell's business partner. After aggressive lobbying by Hunt at the state capitol in Austin, the company received a corporate charter from the State of Texas on February 11, 1860. The charter allotted five years to build the toll bridge. Toll fees were seventy-five cents for a coach and four mules, and ten cents for a horse and rider.[3]

Although the West Fork Bridge Company received their state charter in February 1860, such approval did not automatically indicate that the promoters had already built their toll bridge, just that they intended to. For example, during the previous month, in January 1860, Archibald C. Hyde of El Paso County received a similar charter for a Butterfield toll bridge, namely, the Pecos Bridge Company at Horsehead Crossing. The state issued Hyde a thirty-year charter for his Pecos River project, but he never built the toll bridge.[4]

West Fork Company officers selected the William C. Anderson Survey four miles east of Cactus Hill for the toll bridge site. The previous owner of this land was none other than Colonel Hunt, who acquired it from Anderson in 1855. The following year, Hunt sold it to Pearce Woodward, his neighbor in Cactus Hill. In the spring of 1860, after receiving their state charter, the company's officers convinced a group of local laborers and investors to help build a 250-foot bridge of cottonwood planks across the West Fork of the Trinity. It is unclear how much of their own money Hunt and the other directors put into the project. In the summer of 1860, Butterfield accepted the rerouting proposal through North Texas. In altering its schedule, the Overland Mail Company would shutter five stage stops: Davidson's in Cooke County, Spring Station in Montague County, Connely's in Wise County, and Earhart's and West Fork (Bean's Crossing) in Jack County.[5]

Census records show that as of June and July 1860, overland stage drivers were still living at Spring Station, Connely's, and Earhart's, indicating that the original route was still in use. Finally, in August 1860, Butterfield implemented its new itinerary. On August 21, Cooke County commissioners in Gainesville approved the immediate adoption of the new route to Decatur in Wise County. Commissioners designated the road as a first-class thoroughfare. First-class road regulations required significantly more maintenance and upkeep than the rougher, second-class roads used in many North Texas counties during this period.[6]

The new Butterfield segment approved by Cooke County commissioners in August 1860 ran southwest from Gainesville to Robert Wheelock's farm at the head of Spring Creek, then to William Downing's house on Blocker Creek, and next to Wiley Jones's homestead on Clear Creek, near the intersection of the Cooke, Wise, and Denton County lines. From 1860 to 1864, Josiah Jones, Wiley Jones's younger brother and neighbor, served as Cooke County overseer of the new Gainesville-Decatur Road.[7]

As part of the route change, commissioners further ordered that from Wiley Jones's homestead, located just south of present-day Leo and Dixon Creek Church, the new road was to go "in the direction of the town of Decatur by the most direct route to the [Cooke-Wise] county line." The most direct route from Wiley Jones's homestead, located just north of the Cooke-Wise County line, to Decatur, is via the Leo, Prairie, and Greenwood Roads (using modern landmarks). In the 1870s, local residents founded the community of Greenwood on the old overland road, two miles northeast of Denton Creek.[8]

Heading southwest from Wiley Jones's ranch on the Cooke-Wise County line, overland coaches crossed Denton and Black Creeks en route to Decatur, the Wise County seat. The town was originally known as Taylorsville, but citizens changed the community's name to Decatur in September 1858, several weeks before Butterfield commenced operations. One traveler passing through the settlement observed, "The little town has a frame Court House in a square surrounded by wooden stores and shanties of recent building, which form nearly the whole of this frontier country town."[9]

Daniel Howell, a local merchant and civic leader, served as Decatur's postmaster from 1858 to 1861. Howell established the settlement's first store on a hill, at the base of which was a sizeable spring that furnished abundant water year-round. Overland Mail employees watered the company's livestock at Howell Springs, which flowed out of a limestone formation. Howell took on Alfred Elmore Allen as his business partner, and they renamed their firm Howell and Allen.[10]

The partners subsequently moved their business a short distance to State Street on the west side of the downtown public square. During the county's formative period, Howell and Allen's General Store served as the post office and community center. The store conducted a lively trade with neighboring Delaware Indians, who sold hides, furs, and moccasins to the merchants in exchange for blankets, fabrics, tobacco, and whiskey. During the Delawares' visits to town, Indians and whites would hold horse and foot races as well as marksmanship matches. Another prominent early Decatur establishment was Bishop and Blythe Mercantile Store, located on Walnut Street on the north side of the square. Absalom Bishop ran the store with his son-in-law, Edward Blythe. Wise County historian Cliff Cates says that the Overland Mail Company utilized Bishop and Blythe's store as its stage stop in Decatur.[11]

From Decatur, the overland road ran west-southwest toward the new toll bridge site at the West Fork of the Trinity River. Work on the bridge was well under way by the summer of 1860, and a small community of merchants and settlers had begun to take root. The first establishments were the Buckhorn Saloon and a general store.[12]

The owners of the toll bridge christened their new settlement West Fork. This was the name listed on their application for a post office, which the U.S. Postmaster General approved on June 19, 1860. The first postmaster was Madison F. Pruit. With work on the toll bridge completed and their new post office established,

West Fork Company officials were now ready for the opening of the new overland route. In August 1860, Butterfield stagecoaches began using the West Fork Toll Bridge.[13]

Over the years, numerous writers have confused antebellum West Fork, Texas, with the later community of Bridgeport, established on the same site in the spring of 1873. Samuel P. Gibbs filed the initial application for a post office at Bridgeport, which the U.S. Postmaster General granted on May 5, 1873. Gibbs served as the town's first postmaster. Coinciding with the opening of its new post office, on May 1, 1873, the town dedicated a new toll bridge. Charles D. Cates and John W. Hale built the new bridge on the same location as the previous 1860 structure. When the Rock Island Railroad came through Wise County twenty years later, in 1893, Bridgeport citizens, worried that they would be bypassed, moved the townsite to its current location two miles to the northeast.[14]

From August 1860 to March 1861, Butterfield stagecoaches crossed the toll bridge at West Fork of the Trinity and steered due west to Cactus Hill, the home of Colonel Hunt. Today, Cactus Hill lies submerged beneath Lake Bridgeport; its location is a short distance northeast of present-day Horse Island. On the west side of the lake, there is a trace of the old overland trail that passes just south of McDaniel Cemetery and runs up Jim Ned Hill to Wizard Wells, just west of the Jack County line. From there, the mail road continued on to Jacksboro, where it rejoined the original Butterfield itinerary.[15]

Butterfield historians Roscoe and Margaret Conkling state that the Overland Mail Company built a new stage stop in 1860 on the site of present-day Wizard Wells, midway between West Fork and Jacksboro, but they provide no evidence for this claim. Undoubtedly Butterfield would have needed a relay station to change out livestock on this twenty-four-mile section of the route. Exactly where this station was, however, remains unknown.[16]

It is important to remember that overland stagecoaches utilized this new road through Cooke, Wise, and Jack Counties just seven of the thirty months that the mail company operated in Texas. The most significant element of this rerouting story has always been the toll bridge at West Fork, near present-day Bridgeport, Texas. The City of Bridgeport, in an effort to attract more tourism dollars, has increasingly promoted its Butterfield legacy and the 1860 toll bridge. This marketing focus is not by accident. Among all the imagery associated with the history of the American West, the stagecoach remains one of the most prevalent and potent symbols.[17]

Decades of Western movies and television programs have permanently etched the enduring popularity of the Old West into our public memory. Western-themed sites continue to rank among the nation's most visited tourist attractions and are a powerful magnet for both foreign and American visitors. California has Sutter's

Mill and the gold rush, Arizona has Tombstone and the OK Corral, and New Mexico has Billy the Kid and the Lincoln County War. Communities across the country continue to cash in on this enduring Wild West mystique and cachet, even in such eastern locales as New Jersey, Maryland, and Florida. Most in demand among the offered entertainment at these sites are shootouts and stagecoach rides.[18]

When Americans think of the Lone Star State, they immediately imagine the West, even though the eastern half of the state is distinctly southern in terms of its environment and culture. Texas's state tourism office, well aware of this western stereotype and its enduring popularity with visitors, deliberately plays to this audience in its promotional materials. Recent western icons adorning state highway maps include a cowboy hat, cowboy boot, horseshoe, and spur. One map cover depicts a cowboy and his horse riding in a car down the open road. The front cover of a state travel guide has a cowboy on horseback on top of a surfboard riding the waves. The state tourism logo is the word "Texas" branded on a leather patch that closely resembles those stitched on the back of Wrangler blue jeans. Clearly, the State of Texas is capitalizing on the potent attraction and influence that the Old West continues to exert on the nation's tourism industry.[19]

Like the state tourism office, communities across Texas are emphasizing their western curb appeal. Alpine, Texas, claims that it is the "Last Frontier," while Abilene promotes itself as the "Friendly Frontier." Abilene also has Frontier Texas, a popular tourist attraction that offers a ride on a "real" stagecoach. Speaking of stagecoaches, Bridgeport, Texas, touts itself as "the Stagecoach Capital of Texas." In 2009, the city applied for and received this official designation from the Texas State Legislature and Governor Rick Perry. The legislature granted the city the special recognition because "[t]he community of Bridgeport, Texas, started from a toll bridge . . . for stagecoaches of the Overland Mail Company." In addition, "heritage and tourism efforts in Bridgeport have been, and continue to be, centered around the stagecoach theme." Texas legislators recognized "the continuing efforts of the city to preserve this picturesque and symbolic part of its history."[20]

In May of each year, Bridgeport holds its main event: Butterfield Stage Days. Downtown Bridgeport features a large mural depicting a Butterfield stagecoach crossing the toll bridge. On the west side of town, civic leaders have placed a "Butterfield Stage" sign welcoming visitors. On the east side is another sign that says, "Welcome to Bridgeport / 'The Stagecoach Capital of Texas.'" Like Colonel Hunt in 1859, the community wants to maximize potential economic benefits from the Butterfield Overland Mail, in this case, heritage tourism dollars. Such shrewd marketing could prove providential. The federal government is currently considering naming the Butterfield Overland Road a national historic trail. Such designation would be a considerable economic boon, enhancing the reputation of Bridgeport and other Butterfield communities as prime "western" tourist destinations.[21]

Bridgeport is hitching its marketing and tourism efforts to its Butterfield legacy, specifically, the 1860 toll bridge. There is, however, more to this toll bridge story. A state historical marker commemorating the old toll bridge at FM 920 and the West Fork of the Trinity reads, "When the Butterfield Overland Mail traversed this area . . . a [bridge] crossing over West Fork of the Trinity was a necessity." This text ignores the fact that from September 1858 to August 1860, Overland Mail Company coaches regularly crossed the West Fork at Bean's Crossing in Jack County. Building a bridge over the Trinity was not really a "necessity." While high water occasionally delayed the mail's crossing at all Texas rivers, at no time did the Overland Mail Company feel compelled to construct bridges over the Brazos, Clear Fork of the Brazos, Colorado, North Concho, or Pecos.[22]

Butterfield's contract with the U.S. Postmaster General stipulated that each trip was to take no more than twenty-five days. Period newspaper records indicate that during the first four months of operations the mail company typically made the journey in twenty-four to twenty-seven days. After fine-tuning the route in late 1858 and adding additional stations, Butterfield significantly improved its performance. From late January 1859 to early August 1860, the trip took twenty-one to twenty-three days. In other words, by the time Wise County residents built the toll bridge at West Fork, the mail company was already running two to four days ahead of schedule. Clearly, high-water delays were not a significant problem. If they had been, the company would have bridged the major rivers in Texas. While the new toll bridge undoubtedly streamlined operations for Butterfield, the only real necessity for the West Fork Bridge in Wise County was financial in nature.[23]

As previously related, during the summer of 1860, directors of the West Fork Bridge Company started construction on the toll bridge. Workers had completed the structure by August 1860, when Butterfield switched to its new North Texas itinerary. From the outset, however, the toll bridge seemed jinxed. Wise County deed records from January 1861 reveal that all was not well at West Fork, Texas; West Fork Company directors had not lived up to their promises to pay the laborers who built the bridge and the investors who had helped fund the project.

In exchange for constructing the span across the Trinity, the West Fork Company had issued Marion Johnson of Cactus Hill a promissory note for $228 payable on January 1, 1861. As of January 23, West Fork directors had still not paid Johnson. The company attempted to placate Johnson by granting him a mechanic's lien on the bridge. The lien was not worth much, however, as the company document explicitly prohibited Johnson from collecting any toll money and stressed that "said bridge shall continue in the hands of said company as though no lien had been given."[24]

The lien's doublespeak failed to placate Johnson and his wife, Elizabeth, who won a ruling in the Wise County Precinct One Justices Court against the bridge company's board of directors. Between February 2 and March 2, 1861, West Fork directors lost three more judgments in the same court to other toll bridge workers and investors they had failed to pay, namely, Amos Grider, Thomas Grider, John B. Williams, John Finley, William H. Foster, N. H. Foster, and John Boyd. The justices further ordered that Wise County Precinct One constable N. A. Crann seize the toll bridge and its assets, which he did at six in the morning on March 15.[25]

On March 28, 1861, as Butterfield was winding down its operations in Texas, Constable Crann sold the West Fork of the Trinity Toll Bridge at public auction in Decatur to the highest bidder. West Fork Company director George Isbell, who was also the Wise County judge, won the bid with $550. Only a few weeks earlier, West Fork Bridge directors, including Isbell and Pearce Woodward, lacked $228 to pay Marion Johnson for building the bridge, yet Isbell somehow found $550 to buy the bridge at auction. A month later, on April 26, Woodward sold Isbell 320 acres of land surrounding and including the bridge for $816.25. How Isbell obtained these funds is unknown. Constable Crann had seized the bridge because of Isbell's, Woodward's, and the other directors' failure to honor their debts.[26]

Then, in a new twist on events, on August 13, 1861, five months after the bridge's seizure for financial default, George Isbell sold the land back to Woodward for the same exact amount, $816.25. Unlike the previous transaction, however, Isbell retained 1 acre out of the 320-acre sale, specifically, the acre encompassing the West Fork Bridge. In retrospect, these transactions raise a question: were the directors running some sort of real estate shell game to avoid paying their creditors, by claiming insolvency and then buying their bridge back at a discount through the bankruptcy process?[27]

Despite the bridge's tarnished financial history, on December 30, 1861, the owners of the West Fork Bridge Company convinced the Texas Legislature to pass further legislation amending their incorporation charter. Company directors apparently retained some measure of influence in Austin. This supplemental act, passed nine months after Butterfield ceased operations in Texas, gave the West Fork Bridge Company exclusive right-of-way for a mile and a half upstream and downstream of the bridge. This right-of-way prohibited anyone from opening a new road or river crossing within the stated distance of the bridge.[28]

Ultimately, the company received scant benefit from the amended charter, and the West Fork saga ended on an ironic note for the bridge's promoters. For all the effort expended in getting the overland road rerouted, Butterfield stagecoaches used the toll bridge for only seven months. In March 1861, Texas seceded, Congress ordered the transcontinental mail line moved northward, and Constable Crann seized the Wise County river crossing. During the Civil War, the bridge fell into disrepair, the cottonwood planks warped badly, and the structure collapsed into the Trinity. By 1867, West Fork's population had dwindled considerably, and the U.S. Postmaster General closed its post office.[29]

In its current efforts to promote the community's Butterfield legacy, Bridgeport, Texas, is evoking the excitement and adventure of overland stagecoach travel on the antebellum frontier. Sometimes, however, commemorating history can be like opening Pandora's box. As western historian Patricia Limerick observes, "Celebrating one's past, one's tradition, one's heritage is a bit like hosting a party: one wants to control the guest list tightly and . . . 'selectively.' To celebrate the Western past with an open invitation is a considerable risk: the brutal massacres come back along with the cheerful barn raisings, the shysters come back with the saints, contracts broken come back with contracts fulfilled." With our detour to Decatur and Bridgeport now complete, we resume our original Butterfield itinerary on Salt Creek Prairie in Young County.[30]

Colonel William Hudson Hunt, leader of the West Fork Toll Bridge project. From Cliff D. Cates, *Pioneer History of Wise County* (St. Louis: Nixon-Jones Printing, 1907).

Detail of August 1860 route change from Gainesville to Decatur and Bridgeport (Caddo Village). From Map #76226, *Charles W. Pressler's 1867 Traveller's Map of the State of Texas*, courtesy of Texas General Land Office Archives, Austin.

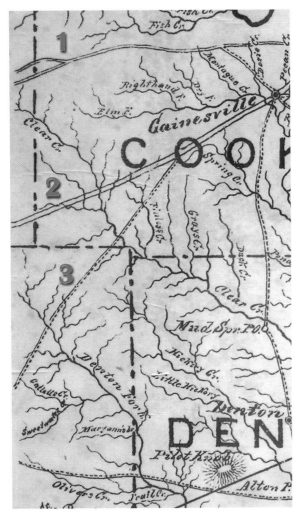

Left: Detail of map of North Texas and Gainesville (circa 1860s) with author-inserted numbers in red. Road #1 is the 1849 California Emigrant Road heading west to the Pecos River. Road #2 is the original Butterfield route (1858–60) through the southeast corner of Montague County. Road #3 is the August 1860–March 1861 Butterfield rerouting from Gainesville to Head of Spring Creek to Decatur, which crossed into Wise County near Wiley Jones's home on Clear Creek. National Archives Cartographic and Architectural Section, College Park, Md.

Above: Melinda Veatch at Greenwood, Texas, on the Gainesville to Decatur Butterfield Road segment. Photograph by the author.

Roscoe Conkling in the 1930s on the Greenwood Road, part of the Gainesville to Decatur Butterfield Road alteration. Conkling Papers, courtesy of Seaver Center for Western History Research, Los Angeles County Museum of Natural History.

Location of antebellum Daniel Howell and Alfred Elmore Allen General Store on State Street, on the southwest side of the Decatur courthouse square. Photograph by the author.

Location of Absalom Bishop and Edward Blythe Mercantile Store (1859–79) on Walnut Street, on the northwest side of the Decatur courthouse square. Wise County historian Cliff Cates says that Bishop and Blythe's Store served as Butterfield's stage stop in Decatur. Photograph by the author.

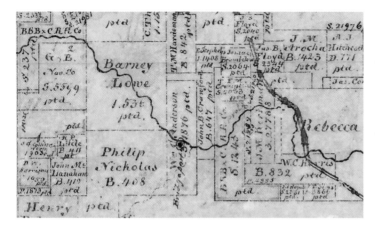

Detail of survey map showing Bridgeport settlement in the William C. Anderson survey, located at the site of the antebellum West Fork Toll Bridge, prior to the town's relocation two miles to the northeast in 1893. Map #4164, *1878 Map of Wise County, Texas,* courtesy of Texas General Land Office Archives, Austin.

Bridgeport "Stagecoach Capital" signage, Highway 380. Photograph by the author.

Bridgeport "Butterfield Stage" signage, Highway 114. Photograph by the author.

Historical marker near the site of the West Fork Toll Bridge. Photograph by the author.

Roland Ely (author's father) at Wizard Wells, Texas. Photograph by the author.

CHAPTER 4

Bedlam at Belknap

Robert Simpson Neighbors and Elizabeth Ann Neighbors. Hand-tinted photograph from about 1851. Robert Neighbors Papers (di_04287), courtesy of Dolph Briscoe Center for American History, University of Texas at Austin.

Heading west along Salt Creek Prairie, Butterfield stagecoaches soon reached Murphy's Station, located near Flint Creek northeast of present-day Graham, Texas. Murphy's Station, twenty-two miles west of Jacksboro, was the first of three stage stops in Young County. The Murphy family, originally from Kilkenny, Ireland, operated the station. Dennis Murphy, Sr., moved to New York in 1832 and supported his family through various jobs, including a stint as a cotton broker. He became a U.S. citizen in 1837. His son Patrick, born in 1826, left New York for Texas in 1854 or 1855 and by 1856 had started farming and ranching in eastern Young County. From 1856 to 1858, Patrick Murphy served as the first sheriff of Young County. In 1857, some of the Murphy clan from New York visited Texas and liked what they saw. Following the visit, Dennis Sr., his daughter, Margaret, and his son Dennis Jr. moved to Young County and joined Patrick in the cattle business.[1]

After the Overland Mail Company commenced operations, the Murphy family signed on to run the Flint Creek stage stop. While the 1860 federal census listed fifty-six-year-old Dennis Murphy, Sr., as the station manager, the owner of the building was his son Patrick. In addition to his Butterfield duties, Patrick Murphy served on the road crew responsible for maintaining the overland route in eastern Young County. Another employee at the stage stop was Edward Cornett, who married Patrick's sister, Margaret, in June 1859. When the overland correspondent for the *Daily Alta California,* J. M. Farwell, arrived at Murphy's Station, he noted that the water served to passengers came from a salt creek and was "very unpleasant to the taste." The briny libation notwithstanding, Farwell "obtained a very excellent breakfast."[2]

From Murphy's Station, the overland route continued sixteen miles to the stage stop at Belknap, the Young County seat. A half mile west of the community was the military outpost Fort Belknap. The U.S. Army established Fort Belknap in June 1851 as part of a new chain of forts designed to protect Texas's ever-expanding westward line of settlement. During 1851 and 1852, the U.S. Army blazed a road linking these new garrisons that ran southwest from Fort Belknap to Fort Phantom Hill to Fort Chadbourne and on to Camp J. E. Johnston on the North Concho River.[3]

Five years later, in the fall of 1857, Young County commissioners began planning a new thoroughfare that would connect the military road at Belknap to the

Overland Mail line in Jacksboro. In February 1858, county officials allocated $150 "for the purpose of cutting and opening The California Overland Mail Company stage road" to Jacksboro. Commissioners specified that all Young County first-class roads, including the Overland Mail route, had to be "at least thirty-five feet wide, stumps cut down to six inches of the surface, all causeways laid out be at least fifteen feet wide."[4]

The road upgrades undoubtedly coincided with the arrival of Butterfield's exploratory parties to Belknap in January and February 1858. The Overland Mail Company, however, did not start building and provisioning its Texas stations until mid-July. In that month, the *Dallas Herald* noted, "Well, at last, and according to promise, the advance guard of the California Stage Company has arrived [at Belknap], and are now camped on the site of the Young County courthouse, i.e., the public square."[5]

The *Herald* continued, "In two or three days, the party who are to establish stands through Texas will be here. . . . [They] are prepared to station their horses, bringing some with them and purchasing others on the route. . . . Last but not *least*, Belknap has been fixed upon as a *point*—and no change will be made for four years any how [*sic*]." The Young County seat soon became more than a point; by late summer Belknap was a regional operations hub for Butterfield. With the arrival of the federal mail line came real estate speculation. "In consequence thereof, lots in the *City of Belknap* have risen from 150 to 200 per cent [*sic*], and you can hear of nothing now but contracts for building houses and the price of lots generally. *Vive la Belknap!*" Cashing in on the boom, Young County commissioners sold numerous town lots in Belknap, offering lenient payment terms of up to one year.[6]

On August 10, Belknap residents noticed two coaches and horses passing through en route to Fort Chadbourne. Several weeks later, the *Herald* reported that "twelve or fifteen stages passed through Belknap . . . [bound] for El Paso accompanied by a train of twenty-five men, one baggage wagon and 250 mules." The Dallas newspaper, singing Butterfield's praises, noted that the national mail line was spurring economic development along the route and predicted that it would "doubtless attract immigration" and "aid powerfully in extending the settlement of the frontier. It will do more than an army . . . in settling the 'Great West' of Texas."[7]

Visitors to Belknap during this period expressed mixed opinions. Waterman Ormsby, whose Butterfield coach passed through in September 1858, observed, "The town has about one hundred and fifty inhabitants, and the houses, most of them, look neat; there are several stores and a billiard saloon and post office." In January 1859, William L'Engle, the new doctor at the fort, described the county seat as "a sort of one horse town . . . a whiskey ranch—nearby are about 150 rowdies and border ruffians." Stopping here in the summer of 1860, overland passenger

William Tallack noted that the community was "a place of considerable notoriety in the annals of border Texan exploits."[8]

Much of this notoriety stemmed from a brutal assassination that occurred in the streets of Belknap in September 1859. Those responsible were two Butterfield employees, none other than Patrick Murphy and his brother-in-law, Edward Cornett, both of whom worked at Murphy's Station. The victim was Robert Simpson Neighbors, federal superintendent of Indian affairs in Texas.

The two years preceding his murder had been terrible for Neighbors. The demands of his job required him to be apart from his wife and children for extended periods of time. Far more disconcerting were the vigilantes who repeatedly threatened his life. In his travels throughout Texas, he often rode horseback on solitary trails, never knowing when or where assailants might strike. Over time, the cumulative stress had become unbearable. Although deeply dedicated to his job, by early September 1859, the fifty-three-year-old Neighbors had had enough. It was time to step down. After he submitted his resignation, his thoughts turned to the prospect of happier days ahead, of returning home to San Antonio and spending time with his family.[9]

On the morning of September 14, Neighbors was at the Belknap post office wrapping up several hours of unfinished paperwork before heading home. After mailing his final reports and correspondence with Postmaster William Burkett, Neighbors and Andrew MacKay, who was visiting in the post office, stepped out into the street. They had not gone more than fifty paces when Patrick Murphy yelled out to Neighbors. Neighbors wheeled round to see Murphy brandishing a gun.[10]

Murphy accosted the federal agent in an accusatory tone: "Neighbors, I understand that you have said that I am a horse thief. Is it so?" Neighbors, moving his hand to his weapon, replied, "No, sir, I never did." Another account said that when confronted about calling Murphy a horse thief, Neighbors replied, "I'll take nothing back." In any case, immediately after this tense exchange, Murphy's brother-in-law, Edward Cornett suddenly appeared from behind a building with a double-barreled shotgun. Cornett placed the shotgun close to Neighbors's right side and blasted him with a twelve-buckshot load, burning a hole in his coat. Neighbors collapsed, exclaiming, "Oh, Lord," and died ten minutes later. The federal agent knew Murphy from previous unpleasant encounters but had never met Cornett.[11]

The killing of Robert Neighbors represented a massive failure of state and federal frontier policy. During the antebellum period, Texas and the U.S. government distrusted each other and frequently worked at cross-purposes. Even worse, in numerous crises, officials did nothing, letting problems fester until they finally erupted in violence. Sensing ripe opportunities amid this volatile vortex, a disparate mix of opportunistic demagogues, vigilantes, horse thieves, military officers, frontier settlers, and Native Americans exploited the situation for personal gain.

The problems dated back to the early 1850s, when the United States and Texas were fine-tuning their respective policies toward Native Americans. Since the nation's founding, incessant European American expansion onto tribal homelands had created conflict between the various groups. Previous strategies for dealing with Indians typically included extermination, removal, or making treaties that neither side upheld. In 1848, the U.S. commissioner of Indian affairs, William Medill, proposed a new idea: the establishment of Indian colonies "in which to gather Indians while the whites filled up the country around them." The Bureau of Indian Affairs enthusiastically endorsed Medill's concept of relocating Native Americans onto reservations where the government would protect them and assist them in becoming self-sufficient, Christian farmers. Such reserves would permit continued expansion, minimize clashes, and further "the great work of regenerating the Indian race."[12]

In the fall of 1853, the U.S. secretary of war, Jefferson Davis, suggested to Texas governor Peter Hansbrough Bell that the answer to the state's frontier problems was the creation of a federal reservation system. Bell and the Texas Legislature agreed, and in February 1854, the state allocated land for two reservations. In April 1854, Medill's successor, George W. Manypenny, instructed Robert S. Neighbors and U.S. Army captain Randolph Barnes Marcy to locate and plat two reserves for the various tribes.[13]

During the summer of 1854, Neighbors and Marcy selected two four-league parcels, each totaling 17,714 acres. About 400 Penateka or Southern Comanches settled on one reserve on the Clear Fork of the Brazos River, situated between Marcy's California Emigrant Trail and the U.S. military road from Fort Belknap to Fort Phantom Hill (later used by Butterfield). Four years later, the Overland Mail Company would locate its Clear Fork Station near the southeast corner of the Comanche Indian Reservation. The second Native American reserve was forty miles to the east, south of present-day Graham, Texas, at the junction of Salt Creek and the Brazos River. About 1,100 members of the Waco, Caddo, Anadarko, Tawacano, and Bidais tribes populated the Brazos Indian Reservation.[14]

In February 1856, the Texas Legislature allocated five leagues of land (22,142 acres) for a third reservation, to be located just west of the Pecos River and intended for the state's western tribes, namely, the Lipan and Mescalero Apaches. The purpose of the reservation was to instruct these Native Americans in "the arts of agriculture and civilization . . . whereby the citizens of the State will be relieved from the continued losses sustained by the predatory incursions of said Indians." Officials at the U.S. Department of the Interior, however, never got past the planning stages for this Pecos River reservation.[15]

By September 1855, the federal government had appointed Captain Shapley Prince Ross as Indian agent for the Brazos Indian Reservation and John Robert Baylor as agent for the Comanche Reservation. Both men reported to Neighbors. Charles E. Barnard, who along with his brother George operated several Indian trading posts in central Texas, secured the appointment as sutler and beef contractor for both reservations.[16]

Baylor lasted in his job until March 1857, when Commissioner Manypenny replaced him with Colonel Matthew Leeper. Leeper assumed his new duties at the Comanche Reservation on May 14, 1857. Although Manypenny did not provide an explanation regarding Baylor's dismissal, there had been questions concerning numerous unexplained absences from the Comanche Agency. In addition, Superintendent Neighbors stated that Baylor had been padding his expense account, "having a good time of it" on the government payroll.[17]

Unwilling to address his personal shortcomings, the ex–Indian agent instead blamed Neighbors for his firing. Baylor's deep and bitter well of ill will toward Neighbors sparked a violent chain reaction that resulted in the superintendent's assassination two years later. Although Butterfield employees Cornett and Murphy were responsible for waylaying the Indian superintendent, Baylor had incited the pair to action. More than anyone else, John R. Baylor bears responsibility for sparking the bedlam that subsequently engulfed Belknap and the Texas frontier. Inept state and federal policy certainly contributed to the chaotic conditions, but Baylor's systematic poisoning of local opinion against Neighbors and the two Indian reservations proved the primary catalyst.

Born in Kentucky in 1822 and later a resident of Fayette County, Texas, Baylor was not one to trifle with. Period photographs reveal a threatening intensity in his gaze. Tall, dark, and brooding, he was no stranger to anger and violence. He also possessed considerable charisma and an enormous ego, fancying himself a natural leader. Above all, Baylor was an intimidating and dangerous demagogue.[18]

Although Baylor was insensitive and misguided concerning many aspects of Native American character and culture, several of his misgivings about the Comanche Reserve proved correct. Foremost among these was his belief that some Penatekas on the Comanche Reservation were joining Northern Comanches, from north of the Red River, in committing depredations on Texas's frontier. Baylor also alleged that Reserve Indians were protecting Northern Comanches on their raids and providing them safe harbor.[19]

Unlike the Brazos Reservation Indians, Penateka Comanches were never enthusiastic about making the transition to farming and ranching. Most Penatekas preferred their traditional, independent lifestyle. Only 400 of the tribe's 1,200 members had settled on the Clear Fork. While Native Americans on the Brazos Reserve enjoyed some measure of success in their agricultural pursuits, those on the Comanche Reserve achieved mixed results. As Gary Clayton Anderson notes, "Comanche men were warriors and hunters, not farmers."[20]

One newspaper article accurately summed up the situation concerning the Comanche Reservation. "Whilst very few of the depredations are committed by Comanches from the Reserve," the paper noted, "it must be conceded that there are bad Indians among them, who are in collusion with the wild Indians, and render them assistance in stealing and concealing stolen property and giving them information." The report concluded, however, that "[t]he great body of the Comanches on the Reserve are well disposed and peaceable." Superintendent Neighbors, well aware of the livestock raiding, called on federal and state officials to enforce the laws and punish all marauders, whether from the reservation or elsewhere. Such enforcement, however, was often nonexistent, sporadic, or flawed in its execution.[21]

On January 2, 1856, the U.S. Army established Camp Cooper at the Clear Fork reservation, three and a half miles upstream from the main Comanche village. Troops stationed at Camp Cooper were to safeguard the reservation and chastise hostile Indians. Over at the Brazos River reservation, protection came from soldiers stationed eleven miles upstream at Fort Belknap. The garrison at Belknap provided assistance until February 23, 1859, when the Department of Texas commander, Brevet Major General David E. Twiggs, ordered the post closed and its troops billeted at Camp Cooper.[22]

Army officers at Cooper and Belknap charged with protecting the Indians held mixed opinions regarding the merits of the two reservations. The more skeptical of these, Brevet Major Gabriel René Paul and Captains George Stoneman, Nathan G. Evans, and Newton C. Givens, all proved recalcitrant in providing Superintendent Neighbors the requisite security for the reserves. The four men held strong biases against Native Americans and believed them incapable of adapting to the white man's way. Neighbors specifically accused Paul, Stoneman, and Givens of conspiring "to inflame the public" against the Reserve Indians. The officers also had personal motives that influenced their conduct: Paul and Givens, in particular, had started cattle ranching as a lucrative sideline to military service. These military men, along with some white settlers in the region, covetously eyed the choice riverfront acreage within the two reservations. If for some reason the Indians were to leave the reserves, the State of Texas would sell the vacant land.[23]

During 1856, public support was largely in favor of the colonizing efforts taking place on the reservations. This goodwill, however, began to erode during 1857, most notably after John Baylor's dismissal in the month of March. Throughout the remainder of 1857, Baylor spent much of his time trying to inflame public sentiment against the Reserve Indians and Neighbors. Gradually, the former Indian agent's vindictive vendetta began paying dividends. By December, Texas governor

Hardin Richard Runnels (1857–59) had received petitions from citizens in several counties calling for Neighbors's removal.[24]

Toward the end of 1857, there was a noticeable increase in the number of Indian raids on Texas's northern frontier, which only reinforced the arguments of Neighbors's critics. The fact that it was not Reserve Indians but "wild" tribes based north of the Red River who were committing most of the depredations was lost upon frontier settlers, who could not distinguish between different bands of Native Americans. To many whites, all Indians looked the same. For some time, Neighbors, Governor Runnels, the Texas Legislature, and officers in the U.S. Army had all been asking the federal government to establish a military outpost in the Wichita Mountains north of the Red River to keep an eye on the tribes and check their raids into Texas. While federal officials agreed with the idea, because of the expense involved, they deferred establishment of a permanent installation near the Wichitas until January 1869.[25]

With the increased raids upon the frontier, the reservations' viability began unraveling in 1858, as Baylor's smear campaign gathered momentum and attracted new converts. These included U.S. Army captain Newton Curd Givens, Texas Ranger lieutenant Allison Nelson, and Oliver Loving (later partner of Charles Goodnight). At a January meeting on the Clear Fork, Baylor and his associates penned three documents: a petition and two letters. The first item, a petition to Comanche agent Leeper, bore the signatures of twenty-eight citizens. The group threatened Leeper that "if there is a man killed on this river and there is the least proof that it was done by the Reserve Indians, that we will attack the reserve with a sufficient force to break it up, regardless of the consequences." A second document from this gathering, a letter addressed to Captain Givens and endorsed by four of the attendees, allegedly offered proof of Reserve Indians' guilt in livestock raids. A third item, inked by several others at the meeting, was a letter to Governor Runnels requesting him to lobby the federal government for Superintendent Neighbors's removal.[26]

James H. Swindells, a physician at Belknap, attended the Clear Fork meeting. In a subsequent letter to Neighbors, Swindells said that he had heretofore assumed that Baylor was an honorable gentleman. After listening to Baylor's speech to the gathering about alleged raids by Reserve Indians, the doctor expressed amazement. "I could not believe that he would tell a deliberate falsehood," he said. "[H]is statements were made with so confident an air, that it carried conviction to all, or nearly all." Swindells continued, "When he said he was authorized to sign certain men's names [on the above three documents] he lied." The doctor said that the gathering proved most instructive, as "the people have been enlightened as to the real character of Baylor."[27]

In a letter to the *Dallas Herald*, Agent Leeper responded to the first document, the threatening petition addressed to him. Leeper said, "[T]he law makes it my imperative duty to expose the nefarious designs of Captain Baylor." Leeper enclosed a deposition from three men whose names were on the petition, stating that their signatures were forged. Next, a fourth person came forward, complaining that he had never signed the second document, the letter detailing alleged Reserve Indian raids, and that his signature was counterfeit. Finally, two additional complainants filed formal depositions stating that they had not signed the third document, the letter to Runnels calling for Neighbors's dismissal. They continued, "[N]or did we authorize anyone to sign our names, and we pronounce the signatures or signing of our names to said document a base forgery."[28]

In a letter to his superior addressing the falsified petition and letters, Superintendent Neighbors noted that much of the hostility toward the reservations and Indian agents was the work of "designing persons." Foremost among these was Baylor. In addition to forging documents, Baylor conspired to manufacture evidence implicating the Reserve Indians. Baylor showed two Texas Rangers a quiver containing authentic Comanche-made arrows, which he suggested they shoot into his neighbor's livestock. Afterward, they would "make trails and drop arrows in the direction of the [Comanche] agency, [so] that it would be charged to the Reserve Comanches."[29]

Baylor responded to the damning evidence against him in his usual fashion, by threatening to harm those who exposed his deceitful and duplicitous nature. To Leeper he replied, "I shall be very glad to terminate the difficulty between us by a resort to some more formidable weapon than the pen." Next, Baylor issued a cryptically veiled threat against Neighbors's well-being, stating, "The citizens of the frontier have determined that should the arduous duty performed by the illustrious Superintendent cause his premature death, they will place a stone to mark the spot where he lies, and inscribe on it *vive le humbug*."[30]

In April 1858, frontier tensions spiked sharply after the particularly brutal massacre of seven white settlers in Jack County. In the latter half of that month, a group of four white men and twenty Indians (some of them Kickapoos) butchered Mr. and Mrs. James B. Cambern and three of their sons, along with their neighbors, Mr. and Mrs. Tom Mason. The attack occurred in Lost Valley, near present-day Jermyn, Texas. The leader of the raiding party was a white man with red hair. Before leaving, the gang took $500 to $600 in gold from the Cambern home. Around this same time, almost one hundred horses disappeared in a "clean sweep . . . in and about Belknap." Locals suspected that the Cambern-Mason killers were involved in the livestock losses.[31]

Some accounts of the massacre mention only Indians, omitting reference to the Anglo participants. The record shows that after the murders the Indians rode northwest toward the Red River with the stolen livestock while the white men fled south toward the Hill Country. The warriors escaped, but in May 1858 a posse that included Oliver and J. C. Loving caught the four outlaws in Lampasas County and brought them back to Jacksboro. There, young Mary Cambern, who had survived the bloodshed, identified the red-haired leader as one of the attackers.[32]

Baylor and his associates quickly capitalized on the Jack County massacre by stoking settlers' anxieties. John Shirley, assistant sutler at the Comanche Agency, reported, "After the outrages a few unprincipled but designing men exerted all their influence to collect a mob and make a descent on the Comanche Agency." The commander of Fort Belknap, Captain Richard W. Johnson, unlike some of his fellow officers, resolved to protect the Reserve Indians and their agents. Johnson informed the mob that if they made a move to attack the reserve his troops would resist them. Facing armed opposition, the vigilantes temporarily stood down, biding their time until a more advantageous opportunity to break up the reservations presented itself.[33]

Texas Ranger captain John Salmon "Rip" Ford, no admirer of Baylor and his ilk, visited the Texas reservations in April 1858 and recorded his impressions. In a letter to Governor Runnels, he wrote, "I should view any combination of circumstances which tended towards the breaking up of this reserve as a serious misfortune to the state of Texas, and a calamity." The Ranger captain, while a firm believer in punishing raiding warriors, also advocated pursuing a balanced policy toward Native Americans. In Ford's nineteenth-century worldview, Indians were humans too, "and entitled to consideration as such, and when they stand out and ask to be relieved from the dogs of barbarism it is a Christian duty in us to extend them a helping hand."[34]

Unable to attack the reservations, John Baylor and his group doubled down in their campaign against Superintendent Neighbors. Baylor's associate, Ranger lieutenant Allison Nelson, told Ford that there were men after Neighbors "who will hurt him, he will be removed." Nelson's threat was not an isolated incident. Down in Waco, Captain J. M. Smith of the Rifle Rangers wrote to Neighbors "as a friend *and a Mason*," warning him that vigilantes were designing to waylay both Neighbors and the Brazos Reserve agent, Shapley Ross, stating that the mob would "rather kill you two than the Indians." Neighbors got the message. He informed his superiors in Washington that he and his agents had armed themselves because "a lawless class of citizens" intended to harm them and that it had now become "unsafe to travel the roads."[35]

In tandem with their threats, Baylor's group mailed numerous letters and petitions to various federal officials calling for Neighbors's dismissal. One of these was from Allison Nelson, who wrote U.S. president James Buchanan, "The very large majority of the frontier population are against the gross abuse of power on the part of your agent." Another communication was from T. C. Alexander, of Meridian, Texas, who asked Buchanan to remove the superintendent and to replace him with Nelson. Alexander felt that "R. S. Neighbors has been remiss in his duties." Baylor also threw his support behind Nelson, writing, "I want Nelson in the place of Neighbors and will do all in my power to aid him." Responding to the barrage of complaints, U.S. secretary of the interior Jacob Thompson in August 1858 appointed Thomas Hawkins of Lexington, Kentucky, to investigate the veracity of the charges leveled against Neighbors and his subordinates.[36]

The federal investigation commenced in the fall of 1858. The results proved most illuminating. After journeying to the Texas frontier, Hawkins requested that the complainants meet with him and voice their concerns in person. Few took him up on his offer. The irony of their absence was not lost upon the federal investigator. He reported, "Thus it will be perceived that most of the persons for whose convenience and in redress of whose alleged grievances a special agent has been sent thousands of miles decline to avail themselves of the opportunity of pouring their complaints into the very ear, so to speak, of the government itself."[37]

Ultimately, Hawkins's final report reflected "a mass of testimony highly favorable" to Neighbors, Ross, Leeper, and the two reserves. A portion of this testimony came from Thomas Lambshead, Butterfield overseer and manager of the company's Texas stations at Mountain Pass and Valley Creek. Writing from his Clear Fork Ranch, Lambshead said that he supported both Neighbors and the reservations. Additional evidence collected from Rip Ford and Ranger lieutenant Edward Burleson proved particularly damning to the Baylor mob. In a sworn affidavit, Ford recalled a conversation with Allison Nelson in which Nelson offered to fabricate evidence against the Reserve Indians. Ford came to see Nelson as someone "endeavoring to subserve his own ends" and someone who "thought it necessary to play a double part to effect his object." Burleson's testimony corroborated Ford's statements. Burleson recalled that Ford had ordered all of his officers to take no part in the controversy surrounding Neighbors and the reservations. Nelson, however, refused to follow orders, and "he consulted with Captain Baylor and seemed to take an interest against the [Indian] agents." Regarding Neighbors's conduct as superintendent of Indian affairs in Texas, Ford said, "The ordeal through which Major Neighbors has passed endorses him. He needs no commendation from any quarter."[38]

Following the conclusion of Hawkins's investigation, President Buchanan in April 1859 reappointed Neighbors as superintendent and Leeper and Ross as his agents. The U.S. Senate confirmed all three appointments. Baylor, Nelson, and their associates' campaign against Neighbors and the Indian reservations had failed. The reappointments rendered Baylor's group apoplectic. In mid-April, Baylor and Nelson, along with Oliver Loving and ten others, sent a threatening message to the three federal Indian agents. "Having learned that you have lately been reappointed," the group wrote, "we take this to make known to you our unqualified disapprobation of your course as agents and to demand your immediate resignations."[39]

After their slanderous vendetta proved unsuccessful in getting rid of Neighbors and the Texas reservations, Baylor and his associates increasingly resorted to violence to achieve their ends. Recent additions to this vigilante mob included Peter Garland, who commanded an unofficial frontier guard based out of Erath County. At daylight on December 27, 1858, Garland and twenty men attacked a group of twenty-seven friendly reservation Indians encamped in Palo Pinto County, a few miles from the Brazos Reserve. The Indian party, led by Choctaw Tom, had been hunting for game in the region for several weeks and had a signed permit from Agent Shapley Ross. Choctaw Tom, a highly regarded resident of Texas for many years, had served as Texas president Sam Houston's interpreter in 1843. In their bloody onslaught, Garland's men massacred seven Indians, including three women. Two other women and three children were critically wounded. One of the victims was Choctaw Tom's wife.[40]

Garland's attack on Choctaw Tom's hunting party and the ensuing fallout proved a pivotal turning point in Texas's frontier history and doomed any chance of success for the Brazos and Comanche Reserves. Rancher Charles Goodnight, an occasional member of the Baylor gang, judged the massacre as a "dirty piece of business. They just wanted to be killing some Indians." Rip Ford, in a letter to Governor Runnels the day after the attack, said, "What this may portend I can not say. There appears to be a determination in certain quarters on the frontier to make war indiscriminately on the Reserve Indians. This may be the beginning." Ford's closing comments proved prescient. "I am disposed," he wrote, "to view the affair as very serious indeed and know not where it may stop." In another report on the massacre, respected frontiersman George Bernard Erath (namesake of Erath County) observed, "It is impossible to convince a respectable minority of the settlers of the differences of disposition and friendly relations" of various Native American tribes.[41]

The events following the December 1858 massacre ushered in one of the more bleak periods in Texas's nineteenth-century history. The marked breakdown of law and order combined with a dearth of state and federal leadership left an embarrassing black mark upon the Lone Star legacy. On January 15, 1859, Robert Neighbors traveled to Waco and filed a formal written complaint against Peter Garland and his accomplices with state district judge Nicholas William Battle. Two days later, Battle reported that the accused men defiantly "stated that they had organized and that no peace officer could arrest them." Information received from Palo Pinto County warned that Oliver Loving was raising a company of men to protect Garland and his gang and that if officials took them into custody, Loving would free them and then "make a general massacre of the [Reserve] Indians." The *Dallas Herald* noted, "Captain Garland and party who killed the Reserve Indians, . . . far from submitting, . . . defy the civil authorities and laugh the law to scorn." Aptly summing up the situation on Texas's frontier, the newspaper observed that "we shall see ere long which is supreme, the law of the country, or the law of mobs."[42]

Judge Battle, one of the few courageous persons involved in this matter, was not intimidated and issued arrest warrants for the group. Facing the prospect of taking the accused into custody, the Palo Pinto County sheriff indicated that he could not and the Erath County sheriff said that he would not. With this evident breakdown of county law enforcement, Battle then deputized Ranger captain Rip Ford, directing him to arrest Garland and his gang. On February 11, Governor Runnels ordered Ford to cooperate with the judicial authority, "giving all the aid in [his] power," and instructing him that he "was justified in the use of all lawful means to effect the object." Runnels stated, "The right of civil authorities to call on the military when resistance is made to due process of the laws cannot be questioned."[43]

On March 3, Runnels repeated his instructions to Ford, directing him to promptly render assistance should he be called upon to help arrest Garland and his men. Runnels then forwarded his note to Ford on to Judge Battle in Waco, saying, "You will see that the military are at your command whenever its services may be found necessary to the execution of the law." Instead of arresting Garland, however, Ford dissembled, issuing carefully parsed reports to the governor justifying his inaction. Ultimately, rather than risking an armed confrontation with Garland's gang, the captain decided to take his Ranger company on a scout for Indians. Ford's remarkable shirking of duty during this crisis represents the nadir of his decades-long, storied public service to Texas.[44]

It soon became clear that no arrests were forthcoming. Baylor, Nelson, Garland, and other vigilantes interpreted these developments as a green light for their activities. It was now open season on the Reserve Indians. In mid-March, news began circulating in the frontier counties of an impending massed attack upon the two reservations. Governor Runnels issued a proclamation putting Baylor's group on notice: "It would be idle and indeed foolish to expect that the officers of the law will wink at such offenses or fail to use its strong arm" to protect the reserves. The governor warned that "the state will use its whole force in bringing offenders to justice."[45]

In truth, however, the State of Texas was not going to protect the inhabitants of the Brazos and Comanche Reservations. Less than a week after issuing his proclamation, Governor Runnels was following Ford's lead and ducking his responsibilities as the state's chief executive. In a letter to General Twiggs, commander of the Department of Texas, Runnels stated, "I have to say I do not after most mature reflection consider it incumbent on the authorities of Texas to furnish means for protection on Indians or Indian territory over which the U.S. Government has exclusive jurisdiction." Twiggs, however, was having none of it, and he immediately shifted responsibility back onto Runnels and Texas authorities. Twiggs's adjutant told the governor that the general considered it "purely a civil matter with which he has nothing to do."[46]

Shortly after his exchange of letters with Runnels, General Twiggs softened his position somewhat and ordered a company of infantry to the Brazos Reserve, "[h]oping their presence will prevent any collision between the Indians and citizens." Twiggs, however, still held firm to his opinion that since "those Indians are within the State and the difficulty with them with the citizens of Texas, I do not think the U.S. troops should interfere in the matter." Despite the general's views, acting secretary of war William Drinkard instructed him to ensure that he had sufficient forces to protect both reservations and that their size was "large enough to overawe and prevent extreme measures."[47]

The additional federal troops arrived on the North Texas frontier just in time. In the last week of March 1859, a hundred men assembled at Rock Creek, fifteen miles below the Brazos Reserve, and another thirty-five gathered at Jameson Peaks in Eastland County. The "lawless band of marauders" planned to unite and attack the Brazos Reservation but found their objective blocked by Captain John Haskell King's First Infantry troops and an artillery piece. Reports indicated that Baylor was part of the mob.[48]

Faced with armed opposition, the vigilantes disbanded, but only temporarily. They vowed to return in six weeks and try again. By early May, rumors of another attempt were percolating throughout area communities. George Barnard, the sutler at both reserves, warned the governor that Baylor and his associates were "making the most inflammatory speeches . . . based upon anything else than the truth." Barnard told Runnels that the group had "the destruction of the reserve at heart and more particularly the killing of Major Neighbors, Captain Ross, and every other white man connected with the reserve." In addition, Baylor, Nelson, Garland, and their accomplices were "offering a reward for Neighbors and Ross's scalps."[49]

That same week, in a firm rebuke of Neighbors and the Texas reservations, a grand jury on May 5 declined to indict Peter Garland and his men for the December 1858 massacre of Choctaw Tom's party. Instead, members of the jury declared that the Indian reserves were "an intolerable nuisance" and that local citizens would "take up arms against the Reserve Indians." With grand juries sanctioning violence and even murder, talk of killing the Indians and their agents was no longer an empty threat. Baylor and his mob were deadly serious, and they had many like-minded allies. By the spring of 1859, some of these allies included Butterfield employees Edward Cornett, Patrick Murphy, and Berry Lewis Ham, along with Jack County tax assessor-collector Harris A. Hamner.[50]

On May 7, two days after the grand jury declined to indict the murderers of Choctaw Tom's party, fifteen whites attacked seven friendly Caddo Indians from the Brazos Reserve, one of who was a federal courier, delivering communications from Fort Arbuckle, Indian Territory, to the Brazos Reservation. The assault occurred in Young County, thirteen miles northeast of the reserve, near the intersection of the overland road and Turtle Hole Creek. The Anglo vigilantes, an ad hoc group calling themselves the Jacksboro Rangers, fired a volley at the Native Americans, who promptly spurred their mounts. Six of the seven friendly Indians managed to escape, but the pursuers cornered the seventh, the federal courier, a man named Fox, who was riding a slow horse. The white men then took Fox to Murphy's Station, the Butterfield stage stop a half mile distant. There station manager Patrick Murphy and the assembled mob interrogated Fox, who showed them his signed courier pass from federal Indian agent Samuel A. Blain at Fort Arbuckle.[51]

Next, the thugs ransacked Fox's courier bag, opening sealed communications between federal agencies. After reading the letters, they grabbed Fox, mounted their horses, and continued east along the overland road toward Jacksboro. After crossing the Young-Jack County line, the outlaws shot their captive in the chest, scalped him, took his personal belongings, and left him for dead a short distance from the Butterfield Road. Agent Ross of the Brazos Reserve noted, "The principle [sic] object the whites seem to have had in attacking the Indian was plunder. They succeeded in getting two guns, some blankets, and six ponies, . . . [and] they carried off the papers sent to me from Fort Arbuckle."[52]

After learning of the Jacksboro Rangers' assault on the seven Indians near Murphy's Station, army lieutenant William Burnet (son of former Texas president David G. Burnet), along with two soldiers and a hundred friendly Indians, marched from the Brazos Agency to investigate. Burnet's party rode to Murphy's Station, interrogated the Butterfield employees there, and rode another twelve miles along the overland road to the place where, just before sunset, they found Fox's corpse. After attending to the body, Burnet traveled another eight miles to Ham Spring, home of Berry Ham, Butterfield overseer and manager of Jacksboro and Fishpond Stations. When questioned by the lieutenant, Ham said that Fox's killers had stopped by just before sundown. One of the men was proudly displaying the dead Caddo's scalp from his saddle horn.[53]

After talking to Ham, Burnet and the Indians rode another five miles to Jacksboro but were unable to locate the outlaws. Two men who had passed by Ham's while Burnet was there had ridden ahead and forewarned the Jacksboro residents. When questioned by the lieutenant, the locals, many of them sympathetic to Baylor, stated they had neither seen nor heard of the killers. Upon learning this, many of the young Native Americans in Burnet's party became enraged. The warriors wanted to attack the town and exact revenge for the lawless attack on Fox's group, "but the Chief and the older men . . . restrained them." Failing in their mission to apprehend the killers, Burnet's posse returned to the Brazos Reserve.[54]

The image of a band of Indians and federal soldiers riding into Jacksboro and interrogating locals incensed Baylor's supporters. To them, the "reprehensible" action "was an outrage of the most dangerous and insulting character, unparalleled, perhaps" in the history of Texas or any other state. Retribution was not long in coming. Baylor and his followers tried to waylay Old Tall Tree, an Indian from the Comanche Reservation, but their attempt proved unsuccessful. The mob, undeterred by this minor setback, only redoubled their efforts. "The country is exceedingly disturbed by lawless rabble," Comanche agent Leeper reported. "They threaten the Indians as well as the white persons in any connection with the Indian service with extermination."[55]

Five days after the brutal murder of the federal Indian courier, Superintendent Neighbors notified his superiors in Washington that despite making every appeal possible to Governor Runnels for assistance, Runnels had "thus far taken no measures to preserve order on the frontier or control the citizens." Because the governor had abdicated his executive responsibilities, lawlessness was pervasive throughout the region. Every frontier county near the reserves was "raising and arming a band of lawless men who term themselves Rangers," who would murder "every Indian they meet, and I fully believe they would murder the [Indian] agents if they had an opportunity."[56]

By the latter part of the month, John Baylor had assembled a group of 250 men and was renewing his plan to attack the Reserve Indians. On the morning of May 23, the lawless horde marched to the Brazos Reserve and confronted the federal troops massed there to protect the reservation and its occupants. After several parlays with the army's commanding officer, it became clear to the vigilantes that the soldiers would not stand down. Rather than risk significant casualties, Baylor withdrew to Marlin's Ranch, eight miles west of the reservation. As the vigilantes left, they grabbed an old Indian, "tied a rope around his neck and then . . . killed and scalped their prisoner." Fifty to sixty Reserve Indians followed the mob to the ranch, exchanging gunfire throughout the eight-mile trip. Once at the ranch, Baylor and his men took refuge in the buildings. One of the Anadarko Indian chiefs, Jim Pock Mark, rode up and openly challenged Baylor to come out and engage him in one-on-one combat. The vigilante leader declined. The firefight continued until sundown, when the warriors finally withdrew to their reservation. Baylor lost two men in the battle, with another three wounded, while the Indians had five wounded and two killed, including the old man lynched by the mob.[57]

As in the case of Peter Garland and the massacre of Choctaw Tom's party, John Baylor would face no consequences for his group's lawless and bloody actions. With the collapse of law and order along Texas's northern frontier, a reign of terror ensued. U.S. Army major George Thomas reported, "All civil authority seems to be at an end. The May term of the District Court of Young County could not be held, the judge and officers fearing to travel through this excited district." Parson Tackett, a Methodist circuit preacher, reported that local residents were intimidated after being threatened by the mob not "to testify in a court of justice against the offenders." Writing to the U.S. district judge in Austin, Neighbors said that "the terror engendered by the imposing force mustered" by Baylor, Nelson, and Hamner had "made every citizen in this county afraid to speak or testify." The Indian superintendent asked the judge to initiate action that would "lead to the arrest and trial of this murderous party under John R. Baylor."[58]

Nine days after the attack on the Brazos Reserve, General Twiggs urgently requested Governor Runnels to "take immediate steps to have Mr. Baylor and his accomplices arrested" to avoid "further outrages upon Indians." Runnels, however, took no action to apprehend Baylor or his men, causing Neighbors to lament, "It is unfortunate at this time that we have in the state of Texas a governor who appears to be afraid to enforce the laws of the state, to arrest criminals or to endeavor to put down a mob." Once again, the message was loud and clear to the lawless element terrorizing the region—they could murder friendly Indians with impunity. The State of Texas would not investigate the crimes or enforce its laws. Both Runnels and his successor, Sam Houston, understood that arresting vigilante killers such as Garland and Baylor risked igniting a violent civil war among frontier citizens. B. A. Fauntleroy of Palo Pinto spoke for many residents when he said, "Whenever Capt. Baylor is killed there will be open war and bloodshed . . . [and people] will surely avenge his death."[59]

The federal government deserved its share of the blame for the tragic events unfolding on Texas's northern frontier. Fourteen months earlier, in March 1858, Superintendent Neighbors had asked the Bureau of Indian Affairs and the Department of the Interior to move the Reserve Indians north of the Red River to Indian Territory as soon as possible to avoid further violent collisions with lawless frontier elements. Federal officials did nothing until events forced them to take action. In the summer of 1859, they finally ordered the closure of the two reservations. Meanwhile, Governor Runnels and General Twiggs were still each trying to assign responsibility for protecting the reservations to the other. In early June, Runnels wrote Twiggs, "I cannot concur as expressed by you that this is 'eminently a state matter.'" Twiggs, for his part, said, "The outrages lately perpetrated . . . were the acts of armed bodies of citizens organized within the limits of Texas and who are now at large in the state and amenable to her laws."[60]

Eventually Runnels took action. In early June, he ordered the Texas Rangers to the frontier, to act as a buffer between the reservations and the vigilantes until the Indians' removal to Indian Territory. Some of these Rangers, under the command of the conceited Captain John Henry Brown, rather than acting with balance and restraint, seemed anxious to have a confrontation with the Native Americans. Superintendent Neighbors warned Brown that should his men interfere with Indians gathering their livestock, as authorized by their agents, that Brown "alone must be responsible for the consequences" if violence resulted. The arrogant Brown, obviously biased against the reservations, was clearly not the best person to charge with their protection. Brown confided to the governor that the reserves were "little better than a den of thieves. As to the pretended civilization of the Indians or any advance in that direction, since their location on the reserve[,] it is simply and palpably untrue."[61]

During the tense weeks leading up to the Indian removal, relations between Neighbors and Brown reached the breaking point. The Ranger captain complained to the governor, "The conduct of Major Neighbors towards me . . . has convinced me that he is a bad and base man." In an insulting letter to Neighbors, Brown wrote, "I have to say that I regret to see an old citizen of Texas who has filled so many offices under the Republic and State . . . descend to personalities which I regard with contempt." The Indian superintendent responded to Brown that he would soon be leaving his federal job and entering private life. As a citizen of Texas, Neighbors reserved the right to defend himself "at the proper time and manner as such against the unjust attacks you appear determined to continue to make upon me."[62]

Matters worsened on July 23, 1859, when Butterfield employee Patrick Murphy encountered three Waco Indians from the Brazos Reserve butchering one of his cows near Murphy's Station. Murphy and a man named Stewart charged the trio with guns blazing. One of the Wacos fell dead while the other two escaped. The following day, July 24, two soldiers and some Indians from the reservation visited Murphy's Station in search of the three missing Wacos. During a visit of the station grounds, the searchers discovered the other two Wacos hiding near Murphy's cow pen. Murphy stated that they were "seeking an opportunity to murder me." He may have been right. With the May 7 murder of the Indian courier, Fox, and the July 23 shooting of the Waco, Murphy's Station and its occupants had acquired an unsavory reputation among Native Americans. Within a month's time, Murphy lost five horses and three cows to thieves.[63]

July 24 was a day punctuated by gunfire. Fifty miles west of Murphy's, on the Clear Fork of the Brazos, some of Brown's Rangers got into a firefight with Indians from the Comanche Reservation. Agent Leeper contained the situation before it escalated further. Six days later, on July 30, the long-awaited Indian removal finally began. Leeper abandoned the Comanche Reserve in Throckmorton County and marched north with his charges to their new home in Indian Territory. The following day, August 1, Agent Ross and Superintendent Neighbors left the Brazos

Reserve in neighboring Young County, en route to the Red River. With Baylor's group still threatening to attack the Reserve Indians wherever possible, the U.S. Army provided the Indian agents with two companies of infantry and two companies of cavalry as escort for the trip north. On August 8, 1859, Neighbors and the Native Americans crossed the Red River and entered Indian Territory. With their exodus concluded, the superintendent exclaimed, "I have this day crossed all the Indians out of the heathen land of 'Texas' and am now 'out of the land of the philistines.'"[64]

Greatly relieved to see the Indians safe, Neighbors left Indian Territory to rejoin his family in San Antonio. By the night of September 13, Leeper and Neighbors were back in Texas, encamped on the banks of the Brazos River. Deep in the Cross Timbers, members of Baylor's vigilante group, including Allison Nelson, Harris Hamner, Peter Garland, Patrick Murphy, and Edward Cornett, all nursed serious grudges against Neighbors and wished him bodily harm. A central Texas newspaper had reported that Baylor publicly threatened to hang Neighbors.[65]

Well aware that his life was in danger, Neighbors nonetheless neglected taking appropriate precautions. On the morning of September 14, he left Leeper in camp and walked alone into Belknap to wrap up some unfinished paperwork. There he encountered Patrick Murphy and Edward Cornett, armed with pistol and shotgun. Minutes later, he lay dead in the dirt street. Army lieutenant William Burnet reported, "The 'Baylor Party' have murdered Major Neighbors[;] . . . the assassination . . . was a most foul and cowardly murder." Patrick Murphy, in a pathetic attempt to shield Cornett, claimed that "some one, (I know not who, but suppose a friend of mine, to prevent my being killed) shot . . . Neighbors." Before making this ludicrous statement, Murphy had posted a $1,000 bond for this "unknown" murderer, namely, Edward Cornett. The thirty-year-old Cornett remained free on Murphy's guarantee for more than nine months, until May 1860, when irresolute authorities finally indicted him for Neighbors's murder. State and county officials had been inexplicably slow to prosecute the high-profile case of the slain federal superintendent, perhaps fearing retribution from Baylor's vigilantes or perhaps because Neighbors had been perceived as an "Indian lover."[66]

Neighbors's removal of the reservation Indians did not stop the chronic raiding in North Texas. Depredations by Comanches and Kickapoos from north of the Red River continued. Even before the removal, however, it became clear that many of the attacks were the handiwork not just of Native Americans but also of white horse thieves. There is overwhelming evidence that a professional gang of Anglo rustlers masquerading as Indians committed numerous crimes along the Texas frontier from 1858 to 1861. The gang's lawless activities included livestock rustling, arson, murder, and kidnapping. Their territory included Colorado, Kansas,

Arkansas, Indian Territory, and Texas. While Kickapoos occasionally cooperated with the white outlaws, Comanches did not.[67]

A September 1858 newspaper article observed, "The existence of a band of robbers in this State, extending across it and into . . . Indian Territory . . . is doubted by few. These scoundrels are in league with the Indians." The report cited the robbery and murder of the wealthy Cambern family in Jack County by white outlaws and their Kickapoo confederates a few months earlier. During this same month, Anglo outlaws stole forty horses from the Brazos Indian Reservation. Pursuers of the thieves "discovered tracks of shod horses on the trail." Seasoned Texas frontiersmen knew that Comanches, both on the reservation and off, did not shoe their mounts.[68]

Over time, the broad scope of the gang's operations came into focus. In June 1858, Ranger captain Rip Ford wrote the governor that white traders north of the Red River were involved in a "nefarious and unholy traffic" with Native American tribes, freely swapping "arms, ammunition, provisions, etc. to the Indians for horses plundered from the people of Texas." One destination for the stolen livestock was Kansas. Another was Bent's New Fort on the Arkansas River (in present-day Colorado). U.S. Indian agent Samuel Blain reported that "lawless white men" living in Indian country north of the Red River were causing much of the trouble and assisting depredating Native Americans in disposing of stolen livestock. Some of these men were jayhawkers who had been recent participants in the "Bleeding Kansas" vigilante violence between proslavery and antislavery factions.[69]

In a May 1860 letter to the U.S. commissioner of Indian affairs, federal Indian agent Matthew Leeper said, "It is the confident belief of many officers of the Army on the frontier . . . that these depredations are the work of a regularly constituted band of thieves and robbers, composed principally of white men clothed with the ordinary trappings of Indians." Leeper noted that the gang's trails "have often been followed and they invariably lead in the direction of Bent's Fort on the Arkansas River." As confirmation of its contents, Leeper's letter bore the endorsements of four army captains and three lieutenants stationed at Fort Cobb, Indian Territory (in present-day Caddo County, Oklahoma).[70]

Comanche warriors raiding in Texas also traded on the Arkansas River and in New Mexico. In December 1859, Samuel B. Watrous of La Junta, New Mexico, reported that "a large portion of the stock stolen from Texas is purchased by traders from New Mexico who penetrate nearly to the frontier settlements of Texas, to supply these Indians with everything they need." Watrous observed that local authorities were well aware of this illicit activity but did nothing to stop it: "This trade is carried on openly and extensively, . . . Comanches come into our settlements and boast of the outrages committed in Texas." During his decade at La

Junta, Watrous had frequently witnessed Comanches bartering with comanchero traders.[71]

Some of these comancheros were Hispanics from the frontier settlements, while others were Native Americans from New Mexico's pueblos, including Santo Domingo, Tesuque, and Santa Clara. The Pueblo Indians and Hispanics had a long trading relationship with the Comanches, dating back more than a century. Several prominent New Mexico merchants bankrolled the comancheros, providing them with trade goods (including the latest firearms), which were then exchanged for stolen livestock. Some of these same merchants held federal contracts to provide the U.S. military with horses, mules, and cattle. Over time, purloined animals from the Texas frontier began appearing in army corrals.[72]

State and federal troops investigating livestock rustling on the Texas frontier reported that several of the thieves' trails led northwest toward the Double Mountains and New Mexico. Comanches traveling to New Mexico from Texas with their stolen herds used several paths. From the 1850s to the 1880s, raiding warriors, comancheros, and occasionally white outlaws used one route from Lubbock County to the Pecos River. An 1864 map published by the U.S. army was one of the first to document this clandestine road's existence. A second Comanche trail led from Borden County to the Texas state line, where it merged with the Lubbock County route and continued on to the Pecos River. Some Indians also utilized a third trail, which ran northwest from present-day Quitaque, Texas, to the Fort Smith–Santa Fe Road on the Canadian River and then westward to the state line and on to New Mexico.[73]

In the summer of 1860, officers at Hatch's Ranch near Las Vegas, New Mexico, detained some Pueblo Indians whom they suspected of being comancheros. Upon investigation, the officers learned that the Tesuque and Santa Clara Indians carried signed passes from U.S. Pueblo Indian agent Silas F. Kendrick permitting them to trade with the Comanches. The commander of the Department of New Mexico, Colonel Thomas Turner Fauntleroy of the First Dragoons, reported that in return for providing the comancheros with "mules and horses stolen from citizens of the United States and Texas," the Indians received "supplies of ammunition and information . . . [on the] movement of the troops." Here then, was one branch of the federal government, the U.S. Army, trying to interdict the Comanche trade at the same time another branch, the Bureau of Indian Affairs, was enabling it.[74]

Comanches traveling into New Mexico from Texas's South Plains, Canadian River, and Panhandle regions often exhibited a bold and arrogant attitude. The Native Americans understood that the U.S. Army's limited presence in Texas and New Mexico precluded any effective threat to their established raiding and trading patterns. Officers at Hatch's Ranch noted that, despite repeated warnings, the Comanches visited Hispanic towns on New Mexico's eastern edge of settlement whenever they pleased. Army threats did not intimidate the Plains warriors. Matters came to a head in the second half of 1860, when several groups from the tribe journeyed to eastern New Mexico to trade with local comancheros.[75]

On July 23, a hundred well-mounted Comanches sauntered into Hatch's Ranch. When the warriors kept advancing, fifty men from the Eighth Infantry opened fire, killing three or four Indians and wounding several others. The remaining Indians quickly left town. Three months later, on October 3, another group of a hundred Comanches rode into Chaperito, three miles from Hatch's Ranch. The Indians leisurely unsaddled and proceeded to spread out their baggage on the town plaza. With only twenty-five men to oppose the Native Americans and most of these green recruits, Captain E. B. Holloway (also of the Eighth Infantry), charged the Comanches. The Indians took cover in some nearby buildings and commenced shooting at the soldiers. Staying out the warriors' range of fire, Holloway and his men captured the Comanches' entire herd of fifty-one animals. Next, they collected the Indians' saddles and baggage, which they burned on the town square.[76]

Although temporarily chastened, the Comanches did not stop trading Texas livestock with the comancheros. From 1858 to 1861, the U.S. Army and the Texas Rangers inflicted serious losses upon various bands of Comanches in New Mexico, Texas, and Indian Territory, but they lacked sufficient forces to follow up with a sustained, coordinated campaign throughout the southern plains that would overwhelm the entire tribe. In fact, neither side possessed the requisite military might to decisively settle the conflict, and the situation remained stalemated until after the Civil War.

During the antebellum period, Comanches, Kickapoos, and white rustlers enjoyed considerable success in their raids on Texas settlements. Among the Anglo horse thieves, however, recurring mistrust threatened to erode that success. In September 1858, some of these cutthroats had a falling-out at Fort Belknap and resorted to gunplay. A report on the fracas noted that a man named Herrington threatened "to make disclosures upon certain parties—he is attacked, but uses a six shooter a little too well to suit his assailant or assailants—one is wounded—the balance leave, they say . . . for Indian Territory." The following month, several highwaymen ambushed John Edmonson on the Butterfield Road near Murphy's Station. Edmonson, who had allegedly assisted in disposing of the gang's stolen livestock, "was shot in the side and arm, and his throat cut, besides being scalped. Notwithstanding the latter sign, it is believed by everyone here that he was killed by a white man."[77]

Arrests by local law enforcement officials proved ineffective in stemming the lawlessness. In December 1858, three accused rustlers escaped from the Young County Jail at Belknap. One of the trio, Hunter, was recaptured after "a well contested foot race" with the jailor, a man named Beard, but the other two, Copeland

and Williams, got away. A subsequent investigation revealed that someone on the outside had smuggled a file into the Belknap jail, which the prisoners then used to file off "the heavy irons with which they were manacled." A newspaper report noted that even the best of jails could not hold horse thieves and that the escape provided "additional confirmation of the existence of a confederated organized band extending through the country, ready to assist and extricate each other from any difficulty." The article concluded, "This is the great reason why so many horse thieves have recently been lynched, as it was known [that] the jails would not hold them, and they would thus go unwhipt of justice."[78]

From its inception, the Young County Jail at Belknap seemed star-crossed. In July 1858, county commissioner Hugh Harper, who held the contract to build the facility, ran into delays after Indian depredations interrupted his work crews. Indian raids had also caused the cancellation of the May 1858 Commissioners Court meeting. When finished, the county lockup proved far from secure. First, there were the three escapes in December 1858. Then, in February 1859, a rustler named William Lankford, under indictment for murder and "branding stock feloniously," effected his getaway. When not busy escaping from prison, Lankford also worked on the road crew charged with maintaining the Butterfield route in Young County.[79]

The systematic pattern of livestock thefts continued. In March 1859 near Belknap, thieves "stole eighty mules out of about two hundred [that] the [Overland Mail] Company had purchased" to restock stations along the line. A month later, in April 1859, locals jailed another man at Pecan Bayou (now Brownwood, Texas) who had stolen 35 to 40 horses in the region. Two other reported hauls, one in Palo Pinto County and the other at Camp Cooper, netted the outlaws 220 horses and mules. In Coryell County, Anglo rustlers were leaving numerous moccasin tracks in local neighborhoods in an attempt to panic residents into fleeing so that the thieves could steal anything left behind. One newspaper observed, "Such villainy can only spring from the blackest of hearts." A few weeks later, on May 23, "fifty horse thieves and notorious desperados" joined ranks with John Baylor in the aforementioned attack on the Brazos Indian Reservation. The horse thieves likely participated in hopes of making off with a sizeable haul of Native American ponies during the mayhem. Baylor, who desperately needed men to augment his ranks, was unconcerned about the character of those serving under him.[80]

Continuing their campaign to terrorize residents and further destabilize the frontier, in November 1859, the Anglo outlaws dressed up as Indians and kidnapped Margaret Murphy Cornett, sister of Patrick Murphy, from northwestern Palo Pinto County. On November 7, Margaret disappeared from her residence at Caddo Village (at present-day Possum Kingdom Lake). After her disappearance, a search party followed moccasin tracks leading away from her house for several miles before losing the trail. Patrick Murphy offered a $1,000 reward for his sister's safe return.[81]

Some locals claimed that former Reserve Indians living north of the Red River had made off with Margaret Cornett, but in fact the gang of white horse thieves had engineered her disappearance. Conclusive evidence documenting their involvement surfaced in January 1860. Fifteen miles below Camp Cooper, a young boy found the body of a murdered man named Page lying in a thicket near the Clear Fork of the Brazos. In one of Page's pockets was a letter. Page, a member of the gang, had recently traveled to the Clear Fork to hand-deliver the letter and to "settle a small matter with some fellows." In the end, however, it was Page who "got settled."[82]

The note found on Page's corpse, dated December 15, 1859, was from Caddo Creek, Arkansas, near present-day Bismark and Arkadelphia. The author, one of the gang's henchmen, wrote, "Dear Chum, . . . I was not aware that you and [Patrick] Murphy was on bad terms when we concocted the arrangement [that is, the kidnapping] in regard to his sister or I would not have anything to do with it as I fear it will end badly should he come to find it out." Young County residents suspected that "Dear Chum" was Edward Cornett, husband of Margaret Murphy Cornett, and that he was part of the rustling ring.[83]

The "Dear Chum" letter continues, "We are happy to know that your party succeeded so well in getting the last drove of horses, etc. from Belknap and that you so completely fixed the affair on the Indians." The writer then inquired as to the progress "the Captain" was making toward raising a regiment of Texas Rangers. "The Captain" was none other than John R. Baylor. In December 1859, Baylor asked Allison Nelson, now a state representative, to visit Governor Houston in Austin and get approval for a new regiment of Rangers. Baylor would be captain and Harris Hamner first lieutenant. If the request for the regiment got approved, the horse thieves would then inform Baylor as to their rustling plans so that he and his Rangers would be sure to be scouting elsewhere.[84]

Nelson forwarded Baylor's request to Governor Houston. Nelson also asked the governor to accept a company of men from Erath County commanded by Peter Garland, leader of the Choctaw Tom massacre. Since the massacre, Garland had been taunting public officials to arrest him. Sam Houston, well aware of whom he was dealing with, declined both Baylor's and Garland's requests. After Baylor's plans fell through, Hamner formed his own unit, the Jacksboro Rangers. Hamner held a barbecue in town to enlist men for his company. The new recruits selected Hamner as captain, Patrick Murphy as first lieutenant, and W. R. Worrell as physician. Second sergeant was Edward Cornett, whom officials had still not indicted for the murder of Robert Neighbors. Butterfield overseer and station manager Berry Lewis Ham enrolled in Hamner's regiment as a private. Reporting on the barbecue, the *Dallas Herald* observed, "No better selections for officers could have been made."[85]

Despite the *Herald*'s glowing endorsement, Governor Houston strongly disapproved of the officer choices and refused to accept Hamner's company into the Texas Rangers. J. M. W. Hall, the Rangers' enrolling officer, traveled to Jacksboro and told locals that the governor would have "no lawless man in the service who cannot or will not . . . respect his authority." Hall pointed out that Hamner had publicly denounced the governor "as a traitor, aider and abettor of thieves and murderers, etc." Defying Houston, Hamner proceeded with his plans and was soon out in the field with his own independent unauthorized militia.[86]

In early December 1859, Hamner and Worrell announced plans to start a newspaper in Jacksboro named the *White Man.* As of December 1, they were still waiting for the printing press to arrive, but they intended to start publishing in January 1860. The first issue of the *White Man* came off the presses on January 21, 1860. During its brief run, the *White Man* published inflammatory, slanderous, and often erroneous reports, many of these aimed at Sam Houston and Native Americans. Noted for its lurid hyped-up stories of frontier depredations, the newspaper promoted a strong vigilante perspective and was a staunch defender of John R. Baylor and his associates. Not surprisingly, by the summer of 1860, Baylor had become coeditor of the *White Man.* Hamner was just as feisty as his newspaper. In 1858, he earned the distinction of being the first person charged in Jack County for assault with intent to murder. By July 1860, seven months after its inaugural edition, the *White Man* had already engendered numerous enemies. On July 29, arsonists burned its office and printing press in Jacksboro, forcing the editors to relocate to Weatherford, Texas. Hamner vowed that "a pack of hell-hounds, . . . the torch of the incendiary . . . and the knife of the assassin" would not force "Baylor, Hamner, Murphy and their friends . . . from the frontier." True to his vow, by September 1860, the *White Man* was back in business.[87]

Another section of the "Dear Chum" letter states, "Tell our friend of the *White Man* [Hamner] above all [to] keep up the Indian excitement . . . [and] also acquaint our friends at Belknap particularly[,]," as "it will be necessary to keep the matter up [that is, terrorizing local residents], . . . even [if we] . . . have to kill or shoot at some fellow." In addition to rustling and murder, arson became a key implement in the gang's toolbox of terror utilized on frontier residents. In several instances, the outlaws and their confederates deliberately torched buildings to panic area citizens. The letter continues, "I think our friend near Camp Cooper is asking too much compensation for the burning down of his stable particularly as he has not succeeded in making that haul on Camp Cooper [of army horses and mules], let me know if they have moved to the Stone Ranch." The Stone Ranch (now part of Lambshead Ranch) was the homestead of army captain Newton C. Givens, a bitter enemy of Robert Neighbors. Givens had died in March 1859, and the horse thieves were using his Clear Fork ranch for their operations.[88]

The "Dear Chum" author signed his letter with the initials "O.L.M." The letters stood for "Old Law Mob," a loose alliance of horse thieves, cutthroats, and opportunistic demagogues who intimidated the frontier populace to further their own ends. The chronic lawlessness they incited proved very effective in keeping locals on edge, silencing any opposition, and overwhelming the meager resources of Texas judges and sheriffs.

Some antebellum Old Law Mob members such as Baylor, Hamner, Nelson, Garland, Murphy, and Cornett liked to pose as white knights or Rangers, but their actions revealed them to be vicious, violent, and far from honest. These men were in league with the horse thieves as a marriage of convenience, one in which each party got what they needed. Having a chronically chaotic, unsettled frontier perfectly suited their nefarious designs. Baylor, Hamner, Nelson, and Garland preyed upon the local populace, incessantly stoking their fears, all the time positioning themselves as trusted, resolute leaders that frightened residents could turn to amid the chaos. The citizens were largely unaware that Baylor and his fellow demagogues frequently manufactured this chaos for their own advancement. Within a short time, the Baylor clique rose to leadership positions in regional militia units.

Baylor was such a megalomaniac that he refused to take orders from anyone else. Twice he declined to serve under Texas Ranger captain Rip Ford. Ford alerted the governor to Baylor's egocentric behavior, noting that "true patriotism and proper regard for the interest of the state would have dictated another course." Baylor confirmed as much in a letter to Allison Nelson, threatening that if the governor would not give him his own Ranger company, "the state could go to the devil and I will do as I have many a time, [and] fight on my hook."[89]

Baylor's armed militias, working in tandem with the O.L.M., proved very effective in cowing potential opposition. Many frontier citizens were "compelled to remain quiet and swim with the current." In a confidential note to Governor Houston, James H. Swindells of Belknap reported that it was too dangerous for a man to speak out "without running the risk of being waylaid or dragged into a quarrel and shot down." Swindells told Houston, "We truly have a 'reign of terror' here." County officials were afraid to take action because they were unsure whom they could depend on for support; Swindells reported, "[W]e do not know our enemies." In an appeal to Houston from neighboring Cooke County, R. W. Scott wrote, "The country is divided into factions and men are arrested and hung without law or trial, such things are horrible. The best man who has an enemy may be arrested by his influence and swept away from friends and family in an hour. Can nothing be done by the Governor?"[90]

The chaos continued. In December 1859, someone set fire to Murphy's Butterfield station and stole several animals. Raiding Indians may have been responsible or it might have been the O.L.M. as part of their campaign to terrify settlers. Perhaps someone wanted to send a threatening message to Murphy. Interestingly, after the blaze, Patrick Murphy deeded all of his material assets to his wife, Anna. His motive for the transfer is unclear. Regardless, in the weeks following, O.L.M. arsonists kept busy.[91]

In a bid to keep the flames of fear fanned along the Texas frontier, members of the outlaw gang deliberately torched several structures at Belknap during the first quarter of 1860. While the town had already been suffering economically from the closing of Fort Belknap, the series of fires greatly accelerated the depopulation of the Young County seat. One traveler noted, "During the previous years there had been eight buildings in town . . . but in the early spring of 1860 a treacherous fire destroyed five of these." The *St. Louis Missouri Republican* published a higher tally: "Eight large stores [were] destroyed at Belknap, owned by Drs. Foote and Throgmorton [*sic*]."[92]

The *Dallas Herald* reported incendiaries at work in Belknap during March and April 1860. On March 27, a white man put a match to the blacksmith shop, and on March 30, "an attempt was made . . . to set fire to a small building at Belknap, occupied by a widow lady and her two sons, but it was discovered, and the incendiary pursued and fired at. He returned the fire, . . . [and] succeeded in making his escape." The correspondent continued, "A man named Anderson was killed near the town of Belknap . . . Sheriff Woolforth [*sic*] had gone to arrest him, on a charge of arson. He attempted to escape, but was followed and killed." Reflecting on the passing of Anderson and other members of the mob, Young County surveyor R. F. Luckett said, "There are very few sorry of their death, especially Anderson."[93]

As the lawlessness continued, frontier citizens continued to harangue Governor Houston with pleas for protection. Although sensitive to their concerns, Houston nonetheless understood that Native American raids were not the only issue. Replying to a petition asking for relief from the attacks, Houston told Ranger lieutenant S. T. Jones, "Reports of Indians . . . committing depredations will not be taken as evidence of the fact[;] it must be clearly established by positive proof." Houston added, "In the counties south of you it has been fully ascertained that white men are committing most of the injuries upon the settlers. The people of the frontier should keep a strict watch upon all suspicious characters as the Executive cannot protect them from *white Indians*."[94]

While the governor fielded as many Texas Ranger companies as possible, there was only so much that he could do, considering the state's limited finances. Houston observed, "The [Texas] Legislature adjourned without leaving me a dollar in the treasury, . . . [I]n other words, the state is bankrupt so I have neither money, arms, or munitions." Regarding assistance from the federal government, President Buchanan informed Houston that he had "a sincere desire in every practical way to meet the wishes of the governor and people of Texas, [but] he conceives he has already performed his whole duty."[95]

Although constrained by his slender budget, Governor Houston was determined to make a breakthrough in the O.L.M. case. In May 1860, he hired P. D. Turner of Old Camp Colorado, Texas, to act as his secret agent in Indian Territory. The governor instructed Turner to proceed to the Wichita Indian Agency and from there to journey out onto the wild prairies to, as Houston instructed, "ascertain where those who steal our horses find a market and with whom they trade." Turner was to "maintain the strictest secrecy as to the object of [his] mission." To help expedite his spy's departure, Houston loaned him several mules for the journey. Unfortunately, Turner proved to be rather timid and never ventured far from the safety of the Wichita Agency and area army camps to fulfill his mission. Turner wrote the governor several notes attempting to justify his lack of progress and to buy more time, but Houston was having none of it. In early August, he pulled the inept Turner off the mission and ordered him to return to Texas with the borrowed mules.[96]

By the time Turner returned, "vigilante committees" in central Texas had apprehended five O.L.M. members and were trailing eight others, including one named Dawdy, who had fled to Arkansas. The outlaws had been stealing livestock in the region and attempting to put the blame on the Indians. This time, however, the gang made the fatal mistake of stealing horses from a Texas Ranger captain. After a vigorous pursuit, the thieves were soon in custody. When confronted with the prospect of a "rope necktie," several prisoners started implicating fellow members of the O.L.M.[97]

Several of these outlaws (notably, Robert Tucker, Aaron Sprigs, Joe Walker, and a man named Covington) had ties to rustling operations in the Belknap area. Although the Rangers tried to spare some of the prisoners who cooperated, locals ended up lynching them with the others. According to Sergeant Buck Barry of the Bosque County Minute Men, "The excitement of the people was too great owing probably to [the thieves] taking horses on Indian credit." Barry said that the swift justice had effected a "general bursting up" of the gang in Erath, Johnson, and Hill Counties. James M. Cox of Hill County wrote Governor Houston that the vigilante committees were now "satisfied that most of the stealing that has been done on our frontier has been done by white men instead of Indians as was supposed by many."[98]

In central Texas, the vigilantes had refused to wait for local law enforcement officials and the Texas courts to take action against the O.L.M. Getting indictments and successful convictions could take years, not to mention the problem of finding a secure jail to hold the prisoners. In marked contrast, Young County locals had been in no hurry to deal with another O.L.M. member, Edward Cornett, who had shotgunned Robert Neighbors at Belknap in September 1859.

Since being freed on bail, Cornett had been active, traveling to Indian Territory and serving as a sergeant in Hamner's Jack County militia. On May 24, 1860, eight months after Neighbors's death, the Young County grand jury finally indicted Cornett for murder. On the same day, Cornett had a violent quarrel with his brother-in-law, Dennis Murphy, Jr. (brother of Patrick). During the argument, Cornett pulled a gun on Murphy and threatened to shoot him. Immediately after the altercation, Dennis Murphy rode into Belknap and reported the incident to the district court. The next day, May 25, the Young County grand jury indicted Cornett for assault and battery against Murphy, and Judge Nathaniel Macon Burford of the Sixteenth Judicial District revoked Cornett's bail. Following his murder indictment the previous day, Cornett had failed to appear in Burford's court to make a plea in the Neighbors case. Perhaps he was too busy arguing with Murphy.[99]

Two of the grand jurors handing down the multiple indictments against Cornett were Dennis Murphy's brother, Patrick, and Young County treasurer George Fisher, both of whom had guaranteed Cornett's $1,000 bail. Immediately after the grand jury's indictment for assault and battery, Judge Burford issued a writ for Cornett's arrest. Young County sheriff Edward Wolfforth asked Texas Ranger colonel M. T. Johnson for assistance in executing the warrant. Johnson sent his son, Captain Thomas J. Johnson, along with eight men. Several citizens also joined the posse, including Patrick Murphy, who was safeguarding his share of the bail bond should his brother-in-law try to skip town.[100]

Like the Murphys, Sheriff Wolfforth's story involved the Overland Mail Company. Both the Murphys and the Wolfforths rented lodging in their homes to Butterfield employees. Wolfforth and his wife, Charity, had four stage conductors, one stage driver, and a clerk boarding with their family. In yet another parallel, Wolfforth had succeeded Patrick Murphy as Young County sheriff. One frontier resident, H. W. Strong, was no admirer of Wolfforth and described him as "a noted character. He always blurted out what he thought or anything he thought someone was trying to hide. He was always ready to expose a dirty piece of business in anyone."[101]

In their search for Cornett, Wolfforth's posse missed apprehending him at the house where he had been staying, but they later cornered the fugitive on the Butterfield Road, midway between Belknap and Murphy's Station. Cornett was heading for Kansas, perhaps to join his O.L.M. confederates. Despite his head start, Cornett was riding a slow horse, which proved his undoing. The posse ordered him to stop, but Cornett spurred his horse onward. Wolfforth ordered his men to fire. Patrick Murphy shot first, wounding his brother-in-law in the leg as well as his horse, which fell to the ground. Freeing himself from the fallen steed, Cornett then tried to escape on foot. Captain Johnson ordered him three times to surrender, but he refused, pulling his gun while sprinting away from his pursuers. Johnson fired one blast from his shotgun at Cornett, "breaking his arm and filling his side with shot. He still ran on, when the Capt. fired the other barrel, killing him instantly." The posse buried him where he fell.[102]

Finally, there remains the question of what sparked the argument between Dennis Murphy and Cornett. Perhaps Cornett told Dennis that he would not stand trial for killing Neighbors. If Cornett fled the state, Dennis's brother, Patrick, would forfeit his bail money, causing financial hardship for the Murphy family. Cornett may also have threatened to implicate Patrick in Neighbors's murder. For his part, Dennis Murphy had likely seen the full text of the O.L.M. letter that several Texas newspapers published in March 1860 and realized that Cornett was involved in his sister Margaret's disappearance. In any case, Cornett's death did not end the problems facing the Murphy clan. In late July 1860, someone torched Murphy's Butterfield station a second time. Not long after, Patrick Murphy left Texas for St. Louis, via the overland road. Before leaving, Patrick sold his cattle ranch to Phillip S. George, a prosperous farmer from Indiana. Murphy's reasons for leaving are not known, but the repeated arson attacks and several newspaper articles published at the time of Cornett's death suggest that there were people after him with scores to settle.[103]

During the Civil War, chronic raids by Indians, renegades, and bandits depopulated much of the Texas frontier. On April 10, 1865, Young County commissioners abandoned the county seat of Belknap because "the clerks [sic] office and court house of said county was [sic] unsafe." Commissioners disbanded Young County and sent the county's records to neighboring Jack County for safekeeping. Residents did not reorganize Young County until April 1874. In the ensuing years, Belknap ceased to exist. The buildings fell into disrepair, and a subsequent landowner plowed under the once-bustling county seat. Today, all that remains is Belknap Cemetery. Robert Neighbors is buried here in a peaceful, pastoral setting, encircled by fields of hay.[104]

From Murphy's Station to Belknap, the story of the Butterfield line through this portion of Young County reveals a violent and unsettled Texas frontier. Baylor, Hamner, Nelson, Garland, Murphy, and the Old Law Mob ultimately won the contest for this section, but in some respects, it was an empty victory. The legacy of the failed Indian reserves continued to haunt the region. Neighbors's murder removed the last vestige of stability on the antebellum Texas frontier. The brutal conduct by Baylor and his vigilante group sparked aggressive Native American reprisals, sending the cycle of violence spinning out of control. Baylor's son, Walker, regretted the murder of his father's nemesis, opining that "the killing of

Major Neighbors was about the greatest misfortune that could have befallen our northern frontier. I think he could have, by his influence over the Indians, prevented largely the horrible murders of men, women and children . . . for many years after his untimely death."[105]

Baylor and his vigilante associates represented a significant element of Anglo frontier sentiment. To these residents, Native Americans had no place in Texas. The frontiersmen wanted the tribes removed or exterminated. Eventually, Baylor ran into serious problems. In November 1862, Confederate secretary of war G. W. Randolph relieved him of his command for issuing an order to exterminate Apache Indians in Arizona. Confederate president Jefferson Davis instructed the secretary of war that Baylor's "infamous crime" required immediate attention.[106]

Writing in his defense, Baylor spoke of his "unsparing hatred of a relentless, merciless, and treacherous foe, and a natural desire to see them utterly driven from the face of the earth." Baylor, "a firm believer in the civilizing effects of slavery as regards to the African race," felt the Indians too wild to successfully enslave. While not officially endorsing Baylor's extermination policies, his superior, Confederate major general John Bankhead Magruder, commanding the District of Texas, proved sympathetic, saying that "these Indians, who I know well as not being better than wild beasts . . . [are] totally unworthy of sympathy."[107]

Like many other Texans, Magruder and Baylor possessed immovable conceptions regarding Native Americans. Making distinctions between various tribes proved too complicated. Faced with such virulent racial attitudes, the North Texas Indian reservations never had a chance. For their part, many of the Comanches, Kiowas, and Apaches had no desire to walk the white man's path. These tribes matched the frontiersmen, blow for blow, in the brutal and bloody struggle for control of the region.[108]

The state and federal governments proved abysmal in their handling of the Brazos and Comanche Reservation troubles. Because of Texas's longstanding hostility toward Native Americans, almost none of its original tribes reside within its borders today. The Cherokees, Caddos, Comanches, Kiowas, and Apaches all live elsewhere. In the last century, other tribes, such as the Tiguas and Alabama-Coushattas, have persevered in numerous legal disputes with state officials over their tribal lands and legal status. The record shows that Texas has a legacy of failed relations with Native peoples, a legacy that it has yet to come to terms with.

John Robert Baylor, the dark demagogue who used both people and circumstances to promote his self-serving ends, died of natural causes in Montell, Texas, in 1894. Harris Hamner moved to California after the Civil War and died in Los Angeles in 1876. He named one of his children John Baylor Hamner. Allison Nelson served as a brigadier general in Arkansas during the Civil War and died of typhoid fever in the fall of 1862 at age forty. Peter Garland moved from Erath County to Hood County, where residents elected him the county's first treasurer in 1867. Garland, who died in 1873, named his son Allison Nelson Garland. After spending time in Missouri, Patrick Murphy moved back to North Texas, where in 1880 he was living in Jacksboro with his son, Patrick Murphy, Jr. It is unknown when and where he died. In a notable affront to Robert Neighbors, the Reserve Indians, and numerous frontier residents, authorities failed to prosecute any of these men for their considerable crimes. Among this band of cutthroats, only Edward Cornett paid for his sins. The others literally got away with murder. Because officials proved unwilling to take action and sometimes cooperated with them, lawless vigilante groups such as the Old Law Mob continued to flourish throughout Texas in the ensuing decades.[109]

Roscoe Conkling at the ruins of Murphy's Station in December 1934. The spring in the foreground provided water for the stage stop. Conkling Papers, courtesy of Seaver Center for Western History Research, Los Angeles County Museum of Natural History.

Margaret Conkling at the ruins of Murphy's Station in December 1934. Conkling Papers, courtesy of Seaver Center for Western History Research, Los Angeles County Museum of Natural History.

Belknap Station ruins, Belknap, Texas, in the 1930s. Conkling Papers, courtesy of Seaver Center for Western History Research, Los Angeles County Museum of Natural History.

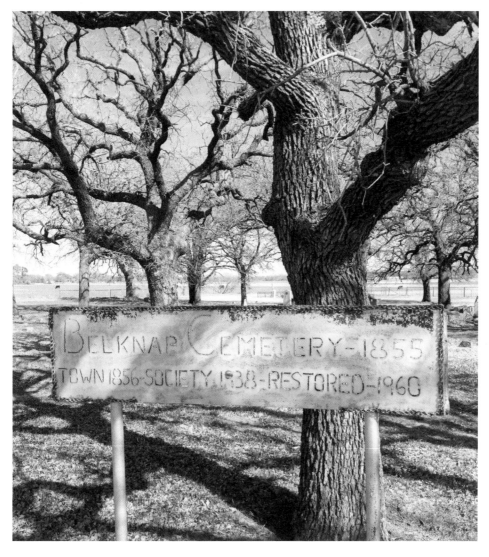

Belknap Cemetery. The cemetery is all that remains of the Belknap community, the former county seat of Young County, Texas. Photograph by the author.

Robert Simpson Neighbors grave at Belknap Cemetery, Young County, Texas. Photograph by the author.

Butterfield marker at Fort Belknap. Photograph by the author.

"Site of Camp Cooper" marker, Throckmorton County, Texas. Photograph by the author.

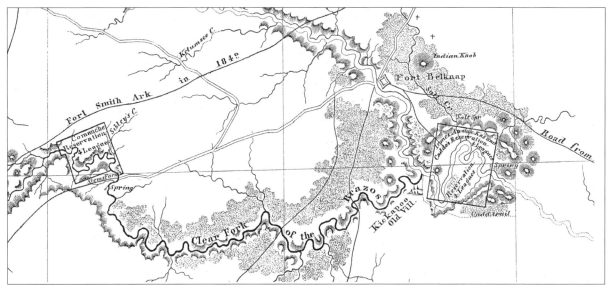

Texas Indian Reservations detail map. The Brazos Reserve (in Young County) is on the right side of map, and the Comanche Reserve (in Throckmorton County) is on the left side. Note Stem's Farm immediately below the Comanche Reserve. Map #76284, *Capt. R. B. Marcy 1854 Map of the Country upon the Brazos and Big Wichita Rivers*, courtesy of Texas General Land Office Archives, Austin.

John Robert Baylor. Photo courtesy
of Jerry D. Thompson.

Harris A. Hamner. Courtesy of Kenneth M. Holtzclaw and Peggy Christian, *San Timoteo Canyon* (Mount Pleasant, S.C.: Arcadia Publishing, 2007).

Texas governor Hardin Richard Runnels. Courtesy of Texas State Library and Archives Commission, Austin, Prints and Photographs Collection (2001/140-1).

Brevet Major General David Emanuel Twiggs, commander of the Department of Texas. Courtesy of Library of Congress, Prints and Photographs Division, Washington, D.C.

Sam Houston.

Texas.

Texas governor Sam Houston. Courtesy of Library of Congress, Prints and Photographs Division, Washington, D.C.

Cambern headstone in Lost Valley, Jack County, Texas. The Cambern-Mason massacre occurred on April 18, 1858. Photo courtesy of Jess and Susan Elmore.

Mason headstone in Lost Valley, Jack County, Texas. Photo courtesy of Jess and Susan Elmore.

THE WHITE MAN.

HAMNER & BAYLOR, Editors.

TERMS: $250 A YEAR.

WEATHERFORD, TEXAS,

Saturday, Sept. 15, 1860.

"THE CONSTITUTION—EQUAL RIGHTS TO EVERY STATE AND EVERY AMERICAN FREEMAN!"

"THE CONSTITUTION AND THE EQUALITY OF THE STATES—THESE ARE THE SYMBOLS OF EVERLASTING UNION. LET THESE BE THE RALLYING CRIES OF THE PEOPLE."
[John C. Breckinridge

FOR PRESIDENT.
JOHN C. BRECKINRIDGE,
OF KENTUCKY.

To Our Friends.

With intense interest, and solicitude, have we looked forward to the present time, when we could again present you with the "WHITE MAN," and, as many of you are not aware of the causes that brought about the suspension of our paper, we feel that an explanation is due you as well as ourselves.

In the first place, our supply of paper gave out, and it was impossible to procure a supply in this country; we therefore went to New Orleans, and bought a year's supply, and just as it was within a days' travel of its destination, some black hearted incendiary set fire to our Office, burning everything connected with it.

Thus we were left with the ashes of a Press, and the consolation of knowing that our last dollar was gone. Discouraged we determined to quit the business—give up. But the earnest solicitations of our friends and their generosity in loaning us the means for purchasing another press, and liberal contributions to rebuild our office, has induced us to continue. We assure

Masthead of *The White Man* newspaper, edited by Harris A. Hamner and John Robert Baylor, published in Jacksboro and later Weatherford, Texas. Historic Newspaper Collection, courtesy of Dolph Briscoe Center for American History, University of Texas at Austin.

Caddew Creek Ark,
December 15th 1859.

Dear Chum,

Yours of the 25th ult. has been duly re-
-ceived and we are happy to know that your party suc-
-ceeded so well in getting the last drove of horses &c from
Belknap and that you so completely fixed the affair on
the Indians but I am now becoming aprehensive as the
last droves were very inferior. Every thing is quiet here at
present except some little grumbling about the last division
as some you know got to much but this was policy as for
the others we can scare them into terms.

Yours &c &c
O. L. M.

Composite view of front and last pages of "Dear Chum"/Old Law Mob letter, one of the more important documents from Texas's frontier period. Texas Adjutant General's Department, Pre–Civil War Ranger Records, 1846–62, courtesy of Texas State Library and Archives Commission, Austin.

CHAPTER 5

From the Brazos to Valley Creek

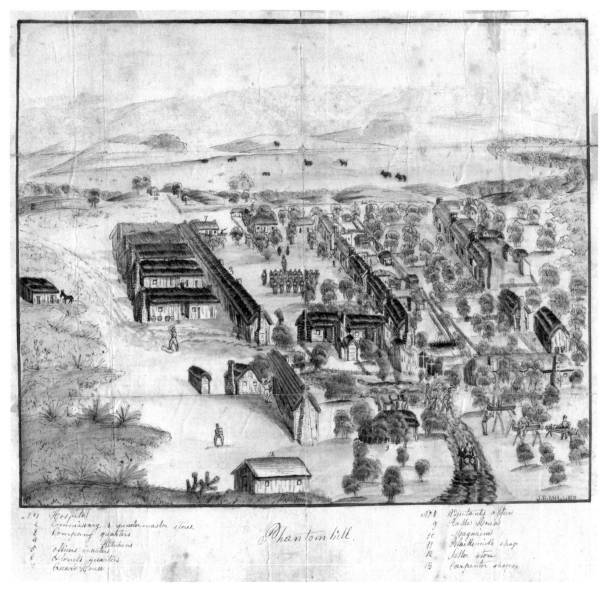

Fort Phantom Hill, watercolor by J. B. Miller, from about 1853. Burleson (Albert Sidney) Papers, 1841–46 (di_04124), courtesy of Dolph Briscoe Center for American History, University of Texas at Austin.

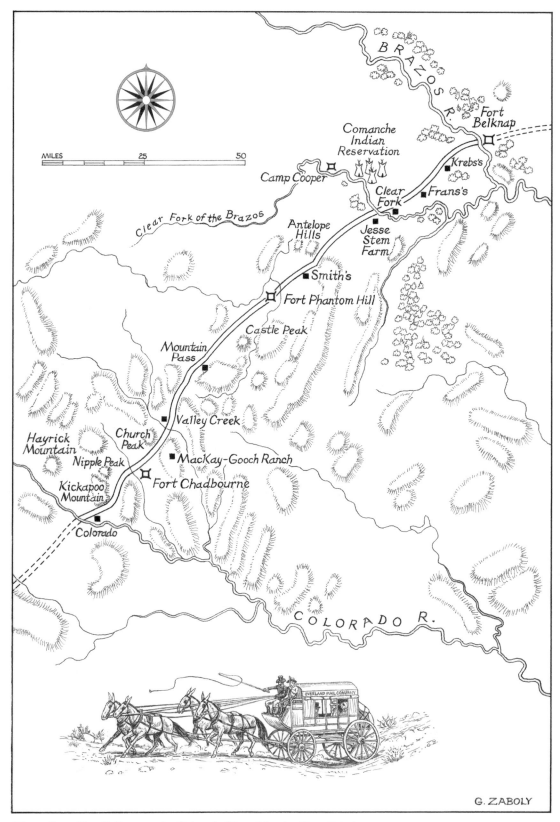

Map 3. From Fort Belknap to the Colorado River. Map by Gary Zaboly.

From Belknap, the Butterfield Road descended to the Brazos River and crossed at a sandbar. Ascending the opposite bank, the trail then turned southwest, heading for the Clear Fork of the Brazos River. For this section of the overland route from Belknap to the Clear Fork, the overseer of Butterfield's day-to-day operations was James Madison "Uncle Matt" Frans. When not out riding the route, Frans worked as tax assessor-collector for Young County. County commissioners appointed him to the position in August 1857, and he served in that capacity until August 1860. Frans supervised three overland stage stops: one in western Young County, Krebs's Station; and two in neighboring Throckmorton County, Frans's Station and Clear Fork Station.[1]

The namesake of Krebs's Station was Benjamin Krebs. Over the years, people have incorrectly cited Krebs's name and nationality. Some spell his last name as "Cribb" or "Cribbs," while others have it as "Kribb" or "Kribbs." Locals often called him a Dutchman, nineteenth-century American slang for someone from Germany, Austria, Switzerland, or the Netherlands. Ben Krebs was born in Switzerland in 1828 and immigrated to the United States in 1850. In October of that year, he became a U.S. citizen and settled in western Wisconsin. Seven years later, in 1857, Krebs moved to Young County, Texas. Upon arrival, he purchased a town lot in the county seat of Belknap. Krebs was a man of modest means who worked as a laborer and farmer to make ends meet.[2]

By June 1860, he was employed by the Overland Mail Company as a stage driver based in western Young County, near present-day Proffitt, Texas. The manager of the Butterfield station where Krebs lived was William A. George of Indiana. George, his wife, Mary, and their two children shared living quarters with Krebs and another Butterfield stagecoach driver, L. B. Carlille of New York. Although George was in charge, over time the stage stop acquired the name Cribbs's Station, after Ben Krebs. Krebs likely owned the station property, as tax records indicate that by 1861, he had purchased 320 acres in the Texan Emigration and Land Company's premium surveys, located in the western part of the county. The land was prime real estate, featuring a sizeable prairie studded with mesquite, along with plenty of post oak timber and water.[3]

Krebs's Station was not on Butterfield's original itinerary. In fine-tuning its mail route and shortening the distance between livestock changes during November 1858, the Overland Mail Company built a new relay point halfway between

Belknap Station and Frans's Station, twenty-one miles distant. The mail company located the log cabin stage stop near a large water hole on Cribb Station Creek. In her 1937 history of Young County, Carrie Crouch notes that "Cribb [*sic*] Station was the first stop west of Belknap on the Butterfield Overland Mail Route where Ben Cribb ran the stable and a store in the pre-war days."[4]

Two newspaper reporters traveling through Texas on the Butterfield in September and October 1858 failed to mention a building on Cribb Station Creek, but when the correspondent for the *San Francisco Daily Evening Bulletin* came through in late November of that year he noted a stage stop between Fort Belknap and Frans's Station called "Clark's." During this period, western Young County had few homesteads and was largely isolated. Travel through the region was hazardous. In late January 1860, two men—William Powell and Colonel Thomas Hunter—made the trip from Belknap to the Clear Fork in a two-horse wagon. About eight miles west of Belknap, they encountered a party of six Indians. The chance meeting surprised both parties, who paused to take stock of each other.[5]

The lull lasted but a few seconds, and the two men quickly found themselves racing for their lives, with the Indians in hot pursuit. Powell and Hunter urgently lashed their horses and sped off westward in the ruts of the Butterfield Road. A newspaper report on the incident said, "Our young friends being unarmed, as well as considering 'discretion the better part of valor,' took to their heels . . . until they arrived at Cribb's [*sic*] Station, a few miles farther." The Native Americans broke off their chase when the two men came under the protective gunfire of station employees. Hunter told the newspaper that during the desperate race for his life, "[t]imes looked rather squally, and I began to think considerably about going under." The newspaper also noted that later that same day, Indians had attacked the Overland Mail stage near Krebs's Station. The warriors shot several arrows at the coach but failed to stop the vehicle.[6]

Because the Overland Mail Company had built Krebs's Station on this remote section of the Texas frontier, Thomas Hunter lived to tell of his harrowing encounter. These stage stops served as fortified, self-contained strongholds in the middle of what was often a raw wilderness. The men and women who risked their lives working at places such as Krebs's faced Colonel Hunter's fears on a daily basis. The specter of Indians overrunning a stage stop, setting fire to the building, and killing and scalping the employees was a real and terrifying prospect for those working at Butterfield stations. Over a three-year period, Comanches and Apaches destroyed several Overland Mail Company stations in the Lone Star State, and some of these more than once.

With the coming of the Civil War, the abandonment of the Butterfield route, and the withdrawal of the federal army from Texas, the isolated and exposed location of Krebs's Station forced its inhabitants to move elsewhere. Ben Krebs stayed in Young County through 1862, but by 1864, he had relocated to Montague County. During that year, Corporal Ben Krebs served in Captain Sevier Shannon's Company B from Montague County, part of the Texas State Troops' Twenty-First Brigade assigned to protect the First Frontier District. In 1865, Krebs married Eliza Ann Taylor Savage and settled six miles south of the county seat of Montague. During the Civil War, his Young County stage stop fell into disrepair. In the summer of 1867, renowned cattlemen Charles Goodnight and Oliver Loving rendezvoused at the ruins of Krebs's Station for the start of their second cattle drive to Fort Sumner, New Mexico. It was on this second ill-fated trip that Comanche Indians mortally wounded Loving on the Pecos River, a few miles south of present-day Carlsbad, New Mexico.[7]

From Krebs's Station it was eleven miles to the next stop, at Frans's, named after Butterfield overseer James Madison Frans. Frans, born in 1814, originally hailed from Virginia, as did his wife, Frances. The couple married in January 1842. After moving to Missouri, they eventually settled in Texas, first in Grayson County and later in Young and Throckmorton Counties. From 1857 to 1859, Frans and his family lived in a two-room log cabin situated on the west side of Middle Kings Creek, near present-day Woodson, Texas. When the Overland Mail Company commenced service in September 1858, Frans's home became a stage stop. Near the cabin were several stables built of log and stone. Station employees lived in the stables but took their meals with the Frans family. At the time, there were no neighbors within an eleven-mile radius.[8]

Daughter Elizabeth Frances Frans, born in 1846, recalled serving meals as a teenager to Butterfield passengers who stopped at the family's cabin. The food, prepared on the fireplace hearth, cost fifty cents per person. Since the overland stages arrived at all hours of the day, Elizabeth often had to get up in the middle of the night to fix dinner or breakfast. Her mother insisted that the children clean the table and wash the plates before going back to bed. Butterfield Division Six superintendent Henry Bates was a regular visitor. The corpulent superintendent and his glass eye impressed young Elizabeth, who would sit in a corner and listen to Bates and her father as they sat before the fire, smoking and conversing.[9]

The rustic setting at Frans's Station failed to inspire one overland passenger, who commented on the landscape's "sterile plainness . . . only varied by clumps of black oaks or weeds and coarse grass, with hardly a house or field to beguile the dreary spectacle." After two years of relative isolation on Middle Kings Creek, Frans and his family likely agreed with this assessment. By the summer of 1860, they had left their namesake stage stop and moved thirteen miles westward to manage another Butterfield station on the Clear Fork of the Brazos.[10]

When Butterfield passenger Waterman Ormsby arrived at the Clear Fork, he commented that the river "was not very clear, but even its muddy waters were a grateful boon for a bath while our horses were being changed at the station on the banks." Ormsby further observed, "Here were in progress of erection a log hut for the station keeper and help, and a corral, or yard, in which to herd the mules and catch them for harnessing. Dr. Birch, the mail agent, had everything in readiness, so that I had to finish dressing in the wagon—so short was the delay." The *San Francisco Daily Evening Bulletin* reporter, stopping here in November 1858, called the stage stop "Jackson's," after Tryal Evan Jackson, Frans's predecessor, who managed the Clear Fork Station from 1858 to 1860. Jackson was a pioneer rancher in the area.[11]

John G. Irwin, a twenty-eight-year-old Irishman, helped Jackson run the Clear Fork station. Irwin was a sergeant stationed at Fort Chadbourne who left the army in 1859 after securing a government contract to supply beef to the garrison at Camp Cooper. Irwin's son, John Chadbourne Irwin, born at Fort Chadbourne in February 1855, remembered Frans succeeding Jackson as station manager in 1860. Reflecting on the Clear Fork's Butterfield period, Irwin noted that the stage station "was located where the old Judge [Cornelius] Stribling ranch house now stands. . . . [The adjacent Stagestand] Creek is named after the old stage line." Irwin said, "The old crossing on the Clear Fork may be seen in the Stribling field; also the old road can be traced north of the station in the Stribling pasture. I remember the old stage coaches quite well as they passed. They drove four to six horses or sometimes mules." At Clear Fork Station, a parade of humanity passed before the wide-eyed child. "The passengers who stepped out of the old stage coach were of all types," Irwin fondly recalled; "prospectors, gamblers, cowmen, and assorted adventurers. The stage driver too was the cussing, whip-cracking fellow the story books picture him."[12]

According to Butterfield historians Roscoe and Margaret Conkling, Clear Fork Station consisted of a log cabin and a small "picket house. There was a spring . . . [but when] the spring went dry . . . [the mail company] put in a well. The log house had two rooms, sixteen or fourteen feet each way. The [round] picket house was used as a kitchen." Henry McCluskey managed the stage stop's livestock and corrals, situated down the hill a short distance below. The present-day Stribling homestead, perched on a hill overlooking the Clear Fork, incorporates some of the original rocks from the old stage stop. The original well, dug by John G. Irwin when the station's spring failed, is still in fine shape. The well, rebuilt in the early 1900s, retains the original rock in its lower half.[13]

Cornelius Kinchelo Stribling acquired the Clear Fork Station property during Reconstruction. Stribling, Shackelford County judge in 1880, was reportedly part of the Vigilance Committee, or Tin Hat-Band Brigade, a clandestine vigilante group that operated in the region before 1874. Another reputed member of this extralegal outfit was former Butterfield station manager Tryal Evan Jackson. Discussing possible links between the antebellum Old Law Mob and the post–Civil War Vigilance Committee, local historian Ben O. Grant notes that while some locals believe the Old Law Mob "ran its course and died out," others claim "that it emerged into what later became known as the Vigilance Committee." In fact, North Texas was a hotbed of vigilante activity from the 1850s through the 1870s, and the Clear Fork region was one of its epicenters. As previously recounted, in early 1860, authorities discovered the "Dear Chum"/Old Law Mob letter in the pockets of a murdered man lying alongside the Clear Fork.[14]

During the Butterfield period, those living along the Clear Fork were a decidedly mixed bunch. Some made their living as freighters and contractors for the U.S. Army and the Overland Mail Company, while others operated stores, saloons, and gambling halls catering to the garrison at Camp Cooper. The army established Camp Cooper in close proximity to the Comanche Indian Reservation in January 1856. Excluding a fourteen-month period, Camp Cooper's location for most of the antebellum period was on the north bank of the Clear Fork, half a mile downstream from its junction with Graveyard Canyon. Lieutenant Colonel Robert E. Lee commanded the garrison from May 1856 to July 1857.[15]

One Clear Fork local associated with Camp Cooper was Young County commissioner Hugh Harper, who held the post sutler contract. Harper ran into trouble with Major Gabriel René Paul of the Seventh Infantry, the commander of Fort Belknap in neighboring Young County. Federal law prohibited all liquor sales within a two-mile radius of Indian reservations. After learning that Harper was selling liquor to both Reserve Indians and his troops, Paul ordered Lieutenant C. B. Stevens to destroy a barrel of whiskey belonging to the merchant. Harper subsequently filed suit against Paul, asking for $10,000 in damages.[16]

Camp Cooper's commander, Captain James Nelson Caldwell of the First Infantry, was also investigating reports of whiskey smuggling and sales. Reports implicated several Clear Fork residents in illegal liquor transactions with both Reserve Indians and soldiers. In their contraband roundup, Camp Cooper troops seized and destroyed ten barrels of whiskey and a quantity of wine. One local home rigorously searched by Caldwell's men belonged to John Maxwell. Maxwell was a frontier character of some notoriety.[17]

In the summer of 1860, a newspaper implicated Maxwell, Harper, and a third man, Rufus Oliphant, in the lynching of an attorney named M. B. King. At the time of King's death, Oliphant was living at the Clear Fork home of Butterfield station manager Tryal Jackson. Maxwell and his accomplices supposedly lynched King because Maxwell's wife, Margaret, had hired the lawyer to initiate divorce proceedings against her husband. In addition to divorcing her husband, Mrs. Maxwell allegedly wanted him murdered. For King, Mrs. Maxwell may not have been the best choice in a client, since her husband was reputedly a member of the Old

Law Mob. Maxwell warned King not to handle his wife's case, but the attorney ignored him. Several days later, Maxwell advised King to leave the area within twenty-four hours. Once again, the lawyer paid him no heed. Soon after, King was lynched.[18]

His body hung from a tree for three days before cow hunters cut him down, laid his body in the creek below, and covered it with brush. John Chadbourne Irwin saw King's remains, "which were never buried but tossed in a ravine." The killers pinned a note on King's body that read "O.L.M.," or Old Law Mob. The *White Man* newspaper reported, "We saw the grave if it can be called such and hope never to see another; every tree within several hundred yards was filled with buzzards and the half devoured body was plainly visible." The *Belton Democrat*, reporting on the killing, apparently approved of King's fate, labeling him an "abolitionist, incendiary, lawyer." The site of his hanging was a short distance downstream from the present-day Highway 283 bridge over the Clear Fork. For some years after, locals called King's final resting place Maxwell Creek.[19]

A second Old Law Mob lynching in the summer of 1860 had ties to a Shack-elford County landmark, namely, Collins Creek, located four miles south of Clear Fork Station. In a note to Belknap merchant Charles Neuhaus, Clear Fork resident John G. Previn reported, "We have had quite an excitement here this week, Mr. Collins was killed on Monday last." John Chadbourne Irwin recalled that this murder followed the circulation of an anonymous letter implicating L. F. Collins (a close friend of John R. Baylor's) in the theft of army livestock from Camp Cooper. According to the *White Man*, a group of ruffians that included several Texas Rangers ambushed Collins, a "notorious horse thief," at his home. The vigilantes, concealed in the underbrush, shot Collins from his horse. The killers then rummaged through the dead man's pockets and ransacked his home, taking more than $8,000 in cash, notes, and bonds. The *White Man*'s editors took a accusatory tone, stating, "That the [Texas] Rangers had a hand in it, there is no doubt, and one of them . . . was detailed . . . to kill Collins." When found, Collins's corpse bore the usual hallmark of an Old Law Mob lynching: pinned to his clothing was a piece of paper with the initials "O.L.M."[20]

Besides Harper, Maxwell, and Oliphant, other persons of interest living near Butterfield's Clear Fork Station included Andrew J. MacKay and John C. Gooch and his brother, Ben Gooch. As previously related, MacKay was with Robert Neighbors on September 14, 1859, when Butterfield employees Patrick Murphy and Edward Cornett waylaid the federal Indian agent. MacKay and John Gooch had relocated to the frontier from Austin and Georgetown in hopes of securing lucrative government deals. In 1860, MacKay, a native of New York, and Gooch, who was from Arkansas, listed their occupations as "speculators." The apt description fit many people floating throughout the region during this period.[21]

MacKay and Gooch shared lodging with Gooch's younger brother, Ben, in George Marquis's home on the Clear Fork. Part of MacKay and Gooch's "speculating" activities involved bidding on U.S. Army supply contracts. During the Butterfield period, they inked agreements to deliver sacked corn and flour to Camp Cooper and hay to Camp Colorado. Ben Gooch, a wagon master by trade, handled deliveries for the firm of MacKay and Gooch. By the summer of 1860, the partnership was prospering. Andrew MacKay listed his assets at $28,000, while John Gooch reported a net worth of $8,000. MacKay and Gooch were active along a large swath of the Texas frontier, and their story continues later at Fort Chadbourne in Coke County.[22]

After leaving Clear Fork Station, Butterfield stagecoaches passed over a steep but traversable grade that led down to the river's east bank. Today, the overland road and the crossing of the Clear Fork are still visible. In wet periods, the chocolate-brown river is deep and wide, with a strong current. During times of drought, however, the watershed can be bone dry. On the west side of the Clear Fork, a short distance from the overland crossing and near the mouth of Lambshead Creek, one can see the ruins of an antebellum structure. The building and surrounding acreage are now part of the well-known Lambshead Ranch near Fort Griffin, Texas.[23]

Watt Matthews, who lived at the ranch most of his life, believed that this Lambshead Creek ruin was once a Butterfield station, and he erected a marker here identifying it as such. Matthews maintained that the mail company built a relay station on the west side for times such as when heavy rains made the Clear Fork impassable and delayed overland traffic. According to his theory, "it made sense to put a stage stand on the east bank and a relay station on the west bank of the river. When the stream was up, travelers and mail . . . could cross by boat or raft and continue their journey by stage from either side."[24]

It is highly unlikely, however, that the Overland Mail Company used this westside structure as a relay station. While high water at the Clear Fork in May and July 1859 delayed overland coaches fifteen and twelve hours, respectively, such instances were far from the norm. Realistically, the infrequency of high-water stages at the Clear Fork crossing did not warrant the expense of building and maintaining an additional station so close to an existing one. Such duplication of service would have been both wasteful and unnecessary. At no other river crossing in Texas did the Overland Mail Company use stations on both banks, and it is improbable that they made an exception here.[25]

Detailed research shows that this structure is the Jesse Stem homestead. Onsite fieldwork dates this Lambshead Creek site to the antebellum period. Stem was a federal Indian agent in Texas until 1853, when he retired and started farming on the Clear Fork. He carefully selected the location of his 640-acre farm, which was ideally suited for agricultural endeavors and situated astride one of Texas's primary east-west thoroughfares. Stem hoped to make a tidy profit from sales to local military outposts. Within a short time, he secured a government contract to supply corn to Fort Belknap.[26]

In April 1854, army captain John Pope and his men stopped at Stem's log house and farm, the first dwelling his party had seen after months of exploring the desolate wilds of West Texas for a federal railroad survey. "It requires an absence as long as ours from all human habitations," Pope remarked, "to realize the sensation this sight created." A few months later, in August 1854, U.S. Indian agent Robert Neighbors and army captain Randolph B. Marcy visited Stem's farm while surveying lands for the two federal Indian reservations in Throckmorton and Young Counties. The pair conversed with area Indian chiefs about the pending reservations at a shaded, cool spring located half a mile downriver from Stem's farm.[27]

When first approaching Stem's homestead, Marcy's companion on the trip, W. B. Parker, noted, "To our surprise, on ascending the opposite [west] bank, the road wound through a large field of oats on one side and corn on the other, and in the distance we saw a house. . . . In this solitary spot, Colonel Stem, late Indian agent, established this rancho." Randolph Marcy also mentioned Stem in his writings, saying, "We were much rejoiced on arriving here to find evidence of civilization in this far Western Indian country. A former agent of the Comanches (Colonel J. Stem) some years since purchased a tract of land here, upon which he determined to open a farm. . . . Thus far the cultivation of this farm has realized handsome profits to its proprietor, and he finds a ready market for his produce at Fort Belknap, at good prices."[28]

While Pope and Marcy rejoiced at seeing Stem's homestead, the building had an aura of tragedy hanging over it. In March 1853, four Wichita Indians, including a mother and child, died here after a heated confrontation with Major Henry Hopkins Sibley and his troops over stolen army horses. Eleven months later, in February 1854, as Stem headed home from Fort Belknap with a wagonload of supplies, marauding Kickapoo Indians waylaid him and another man. The Kickapoos "shot at them, but missing, clubbed their rifles and beat them to death, then stealing what was most valuable, made their escape." Ironically, Stem, an Ohioan and close friend of future president Rutherford B. Hayes, had come to Texas in 1851 for his health.[29]

There are several graves near the former Indian agent's house at Lambshead Creek, but Stem's is not among them. The army originally buried him at Fort Belknap but in 1910 removed his remains to Washington, D.C., and reinterred him with full military honors. Stem's murder provides a poignant reminder of the harsh realities confronting idealistic pioneers who came to the Texas frontier to make their fortune. While some of these early settlers became wealthy, many more ended up eking out a marginal existence, while others, such as Jesse Stem, lost their lives.[30]

Because Stem died in 1853, one remaining question concerning Stem's Ranch is, who was living at his house and tending the crops that Marcy and Parker observed in 1854? The answer lies in a May 1856 letter, in which one Thomas Lambshead states that he had moved to his "Clear Fork Farm" in 1854. At this time, there were no other known buildings in the area, as shown in the Peters Colony and Marcy-Neighbors maps from 1854. In these three maps, Jesse Stem's farm is the only habitation near the Clear Fork crossing. The federal government did not construct the log buildings for the Comanche Indian Agency across the river, on the east side of the Clear Fork, until the fall of 1855. Thomas Lambshead leased this ranch from Stem's widow beginning in 1854. Stem's Ranch is on Lambshead Creek, named after Thomas Lambshead, and this site is now part of the historic Lambshead Ranch. In 1856, Young County commissioners designated Thomas Lambshead's home as the site for all Precinct Three elections, with future Butterfield station manager Tryal Evan Jackson serving as election judge.[31]

Thomas Lambshead's story is both a compelling and a bittersweet frontier saga. His immigrant story follows an arc, of moving from England to a fresh start in Texas full of promise and hope. This frontier narrative concerns two English families: Thomas Lambshead and his nephew, William; and Thomas's wife, Eliza, and her brother, Samuel Hammick. Thomas Lambshead was born around 1805 in Ilsington, Devon County, England. By 1841, he was living with his brother John and his family, which included nephew William, age four. By July 1848, Thomas had married Eliza Elizabeth Hammick and immigrated to the Peters Colony in North Texas. In May 1850, colony land agents issued him a grant for 640 acres on Paint Creek in Throckmorton County. Samuel Hammick joined the Lambsheads in Texas. Peters Colony records indicate that Hammick, a single man, came to the colony by July 1848 and in May 1850 acquired a 320-acre parcel bordering the north part of Lambshead's Paint Creek acreage.[32]

Lambshead and Hammick selected their grants based on their close proximity to both Paint Creek and the only major route through the region at the time, Marcy's California Emigrant Road, originally blazed by gold rush Argonauts in the spring of 1849. In an unfortunate twist of fate for Lambshead and Hammick, the California Emigrant Road never became popular, because of the lack of military protection, scarcity of water, and harsh conditions along the route. In late 1851, eighteen months after Lambshead and Hammick chose their properties, the U.S. Army laid out a new military road from Fort Belknap to the North Concho River. This new route, later used by Butterfield, passed some miles to the south of Paint Creek, bypassing Lambshead's and Hammick's parcels. As a result, their land values never appreciated. Eliza Lambshead received only $33 for both parcels (960 acres combined) when she sold them in 1868. Ten years earlier, in 1858, Young County tax collector and Butterfield overseer James M. Frans had appraised the same acreage at $480.[33]

In 1850, Lambshead, Eliza, and their baby girl were living in Navarro County, Texas, where he worked as a farmer. Sadly, their daughter did not survive. In their early years in Texas, Lambshead and his family lived close to the margins. The federal census for 1850 shows the family with no material assets. In 1851, Lambshead's financial situation had improved slightly: by then, Thomas owned three horses and twenty cattle.[34]

By 1853, Lambshead and his family no longer resided in Navarro County and were en route to or already living in Throckmorton County. By 1854, Thomas had settled at Jesse Stem's Clear Fork farm. The following year, in 1855, he hired nine men to assist with the farming operations. Three years later, in January 1858, Thomas Lambshead was one of the founders and first county commissioners of Throckmorton County. By that time, his financial situation had markedly improved. Besides the crops on his Clear Fork farm and 640 acres on Paint Creek near Camp Cooper, the Englishman also owned five slaves, five horses, and 455 cattle, for a total net worth of $5,190. In 1858, wanting to maximize his earnings from the booming frontier economy, Lambshead secured the federal beef contract for Camp Cooper.[35]

After four years on the Clear Fork, in the summer of 1858 Lambshead expanded his business operations by accepting employment with the Overland Mail Company as overseer of the portion of the route between the Clear Fork and Fort Chadbourne. This section included four Butterfield stations, namely, Smith's, Phantom Hill, Mountain Pass, and Valley Creek. It seemed that Lambshead's years of backbreaking work were finally starting to pay off. Compared to many on the frontier, he was now a man of means. In August 1858, he signed a $600 contract with Belknap merchant Conrad Neuhaus for 10,000 pounds of flour for the Butterfield stations at Phantom Hill and Mountain Pass. Neuhaus was also to furnish "a quantity of good common whiskey to said [stage] stands as may be called for, at the rate of $1.50 per gallon." Regarding payment for these Butterfield supplies, Lambshead agreed "to pay Newhouse [sic] for the flour, whiskey, and all other articles which may be called for, at the expiration of every quarterly term of the Overland Mail Company." In addition to his duties as section overseer, in the summer of 1858 Thomas Lambshead assumed responsibilities as station manager at Valley Creek (near Shep, Texas), while his nephew, William, worked at Mountain Pass (near Merkel, Texas).[36]

When Lambshead moved out near the one hundredth meridian to oversee Butterfield operations, he entered Comanche territory. Unlike the more compliant

Penatekas who settled on the Comanche Reserve near Lambshead's Clear Fork farm, other Comanches living beyond the one hundredth meridian had no desire to walk the white man's road. Examples of the tribe's pervasive presence in this part of Texas include local landmarks such as Comanche Springs, Comanche Pass, and the Great Comanche War Trail. On this section of the frontier, Comanche power was still alive and well. The tribe actively battled whites for control of the region and enjoyed relative military parity with the U.S. Army. Lacking superior numbers, neither group could dominate the other.[37]

In antebellum West Texas, the best that the U.S. Army could ever achieve was a standoff with Comanches and Apaches. At the same time, while Native Americans often raided frontier communities at will, they proved unable to halt the ever-advancing westward line of European American settlement. With conditions essentially stalemated, whites, Hispanics, and African Americans living west of the Clear Fork knew they could not depend on the State of Texas or the federal government to protect them. Government contractors, settlers, and Butterfield employees such as Thomas Lambshead understood that they were on their own. The Lambshead story continues later, farther to the west in Taylor County.

From the Clear Fork of the Brazos, it was twenty-six miles to the next stop on the overland itinerary, at Smith's Station in neighboring Shackelford County. Butterfield passenger Waterman Ormsby, who passed through in September 1858, recalled that his stagecoach driver for this leg of the route was a stout lad named "Big Dick." Dick regaled Ormsby with lurid tales of his times as a canal boatman, bragging that he was "three days 'on the canal and never saw land, because he was drunk in the hold'—and various other things."[38]

As mail road steered southwesterly toward the North Concho River, it continued following the trail blazed by the U.S. Army in late 1851. After crossing over to the west bank of the Clear Fork, the trail intersected Lambshead Creek and followed along the stream's north bank for more than four miles. After passing into Shackelford County, Ormsby noticed a gradual transition in the environment, where Texas's timbered country gave way to the southern Great Plains. Within this 220-mile transition zone, which stretched from Gainesville west to Fort Chadbourne, the environmental and cultural aspects of the Old South yielded to those of the American West. Beyond Fort Chadbourne, the Lone Star State had more in common with the West than it did with the South.[39]

Ormsby's initial impression of the southern plains, seen through his Butterfield window, was none too favorable. Describing the West Texas scenery near present-day Albany, Texas, Ormsby commented on the "rolling plains, covered with . . . grass and mesquite—a sorry landscape, I assure you." Another antebellum traveler passing over this portion of the road also judged the land to have few natural assets of value or potential for development. He found the environs "a tedious succession of barren and rocky hills, covered with short green grass of very poor quality. . . . [A] more inhospitable unpromising region for grazing one could hardly expect to see." A third visitor, J. M. Farwell, reporter for the *Daily Alta California,* rode a Butterfield coach through this same section six weeks after Ormsby but observed entirely different aspects of these western lands, remarking upon the abundant herds of pronghorn as well as numerous deer and flocks of turkeys, ranging from twenty to forty in size.[40]

En route to Smith's Station, the mail road crossed Fish Creek and Bluff Creek. From Bluff Creek, stagecoaches continued several miles farther before halting at Chimney Creek, the site of Smith's Station. The stage stop was situated in a grassy flat beside the creek. The watershed likely received its name from the Butterfield station's stone chimney, a facsimile of which the current landowner has reconstructed on the original site. When Waterman Ormsby arrived at Smith's Station, Overland Mail Company employees were completing a brush corral to hold the horses and mules. The Butterfield crew, who were living in tents, had not started work on erecting the station house. With few trees in the vicinity, the mail company opted to build a rock structure. A nearby quarry that supplied the limestone for the station is on the west side of the stream. The Chimney Creek site affords a dependable water supply. For much of the year, one can find large pools of water along the watershed. In addition, there is a "fine spring" located a short distance above the stage stop, behind a more recent ranch house. Ormsby's visit to Smith's Station was brief; while the hostlers swapped out the coach's animals, he and his driver, Big Dick, bolted a quick meal. The bill of fare was "cake cooked in the coals, clear coffee, and some dried beef cooked in Mrs. Smith's best style."[41]

From Smith's Station, the overland route crossed Chimney Creek, heading southwest to the Shackelford-Jones County line. Near the county line the trail intersected Deadman Creek. Exactly when Deadman Creek received its name is unclear. Maps of the region from 1858 through 1879 show the stream's original name as Willow Creek. Uncle Will Foster, who built his home along the watercourse in 1881, recalled that locals were already calling it Deadman Creek when he moved there. A 1928 Abilene newspaper article said that since the Civil War, the "treacherous stream" had claimed the lives of eight people. The first alleged victim was an army express rider who fell off his horse into the stream near the county line and froze to death. Local residents found the soldier's icy body the next morning. The reporter noted that the most recent drowning in the creek's "turbulent water" occurred in 1921. Another account states that "the body of an unidentified man was found in the road near the crossing, where it was buried and where the grave may still be seen [as of 1947]." Continuing westward from Deadman Creek, the overland road crossed Elm Creek before reaching Fort Phantom Hill, the next Butterfield stop, twelve miles from Smith's Station.[42]

The U.S. Army established Fort Phantom Hill on November 14, 1851, on a ridge between the Clear Fork of the Brazos River and Elm Creek, a short distance south of their confluence. Major John Joseph Abercrombie served as the first commander. The fort's original name was Post on the Clear Fork of the Brazos. The setting provides a commanding view of the neighboring terrain. When first seen from afar, the location appears to be on a mound. This initial perspective, however, is an apparition. When one arrives at the fort, this rise disappears and the terrain flattens out. The apparent knoll is a mirage, a fleeting, phantom hill. This topographical mirage explains why Brevet Major General Persifor F. Smith called it Phantom Hill in the fall of 1851 after selecting the site.[43]

The army's site selection process regarding Phantom Hill is typical of federal bureaucratic bungling on the antebellum Texas frontier. General Smith rushed to judgment on his choice of locales, not taking the time to fully evaluate potential drawbacks. Smith based his decision on one visit, an impression that failed to consider typical, year-round conditions and climate. When considering locations in West Texas, the army often failed to ask several basic questions. Did the setting offer an ample supply of water, timber, and arable soil? Had the army acquired legal title to the land? In many instances, the federal government neglected to secure title to a parcel before announcing its selection. Savvy Lone Star businessmen such as Samuel Maverick and John James often anticipated federal plans, snapping up title to "the sites with the best water and best timber in advance of the army's movements of forts into West Texas."[44]

Because of chronic poor planning, the U.S. Army frequently ended up paying rent for land on which it located forts. In addition to Maverick and James, other enterprising real estate speculators acquired acreage adjacent to military installations, forcing the federal government to lease these lands for requisite resources such as water, timber, and hay. Ironically, in 1851, General Persifor F. Smith made a plea for better federal foresight and planning regarding frontier outposts, arguing that the government should "make some arrangement for the purchase of sites for posts in Texas including land for wood and pasture." He noted that typically, "as soon as a post is established the land and all about it is entered in the Texas land office and exorbitant prices asked for rent, wood, and grass." Army officials ignored Smith's warning, and as a result, the military encountered lawsuits and controversy over leases and titles in West Texas.[45]

During the time the army garrisoned Fort Phantom Hill, various Comanche groups visited the post to trade. Emma Johnson Elkins, who lived at the fort as a young girl, recalled that the Indians mostly begged and stole and would kill anyone they caught off-post. Troops at Phantom Hill understood that they faced a formidable Comanche presence in the region. Adopting defensive measures, the soldiers dug an eight-foot-wide trench around the fort and placed artillery in the middle of the parade ground pointing outward. Elkins said that the garrison completed their work just in time, for a few days later, Buffalo Hump and 2,500 Comanches came within view. Upon approaching the outpost, however, and "seeing the preparations for their reception, it was too much for the noble red men, and they passed on with scowls and angry looks, going in a westerly direction."[46]

Menacing Comanches and land disputes were but a few of the problems plaguing federal efforts on the Texas frontier. Upon arriving at Phantom Hill, Major Abercrombie quickly determined the location's unsuitability for a military outpost. The major sent a request asking to halt construction, but General Smith was away from his office and unavailable. Not wishing to disobey a direct order, Abercrombie had no choice but to proceed. Because of the unfortunate location, it is no surprise that the military used Phantom Hill as a permanent outpost for only two and a half years before abandoning it. One officer stationed at Phantom Hill, Lieutenant Clinton Lear, bemoaned, "Everybody is disgusted. . . . I cannot imagine that God ever intended for [the] white man to occupy such a barren waste."[47]

The most pressing issue facing Major Abercrombie at Phantom Hill was the paucity of natural resources. In the vicinity of the post, most of the scrawny and irregularly shaped scrub oak, post oak, and blackjack trees were unsuited for building purposes, requiring the post commander to cut and haul wood from up to forty miles away. By 1853, construction crews had finished ten officers' quarters and five jacal barracks for the enlisted men. In late August of that same year, army inspector Brevet Lieutenant Colonel W. G. Freeman characterized the post as poorly constructed and of a "temporary character." He described the new barracks as already "dilapidated" and their thatched roofs unsound, and he predicted that the structures would probably collapse during the first severe winter storm.[48]

Phantom Hill's water supply was also problematic. It had a high salt content, which rendered it "brackish and bitter." General Smith had been aware of complaints regarding the water prior to selecting the site, but the "stubborn general was unmoved by the suggestion that the waters of the Clear Fork were saline" and declared that the post was surrounded by "fine running streams." Occasionally, soldiers on water detail would find a dead buffalo decomposing in their Clear Fork water supply. Often Elm Creek dried up completely, forcing the garrison to transport water in wagons from a spring four miles distant. In addition, the surrounding grasslands that the fort harvested hay from were soon exhausted. Major Abercrombie resorted to hauling forage to Phantom Hill from a considerable distance. Numerous outbreaks of scurvy among the troops also proved vexing. The post surgeon recommended raising more vegetables to supplement the garrison's limited diet. The local soil, however, was "poor and shallow" and ill suited for farming. Eventually, a combination of factors, severe climate, poor housing, salty water, and inadequate diet led to serious health problems among the troops stationed at

Phantom Hill. During one year, more men were sick in the hospital than available for active duty.[49]

During his official inspection in August 1853, Lieutenant Colonel Freeman described Phantom Hill's location as "uninviting," commenting that "no post visited, except Fort Ewell, presented so few attractions." One military historian says that over time these unresolved issues with the fort's water supply and the garrison's poor health led to a marked increase in dissension among the soldiers. Finally, the army admitted its mistake and ordered Phantom Hill's closure. On April 6, 1854, the new commander, Lieutenant Newton C. Givens, and his garrison of forty-two men marched away from the accursed post. Sometime between April and November 1854, arsonists struck Fort Phantom Hill. Exactly who torched the site is unknown. Possible suspects include the departing soldiers, who despised the fort and wanted to ensure that they would never be posted there again. The more likely scenario is that Comanches fired the abandoned buildings. A member of a federal wagon train passing by Phantom Hill in September 1857 reported that the post was "burned and razed by the Comanche Indians almost immediately after its evacuation (such is our information)."[50]

Historian Mildred P. Mayhall concurs with this view and believes that Penateka Comanches under the chiefs Sanaco, Yellow Wolf, and Buffalo Hump set fire to the structures. Mayhall says that the Comanches "had long resented this fort placed across their main line of passage." The army's military road from the Clear Fork to the North Concho, and the frontier outposts astride it, encroached on lands long used by Native Americans for seasonal hunting and camping. Surveying the charred ruins at Phantom Hill in 1857, one visitor reflected, "Nothing now remains of all the life and bustle which once thronged the precincts of . . . [the fort]. Bare and mouldering walls[,] blackened and crumbling chimneys[,] and here and there the 'fragment of a [knife] blade' reveal the site of the post."[51]

Perhaps the person hurt most by Phantom Hill's closure was post sutler J. J. Thibault. A native of Philadelphia, Thibault went to California during the gold rush and made a small fortune totaling $30,000. After returning to Philadelphia to marry his fiancée, he received news that a fire in San Francisco had burned all his assets, leaving him almost destitute. After casting about for some kind of employment in the West, Thibault landed a federal appointment as sutler at Fort Phantom Hill. Banking all he had on the frontier economy, the Pennsylvanian took out a line of credit, purchased a considerable supply of goods, and arrived at the post ready to start business. A short time after he opened his store at Phantom Hill, the garrison received orders to abandon the fort. With no outlet to sell his wares, Thibault loaded his goods onto an ox train consisting of eleven wagons, and with his bride, their new baby, and several hired men, he headed west for El Paso. By the time he got on the road, the fort's soldiers had already marched away, leaving Thibault and his caravan alone on the frontier. Shortly after his departure from Phantom Hill, a group of Comanches intercepted his ox train and demanded gifts. After receiving three barrels of whiskey, the Indians allowed him to continue.[52]

Some days later, a band of Mescalero Apaches attacked his caravan in the Guadalupe Mountains, on the same road later used by Butterfield stagecoaches. The Apaches murdered several of his men and took all of his livestock, except an ox and a mule. The raid cost him eighty oxen, twenty-five milk cows, and several horses, or roughly $3,000, the equivalent of six years' wages for the average Texan during this period. Leaving his goods in Guadalupe Pass, Thibault hitched a mule to a wagon, and with his wife, baby, and a Mexican boy, he rode on to El Paso, a hundred miles distant. After opening a store in nearby Socorro, Texas, with goods salvaged from the raid, Thibault made some of his money back, only to go bankrupt in a bid to secure the corn contract for Fort Bliss. A short time later, his wife took ill and, upon expiring, fell over, her lifeless body fatally smothering their infant. Almost insane with grief, Thibault left Texas for New Mexico's copper mines, where he reportedly made yet another fortune. If ever there was a star-crossed episode in the history of the federal frontier economy, it must be Fort Phantom Hill and its hapless sutler, J. J. Thibault.[53]

Even bad luck, abandonment, and arson could not prevent Phantom Hill from playing a continuing role in the daily life of antebellum West Texas. The old post's strategic position on the Fort Belknap to North Concho military road ensured its continued use by army patrols, travelers, and the Overland Mail Company. As Martha Doty Freeman points out, this important Texas thoroughfare was "a cultural, military, and economic highway that fed soldiers, traders, government explorers, immigrants, and the mail into the greater Southwest region."[54]

Although much of Phantom Hill's infrastructure burned in the 1854 fire, Butterfield employees renovated several surviving structures in the summer of 1858. The Overland Mail Company used one stone building as the station house and the post magazine as a storehouse. In addition, Phantom Hill's stable was still operational, as was an eighty-foot-deep well "twenty feet in diameter, which . . . had seventeen feet of water in it." A lone couple, the Burlingtons, managed the stage stop at the abandoned post.[55]

Waterman Ormsby, much impressed with this husband and wife team, observed that the courageous couple was utterly alone and exposed, "hundreds of miles from any settlement, . . . fearless of the attacks of blood-thirsty-Indians." Noting the station's location astride the Comanche trail, Ormsby spoke admiringly of Mr. Burlington, calling him "as brave a man as ever settled on a frontier." The newspaper reporter offered a strong rebuke of the U.S. Army and the Overland Mail Company for providing scant protection for these isolated stations and their occupants. Ormsby lamented that such negligence invited Indian attack and was tantamount to "trifling with human life." The stage stop certainly needed additional protection, as evidenced several months later in February 1859, when Comanches stampeded twenty-eight Butterfield mules "at the moment the coach was driven up to the station building." The following week, another band of Comanches made off with almost fifty horses from the station's corrals.[56]

In September 1859, Albert Richardson passed through Phantom Hill on a west-bound Butterfield stagecoach, arriving here at sunrise. Richardson commented on the numerous prairie dog towns, the barren terrain punctuated with cactus and mesquite, and the old post's "white ghostly chimneys." In December 1860, while traveling to St. Louis on his wedding trip, reporter Henry Dwight Barrows's stage-coach stopped at Phantom Hill. The newlywed remarked that the lone chimneys and burned buildings here reminded him of the "ruins of an ancient city." Barrows described the lonely setting as an "oasis in the desert," where he and his fellow Butterfield passengers enjoyed a sumptuous feast of buffalo and venison before a warm and cheery fire.[57]

Heading southwest to the next station at Mountain Pass, thirty miles distant, the Butterfield Road stayed between the Clear Fork and Elm Creek watersheds. The overland trail passed by East Peak and Castle Peak, also called Abercrom-bie Peak, namesake of Phantom Hill commander Major J. J. Abercrombie. Head-ing southwest, the road entered Mountain Pass, also known as Abercrombie Pass and Comanche Pass. Mountain Pass runs through the 2,400-foot Callahan Divide. The divide, which lies halfway between the Clear Fork and Colorado watersheds, was formerly known as the Abercrombie Range, yet another natu-ral feature named for the popular army major. Describing this impressive range, Waterman Ormsby observed, "At a distance they resembled the turrets and abut-ments of a lofty fortress. They could be seen for thirty or forty miles of our road." Today, drivers on Interstate 20 can see the Callahan Divide off in the distance south of Merkel, Texas.[58]

Mountain Pass Station sits on a hill, overlooking a fine spring. Today the spring is an enclosed pond, ringed by tall rushes. During the 1930s, the owner of the property, Sam Butman, Sr., told Butterfield historians Roscoe and Margaret Con-kling of his many visits to the stage stop in the 1880s. When Butman first saw the spring below the stage stop, it was "a shallow well . . . eight feet deep" and the water "flowed over the top of the well and down the branch [or creek]." Regard-ing the station buildings, Butman recalled, "At that time the chimneys were partly standing [and] the cedar log houses had been burned" by Indians. Butman also remembered seeing several graves of persons killed by raiding Native Americans a short distance east of the stage stop. When the Conklings visited Mountain Pass in May 1931, the station was "gone except for a few blocks of sandstone." Since the Conklings' visit, more recent landowners have bulldozed the site while doing fence work. Today, one can still see rocks from the old building and a scattering of period artifacts.[59]

In late September 1858, Waterman Ormsby observed two men named Lambshead working at Mountain Pass and Valley Creek, the next Butterfield station to the west. Thomas Lambshead had recently moved here from the Clear Fork with his nephew, William. Thomas ran the Valley Creek stage stop while William worked at Mountain Pass. In the spring of 1860, the *Dallas Herald* reported that William Lambshead, Shadrach Styer, and James Hamby were handling operations at Mountain Pass Station.[60]

When Ormsby's Butterfield coach stopped at Mountain Pass, an elderly African American woman served him a breakfast of "coffee, tough beef, and butterless short cake." The New York reporter commented on his hostess's appearance, saying that "if cleanliness is next to godliness, [she] would stand but little chance of heaven." Ormsby further remarked, "There is an old saying that 'every man must eat his peck of dirt.' I think I have had good measure with my peck on this trip, which has been roughing it with a vengeance." In marked contrast, *Daily Alta California* reporter J. M. Farwell enjoyed his visit here. Arriving at two in the morning in early November 1858, Farwell savored "a good meal of beef-steaks, eggs, coffee, and the like."[61]

Besides the bill of fare and accommodations along the route, another matter frequently discussed in period accounts was the efficiency of mail company operations. While breakfasting at Mountain Pass, Farwell met Henry Bates, Butterfield's superintendent for Division Six, between Red River and Fort Chadbourne. The correspondent, clearly impressed by a supervisor willing to work both day and night, noted that Bates "was making vigorous exertions to perfect the condition of the sections under his superintendence, as well as the improvements of the roads." However, Bates also had his detractors. In October 1859, a St. Louis correspondent relayed several complaints about the level of service along the line: "On this part of the route passengers commonly begin to swear." Coaches were overloaded and passengers crammed together, "like goods in the hold of a steamboat." Travelers also had to deal with "impudent" drivers and "utterly incompetent" conductors."[62]

Passengers also debated the hazards of overland travel. What one person might experience as mundane, another might perceive as life threatening. Commenting on his coach's easy passage down the Callahan Divide, J. M. Farwell said that the place could hardly be called a "pass," as the road was so smooth and the coach's rate of speed through it so fast. The occupants of a July 1860 eastbound coach might have differed with Farwell. A Celerity wagon with seven passengers, a driver, and a Butterfield conductor named Stout ran into serious trouble soon after leaving Mountain Pass Station. When the reinsman cracked his whip, the horses took off at a fast clip. Upon reaching the brow of the pass, the driver tried to apply his brakes before descending down the gorge. The brakes failed, forcing the vehicle's operator to take drastic measures. He turned the horses toward the side of the hill and drove the coach off the road. The wagon then hit a tree, "literally smashing the coach in pieces, killing one man . . . and injuring every other person in the stage to a more or less extent." The dead man was a cattle drover from Missouri named MacKay on his way to California. A newspaper report said that the conductor, Mr. Stout, who also served as a company road agent, "was severely cut on the face, his nose being completely flattened . . . [and also] complains of internal injuries." The fatal accident delayed overland mail service for thirty hours. In an odd twist of fate, MacKay had convinced the original ticket holder, a man from Iowa, to relinquish his seat on the ill-fated coach so that MacKay could ride with a friend.[63]

Butterfield passengers and employees faced not only transportation hazards but also injury or death from raiding Comanches. On nineteenth-century maps and illustrations, this Callahan Divide landmark typically appears as "Mountain Pass" or "Comanche Pass." Travelers called it Comanche Pass for good reason. A Texas Ranger's report to Governor Houston in 1860 said that depredating Indians frequented the gap. As in the case of Fort Phantom Hill to the east and Fort Chadbourne to the west, the Butterfield station at Mountain Pass sat astride a major Comanche trail. In 1856, a Comanche warrior ambushed an army express mail rider near the spring here. The Comanche's "intent was murder or robbery," but he soon "found that killing people was a game that two could play at and who lost his own life instead of taking that of another." After this 1856 attack, the valley's watershed acquired the name Comanche Creek. In November 1858, *Daily Alta California* reporter Farwell called it Comanche Springs.[64]

In January 1859, Indian raiders ran off eight mules just before the overland mail arrived at Mountain Pass Station. A few weeks later, a Butterfield employee killed a Comanche near the stage stop an hour before the coach came through. A report of the incident noted, "Four Comanches were skulking near the place for the purpose of running off some stock in care of a Mexican herdsman. The latter concealed himself and fired as the Indians approached, shooting one down, and then retreated in some haste." In March 1859 at Mountain Pass, "Indians killed a Negro man who was in the Company's employment." The increased frequency of deadly attacks at Mountain Pass and other stations in West Texas prompted the Overland Mail Company that same month to issue additional Sharps rifles and ammunition to its employees.[65]

Despite the issuance of more arms, however, the Indian raids continued. At three in the afternoon of April 12, 1860, fourteen Indians, likely Comanches, raided Mountain Pass Station. A newspaper account reported that Shadrach Styer, James Hamby, and twenty-three-year-old William Lambshead (Thomas Lambshead's nephew) were two hundred to three hundred yards from the stage stop when the attack commenced. The warriors shot and scalped Styer and Hamby, and "Lambshead, when last seen, was passing over the brow of a hill twenty or thirty yards in advance of his pursuers; his body has not yet been found." Next the raiders turned their attention to the stage stop, "which was defended by one man, and shot several arrows into the door." A short time after the Indians departed with five Butterfield mules, Styer appeared at the station entrance, "scalped and dripping with gore, presenting a truly horrid spectacle." He lasted another ten minutes before expiring.[66]

Mountain Pass's use as a stage stop did not end when Butterfield ceased operations in Texas in March 1861. In February 1869, Ben Ficklin's company repaired the old station when it revived this section of the overland line for passenger and mail service from Fort Concho, Texas, to Fort Smith, Arkansas. Chronic Native American depredations prompted the U.S. Army to establish a picket at Mountain Pass Station. On February 15, 1870, six African American soldiers from the Twenty-Fourth U.S. Infantry arrived at Mountain Pass to relieve the guard stationed there. Shortly thereafter, seventy-five Comanches swept down on the station. Despite the twelve to one odds, the troops made a determined stand, killing three Indians and driving off the rest. Before leaving, the raiders made off with five mules and one horse from the station's corral.[67]

Eleven months later, on New Year's Day in 1871, eighteen Texas Rangers and cowboys battled another band of Indian raiders in the gorge. After stealing horses from Coleman County, the warriors made for the pass, where Ranger captain James Swisher, rancher Sam Gholson, and their posse confronted them. The Indians, numbering less than twelve, retreated up the sides of the gap, and an all-day battle ensued. When night fell, the warriors abandoned their stolen horses and made their escape. The casualties numbered one Indian killed, with one cowboy and one raider wounded. Later that same year, in August 1871, an army private lost his life while guarding the station. Throughout its use as a stage stop, from 1858 to 1872, Mountain Pass consistently ranked as one of the deadliest sites on the entire Texas route.[68]

At the south end of Mountain Pass, the Butterfield Road veered southwesterly toward Elm Creek. During the 1870s, Taylor County ranchers began utilizing the Elm Creek drainage. In late 1874, M. C. Lambeth, one of the first settlers in the county, wintered 3,700 cattle at Elm Creek. Lambeth recalled that he traveled to Taylor County via the Butterfield Trail, an example of the road's continued use and enduring historical significance. After fording Elm Creek, the overland route crossed Cottonwood Creek before coming to the Falls at Valley Creek, near present-day Shep, Texas.[69]

Valley Creek Station, located at the falls, is fifteen miles from Mountain Pass. In September 1858, Waterman Ormsby found station keeper Thomas Lambshead tending a flock of three hundred sheep here. Lambshead was raising the sheep to sell to the U.S. Army at nearby Fort Chadbourne. The Valley Creek sheep venture in Taylor County augmented his growing cattle and farming operations on the Clear Fork near Camp Cooper. As Michael L. Tate notes, "[T]he delivery of beef, mutton, and other foods to military posts" ranked among the most profitable federal contracts available to citizens on the frontier.[70]

At Valley Creek, Thomas Lambshead enjoyed one of the more scenic locales for this section of the mail road. In 1857, one visitor commented favorably on the tranquil and rustic setting. Relaxing on its banks, he found Valley Creek most pleasant to behold, with its gleaming, "dancing waters, . . . full of fine fish[,] . . . overhung and shaded by willows and . . . forest trees." Today, the ambiance at Valley Creek is a far cry from its former pastoral surroundings. The shaded, well-watered nineteenth-century oasis no longer exists. Later settlers decided that a more profitable use of the natural resources would be to dam both forks of the stream behind spillways. A former landowner bulldozed the old mail station to enlarge his field and maximize crop yields. The restful stream and its pools are dry, the fish gone, and the falls of Valley Creek long silent.[71]

Ultimately, Thomas Lambshead's years of backbreaking work came to naught. During the Civil War, Indian raids devastated western Texas, and the line of settlement in many places retreated 150 miles to its former position in 1849. Like hundreds of other frontier families, Thomas Lambshead and his wife, Eliza, abandoned their holdings and moved eastward. The Lambsheads relocated to Austin, where in September 1863, Thomas became a clerk to Confederate captain G. H. Leigh, assistant commissary of subsistence.[72]

Thomas and Eliza subsequently moved to Bryan, Texas, where Thomas died on September 27, 1867. The following year, Eliza signed a deed selling both the Lambshead and Hammick Paint Creek properties. In the deed, Eliza stipulated that she was the only living heir for both her husband and her brother, Samuel Hammick. Tax rolls for Brazos County, Texas, show Eliza Lambshead almost impoverished. Her only material asset was a one-acre parcel worth fifty dollars. Whatever money Thomas and Eliza had prior to the Civil War was long gone by 1868. Eliza left Brazos County in 1869 and returned to England, where she settled in Pinhoe (near Exeter). She lived another thirty-seven years. Eliza Lambshead died in Devon, England, in 1906 at the age of eighty-five.[73]

The Lambshead frontier saga had traveled its full arc. Upon their arrival in Texas in 1848, the couple, filled with hope and a fresh start in the Peters Colony, worked hard for the next decade. Their early years were tough. They earned a negligible income, owned little property, and lived close to the margins. They lost their infant daughter. Despite such hardships, the promise of a fresh start in new lands lured other family members from England to Texas. Eliza's brother, Samuel, was the first to come, followed by Thomas's nephew, William.

Finally, it seemed that their hard work was beginning to pay off. Thomas was a founder of Throckmorton County and one of its first county commissioners. He secured a military beef contract and increased his cattle herd. He purchased five slaves to help with the farming and ranching. Next, the Overland Mail Company hired him as a section overseer and manager for two of its stations in Taylor County. At Valley Creek, he expanded his business ventures to include raising sheep for sale to the U.S. Army.

Then the dream began to sour. Comanches killed nephew William Lambshead at Mountain Pass. Texas seceded. Butterfield moved its operations northward to the Central Overland Route. The U.S. Army canceled its contracts and abandoned its frontier outposts. Relentless Indian raids forced the Lambsheads to abandon their hard-earned frontier investments and move to Austin. By 1868, Eliza had lost both her husband and her brother. Reduced once again to near poverty, she abandoned her hopes for a new life and a fresh start on the Texas frontier. For Eliza Lambshead, the dream was over. Facing a depressed post–Civil War economy in Texas, she sold her remaining assets for a fraction of their original value and returned home to England, where she spent her remaining years as a widow.

Roscoe Conkling in the 1930s, on trace of Butterfield Road leading from Fort Belknap to Brazos River crossing. Conkling Papers, courtesy of Seaver Center for Western History Research, Los Angeles County Museum of Natural History.

Ben Krebs of Krebs's Station in Young County, Texas. Photo courtesy of William Preston Krebs.

Ben Krebs's grave at Newport Cemetery, Carter County, Oklahoma. Photograph by the author.

BEN KREBS
DEC. 28 1828
FEB. 21 1901

Ruins of Krebs's Station. Photograph by the author.

Stone from Krebs's Station. Photograph by the author.

Krebs's Station water hole on Cribb Station Creek. Photograph by the author.

Krebs's Station artifacts. Photograph by the author.

James Madison Frans of Frans's Station and Clear Fork Station. Conkling Papers, courtesy of Seaver Center for Western History Research, Los Angeles County Museum of Natural History.

Frans's Station ruins. Photograph by the author.

Frans's Station artifacts. Photograph by the author.

Left to right: John Chadbourne Irwin, Elizabeth Frans Thorp (Frans's daughter), and Judge J. A. Matthews of Lambshead Ranch, in August 1932 at Stribling homestead, formerly Clear Fork Station site. Note the old Butterfield station well behind Judge Matthews. Conkling Papers, courtesy of Seaver Center for Western History Research, Los Angeles County Museum of Natural History.

Joe Allen at Clear Fork Station well, Stribling homestead. Photograph by the author.

Butterfield/military road crossing of Clear Fork of the Trinity. Photograph by the author.

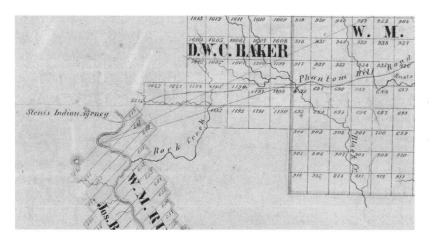

Detail of survey map showing Stem's Ranch ("Indian Agency") and 1851 U.S. military road from Fort Belknap to North Concho (Phantom Hill Road). Map #83007, *1854 Map of the Surveyed Part of Peters Colony, Texas* (western part), courtesy of Texas General Land Office Archives, Austin.

Ruins of Jesse Stem–Thomas Lambshead ranch, Lambshead Creek, Throckmorton County, Texas. Photograph by the author.

Building outline of Jesse Stem–Thomas Lambshead homestead. Photograph by the author.

Artifacts from Jesse Stem–Thomas Lambshead ranch site. Photograph by the author.

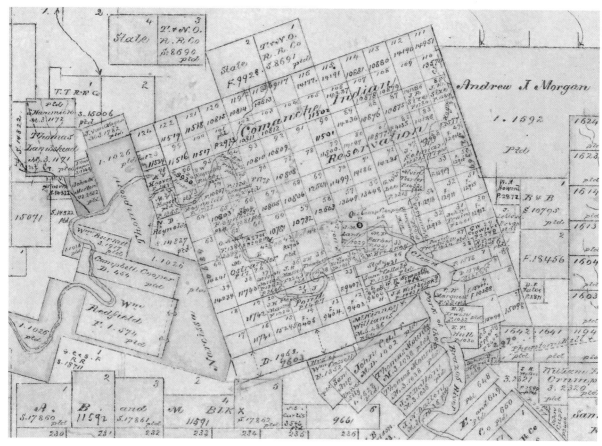

Detail of survey map showing Samuel Hammick and Thomas Lambshead Surveys (*upper left*), Old Camp Cooper (*center*), and Comanche Indian Reservation. Map #4079, *March 1880 Map of Throckmorton County, Texas*, courtesy of Texas General Land Office Archives, Austin.

Smith's Station on Chimney Creek, Shackelford County, Texas. The landowner reconstructed the chimney. Photograph by the author.

Chimney Creek, which provided water for Smith's Station. Photograph by the author.

Smith's Station artifacts, located by Joe Allen during a field study for the landowner. Photograph by the author.

Fort Phantom Hill Butterfield Station in the 1930s. Conkling Papers, courtesy of Seaver Center for Western History Research, Los Angeles County Museum of Natural History.

Fort Phantom Hill magazine in the 1930s, used by Butterfield as a storehouse. Conkling Papers, courtesy of Seaver Center for Western History Research, Los Angeles County Museum of Natural History.

Author at Mountain Pass, Taylor County, Texas. Photograph by Roland Ely.

Mountain Pass Station ruins and artifacts. Photograph by the author.

Roland Ely at Mountain Pass Station spring and water hole. Photograph by the author.

Mountain Pass Station artifacts collected by Barry Scott. Photograph by the author.

Garland Richards (*left*), friend (*center*), and Joe Allen (*right*) at site of Valley Creek Station, Taylor County, Texas. Photograph by the author.

Rock from the station building, pushed by the landowner into Valley Creek. Photograph by the author.

Margaret Conkling and landowner in November 1938, in Butterfield/military road crossing of Valley Creek. Conkling Papers, courtesy of Seaver Center for Western History Research, Los Angeles County Museum of Natural History.

From Fort Chadbourne to the North Concho

Comanche Moon, Tom Lovell. Oil on canvas, 1971. Courtesy of Abell-Hanger Foundation and the Permian Basin Petroleum Museum, Library, and Hall of Fame, Midland, Texas (where the painting is on permanent display).

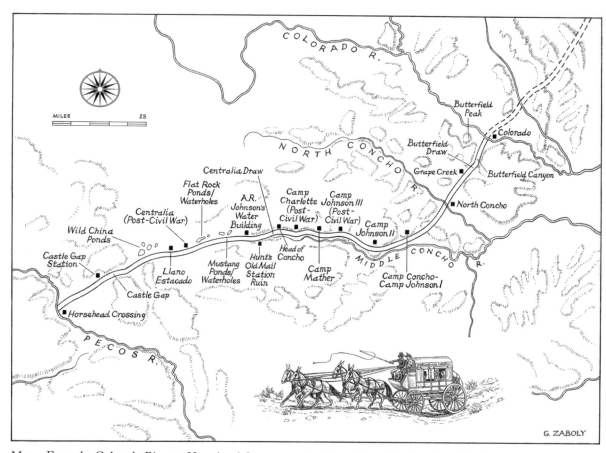

Map 4. From the Colorado River to Horsehead Crossing on the Pecos River. Map by Gary Zaboly.

Upon leaving Valley Creek, the Butterfield Road passed through a wide saddle between two hills and entered Nolan County. Next, the trail cut southeast of Church Mountain and ventured into Runnels County briefly before crossing into Coke County. A short distance from the Coke County line is Fort Chadbourne, the next Butterfield station, twelve miles from Valley Creek. Fort Chadbourne was the last military outpost on the route until Fort Stockton, 215 miles to the west. The Overland Mail Company station here was on the north side of the enlisted men's barracks. Employees quarried sandstone blocks for the building from nearby Oak Creek. The postmaster at Chadbourne, George Leigh, was also one of the fort's sutlers.[1]

In the fall of 1860, an eastbound stagecoach carrying William Tallack made a brief stop at the frontier outpost. "To-day [sic] we reached Fort Chadbourne, and breakfasted at the first inclosed [sic] farm we have seen since leaving California," Tallack wrote, "and at the same time met with the first appearance of slavery in our route, as a regular institution." The bill of fare at the Chadbourne stage stop left something to be desired. Tallack noted, "Our table and food were black with clustering flies, which crowded even into our tea, and had to be spooned out."[2]

The U.S. Army established Fort Chadbourne on October 29, 1852. Before its construction, the nearest federal outpost for this section of West Texas had been forty-three miles to the southwest, on the North Concho River. The army named the North Concho site for Captain Joseph Eggleston Johnston, who reconnoitered the military road from Fort Belknap to the North Concho in the fall of 1851. Soldiers first garrisoned Camp J. E. Johnston on March 15, 1852. The setting, situated on a high bluff overlooking the river, seemed ideally suited for a military encampment. Within a few weeks, however, the post's location proved problematic, and both enlisted men and officers began voicing strident objections.[3]

Camp Johnston's unsuitable locale once again raised questions about the army's erratic and slipshod site selection process. As in the case of Fort Phantom Hill, there was a shortage of timber at Camp Johnston. The available wood was scrawny and poorly suited for building. Assessing his surroundings, camp commander Colonel John Garland stated that "it had been a mistake to think that even half a regiment could be sheltered on the North Concho . . . [as] even Indians would have shunned" it. During the summer of 1852, severe weather and flooding endangered the outpost. Violent hailstorms and high winds blew over tents and stripped the trees of their leaves. During one such episode, a group of terrified chickens belonging to one soldier sought shelter inside his tent. Compounding Garland's frustrations, in early October 1852, a group of Comanche warriors swept down on the encampment and made off with numerous horses.[4]

After only a few months at Camp Johnston, the army began scouring the surrounding countryside for a more suitable location. The post sutler, Richard Austin Howard, lobbied Colonel Garland to have the federal government select Kickapoo Springs in Concho County as the new site. Howard, a former soldier and surveyor turned merchant-businessman, was part owner of Kickapoo Springs, situated on the Upper Emigrant Road from San Antonio, and stood to make a tidy sum on leasing the land to the government. Whenever the federal government made a move on the frontier, land speculators, contractors, and merchants were not far behind.[5]

Finally, in October 1852, General Persifor F. Smith selected a new position for the federal outpost, forty-three miles to the northeast in Coke County, where Johnston's military road crossed Oak Creek. The army named the site Fort Chadbourne, after Lieutenant Theodore Chadbourne, who died in May 1846 during the Mexican War battle of Resaca de la Palma. In April 1857, the well-connected Richard Howard secured the position as post sutler at Chadbourne. Howard was a close friend of several prominent army officers in Texas. The sutler lived on post with his wife and stocked his store with a wide assortment of provisions and goods freighted in from Fredericksburg and San Antonio. He and his partner, George H. Leigh, proved popular with the troops, and in April 1860, a review board at Chadbourne reappointed the firm of Howard and Leigh as post sutler.[6]

As with Jesse Stem and Thomas Lambshead, the prospect of lucrative government contracts, jobs, and various business opportunities drew all types of persons to the West Texas frontier. Two such people locating near Fort Chadbourne were Andrew J. MacKay and John C. Gooch, whose financial interests stretched from the Clear Fork to Fort Chadbourne and beyond. During the antebellum period, McKay and Gooch actively solicited government contracts. Through their persistent efforts, the pair secured agreements to deliver hay, corn, and flour to several regional outposts. In addition to their operations at Camp Cooper and the Clear Fork, the partners capitalized on the Fort Chadbourne market. MacKay and Gooch established a ranch seven miles to the east-northeast, near an important crossroads on Fish Creek. Their property lay on the Fort Chadbourne–Camp Colorado road and not far from the Fort Chadbourne–Fort Gates road. While half of their ranch was hilly, rocky terrain, the other half was flat, with rich bottomland soil, and ideally suited for farming. Even today, their Runnels County property is still prime agricultural acreage. In November 1853, Andrew MacKay purchased the 640-acre Fish Creek ranch near Fort Chadbourne for $125 from his friend William C. Dalrymple. Three years earlier, in 1850, MacKay had been living at Dalrymple's home in Williamson County, Texas, while working as a trader.[7]

The person handling the Dalrymple-MacKay land sale in 1853 was Benjamin Gooch, the Williamson County clerk. Benjamin Gooch's nephew was none other than John C. Gooch, MacKay's business partner. John enlisted his brother Ben F. Gooch to assist in the firm's day-to-day operations. Soon after moving to the Texas frontier, MacKay and Gooch began bidding on multiple supply contracts for the U.S. Army. In 1851, MacKay inked an agreement to supply corn to Fort Gates. In 1854, Gooch secured the corn and beef contracts for Fort Chadbourne. Gooch and MacKay's Fish Creek ranch was in an ideal setting for farming and ranching, but its remote, exposed position seven miles from Fort Chadbourne left it vulnerable to Indian raids. In July 1854, Comanches made off with the ranch's entire cattle herd.[8]

Persevering through such setbacks, within two years the partners had once again secured the Chadbourne corn contract, at more than double the previous price. In 1859, they landed a lucrative agreement to provide hay for the post. The next year, the government renewed their hay contract with an even larger order at significantly higher prices. By the summer of 1860, MacKay had become a wealthy man from his numerous frontier investments. Despite the demands of his business, he still found time to pen a letter praising the Butterfield Overland Mail and its benefits to the Fort Chadbourne community. MacKay noted that the enterprise was "succeeding admirably" and that he received the St. Louis paper in eight days and the New York paper in ten, which was "rather good for these western wilds and few inhabitants."[9]

While some like MacKay and the Gooch brothers came to West Texas in hopes of landing government contracts for beef, timber, forage, and freighting, others sought to capitalize on the soldiers' paychecks, opening off-post stores, saloons, and brothels. At Fort Chadbourne, these businesses located at "The Flat," an area just below the post next to Oak Creek. Another group seeking opportunities for trade on the antebellum frontier was Native Americans. In February 1853, Delaware Indians brought thirty animal skins to sell at the fort. By March and April, Comanches and whites were conducting a brisk business at Chadbourne.[10]

The Indians traded deerskins, moccasins, dolls, headdresses, and even picture art. Frontier traders scrambled to meet the strong demand among white collectors for Native American clothing and accessories such as ornamental beadwork. In October 1854, the U.S. Army issued strict orders regulating the trade between whites and Indians at Fort Chadbourne. In particular, under no circumstances were Native Americans allowed to trade for liquor, firearms, or ammunition. Lieutenant Alfred Pleasonton warned potential transgressors, "The penalties in each case are very great, and will be enforced."[11]

Indians and whites reached a détente of sorts while trading at Chadbourne, but off post, the fort's residents became potential prey. In September 1854, marauding warriors shot thirteen arrows into Private Matlock of Company F, Second Dragoons while he was enjoying a midnight bath in Oak Creek below the fort. Post surgeon Ebenezer Swift noted that Matlock had six arrows "sticking in his back, . . . Two others entered the cavity of the thorod [*sic*] and two the abdomen." Post commander Captain Patrick Calhoun predicted that the private would die, but Matlock recovered.[12]

Reporting on the attack, one period newspaper expressed "deep concern for the safety" of Chadbourne's tiny garrison, noting "that there are some four or five hundred Comanches surrounding the fort." To deter the Indians, the army had only fifty men and "many of these not worth much." Butterfield passenger Waterman Ormsby observed that the post's commander had implemented defensive safeguards at the fort when he arrived in September 1858. Ormsby noted that Chadbourne was "almost surrounded by a sort of barricade which was built a few years since in anticipation of a sweeping attack by the Indians—which did not come off." Albert Richardson, a Butterfield passenger traveling through a year later, remarked that "the Comanches regard our soldiers [at Fort Chadbourne] much as they would a company of children armed with pop-guns and penny whistles." Because of their numerical superiority, the Comanches could have at any time easily overrun Fort Chadbourne, but they chose not to because of the economic advantages the fort offered, namely, opportunities for trading and raiding.[13]

In July 1858, when the Overland Mail Company arrived in Texas to construct and provision stations along the line, Fort Chadbourne became a regional operations hub. The remote outpost served as the dividing line between Butterfield's Division Six, which ran from Fort Chadbourne eastward to the Red River, and Division Five, which spanned the western section of Texas, between Fort Chadbourne and El Paso. Henry Bates managed Division Six, while James Glover (later replaced by Henry Smith) supervised Division Five.[14]

In early August 1858, the Overland Mail Company deposited two coaches and livestock at Fort Chadbourne in preparation for the route's inaugural run in September. At the end of August, a caravan of twelve to fifteen Celerity coaches, twenty-five men, and 250 mules passed through Fort Chadbourne en route for El Paso. Although better suited to the dry and dusty environs than the heavier, all-wood Concord stagecoaches, the Celerity canvas-topped wagons were similarly susceptible to mechanical problems. In January 1859, an eastbound wagon broke down fifty miles west of Fort Chadbourne. Butterfield agents left the passengers, all from San Francisco, at the scene of the accident and carried the mail on horseback on to the fort. At Chadbourne, the employees put the mail on another coach and continued the trip eastward. The replacement stagecoach got within forty miles of Fort Smith before "the tongue of the vehicle was broken and the mail a second time put upon horseback."[15]

In February 1859, the Overland Mail Company slipped more than a day behind schedule after an eastbound coach overturned near the Colorado River, south of Fort Chadbourne. While Butterfield employees were fixing the vehicle, the westbound stagecoach arrived and promptly "capsized near the same place." One passenger in the second coach suffered a broken shoulder, while another received several serious gashes on his face. After completion of the repairs, the eastbound Celerity wagon resumed its journey. Near Bolivar, Missouri, at eight o'clock at night, a highwayman stopped this same ill-fated coach, while his "accomplices" rifled the contents of the vehicle's boot, or storage compartment. A newspaper report of the incident noted, "The mail coaches have been stopped on several occasions previously, and the 'boot' has been found cut open." Some writers have claimed that Butterfield never transported precious metals, but this is incorrect. Company road agent W. H. Pardee stated that in December 1858, he carried "a large amount of gold and silver coin . . . to distribute, as directed, between St. Louis and Tucson."[16]

Butterfield property presented a tempting target not only for Anglo outlaws but also for Native American raiders. In January 1859, Comanches stole "a large number of animals" from the overland corrals at Fort Chadbourne and neighboring stations. In March 1860, another group of Comanche raiders killed a company blacksmith near the fort.[17]

Upon leaving Fort Chadbourne, the overland road through Coke County struck a southwesterly course for the next fifteen miles, en route to the next stop, at Colorado Station. After crossing Oak Creek, the Butterfield Trail passed east of Nipple Peak, Kickapoo Mountain, and Hayrick Mountain, crossing Turkey Creek and Cow Creek before reaching the Colorado River When Waterman Ormsby passed through in September 1858, the Overland Mail Company had not yet built a stage stop on the north bank of the river. A few weeks later, however, correspondents for both San Francisco newspapers mentioned Colorado Station.[18]

Albert Richardson arrived here on the night of September 29, 1859, and the river was flooding, forcing the coach to halt until the waters receded. As there was no room in the cramped station, he and his fellow passengers passed the night in their canvas-topped coach. Richardson lamented, "The vehicle's roof was like a sieve, and cold pitiless rain deluged us all night." The morning was only somewhat better. Richardson commented, "Awoke cold and rheumatic; but . . . breakfasted heartily upon pork and mesquite beans; and dried our clothes before the fire." After waiting two days for the rain-swollen river to subside, Richardson's coach finally made it across to the south side, but not before "the strong current swept our six little mules several yards down the stream, and compelled them to swim." Capturing a bit of the western frontier flavor, Richardson recalled that when his Celerity wagon exited the river bottom, its wheels ran over several rattlesnakes lounging in the overland trail. Seeing the crushed rattlers in the roadbed prompted Richardson to remark that "their flesh was a favorite dish with old plainsmen."[19]

Today, the remnants of the Butterfield station, an "adobe hut" on the north bank of the Colorado, lie in a plowed field overlooking the river. As occurred at Valley Creek, farming and ranching operations on the Colorado took precedence over preserving the region's early history. Walking across the field, one can still find pieces of quarried sandstone, old bottle fragments, bullets, square nails, pottery shards, and hatchet blades from the old station. At the southern edge of the field, a wide V-shaped opening in the dark red bluff marks the passage used by Butterfield coaches in their descent to the Colorado River crossing.[20]

From the Colorado south to the North Concho River, the Overland Mail Company continued following Captain Johnston's military road from Fort Belknap. In September 1858, while en route to the North Concho, a nervous Waterman Ormsby closely questioned the driver of his coach, J. B. Nichols, regarding the direction and safety of the route. Nichols exhibited a laconic and detached manner. Ormsby asked, "Do you know the road?" Nichols replied, "No." Ormsby pressed the man for more information. "How do you expect to get there?" Nichols answered, "There's only one road; we can't miss it." As they were driving at night through the heart of Comanche country, Ormsby queried, "Have you any arms?" An unconcerned Nichols replied, "No, I don't want any; there's no danger."[21]

For the next leg of the journey, to Grape Creek Station, the overland trail generally kept between Buffalo Creek on the east and Cement Creek on the west. Dominating the horizon is a prominent 2,100-foot conical-shaped hill that appears on county and federal maps as Butterfield Peak. The mail road passed just south of Butterfield Peak and Cement Creek. A government wagon train camped at this spot in September 1857, in the shadow of adjacent Cement Mountain. The setting's dramatic scenery captivated the imagination of the caravan's chronicler, who observed, "Towering immediately above . . . is a lofty hill with a castellated turret crowning its summit[,] the picturesque and massive proportions of which seem as though they might be the results of the labors of giants working out the designs of Titanic architects."[22]

Passing between Cement Mountain and two other conical hills lying to the west, the Overland Mail Road entered Butterfield Canyon. The name "Butterfield Canyon" appears on federal, state, and county maps, another instance of the mail road's lasting legacy. The canyon leads up to the top of a sizeable 2,400-foot divide that separates the Colorado and Concho River watersheds. When Ormsby's coach attempted this precipitous ascent at nighttime, one of the mules "could neither be coaxed [n]or driven up, so we had to camp until morning, when, after much difficulty, we ascended the hill." Today, the old Butterfield Trail up the divide is still in use as a working ranch road, although the last section is very steep and extremely rough and best traversed on foot. At the top of Butterfield Canyon, the road passed by Buffalo Spring, the source of Buffalo Creek, which empties into the Colorado River eleven and a half miles to the northeast.[23]

On the western side of the divide, the overland road entered a valley running to the southwest, shown on maps as Butterfield Draw. In all of Texas, Coke County enjoys the unique distinction of having the most natural features named after the Butterfield Overland Mail. The mail company erected its next station, Grape Creek, at the first source of permanent water in Butterfield Draw. This never-failing spring, located under a rock ledge on the south side of the draw, flows into East Grape Creek a short distance downstream. The station site near the spring and a beautiful grove of live oaks is one of the prettiest settings along the Texas portion of the route.[24]

In 1857, the Leach Wagon Train, a federal road-building expedition, was one of the first to take note of the choice site. As in the cases of Mountain Pass and Valley Creek Stations, the Overland Mail Company likely consulted the Leach report when locating its Grape Creek stage stop. An entry in the expedition's diary describes the spring here: at the bottom of "a heavy ledge of rocks . . . lies a magnificent reservoir of water as clear as crystal." While camped for three days in Butterfield Draw, the Leach party caught copious quantities of catfish, trout, perch, and even soft-shelled turtle. The wagon train's diarist, obviously enchanted with Grape Creek, noted that the stream "either sleeps quietly in deep dark pools beneath over-reaching boughs . . . or flashes merrily over a rocky chasm to rest again in another mimic lake." The writer also observed abundant game near their camp. "We momentarily caught glimpses of herds of deer and antelope which as they bounded lightly along at the first sight of their natural enemy, man, lent grace and animation to this lovely scene where nature itself seems moved into amorous silence by the charms which the Almighty has lavished upon this favored spot." Unlike other Butterfield locales in West Texas, Grape Creek's natural advantages remain much the same today as they did before the Civil War. Later landowners utilized the land for farming and ranching without sacrificing its core environmental and historical assets.[25]

When the first Butterfield coach arrived at Grape Creek on the morning of September 24, 1858, with Waterman Ormsby the lone passenger on board, the stage stop was still under construction. Overland Mail employees were living in tents inside a corral "built of upright rough timber, planted in the ground." Wary of Indian attacks, the men working at the station alternated guard duty every two hours. Henry Roylan was the first of several managers at Grape Creek Station and occasionally drove company stagecoaches. Period accounts call this stage stop "Roylan's," "Ryland," and "Grape Creek."[26]

On Halloween 1858, "a strolling band of seven Comanches" entered the station corral in broad daylight and made off with seven mules and a horse while three employees at the adjacent stage stop stood by and made no attempt to stop them. Butterfield passenger J. M. Farwell, the correspondent for the *Daily Alta California*, noted that "the men said they would have offered resistance, but had no arms." Farwell retorted that "they were well armed, but lacked courage."[27]

In early 1861, thirty Comanches swept down on Grape Creek and stole all of the station's livestock. The head of the raiding party, who exuded a haughty and arrogant attitude, subsequently examined the stolen mules and horses. Supremely confident in his numerical and tactical superiority, he returned to the stage stop and lodged a complaint with Butterfield employees about the poor quality of the animals. The Comanche leader barged into the station house and admonished those inside that he expected a better grade of stock to be on hand when he returned in a month or he and his men would kill them. Before leaving the building, he grabbed a fine blanket on the bed, turned around, and then stormed out.[28]

True to his word, the chief and his band visited the stage stop again the following month. Angry after finding only a "wagon team and one or two ponies" in the corrals, the warriors launched a full-scale attack on the Grape Creek building and its occupants. The Comanches first set fire to the log cabin. Forced to flee the burning station, manager Joel Pennington, his wife, brother-in-law Charles Cox, and Elijah Helms ran outside, where the Indians were waiting. In their opening salvo, the Comanches blew off part of Pennington's face with a shotgun blast, "breaking both jaws." Helms and Cox returned fire, forcing the raiders to withdraw. Helms's cool and courageous conduct during the attack saved Pennington and his wife "from being scalped." After rescuing Pennington, Helms and Cox transported him to Fort Chadbourne, where the post surgeon, Jesse Denson, attended to his "horrible" facial wounds. Pennington had recovered sufficiently by early March 1861 to return home to Fort Mason, Texas.[29]

The struggle between the Overland Mail Company and Comanches for control of Grape Creek and its resources is typical for this section of the frontier. The only military outpost on the overland road between the Clear Fork and the Pecos River was Fort Chadbourne. During the Butterfield period, the number of troops at Fort Chadbourne never exceeded ninety-four. From August 1859 to April 1860, the garrison numbered in the sixties, hardly an intimidating deterrent for raiding Comanches.[30]

The charred logs from Grape Creek Station decomposed long ago. Today, only the building's foundation stones and an assortment of period artifacts mark the picturesque location of the old overland stage stop, next to the still-flowing sylvan spring amid beautiful live oaks. En route to the North Concho River, Butterfield stagecoaches continued on Captain Johnston's military road. The twelve-mile journey to the next stage stop on the North Concho was a gradual descent over mostly level terrain, an easy passage for Celerity wagons. Several miles south of Grape Creek Station, near Ruby Point, are the remnants of a sizeable nineteenth-century military and civilian campground. Shortly after passing the camp, the Butterfield Road veered to the southwest, striking the North Concho on the outskirts of present-day Carlsbad, Texas.[31]

When the Overland Mail Company published its original itinerary, it included no listing for a North Concho stage stop. In late September 1859, however, Butterfield passenger Albert Richardson remarked that he "dined at the North Concho." He related that during dinner, "Our spirited little landlady, reared in eastern Texas, gave us a description of an attack made by a hundred and twenty Comanches three weeks before." As the warriors approached, she and her husband barricaded themselves in the log station house. Grabbing their rifles, the couple launched a fusillade at the attackers, keeping them at bay. Despite the couple's well-placed rifle fire, the Comanches still managed to drive off all of the mules and cattle from the corral. The raiders then departed, leaving "a dozen of their iron-pointed feather-tipped arrows . . . still sticking in the [cabin's] cottonwood logs" as a memento of their visit.[32]

Only a few hours before this attack, the husband had been riding to the North Concho Station when a group of Comanches spotted him. A two-mile chase ensued. Thanks to his fleet-footed horse, the station keeper managed to stay ahead of his pursuers, who were shooting arrows at him, one of which went through his hat. The husband "laughed heartily" while recounting the story to Richardson, "but his little wife was only angry, declaring vehemently that they would not be driven out of the country by worthless Red-skins [sic]."[33]

Over the years, most writers have overlooked the North Concho Station and its history. The stage stop sits in a field on the north bank, next to the Butterfield river crossing. Sometime after the Comanche attack in 1859, the mail company replaced the cabin with a more secure stone structure. Since the 1880s, landowners have greatly altered the site's appearance, plowing over the ruins and scattering slabs of limestone and artifacts over a wide area. At the southern edge of the plowed field, one can still see an excellent trace of the overland road as it winds its way down the riverbank to the North Concho.[34]

Fort Chadbourne, Texas, January 1854, Charles Shuchard. From *Survey of a Route on the 32nd Parallel for the Texas Western Railroad, 1854: The A. B. Gray Report*, courtesy of Texas State Library and Archives Commission, Austin, Prints and Photographs Collection.

Detail of survey map showing the Fort Chadbourne road system. The road running southwest from Church Mountain through the fort is the Butterfield/military road. The road running south and then east is the road to Fort Gates. MacKay-Gooch Ranch is near the intersection of Fort Gates Road and Fish Creek. The road heading south/southeast goes to San Antonio. Map #4003, *May 1867 Map of Runnels County, Texas*, courtesy of Texas General Land Office Archives, Austin.

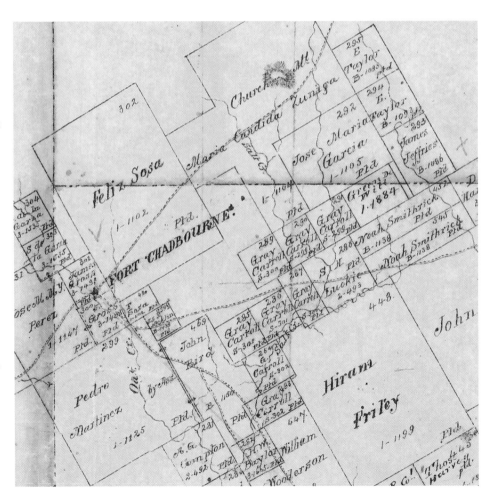

Garland and Lana Richards, Fort Chadbourne Foundation. The Richardses have worked tirelessly for decades to restore the fort. Photograph by the author.

Restored Butterfield station at Fort Chadbourne, Coke County, Texas. Photograph by the author.

Restoration of enlisted men's barracks at Fort Chadbourne in 2002. Photograph by the author.

Historic graffiti at Fort Chadbourne from October 1858. Photograph by the author.

Lana Richards pointing out wheel ruts carved in sandstone by wagons and coaches along the Butterfield/ military road from Fort Chadbourne to the Colorado River. Photograph by the author.

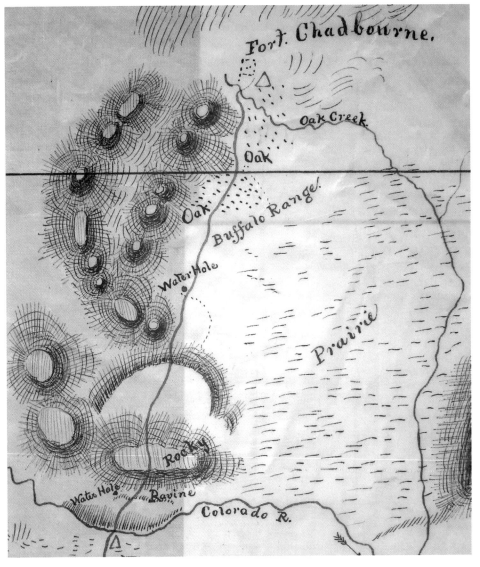

Detail of map showing the Butterfield/military road from Fort Chadbourne to the Colorado River. From Lieutenant Colonel E. J. Strang, *Topographical Sketch of the Road from Fort Stockton to Fort Chadbourne, October and November 1867*, National Archives Cartographic and Architectural Section, College Park, Md.

Site of Colorado Station, Coke County, Texas. Rock from the station building is visible in the foreground. Photograph by the author.

Detail of Colorado Station rocks and artifacts. Photograph by the author.

Cumbie Ivey at Butterfield/military road trace leading down to the Colorado River crossing. Photograph by the author.

Wayne McCabe in front of Butterfield Peak, Coke County, Texas. Photograph by the author.

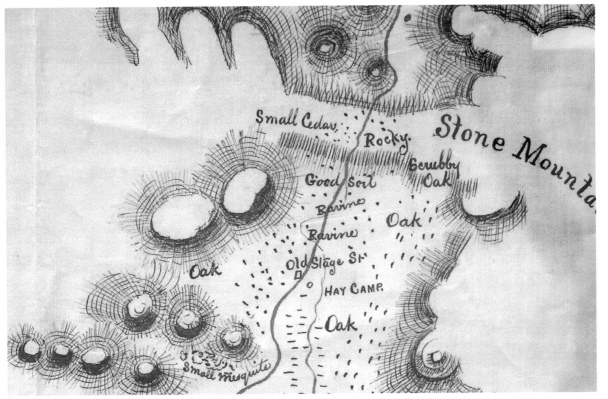

Detail of map showing the Butterfield/military road from Butterfield Peak to Grape Creek Station ("Old Stage St").
From Lieutenant Colonel E. J. Strang, *Topographical Sketch of the Road from Fort Stockton to Fort Chadbourne, October and November 1867*, National Archives Cartographic and Architectural Section, College Park, Md.

Joe Allen on Butterfield/military road in Butterfield Canyon, Coke County, Texas. Photograph by the author.

Roscoe Conkling (*right*) standing in the overland road at the top of Butterfield Canyon with John Abe March (*left*) and his young son, Jock March (*center*), in July 1933. Conkling Papers, courtesy of Seaver Center for Western History Research, Los Angeles County Museum of Natural History.

Patrick Dearen (*left*) and Hugh Stone (*right*) in Butterfield Draw, Coke County, Texas, with the Butterfield/military road visible on the right side. Photograph by the author.

Ruins of Grape Creek Station, Coke County, Texas. Photograph by the author.

Artifacts from Grape Creek Station. Photograph by the author.

Close-up of Grape Creek Station artifact (note "St. Louis" on metal plate). Photograph by the author.

Grape Creek Spring, the water source for the stage stop. Photograph by the author.

North Concho Station ruins, Tom Green County, Texas. Photograph by the author.

North Concho Station artifacts. Photograph by the author.

Trace of Butterfield Road leading down to crossing of the North Concho River. Photograph by the author.

North Concho River site of 1852 Camp J. E. Johnston, named after army captain Joseph Eggleston Johnston, who laid out the 1851 military road from Fort Belknap south to the North Concho. From 1858 to 1861, the Overland Mail Company utilized Johnston's road. Photograph by the author.

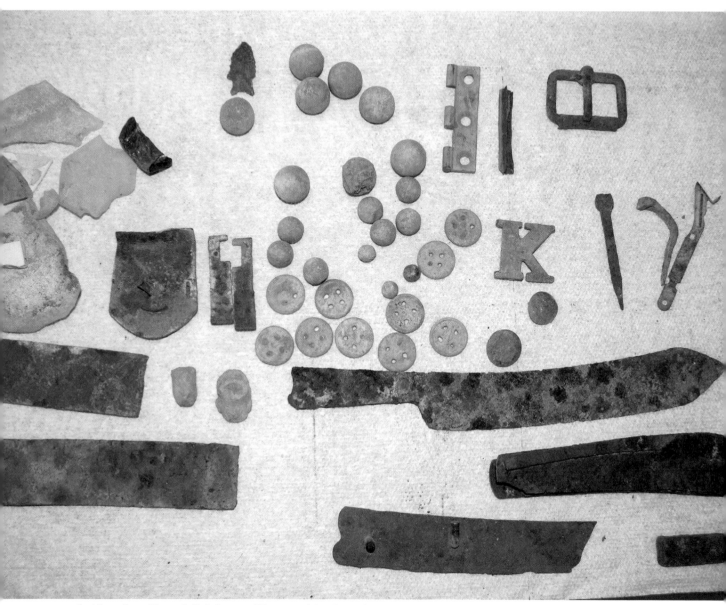

Artifacts from Camp J. E. Johnston. Photograph by the author.

CHAPTER 7

From the North Concho
to Horsehead Crossing

Horsehead Crossing on the Pecos River, Tom Lovell. Oil on canvas, 1975. Courtesy of Abell-Hanger Foundation and the Permian Basin Petroleum Museum, Library, and Hall of Fame, Midland, Texas (where the painting is on permanent display).

After fording the North Concho, the Butterfield Road branched off from the federal military road, which continued on to Fort Mason. For the next 15 miles down to the Middle Concho River, stagecoaches traversed a fresh track opened by the mail company in the summer of 1858. Shortly after striking the Middle Concho, the new route joined the 1849 Upper Emigrant Road from San Antonio and Fredericksburg. From the Middle Concho westward to Horsehead Crossing on the Pecos River, the Overland Mail Company followed this older overland route, first explored by Lieutenant Francis Theodore Bryan of the U.S. Topographical Engineers during June and July 1849. As Butterfield stagecoaches crossed West Texas's rugged terrain, their pace was by no means rapid. Throughout the 414-mile section between Fort Chadbourne and El Paso, the company's Celerity wagons averaged only 2.7 miles per hour, the slowest rate of travel along the entire St. Louis to San Francisco route. In comparison, from El Paso to Tucson, the typical speed was three times faster, at 9 miles per hour.[1]

The first station on the Middle Concho was near West Rocky Creek, not far from present-day Arden, Texas. Period timetables and newspaper reports listed the station first as Camp Concho and later as Camp Johnson or Johnson's Station, after Adam Rankin Johnson, Butterfield's overseer for this section of the mail road. Johnson and his brothers, Thomas and Ben, who assisted with stagecoach operations, were Kentucky natives who migrated to Burnet, Texas, in the 1850s. The Johnson brothers are among the more successful stories from the antebellum federal frontier economy. The Johnson family adroitly diversified their operations to maximize potential revenue from both federal and state governments. Whether surveying, freighting, operating a string of overland stations, or serving in the Texas Rangers, the three brothers understood the mechanics of making a living on the frontier.[2]

From 1859 to 1861, Adam Rankin Johnson oversaw operations for several Overland Mail Company stage stops, namely, Johnson's Station, Camp Mather, Head of Concho, Llano Estacado, Castle Gap Station, Horsehead Crossing, Van Horn's Wells, and Eagle Spring. When not attending to overland business matters, Johnson served as a state land surveyor in central and West Texas and occasionally as an Indian fighter in the Texas Rangers. Many of the men who worked for Johnson at these Butterfield stations also worked on his survey crews and participated in the same Indian fights. In addition to brothers Thomas and Ben, other regulars in Johnson's frontier group were James O. Nored from Burnet, Texas, surveyor Oscar Call of New York, and Neil Helm of Missouri, whom Johnson called his "right-hand man."[3]

During the antebellum period, Johnson filed land claims for several sites upon which Butterfield established stations, namely, Head of Concho, Leon Holes, and Barilla Spring. He also filed a claim for Mustang Waterholes, the only semireliable water source on the 79-mile stretch of the parched Llano Estacado region between Head of Concho and the Pecos River. The Llano Estacado, or Staked Plains, of northwestern Texas are "palisaded" tablelands that constitute the southern end of the high plains, encompassing 32,000 square miles and thirty-three Texas counties.[4]

Persistent Indian incursions along the overland route provided Johnson and his men with a firsthand education about life and death on the Texas frontier. Many of the lessons they learned were similar to those absorbed by American troops a century earlier while fighting Native Americans during the French and Indian War. Soldiers in that conflict later employed the same tactics against the British during the Revolutionary War. Likewise, Adam Rankin Johnson recalled that many of the stratagems he learned about subterfuge, survival, and guerilla warfare while fighting Comanches and Apaches on the Texas frontier he later put to good use against Union troops during the Civil War. Reflecting upon Native American military tactics in antebellum Texas, Johnson observed, "The red man had by this time learned to respect the courage and strategy of the pale-faces." To minimize casualties, Comanche raiders would rarely risk a frontal assault unless assured of "advantage in position as in numbers." Several of Johnson's Butterfield colleagues agreed. Henry Skillman, Bradford Daily, and Henry Ramstein, all well versed in frontier affairs, noted that Comanches often preferred to set a trap, arranging "an ambuscade by which an assault can be made with sufficient security."[5]

According to Johnson, from 1859 to 1861, a band of Comanches numbering 150 frequently raided his Overland Mail Company stations from the Middle Concho to the Pecos. At sunrise one morning in early September 1859, one hundred Indians, thirty on foot and seventy mounted on horseback, swept down on Camp Johnson. Armed with guns and bows and arrows, the raiders launched an assault on the station house. After this opening skirmish, the lead warrior approached the stage stop and speaking "good English, demanded the horses in the corral." The building's occupants—two children, a woman, and four men—directed the Comanches to take the livestock but insisted that the Indians stop firing on the station house. The warriors "took nine mules and a horse, and killed a . . . [steer] and ate it, but kept firing on the house, after which they went off."[6]

Just before midnight, some hours after the raiders departed, the eastbound stage arrived at Camp Johnson. The woman and children boarded the coach, while the men from the station walked behind. The group set out for the next stop eastward. A newspaper account of the attack noted, "Two little pigs at the station followed the party the whole distance as they also had been scared by the Indians. Another station was robbed in the vicinity a few days before."[7]

A Butterfield passenger named Woods riding to San Francisco reported the situation along the Middle Concho as precarious and stated that the Comanches had "declared war against the whites." Traveling along this watershed on a chilly winter night west of Camp Johnson, Woods's coach passed between two ominous fires blazing on either side of the road, the scene eerily deserted, with not an Indian in sight. Woods breathed a sigh of relief after his coach safely ran this nocturnal Comanche gauntlet and proceeded on to the next station, Camp Mather. Camp Mather, thirteen miles distant, was located near the intersection of North Liveoak Draw, Bradford Draw, and the Middle Concho.[8]

The station's namesake was a Butterfield line agent named Mather who worked for Division Five superintendent James Glover. This stage stop, not included on the original Butterfield itinerary, appears on the last published overland schedule from 1861. Camp Mather is also on several military scouting maps from the period. Agent Mather apparently had a short fuse. When Waterman Ormsby first met him, Mather was upset over several wild and unruly mules that resisted being hitched to the stagecoach. Ormsby commented, "Both of the leading mules having escaped," Mather became quite agitated, and said that "every one should go to the devil, and . . . that he did not care a damn for anyone."[9]

After heading westward from Camp Mather, overland coaches journeyed almost seventeen miles before reaching Head of Concho Station, situated at 2,400 feet in elevation on the headwaters of the Middle Concho River. The locale, the last permanent water for seventy-nine miles (until the Pecos River), served as a regional operations hub and supply base for the Overland Mail Company. Butterfield leased the property from the owner, Adam Rankin Johnson. In October 1859, Johnson sold the parcel to Louis Shellenberger of Fort McKavett, Texas. The mail company built a substantial rock station here near a deep water hole that provided an ample supply of water for both employees and livestock. Describing the setting, one traveler noted the "low arid hills" surrounding the stage stop. The land, "destitute of all timber," was "perfectly dry and dusty." Head of Concho also served as a beef depot. The steady demand for cattle on the Texas frontier encouraged local ranchers and overland employees to raise livestock to sell to the mail company and the military. *San Francisco Daily Evening Bulletin* reporter Baer, riding eastward in late 1858, observed that the station keeper at Head of Concho "had one hundred head of cows grazing in the vicinity. Let him look out and be wide-awake, or the Camanches [*sic*] will have them before spring!"[10]

Indeed, Comanche raiding on the Middle Concho proved so troublesome during this period that it seemed the Indians "and the employees of the Mail Company [were] virtually at war." The same correspondent reported that Butterfield was "building strong station-houses, . . . provided with ten to twenty guns each." Constructed of quarried limestone blocks, Head of Concho Station proved virtually impregnable to Comanche attacks. Overland Mail employees, however, were always vulnerable when going in or out of the stage stop, typically on forage detail or tending to the livestock.[11]

In December 1858, sixteen raiders attacked the station's hostlers five hundred yards from the station, making off with twenty-seven mules and horses. Since the men were all on foot, they could not mount any pursuit. In the six weeks preceding this raid, Comanches had taken thirty-four mules and horses from the stage stop's corrals. On June 19, 1860, twenty-five Comanches trapped Head of Concho station manager J. W. Shephard outside the station. Making a final stand with a rifle and a Colt revolver, Shephard downed the lead warrior's horse with a shot from his rifle and "fired his pistol some four times, when he was shot down and scalped. The body was entirely stripped of all clothing."[12]

After killing Shephard, the Comanches turned their attention to the station's hostler, a twelve-year-old Mexican boy, who was tending to some grazing mules. The young lad made a desperate dash for safety on his pony, with the Indians in hot pursuit. A newspaper reported, "The Mexican acting upon the principle that a good run was better than a bad stand made good his escape." The youth quickly realized that his pony, shod with metal horseshoes, moved faster over broken terrain than did his pursuers' unshod horses. Butterfield overseer Adam Rankin Johnson said that the hostler "saved his life by his coolness and courage" by deliberately seeking "out in his flight the rocky ridges and, by circling around the Indians, [he] finally . . . reached the [station] house in safety."[13]

Although the marauders failed to corner the livestock tender, they still managed to run off ten mules and one horse from the station. The loss of all company livestock caused a seven-hour delay in overland mail service, until Butterfield sent replacement mules to the besieged stage stop. William Tallack, riding east on a stagecoach in the summer of 1860, likely arrived at Head of Concho during this same time. Tallack recalled, "At this station a week ago, a man was scalped by the Indians." Overland Mail employees buried the slain station manager, Shephard, next to the stage stop. Shephard, who left behind a wife and three children in Kansas, had come to the Texas frontier to make his fortune but instead lost his life.[14]

Only five days after this Comanche raid, another tragedy struck Head of Concho Station. Louis Shellenberger, the landowner, had assumed management of the stage stop after Shephard's death. On the morning of June 24, 1860, the new station manager shot his wife. Both Shellenberger and his wounded spouse claimed the shooting was an accident, but some people familiar with the couple suspected otherwise. According to reports, Mrs. Shellenberger "had been very cruelly treated and beaten by her husband recently," causing neighbors to form "the impression of his guilt in the act of shooting." The wife was "in an advanced state of pregnancy," a newspaper noted, and her wound so severe that there was little confidence in her recovery.[15]

Nine months after the shooting, in the spring of 1861, the Overland Mail Company abandoned Head of Concho Station. After the Civil War, however, Ben Ficklin's San Antonio–El Paso stage line utilized the site. In August 1869, Brevet Lieutenant Colonel Thomas B. Hunt passed through and noticed a new stage stop on the headwaters of the Middle Concho, a short distance from Butterfield's "old stone breastwork and abandoned house." Hunt noted the name of the station keeper as "Shallinburger." This was likely Louis Shellenberger, who still owned the property.[16]

When Waterman Ormsby's coach arrived for breakfast at Head of Concho in late September 1858, there was no station house, and employees were living in tents. Nearby was a makeshift brush corral holding a substantial number of mules. "The good natured Dutchman [German] who officiated as cook quickly ranged the tin cups and plates and got us some broiled bacon, shortcake, and coffee," Ormsby noted, "which was considered quite an aristocratic meal for so early a settlement, and which our long ride certainly made acceptable, however different from New York fare." Commenting on the hostlers' attempts to hitch a new team of animals to the coach, Orsmby disdainfully observed that the "greasy Mexicans" came close to strangling them with their lariats and that each mule was almost exhausted "before his work had commenced."[17]

By this stage of his trip across West Texas, Ormsby's impressions of the land had changed noticeably. While traveling along the overland road, "literally baked hard in the scorching sun," he began observing subtler and more favorable aspects of the environment. Ormsby seemed almost surprised at the abundance of wildlife, remarking on the pronghorns, quails, prairie dogs, and snakes. Upon spying an immense rattlesnake, his driver, a hard-boiled fellow "of Herculean frame" named "Baby" Jones, stopped the coach. After harassing the reptile with a stick, Jones killed it and twisted off its large rattle, handing it to Orsmby. Once under way again, the New York reporter reclined in his solitary coach and peered out the open window while a "decidedly cool and delicious breeze refreshed" him. "It was just after sunrise that we entered the desert road," he wrote, "and I was agreeably surprised to see, instead of a tedious sea of parched sand, a variety of curious though weird vegetation."[18]

One notable plant that commanded Ormsby's attention was the Spanish bayonet yucca. Often growing to the size of a man or taller, the Spanish bayonet's silhouette, when seen at night, could be terrifying. In several eerie nocturnal encounters during his trip across western Texas, Ormsby mistook these yuccas for lurking Comanches. Numerous reports of bloody depredations up and down the line had instilled a healthy fear of Indians in the reporter, helping to fuel his vivid imagination.[19]

The trip from Head of Concho to the Pecos River required crossing a seventy-nine-mile stretch of desert noted for its unreliable water holes. Originally, Butterfield had allocated extra mules for this segment to change out as needed, but this arrangement proved imperfect. In early 1859, Comanches attacked the company's mule train, making off with thirty-two animals. To address these attacks and the persistent problem of dependable water, the Overland Mail Company built Llano Estacado Station (also known as Staked Plains Station), thirty-one miles from Head of Concho.[20]

One visitor to this new stage stop was William Tallack. He described the surrounding scenery as a "long and very barren tract of table-land." Tallack enjoyed the wide-open spaces, commenting favorably on the "airy ride in these clear upland regions." After spending hours aboard his stagecoach, he arrived at Llano Estacado with a hearty appetite. "On dismounting at the station," Tallack recalled, "we found a good dish of dried apples stewed, fresh steaks, and hot coffee, and never ate a breakfast with a keener relish." Another overland passenger passing through, *Daily Alta California* reporter J. M. Farwell, found himself pleasantly surprised with the western setting. "I had imagined that this was a barren and sterile waste. Nothing is more erroneous," Farwell said; "it is one of the pleasant features of the whole journey." Not everyone shared Tallack's and Farwell's environmental assessments. Albert Richardson, traveling aboard a westbound Butterfield coach in October 1859, described the Staked Plains as a "shoreless ocean of desolation[,] . . . an utter sand-waste with a few shrubs of cactus."[21]

Commenting further on one variety of the region's vegetation, known as soap-tree yucca, Richardson reported that it was favored among Mexicans for "washing their persons and clothing; but generally they cherish strong antipathy to *all* soap." Continuing in this same biased vein, he said, "Most of them would be improved by spending half an hour under a pump-spout, with a vigorous man at the handle." Echoing this low opinion of the region and some of its inhabitants, a correspondent named Smith traveling through on the Butterfield Road in early 1859 judged this part of the Lone Star frontier as worthless and ill suited for white settlement: "Leave the deserts to the Comanches and Apaches," he said, "for if Texas is a 'God-forsaken country,' the 'Llano Estacado' is a little more so, if not considerably."[22]

The Overland Mail Company established Llano Estacado Station on the north bank of Centralia Draw. The nearest dependable water was twenty miles eastward, at Mustang Waterholes. Closer were Flat Rock Ponds, six miles to the east, but these were seasonal and often unreliable. During the antebellum period, Flat Rock frequently disappointed overland travelers. When U.S. boundary commissioner John Russell Bartlett stopped here in October 1850, the ponds were "quite dry" and there were no "indications that there had been any [water] there for months." When the Overland Mail Company began stocking the line in the summer of 1858, it quickly became apparent that the lack of water along this section posed a formidable problem. Without water for the employees and livestock, neither the stations nor the stagecoaches could operate.[23]

To surmount this obstacle, in 1859 Butterfield superintendent Henry Smith agreed to pay $4,500 a year to haul water from Mustang Waterholes to Llano Estacado Station. The recipients of these funds were the Johnson brothers, Adam, Ben, and Thomas. Although the Johnsons received what seemed very generous compensation, the work was exceedingly dangerous and sometimes fatal, since it meant operating in the heart of Comanche territory. The Comanches also depended on these water holes. The tribe fiercely resisted Butterfield's expansion onto their lands and the company's commandeering of their natural resources.[24]

Throughout the centuries, Native Americans have utilized Mustang Waterholes and Centralia Draw. Along some of the rock ledges overlooking the drainage, one can see mortar grinding holes and stone breastworks that served as Indian lookouts. Numerous pieces of worked flint litter the ground at several of these overlooks near New Pink Draw. After the Mexican War, forty-niners traveled this route to the gold fields in California. Various mail lines including Butterfield followed in their tracks, utilizing the trail from the late 1850s until the 1880s. During the Roaring Twenties, early automobile traffic used the overland road as an east-west thoroughfare from San Angelo to Stiles and beyond. County officials placed mileage markers at various intervals along the route. Locals continued driving parts of the Centralia route until World War II.[25]

Situated in Centralia Draw twelve miles west of Head of Concho, Mustang Waterholes consists of several sets of ponds spanning two miles. Scouting the road from San Antonio to El Paso in July 1849, Lieutenant Francis T. Bryan stopped at the western group of ponds near North Creek Draw, noting "two water-holes of large size." Describing the country along Centralia Draw, Bryan found it "extremely destitute of wood [and] . . . extremely dry" and the grass "very indifferent." In October of the following year, when John Russell Bartlett traveled through, "not a particle of water was to be found" at the ponds. Recording his impressions of the land, Bartlett said, "Every thing bore the appearance of extreme barrenness; not a tree could be seen . . . [in] this desert region." Passing through en route to California, C. C. Cox remarked, "This portion of Texas is exceedingly poor, and so barren that . . . it will *always* remain uninhabited."[26]

Realizing that Mustang Waterholes was the only semipermanent source of water on this section of the route, Adam Rankin Johnson moved quickly to purchase the acreage encompassing the water holes. In March 1859, he paid W. B. Coffee of Burnet, Texas, thirty dollars for the 153-acre parcel. The transaction meant little to Native Americans, who had claimed these lands long before Johnson arrived on the scene. In January 1859, Comanches attacked one of Johnson's water wagons at the ponds. During the raid, "many arrows were shot at the party, fortunately without wounding them, and when they replied with their guns, the Indians took to flight." Johnson wrote, "The constant raids of this band of Indians . . . made it exceedingly dangerous and very difficult" for his men. Indian depredations cost Johnson several ox teams and numerous delays in delivering water to Llano Estacado Station.[27]

Fed up with the relentless Comanche assaults upon his water crews, in the fall of 1859 Johnson erected a limestone water depot at Mustang's eastern water hole to provide refuge for his employees. On October 21, Comanches attacked Johnson's crew while they were working on the building. The Indians surprised two men hauling stone from a nearby quarry and proceeded to scalp and kill them. One of the slain men, Myers, was from Collin County, Texas, while the other, David Gilbert, came from "Grape Vine Prairie, Dallas County." Apparently, the mail company owed Gilbert a considerable amount of back pay, which had caused him to quit some months before the attack. Gilbert had "started to go to Arizona, became discouraged, turned back, and came as far as Mustang Pond," where he found a job working for Johnson. Another report noted, "Our red and warlike bretheren [sic], the Comanches[,] have been very troublesome of late."[28]

Despite the chronic raiding, Johnson pressed ahead and finished the construction of the limestone storehouse. Shortly after the building's completion, Comanches struck again. One hundred and fifty warriors surrounded Johnson's brother Thomas and three other men at the water holes with their wagon team. The water crew made a frantic dash for the rock depot and once inside bolted the wooden door shut. The Indians then killed the oxen hitched to the water wagon and, in plain view of the storehouse, "coolly barbecued their stolen meat and engaged in a great feast."[29]

A Butterfield stage heading west alerted Johnson at Llano Estacado Station of the siege under way at Mustang Waterholes. After gathering several men and a new wagon team, Johnson set out to rescue his water crew. Upon arrival, he quickly realized that he was vastly outnumbered. The resourceful overseer decided that employing subterfuge was his best chance at liberating the occupants of the rock depot. "Indians are both superstitious and timorous," Johnson remarked, "when any strange, unusual expedient is employed to frighten them." The rescue party moved quietly up to within several hundred yards "of the feasting warriors, rioting in fancied security."[30]

Johnson ordered his men driving the water wagon to "make a great uproar by shouting loudly and rattling the empty water barrels while driving at a gallop" past the Indians' camp to the storehouse. While keeping the raiders occupied on one front, Johnson and several others circled around, firing their guns and making as much noise as possible. Believing themselves under attack from several directions at once, the Comanches withdrew, allowing Johnson to liberate the depot. The rock storehouse had more than passed the test. Today, ruins of the old building are scattered down the hillside toward the pond below. Above, a lone windmill marks the spot where Comanches once battled Butterfield employees for control of this historic water hole.[31]

Out on this isolated frontier, the Overland Mail Company provided not only security but also a sense of community and connection, linking the region's residents to the rest of antebellum America. As stagecoaches passed stations, forts, and settlements along the western frontier, they delivered the most recent newspapers from New York, St. Louis, and San Francisco. Despite the remote locale, Butterfield employees demonstrated a firm grasp of national news and politics.

In October 1860, the proprietor of the Staked Plains stage stop conducted an informal poll of passengers that revealed an overwhelming preference for John Breckenridge as the country's next president. The station manager remarked, "There are some four hundred voters on this division of the road, and Bell and Douglas both will not get twenty-five of them." Abraham Lincoln, immensely unpopular in Texas, was not on the state ballot.[32]

Commenting on local conditions at Llano Estacado, the station manager complained of the scant protection provided by federal and state officials for Texas's western frontier. "There are plenty of Indians out here, and they commit all kinds of depredations with impunity." The station keeper asked, "Can you inform me why [some protection does] . . . not come out this way?" Locals kept authorities in "direct communication" and informed them "every week of the Indian robberies." The negligible security provided by Washington and Austin compelled frontier residents to fend for themselves. By the time they reported a raid, the Comanches were long gone.[33]

To Adam Rankin Johnson, it must have seemed that he encountered depredating Indians more often than U.S. troops or Texas Rangers. On several occasions after returning from trips back home to Burnet, Texas, Johnson found that "the redskins had stripped several stations of their stock and killed all of my . . . oxen that had been kept for supplying the people of the several plains' stations." West Texas appeared to be teeming with Comanches. He noted, "Whole families were scalped; many of the settlers deserted the country, fleeing as from a pestilence." During his time on the frontier, Johnson survived several close scrapes with this tribe, which helped form his impressions regarding Native American character.[34]

During one encounter, he wounded a warrior with a blast of buckshot. While searching for the injured brave the following day, Johnson found him in some dense brush with his leg buried in the ground to staunch the flow of blood. Surveying his cornered quarry, Johnson assumed a condescending attitude. "Though the Indian has not the courage of the pale-face in battle," Johnson reflected, "he is superior to him in stoical, quiet endurance of pain." The wounded Comanche "asked for no quarter" and raised his weapon to fire at Johnson and his men as they approached, whereupon the posse "mercilessly" shot him "to pieces."[35]

Despite the persistent raids, Johnson and his brothers succeeded in keeping the water wagons operating regularly between Mustang Waterholes and Llano Estacado Station. At Llano Estacado, Johnson built a large stone cistern to hold the water transported from the water holes. Employees attached the cistern to the west wall of the stage station, which was another stout limestone fortress similar to Head of Concho Station. Under Johnson's able supervision, Llano Estacado Station surmounted both environmental and manmade obstacles. Despite its arid location in the midst of Comanche territory, completely isolated and miles from the nearest water, the Staked Plains stage stop proved a success.[36]

When Butterfield abandoned its Texas operations in 1861, travelers continued using the overland road, which served as an east-west thoroughfare well into the twentieth century. During the Civil War, hundreds of disillusioned Texans left the state and headed west along the Butterfield Trail to a new life in California. One family that was part of this westward exodus lost their infant daughter to diphtheria while camping at Llano Estacado Station. On May 23, 1864, the parents of eighteen-month-old Mary Alice Forseman buried her twenty yards southeast of the Butterfield station house. Today, her headstone lies hidden among clumps of brush, out on the desolate, windswept plains of West Texas.[37]

Continuing westward, the journey from Llano Estacado Station to the Pecos River was a long and dry forty-eight-mile stretch with no reliable water. Nineteen miles into the trip, travelers reached Wild China Ponds, a collection of water holes noted for their fickle supply. The site's name comes from chinaberry trees that once grew nearby. In 1849, Lieutenant Francis T. Bryan stopped here and found the ponds "entirely dry." Despite his thirst, the large herds of wild mustangs nearby impressed him. The following year, after finding no water first at Mustang Waterholes and then discovering Wild China Ponds "destitute of water," U.S. boundary commissioner John Russell Bartlett became incensed, taking period cartographers to task. "Great mischief is caused by marking such places on the maps," he vented, noting that if his party had known of these ponds' temporary nature, they could have taken precautions and not suffered so severely.[38]

Indeed, during some dry years, this desert country became a killing zone. C. C. Cox, traveling to California in 1849, said, "I never saw the earth so dry as it is in this district, vegetation is completely burned up, and every water hole is dry as a 'bone yard.'" Bartlett recounted that he later encountered several people who "were loud in their denunciation of those who had advised them to take this road, and more so of those who furnished them maps, which deceived them as to the watering-places." Bartlett said that one group, without water for three days between Head of Concho and the Pecos, "came near perishing. Many of their mules and cattle died." In marked contrast, in 1869, Lieutenant Colonel Thomas Hunt and his wagon train proved more fortunate, passing through during a wet season. At Wild China Ponds, he found plenty of water for his men and livestock.[39]

Because of emigrants' limited knowledge and inadequate preparation, they and their livestock often suffered unnecessarily. Traveling across the Staked Plains in the spring of 1849 with no guide, and only a map and a compass to rely upon, John Theophil Strentzel's 135-person wagon train ran out of water and came close to perishing. "Our teams became so exhausted that they began to reel and stagger, seeming ready to drop down," he said. "[W]e had almost given up in despair." Luckily, the group's scouts located several pools of water ahead, and the partici-pants in the California-bound caravan survived their trip through this section. Strentzel recalled, "The joy and gratitude of that moment no one can ever under-stand, unless they have passed through the same, or a like experience."[40]

In 1858, another westward-bound emigrant train with a large herd of cattle left the overland road and struck out over the Llano Estacado in search of a shortcut. The group soon depleted their water supply and, to save themselves, left behind three thousand cattle to perish on the parched plains. Traveling across the Llano Estacado in a Butterfield stagecoach that same year, Waterman Ormsby witnessed distressing scenes of suffering cattle along the overland road, of "almost living skel-etons, gradually dying of thirst. . . . [S]ome were standing, others lying, and others just gasping in the agonies of death—a sight almost enough to sicken the stoutest heart."[41]

Ormsby said that for as "far as the eye could reach along the plain[,] . . . decayed and decaying animals, the bones of cattle and sometimes of men (the hide drying on the skin in the arid atmosphere), all told a fearful story of anguish and terrific death from pangs of thirst." For the New York reporter, the sobering sight of "grim skeletons warning the traveller of the dreadful dangers of the desert" provided silent but graphic testimony as to "the eternal laws of nature" on Texas's western frontier. He estimated that the scarcity of water in the region forced some drovers to abandon one-half to two-thirds of their herds by the side of the road.[42]

Many of these herds were part of cattle drives heading to California. After the discovery of gold at Sutter's Mill in January 1848, some cattlemen hoped to get rich by selling Texas beef to hungry gold miners. "Even though California already had its cattle ranches," J. Evetts Haley notes, "Texas cowmen, still virtually without a market, were tempted by what logic or chance report suggested might be a profitable one for their cattle." Some of these reports were nothing more than hearsay.[43]

One oft-told tale concerned a Texas cattleman named Trimmier who supposedly received one hundred dollars a head for his herd in California. Although there was no basis in fact for the story, Texans anxious to sell their cattle wanted to believe it. Dreams have always been a powerful motivator in the history of the American West. According to Haley, the Texas cattle trade to the West Coast peaked in 1854. The following year, Lone Star cattle sold in California markets for only six to seven dollars a head. Ultimately, getting rich from western cattle markets proved as illusory as striking it rich in the gold fields.[44]

The last stretch of the Staked Plains passage from Wild China Ponds to Horsehead Crossing on the Pecos River spanned twenty-nine miles. A little more than halfway to the Pecos was Castle Gap. This noted West Texas landmark received its name from the surrounding cliffs, "which sometimes assume the appearance of castles." Castle Mountain, 3,141 feet in elevation, bounds the canyon to the north, while King Mountain, also 3,141 high, is to the south. Butterfield constructed Castle Gap Station, a small limestone structure, at Castle Gap's western entrance. During the nineteenth century, the locale both impressed and intimidated visitors. While traveling through with a cattle herd, Stephen Powers pronounced it "a pass of peril, of awful and sublime grandeur."[45]

Riding in a wagon train bound for California, Maria Shrode described the canyon as "the grandest scenery that I ever saw in my life." Other aspects of her surroundings, however, mitigated her favorable impression. "If it had not been for the bones of dead cattle strewed round in every direction," Shrode remarked, "I could have enjoyed the romantic scenery." Ruth Shackelford, part of another wagon train, saw hundreds of rotting beeves. "Every now and then we would pass a pile of dead cattle seven or eight in a pile," Shackelford recalled, "and it being a very warm evening it was not a very pleasant trip I can tell you." Her party resorted to holding camphor-impregnated handkerchiefs over their noses to mask the stench of rotting carcasses.[46]

In 1857, a federal road-building expedition passed through Castle Gap and found the rough trail along the canyon floor both jarring and precipitous. The diarist for the wagon train observed that the rugged gorge possessed "something of the romantic in the general appearance. . . . Rocky walls some hundreds of feet in height, hem in and overhang the traveler." The writer viewed the chasm, long known as a favored ambush site for raiding Indians, as menacing. As the caravan wound its way down the ravine, he nervously anticipated "the shrill war whoop" of Comanches, noting, "[T]he eye and ear are on the *qui vive* for some such manifestation of the ancient feud which these dusky devils bear to the white race."[47]

Although the wagon train encountered no Native Americans on its trip through the canyon, such fears were well founded. At Castle Gap, the overland road joined a major Indian thoroughfare known as the Great Comanche War Trail. For decades, the Comanches had utilized this trail on their raids south into Mexico. In March 1849, army lieutenant William Henry Chase Whiting intersected this road while exploring a route from San Antonio to El Paso. Whiting said that the "large Comanche warpath . . . filled us with astonishment. Close together, twenty-five deep worn and much used trails made a great road." H. O. Hooper, heading west to California that same year, observed, "We were on an Indian trail which had been traveled a great deal; the bones of horses and cattle scattered over the ground nearly the whole length of it."[48]

Emigrant and stagecoach traffic through the Pecos region presented attractive targets for raiding Indians. For Butterfield employees living at Castle Gap, the nearest military protection was forty-seven miles to the southwest, at Fort Stockton. Army patrols were infrequent, and Overland Mail personnel at Castle Gap Station typically fended for themselves. *San Francisco Daily Evening Bulletin* reporter Baer arrived at "the Comanche Pass in the Castle Gap range" escorted by three Butterfield guards on horseback, all of them "armed to the teeth with knives, revolvers, and rifles."[49]

At Castle Gap Station, good water was in short supply. A small seep spring in the canyon grudgingly issued a small discharge. When Lieutenant Francis T. Bryan came through in 1849, he discovered "a little dirty and brackish water, which sufficed to water our mules, but was unfit for any other purpose." During a visit in 1869, Lieutenant Colonel Hunt observed "a few alkaline waterholes filled with dead cattle. The water is totally unfit to drink for man and beast." In 1878, an army captain and his men sampled the canyon's water holes. The captain remarked, "The water is of a very bitter quality, evidently caused by surface wash and bird manure. It made some in the party sick to the stomach." With no dependable water source at Castle Gap, the Overland Mail Company eventually resorted to hauling casks of water from the Pecos River, twelve miles distant.[50]

After the Overland Mail Company ceased operations in Texas, the military utilized Castle Gap Station. Following the Civil War, the U.S. Army picketed men at the stage stop to protect both stagecoaches and cattlemen. State maps from the late 1870s and early 1880s show a military sub post at Castle Gap. Ben Ficklin's San Antonio–El Paso Mail line ran coaches through the gorge until the summer of 1868, when the mail company blazed a new road leading southwest from Llano Estacado Station to Pontoon Bridge on the Pecos.[51]

Even after the San Antonio mail line stopped running and the army abandoned its sub post at Castle Gap, locals continued to use the overland road and stage station. C. C. Childress, passing through the canyon with his parents in 1887, paused at the stage stop to water their horses. Childress recalled, "There was a house standing there and [someone] was using it. It was made out of dirt and little chunk rocks." An 1884 land survey of the gap's west end mentioned "the old stone fort formerly used as a stage stand."[52]

After the Mexican War, a parade of forty-niners, stagecoaches, outlaws, cowboys, and Indians passed through Castle Gap, forever etching the setting into the lore of the Old West. Many of the legends concerning Castle Gap are fictitious. One unsubstantiated story concerns the holdup of a Butterfield stagecoach here in 1860. Outlaws hiding on a ledge overlooking the steep canyon ambushed the coach and killed all its occupants. After ransacking the coach's strongbox, the bandits allegedly stashed some of their plunder in a nearby cave. The most famous Castle Gap treasure tale involves the Austrian archduke Maximilian, who served as the emperor of Mexico from 1864 to 1867, when a Mexican firing squad cut short his reign. Before his capture, however, the emperor supposedly sent his valuables north on a wagon train.[53]

After crossing the Rio Grande at Presidio, Texas, the caravan reached Castle Gap, where the teamsters peeked under the wagons' canvas tarps and discovered Maximilian's treasure. The men hid their loot in Castle Gap and then fell to quarrelling among themselves. A lone survivor fled north and never returned to retrieve the cached riches. Over the past century, treasure hunters searching for the emperor's fortune irrevocably damaged many of the prehistoric and historic sites in Castle Gap. One seeker even used a backhoe to dig out an enormous trench in the west end of the canyon. Treasure hunters also damaged much of the Butterfield station, knocking down its walls and greatly altering the site. Today little remains of the stage stop, just a low outline of the foundation and a scattering of cut limestone rock. The building's importance, however, remains undiminished. Castle Gap Station, with its isolated and precarious position, maintained daily operations and served as the vanguard of federal expansion into the region. Today, the ruin is the oldest European American site in Upton County.[54]

From Castle Gap Station it was twelve miles to Horsehead Crossing on the Pecos River. Whenever a wagon train or cattle drive left Castle Gap for the Pecos, the race was on to get to water as fast as possible. Along the overland route in Texas, this particular stretch was notably lethal. The trail ran across "a heavy sandy plain" that made for hard pulling for stagecoaches and wagons. The road was often "full of dead cattle." H. O. Hooper, recalling his experience in 1849, wrote, "I will not attempt to describe the agony of thirst that is about to kill, or the joy of the thirsty one at the sight of water; no one can understand until he has experienced it." Many thirst-crazed livestock and even some people never reached the banks of the Pecos. William P. Huff, traveling to the California gold fields in June 1849, found a note penciled on a mule skull at the western end of Castle Gap. The macabre warning, left by another forty-niner party, said that they were without water for two days and that six of their group had died.[55]

Struggling through the deep sand to reach the river, some wagons had to have two teams of animals hitched to them to complete the journey. Once out on this plain, emigrants and cattle drovers found it difficult to control their livestock. The animals, many of them literally dying of thirst, caught scent of the Pecos River from many miles off. Sometimes it proved impossible to prevent a cattle herd from stampeding to the water in a disorganized mass.[56]

From a distance, the Pecos River would have looked like a snake winding its way through a barren, treeless plain. The Pecos's steep, sterile banks would have blended into the bland and dreary landscape, providing no warning of the river's location to approaching man or beast until they happened upon it, often unexpectedly. Stampeding livestock, desperate for a drink, would often run like lemmings to the river, pitching over the riverbank and drowning in the water's swift current. "Scarcely wider than a canal, deep, with its banks very steep, it swept down in its swift and swirling flood innumerable cattle and horses which had struggled so bravely and uncomplaining [through the Staked Plains] only to perish at the last."[57]

Livestock that did not drown in the river often became mired in the quicksand. Pulling a stranded cow from the river bottom was no easy task and herders often left livestock to die. Ruth Shackelford recalled that her wagon train filled its water barrels "with nasty, dirty water. We can see the dead cattle floating down while we are dipping up the water and see them lying on the banks all over." Shackelford lamented that she would be drinking from these water barrels for the next few days as she traveled east on the overland road across the Staked Plains.[58]

Lieutenant Colonel Hunt described the Pecos as "forty feet wide [and] four and a half feet deep, [with] banks ten feet high" and noted that "the bottom is quicksand, [the] current rapid." On occasion, the Pecos's strong eddies claimed the lives of unfortunate travelers. In June 1849, a gold rush emigrant named Bradshaw drowned while swimming in the murky waters. After a futile, two-day search for his body, the remaining members of Bradshaw's caravan continued their journey westward.[59]

Few travelers formed favorable impressions of the Pecos River and the surrounding landscape, which was "hideous with bleaching skeletons." Passing through en route to California in 1849, William P. Huff called the Pecos country "a solitary waste . . . without a single redeeming quality to invite the settler or the emigrant to tarry." Huff judged the region unsuitable for agriculture. "The soil is poor, pebbly, and utterly worthless," he wrote, and "the face of the country is barren and uninteresting." Lewis B. Harris, another Argonaut heading to the gold fields, remarked that he "would not pay taxes on a league of it" even if the government gave it to him. "We have had nothing but one steady stream of dust and sand since we struck [the valley]," Harris complained, "and the sand now covers my ink as I write, so as to make a sand box superfluous." John Murchison, trekking with another gold rush outfit in 1849, characterized it as "a poor and barren country" with "[t]he surface in many places crusted over with salt." Robert Beeching, journeying west that same year, described the valley as "a boundless waste of country."[60]

After camping on the Pecos for several days, Ruth Shackelford called the river a "nasty, dirty, muddy, ugly stream. Everything within two or three miles is burned up with alkali and the dead cattle lay thick on the banks of the river." Pausing at the water's edge, Stephen Powers found the Pecos "appalling in its ghastliness. Many great droves had arrived before us," Powers recalled, "and thousands upon thousands of cattle lay dead about the Pecos, while all the road was white with fleshless bones." Along the banks of the river lay pools of deadly alkali water. Instead of continuing on to the Pecos, many cattle in their desperate headlong dash to water stopped first at these "glittering pools of alkali and quaffed the crystal death, falling where they stood."[61]

Visitors uniformly judged the Pecos Valley unfit for settlement, possessing no natural resources, excluding salt, suitable for development or profit. Comanches and Apaches passed through here while raiding but rarely lingered. To European Americans and Native Americans alike, this truly was a cursed land. Unlike other locales along the overland road offering choice water, timber, game, or grazing, the Pecos Valley had nothing worth fighting over. Exploring the region in 1849, Lieutenant William Henry Chase Whiting remarked, "Few landscapes can be conceived more bleak and utterly desolate, in its monotonous and somber features [and] its destitution of trees and foliage, than the Pecos country affords. Even game seem to shun it." Visiting the Pecos a few months after Whiting, Captain Samuel Gibbs French observed, "The antelope and wolf alone visit its dreary, silent, and desolate shores. It is avoided even by the Indians."[62]

The overland road (and the Comanche War Trail) crossed the Pecos River at Horsehead Crossing. The name of the ford, according to Lieutenant Francis T. Bryan in 1849, came "no doubt from the number of horses' heads [skulls] which lie scattered near." To Stephen Powers, Horsehead Crossing was "the very abode and throne of Death, for even the cayote [sic] and the raven avoid it and leave the carcasses to waste away ungnawed." Such was the setting the Overland Mail Company encountered in the fall of 1858, when it established operations on the east bank of the river a short distance upstream from Horsehead Crossing. With no timber or stone readily available, the mail company built its station here out of adobe. Butterfield employee J. M. Browne says the stout structure had no windows and only one door. The stage stop and corrals were located "in a horseshoe bend of the river, the house being at the front of the narrow neck which formed the heel of the horseshoe." Charles Ranner served as the station keeper.[63]

Unlike at Llano Estacado or Castle Gap Station, there was an ample supply of water at Horsehead Crossing. Its palatability, however, was debatable. Regarding the Pecos River, Captain French observed, "Its waters are turbid and bitter, and carry, in both mechanical mixture and chemical solution, more impurities than perhaps any other river" in the region. William P. Huff said the water was as "bitter and salty . . . as the briny deep." In 1849, David Demarest's party began "to feel somewhat weak from purging caused by drinking the alkali water." Michael Baldridge, part of an expedition to California in 1850, recalled, "Our animals and men . . . suffered considerably from drinking the muddy water of the Pecos." Having endured great hardships during their passage through the Staked Plains, most travelers of the period likely agreed, however, that barely potable water was better than no water.[64]

When Butterfield passenger Waterman Ormsby reached Horsehead Crossing on September 26, 1858, with his driver, "Baby" Jones, he made no mention of the adobe station house. Ormsby, however, did reiterate his contempt for the Hispanics employed by the mail company. At Horsehead, he found "fifteen Mexicans, or 'greasers' as they are more commonly called." Ormsby commented, "A more miserable looking set of fellows I never saw. They stood shivering over the fire and had to be fairly driven off to get things in readiness for our immediate departure." The New York reporter, like many other European Americans during this period, had little appreciation for the multicultural western frontier. In the West, many Mexican Americans worked for Butterfield and the U.S. Army as hostlers, cooks, freighters, and contractors. Tejanos, like Anglos, capitalized on the benefits of the regional economy. Some Hispanics in antebellum West Texas prospered in their business endeavors—people such as Gregorio García, Jesús and Martín Luján, Agapito Apodaca, and Calisto Olguín of El Paso County.[65]

The stage stop at Horsehead Crossing, like other Butterfield stations in this section, depended on Head of Concho as their supply depot. Although some native grasses grew around the stage stand at Horsehead, many animals would not eat these, because of their heavy alkali encrustation. As a result, the mail company hired forage contractors to deliver the requisite hay and corn to regional supply depots such as Head of Concho. On one 1860 trip to reprovision Horsehead Crossing Station, manager Charles Ranner rode with Adam Rankin Johnson on the supply wagon, driven by Johnson's brother Thomas. When the group got within two miles of Head of Concho, they ran into a Comanche ambush. Johnson immediately recognized the leader of the raiding party, which numbered 150. "The old white-haired chief . . . was well known," Johnson recalled, "as he had taken part in all the raids on the mail line." The Butterfield men used their wagon and its contents as a breastwork to shield them and waited for the Comanches to advance. Sensing that they would likely sustain considerable casualties attacking the wagon, the warriors withdrew. Reflecting on the engagement some years later, Johnson said, "I always considered the little Louisiana creole, Charlie Ranner, as the hero of this occasion."[66]

On another trip while supervising the western end of his section, Johnson hitched a ride on a Butterfield coach. Johnson and the coach's driver, Mr. McFarland, reached the Pecos River, where they "discovered a large band of Indians moving swiftly toward us." Johnson shouted to the coach conductor to quickly close the curtains to prevent the warriors from determining how many passengers were in the vehicle. McFarland then pulled the Celerity wagon into a horseshoe bend of the river and waited for the raiders to approach. The leader of the marauding Indians, once again the "old gray-headed chief, who was well known on the mail line," approached the overland stage. While Johnson and the driver covered the chief with their drawn pistols, McFarland, "who spoke their language," asked what the warriors wanted. The leader demanded gunpowder and tobacco, but McFarland gave him only tobacco and told the chief to leave. "The temptation to shoot down this Indian was almost irresistible," Johnson said, "for he was known to have murdered quite a number of men on the mail line." Greatly outnumbered, however, Johnson and McFarland restrained themselves from killing the chief, "being glad to get to the station [at Horsehead] in safety in the face of such great odds."[67]

In August 1858, when Butterfield was still organizing its operations here, fifteen warriors crossed the river, driving five hundred stolen horses. A newspaper account noted, "There being only three whites [at Horsehead], no effort could be made to overhaul the Indians." In September, three hundred Native Americans attacked a cattle train on the Pecos, making off with five hundred cattle. Four months later, on a moonlit night in January 1859, ten to fifteen Comanches attempted to ambush the stage near Horsehead Crossing. Spotting the silhouettes on the horizon, the Butterfield driver and conductor grabbed their guns and squeezed off several rounds at the lurking marauders, who rode off without returning fire. In June of the same year, the U.S. Army provided one of its infrequent but welcome assists on the Pecos, when Captain Albert Brackett "killed four Indians . . . who had been plundering settlers near the Horse Head crossing on the Pecos." A few months later, in mid-September 1859, "some one hundred Comanche Indians . . . stole all the stock and destroyed the property at the [Horsehead] station." In late September 1860, raiders made off with eight Butterfield mules from Horsehead, but the animals "were subsequently recaptured by the station men, who took them from the camp of the Indians by stratagem."[68]

Survival on this isolated frontier often depended upon such guerilla tactics. It is no surprise that Adam Rankin Johnson, Butterfield's overseer for this part of the route, earned the nickname "the Swamp Fox of Kentucky" during the Civil War. Johnson mastered the art of subterfuge while fighting Comanches and Apaches in

West Texas. The success of Butterfield operations on this section of the route was due in large part to the efforts of Johnson and his men.[69]

Ultimately, it was the U.S. Postmaster General and the Overland Mail Company that jump-started development of this portion of Texas's nascent frontier. From the Colorado River to the Pecos River, Butterfield served as the primary economic engine and the advance agent of European American settlement. The mail company built and provisioned eight mail stations and staffed them with its own security force armed with Colt Navy revolvers, Sharps rifles, and plenty of ammunition. Considering the Overland Mail Company's impact upon the region, an apt description for this part of antebellum West Texas would be "the Butterfield Frontier."

Adam Rankin Johnson in 1863. From Adam R. Johnson, *The Partisan Rangers of the Confederate States Army*, edited by William J. Davis (Louisville, Ky.: Geo. G. Fetter, 1904).

Detail of map showing Camp Johnson ("Old Stage St.") on the Middle Concho River and the junction of the Butterfield Road (in red) with the 1849 Upper Emigrant Road leading southeast to Green Mounds, Kickapoo Springs, Fredericksburg, and San Antonio. From Lieutenant Colonel E. J. Strang, *Topographical Sketch of the Road from Fort Stockton to Fort Chadbourne, October and November 1867*, National Archives Cartographic and Architectural Section, College Park, Md.

Roscoe Conkling in August 1932 at the second Camp Johnson site, near Dry Creek and the Middle Concho River. Conkling Papers, courtesy of Seaver Center for Western History Research, Los Angeles County Museum of Natural History.

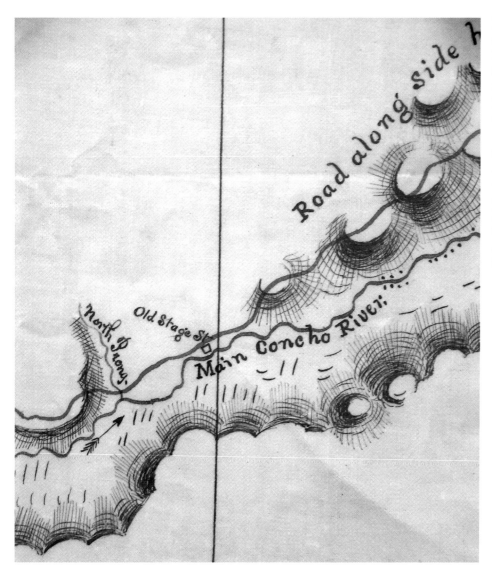

Detail of map showing Camp Mather ("Old Stage St") on the Middle Concho River. From Lieutenant Colonel E. J. Strang, *Topographical Sketch of the Road from Fort Stockton to Fort Chadbourne, October and November 1867*, National Archives Cartographic and Architectural Section, College Park, Md.

Head of Concho Station ruins. Photograph by the author.

Detail of wall from Head of Concho ruins. Photograph by the author.

Ranch foreman at Hunt's "Old Mail Station" site. Photograph by the author.

Hunt's "Old Mail Station" water hole. Photograph by the author.

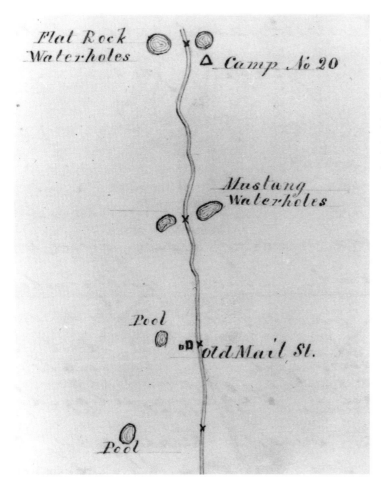

Detail from 1869 map showing the overland road heading west from Hunt's "Old Mail Station" ("Old Mail St.") to Mustang Waterholes and Flat Rock Waterholes/Ponds. From "Journal Showing the Route Taken by the Government Train from Austin, Texas to Ft. Craig, New Mexico," by Brevet Lieutenant Colonel Thomas B. Hunt, National Archives Cartographic and Architectural Section, College Park, Md.

Joe Allen in Butterfield Road trace near Mustang Waterholes. Photograph by the author.

Ruins of Adam Rankin Johnson's water depot building at the eastern end of Mustang Waterholes. Photograph by the author.

Joe Allen (*left*) and ranch foreman (*right*) at the western end of Mustang Waterholes. Photograph by the author.

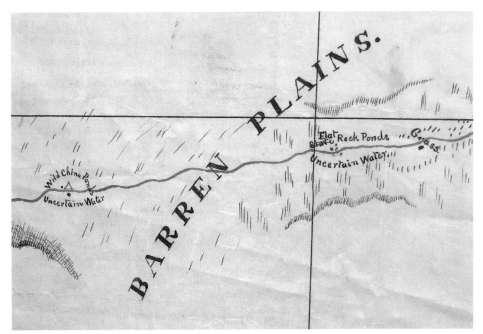

Detail of map showing the Butterfield Road from Flat Rock Waterholes/Ponds to Wild China Ponds. From Lieutenant Colonel E. J. Strang, *Topographical Sketch of the Road from Fort Stockton to Fort Chadbourne, October and November 1867*, National Archives Cartographic and Architectural Section, College Park, Md.

Flat Rock Waterholes/Ponds in Centralia Draw. Photograph by the author.

Ruins of Llano Estacado Station (Staked Plains Station). Photograph by the author.

Llano Estacado Station artifacts. Photograph by the author.

May 23, 1864, grave of Mary Alice Forseman at Llano Estacado Station. Photograph by the author.

Wild China Ponds in October 1930. Conkling Papers, courtesy of Seaver Center for Western History Research, Los Angeles County Museum of Natural History.

Roscoe Conkling in October 1930, in Butterfield Road trace at Wild China Ponds. Conkling Papers, courtesy of Seaver Center for Western History Research, Los Angeles County Museum of Natural History.

Author in Butterfield Road trace between Wild China Ponds and Castle Gap (*behind author*). Photograph by Joe Allen.

Ruins of Castle Gap Station at Castle Gap. Photograph by the author.

Artifacts from Castle Gap Station. Photograph by the author.

Charles Armstrong in Butterfield Road trace, Castle Gap Canyon. Photograph by the author.

Roscoe Conking in October 1930, in Butterfield Road trace, west side of Castle Gap. Conkling Papers, courtesy of Seaver Center for Western History Research, Los Angeles County Museum of Natural History.

Detail from 1869 map showing overland road heading west. Note Castle Gap Station ("Old Mail St.") at Castle Gap ("Castle Mountains") and Horsehead Crossing Station ("Old Station") at the river. Also note the markings for multiple crossings at Horsehead, one for the ferry and another upstream, between the Butterfield station and the ferry. From "Journal Showing the Route Taken by the Government Train from Austin, Texas to Ft. Craig, New Mexico," by Brevet Lieutenant Colonel Thomas B. Hunt, National Archives Cartographic and Architectural Section, College Park, Md.

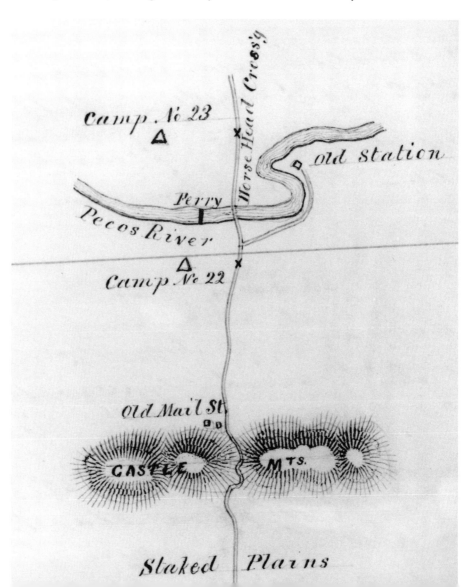

John Crain (*left*) and Charles Armstrong (*right*) at Horsehead Crossing marker on west side of Pecos River. Photograph by the author.

Left to right: Travis Roberts, Jr., Betty Hargus, Bill Hargus, Joe Allen, Patrick Dearen, Tom Beard, and unidentified person at ferry crossing site at Horsehead Crossing, west side of river. Photograph by the author.

Upstream ford at Horsehead Crossing, between mail station and ferry crossing, east side of river. Photograph by the author.

The Upper Road to El Paso

Captain Pope's Well, Tom Lovell. Oil on canvas, 1972. Courtesy of Abell-Hanger Foundation and the Permian Basin Petroleum Museum, Library, and Hall of Fame, Midland, Texas (where the painting is on permanent display).

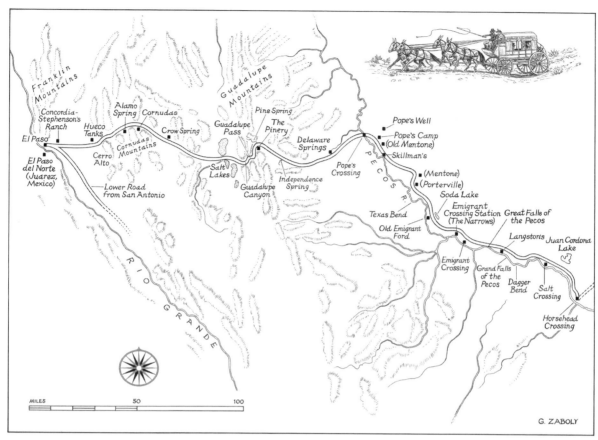

Map 5. From Horsehead Crossing to El Paso via the Upper Road. Map by Gary Zaboly. The map shows the mail road on the south bank of Delaware Creek heading to Delaware Springs. In fact, it ran along the north bank.

From Horsehead Crossing on the Pecos, Butterfield stagecoaches turned upstream, traveling the river's east bank to the New Mexico line at the thirty-second parallel. As the overland road wound its way up the Pecos Valley, it followed a trail originally blazed by the U.S. Army in May 1855. In that month, Captain John Pope's caravan of engineers and soldiers established a camp four miles south of the thirty-second parallel on a bleak and barren bluff overlooking the Pecos. Army officials had sent Pope to the western frontier to drill for water on the Llano Estacado.[1]

Pope was no stranger to the thirty-second parallel or the Pecos River. In 1854, U.S. secretary of war Jefferson Davis had ordered him to explore the thirty-second parallel from the Rio Grande eastward to the Red River to determine its suitability for the nation's first transcontinental railroad. Davis and other southerners favored this route. The captain conducted his railroad survey from February to May 1854. During March of that year, the survey party explored the Pecos River and the Llano Estacado. In October, Pope filed a highly favorable report recommending the thirty-second parallel for the national railroad. The only drawback was the lack of water in the Llano Estacado section. To solve this problem, Pope recommended drilling a series of artesian wells in the region.[2]

Pope and Davis understood West Texas's environmental realities. Without dependable water, infrastructure development and settlement would be limited for the foreseeable future. Well into the twentieth century, the State of Texas lacked the financial resources necessary to tackle such large-scale problems. As a result, the federal government took the lead in establishing West Texas's transportation and hydraulic networks. Captain Pope's $100,000 artesian well experiment in the Pecos Valley marked the first of several attempts by Washington to stimulate development of a regional hydraulic system.[3]

During the nineteenth century, many people—including Pope—believed that American Manifest Destiny, ingenuity, and scientific expertise could overcome a myriad of challenges, including Mother Nature's environmental limitations. Scientifically based irrigated agriculture would make the western desert bloom like a rose, creating a man-made Garden of Eden. Drilling artesian wells on Texas's western frontier would reclaim "large districts of country, at present unproductive, to the use of the agriculturalist." To the period mind-set, western Texas and portions of the American West were little more than wastelands, an "unproductive . . . solitude." Captain Pope remarked that "without some means of supplying water by artificial arrangements, a vast region of country, equal in extent to the whole region east of the Mississippi, must forever be lost to the government for any useful purpose whatever."[4]

By 1855, the U.S. War Department had secured funding for the project, and Jefferson Davis instructed Pope to proceed immediately to the Pecos and commence drilling operations. From the start, Pope's project seemed jinxed. At his drilling site on the thirty-second parallel several miles east of the Pecos, equipment broke down and well holes caved in. The salty river water, with its high sediment load and numerous impurities, corroded the boilers supplying the steam engines, causing them to burst. The weather turned bitterly cold, creating much hardship for both animals and men. Eventually the $100,000 congressional appropriation ran out.[5]

In September 1858, Pope abandoned his project, with little to show for his three-year effort. Back in the nation's capital, people mocked the captain and his Staked Plains drilling endeavor, calling it "Pope's Folly." Pope's experiment was the first in a long succession of boom-bust projects that attempted to exploit West Texas's natural resources. In addition to irrigation endeavors, other cyclical industries in the region have included farming, ranching, mining, real estate, and oil. Patricia Limerick notes, "Cycles of prosperity and recession have long characterized the American economy," and the West provided "the prime example of the boom/bust instability of capitalism."[6]

From the 1850s to the 1980s, countless attempts to transform West Texas's arid lands into an agricultural success story have largely failed. Along the old Butterfield Road, in one community after another, irrigation's bankrupt legacy provides a common narrative. Pope himself is partly responsible for the ruinous trajectory that has proven an environmental debacle, leading to the despoilment and destruction of irreplaceable natural resources. Since Pope's time, irrigation boosters have rechanneled the Pecos, carving out canal networks stretching hundreds of miles. These endeavors destroyed many prominent natural and historic landmarks, including waterfalls. In addition, irrigationists aggressively pumped the region's aquifers, adversely impacting numerous springs (some of these being former Butterfield sites) that were once a vital part of the regional ecosystem.[7]

In his survey of the thirty-second parallel, Captain Pope showed little understanding of the area's agricultural realities. "The soil . . . proves to be fertile and of easy cultivation. It can be irrigated from many points of the river," he wrote authoritatively, without ever having raised a crop here. In fact, nineteenth- and twentieth-century farmers discovered that over time high salinity levels in the river water and in the soil "salted up" their acreage, greatly curtailing crop yields. Nonetheless, throughout his 1854 exploration of the Pecos, Pope continually praised the river's agricultural advantages. He boasted that the Pecos valley was "capable of extensive culture" and could "be easily irrigated, and would, no doubt, amply repay the outlay and labor." Pope's optimism would fade, however, and by September 1858, he had abandoned his brash boosterism.[8]

Future Pecos-area farmers would have been wise to take note of his disillusionment and of his grudging acceptance of man's inability to overcome environmental realities. "It is with deep regret, therefore, . . . [that] I am forced to terminate these experiments," Pope said, "[to] reclaim any large portion of this country to the uses of agriculture." For Pope there was no point in trying to adapt to the land and live within its natural limits. If man could not bend West Texas to his will and transform it through irrigation, the region was worthless and uninhabitable. Texas's arid lands "must forever be lost . . . for any useful purposes . . . [and] all hope of settlement."[9]

In retrospect, "Pope's Folly" was not the captain's failure to drill successful wells, which later drillers accomplished, but the arrogant and erroneous belief that humans, with enough scientific knowledge, technology, and investment capital, could surmount the West's natural limitations. Donald Pisani notes, "At all levels of government, water policy exemplified the American will to order and dominate the physical world, an almost primal impulse to 'complete' an evolutionary process dictated by God or culture." It has taken 150 years for this bankrupt irrigation ideology to run its course in the region. When asked whether Mother Nature ever intended man to establish large-scale farming operations in western Texas, Loving County judge Skeet Lee Jones replied, "Not out in this desert, no." Jim Ed Miller, former manager of the Pecos River's Red Bluff Power and Control District, agrees: "What people should have done maybe was never farm to start with. 'It's not nice to fool Mother Nature.'"[10]

Ultimately, Captain Pope proved unable to transform Texas's arid frontier into a man-made Garden of Eden. Nor could he and Jefferson Davis convince Congress to locate the transcontinental railroad along the thirty-second parallel. Sectional divisions created a stalemate in Congress over the selection of the route. A major factor contributing to the congressional deadlock was the Butterfield Overland Mail. In 1857, the U.S. postmaster general, a southerner named Aaron Brown, picked a southern mail route from St. Louis to California that ran through Texas. Brown, Davis, and others in the southern faction hoped that the southern mail road would pave the way for establishing the national railroad over the same line. A period newspaper observed, "The successful operation of this stage line, and the settlements made along it, may have a great influence on the future location of a railroad."[11]

Some northerners feared that a southern transportation network would expand the South's influence westward. Brown's selection of an overland mail road through Texas infuriated the northern faction in Congress, who felt hoodwinked by the postmaster general. Following their bitter experience with the overland mail, northerners vowed that they would not lose again with the railroad. As a result, on the eve of the Civil War, the route of the nation's transcontinental railroad remained unresolved.[12]

With his railroad route out of favor and his artesian experiment out of funding, Pope abandoned his Pecos River headquarters, leaving behind a collection of adobe and limestone buildings. In September 1858, the Overland Mail Company took over the site, transforming it into a stage stop named Pope's Camp, after the army captain. Like Pope, Butterfield experienced frustration and failure along the Pecos River and the thirty-second parallel. Sparse military protection and inadequate water supplies plagued sections of the Upper Road from Horsehead Crossing westward to the Guadalupe Mountains, Hueco Tanks, and El Paso. Already shouldering considerable economic and environmental limitations along the route from the Middle Concho to Horsehead, the mail company could simply not afford to extend these problems to El Paso. By the spring of 1859, Butterfield realized it needed to take corrective measures. Within nine months of taking possession of Pope's Camp, the mail company abandoned the Upper Road in favor of the alternative Lower Road to El Paso.[13]

The first westward-bound Butterfield stagecoach left Horsehead Crossing at 4:30 a.m. on Sunday, September 26, 1858. Waterman Ormsby was still the lone passenger. "Baby" Jones, who had driven Ormsby's coach across the Llano Estacado, stepped off the box at Horsehead for a well-deserved rest. The new reinsman from the Pecos to El Paso was Henry Skillman. Originally from New Jersey and raised in Kentucky, Skillman was the quintessential West Texas frontiersman. A former army scout and stagecoach driver on the San Antonio to Santa Fe route, Skillman was an expert on West Texas's geography. Besides driving a stagecoach for Butterfield, in 1858, Skillman also served as the beef contractor for Fort Bliss in El Paso County.[14]

Describing Skillman's colorful appearance, Waterman Ormsby noted, "Captain Skillman, an old frontier man . . . [is] about forty-five years of age, in appearance much resembling the portraits of the Wandering Jew, with the exception that he carries several revolvers and bowie knives, dresses in buckskin, and has a sandy head of hair and beard." Skillman made a distinct impression on the young reporter. Ormsby observed that his driver "loves hard work and adventures, and hates 'Injuns,' and knows the country about here pretty well."[15]

Heading upstream from Horsehead Crossing with Henry Skillman at the reins, it was not long before Ormsby was lamenting the deplorable condition of Pope's Road up the east bank of the Pecos. The reporter complained that the trail was "full of stumps and bunches of weeds which made it by no means pleasant riding in the thorough braced wagons, for the jolting was almost interminable and insufferable, and I frequently wished that Captain Pope could experience my ride over his road."

One hundred fifty years later, the road is much the same, with weeds, stumps, and bumps galore.[16]

Seven and a half miles above Horsehead, Butterfield stagecoaches intersected the Salt Road, long significant in West Texas's history. The Salt Road, an important regional artery, linked Juan Cordona Lake, a major source of high-quality salt, to outside commercial markets. The Salt Road ran southwest from Juan Cordona Lake to Salt Crossing on the Pecos. After crossing over to the west side of the Pecos, the trail split into several branches that continued on to the Trans-Pecos region and Mexico. During the eighteenth and nineteenth centuries, Indians and Hispanics freely utilized Juan Cordona Lake and other regional salt deposits. After the Mexican War, however, competing worldviews increasingly clashed along Texas's contested frontier over questions of public and private ownership and the best use of natural resources.[17]

Beginning in the 1850s, Anglo-Americans snapped up valuable area assets such as freshwater springs, timber, salt, and other minerals. The new owners viewed their acquisitions as commodities to be bought and sold and not to be used free of charge. During this period, salt was not as plentiful or as cheap as it is today. R. D. Holt notes that the average Texan consumed fifty pounds of salt per year. Prior to canned goods and refrigerators, "salting and smoking were the only methods known for curing meat[,] and meat was of first importance" to the settlers' diet. Holt says that it took 100 pounds of salt to cure 1,000 pounds of pork and 112 pounds of salt per 500 pounds of beef. Early pioneers also utilized salt to preserve and cure animal hides.[18]

Over the years, frequent visitors to Juan Cordona Lake included salt freighters such as August Santleban of Castroville, Texas. While stopped at Juan Cordona, Santleban always kept a sharp eye out for Native American raiders. Before harvesting any salt, Santleban posted a guard around the perimeter. "The water of the lake, which covers an area of about fifty acres of land," Santleban recalled, "was only about eighteen inches in depth, and its surface was a glittering sheet of white salt about four inches thick." It took three days to fill each wagon with three feet of salt. For fifty thousand pounds of salt, Santleban received $2,500, or a wholesale price of five cents a pound. Mexicans hauling salt to Chihuahua, Mexico, where "they found a ready market," typically charged "$12 a fanega of 240 pounds, and at that price it was remunerative." In 1852, at Camp J. E. Johnston on the North Concho, the U.S. Army paid salt contractors twenty-five cents a pound. In 1860, Overland Mail Company agents in Texas typically paid thirty to thirty-five cents per pound.[19]

Heading upstream from Salt Crossing, the Butterfield Road followed the river's numerous bends for another twenty-two miles before reaching Langston's Station, the next stop, near Dagger Bend. At Dagger Bend, located northeast of present-day Imperial Reservoir, the Pecos River makes a V-shaped turn. Langston's Station was located on the upper part of the bend near Ward County Road 373, about four miles from the present-day town of Grandfalls, Texas. When Waterman Ormsby came through in September 1858, there was no stage stop at Dagger Bend. Within a few weeks, however, the rigors of the route had forced the mail company to add another relay station. According to period accounts, searing heat, sandy roads, and the long distances between stations were causing many mules to collapse.[20]

Daily Alta California reporter J. M. Farwell, traveling east on the Butterfield, stopped at Dagger Bend in early November 1858 and mentioned a just-completed station where workers swapped out a fresh set of mules for his coach. *San Francisco Daily Evening Bulletin* correspondent Baer called the site Langston Station, likely named for its manager. Baer noted that the mail company used six mules "in dragging" the passengers to Langston's and that "the road was quite sandy and fatiguing, and two of the mules gave out." W. R. Owen, who started working cattle on the Pecos in 1875, recalled seeing the old Butterfield stage stand at Dagger Bend. When driving cattle on the east side of the Pecos, Owen said that cowboys always halted their herds here, where there "was a big watering."[21]

As was the case for many of the sizeable bends along the snakelike Pecos, the Overland Mail Company bypassed much of Dagger Bend. The Butterfield Trail steered almost due west from the Crane-Ward County line across the top of the bend, striking its far side above Grand Falls of the Pecos. At one time, travelers considered Grand Falls, two and a half miles south-southwest of modern Grandfalls, Texas, one of the finest waterfalls in this section of the river. Visiting Grand Falls in July 1849, army lieutenant Francis T. Bryan said, "The water tumbles over several steps of rocks. The total fall is about ten feet." Bryan recorded that the water here was five feet deep and the gravel river bottom "firm and hard." Stopping here twenty-one years later in August 1870 with an emigrant wagon train, Maria Shrode remarked that she "saw a grand sight at the falls of the river. The water falls about ten feet in six rods [that is, over a distance of seventy-five feet]."[22]

In the 1890s, Grand Falls of the Pecos "met with disaster when one Horace Smith built a race [or channel] around the falls in order to get power for a gin." E. W. Sweatt, whose family was one of the first to settle in the area, recalled, "The headworks to the race gave away from floodwaters about 1900 and the river changed its course through the race cutting around the falls. The loss of the . . . falls was very disastrous to the community."[23]

Before irrigation and flood control projects on the Pecos, the river occasionally overflowed its banks, inundating low-lying areas for a considerable distance. In such sections, Butterfield coaches avoided potential quagmires by running along the edge of the foothills. Even during dry spells, the Pecos route proved inconvenient. Passenger Orsmby complained about the "weary and dusty road . . . inhaling constant clouds of dust and jolting along almost at snail's pace."[24]

Another common complaint about the Pecos passage concerned the river water served to passengers at stage stops. *Daily Alta California* reporter Farwell, who, like Ormsby, had Henry Skillman as his driver, described the Pecos water as "almost red in appearance, and hardly drinkable." Skillman informed Farwell that the river cut through deposits of copper, saltpeter, and gypsum and that the water was "considered to be healthy in its effects." If "healthy in its effects" meant acting as a strong laxative, then Skillman was certainly correct in his description.[25]

Nine and a half miles upstream from Grand Falls, the Butterfield Road passed Great Falls of the Pecos, another major waterfall along this section of the river. Great Falls, also called Pecos Falls, was just upstream from the present-day FM 1776 Pecos River bridge and served as the dividing line between Reeves and Pecos County on the west side of the river. Butterfield employee J. M. Browne described the location as "one of the prettiest falls ever seen in a river, not so very high, but the whole river is poured down in an unusually narrow space, . . . a deep cleft." Browne enjoyed the picturesque setting because it provided a welcome break from the "monotony of awful stillness characteristic of the region. The roar of the water is easily heard ten miles away." On both sides of the river were inviting, grassy plateaus "as beautiful . . . as one might see in a lifetime."[26]

While Browne admired the beauty of the cascade, he was also appraising its commercial potential. "I have many times thought in looking at this cataract what a fortune and blessing it would be in any settled country as water power." He believed that "[o]ne great water wheel, on a sixty foot shaft, would secure it, and in such power as would run the machinery of a considerable manufacturing city."[27]

Stopping here in the 1870s, army lieutenant Thomas C. Davenport estimated that the Great Falls of the Pecos was about six feet in height. At this point, the river was thirty yards wide and with low banks. According to Browne, a short distance downstream from the falls, near today's FM 1776 bridge, was a river ford known as Indian Crossing, "so named because it was used by the Indians in their raids towards the settlements about the lower Rio Grande." Indian Crossing was wider and shallower than Horsehead Crossing.[28]

Indian Crossing linked parallel roads running on both sides of the Pecos with a third road leading south-southeast to Santa Rosa Spring, Monument Springs, and Comanche Springs at Fort Stockton. On the north side of the river, overlooking Great Falls, are the ruins of an old adobe town, likely a failed farming community dating from the 1870s. During the early 1890s, local resident Lee Hardeman built a brush diversion dam at the falls to channel river water into his irrigation company's network of canals. In 1894, a big flood swept downriver, and Hardeman became concerned that the deluge would destroy his irrigation project. Wanting "to relieve the pressure against his dam," he had one of his workers "plow furrows across a bend in the river to let a little excess water go through."[29]

The plowing yielded unexpected consequences. To Hardeman's "amazement, the river changed its course around the dam and left the Great Falls . . . high and dry." E. W. Sweatt said that the loss of Great Falls "was the hardest on the settlers as the canal had to be extended two miles up river and a new dam constructed to divert the water," at a time "when no one had any money." Residents subsequently abandoned the nameless adobe settlement overlooking Great Falls. Since irrigated farming projects silenced both Grand Falls and Great Falls more than a century ago, the Pecos has coursed downstream from its upper Texas reaches to Horsehead Crossing uninterrupted in its sinuous "monotony of awful stillness."[30]

In the nineteenth century, Great Falls of the Pecos, well known for its natural assets, also enjoyed a sinister reputation. Both before and after the Civil War, the Pecos Valley served as a major corridor for raiding Comanches driving stolen livestock and captives en route to meet comanchero traders from New Mexico. Historians previously assumed that the comanchero trade ended after the U.S. Army defeated the Comanches in the Red River War of 1874–75. On June 2, 1875, the last Comanche holdouts, the Quahadi band under Chief Quanah Parker, surrendered to Colonel Ranald S. Mackenzie at Fort Sill's Comanche Reservation.[31]

Army reports, however, reveal that in the spring of 1878, while scouting on the Pecos along the old Butterfield Trail, Captain Alexander Keyes of the Tenth Cavalry made a startling discovery when he stopped at the adobe town at Great Falls. "I am inclined to believe that 'the falls' is a rendezvous for horse thieves and Indian traders [or comancheros]," Keyes said. "[H]orses known to have been stolen by Qua-ha-da [sic] Comanches from New Mexico in 1875 have been seen at this settlement." Keyes's report reveals that comancheros may have continued their clandestine trade into the late 1870s.[32]

Continuing upriver, from Great Falls it was sixteen miles to the next overland station. Various itineraries list this site as Emigrant Crossing Station, even though it was five miles above the actual Emigrant Crossing, where the 1849 California Emigrant Road from the Red River struck the Pecos. One person who traveled this gold rush route westward to the Pecos River was Lieutenant Nathaniel Michler, of the U.S. Topographical Engineers. Michler and his command started their journey from Fort Washita, Indian Territory, on November 9, 1849. Crossing the Red River into Texas, they passed through northern Young County, past Big Spring, Mustang Springs, and the Sand Hills, before reaching Emigrant Crossing on December 30. At the ford, Michler noted the barren appearance of the Pecos. There was "nothing to indicate its presence but a line of high reeds growing upon its banks." He found the river to be "a rolling mass of red mud," forty feet wide and too deep to safely cross. Michler and his command marched forty miles downriver along the east bank to Horsehead Crossing before heading east to San Antonio.[33]

Four years later, in March 1854, another federal surveying party reached Emigrant Crossing, this one led by Captain John Pope. After passing west to east across the Pecos, the army captain spoke disparagingly of the ford. "This is an extremely bad crossing; our oxen swam for upwards of thirty feet to the opposite bank," Pope wrote. He continued, "[I]t would be utterly impossible for wagons to cross without rafting." From a practical point of view, Emigrant Crossing presented "many difficulties—soft bottom, deep stream, and on the east side, miry banks."[34]

A short distance downstream from Emigrant Crossing, newspaper publisher Barney Hubbs of Pecos, Texas, and two others found a mass grave dating from the nineteenth century. According to Hubbs, in 1924, local rancher Earl Ligon discovered a human skull on a bluff overlooking the west bank of the river. Ligon, Reeves County sheriff E. B. Kiser, Hubbs, and several others went back out to the Pecos to investigate further. They eventually discovered the remains of eighteen people. "Coyotes had dug up their skeletons," Hubbs said. Authorities speculated that the deceased were emigrants who had been crossing the Pecos when Indians swept down upon them and massacred the entire group. Hubbs noted that the warriors had taken "everything they wanted in the way of bedding and blankets and so forth, then just burned the rest . . . and left the bodies out on the ground." After concluding his investigation, Sheriff Kiser had workers reinter the eighteen skeletons at the massacre site.[35]

Long after the California gold rush, Michler's reconnaissance, and the emigrant massacre, travelers and ranchers continued using Emigrant Crossing. In 1931, Judge T. B. Anderson of Barstow, Texas, said that locals had "found old pieces of iron, [and] parts of old wagons, etc." at the site. Well into the twentieth century, cowboys were crossing their herds here on their way through the Pecos River country. One old time cowpuncher, Jim Witt, said that he first used the ford in the late 1920s. "It was shallow, less than knee-deep to a horse, it was a little bit gravelly; it wasn't boggy." Witt remembered that he "could still see those old wagon tracks, pretty deep, washed out." After crossing over to the west side, his cattle would head straight for the old Bateman well, a half mile distant, to drink their fill. The cattle always preferred the "real good water" at Bateman to the brackish and salty Pecos. Today at Emigrant Crossing, one can still see well-defined channels on both sides of the river carved out by countless wagon wheels and livestock hooves.[36]

Butterfield's Emigrant Crossing Station was located five miles upstream from this historic ford, at a sharp bend in the river known as the Narrows. The site is downstream from where Quito Draw empties into the Pecos. Here the surrounding Quito Hills on the east bank crowd in close to the river, leaving only a small gap to pass through. The manager of Emigrant Crossing Station was a Mr. Wiley.

Wiley, originally from Ohio, was a "quite a character . . . [a reckless] dare-devil . . . [with] a splendid physique." Although he was a Yankee, Wiley disliked northerners, saying they lacked mettle. "They are scared half to death of the Indians . . . and if I should get into trouble they would simply be in the way," he remarked; "[Y]ou can't rely on them in a pinch."[37]

Wiley and his crew situated the stage stop against a hill. Overland Mail Company employee J. M. Browne recalls that the "hillside was dug away for quite a distance, and an adobe house and corral was built, the bluff side of the hill forming one side of the house, and two sides of the corral." The men constructed the station roof of sturdy poles, grass, and brush, topped off with a deep layer of soil, "which had been scraped and dragged on it from the hill, so that one could walk straight off the hill on[to] the roof of the house." Browne says that the entrance to the mules' corral was "at one side or corner of the house, so that Indians might not steal them without first having used the rest of us up in a fight." A sizeable porthole in the station door, large enough to shoot out of, overlooked the corral.[38]

Emigrant Crossing Station was still under construction when Waterman Ormsby's stagecoach pulled up at night in late September 1858. "The three Americans in charge of the station had, with the assistance of half a dozen 'greasers,'" Ormsby noted, "built a very fine 'adobe' corral and had started a house of the same material." The station's employees were confident that despite their isolated locale, "they could defend . . . against a whole tribe of Indians." Despite such brash claims, one thing was certain—Emigrant Crossing Station could not depend on the U.S. Army for protection.[39]

The nearest military outposts, Forts Stockton and Bliss, were almost one hundred and two hundred miles distant, respectively. In June 1859, Fort Stockton listed an aggregate strength of 72, and Fort Bliss, 86. By 1860, the situation had not improved, with Fort Stockton reporting only 79 men present for duty and Fort Bliss 43, hardly an intimidating presence. General Twiggs, commanding the Department of Texas, freely acknowledged that some "portions of the frontier [were] in some measure unprotected." Twiggs claimed his options were limited, stating, "That is all I can do with the present force."[40]

Following the Civil War, cattlemen and soldiers frequently referred to Emigrant Crossing Station as Adobe Walls, after the ruins of the adobe stage stop. Jim and Lish Carter utilized the Butterfield site as headquarters for their cattle operations. The Goodnight-Loving Trail, named for cattlemen Charles Goodnight and Oliver Loving, passed through the Narrows following the ruts of the overland road upstream to the thirty-second parallel. In June 1867, Goodnight and Loving started their second, ill-fated, cattle drive westward from the ruins of the Butterfield stage stop, Krebs's Station, in western Young County.[41]

Several weeks into the drive, Loving and a wrangler named "One-Armed" Bill

Wilson rode on ahead of Goodnight to arrange the sale of the herd to government beef contractors at Fort Sumner, New Mexico. Some days later, in the latter half of July 1867, Goodnight unexpectedly found Wilson at the Narrows, half-naked, barefoot, and starving in a cave. Wilson recounted that shortly after he and Loving left Goodnight and the herd, Comanches attacked them upstream just south of present-day Carlsbad, New Mexico, seriously wounding Loving. After assessing Loving's injuries, Wilson set out downriver to get help from Goodnight, who was trailing behind with the cattle herd. When Goodnight found Wilson at the Narrows, his clothes were as red as the sediment-laden Pecos River water. Goodnight said that Wilson "was the most terrible object" he had ever seen. Wilson's "eyes were wild and bloodshot, his feet were swollen beyond all reason, and every step he took left blood in the track." Loving subsequently died from his wounds on September 25, 1867, at Fort Sumner, New Mexico.[42]

With the arrival of the barbed-wire fence and the railroad, large-scale cattle drives such as those by Goodnight and Loving gradually faded. In another example of changing land use and priorities, after the turn of the century, construction of the Big Valley Dam obliterated Emigrant Crossing Station, formerly the oldest European American building in Ward County. The dam, another boom-bust irrigated farming endeavor, controlled the flow of river water into the Big Valley Irrigation Canal, which ran downstream to Grandfalls, Texas. In several places, this canal parallels the old overland road. Initially, Ward County irrigated-farming ventures prospered, but over time soil and water salinity combined with periodic droughts created serious if not insurmountable problems.[43]

In 1927, the county had 27,493 acres under irrigation, but by 1984, only 284 acres remained. Many Ward County farmers experienced personal and financial "heartbreak over the failure of irrigation and agriculture." Future prospects for irrigated farming remain "dreary." Today, the Big Valley Dam is in disrepair. The only visible remains of Butterfield's Emigrant Crossing Station are several trash dumps containing lead-lined cans and beer bottles from the period. Here at the Narrows, four layers of history overlay one another: Captain Pope's road, the Overland Mail Road, the Goodnight-Loving Trail, and finally the Big Valley Irrigation Canal.[44]

After exiting the Narrows, the Butterfield Road temporarily left the Pecos River, heading northwest through the Quito Hills. The trail passed two miles above present-day Barstow, Texas, and skirted the northern edge of Soda Lake, another prominent natural landmark. Soda Lake, a large saline deposit similar to Juan Cordona Lake, is a mile and a half long and a third of a mile wide. At Soda Lake, the overland road intersected a trail blazed nine years earlier, in September 1849, by army captain Randolph Barnes Marcy. Marcy, part of the U.S. Topographical Engineer Corps, was on his way back to Fort Smith, Arkansas, from Doña Ana, New Mexico, and camped two nights at the lower end of Soda Lake. Two decades later, in August 1870, an emigrant wagon train stopped at Soda Lake. A member of the party, Maria Shrode, wrote in her journal, "There had been rain the day before and the shore was nearly as smooth as glass. The children all got out and walked and ran foot races and capered along at a fine rate."[45]

In 1932, Ozark Chemical Company of Tulsa, Oklahoma, built one of the nation's first sodium sulfate plants at Soda Lake. Over the ensuing years, the company processed "millions of tons" of salt from the lake, shipping it in railroad cars to market. Soda Lake's abundant saline deposits, created millions of years ago during the Permian period of Texas's geologic history, eventually ran out. In 1970, the company closed the plant and laid off its Ward County employees. Today the desolate and depleted Soda Lake has few visitors, except for the occasional ATV or dirt bike.[46]

After leaving Soda Lake, the overland road rejoined the Pecos River before heading on to Skillman's Station, thirty-five miles from the Narrows. The Butterfield Trail entered Loving County at Texas Bend on the Pecos, almost four miles due south of the present-day county seat of Mentone, Texas. The ruts of the mail road pass by the ruins of Porterville, an abandoned irrigated farming community founded in 1906. Porterville lasted for two decades before the briny river water forced farmers to abandon their salted-up acreage.[47]

During the antebellum period, there were only a handful of people (all Butterfield employees) living in what is now Loving County. Today, the situation is little changed. This has always been an empty country. The locals like the solitude. For many years, Loving County has had the distinction of being the least populated county in Texas, and according to *National Geographic*, it is "the least populated county in the 48 contiguous United States." In 2012, the U.S. Census Bureau listed seventy-one residents in the county, a decline from eighty-two in 2010.[48]

When Waterman Ormsby came through here in September 1858, Butterfield employees had not yet constructed Skillman's Station (namesake of Butterfield stage driver and section overseer Henry Skillman) on the Pecos below Narboe Point. Within weeks, however, a station house appeared on a high sandy bluff overlooking Narboe Bend, where the river makes a major bend to the west. Both J. M. Farwell of the *Daily Alta California* and Baer of the *San Francisco Daily Evening Bulletin* mention stopping at Skillman's in late October and November 1858. Skillman's Station was an adobe structure similar in size to those at Horsehead Crossing Station and Emigrant Crossing Station. The station site at Narboe Bend was a short distance upstream from a river ford known as Narboe's Crossing. Locals named these Loving County landmarks near present-day Mentone, Texas, after members of the Narboe family. John P. Narboe, John Narboe, Jr., Paul M. Narboe, and Peter Narboe emigrated from Norway to the United States in 1832 and later came to Dallas County, Texas, as Peters Colony emigrants. Historic graffiti at Hueco Tanks State Park and Historic Site reveals that a J. Narboe was traveling the Upper Road in July 1856.[49]

Skillman's Station, where overland passengers disembarked for a welcome rest and meal, was a cut above the average stage stop that offered marginal, substandard fare. On occasion, food served to Butterfield sojourners was rancid, spoiled, or thoroughly unappetizing. In some instances, however, the cooks at these stage stops were superior and provided a bright spot along the route. Farwell, the *Daily Alta California* reporter, found Skillman's Station to be such a place, remarking that he had an excellent dinner here before reboarding his stagecoach heading east. The stage stop had little else to recommend it, as the surrounding terrain was neither inspiring in its vistas nor inviting in its bleak, dusty desolation.[50]

During May 1859, this section of the Pecos River experienced a sizeable, if temporary population boost. For two weeks, a group of state and federal officials conducting a boundary survey camped along the east bank of the Pecos, from Pope's Camp south to Skillman's Station. The $80,000 survey of Texas's northern and eastern boundaries with New Mexico, although eventually completed, was not a rousing success. A survey error locating the 103rd meridian mistakenly allocated Texas more than 600,000 acres from New Mexico. Additionally, ego clashes between Texas and U.S. commissioners careened out of control, culminating in a particularly acrimonious squabble near Skillman's Station. The spat provides another example of the periodically testy relationship between state and federal officials during this period.[51]

On May 10, William Read Scurry, head of the Texas delegation, rode a Butterfield stagecoach to the federal commission's camp near Skillman's. Upon arrival, Scurry launched into a heated discussion with U.S. commissioner John H. Clark, leader of the boundary survey. On May 11, the day after this rancorous confrontation, Scurry informed Clark that he and his men were pulling out and refused to participate further in the survey. Scurry's principal assistant was Anson Mills, an El Paso County surveyor. Mills also worked as a Butterfield contractor, overseeing construction of the company's El Paso station, which occupied an entire city block.[52]

Discussing the ill-fated boundary survey in his memoirs, Mills was complimentary of Scurry but critical of Clark. "Major Scurry was a most genial companion," Mills wrote, while "Mr. Clark was ambitious in his assumption of highly scientific attainments and overbearing to those he deemed not his equal in such acquirements." Mills proved less than forthcoming, however, omitting salient details concerning Scurry's behavior as well as his own. Clark informed U.S. secretary of the interior Jacob Thompson that Scurry had been in the field with the surveying commission on only two occasions. Apparently, the head of the Texas delegation spent most of his time "in private business in El Paso to the neglect of the business that it was his duty to perform" with Clark. Scurry was angling to enrich himself by locating choice acreage along the survey route that he could later sell; "but not being able to make a fortune out of it, as he expected and frequently expressed," he abandoned his responsibilities to the State of Texas.[53]

Similarly, Anson Mills completely ignored Clark "as chief of the [surveying] party [and] . . . was entirely deficient as to the duties of his position." Moreover, Mills unleashed a xenophobic tirade against Clark's lead surveyor, John E. Weyss. While out in the field, Mills twisted off on Weyss, saying, "God damn you sir, you are a God damned liar; you are a damned Dutchman [that is, a German]; you never was nor is a gentleman; you God damned foreigner." In El Paso, Texas, both Anson and his brother, W. W. Mills, had reputations for being volatile and abrasive. In his self-serving autobiography published in 1918, Anson Mills omits any mention of the undignified and ungentlemanly behavior he exhibited toward Weyss.[54]

Following the Texas commission's withdrawal on May 11, 1859, Clark and the federal delegation continued eastward with their boundary survey. As Clark's crew marched off, Butterfield employees on the Pecos returned to their solitary routine. Besides the four or five people working at Skillman's, the only other area residents were those living at Pope's Camp, the next station, twenty-five miles upriver. On the way to Pope's Camp, the mail route bypassed a big, lazy curve in the Pecos and cut cross-country toward Tunstill Bend. Five miles upstream from Skillman's, in the ruts of the overland road, are the ruins of a now-forgotten ghost town. In Loving County, much of the former and current development is on or near the Butterfield Trail. The ruins are all that remain of Old Mentone, one of the more intriguing Pecos River boom-bust sagas.[55]

The history of Old Mentone starts in 1893 with the Loving Canal and Irrigation Company. In that year, six men created a corporation to construct canals from the Pecos River to irrigate adjacent farmland. The company platted town lots and established mail service to the site via the old overland road. Within months, 150 persons signed a petition to split off from Reeves County and create Loving County. Reeves County commissioners approved the petition and ordered an election for organizing the new county and electing officials. Eighty-three people voted in the July 1893 election, which also designated the partially developed townsite of Mentone (now Old Mentone) as the county seat. The new commissioners court issued $6,000 in bonds to cover construction of a county courthouse. Officials also approved selling four leagues of land to help finance operations.[56]

By the close of 1893, several workers and a few families were living in a makeshift community astride the old Butterfield Road, on a high bluff overlooking the river valley. A few adobe homes soon took shape, a general store opened for business, and the workers completed an irrigation dam on the Pecos below the townsite. In early 1894, however, three county officials "disappeared without [a] trace," leaving behind a wake of forgery and fraud that doomed the fledgling county. With no additional funds, work stopped on the new courthouse and residents drifted away. By the spring of 1894, only two people remained. In 1897, the State of Texas nullified the organization of Loving County and reattached it to Reeves County.[57]

Walking along the ruts of the Butterfield Trail at Old Mentone today, one can still see remnants of a well, abandoned homesites, scattered trash, and the rock foundation of the first county courthouse. Several decades ago, Loving County judge Skeet Lee Jones found a rusting abandoned safe on the river below the townsite. Old-timers told Jones that the missing county officials cleaned out the safe and dumped it on the riverbank prior to absconding. The current landowner hauled away the antique safe and now uses it as a planter at his ranch house, an apt epitaph for Old Mentone.[58]

In 1931, 130 people signed a petition to reorganize Loving County. After receiving permission, residents in June of that year established a county government, giving Loving County the distinction of being the last county organized in Texas. County officials chose a new county seat, once again called Mentone, eleven miles downstream from Old Mentone and half a mile north of the overland road.[59]

More than eight decades after its reorganization, Loving County still struggles to survive. In 1933, the county had 600 residents. In 1940, there were 285. Today there are 71. In 1931, Mentone had five cafés, five gas stations, two hotels, two drugstores, two recreation halls, two barbershops, and a dance hall. Now only a county courthouse and annex and one small convenience store remain. Loving County is barely hanging on. Recent increases in area oil and gas production are helping the local economy, but how long the upturn will last is anybody's guess. From Captain Pope's time to today, the Pecos Valley has always been a boom-bust region.[60]

The next Butterfield station, thirty-one miles above present-day Mentone, is Pope's Camp. The site, four miles below the New Mexico line, served as Pope's headquarters for his artesian drilling experiment from May 1855 until September 1858. Situated up and away from the river, the setting commands an excellent, broad view of the Pecos Valley. Pope selected the location because of its proximity to a spring, which provided freshwater more palatable than that of the river below. Occupied by the Overland Mail Company in September 1858, Pope's Camp was one of the more elaborate stations on this section of the mail route. The buildings featured both adobe and limestone construction. Workers quarried the limestone from a quarry half a mile downstream.[61]

Butterfield passenger Waterman Ormsby described the buildings at Pope's Camp as being "built of adobe in a substantial manner, . . . [they] form quite a little town." One historian noted, "When one considers the isolation and nakedness of the location . . . [the camp] was almost luxurious." For protection against Indian attacks, a limestone breastwork encircled the complex. The site even featured stone walkways and a flagpole.[62]

When Ormsby arrived here on a clear moonlit night in late September, he "stopped just long enough to get some supper of shortcake, coffee, dried beef, and raw onions." A few months after Ormsby passed through, the Comanches paid a visit to Pope's Camp. A January 1859 account said that a group of warriors stole twenty-seven mules from the Overland Mail Company's corrals. "When the stage arrived there the station men were all out hunting for their lost stock," the report noted, "and the coach was compelled to keep on forty miles further with the same team for want of a relay."[63]

At Pope's Camp 150 years ago, one could clearly see the majestic outline of the Guadalupe Mountains, sixty-four miles to the west. Today, because of increased air pollution, this is often not the case. Virtually every traveler of the antebellum period mentioned the rugged beauty and grandeur of the Guadalupes, including Guadalupe Peak, at 8,751 feet the highest point in Texas. From Pope's Camp westward to Delaware Springs, the next Butterfield station, thirty-eight miles distant, the Guadalupes dominated the horizon. En route to Delaware Springs, stagecoaches forded the Pecos and turned westward.

The ford was at Pope's Crossing, two miles above Pope's Camp in present-day Tucker Draw. A November 1858 report said that the mail company had installed a ferry here. A short distance east of the crossing are the ruins of an old yellow and red sandstone homestead belonging to the noted "gentleman gunfighter" of the Old West, Robert Clay Allison. After hanging up his guns in the early 1880s, Allison started ranching at Pope's Crossing. He died on July 3, 1887, a few miles from home, when he fell out of his wagon while drunk. Allison's gravestone in Pecos, Texas, reads, "He never killed a man who did not need killing."[64]

From Pope's Crossing, the mail road struck Delaware Creek and ran along its north bank to its headwaters at Delaware Springs, in present-day Culberson County. Captain Randolph Marcy stopped here in mid-September 1849 and discovered a spring that "bursts out of a solid limestone rock in a volume of sufficient magnitude to drive an ordinary sawmill." He declared it "as pure, sweet water as I ever drank." A second spring at the site, strongly impregnated with sulfur and hydrogen, tasted "like the Kentucky 'Blue Lick Water.'" The captain also sampled a third spring, which was "strongly sulphurous, leaving a thick incrustation of sulphur upon the rocks for many yards from the source." Marcy mused that one day Delaware Springs's mineral waters might become the nucleus of a fashionable health spa and resort for the wealthy, like that at Saratoga Springs, New York. He found the climate "delightful, the atmosphere perfectly elastic and pure, and the temperature . . . delicious."[65]

When Ormsby arrived here in late September 1858, Butterfield had yet to construct its station. His driver, Henry Skillman, stopped their coach at sunrise to

THE UPPER ROAD TO EL PASO

cook breakfast. Ormsby reported that they made a fire of buffalo chips to cook their breakfast of "jerked beef, . . . raw onions, crackers slightly wormy and a bit of bacon." Commenting on the rigors of overland travel via stagecoach, Ormsby shared that "[t]he stomach . . . does not long remain delicate after a few days of life on the plains."[66]

Daily Alta California reporter J. M. Farwell came through on a Butterfield coach a month later, and there still was no station here. Overland Mail Company employees eventually constructed Delaware Springs Station in early November 1858. When *Daily Evening Bulletin* correspondent Baer stopped here later that month, he mentioned the station and its manager, a man named Cooper.[67]

Butterfield's stage stop, located a short distance from the springs, was a six-foot-high stone fortress, measuring twenty-six by forty feet and comprising two rooms, a chimney, a fireplace, and at the back, an attached corral for livestock. Mail company employees needed a fortress for protection. A newspaper report from February 1859 noted that "the Comanches had been in and run off eleven mules" from the station's corral.[68]

The newspaper account may have erred, because the depredating Indians could also have been Mescalero Apaches. The Pecos River served as a fluid boundary between Comanche and Apache territories. Although the two tribes ranged on both sides of the river, typically the Pecos River westward to the Rio Grande was Mescalero territory. Members of the tribe, which numbered about 1,000–1,500 in the nineteenth century, were hunter-gatherers who supplemented their diet by farming. One of their food staples, from which their tribal name derives, was the mescal plant, a type of agave, which they harvested and roasted in rock ovens. Morris Opler notes that the Apaches' "almost total dependence . . . on a hunting and gathering economy in territory that ranged from high elevations to semidesert lowlands dictated a dispersion of population over a large expanse of land and a decided premium on mobility."[69]

Like the Comanches, the Mescaleros possessed no central tribal authority or chief. While regional bands had leaders, "the tribal bond was loose" and "concentrated leadership and direction were lacking." Opler says, "There was no mechanism for uniting the entire tribe for a common venture or to face a common danger." This absence of central unity or organization proved a liability when the U.S. Army mounted large-scale, coordinated assaults against the Apaches' regional strongholds during the antebellum period. Although the army came close to subduing the Mescaleros on several occasions, the lack of a sustained military campaign and an erratic federal Indian policy gave the tribe time to regroup.[70]

During the nineteenth century, American soldiers and settlers put increasing pressure on the Mescalero Apaches and gradually reduced the size of their traditional range, which "meant [the] inevitable disruption of their economy and untold hardship." Opler says, "The depletion of the game by the buffalo hunters, surveyors, soldiers, and settlers . . . made the situation even more acute and desperate." In 1855, U.S. commissioner of Indian affairs George Manypenny noted that the rapid decrease in available game had reduced the Mescaleros "to a state of destitution as to compel them to plunder or steal from our citizens or starve." Manypenny's analysis included a grim forecast. "Under the existing state of things," he observed, "they must rapidly be exterminated by the whites or become extinct."[71]

Although the depletion of game certainly accelerated Mescalero depredations after 1849, "historical data for the American period strongly suggest that plunder from raiding was important for Mescalero subsistence." In other words, raiding served a significant tribal function. In interviews conducted with Mescaleros during the 1950s, Harry Basehart found that "the importance of the roles of warrior and hunter as avenues for achieving prestige in the 'old days' . . . [was still] emphasized." The Mescaleros, like the Comanches, also carried on an illicit trade with New Mexico comancheros. Gold rush Argonaut C. C. Cox recalled that in June 1849 near Pope's Crossing, his forty-niner party crossed paths with some "Mexicali [*sic*] traders who [were] . . . on their return to Santa Fe with a drove of horses and mules purchased of the Apache Indians."[72]

The Mescalero worldview regarding land and natural resources mirrored that of the Comanches. Basehart said, "All living things on the land, animal or vegetal, were available equally and freely to all Mescalero." Tribal members could travel freely throughout the traditional Mescalero range at any time of the year. The Mescalero term for "our country" meant "equally for all; . . . trespass was meaningless where members of the tribe were concerned." In the Trans-Pecos region, the Mescaleros had semipermanent camps near choice locales offering water, grazing, and game. The Guadalupe, Davis, Chisos, Quitman, Sierra Diablo, and Eagle Mountain ranges ranked among their favored campsites in the area.[73]

For Mescalero Apaches, the Guadalupe Mountains, twenty-four miles west of Delaware Springs, were a revered place. Harry Basehart said, "These holy mountains were pre-eminent sources of supernatural power, and were approached with respect and prayer by all Mescaleros." The Apaches called Guadalupe Peak, the highest point in Texas, "Rock Nose." Mescaleros considered this pinnacle the most sacred mountain in their territory. It also served as a tribal center. Basehart noted, "There were always some Mescalero groups present at [the] Guadalupe[s]." In interviews, Apache elders said they considered Rock Nose "as being a holy place" and that "people go to that mountain and . . . pray for all the good things." At the summit of a natural staircase on the peak's west side was a secret cave where Mescalero warriors "might secure great supernatural power if they demonstrated

THE UPPER ROAD TO EL PASO

sufficient . . . [bravery] to withstand a series of ordeals." Such powers would make an Apache more powerful in battle with his enemies and held in greater esteem by his peers.[74]

Throughout the years, the imposing profiles of Guadalupe Peak and the adjacent El Capitan have never failed to inspire. In June 1849, C. C. Cox called "[t]he majestic Guadalupe [*sic*], nature['s] grandest spectacle, a wall as if it were extending from earth to heaven, grand beautiful sublime." Encamped at the base of the mountains, Cox praised "[i]ts marble cliffs, the soft transparent clouds that veil its front, the halo of purple vapor that encircles its summit. . . . What more could the artist want to call forth the genius of the soul[?]" Upon viewing the range in 1858, Waterman Ormsby remarked, "It seems as if nature had saved all her ruggedness to pile it up in this colossal form of the Guadalupe Peak. . . . The wild grandeur of the scene . . . is beyond description."[75]

In late September 1858, five miles shy of the next station, at the Guadalupes, the mules pulling Ormsby's coach stopped in their tracks and refused to go farther, compelling driver Henry Skillman to beat them with rocks the rest of the way. The Overland Mail Company located Pinery Station at the base of the Guadalupes, near Pine Springs and a fine stand of timber. Employees built a stout limestone fortress and an adjacent corral of pine. The Mescaleros called Pine Springs "Hidden Water." During the first half of the nineteenth century, Mexican soldiers reportedly "attacked a large Mescalero camp here during a puberty ceremony . . . [killing] two Mountain Spirit dancers . . . including the son of Jianatsa (Cadete), a noted leader." When Ormsby and Skillman stopped at the Pinery, manager Henry Ramstein served them a dinner of venison pie and baked beans before the pair climbed aboard their coach to resume their trip westward.[76]

J. M. Farwell, the *Daily Alta California* correspondent, also had dinner here while Butterfield employees hitched up fresh mules to his coach. *San Francisco Daily Evening Bulletin* reporter Baer had a difficult time reaching the Pinery. When the mules pulling his eastbound stagecoach got bogged down in the salt lakes and sand dunes on the west side of the Guadalupes, the driver ordered the passengers to dismount to lighten the load. Then, while climbing uphill to the Pinery, a freezing blizzard engulfed the weary pedestrians. Baer said, "The bitter wind blew directly in our faces, and made us shiver, complain and swear at a terrible rate." He described the trek as "one of extreme suffering." By the time the hapless travelers reached the overland station, they had walked almost ten miles.[77]

For westbound passengers, the descent from Guadalupe Pass was both mesmerizing and terrifying. "It is enough to make one shudder to look at the perpendicular side of the cañon," Ormsby noted, "and think what havoc one mischievous man could make with an emigrant train passing through the cañon." Gazing through his stagecoach window at the massive mountains looming overhead, the New York reporter reflected, "The great peak towers as if ready any moment to fall, while huge boulders hang as if ready, with the weight of a rain drop, to be loosened from their fastenings and descend with lumbering swiftness to the bottom, carrying destruction in their path."[78]

Nature was not the only potential hazard here. Guadalupe Canyon lay in the heart of Mescalero Apache territory. Grim reminders of this reality confronted Ormsby and other Butterfield passengers halfway down the gorge, where they encountered the grave of José María Polancio. Apaches waylaid Polancio, a scout for army captain James Longstreet, on February 1, 1855. Soldiers found Polancio stripped naked with seven arrows protruding from his body. Longstreet's men wrapped Polancio in a buffalo robe and buried him in a rock grave. The Indians returned, however, and dug up Polancio's corpse. They shot the cadaver full of arrows, scalped it, and stole the buffalo robe. After discovering the desecration, Longstreet's men interred the hapless scout a second time. The Apaches were sending a strong message: digging up Polancio's body and mutilating it was a deliberate taunt and sign of disrespect. The Indians, through this scornful grim reminder, were clearly communicating that they, not the soldiers, were the masters of these lands.[79]

A short time after passing Polancio's grave in Guadalupe Canyon, Ormsby's westbound coach encountered the first Butterfield stage heading east from San Francisco. It was a historic occasion when, at sunset on September 28, 1858, the Overland Mail Company linked America's east and west together for one brief moment. Upon reaching the bottom of the canyon, Ormsby's coach turned northwest, passing the northern spur of the Patterson Hills before entering the surreal world of sand dunes and salt lakes on the Guadalupes' west side. "The sudden transition in the descent from the salubrious timbered region on the summit of Guadalupe Pass," Roscoe and Margaret Conkling noted, "to the arid and sterile region of the Salt Basin, is almost startling to the senses of the traveler."[80]

En route to the next station, at Crow Spring, the Butterfield road steered northwest toward the thirty-second parallel and the Texas–New Mexico line. Describing the vista, the Conklings wrote, "One has the impression of . . . venturing out over a trackless frozen sea . . . among white and glistening dunes of decomposed gypsum, and across flats of glistening crystalline salts that in the dazzling glare and quivering heat of mid-day sometimes appear like alluring pools of blue transparent water, an illusion that appears and disappears." In the summertime, the searing desert heat turned the sand dunes and salt lakes into an oppressively bright and brutal furnace. Travelers and stagecoaches tried to get over this stretch of trail as quickly as possible. To those passing through at nighttime, however, the west side of the Guadalupes became intriguing and mysterious. "Under a full moon the aspect of this silent white land is even more fantastic, ghastly and unnatural," the Conklings observed, "conveying something of the impression of [a] . . . lunar landscape."[81]

Northwest of the sand dunes, the terrain transitions into a series of salt lakes. In the spring of 1849, Hispanics in San Elizario, Texas, told army lieutenant William H. C. Whiting of several salt trails leading northeast from the Rio Grande to the Guadalupe "Salinas, or Salt ponds, whence much of the salt consumed in Chihuahua is derived." Captain Randolph Marcy traveled east through the Salt Lakes six months later on his way to Fort Smith, Arkansas. He noted that the lakes "had been formerly resorted to by the Mexicans for salt; but that since the Indians had become hostile, they did not venture to go there." Harry Basehart said that Mescalero Apaches often journeyed to the Guadalupes to gather salt and that "the procedure necessitated only a short stay at the salt deposit; both men and women participated in the work." To facilitate transport back to their camps, Mescaleros typically loaded their salt onto animal hides shaped into carrying sacks.[82]

Captain Marcy noted that the Guadalupe Salinas supplied much of the salt used in New Mexico and several states in Mexico. After sampling several specimens, the army captain declared that they possessed a "very strong saline taste, and equal to the best Turk's island salt." In the immense salt basins west and south of the Guadalupes, "the salt is deposited in a pure state upon the bed of the lake, about six inches in thickness," Marcy observed, "and when the water becomes low and recedes from [the] high-water mark, it can be shoveled up in large quantities." Lieutenant Whiting learned that residents of San Elizario judged the Guadalupe deposits superior in quality to those found at Juan Cordona Lake on the Pecos. In 1866, Samuel Maverick filed a claim for 960 acres in the Guadalupe Salt Lakes, located eighty-five miles east of El Paso. A decade later, Charles Howard acquired Maverick's property and in July 1877 filed a claim for another 3,200 acres north of Maverick Lake. Howard's attempt to corner the Trans-Pecos salt market sparked the acrimonious and violent Salt War of 1877. When Howard attempted to block access to the lakes, violence erupted between Hispanics and Anglos in San Elizario.[83]

After passing through the northern part of the Guadalupe salt basin, the overland road approached the thirty-second parallel at the New Mexico line. Just below the boundary, Butterfield constructed a station of gypsum blocks, adjacent to an important and never-failing regional water source, Crow Spring. The spring, twenty-eight miles northwest of the Pinery, fed a small lake that crows liked to frequent. This was the last permanent water for ninety-four miles, until the overland road intersected the Rio Grande.[84]

When Ormsby visited Crow Spring in September 1858, Butterfield had yet to construct a station here. Several weeks later, however, two California reporters mentioned stopping at Crow Spring Station. Both newspapermen took a meal at the stage stop: one had breakfast, and the other dinner. Mr. Baer of the *San*

Francisco Daily Evening Bulletin was scathing in his remarks concerning the locale, noting, "Crow Spring . . . is a most miserable apology for a station, or anything else in the way of a habitable abode." Baer observed that the station manager, a Mr. Wright, employed Mexican attendants "of the *vaquero* class. The mules—some 20 at this point—feed principally on alkali grass—are in bad condition. . . . The springs, or water therein, is extremely brackish, and purges to excess, when drank in any quantity." Another visitor questioned whether the "alkali mud hole can by courtesy be called a spring."[85]

As late as the 1930s, ranchers depended on Crow Spring year-round. Today, the spring is dry, the lake is empty, and the crows are long gone. Aggressive irrigation pumping by agricultural interests in nearby Dell City has markedly lowered the water table, causing Crow Spring to quit flowing. Across the Trans-Pecos, this is a common and controversial problem. Since World War II, excessive pumping of regional aquifers has killed numerous springs, destroying the environmental and historical significance of these sites.[86]

Irrigated agriculture is not the only industry adversely impacting the region's environment. Persistent overstocking of the range by cattlemen has decimated area grasslands. Following the Civil War, pasturage in West Texas was "often as high as a horse's back." Paul McCombs's 1885 railroad survey in Hudspeth County west of Crow Spring and the Guadalupe Salt Lakes details thousands of acres of "fine" and "good" black grama grass. This would soon change. The completion of the Southern Pacific and Texas and Pacific railroads across West Texas in the 1880s heralded the end of the public domain free-range system. "Cowmen began . . . to realize that they could not depend much longer on 'free grass'" before the open range was sold and fenced off. As a result, "every man was seized with the desire to make the most that was possible out of his opportunities while they lasted."[87]

Cattlemen carelessly overstocked the grasslands, not understanding that "as they advanced westward into dryer areas, how much less was the carrying capacity of the ranges there than farther east in regions of more abundant rainfall." During this period, "it was every man for himself, and he was the best man who could put the most cattle on the ranges to eat the most of the free grass." By 1900, overgrazing had reduced the carrying capacity of regional grasslands by 40 percent. A 1975 federal report revealed that 50–75 percent of the range in Culberson and Hudspeth Counties was only in fair condition, while the remainder was in poor condition. Extensive overgrazing has thinned much of the once-abundant grama, bluestem, and tobosa grasses, long since replaced by creosotebush, mesquite, and other invasive brush. Driving across vast swaths of the Trans-Pecos today, one can see first-hand the results of excessive overstocking and overgrazing, "another example of the transformation by human agencies of a fertile land into a desert waste."[88]

Whether it is grasslands or water aquifers, because of man's poor stewardship,

West Texas's resources are under serious stress or in marked decline. Eventually, natural consequences will compel residents to adapt. Throughout history, a hallmark of this fragile, arid environment has been a scarcity of resources. During the antebellum period, man had no choice but to live within the region's carrying capacity. To successfully live in balance with scarcity, people had to adjust their lifestyles. After the Civil War, some farmers and ranchers refused to adapt to western environmental realities and exceeded the land's carrying capacity. Nature eventually forced them to move elsewhere.

During 1858 and 1859, regional water shortages plagued Overland Mail Company operations from Crow Spring to El Paso. A prolonged drought forced Butterfield to transport barrels of water from Crow Spring to the next two stations. The first of these was thirty miles to the west, at Cornudas, part of the Cornudas range, which includes Wind, Flat Top, San Antonio, Washburn, Chatfield, Alamo, and Cornudas Mountains.

Butterfield built its stage stop a short distance from the base of the visually arresting Cornudas Mountain, a twisted and tortured-looking geological oddity. Over the centuries, Native Americans have etched hundreds of petroglyphs around the base of the mountain. Near the stage stop are five graves. Passing through here on May 25, 1880, army lieutenant M. M. Maxon reported seeing the grave of a man from Company G of the Texas Rangers. The deceased soldier, a former Russian nobleman who had joined the Rangers, lost his life on August 9, 1878, when Apaches attacked Ranger lieutenant John B. Tays's detachment on the old overland stage road at Cornudas.[89]

One water source at Cornudas was on the west side of the mountain, in a series of rock basins that hold rainwater. The primary water supply for the station, however, was Thorn's Well, named for Lieutenant Herman Thorn, who found a spring here in 1849 while escorting an emigrant train. William P. Huff, who stopped at Cornudas in July 1849 on his way to the California gold rush, recalled that Thorn had dug a well about four to five feet in depth. Huff said that although the water in it had a "slight muddy tinge, it is cool and palatable." The entrance to the well is a narrow, fifty-foot passage that leads to a marvelous hidden grotto inside the mountain. Indian pictographs and historic graffiti decorate the walls. Outside the grotto, someone has carved "Thorne's [sic] Well" into the rock along with several other names, including a Frank Gentry from 1852.[90]

Lieutenant Francis T. Bryan visited here in July 1849, while reconnoitering the Upper Road. "Outside of the mountain, several wells have been dug by California parties. . . . Inside the mountain, in a cavern," he noted, "there is a fine large well of pure water; this is full to overflowing; the water is very cold and of good flavor." A few months later, Captain Randolph Marcy "found a well fifteen feet deep, filled to the top with beautifully pure water." During some years, however, the water supply at Cornudas proved intermittent. When John Russell Bartlett visited here in November 1850, Thorn's Well was dry. Bartlett made note of the oxen carcasses near the entrance to the grotto, apparently felled from lack of water. When *Daily Alta California* reporter Farwell reached Cornudas in late October 1858, there was no water and the mail company was hauling kegs of water from Crow Spring to supply the station, a round trip of sixty miles.[91]

In hopes of alleviating the water shortages in this section, in late 1858, the mail company added another station to its itinerary nine miles to the west, at Cotton-wood or Alamo Spring. At the base of Alamo Mountain, Butterfield built another large stone fortress. Accessing the spring necessitated a half-mile hike up the side of the mountain. Lieutenant Bryan complained that the water was "quite difficult to get at, on account of the steepness of the mountain." When Bartlett stopped here, he counted seven springs on the mountainside and commented on their good quality. Marcy reported that three cottonwood trees marked the spot, "with an Indian trail leading to it."[92]

Marcy also noted that the area was "a favorite place of resort for the Apaches, who come here when travelers are seen approaching, hide themselves in the caverns of the mountains, and rob them of their horses." At Alamo Mountain, as at Cornudas, there are numerous Indian petroglyphs and many examples of historic graffiti etched into the rocks, testimony to man's lengthy use of this site. Ultimately, Alamo Spring, with an average daily flow of only a few gallons, never provided enough water for mail company operations. Today, there are no live cottonwoods at the spring, but the decayed trunks of several dead trees still mark its location.[93]

Leaving Alamo Spring Station, the Butterfield Road steered southwest, back across the Texas state line, en route to the next prominent landmark, Cerro Alto. The overland route ran around the north side of this sizeable mountain and followed a steep gorge to the level lands below. To assist in guiding coaches down this rugged canyon, the mail company built several series of retaining walls on either side of the road.[94]

Daily Alta California reporter Farwell passed around the north side of Cerro Alto at night. When his driver stopped the vehicle, with pistols drawn, Farwell fully expected to see their path blocked by Apaches. A sigh of relief came soon after. In the dim light, they discerned an approaching stagecoach. Inside the coach was James Glover, Butterfield's Division Five superintendent. After the journey was resumed, it was not long before the jarring, boulder-strewn route forced Farwell's Celerity wagon to pause a second time. "All were obliged to leave the coach and walk up the mountain. This I consider the worst hill on the road thus far," he observed, "being very steep, very high, and the way lying directly up the face of an almost smooth ledge."[95]

Unlike Farwell, Orsmby's driver, Henry Skillman, did not compel him to get out and walk this section. The New York correspondent wrote that he felt some apprehension until his coach cleared the bottom of the pass. "I much feared we could not descend in safety; but our driver seemed to know every stone," Ormsby noted, "and we whirled along on the very brink of the precipices with perfect safety, though the night was quite dark." After exiting the bottom of Cerro Alto's north canyon, the mail road ran straight to Hueco Tanks, twenty-seven miles from Alamo Spring, and the last station before El Paso. The *huecos,* or holes, are natural collection basins for rainfall. In years of severe drought such as 1858, there was no water in the tanks.[96]

The intermittent supply at Hueco Tanks forced the mail company to haul barrels of water from the nearest dependable source, in this case, the Rio Grande, a sixty-mile round trip. Upon his arrival here, Waterman Ormsby discovered, "To our consternation the station keeper [Mr. Losiez] pointed to two eight gallon kegs, saying, 'that is all the water we have left for a dozen men and as many head of cattle.'" The reporter mentioned that the company would have to abandon Hueco Tanks Station unless it could find a convenient and dependable supply of water. In February 1859, a correspondent for the St. Louis paper experienced similar problems, remarking, "Generally, water is so scarce at these points that the company have contemplated changing the line of their route."[97]

Adjacent to the station site at Hueco Tanks are rock shelters containing a wealth of Indian rock art and historic graffiti. During the nineteenth century, station employees, soldiers, cowboys, and emigrants stopped to write their names on the walls. All three of the overland correspondents dined here in 1858, and two of them reported their meal as excellent. One writer feasted on venison, beans, and apple pie, a menu far superior to typical Butterfield fare. *Daily Evening Bulletin* reporter Baer mentioned meeting Henry Skillman here and "found in him a very intelligent and agreeable person." Upon leaving Hueco Tanks Station, the mail road steered southwest toward El Paso. At Concordia, near the present-day El Paso Airport, the Upper Road merged with the Lower Road from San Antonio and Fort Stockton.[98]

Since September 1858, the Overland Mail Company had operated along the Upper Road amid the most trying conditions. Company directors stoically dealt with the constant threat of Indian depredations and ongoing drought, taking these hardships in stride. Despite the considerable difficulties, Butterfield managed to meet its obligations and remain on schedule, with the average transcontinental trip taking twenty-three days. Ultimately, though, the absence of military protection for the Upper Road stations and the chronic water shortages compelled the Overland Mail Company to change its route in 1859. Beginning in late May, Butterfield employees moved operations southward onto the Lower Road.[99]

A major incentive for the company's route change was the U.S. Army's greatly increased visibility along the Lower Road west of the Pecos River. In September 1858, the military established Fort Quitman six miles below the junction of the Lower Road and the Rio Grande. Four months later, in January 1859, troops established Camp Stockton (later Fort Stockton) at Comanche Springs, astride the Comanche War Trail. These two new outposts—along with the existing Fort Davis, Texas (1854), and Fort Bliss at Magoffinsville, Texas (1854)—provided a federal military presence along the Lower Road that was sorely lacking on the Upper Road. By June 1859, Butterfield's new route from Horsehead Crossing to El Paso via Fort Stockton was in full operation. The Overland Mail Company's abandonment of its Upper Road infrastructure marked the end of a regional boom-bust cycle, one that had started in May 1855 with Captain Pope and his artesian wells.[100]

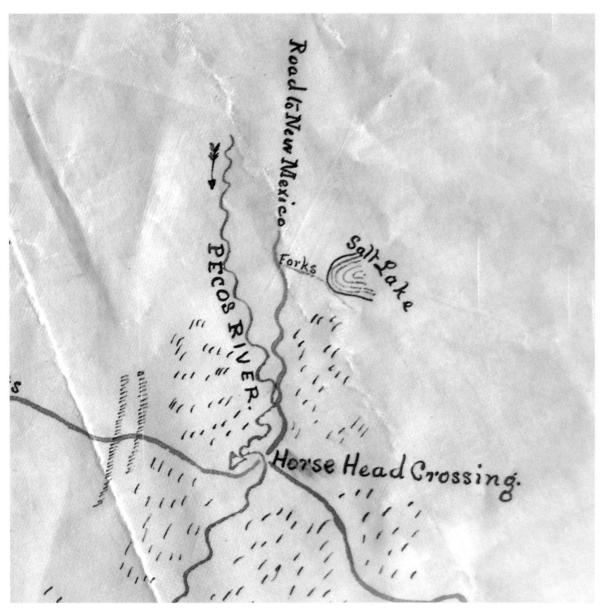

Detail of map showing Juan Cordona Lake ("Salt Lake") and the Butterfield Upper Road intersection with the Salt Road, leading to Juan Cordona. The Salt Road continues west to the Pecos River and beyond. From Lieutenant Colonel E. J. Strang, *Topographical Sketch of the Road from Fort Stockton to Fort Chadbourne, October and November 1867*, National Archives Cartographic and Architectural Section, College Park, Md.

Salt Road Crossing of the Pecos River. Photograph by the author.

Detail of survey map showing Grand Falls of the Pecos. Note the Grandfalls, Texas, townsite northeast of the river. Map #63110, *August 1902 Map of Ward County, Texas,* courtesy of Texas General Land Office Archives, Austin.

Ruins of Langston's Station near Dagger Bend of the Pecos River. Photograph by the author.

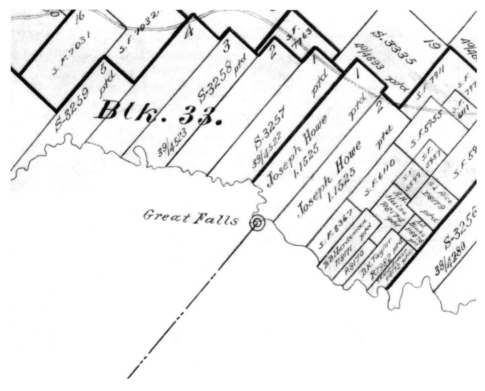

Detail of survey map showing Great Falls of the Pecos. On the west side of the river, Great Falls serves as the boundary line anchor between Pecos and Reeves Counties. Map #63110, *August 1902 Map of Ward County, Texas*, courtesy of Texas General Land Office Archives, Austin.

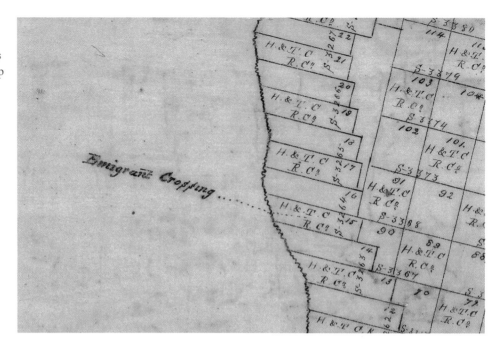

Detail of survey map showing Emigrant Crossing of the Pecos in Ward County. Map #10110, *June 4, 1873 Ward County Rolled Sketch 22*, courtesy of Texas General Land Office Archives, Austin.

Doug Fernandes standing in trace of California Emigrant Road from Preston, Texas, leading to Emigrant Crossing of the Pecos in Ward County. Army lieutenant Nathaniel Michler visited this crossing in 1849, as did Captain John Pope in 1854. Photograph by the author.

Jim Ed Miller, whose ancestors helped settle Barstow, Texas, at Ward County side of Emigrant Crossing of the Pecos. The Emigrant Road into Reeves County is across the river. Photograph by the author.

Site of Emigrant Crossing Station at the Narrows, with the ruins of the Big Valley Canal headgate spanning the Pecos River visible. Photograph by the author.

The Narrows, with the green outline of the Pecos River visible on the left, and the Butterfield Road wrapping around the base of the hills. Photograph by the author.

Detail of map showing Little Falls of the Pecos ("Falls") and "Old Emigrant Ford." This ford, at present-day Barstow Dam, is at or near where Captain R. B. Marcy crossed the Pecos in September 1849 on his way back to Fort Smith, Arkansas, via Preston, Texas. Map #10427, *Ward County Sketch File 6, Sketch of Ward County Irrigation Lands*, courtesy of Texas General Land Office Archives, Austin.

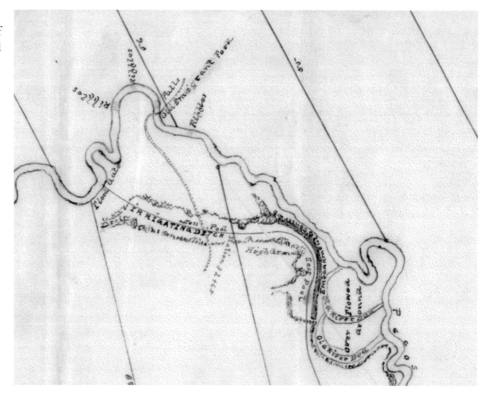

Barstow Dam near Barstow, Texas, at or near where Marcy crossed the Pecos River in September 1849. Photo courtesy of Patrick Dearen.

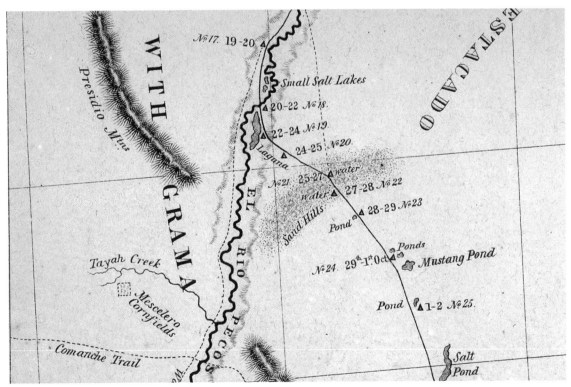

Note the top center area, detailing Marcy's crossing of the Pecos and "Laguna" (Soda Lake in Ward County), where Marcy camped from September 22 to 24, 1849. Detail from *1849 Topographical Map of the Road from Fort Smith, Arkansas to Santa Fe, N.M. and from Dona Ana, N.M. to Fort Smith by Capt. R. B. Marcy*, courtesy of Virginia Garrett Cartographic History Library, Special Collections Library, University of Texas at Arlington.

Patrick Dearen (*left*) and Loving County judge Skeet Lee Jones (*right*) at the site of Skillman's Station. Photograph by the author.

Narboe Bend of the Pecos River (dry during this visit), site of Skillman's Station. Photograph by the author.

Artifacts from Skillman's Station site. Photograph by the author.

Patrick Dearen in Butterfield Road trace heading to Narboe Point. Photograph by the author.

Skeet Lee Jones and rock
foundation line of first Loving
County courthouse at site of Old
Mentone on Butterfield Road.
Photograph by the author.

Skeet Lee Jones (*left*) and ranch foreman (*right*) by an old abandoned safe found by Jones on the banks of the Pecos
River. The safe was supposedly dumped by Old Mentone promoters who absconded with funds. Photograph by the
author.

Harvey Hicks (*left*) and Skeet Lee Jones (*right*) at ruins of Pope's Camp, Red Bluff Lake, Texas. Photograph by the author.

Roscoe Conkling in August 1931 at the ruins of Pope's Camp, prior to the flooding of the site by Red Bluff Lake. Conkling Papers, courtesy of the Seaver Center for Western History Research, Los Angeles County Museum of Natural History.

Ruins of Clay Allison homestead, Red Bluff Lake. Photograph by the author.

Pope's Crossing on east side of Pecos River, Red Bluff Lake. Photograph by the author.

John Pope. Courtesy of Library of Congress, Prints and Photographs Division, Washington, D.C.

Delaware Springs Station ruins in December 1933. Conkling Papers, courtesy of the Seaver Center for Western History Research, Los Angeles County Museum of Natural History.

Ruins of the Pinery Station, Guadalupe Mountains National Park, Texas. Photograph by the author.

Patrick Dearen (*left*) and Joe Allen (*right*) at Pinery Station. Photograph by the author.

Margaret and Roscoe Conkling in September 1931 at Pinery Station sign. Conkling Papers, courtesy of the Seaver Center for Western History Research, Los Angeles County Museum of Natural History.

Margaret Conkling (*far left*) and Roscoe Conkling (*far right*) in the 1930s with a group commemorating the Guadalupe Canyon grave of José María Polancio, an army scout for Captain James Longstreet, who was killed by Mescalero Apaches in 1855. Conkling Papers, courtesy of the Seaver Center for Western History Research, Los Angeles County Museum of Natural History.

Former Guadalupe Mountains National Park superintendent Larry Henderson on Butterfield Road trace, Guadalupe Mountains National Park. Photograph by the author.

Larry Henderson on Butterfield Road trace, west side of Guadalupe Mountains. Photograph by the author.

Guadalupe Mountains and Salt Lakes. Photograph by the author.

Crow Spring in May 1931, when it was still flowing. Conkling Papers, courtesy of the Seaver Center for Western History Research, Los Angeles County Museum of Natural History.

Crow Spring Station artifacts. Photograph by the author.

Butterfield Road trace heading west to the Cornudas Mountains in the distance (*upper left*). Photograph by the author.

Ruin of Butterfield station at Cornudas Mountain, New Mexico. Photograph by the author.

Detail of Cornudas Station. Photograph by the author.

Bobby Jones at entrance to Thorn's Well, Cornudas Mountain. Photograph by the author.

Thorn's Well. Photograph by the author.

Indian pictograph at Cornudas Mountain. Photograph by the author.

Ruins of Alamo Spring Station at Alamo Mountain, New Mexico. Photograph by the author.

Detail of station wall
at Alamo Spring.
Photograph by the
author.

Joe Allen at grave near Alamo Spring Station. Photograph by the author.

Historic rock graffiti on Alamo Mountain near Alamo Spring. Photograph by the author.

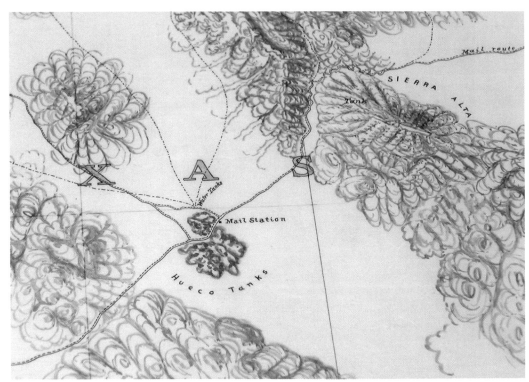

Detail showing the section of the Butterfield Road around the north side of Cerro Alto ("Sierra Alta") and leading to Hueco Tanks Station ("Mail Station"). From *1859 Texas–New Mexico Boundary Survey Map*, National Archives Cartographic and Architectural Section, College Park, Md.

Butterfield ruts on the way from Alamo Spring Station to Cerro Alto in the 1930s. Conkling Papers, courtesy of the Seaver Center for Western History Research, Los Angeles County Museum of Natural History.

Roland Ely in
Butterfield Road trace
in Cerro Alto canyon.
Photograph by the
author.

Hueco Tanks State Park and Historic Site, El Paso County, Texas. Courtesy of the Lyda Hill Texas Collection of Photographs in Carol M. Highsmith's America Project, Library of Congress, Prints and Photographs Division, Washington, D.C.

Tank at Hueco Tanks State Park and Historic Site. There are also numerous rainwater basins (*huecos*) in the rock formations. Courtesy of the Lyda Hill Texas Collection of Photographs in Carol M. Highsmith's America Project, Library of Congress, Prints and Photographs Division, Washington, D.C.

Historic and modern graffiti at Hueco Tanks State Park and Historic Site. Note "G.W. Baylor," possibly indicating Texas Ranger George Wythe Baylor, brother of John Robert Baylor. George Baylor was at Hueco Tanks in the spring of 1880. Courtesy of the Lyda Hill Texas Collection of Photographs in Carol M. Highsmith's America Project, Library of Congress, Prints and Photographs Division, Washington, D.C.

CHAPTER 9

The Lower Road to El Paso

From Horsehead Crossing to Van Horn's Wells

Saving the Mail, Charles Schreyvogel. Oil on canvas, 1900. Permanent Art Collection, courtesy of National Cowboy and Western Heritage Museum, Oklahoma City (1974.024).

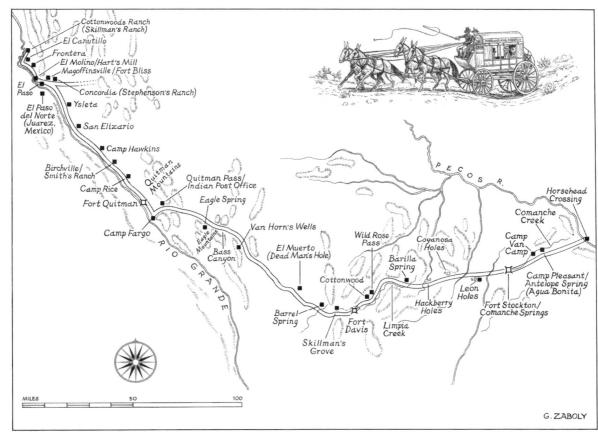

Labels on map:

Cottonwoods Ranch (Skillman's Ranch)
El Canutillo
Frontera
El Molino/Hart's Mill
Magoffinsville/Fort Bliss
El Paso
Concordia (Stephenson's Ranch)
Ysleta
El Paso del Norte (Juarez, Mexico)
San Elizario
Camp Hawkins
Birchville/ Smith's Ranch
Quitman Mountains
Quitman Pass/ Indian Post Office
Camp Rice
Eagle Spring
Fort Quitman
Eagle Mountains
Van Horn's Wells
Camp Fargo
RIO GRANDE
Bass Canyon
El Muerto (Dead Man's Hole)
Wild Rose Pass
Coyanosa Holes
PECOS R.
Horsehead Crossing
Comanche Creek
Camp Van Camp
Barilla Spring
Cottonwood
Barrel Spring
Fort Davis
Limpia Creek
Hackberry Holes
Leon Holes
Camp Pleasant/ Antelope Spring (Agua Bonita)
Fort Stockton/ Comanche Springs
Skillman's Grove

MILES   50   100

G. ZABOLY

Map 6. From Horsehead Crossing to El Paso via the Lower Road. Map by Gary Zaboly.

S witching to the Lower Road afforded Butterfield better military protection and a more dependable water supply, but the expense of abandoning its Upper Road infrastructure, as well as establishing, supplying, and manning fifteen new stations on the Lower Road, created an additional financial burden that the company could ill afford. As the second half of 1859 wore on, the Overland Mail Company's board of directors faced an impending fiscal crisis that required immediate action.[1]

Although Butterfield's contract was a hefty $600,000 per year, the federal government was unable to honor its financial obligations after March 1859, when Congress deadlocked over the annual post office appropriation bill. As a result, Butterfield's cash flow dried up, forcing it to borrow heavily. Confidential credit reports from March 1860 noted that the Overland Mail Company "was a little embarrassed before the Post Office Appropriation Bill was passed, but is now in funds and will soon have $300,000 due from [the] government." The delays ultimately proved costly. In April 1860, company secretary Alexander Holland reported that "the failure of the Government to pay the mail contractors for the past year has entailed upon us a loss of $65,000."[2]

Mounting debts, including postal revenue losses and the alteration of its Texas itinerary, eventually precipitated the removal of Overland Mail Company president John Butterfield. A study of the company's financial operations by W. Turrentine Jackson reveals that "[f]rom the beginning [1857], Wells, Fargo & Co. served as the 'banker' for The Overland Mail Company . . . making loans on an unsecured basis for the development of the mail enterprise." Three of the four major shareholders in the Overland Mail Company also served as directors of Wells, Fargo and Company. At an August 1859 board meeting of the Overland Mail Company, two sitting Wells Fargo directors raised concerns about "management and excessive expenditures." By the spring of 1860, their concern proved even greater when an accounting showed that the Overland Mail Company owed Wells Fargo $162,400 in loans.[3]

The situation came to a head at a subsequent board meeting in March 1860 when Wells Fargo made clear that all advances made to the Overland Mail Company would thenceforth need to be secured with collateral. Wells Fargo demanded that the Overland Mail Company assign all of its physical assets as collateral to guarantee these loans. Wells Fargo also threatened that if the mail company did not meet their demands, they would file a foreclosure action against it. At another board meeting on March 20, 1860, the directors reached a compromise. Wells Fargo "would withdraw its foreclosure action provided changes were made in the Board of Directors and John Butterfield removed as President of The Overland Mail Company." The following day, by a vote of six to one, the board installed William B. Dinsmore as the new president. Wells, Fargo and Company now controlled the Overland Mail Company. Ironically, John Butterfield was no longer in charge of the stage line that bore his name, the Butterfield Overland Mail.[4]

To see how these changes affected company operations in Texas, we return to Horsehead Crossing on the Pecos River. After the route's May 1859 alteration, the overland road no longer went upriver but instead crossed the Pecos at Horsehead and continued on to Fort Stockton, where it joined the Lower Road to El Paso. From June 1859 through March 1861, the Overland Mail Company operated a ferry at Horsehead to shuttle passengers across the Pecos to waiting coaches on the opposite bank. In September 1859, the ferry consisted of a wagon body attached with ropes. Butterfield passenger Albert D. Richardson, traveling west in October 1859, said he crossed "the swollen river in a skiff." William Tallack, riding in an eastbound coach in 1860, arrived at Horsehead at three in the morning and availed himself of a quick moonlight wash in the Pecos "whilst the ferry-boat was getting ready."[5]

Besides the Butterfield station and ferry at Horsehead Crossing, there were few business opportunities along this isolated section of the antebellum frontier. This fact did not stop some speculators from exploring new schemes for profit. In late 1859, El Paso County business partners Jarvis Hubbell and Archibald Hyde seized upon the idea of making money from overland traffic across Pecos River by erecting two toll bridges. Hubbell would capitalize on travel between San Antonio and El Paso with a bridge across the Pecos near Fort Lancaster, while Hyde would capture Butterfield traffic with a bridge at Horsehead Crossing.

After Hyde and Hubbell presented their articles of incorporation to the Texas Legislature on January 7, 1860, lawmakers approved both the Pecos Bridge Company and the Horsehead Crossing of the Pecos Bridge Company. The legislation permitted the partners to operate the toll bridges for a period of twenty-five years. At the Horsehead Crossing Bridge, the toll would be fifty cents for a stagecoach, seventy cents for a six-mule wagon, five cents per pedestrian, and one cent per head of livestock. Hyde and Hubbell's business scheme to take advantage of the overland traffic seemed a grand idea on paper, but ultimately the two men failed to raise the necessary capital for construction of their bridges. Like so many other Pecos River boom-bust enterprises over the past 150 years, plans for the toll bridges failed to materialize.[6]

Once on the west side of Horsehead Crossing, Butterfield stagecoaches steered southwest over a mostly level plain for twenty-three miles to the next stage stop, Camp Pleasant, located at Antelope Spring. On this section, from the Pecos River to Fort Stockton, the mail road paralleled the Great Comanche War Trail. Albert Richardson noted that soon after crossing the Pecos, his coach "struck the old trail of the Comanches to the City of Mexico. Eight beaten paths side by side indicated the frequency of their bloody raids into northern Mexico, for cattle, horses and children." Antelope Spring, also known as Agua Bonita (pretty water), lay eleven miles northeast of Fort Stockton. One traveler, Stephen Powers, called the water hole a "peculiar" desert spring that wept "brackish tears." The grass around the spring proved "unprofitable for man or beast, and the ground [was] moist-looking or glistening with sweat of salt—a muriatic winter in the summer heats."[7]

Ruth Shackelford's wagon train camped here in June 1868, and she found the water "so salty" that she could "hardly cook with it." Shackelford said she "tried to boil some beans but could not boil them soft." Her coffee was so briny that she "could barely drink it." The grass around the waterhole was so "dried up with alkali" that it cracked underneath her feet. Stopping at Camp Pleasant a year later, Lieutenant Colonel Thomas Hunt expressed similar sentiments. Hunt remarked, "Beautiful permanent springs, but very strong with alkaline, grass the same." Today, Camp Pleasant lies in ruins. Rocks from the station house scatter the ground near the water hole. The briny oasis that travelers rested at no longer exists. Antelope Spring is now dry and overgrown with brush. Widespread pumping of area aquifers for irrigated agriculture has killed many Trans-Pecos springs. The situation at Antelope Spring and at other historic water sources along the old overland road vividly illustrates the divergent cultural concepts among various groups living in the region regarding property, ownership, and use of natural resources.[8]

Near Camp Pleasant is another once-flowing spring, Casa Blanca. Immediately adjacent to it are the ruins of a military encampment dating from the Butterfield period. Known as Camp Van Camp, this temporary outpost nine miles northeast of Fort Stockton served as a base of operations for U.S. Army scouts in West Texas during 1859. Company E of the Second Cavalry spent five weeks here from late April to early June. During this same period, Company I of the Second Cavalry was exploring the Comanche War Trail south from Comanche Springs to the Big Bend and the Rio Grande. After the scout, Company I took a two-week break at Camp Van Camp before leaving in early June for an expedition to Fort Stanton, the Guadalupe Mountains, and the now-abandoned Upper Overland Road. By the end of July, the men were back at Camp Van Camp for a well-deserved rest. Company I rode off at the end of August 1859 to a new posting in Kerr County, and Camp Van Camp gradually faded into obscurity.[9]

For the remaining nine miles to Comanche Springs and Fort Stockton, the Overland Mail Road paralleled both the Comanche War Trail and Comanche Creek. The headwaters of Comanche Creek are at Comanche Springs, historically one of the most important water sources in arid West Texas, used by both Indians and European Americans. Native American warriors "brought captive Mexican women and children, and the scalps of their fathers and brothers, along with herds of stock," to rest at Comanche Springs, "leaving a trail chalked with the parched bones of dead animals and captives."[10]

The U.S. Army established Camp Stockton at Comanche Springs on January 17, 1859, specifically to deter such Indian activity in the region. The military named the outpost in honor of Lieutenant Edward Dorsey Stockton of Company A, First Infantry, who died in San Antonio on March 13, 1857, from acute respiratory inflammation. On December 1, 1859, the post commander, Captain Stephen Decatur Carpenter of the First Infantry, requested that the army officially change the name from Camp Stockton to Fort Stockton, and on April 30, 1860, U.S. secretary of war John Floyd approved the request. When Carpenter filed the camp's first official post return in April 1859, he listed only fifty-one men present for duty. By January and February 1861, the number had dropped to forty-one. Fort Stockton's soldiers engaged Indians in combat only one time during the entire antebellum period.[11]

On May 10, 1859, concurrent with Butterfield's move to the Lower Road, the postmaster general ordered the opening of a post office at Camp Stockton, Texas, and the appointment of F. W. Greene as postmaster. Greene lasted only three months; in August 1859, Leonard Pierce became the new postmaster. Official returns for the fort that same month included the notation, "Post office established here via 'the St. Louis and California mail.'" As in many communities across America at this time, there was some jockeying at Fort Stockton for federal postmaster appointments and the coveted income generated by such positions.[12]

The U.S. Postmaster General committed a technical error when establishing the post office at Fort Stockton by mistakenly designating it in Bexar County, Texas. In 1859, Fort Stockton was part of Presidio County, which the Texas Legislature had carved out of the Bexar Land District in 1850. Until local citizens organized Presidio County (in 1875), the legislature ordered it attached to El Paso County for judicial purposes. In July 1859, the postmaster general compounded his problem by naming John D. Holliday as postmaster of Fort Comanche (at Comanche Springs) in El Paso County. With Holliday's appointment, there were two post offices serving the same small community. The confusion continued for a year, until January 19, 1860, when Postmaster General Joseph Holt discontinued the post office at Fort Comanche. On the same day, Holt appointed Holliday as the new postmaster at Fort Stockton after the previous appointee, Leonard Pierce, failed to post the position's requisite bond.[13]

Besides correcting this duplication of service, Holt also addressed overlapping mail routes in West Texas. The Overland Mail Company's move to the Lower

Road and Fort Stockton created a redundancy in regional mail contracts: Butterfield's Route 12578 and George Giddings's Route 8076 from San Antonio, Texas, to San Diego, California, both served the Fort Stockton to El Paso segment. Given Holt's well-known dislike for expensive overland mail contracts that bled red ink, this redundancy was certain to be short-lived. The *New York Times* opined that Giddings's line was of little import and "could easily be dispensed with." The language in Butterfield's contract prohibited Holt from curtailing the Overland Mail Company's service, but Giddings's contract contained no such provisions. Giddings never stood a chance against the mighty Butterfield. Postmaster General Order Journals refer to Butterfield as the "great" Overland California Mail Route and the "great" Overland Mail Line, an adjective never used to describe Giddings's Route 8076. Concurrent with Butterfield's relocation to the Lower Road, Holt started whittling away at Giddings's line.[14]

On April 14, 1859, the postmaster general cut Route 8076 from a weekly service to twice a month. Next, on February 1, 1860, Holt ordered Giddings to discontinue service west of El Paso. Finally, on March 12, 1860, he instructed Giddings to stop all service west of Fort Stockton. The beneficiary of these cuts was the Overland Mail Company. In July 1860, Holt signed a $25,000 contract with company superintendent E. S. Alvord to supply weekly mail service between Fort Stockton and El Paso, designated as Route 8817.[15]

After Holt curtailed Giddings's mail contract, the contractor's revenue plummeted from $196,448 a year in January 1859 to $70,000 a year in July 1860. With Route 8076 cut to the bone, Giddings petitioned Congress to provide financial redress for his unexpected and undeserved losses. Congress proved sympathetic and on March 1, 1861, ordered the postmaster general to reimburse Giddings $70,000 for damages and additional pay. On March 13, 1861, Holt's successor, Montgomery Blair, issued the order for payment.[16]

After the postmaster orders and route changes, Butterfield and Giddings found that they could save money by cooperating on mutually beneficial business arrangements. For the Overland Mail Company, providing effective mail service from Fort Stockton to El Paso required fifteen stage stops. George Giddings had previously established a number of stage stops along the Lower Road for Route 8076. Some of these he built, while others he rented from local landowners. Rather than incurring additional debt by building all-new stations throughout this section, Butterfield approached Giddings and the landowners about leasing options. Ultimately, the Overland Mail Company built several stations along the Lower Road while sharing others with Giddings.[17]

George Giddings had established a stage stop at Comanche Springs in January 1858. Both the station and the springs were located in Survey 150. The owner of

Survey 150 was John D. Holliday, postmaster and post sutler at Fort Stockton. Holliday also served as the local agent for Giddings's San Antonio–San Diego Mail Line and managed the stage stop at Comanche Springs.[18]

Besides cuts to his mail contact, Giddings also suffered considerable losses while operating in the heart of Comanche and Apache territory. For example, at Comanche Springs Station, warriors in March 1858 made off with eighteen mules worth $2,700. In a subsequent attack, raiders stole another twenty-two mules, valued at $3,300, from the company's corrals. To resolve these recurring raids, Giddings turned to the federal government. While in San Antonio, Giddings lobbied General Twiggs, the commander of the Department of Texas, to post a garrison at Comanche Springs. His request proved successful. In a May 1860 letter, army quartermaster Major General T. S. Jessup wrote that the "San Antonio and San Diego Mail Company had already made a relay station" at Comanche Springs, and he believed that "General Twiggs was influenced in a measure to establish a post upon the representation of one or more of the proprietors or agents of said company."[19]

Jessup claimed that Giddings had promised the government free rent if it built a fort at Comanche Springs. The army located its outpost near the stage stop on John Holliday's Survey 150. Astute in business, Holliday had also purchased adjacent parcels 151 and 160 along Comanche Creek, effectively giving him control over much of the local water supply. Despite Giddings's alleged assurances, Holliday later demanded a rental fee from the military for leasing the fort's acreage. Eventually, the two sides reached an understanding. By 1860, Holliday had secured army contracts for supplying beef, hay, and wood to Fort Stockton. Holliday's multiple arrangements essentially gave him a business monopoly in this nascent West Texas community. The case of Comanche Springs and Fort Stockton is a prime example of frontier entrepreneurs such as Holliday working the federal system to their maximum benefit.[20]

During the antebellum period, Comanche Springs was the preeminent oasis for travelers in the Trans-Pecos. Robert Eccleston, journeying to California in 1849, crossed Comanche Creek, calling it "a beautifully clear stream," and camped at Comanche Springs, where, he said, "the water is the finest we have got a hold [of] in some time." Like European Americans, Comanches and Apaches also prized Comanche Springs as one of the most valuable resources in the region. "This is . . . the greatest Indian encampment that it has been our luck to stop at," Eccleston noted. He continued, "The ground is literally strewn with horse dung and bones." Eccleston saw a buffalo skull with horns, as well as the bones of countless mules. One of his fellow travelers "found the skull of a young Mexican girl, with a hole either from an arrow or bullet. Her wisdom teeth were just appearing through the gums."[21]

Lieutenant William H. C. Whiting camped at Comanche Springs in March

1849 and described the spring as "a clear gush of water which bursts from the plain . . . and soon swells in a clear running brook abounding in fish and soft-shell turtles." The lieutenant, like many visitors here, found the water "pleasant to the taste, extremely limpid, . . . and highly mineral in its character." The observant Whiting also noted the scarcity of wood at the well-used campground. Sojourners had stripped all of the surrounding mesquite, forcing the army lieutenant to venture more than half a mile distant to find sufficient wood for cooking.[22]

Upon stopping here four years later, in May 1853, Julius Froebel remarked, "In the plain, several strong springs, rising in a space of a few hundred feet, form a stream, in the deep and clear waters of which we caught a quantity of cat-fish." Such beautiful, life-sustaining resources attracted both prey and predators. Returning here in January 1854, Froebel "found four human skeletons, and at a little distance a fifth." Froebel later learned that the bones belonged to several men heading to California that Comanches waylaid at the springs. Encamped here three years later, in 1857, a member of a federal wagon train observed that Comanche Creek was "a beautiful stream some ten or fifteen yards wide [and] about ten feet in depth, clear as crystal."[23]

Comanche Springs maintained a vigorous output throughout the remainder of the nineteenth century. In 1899, its eleven major and minor flows discharged 30,115 gallons per minute. From 1923 until 1947, with the advent of aquifer pumping for irrigated agriculture, the figure declined to, but then held steady at, 19,020 gallons per minute. After World War II, intense pumping at Leon-Belding, eight miles west of Fort Stockton, caused Comanche Springs to stop flowing. Since 1962, the springs have mostly stayed dry. Downstream, Comanche Creek dried up. Farmers along the creek watched their crops wither and fail.[24]

Gunnar Brune, Texas's foremost expert on natural springs, notes that in Pecos County and Fort Stockton, irrigation pumping has caused area groundwater levels to drop 400 feet, "and nearly all the springs in the county have dried up." Brune says, "The failure of Comanche Springs was probably the most spectacular example in Texas of man's abuse of nature." The centerpiece of Fort Stockton's heritage and identity, the invaluable resource that originally attracted both Indians and European Americans has largely disappeared, and "something very vital to Fort Stockton has been lost." Today, Comanche Springs and Comanche Creek remain dry much of the year. Whenever pumping slows at Leon-Belding, however, both the springs and the creek come back to life.[25]

The irrigation operations at Leon-Belding have also affected Leon Holes, Butterfield's next station, nine and a half miles west of Fort Stockton. Like Comanche Springs, Leon Holes was historically one of the Trans-Pecos's most valuable sources of never-failing water. The water holes also served as an important nineteenth-century regional crossroads. At Leon Holes three roads converge: the overland road continues on to Fort Davis, while another trail goes southwest to Presidio, Texas, and the Rio Grande and a third heads northwest to Toyah, Texas. The Overland Mail Company built its station here near "two bodies of water welling up from the bosom of the earth forming two pools," measuring twenty-four feet deep and fifty feet wide. One visitor noted, "The water runs from one spring to another, and finally, in the course of a half mile, sinks into the earth."[26]

Lieutenant William H. C. Whiting rested at Leon Holes in March 1849 and remarked, "This spring when found is a gem, . . . its sides sloping down like an inverted cone, but clear as the water is, we could not see the bottom." Stopping here a few months later, Captain Samuel Gibbs French said that the area around the springs smelled like sulfur. The ground around the holes was "bare, and covered with finely crystalized salt, which at a distance appear[ed] like snow." Freighter Julius Froebel, who visited here in 1853 and again in 1854, observed the rushes, reeds, and bogs bordering the two water holes, which contained "numerous turtles." Period travelers variously described the water as "clear, impregnated with sulphur and very pleasant to [the] taste" or "quite good" and "clear but brackish." Ruth Shackelford voiced a decidedly different opinion when her wagon train camped here in 1868: "This is a dry alkali place with no wood and very poor grass." She complained, "[T]he water is so salty [that] we cannot have good coffee or tea."[27]

Thirty-five-year-old Nicholas Johnson of Alabama, along with his thirty-one-year-old wife, Emma, and their two daughters, Larch and Jaus, aged eleven and nine, ran the Butterfield station at Leon Holes. An overland stagecoach carrying William Tallack stopped here for dinner in 1860, and the passengers enjoyed "some excellent bread, the best on the route." At Leon Holes, "there was a refinement about the spot very different from the rugged aspect of the generality of Overland stations and their inmates," Tallack observed. He continued, "[T]his was owing to the presence of a cheerful matronly woman (the wife of one of the station keepers), and two gentle girls, her young daughters, bright 'prairie flowers' not often seen in these rough Far-Western wilds."[28]

With the increased traffic along the overland road from cattle drives, wagon trains, and stagecoaches, Leon Holes became an attractive target for Native American raiders. Major General Zenas Randall Bliss recalled that during the 1850s, four hundred Comanches en route to Mexico stopped a wagon train at the springs. After receiving payment of two oxen, the Comanches permitted the freighters to resume their journey. In August 1858, fifteen Comanches cornered nine cowboys driving six hundred head of cattle to California. The Indians captured two hundred beeves and twenty horses, as well as killing and scalping "two white men and two Mexicans" before plundering the party's wagon.[29]

In the summer of 1860, Butterfield overseer Adam Rankin Johnson stopped at Leon Holes Station for dinner. While Johnson and the other employees ate their meal, a band of Indians swept down upon the livestock herder outside the station. The raiders "would have killed him but for the prompt action of Captain Helm," Johnson said, "who ran among them firing right and left with his six-shooter, killing a horse and wounding one of the Indians." The occupants of the station had by then opened fire on the attackers, and the warriors quickly retired, but not before emptying the station's corral of all its mules and horses. Johnson, always a good judge of valuable real estate, had filed a claim on the Leon Holes acreage a few weeks before the raid.[30]

In September 1860, "a party of Mexican guerillas" stole thirty-five mules from the Butterfield corrals at Leon Holes. In a subsequent depredation during December 1860, Native American raiders made off with another twelve mules from the stage stop, for a net loss of $1,800. Three months later, in March 1861, a group of warriors massacred a family near Leon Holes. The family had stopped to repair one of their two wagons, when the Indians swept down on them. After slaughtering the parents and children, the Indians set fire to the wagons and the corpses.[31]

In the 150 years since Butterfield operated its station here, irrigated farming has significantly altered this historic site. In 1948, Leon Holes had a flow of almost 12,680 gallons per minute. By 1960, the discharge was zero. Today, Leon Holes is often dry, "filled with sediment from man-made soil erosion" and ringed with a profuse growth of salt cedar. Since 1855, Captain Pope and countless others have tried to reclaim this desert region for agriculture. The resultant environmental cost has been steep. Out of fifty healthy, flowing springs in Pecos County in the 1850s, only a handful survive today. Gunnar Brune notes that after "thousands of years of years of beneficial use by mankind," the county's "beautiful springs have been sacrificed in the name of *progress*."[32]

After leaving Leon Holes and heading west toward Fort Davis, the Overland Mail Road passed several water holes in Coyanosa Draw before coming to Hackberry Holes, twenty-two miles distant. Although nineteenth-century travelers could not be finicky about the quality of water they found in the parched Trans-Pecos, the rank, muddy water at Hackberry Holes would make even a thirst-crazed man think twice. The next Butterfield station, fifteen miles west of Hackberry, was at Barilla Spring in present-day Jeff Davis County. Travelers named Barilla (or Varela) Spring after Francisco Varela of El Paso County, who operated an El Paso–San Antonio freighting service. Barilla Spring, located in a narrow canyon a short distance above the station, offered a dependable and ample supply of good, clear water.[33]

At numerous sites, including Barilla Spring, the Overland Mail Company deliberately placed its stations away from local water sources to allow Native Americans access. Butterfield overseer Adam Rankin Johnson said that when he traveled through the region, he always camped a short distance from water. After stopping at a water hole east of Fort Stockton one night, and "[k]nowing that the . . . [Indians] would visit the springs, a common camping ground," Johnson withdrew "to a rocky ridge that was at a convenient distance from this watering place." He advised two families traveling to California to do the same, but they declined his suggestion and camped at the springs. Before sunrise the next morning, fifty warriors attacked the emigrants, wounding them and capturing one of their wagons.[34]

Despite the mail company's efforts to provide access to regional water holes, Apaches and Comanches still resented interlopers on their lands. During the antebellum period, Apaches kept a close watch for trespassers and sometimes interdicted their movements. In late February 1854, eighty to one hundred Mescalero Apaches stopped Julius Froebel's wagon train close to the future Butterfield station site at Barilla Spring. The Apaches, led by Marcos and Soldadito, blocked Froebel's party en route to the spring to refill their water casks. The warriors rode across the trail in front of the wagon train "and stuck a lance into the ground, as a sign that . . . [the travelers] were not allowed to proceed." Upon closer examination, Froebel saw that the lance contained part of an old sword with Spanish writing on the blade that read "Por el Rey Carlos III." Adorning another part of the lance was a strand of "long blond hair" belonging to "a white woman they had murdered [that] was fluttering . . . in the wind."[35]

The Apaches demanded a parlay with the wagon teamsters. Chief Marcos spoke: "Your waggons [sic] roll over the country like thunder. We have seen you from our mountains crossing the plains." Marcos promised the men no harm, saying, "Don't you think that we could have plundered you and killed many of you? We have watched you for many days, and have been in your neighbourhood." The Apaches desired only a large gift of tobacco, and after receiving it, they allowed Froebel's party to proceed on to Barilla Spring. Encamped at the spring a few hours later, Froebel reflected, "After the excitement of the day . . . we passed a tranquil night at our watering-place, which refreshed and rested both man and beast."[36]

The Apaches proved less lenient with mail contractor George Giddings at Barilla Spring the following year. In December 1855, raiders made off with a considerable haul: 160 mules worth almost $26,000. Another major loss occurred in October 1859, four months after Butterfield began sharing the station with Giddings. The theft occurred while the station herder was taking his dinner break. After tethering the grazing animals to some mesquite trees, the herder went inside the stage stop. Ten minutes later, as he was eating his meal, a group of Indians swept in and cut the animals loose. The station employees gave chase with guns blazing, but to no avail. The Indians got away with all the Overland Mail Company and San Antonio–San Diego Mail Company's livestock. In March 1861, warriors stole another eighteen mules from the Butterfield and Giddings corrals here, for a loss of $2,700. The owner of the 160-acre Barilla Spring parcel, which included the overland station and water hole, was none other than Butterfield overseer Adam Rankin Johnson.[37]

Heading onward to Fort Davis, twenty-nine miles distant, the overland road followed Limpia Creek upstream to the next stop, Cottonwood Station. En route, Butterfield coaches first traversed Wild Rose Pass, one of the most scenic locales on the entire Texas route. In March 1849, Lieutenant William H. C. Whiting gave this canyon its name, noting, "Wild roses, the only ones I had seen in Texas, here grew luxuriantly. I named the defile 'Wild Rose Pass.'"[38]

Julius Froebel traveled through this section in February 1854 and observed, "A mountain scenery of the strangest character. In general, the Limpia passes are among the most interesting things in nature I have ever seen." The German teamster continued, "I was struck by the wonderful harmony and unity of the . . . elements which compose the landscape." Bishop George Foster Pierce's stagecoach passed up the canyon in May 1859. "We got through as the sun was setting; and on the right was a long broken ridge of mountains, with steep rocks shooting up like steeples and spires," Pierce remarked, "and above were clouds, rolling and tossing with the wind—the reflected light likened them to smoke and flame ascending from a city on fire."[39]

The valley may have been beautiful, but it was also dangerous. Butterfield passenger Albert Richardson recalled an incident in Wild Rose Pass when Apaches waylaid the mail train from San Antonio. Mescaleros killed the driver, plundered the coach, and made off with the livestock. Pausing a few miles on, the Indians lay on the ground to look at several illustrated newspapers they had taken from the mailbags. Having never before seen engraved illustrations, the Apaches became so engrossed in studying them that they failed to notice the rapid approach of a cavalry patrol, which "dashed in among them, killing fourteen and routing the rest." Richardson said, "The Apaches believed the papers had revealed their whereabout [sic]; and still supposing that pictures can talk they avoid them with superstitious dread." As with all who journeyed through here, the scenery made a profound impression upon Richardson. "Sunrise overtook us in Limpia Canyon," he noted, "whose rocky walls, a thousand feet high, have been sculptured by water into fantastic figures."[40]

After exiting Wild Rose Pass, coaches paused at Cottonwood Station, eighteen miles from Barilla Spring. George Giddings established this station in 1858 for his San Antonio–San Diego Mail Line. The Overland Mail Company began sharing the site with Giddings in June 1859. In the latter part of that month, Indians targeted the Butterfield corrals here, making off with eight mules and one horse. In the spring of 1861, a newspaper reported that Indians in the area were "as thick as blackbirds." One hundred fifty years later, a few cottonwood trees still mark the site. All that remains of the overland station are some rock foundations scattered over a cattle pasture and an adjacent rock-lined well, twenty feet in depth.[41]

From Cottonwood Station, the "very rough" overland road crisscrossed Limpia Creek twenty-three times en route to the next stage stop, Fort Davis, home to the largest military garrison in the antebellum Trans-Pecos. The army established the outpost in October 1854 in the heart of Mescalero territory to deter Apache depredations. In 1859, Fort Davis had a garrison of 112 men, and in 1860, 130, sufficient numbers to defend the fort and adjacent community but not enough to curtail Indian depredations in the region. By the eve of the Civil War, Department of Texas commander General Twiggs had given up any hope of mounting an effective offensive campaign against Comanches and Apaches in West Texas. Robert Wooster says, "Twiggs admitted as much, ordering his command 'to resort to the defensive system again.'"[42]

Fort Davis, located in present-day Jeff Davis County, served as one of the epicenters of the federal frontier economy in the Trans-Pecos. "The entrepreneurs who came to Fort Davis to make their fortunes," Wooster observes, "sought to capitalize on the chance to begin anew." Fort Davis, like the rest of the American West, was prone to boom-bust cycles. "Men and women who came to the region often found their fortunes to be closely linked to the interest of a faraway government," Wooster says. He continues, "[N]ot surprisingly, private entrepreneurs alternately profited from and criticized the ebbs and flows of public subsidies."[43]

Butterfield overseer and stagecoach driver Henry Skillman had originally filed a claim on the acreage containing Fort Davis, A. S. Lewis Survey Six. Skillman's claim evaporated when John James of San Antonio secured legal title to the property. In 1854, James signed a twenty-year lease with the government to rent the land for $300 per year. James received an additional $1,000 from the army for cutting timber on his acreage above the fort. James proved adept at snapping up choice parcels in West Texas. Besides his holdings in Fort Davis and the Texas Hill Country, James also acquired Juan Cordona Salt Lake (and its salt) on the Pecos River, Camp Van Camp on Comanche Creek, and after the Civil War, much of the watered lands around Fort Stockton. James and his brother-in-law, James Sweet, owned one of the largest mercantile stores in San Antonio and West Texas: James R. Sweet and Company. Period credit reports noted that John James was "a large landholder and . . . a very shrewd man." In 1860, the wealthiest resident of Fort Davis was the forty-year-old post sutler and postmaster, Alexander Young of Pennsylvania, with a net worth of $22,000. Young also ran a "country store" and held the government corn and wood contracts. Financial reports said that Young was "honest" and his "credit A No. 1" and that he was "doing a good business."[44]

The Butterfield station at Fort Davis was located on the southwest side of the post next to the overland road. George Giddings's stage stop, however, was at a different location. Giddings's La Limpia Station was a mile north of the fort, at Painted Comanche Camp on Limpia Creek. Painted Comanche Camp acquired its name from early explorers such as Lieutenant William H. C. Whiting, who rested here in March 1849. Whiting described stopping in a grove of "lofty" cotton-wood trees, many of which featured drawings he described as "rude sketches of the Comanche." Near Giddings's stage stop was a civilian settlement called La Limpia. Prominent residents of La Limpia included Alexander Young, grocer Daniel Murphy, merchant Patrick Murphy, and farmer Dietrick Dutchover.[45]

In 1860, the composition of Presidio County's six hundred residents (which included Forts Davis and Stockton) was 55 percent Hispanic, 16 percent Northern, and 5 percent Southern, with military personnel constituting the remaining 24 percent. Among federal troops stationed on the frontier, Fort Davis was one of the favored stations in Texas. Situated almost a mile above sea level, the site boasts an excellent climate and outstanding scenery. Zenas Bliss, who served as a lieutenant here from 1855 to 1858, said, "The post was the most beautifully situated of any that I have ever seen."[46]

Westward from Fort Davis, it was twenty-three miles to the next overland station, Barrel Spring. En route, the Butterfield Road passed Nine Mile Hill and Point of Rocks, a well-known landmark situated at the twelve-mile mark. Four miles onward, the mail road went through a beautiful stand of live oak trees known as Skillman's Grove, named after noted Butterfield stage driver Henry Skillman of Kentucky. The site got its name after a band of raiding Native Americans attacked Skillman's mail coach here. The advancing Indians quickly withdrew after Skillman opened fire on them with his Sharps rifle. Believing themselves safely out of rifle range, the warriors were subsequently surprised when the seasoned frontiersman picked off one of their party from a considerable distance. Skillman was fond of his liquor and loved to regale listeners with this story while imbibing at local watering holes. Zenas Bliss recalled that after each drink, the tale grew more incredible, until Skillman's sharpshooter skills seemed almost superhuman. On one occasion, a lieutenant named Taylor grew weary of the braggadocio and poured a pitcher of cold water over Skillman's head. Skillman responded, "Taylor, you can do that because you are from Kentucky."[47]

From Skillman's Grove, it was another seven miles to Butterfield's Barrel Spring Station, situated at 5,500 feet. Visiting here in 1869, Lieutenant Colonel Thomas Hunt found the mail station at the mouth of a canyon. The Butterfield stage stop featured eleven-foot-high walls and a courtyard that included two rooms and the corral. Outside, on either side of the gated entrance, were another two rooms. Over the years, Indian raids periodically decimated the building, forcing mail contractors to rebuild it three times. Barrel Spring was due north of the station, a quarter of a mile up the canyon. Hunt noted that the spring afforded a "good supply of water." The site's unusual name derives from a wooden barrel that station employees placed at the source to collect water. Later landowners placed a permanent circular enclosure around the spring. Harriet Bunyard, who passed through here with a wagon train in 1868, was unimpressed with the locale, describing it as "not [a] very nice place to camp." Barrel Spring, which lies just off modern Highway 166, still flows today, but little remains of the adobe station house, excluding a few foundation stones and period artifacts.[48]

In 1860, William Tallack's Butterfield coach passed through this section of the route with a feisty crew aboard. The passengers, stiff from sitting in the same position for hours on end, decided to try some new seating arrangements. To create more leg room, those in the front of the Celerity wagon pushed the mailbags to the back. One of those occupying the rear of the vehicle, a passenger nicknamed "Texas," took offense at sharing his cramped space with the mailbags. Ignoring Texas's complaints, one of those up front continued moving sacks to the rear and, pointing to his pistols, said there would be a problem "unless his arrangement was agreed with." This threat incensed Texas, who immediately grabbed his own pistol and declared, "Well, if you talk about 'trouble,' I can, too; and, as to that matter, I'd as lief [gladly] have 'trouble' as anything else." Tallack recalled that this "declaration and its accompanying gestures," so characteristic of the Lone Star passenger, "immediately made the first complainant 'draw in,' and exercise his 'prudence as the better part of valour.'"[49]

The next overland station was fifteen miles west of Barrel Spring, at El Muerto, or Dead Man's Hole. The dramatic, rugged scenery at El Muerto Peak reminds the visitor of the setting at Barilla Spring Station, east of Fort Davis. John C. Reid, who stopped here in early November 1857, recounted the story of how the place received its name. Reid said it was a water hole "of notoriety, and named from the remains of a man, who had been shot, having been found in it." Stagecoach passenger Bishop George Foster Pierce opined that it was "a most revolting name for a spring of the best water on the route."[50]

El Muerto Station lay in the heart of Mescalero Apache territory. In late December 1854, a band of Apaches attacked Henry Skillman and several employees of the San Antonio–Santa Fe mail line here. After an intense firefight, the raiders eventually withdrew. A newspaper account stated, "Captain Skillman has a fine gun, with which he considers he has a 'dead thing' on any Indian [at] three hundred yards, and in this fight he is said to have killed three in that distance." Three years later, in January 1858, Mescaleros destroyed George Giddings's El Muerto Station and all its contents, making off with twenty-six mules. The total loss to Giddings's operation was more than $6,000.[51]

A year and a half later, in August 1859, a band of eight Native Americans stole nine mules and a horse from the overland mail corrals here. Station manager Henry Ramstein, formerly at Butterfield's Pinery Station on the Upper Road, told the commanding officer at Fort Davis that the culprits were Mescaleros from the Guadalupe Mountains. In September 1859, Apache raiders took an additional forty mules and several cows. In December 1860, another group of warriors struck El Muerto, waylaying Ramstein while he was out gathering forage for the livestock. "Indians crept up behind the wagon on which Ramstein was riding and shot him through the heart. . . . Ramstein was found dead on the hay."[52]

Renowned stagecoach driver and frontiersman "Bigfoot" Wallace ran into trouble here after stopping to rest his livestock and mend his pants. Wallace was sitting by a pool of water under the spring, which issued from a rock bluff overhead. As he stitched up his buckskin clothing, he heard a piece of gravel come loose from above and splash in the water. Glancing up, he spied an Indian on the bluff observing him. Wallace "grabbed his mail bags in one hand and his weapons in the other and . . . started for El Paso and carried the mail through on foot and without any pants on." Over the years, El Muerto served as a stage stop for all of the major mail companies. The building's adobe walls have long since melted, but a large rock corral remains. A short distance from the corral, the spring in the rocks still produces cool, clear water.[53]

From El Muerto it was thirty-three miles to the next station, Van Horn's Wells. Van Horn's Wells is located in the southwest corner of present-day Culberson County. The name of the wells and the adjacent Van Horn Mountains come from Brevet Major Jefferson Van Horne, Third Infantry, who passed through here in the summer of 1849 on his way to El Paso. The setting was far from ideal. One visitor here remarked, "No man unless outlawed would consider it a desirable location to remain at." The water hole here, although permanent, issued only a marginal flow. When Julius Froebel's party arrived here in March 1854, they found the well empty—previous wagon trains had used up all the water. "All around[,] cattle left behind by preceding caravans lay dying with thirst," Froebel recalled. "It was indeed a melancholy spectacle."[54]

The German freighter's experience was not unique. The water supply at these desert seeps was enough to supply a small band of Indians and their horses but not wagon trains and hundreds of animals. Before pushing on to the next watering hole, Froebel remarked on the tableau of dying cattle that surrounded him. "Many of the poor beasts, still alive, had their eyes dried up and their tongues hanging out of their mouth: we shot several of them, in passing, out of mere compassion."[55]

The station at Van Horn's Wells, located at the base of the Van Horn Mountains, was a favored site for Apache depredations. In a March 1857 attack, warriors stole eighteen mules from George Giddings's station and corrals. In January 1858, Apaches took twenty-six mules and company equipment. Before leaving, they killed an employee and torched the station, destroying seventy-five tons of hay and 125 bushels of corn. Giddings's local agent, state senator Archibald Hyde, subsequently rebuilt the stage stop at a cost of $1,500. Fort Stockton entrepreneur John D. Holliday, always on the lookout for valuable real estate, filed a claim on Van Horn's Wells in February 1859.[56]

By 1860, Indian attacks had become so pervasive upon the station here and at Eagle Spring, the next stop westward, that the Overland Mail Company asked Adam Rankin Johnson to oversee operations at these two Trans-Pecos hot spots. Employing his frontier guerilla tactics once again, Johnson set a trap for raiding Mescaleros at Van Horn's Wells. Placing two lifelike dummies on the corral walls, Johnson, his brother Ben, and Captain Neil Helm secreted themselves on top of the ridge overlooking the station. At sunrise, the trio noticed seven Apaches approaching on one side of the station and sixteen more on the other. The three men let loose a volley from their heights and followed with a mad dash toward the warriors, firing all the while. The Mescaleros rapidly retreated, leaving three dead. During his tenure managing multiple stations across the Butterfield frontier in Texas, Adam Rankin Johnson consistently proved himself one of the mail company's most capable employees.[57]

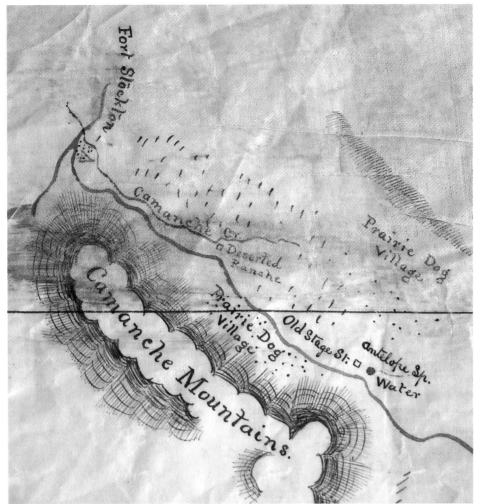

Detail of map showing the Butterfield Road to Camp Pleasant at Antelope Spring and Fort Stockton. From Lieutenant Colonel E. J. Strang, *Topographical Sketch of the Road from Fort Stockton to Fort Chadbourne, October and November 1867*, National Archives Cartographic and Architectural Section, College Park, Md.

Mary Williams at ruins of Camp Pleasant at Antelope Spring. Photograph by the author.

Water holding tank at
Antelope Spring (now
dry). Photograph by
the author.

Ruins of Camp Van
Camp, a temporary
army outpost
used during 1859.
Photograph by the
author.

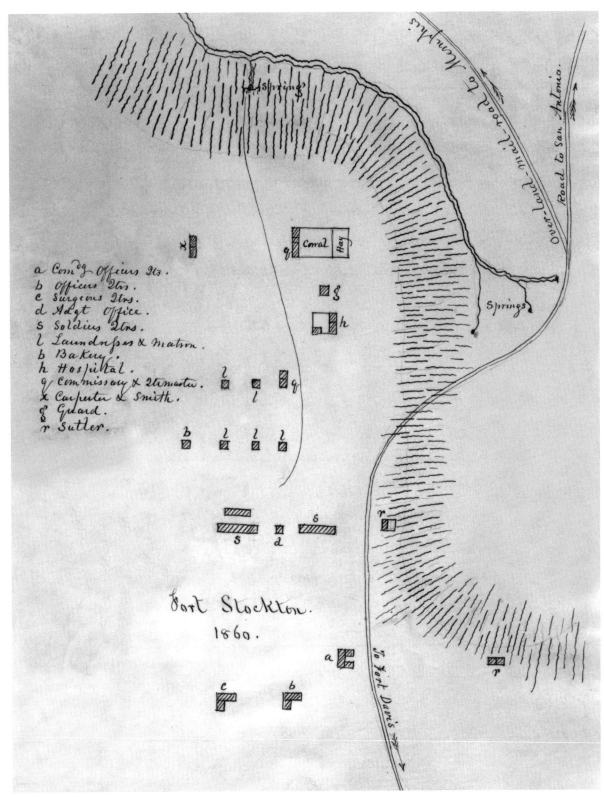

a Com'dg Officers Qrs.
b Officers Qrs.
c Surgeons Qrs.
d Adjt Office.
s Soldiers Qrs.
l Laundresses & matron.
b Bakery.
h Hospital.
q Commissary & Qtermaster.
x Carpenter & Smith.
g Guard.
r Sutler.

Fort Stockton.
1860.

November 1860 sketch of Fort Stockton at Comanche Springs by Colonel J. K. F. Mansfield. The Butterfield station was likely the building marked "r" in the middle of the sketch, while sutler John D. Holliday's store was probably the second building marked "r," in the lower right corner. National Archives copy courtesy of Jerry D. Thompson.

Comanche Creek ford at Fort Stockton in post–Civil War period. Courtesy of Annie Riggs Memorial Museum, Historic Fort Stockton, Fort Stockton Historical Society, Texas.

Ladies reposing at Comanche Springs in post–Civil War period. Courtesy of Annie Riggs Memorial Museum, Historic Fort Stockton, Fort Stockton Historical Society, Texas.

Bath houses on Comanche Creek, Fort Stockton, in post–Civil War period. Courtesy of Annie Riggs Memorial Museum, Historic Fort Stockton, Fort Stockton Historical Society, Texas.

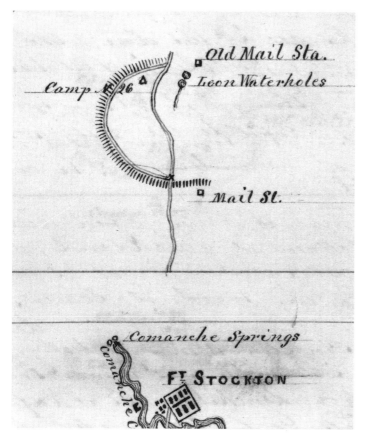

Detail from 1869 map showing overland road from Fort Stockton and Comanche Springs to Butterfield station at Leon Holes ("Old Mail Sta."). The post–Civil War mail station is below, on the east side of the hill ("Mail St."). From "Journal Showing the Route Taken by the Government Train from Austin, Texas to Ft. Craig, New Mexico," by Brevet Lieutenant Colonel Thomas B. Hunt, National Archives Cartographic and Architectural Section, College Park, Md.

Leon Holes in the 1930s. Conkling Papers, courtesy of the Seaver Center for Western History Research, Los Angeles County Museum of Natural History.

Hackberry Holes, Pecos County, Texas. Photograph by the author.

Artifacts from Butterfield Road near Hackberry Holes, including post–Civil War army telegraph insulator. Photograph by the author.

Ruins of Barilla Spring Station, looking south, Jeff Davis County, Texas. Photograph by the author.

View of station ruins looking north up Barilla Spring Canyon. Photograph by the author.

Mary Williams on trace of Butterfield Road in Wild Rose Pass. Photograph by the author.

Mary Williams (*right*) and Mildred Nored (*left*) at rock ruin in Wild Rose Pass. Photograph by the author.

Joe Allen at Cottonwood Station. Photograph by the author.

Rock-lined well at Cottonwood Station. Photograph by the author.

Jennifer Sproul Whitesell at site of Painted Comanche Camp and the adjacent La Limpia settlement. Photograph by the author.

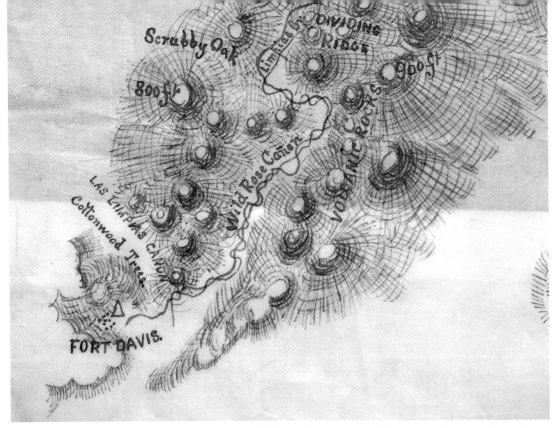

Detail of map showing Butterfield Road through Wild Rose Pass. Painted Comanche Camp and the adjacent La Limpia settlement were located in the area bounded by "Cottonwood Trees" (*left*) and "Las Limpias Cañon" (*right*). From Lieutenant Colonel E. J. Strang, *Topographical Sketch of the Road from Fort Stockton to Fort Davis, October 1867*, National Archives Cartographic and Architectural Section, College Park, Md.

Watercolor of George Giddings's San Antonio–El Paso Mail Station at La Limpia during the 1850s. From *Overland Mail Station*, by Captain Arthur Tracy Lee (91.218.19), courtesy of the Rochester Historical Society, Rochester, N.Y.

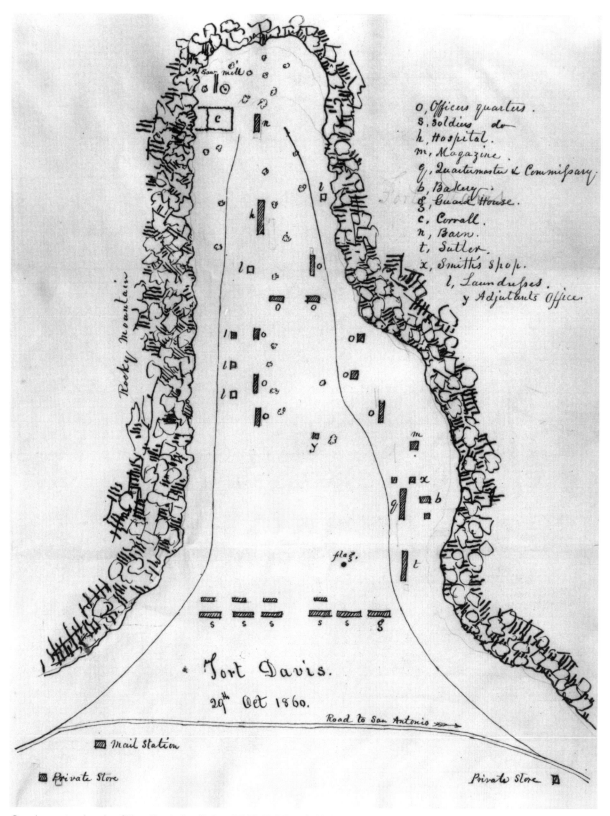

October 1860 sketch of Fort Davis by Colonel J. K. F. Mansfield. Note Butterfield station ("Mail Station") in lower left corner. National Archives copy courtesy of Jerry D. Thompson.

Watercolor of Fort Davis, Texas, during the 1850s. From *Fort Davis, Texas*, by Captain Arthur Tracy Lee (91.218.3), courtesy of the Rochester Historical Society, Rochester, N.Y.

Watercolor of army life at Fort Davis during the 1850s. From *Canyon, Fort Davis—1*, by Captain Arthur Tracy Lee, courtesy of the Department of Rare Books, Special Collections and Preservation, University of Rochester River Campus Libraries, Rochester, N.Y.

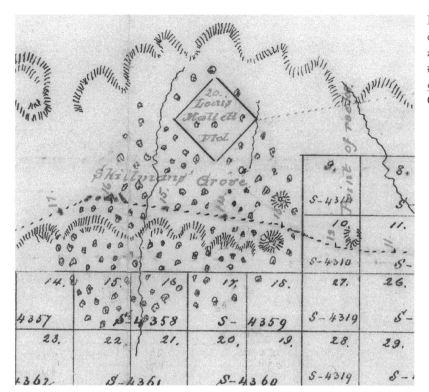

Detail of survey map showing overland road to Point of Rocks and Skillman's Grove. Map #27920, *Presidio County Sketch File 9*, courtesy of Texas General Land Office Archives, Austin.

Margaret Conkling at Barrel Spring in the 1930s. Conkling Papers, courtesy of the Seaver Center for Western History Research, Los Angeles County Museum of Natural History.

Ruins of Barrel Spring Station in the 1930s. Conkling Papers, courtesy of the Seaver Center for Western History Research, Los Angeles County Museum of Natural History.

El Muerto/Dead Man's Hole Station, Jeff Davis County, Texas, in the 1930s. Conkling Papers, courtesy of the Seaver Center for Western History Research, Los Angeles County Museum of Natural History.

Detail of adobe station walls at El Muerto/Dead Man's Hole Station in the 1930s. Conkling Papers, courtesy of the Seaver Center for Western History Research, Los Angeles County Museum of Natural History.

Marker for "Van Horn [sic] Wells" (erected in 1936) with the Van Horn Mountains in background. Rocks from the overland station can be seen behind the marker. Photograph by the author.

Ruins of Butterfield station at Van Horn's Wells. Photograph by the author.

Margaret Conkling at Van Horn's Wells water collection tank in the 1930s. Conkling Papers, courtesy of the Seaver Center for Western History Research, Los Angeles County Museum of Natural History.

CHAPTER 10

From Van Horn's Wells to El Paso

The Apaches!, Frederic Remington. Oil on canvas, 1904. Courtesy of Sid Richardson Museum, Fort Worth, Texas.

Eleven miles northwest of Van Horn's Wells, the overland road passed through a canyon en route to Eagle Spring. Butterfield stagecoaches paused briefly here so that the mules could drink from a spring that issued from a rock outcrop. This Carrizo Mountains landmark, just west of the Hudspeth-Culberson County line, was a notorious locale for Apache ambushes. The site received its name, Bass Canyon, in January 1869 after warriors waylaid stage driver James Bass and passenger Jarvis Hubbell. Hubbell was a person of note in early El Paso history, serving as postmaster, district surveyor, real estate speculator, and Confederate spy. Several days after the attack, occupants of another coach passing through the canyon found Bass's body "in a perfectly nude state and horribly mutilated, either by the red savages or the wolves." A search party subsequently turned up a slipper that Hubbell had been wearing but failed to locate his corpse.[1]

Perhaps the most infamous spot on the Lower Road for Indian attacks was at Eagle Spring, eleven miles to the west. The Butterfield station, located in a canyon on the north side of the 6,915-foot Eagle Mountains, sits in a beautiful yet ominous setting. The absolute silence here is unnerving. The imposing Eagle and Panther Peaks, looming overhead, seem to menace the visitor. Bishop George Foster Pierce described the feeling here in May 1859, while traveling through on a stage. "Eagle Mountain . . . is awful in its grandeur. . . . Three graves mark the spot where . . . emigrants were slain. It is a place in which to be sad," the bishop reflected. "When you look around and see the hiding-places from which the treacherous savage might wing his arrow or send his death-dealing bullet, you feel a little nervous." In October 1859, a St. Louis reporter called the site "the most bleak and cold locality on the line . . . the very picture of desolation."[2]

In July 1854, a group of cattlemen lost 200 head to Mescalero Apaches in a raid near Eagle Spring. In December 1855, Indians stole 15 mules from the station built by George Giddings for his San Antonio–Santa Fe mail line earlier that year. The following June, warriors made off with 18 mules, wrecked the stage stop, burned all the forage, and killed three men. In November 1857, a band of Apaches waylaid John C. Reid's wagon train at Eagle Spring, wounding several in his party.[3]

In December 1858, Apaches took 12 mules and destroyed the station and all of its contents a second time. In February 1860, Apaches ambushed P. Sandoval's wagon train here, taking 450 mules worth $34,000, leaving Sandoval to make his way home on foot. In late 1860 or early 1861, raiding Indians decimated the

Butterfield-Giddings station at Eagle Spring, taking 12 head of livestock, killing two men, and burning the stage stop. Butterfield stage driver David Koney arrived on the scene shortly after the attack and helped bury the slain employees. Today, the walls of the old Overland Mail station no longer stand, but one can still see remnants of the stacked rock corral.[4]

Eagle Spring, which flows from a sandstone formation, is located a short distance up the canyon from the stage stop. When Lieutenants William H. C. Whiting and William F. Smith's expedition stopped here on their reconnaissance of the Lower Road in 1849, they described the water hole as more seep than spring. "The water did not run, but merely oozed out of the ground," they noted. Anticipating a skimpy supply, the lieutenants had staggered the arrival times of their wagons to ensure that there would be enough water for all the livestock. Despite their precautions, "water was not found sufficient for one-third of the animals: consequently, they had to travel seventy miles without water." In the 150 years since Whiting's and Smith's visit, Eagle Spring's flow has remained marginal. In 1976, the water hole yielded 2.37 gallons per minute. At some point, a landowner built a rectangular limestone enclosure around the spring to contain runoff. The tank is now abandoned and in disrepair, but it still holds water.[5]

Heading west from Eagle Spring to the Rio Grande, a distance of thirty-two miles, the overland road wrapped around the northwest side of the Eagle Mountains, en route to Devil Ridge, so named for raiding Apaches that frequented the area. From Devil Ridge, the trail continued on to Rocky Ridge. At the southern end of Rocky Ridge, Butterfield coaches crossed a sandy wash containing a seasonal water hole known as Tinaja de las Palmas. On July 30, 1880, Rocky Ridge and the tinaja featured prominently in a fierce battle between black regulars in Colonel Benjamin Grierson's Tenth Cavalry unit and 125 warriors under Apache chief Victorio.[6]

Leaving Tinaja de las Palmas, the overland road crossed Red Light Draw before entering a remote canyon in the 6,689-foot Quitman Mountains. This rugged, desolate ravine, known as Quitman Pass or Quitman Canyon, was a frequent haunt for depredating Mescaleros. Tejanos called it Puerto de los Lamentos, while Americans knew it as Calamity Pass. German freighter Julius Froebel journeyed over the route in March 1854. Along the road, he saw "hundreds of oxen perishing from thirst, which had been left behind." Upon reaching Quitman Pass, he noted, "The defile is only three miles long, but the road through it is so difficult for large waggons [sic] with long teams, that it took us ten hours to pass through it." At the midpoint of the gorge, the freighter's caravan halted at Apache or Indian Post Office, "a rounded rock covered with Indian hieroglyphics."[7]

Travel through Quitman Canyon has always been an unsettling experience. In 1868, Stephen Powers described his passage. "Four miles the wheels ground and grided and screeched along the gravelly arroyo which runs through the pass into the valley of the Rio Grande," Powers observed. "It is a savage and bristling hole, with every stone in it stained with blood, and we went through with bated breath and every man with his musket on his shoulder." Thirteen years later, in 1881, army corporal Emil Bode made the same journey. "Strange feelings take possession of a man when he is about to pass a place where death may meet him at every step. We kept our eyes suspiciously on every stone, expecting to see a gun or hear the report of a rifle." Even today, the desolate drive from Sierra Blanca to the Rio Grande via Quitman Pass is an edgy experience, whether by moonlight or in broad daylight.[8]

Travelers running the gauntlet through Quitman Canyon were uniformly grateful to reach its southern end and the Rio Grande valley below. Butterfield named its station at the mouth of the canyon Camp Fargo, in honor of company director William G. Fargo. Several period maps identify this site as First Camp on the Rio Grande, since this is where travelers first hit the river after the parched and dusty trip from Eagle Spring. Camp Fargo's location was directly in the middle of a historic international corridor, which is still in use. On the American side of the Rio Grande, two canyons in the Quitman Mountains, Quitman Pass and Smuggler's Gap, feed into this corridor. Heading south across the river, trails from Quitman Pass and Smuggler's Gap lead into the interior of Mexico through a notch in the 6,500-foot Sierra Escanton.[9]

Over the centuries, Apaches, bandidos, drug smugglers, and illegal immigrants have utilized these two Quitman Mountain passages. Today, the U.S. Border Patrol has an active presence here and keeps a close watch on all traffic through the area. It was quite a different scene, however, for Butterfield passenger Albert Richardson in October 1859 when his Butterfield coach stopped at Camp Fargo for breakfast. The only signs of life amid the desolate solitude were "[t]hree dirty blanketed barefoot men smoking cigarettes, [who] shivered over the fire on the river bank, where two Mexican women cooked our breakfast of frijoles."[10]

In December 1860, a group of Indian warriors ran off thirty-two mules and twelve horses from Camp Fargo's corrals and destroyed the station house and a large supply of forage. In January 1861, two groups of Apaches attacked the stage stop, taking sixty-eight head of livestock, including two six-horse teams of fine racing horses. Some of the raiders menaced the station from the river, while the remainder advanced from Quitman Canyon. A station employee recalled that the Indians "commenced shooting and hollering, and came rushing in, and killed anyone they could. They killed a Yankee feller by the name of Billy Fink." Depredating Native Americans likely considered Camp Fargo, with its isolated position and meager defenses, ripe for plunder.[11]

From Camp Fargo, the next stop on the overland itinerary was five and a half miles upriver, at Fort Quitman. Coaches paused only to drop off and pick up mail at the Quitman post office, as the Overland Mail Company had no stage stop here. Passenger Albert Richardson observed that the post's whitewashed adobe walls looked like marble. Established in September 1858, Fort Quitman proved problematic from its inception. This was in large part because of its abysmal setting. An army inspector originally advised building Fort Quitman upriver at the Camp Fargo site, but political lobbying in Washington and in Texas likely changed the location.[12]

Army inspector Colonel J. K. F. Mansfield alluded to this when he visited Quitman in November 1860. "It is to be regretted [that] this post was not established where the road first strikes the Rio Grande from the east," Mansfield said, "as that point is the first water west of Eagle Springs, 33 miles distant & here the emigrant & traveller first wants protection in rushing to the water." The colonel noted, "I recommended in 1853 the establishment of a post at the point where the road from the east first strikes the Rio Grande. The mail station has since been placed there, some 2 or 3 men only to keep it." Once again, instead of selecting a suitable site for its outpost, the army chose what some considered the most abysmal setting in Texas.[13]

Despite the dreadful locale, there was still money to be made, even at Fort Quitman. Pyron and Cochran secured the beef contract for the post for 150 head of cattle. Simeon Hart, of El Paso, landed a contract for forty thousand pounds of flour. George Lyles, the Butterfield station manager upstream at Smith's Ranch, held the hay contract at Quitman for seventy-five tons of grama grass. The garrison here posed no threat to Native Americans in the Trans-Pecos. In 1859, total strength stood at seventy-two men, and by the following year in 1860, it had plummeted to thirty-two.[14]

Residents of Fort Quitman universally condemned the post as unsatisfactory and even downright horrible. The blowing sand, swarms of mosquitoes, flies, rattlesnakes, brutal heat, and warm, muddy river all combined to render the site most unpleasant. One-time commander Zenas Bliss called it "the worst post that I have ever been stationed." Lieutenant Colonel Thomas Hunt described it as "a very gloomy looking place." Bishop George Foster Pierce remembered it as "[a] few adobe houses and some rude stick tents, deep sand, and broad sunshine, as hot as I ever felt." When Pierce's coach pulled up at the fort, a man hurried out and approached the bishop to converse. The gentleman told Pierce that he wanted to "escape from . . . 'this *God-forsaken* country'" as soon as possible.[15]

As previously mentioned, not only was the army notorious for its poor site selection process but also it often neglected to secure title to the lands on which it located outposts. This lax oversight led to numerous lawsuits by real estate speculators who had already filed legal claims to the acreage. The Fort Quitman title dispute is an excellent example. In April 1858, five months before the army established Fort Quitman, business partners Archibald Hyde, William Ford, and Jarvis Hubbell of San Elizario, Texas, staked their claim to the site, along with several adjacent parcels. The trio sought to maximize potential business opportunities in the vicinity by renting out land to the army, military employees, contractors, merchants, and saloonkeepers. Like everything else at this jinxed locale, however, things did not work out as planned. A lawsuit over title to the land dragged on for decades. In the end, none of the three men ever realized the riches they dreamed of back in 1858 when they schemed to create their regional monopoly.[16]

Even running the post office, usually a plum federal appointment on the frontier, seems to have been an unpopular job at the wretched Fort Quitman. Bartholomew DeWitt, post sutler at Quitman, also served as its first postmaster, beginning in November 1858. DeWitt, who had previously been postmaster at Camp Hudson on the Devil's River, left there in September 1858 to assume his new duties at Quitman. In June 1860, DeWitt resigned as Quitman's postmaster, and the postmaster general replaced him with James Mason. Mason declined the position, however, and in December 1860, the federal government appointed J. A. Lempert to the position. Lempert, DeWitt's clerk at the sutler's store, also refused the appointment. Finally, in late January 1861, the postmaster general tapped Alexander Brand to run the post office. There is no record of whether Brand actually worked at Quitman, given Texas's secession vote in February 1861 and the removal of the Butterfield line in early April. If ever there was a miserable frontier outpost, it must be Fort Quitman.[17]

From Fort Quitman, it was an eighteen-mile ride to the next station, at Camp Rice, near modern McNary, Texas. In between Fort Quitman and Camp Rice, there was a turnoff for a road leading northeast to the Guadalupe Mountains Salt Lakes. At Camp Rice, forty-seven-year-old J. G. Thomas of Tennessee was the station keeper, assisted by his wife, Mary, and their children. When not running the stage stop, Thomas farmed and practiced law. George Wythe Baylor, brother of John Robert Baylor, claimed that the station's name was actually Camp Rife, after Captain Thomas C. Rife. Rife, born in Louisiana in 1823, served as a sergeant in Lane's company of Texas Mounted Volunteers during the Mexican War. After the war, he lived in San Antonio, where he married his first wife, Mary Ann, in October 1853. After stints as an army scout and a Texas Ranger, he worked for Henry Skillman and George Giddings as a stage driver. During the Civil War, he was a key member of Henry Skillman's Confederate spy company and escaped into Mexico when Union forces attacked this group at Spencer's Ranch in April 1864, killing Skillman. After the war, Rife worked as a policeman in San Antonio and as custodian of the Alamo. He died in San Antonio in 1894. Camp Rice also served as a stage station on Ben Ficklin's San Antonio–El Paso Mail Line after the Civil War. Lieutenant Colonel Hunt stopped here in September 1869, remarking that the terrain around the stage stop was "undulating and sandy" and studded with mesquite. It remains much the same today.[18]

The next stop, thirteen miles distant, was at Birchville, named after James

Birch. In 1857, Birch held the federal contract for Mail Route No. 8076, from San Antonio, Texas, to San Diego, California, before his untimely death at sea in September of that year. Following Birch's demise, the postmaster general named George Giddings as the new mail contractor for Route 8076, effective January 1858. Locals also called this settlement Smith's Ranch, after William T. "Billy" Smith who lived here. In October 1857, a member of a federal road-building crew heading westward mentioned stopping at "'Smith's Ranch'—Birchville on the Rio Grande" to purchase corn.[19]

Phocion Way, passing through on a stagecoach in June 1858, recalled that "Billy" Smith boarded his coach at Birchville and rode with him to El Paso. Way said that Birchville-Smith's Ranch was "on the bank of the Rio Grande . . . immediately opposite San Ignacio, an old Mexican town." Way enjoyed a mug of coffee and a meal of lamb during his stay at the station, which encompassed "2 or 3 adobe houses and a corral for confining horses and mules." Fred L. Pierpont served as the first and only postmaster at Birchville, beginning in April 1858. The postmaster general discontinued the post office in February 1859. Although the post office closed, the stage stop stayed open. Butterfield utilized Smith's Ranch as a station from June 1859 through March 1861.[20]

Billy Smith, one of El Paso's early pioneers, operated the stage stop here with business partner George Lyles. Smith had arrived early on the scene and acquired some of the area's most valuable real estate. At one time, he owned much of Ponce's Ranch, which today constitutes downtown El Paso, Texas. Smith started out as a wagon teamster in 1849. During the 1850s, he became one of the area's prominent freighters, expanding his fleet of wagons to capitalize on the trade between San Antonio and New Mexico. In the mid-1850s, Smith secured federal contracts to supply corn and beef to Fort Bliss at Magoffinsville. In 1856, the army hired him to transport military supplies to various posts in New Mexico. Smith occasionally worked as an El Paso County election judge, and his ranch served as one of the county's polling places. Anson Mills, a surveyor and Butterfield contractor in El Paso, characterized "'Uncle Billy' Smith [as] an illiterate Kentuckian . . . generous, but unbusiness-like."[21]

Smith's associate, George Lyles, a thirty-two-year-old grocer from Virginia, served as Butterfield's station keeper at Smith's Ranch. Besides his work for the Overland Mail Company, in 1856 and 1858 Lyles held the wood contract for Fort Bliss and, in 1858, the hay contract. In 1860, he supplied beans to Fort Bliss and forage to area stage stations. Both Smith and Lyles were well off in comparison with many of their neighbors. Smith's Ranch also served as a stage stop on Ben Ficklin's line after the Civil War. When Lieutenant Colonel Hunt passed through in September 1869, he called the site "Pierpont's Ranch and Mail Station," after station manager and former Birchville postmaster Fred L. Pierpont, who was living here at that time.[22]

Not much is known about the next Butterfield station, Camp Hawkins, fourteen miles upriver (located near modern Fabens, Texas). Various mail companies used the site off and on as a stage stop from the late 1850s until 1880. Hawkins's identity remains undetermined, but he likely served as the first station keeper. When Lieutenant Colonel Hunt visited here in mid-September 1869, he found the station abandoned. Ben Ficklin's mail company eventually rebuilt the adobe and wood structure at a cost of $1,000. Texas Ranger captain George Baylor recalled passing by Hawkins Station in October 1879. In 1880, with the railroad rapidly approaching El Paso, contractor Charles Bain put his entire San Antonio–El Paso mail line up for sale. Appraisers assessed the value of Hawkins Station at $200. The coming of the railroad forced Bain and other stagecoach contractors to take any offer received, however low.[23]

The next three settlements upriver, San Elizario, Socorro, and Ysleta, are among the oldest in Texas, and during the antebellum period they were home to most of El Paso County's Hispanic population. San Elizario, founded in 1789 and ten miles upstream from Hawkins, had 1,200 residents by 1849. In 1869, Lieutenant Colonel Hunt described the community as a "Mexican adobe town . . . supported entirely by the irrigations of their land" from the Rio Grande. Edwin B. Lafayette served as the local postmaster from April 1855 until April 1861, when Fred L. Pierpont succeeded him. George Giddings operated a mail station in San Elizario starting in 1855. Butterfield stage driver David Koney recalled that Pierpont owned the San Elizario station and that Giddings leased it for his mail line. After June 1859, the Overland Mail Company also utilized the stage stop. Eventually, Giddings bought the station from Pierpont in April 1862 for $200. Besides working as station keeper and postmaster, Pierpont was also a prominent San Elizario merchant and prosperous enough to afford a cook and two servants.[24]

William Ford, a merchant, and Archibald Hyde, a state senator and two-term El Paso County judge, worked as Giddings's agents on the section of the overland route from San Elizario to El Paso. Ford, who also served as El Paso County sheriff in 1854, recalled that before the Civil War, he lived at the San Elizario stage stop. Hyde and his roommate, district land surveyor Jarvis Hubbell, were Ford's next-door neighbors, friends, and business partners. Hubbell and Hyde had come to El Paso County from Connecticut. In May 1850, Texas governor P. H. Bell appointed the two men as the county's first notary publics. Hubbell became El Paso's first postmaster in 1852, and Hyde succeeded him in 1855.[25]

Although San Elizario, the county seat of El Paso County, had more than 1,200 residents, such numbers did not deter Mescalero Apaches from stealing the settlement's livestock. In early February 1859, warriors swept into town and made off with fourteen beeves and several mules. On February 3, Lieutenant Henry Martyn Lazelle of the Eighth Infantry and thirty men of the Regiment of Mounted Riflemen set off from Fort Bliss in pursuit. The following day, several local citizens joined Lazelle's outfit. The raiders' trail led northeast toward Butterfield's Alamo Spring Station in the Cornudas Mountains. After journeying more than eighty-five miles without water, Lazelle's party reached the station's spring at Alamo Mountain and briefly rested before resuming their chase. On February 10, Lazelle reached the entrance to Dog Canyon in New Mexico's Sacramento Mountains.[26]

Proceeding up the canyon, the party encountered thirty Mescaleros. After further investigation, Lazelle discovered eleven fresh beef hides and two mule hides drying on the ground. He noted, "[T]he offal and refuse of the cattle were strewn about and everything indicated that they had recently been slain." After assessing his group's encircled position within the canyon, the lieutenant withdrew, determining to strike the Indians the following day. The next morning, Lazelle reentered the canyon and launched his attack. He soon found himself outnumbered three to one, and after an intense firefight lasting more than two hours, the lieutenant retreated down Dog Canyon once again. In the battle, the Apaches killed four soldiers and badly wounded Lazelle with a shot through the lung. Seven other men received serious wounds. The Mescaleros lost nine, with "a larger number wounded." During the engagement, the Apaches came close to overwhelming their pursuers, and Lazelle was fortunate that his detachment was not shot to pieces. The Dog Canyon fight demonstrated yet again that the U.S. Army's troop strength in the Trans-Pecos was too small to be an effective deterrent to Native American raiding.[27]

The Apaches continued their depredations in San Elizario. In May 1860, Mescaleros attacked the overland stage stop, making off with fifteen mules. State Senator Archibald Hyde recalled another raid before the Civil War in which Apaches destroyed the stage stop. Hyde described the station here as a stone building with three rooms and a corral at the back for the animals.[28]

Continuing upriver from San Elizario, Butterfield coaches next passed through Socorro, seven miles distant. Established in 1682, Socorro had a population of 760 by 1860. Because the town had no post office or station, stage drivers continued on to Ysleta, three miles farther. A group of Tigua Indians had settled Ysleta in 1680 in the aftermath of New Mexico's Pueblo Revolt. By 1860, the town had 800 residents. At Ysleta, overland coaches stopped at the post office only to drop off and pick up the mail. There was no overland station here. The town's postmaster was Henry L. Dexter, who also served as El Paso County judge from 1856 to 1858.[29]

En route from Ysleta to downtown El Paso, overland traffic passed through Concordia, also known as Stephenson's Ranch. Concordia, situated ten miles west of Ysleta, served as an important regional crossroads, where the Lower Road from San Antonio and Fort Stockton merged with the Upper Road from the Pecos River and the Guadalupe Mountains. Hugh Stephenson, the namesake of Stephenson's Ranch, was a merchant from Kentucky. Stephenson was one of the county's earliest settlers and one of its wealthiest. Born in 1798, he arrived in the area in the 1820s and became active in the trade between Chihuahua and Santa Fe. In August 1828, he married Juana María Ascárate, the sole daughter of Juan and Eugenia Ascárate, who was "heir to a considerable fortune in land, cattle, and mines." During the 1830s, Hugh and Juana Stephenson built a "great house called *La Casa Grande el Alto* in their own little community of Concordia." Concordia was also home to Butterfield overseer and stage driver Henry Skillman, who lived in Survey 6 with his common-law wife, Rufina Vigil. When not working for Butterfield, Skillman supplied beef to the troops at Fort Bliss.[30]

After leaving Concordia, overland coaches journeyed three miles to the stage stop in downtown El Paso. The mail station, Butterfield's largest in Texas, occupied much of Block 34, fronted on the west by El Paso Street and on the north by Overland Street. The citizens of El Paso donated Block 34 to Butterfield as an inducement for the company to make a substantial investment in El Paso and its development. The gamble paid off. In the summer of 1858, the Overland Mail Company hired Anson Mills of Indiana, a recent arrival in town, to oversee construction of its regional operations hub. Twenty-eight-year-old Arthur Warnick of New York served as Butterfield's local agent, overseeing the company's affairs in El Paso.[31]

Anson Mills says that the El Paso station, located at the midpoint of the St. Louis to San Francisco route, "was called the halfway house," and "the Superintendent and Conductors lived there." The building included one hundred stalls for company livestock. Block 34 also featured the fashionable Frontier Hotel. Promotional materials announced that the hotel had "taken the new, large, and commodious building lately erected by the Over Land [*sic*] Mail Co., [and] respectfully solicits a share of the patronage of the surrounding and traveling public." Butterfield advertised its facility as offering "every inducement to the weary passenger as a recruiting point—being the halfway house of the terminal of the great overland mail company."[32]

The Frontier Hotel offered among the finest, if not *the* finest, lodging along the entire Butterfield line in Texas. The facility's numerous amenities presented a jarring contrast to those available at the rude, primitive hovels the company operated in more-remote locales. After experiencing the rough-and-tumble aspects of western Texas for more than a week in a stagecoach, many passengers likely welcomed the Frontier Hotel as an oasis of civility amid the raw frontier environs. The establishment's proprietor and leading promoter was thirty-six-year-old Luther Sargent of Vermont.[33]

Sargent boasted that the Frontier was "well fitted up, [with] large airy rooms, the table supplied with the best the market affords, and careful servants, while the proprietor is always in attendance," and a "fine bar well supplied with choice liquors is also connected with the house." Emphasizing El Paso's antebellum reputation as a major "continental crossroads," his hotel's advertisement noted, "Stages leave the office twice a week, for St. Louis and San Francisco, and once a week for Santa Fe, San Antonio, Chihuahua, and the City of Mexico."[34]

Since the Spanish period, travelers have used El Paso del Norte, Mexico (now Juárez), and later, El Paso, Texas, as a place to rest and reprovision before continuing their journeys. Prior to the Mexican War, much of this traffic was typically between Chihuahua, Mexico, and Santa Fe. After the Mexican War and the California gold rush, a major east-west corridor quickly developed on the north side of the Rio Grande through American El Paso, established in 1849. The U.S. Army's explorations of the Upper and Lower Roads through West Texas that year cemented El Paso's prominent geographical location.[35]

By the early 1850s, American El Paso had become an important commercial and mercantile center. For Butterfield, the community's location at the midway point on the St. Louis to San Francisco overland route made the city a natural choice for a regional operations and supply hub. The Overland Mail Company's significant presence here greatly enhanced the city's growing reputation, "exerting a far greater impact on the El Paso area than any other until the arrival of the railroad." Anyone consulting a U.S. map during the antebellum period could see that one day El Paso would become a major rail crossroads, which it did in May 1881.[36]

Some of those perusing national maps included Captain John Pope and his superior, Secretary of War Jefferson Davis, who believed that the thirty-second parallel offered the best course for the nation's transcontinental railroad. El Paso County was on the thirty-second parallel. El Paso historians Rick Hendricks and W. H. Timmons say that Pope and Davis's "views became gospel for the merchants of the El Paso area . . . who never ceased to dream of a transcontinental railroad connecting East and West through El Paso."[37]

After Postmaster General Aaron Brown selected a southern route for the nation's overland mail, some southerners believed that a transcontinental railroad over the same line was predestined. One such person was John C. Reid, who understood the matter firsthand, having traveled overland to El Paso in 1857. Regarding the national railroad, Reid argued that the various surveys conducted showed "beyond all doubt that the route near the 32nd parallel of latitude is altogether practicable, and possess[es] advantages over all others."[38]

Reid, like Postmaster General Brown and Jefferson Davis, was a southerner. Reid argued that a transcontinental railroad along the thirty-second parallel would allow the South and "the pro-slavery element" to expand westward. The number of southern senators in Congress would increase. The South would gain Pacific ports and direct trade with Asia. Hendricks and Timmons say that Reid's "persuasive arguments in support of a southern transcontinental railroad," which were published in 1858, "provided the El Paso leadership in 1860–61 with a rationale for casting its lot with the Confederacy."[39]

Many of the prominent Anglos in El Paso County were merchants, contractors, freighters, or in service-related industries. Any increase in transportation, traffic, and commerce through the region would directly benefit them. The wealthiest and most powerful among these was a group of ardent secessionists led by Simeon Hart, James Wiley Magoffin, and several others. Hart, originally from New York but raised in St. Louis, had married the daughter of Don Leandro Siqueiros, a "wealthy flour miller" in Santa Cruz de Rosales, Mexico. Siqueiros provided his Anglo son-in-law with important social connections and economic capital to jumpstart his milling business.[40]

Hart, like Hugh Stephenson at Concordia, did well in marriage. One should note, however, that Hart's union with Jesusita Siqueiros and Stephenson's with Juana Ascárate benefitted all concerned. Historian Raúl Ramos says that "both Anglo-Americans and Mexicans appeared to manipulate nuptials for mutual social or economic advancement. Elite Tejano families stood to gain from the cultural bridges with Anglo society or [societal] protection provided by an Anglo son-in-law, while Anglo men received inheritances of land or commercial legitimacy among Tejanos and Mexicans."[41]

By late 1849, Hart had established a flour mill on the Rio Grande at El Molino, or Hart's Mill, a mile and a half upriver from El Paso, Texas. Until he expanded operations in 1854, much of the flour that Hart sold in the region he imported from his father-in-law's mill in Mexico. From 1852 to 1854, Hart served as El Paso County judge. Soon he held many of the major army contracts in New Mexico and West Texas for flour and other supplies. Although Hart could be "generous and charming," he "possessed intense convictions and displayed a rancorous disposition toward men he disliked. More than once he became involved in street brawls." In 1860, the forty-four-year-old Hart was the richest person in El Paso County, with a net worth of $350,000.[42]

After Hart, the second-richest person was fifty-nine-year-old James Wiley Magoffin, a native of Kentucky. By the 1830s, Magoffin had become a successful merchant and freighter in Saltillo, Mexico. He subsequently moved his commercial interests to Chihuahua, where in 1839 he married María Gertrudis de los Santos Valdés. Prior to their wedding, the couple had been carrying on an extramarital affair while Valdés was still married to her first husband, José Marcos Farías.[43]

During the 1840s, Magoffin expanded his freighting business to capitalize on the overland trade between Chihuahua, Santa Fe, and St. Louis. After the Mexican War, Magoffin moved his base of operations to El Paso County, Texas, where he established himself at Magoffinsville. During the county's formative years, he acquired a number of prime real estate holdings. Some of these he leased to the U.S. Army on an annual basis. During the antebellum period, Magoffin served as post sutler at Fort Bliss. In 1860, his net worth was $100,000.[44]

Hart, Magoffin, Stephenson, and other Anglo-Americans were a minority in antebellum El Paso County. To take control economically and politically, they understood the need to cultivate "the better classes—that is . . . indigenous elites" to help them dominate the majority Hispanic population, most of whom were poor peons. Typically, these elites were the leading businessmen or alcaldes of local towns such as San Elizario, Socorro, and Ysleta.[45]

For Mexican Americans living along the Rio Grande frontier, life was fluid, requiring constant adaptation and adjustment of their identities, loyalties, and priorities. In the span of several decades, Tejanos had lived first under Spanish rule, in 1824 had become Mexican subjects, and then, in 1848, had become citizens of the United States. During the first half of the nineteenth century, the American economy increasingly pulled residents of northern Mexico into its orbit. By midcentury, many Mexicans and Tejanos along the Rio Grande frontier desired to participate in the economic advantages presented by American markets.[46]

To successfully navigate the American system, however, local Hispanics had to carefully calibrate their political and economic alliances. The new international boundary "forced them to reconsider the meaning of their racial and national identities. . . . Differing strategies developed as individuals attempted to make sense of the shifting local circumstances" and their place in the region. For example, Tejanos in El Paso County did not own African American slaves, nor did they think much about southern ideology and culture. Nonetheless, they wanted to maximize their financial opportunities, and that meant sometimes aligning themselves with Anglos who controlled local markets, employment, and politics, people such as Simeon Hart and James Magoffin.[47]

In El Paso County, Tejano society was "rigidly classified." Mexican American elites clearly saw themselves as superior to the peons. As a result, these elites often allied themselves more with the interests of the Anglos than with those of their own race. Mexican American politicians, however, "were no mere lackeys." In return for delivering Tejano votes and compliance, they were able to secure concessions from the Anglos, including employment and protection for their communities. Additionally, Anglos awarded elites positions of authority in local government, such as county commissioner and county clerk.[48]

During the antebellum period, Anglos and elites believed that most Hispanics were incapable of governing themselves, let alone voting responsibly. A revealing window on local Anglo and Tejano elite attitudes is contained in an October 1851 statement from the district grand jury. The jury, which included such prominent citizens as Archibald Hyde, William Ford, Charles Hoppin, Louis Dutton, Gregorio García, and Jesús Luján, stated that in their opinion, "[a] large portion of the inhabitants of the two counties of El Paso and Presidio are composed of a class of individuals . . . [who] are unguided . . . [and] wholy [sic] incapable of self judgement [sic]." The grand jury recommended that these Mexican American peons be placed in an apprentice system similar to what the British used in the West Indies. The jurors believed that these impoverished Tejanos were ignorant and in need of supervision and guidance, "as it will take years for them to be taught sufficiant [*sic*] for them to provide for themselves."[49]

To Anglos, Tejanos of this class were not only politically incompetent but also misguided concerning regional resources. Many Mexican Americans in the Southwest viewed natural assets such as water, salt, grasslands, and timber as communal, for the greater good. Anglos, however, looked upon these same resources as potentially enriching, commodities they could buy and sell.

An illustrative example of these conflicting worldviews is the 1854 San Andreas Salt War, pitting James Wiley Magoffin and several of his El Paso County associates against Hispanic residents of Mesilla and Las Cruces, New Mexico. In the summer of 1852, Magoffin secured control of San Andreas Salt Springs, on the east side of the San Andreas Mountains. Under Spanish and Mexican law, residents had "the right to gather salt free of charge or tax," and regional salt deposits "were reserved for the benefit of all men." For generations, New Mexicans had been harvesting salt at San Andreas. Magoffin, however, now wanted them to pay a tax on all salt collected on his property. After his collection efforts proved unsuccessful, Magoffin asked El Paso County sheriff William Ford for assistance in stopping salt harvesting at the springs.[50]

Although this mineral deposit was located in New Mexico, where Ford had no legal jurisdiction, in January 1854, the sheriff and twenty-eight men confronted a caravan of 125 New Mexican teamsters and their twenty-six carretas near Chinos. Ford's posse included Magoffin, brother Samuel Magoffin, brother-in-law Gabriel Valdés, Hugh Stephenson's son-in-law Frederick Percy, William "Bigfoot" Wallace, and William "Clown" Garner. A firefight quickly broke out, in which three men died. The Texans scurried back to El Paso County, and subsequent efforts by the Territory of New Mexico to prosecute Magoffin and his associates proved futile.[51]

Anglos such as James Magoffin embraced private landownership and sought to monopolize acreage containing valuable commodities. In regard to natural resources, European Americans on Texas's western frontier were typically more interested in their own material gain than the greater good of the community. Oscar Martinez notes that after the Mexican War, Anglo "newcomers often disregarded local rules and traditions in their drive to acquire property," inflicting significant losses upon Hispanics "in communally-held farm land, timber, and salt." Martinez could also have included acequias.[52]

Acequias, or communal irrigation canals, had been in use in the El Paso area since the late seventeenth century. Under Spanish and Mexican law, anyone who helped build and maintain these canals received the right to use them. In addition, those who used the ditches also had a say in their regulation. After the Mexican War, this custom continued in New Mexico but not in Texas. In the El Paso area, Anglos and Tejano elites moved quickly to gain control of community acequias.[53]

In 1851, a grand jury asked the governor of Texas to grant El Paso County permission to form a board of commissioners who would then appoint "suitable persons" to apportion or regulate the water systems. The commissioners would receive compensation for their service. It seems fairly obvious who would constitute this acequia board: prominent Anglos and Tejano elites. The grand jury's petition received a favorable response from Austin. In 1852, the State of Texas placed these communal water systems "under the control of county courts." During the antebellum period, the county had a series of acequia networks: at San Elizario and Ysleta in the Lower Valley, at Magoffinsville and downtown El Paso, and at Canutillo and Cottonwoods Ranch in the Upper Valley near the New Mexico line.[54]

Besides Canutillo and Cottonwoods Ranch, El Paso County's Upper Valley included a third settlement, at Frontera. From El Paso, it was six and a half miles up the Rio Grande to Frontera. Established in August 1848 by T. Frank White, Frontera was located next to the present-day railroad tracks at the intersection of Doniphan Road and Sunland Park Drive. White built a trading post and customs house here at Mule Ford on the Rio Grande, one of several local crossings on the Chihuahua–Santa Fe Trail. From El Paso to Mesilla, New Mexico, the Santa Fe Trail and the overland road to California (used by Butterfield) followed the same route. At Mesilla, the overland road branched off to the west, while the Santa Fe Trail continued north.[55]

Frontera sat at the southwestern end of the Sierra del Puerte (now the Franklin Mountains), directly across from the 4,700-foot Cerros de Muleros (now Sierra de Cristo Rey). When Lieutenant William H. C. Whiting of the U.S. Topographical Engineers stopped at Frontera during his reconnaissance of West Texas in April 1849, he remarked favorably on the location: "Here is a suitable ford; a branch of the great road leaves the left bank of the river by it and continues through . . . [El Paso del Norte, now Juarez, Mexico,] to Chihuahua." The lieutenant viewed the ford downstream at El Paso, Texas, as inferior, noting that traders and freighters preferred the crossing at Mule Ford. "I find the position [at Frontera] suitable for defense and eligible as a military post," Whiting wrote, and "these considerations have induced me to recommend it as a site for the encampment and permanent location of the troops destined for [El] Paso."[56]

Despite Whiting's recommendations, in January 1854 the army established its permanent outpost a mile downstream from El Paso, Texas, at Magoffinsville. Two months later, the military officially named the site Fort Bliss, after Captain William Wallace Smith Bliss. By this time, Frontera's fortunes had waned. The location at Mule Ford never caught on, and economics forced Frank White to close his trading post in 1850. During 1851, the federal government leased Frontera and established an astronomical observatory there while working on U.S. and Mexican boundary surveys in the area. In 1852, White received a charter from the Texas Legislature to construct a toll road at the crossing from Frontera, Texas, to El Paso del Norte, Mexico, but the project never got beyond the planning stages. The Rio Grande temporarily dried up, and White's agricultural pursuits proved a failure. In 1854, he moved away, and Apaches torched the abandoned buildings. In April 1855, White sold his property to Henry Dexter for $260. After the Civil War, the Dexter family used Frontera as a ranch and mail station. Although White had disappeared from the local scene by the late 1850s, he made important contributions to early El Paso County history through his service "as the first magistrate of Anglo-American El Paso, the proprietor of its first mercantile establishment, and the first American collector of customs" in the region. Today, the Frontera site no longer exists. The railroad and development along Doniphan Drive have obliterated all traces of this pioneer settlement.[57]

From Frontera, the overland road led six and a half miles north to Canutillo, the next settlement in El Paso County's Upper Valley. Development of the Upper Valley started in 1824 with a farming operation at El Canutillo, "a crescent-shaped *playa* lake" a short distance north-northwest of the present-day Borderland Bridge on Doniphan Drive. The landowners raised crops here until 1833, when Apache raids forced them to abandon their lands. The old ranch buildings lay deserted until the spring of 1850, when James Wiley Magoffin laid claim to the property. Magoffin believed the acreage to be vacant and began homesteading the parcel. He "proceeded to improve and cultivate" and "constructed improvements thereon valued at two thousand dollars." Stopping here in April 1851, U.S. boundary commissioner John Russell Bartlett noted, "A large piece of bottom land has just been ploughed up and put under cultivation, by Mr. Magoffin, . . . the only cultivated spot between El Paso and Las Cruces."[58]

Like the ranch's former occupants, however, Magoffin discovered that the Apaches did not recognize his claim to their traditional tribal lands. During one raid on the Canutillo Ranch in March 1852, Indians stole all of Magoffin's cattle, killed a ranch hand, and took a sixteen-year-old boy captive. Four months later, sixty warriors attacked Canutillo, "taking all the outfit . . . [that Magoffin] had there for farming purposes, [including] Cows, Calves, etc." The Canutillo raids were part of a notable spike in regional depredations dating from September 1851, when the federal government withdrew its troops from El Paso County. Indian attacks would ravage the region until 1854, when, following a chorus of complaints from area residents, the U.S. Army finally established Fort Bliss at Magoffinsville.[59]

Magoffin's claim to the old Canutillo Ranch sparked a lawsuit that was not resolved until 1886. In the summer of 1860, José Sánchez, Guadalupe Miranda, and

Romulo Barelo, who had an interest in the property, hired Anson Mills to survey the grant, in return for which Mills received one hundred acres. In late 1860 or early 1861, Mills and his two brothers, William Wallace and Emmett, constructed their ranch, Los Tres Hermanos, on this hundred-acre parcel near El Canutillo. Mills said the building, which cost $1,000 to $1,200 to erect, was to have been a Butterfield station. "I built it for the Stage Company by agreement," he recalled, "but it was just before the war broke out and they never occupied it." Mills's account is confirmed by the last overland mail itinerary, published in April 1861, which lists a stage stop at Canutillo. Today the long-forgotten, crescent-shaped lake is still visible in a small field. The current channel of the Rio Grande has washed away all evidence of the old 1824 ranch.[60]

The Butterfield station near Canutillo was to have replaced the mail company's rough-hewn and dilapidated stage stop seven miles to the north, at Cottonwoods Ranch, near present-day Anthony, Texas, and the New Mexico line. Located twenty miles north of El Paso, Cottonwoods Ranch was originally a station on George Giddings's San Antonio–San Diego Mail Line. Phocion R. Way's stagecoach stopped here in June 1858 for breakfast. Way called the station "Skillman's Ranch," after Henry Skillman. Before joining Butterfield in the summer of 1858, Skillman had driven stagecoaches for both Giddings and his own mail route.[61]

The idyllic setting at Cottonwoods Ranch, also known as Los Alamos and Los Alamitos, made the site a popular campground during the 1850s and 1860s. A fine grove of cottonwood trees encircled a large water hole. The Giddings-Butterfield station here was little more than a filthy hovel. Phocion Way described it as "an odd looking ranch made of poles and mud, and without windows. It is occupied by two or three hard-looking white men and a Mexican man and woman, 5 or 6 dogs, and an old turkey gobbler." J. A. Lucas, who worked on Giddings's mail line, recalled visiting Cottonwoods Ranch in 1860. He noted, "It was constructed of poles set up endwise, covered with mud and dirt. It had a dirt roof. Corral and stables were built in a similar manner. It could not have cost more than $150 altogether."[62]

Today, all of the land surrounding the old Cottonwoods Ranch site is under cultivation. Thick brush and trash obscure the now-dry water hole. Nothing remains of the pole structure or corrals, but the beautiful cottonwood grove still stands. A careful search of the plowed acreage just west of the stage stop and water hole unearthed metal artifacts marking the distinct line of the Butterfield Road as it heads to the New Mexico line a short distance to the north. It is here at the New Mexico line, just north of present-day FM 1905 (West Washington Street), that our overland journey across Texas concludes.[63]

Bass Canyon, near the Culberson-Hudspeth County line. Photograph by the author.

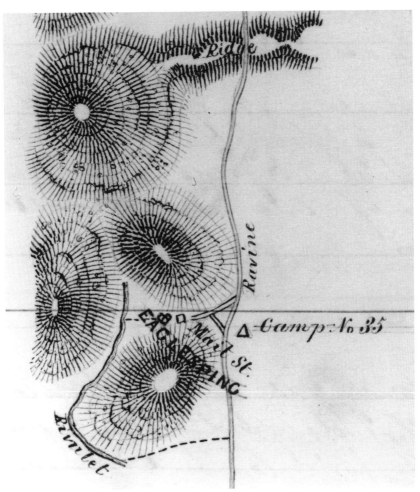

Detail from 1869 map showing overland road and Eagle Spring Station ("Mail St."). From "Journal Showing the Route Taken by the Government Train from Austin, Texas to Ft. Craig, New Mexico," by Brevet Lieutenant Colonel Thomas B. Hunt, National Archives Cartographic and Architectural Section, College Park, Md.

"Eagle Springs [*sic*] Stage Stand" marker (erected in 1936), Hudspeth County, Texas. Panther and Eagle Peaks are in the background. Photograph by the author.

Eagle Spring and rock-lined tank, which still holds water. Photograph by the author.

Stacked rock corral walls at Eagle Spring Station. Photograph by the author.

Butterfield Road crossing of Tinaja de las Palmas at the south end of Rocky Ridge, Hudspeth County, Texas. Photograph by the author.

One of the rock breastworks atop Rocky Ridge that featured in the July 30, 1880, firefight at Tinaja de las Palmas between Colonel Benjamin Grierson's Tenth Cavalry and Apache chief Victorio. Note the Butterfield Road at the top of the picture, wrapping around the ridge. Photograph by the author.

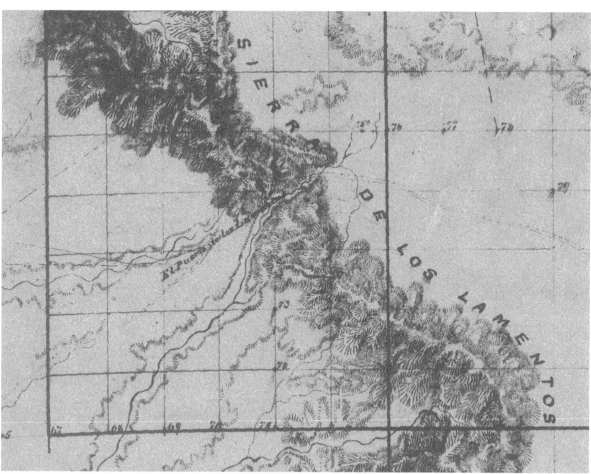

Detail of map showing the Butterfield Road through the Quitman Mountains ("Sierra de los Lamentos") and Quitman Pass, also called Calamity Pass ("El Puerto de los Lamentos"). Map #65333, *1879 Map of the Texas & Pacific Railway Reserve West of the Pecos River*, courtesy of Texas General Land Office Archives, Austin.

Apache or Indian Post Office in the middle of Quitman Canyon. Photograph by the author.

Patrick Dearen walking Butterfield Road trace in Quitman Canyon. Photograph by the author.

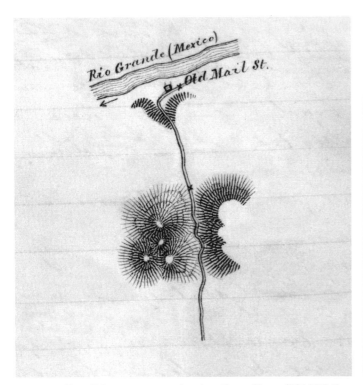

Detail from 1869 map showing Camp Fargo ("Old Mail St."). From "Journal Showing the Route Taken by the Government Train from Austin, Texas to Ft. Craig, New Mexico," by Brevet Lieutenant Colonel Thomas B. Hunt, National Archives Cartographic and Architectural Section, College Park, Md.

Gary Williams (*left*) and Joe Allen (*right*) at Camp Fargo site, Hudspeth County, Texas. Photograph by the author.

Gary Williams in Butterfield Road trace near Camp Fargo. Note the stacked rocks on the side of trail. Photograph by the author.

James Irby walking west toward Fort Quitman in trace of Butterfield Road. Photograph by the author.

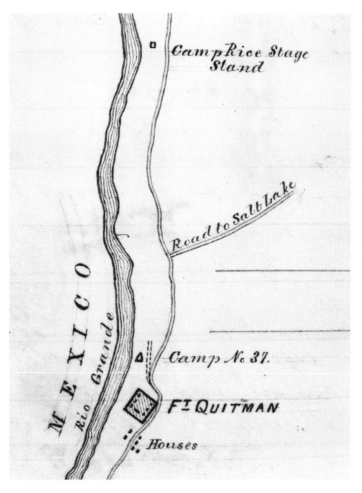

Detail from 1869 map showing Fort Quitman and Camp Rice Station upstream. From "Journal Showing the Route Taken by the Government Train from Austin, Texas to Ft. Craig, New Mexico," by Brevet Lieutenant Colonel Thomas B. Hunt, National Archives Cartographic and Architectural Section, College Park, Md.

Adobe ruins of Fort Quitman in the 1930s. Conkling Papers, courtesy of the Seaver Center for Western History Research, Los Angeles County Museum of Natural History.

Ruins of Camp Rice Station, Hudspeth County, Texas. Photograph by the author.

Trace of Butterfield Road at Camp Rice. Photograph by the author.

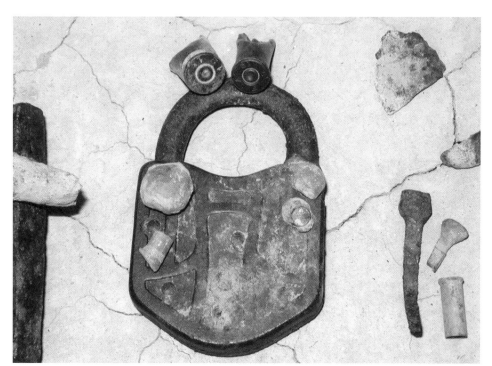

Padlock, bullets, and horseshoe nails from Camp Rice. Photograph by the author.

Remnants of canteen and rifle at Camp Rice. Photograph by the author.

Detail from 1869 map showing Pierpont's Ranch Station, called Birchville-Smith's Ranch during the antebellum period. From "Journal Showing the Route Taken by the Government Train from Austin, Texas to Ft. Craig, New Mexico," by Brevet Lieutenant Colonel Thomas B. Hunt, National Archives Cartographic and Architectural Section, College Park, Md.

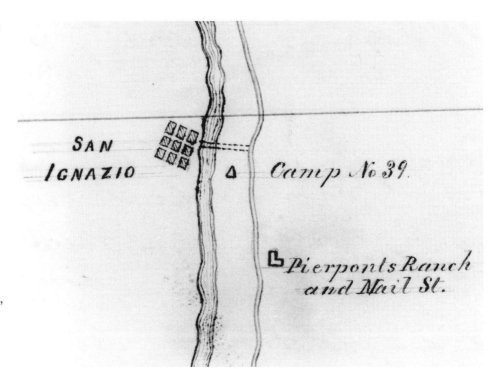

Later adobe ruin at the site of Birchville-Smith's Ranch. Photograph by the author.

Butterfield Road trace at Birchville-Smith's Ranch. Photograph by the author.

Portrait of William "Billy" Smith, namesake of Smith's Ranch. Courtesy of El Paso Museum of History, El Paso, Texas.

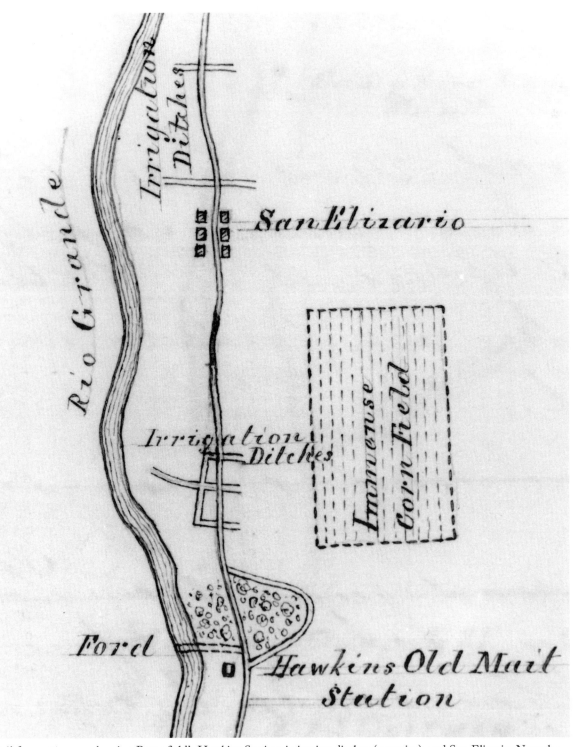

Detail from 1869 map showing Butterfield's Hawkins Station, irrigation ditches (acequias), and San Elizario. Note the loop road, used during wet weather, to the right of Hawkins Station. From "Journal Showing the Route Taken by the Government Train from Austin, Texas to Ft. Craig, New Mexico," by Brevet Lieutenant Colonel Thomas B. Hunt, National Archives Cartographic and Architectural Section, College Park, Md.

Later building on site of Hawkins Station. Photograph by the author.

Hawkins loop road today. Photograph by the author.

San Elizario Chapel. Courtesy of Library of Congress, Prints and Photographs Division, Washington, D.C.

Ysleta Mission. Courtesy of the Lyda Hill Texas Collection of Photographs in Carol M. Highsmith's America Project, Library of Congress, Prints and Photographs Division, Washington, D.C.

Concordia Cemetery, in the remaining portion of Stephenson's Ranch, home to Hugh Stephenson and his wife, Juana María Ascárate Stephenson, as well as Henry Skillman and his common-law wife, Rufina Vigil. Courtesy of the Lyda Hill Texas Collection of Photographs in Carol M. Highsmith's America Project, Library of Congress, Prints and Photographs Division, Washington, D.C.

James Wiley Magoffin, namesake of Magoffinsville and sutler at Fort Bliss, Texas. Portrait by Henry Cheever Pratt. Courtesy of Magoffin Home State Historic Site, El Paso, Texas, Texas Historical Commission.

Site of El Paso's Butterfield Station, bounded by Overland Street on the north and El Paso Street on the west. Photograph by the author.

Detail of Overland Mail Company's Block 34, from October 1883 Sanborn Fire Insurance map of El Paso, Texas. Courtesy of the University of Texas Libraries, University of Texas at Austin.

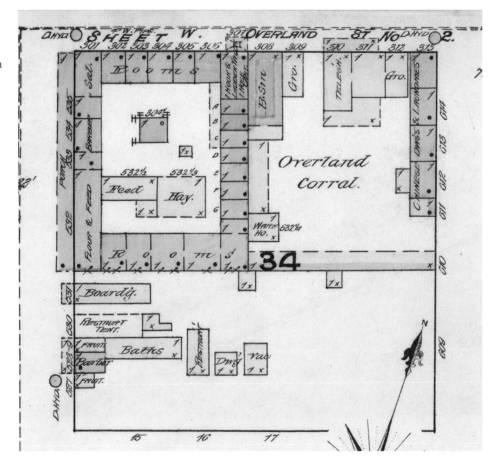

Simeon Hart (Hart's Mill/El Molino) and family. Courtesy of University of Texas at El Paso Library, Special Collections Department, Cleofas Calleros Papers (MS 231).

Ruins of Hart's Mill/El Molino in 1936. Courtesy of Library of Congress Prints and Photographs Division, Washington, D.C.

Detail of 1869 map showing El Paso County's Upper Valley settlements at Frontera ("Ranche [*sic*]" and "Mail St.," *bottom*), El Canutillo ("Ranche [*sic*]" and "W.H." [water hole], *center*), and Cottonwoods Ranch/Skillman's Ranch ("Cottonwood Ranche [*sic*]" *top*). Cottonwoods Ranch is not in New Mexico; it is just south of the state line. From "Journal Showing the Route Taken by the Government Train from Austin, Texas to Ft. Craig, New Mexico," by Brevet Lieutenant Colonel Thomas B. Hunt, National Archives Cartographic and Architectural Section, College Park, Md.

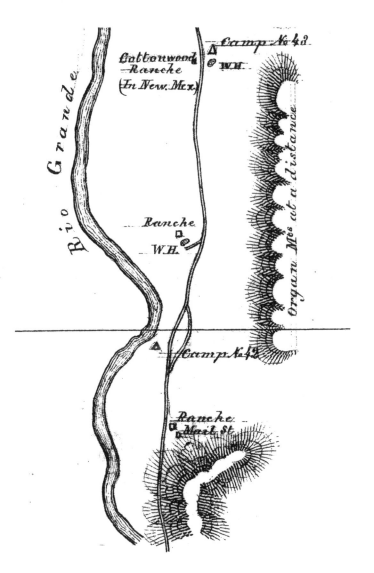

Site of Frontera, on railroad at intersection of Doniphan Road and Sunland Park Drive. Photograph by the author.

Site of El Canutillo, near Borderland Bridge and Doniphan Drive. Photograph by the author.

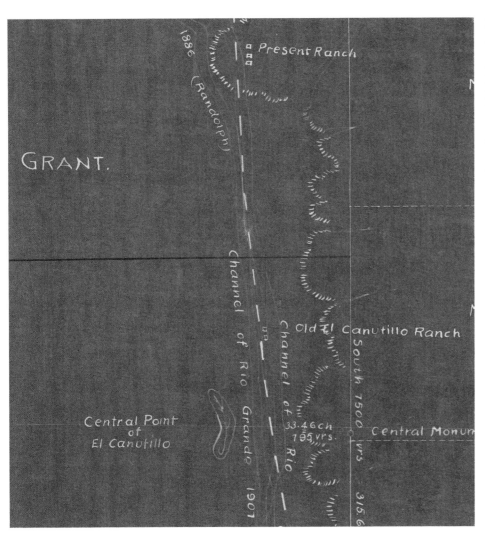

Detail from 1908 map of El Canutillo (the crescent-shaped lake), old ranch, and later ranch. From Map #8858, *El Paso County Rolled Sketch 31*, courtesy of Texas General Land Office Archives, Austin.

Site of Cottonwoods Ranch/Skillman's Ranch, just south of the Texas–New Mexico state line. Photograph by the author.

Sketch labeled as "Skillman's Ranch near El Paso, NM," by Phocion Way. Heading west, Cottonwoods Ranch/ Skillman's Ranch is the last Butterfield station in Texas. Courtesy of Arizona State Library, Archives and Public Records, History and Archives Division, Phoenix.

The End of the Line

SURRENDER OF EX-GENERAL TWIGGS, LATE OF THE UNITED STATES ARMY, TO THE TEXAN TROOPS IN THE GRAN PLAZA, SAN ANTONIO, TEXAS, FEBRUARY 16, 1861.—[SEE PAGE 182.]

Department of Texas commander General David E. Twiggs surrenders all federal military posts and public property in Texas to Secession Convention commissioners in San Antonio after eleven days of negotiations, lasting from February 8 to February 18, 1861. From *Harper's Weekly*, March 23, 1861, courtesy of Texas State Library and Archives Commission, Austin, Prints and Photographs Collection (1965/036-09).

From its inception, the Overland Mail Company faced major stresses from within and without. While the company was able to address mounting debt and internal power struggles, it could not overcome significant external impediments, in particular, America's growing sectional divide. On December 20, 1860, South Carolina became the first state to leave the Union. Two months later, in February 1861, Texas voters approved secession by a three-to-one margin. According to the state's official Secession Ordinance, Texas's first and foremost reason for leaving the Union was to ensure the "holding, maintaining, and protecting [of] the institution known as negro slavery—the servitude of the African to the white race, and which her people intended should exist in all future time." While most Texans favored disunion, along the Lone Star frontier southern identity encountered stiff headwinds. Residents of counties between the ninety-seventh and one-hundredth meridians possessed mixed feelings about secession. This section, best described as a regional transition zone, is where the culture and environment of the Old South collided with those of the American West.[1]

Within this zone, citizens held conflicting opinions regarding Southern ideology and leaving the Union. While some counties voted for secession, others (namely, Blanco, Burnet, Cooke, Gillespie, Grayson, Jack, Mason, Medina, Montague, and Uvalde) did not. In fact, the farther west in Texas that one went, the less secessionist the population. West of the one-hundredth meridian (specifically, in Presidio and Maverick Counties), the vote was strongly against disunion. Continuing westward, into neighboring New Mexico Territory, unionist sentiment was even more prevalent.[2]

Amid this prevailing western trend is one glaring exception: El Paso County. The county's lopsided election result, with 871 in favor of secession and 2 opposed, represents a distinct regional anomaly. Over the years, some writers have cited this tally as proof of a fervent, prosecession population in El Paso. Walter Buenger mentions the "town's rabid support of secession." C. L. Sonnichsen writes that "almost everyone" in El Paso was "deeply and passionately Southern" and that "El Paso was as Southern as Savannah."[3]

Some of these previous studies, however, have largely ignored the issues of voter intimidation, fraud, and regional identity in their discussions of El Paso County's secession vote. While residents of the rest of Texas cast their ballots on February 23, 1861, El Paso County received an exclusive waiver to hold its vote five days earlier, on February 18. The waiver allowed county officials enough time to send in their tally to Austin, as the Texas secretary of state required certification of all county election returns on or before February 26. On March 2, state officials would count all the votes and formally certify the election results.[4]

In his report on the February 18 vote, El Paso County judge Henry Gillett noted, "There are two or three precincts yet unheard from, the returns of which I will have the honor of forwarding as soon as received." Despite such promises, the prosecessionist Gillett sent in no further election updates regarding unreported precinct returns. One of the missing precincts was Precinct Six, which encompassed Presidio County, El Paso's adjoining neighbor to the east. Created by the state legislature in 1850, Presidio County was only partially organized by 1861. Until local residents fully organized the county (in 1875), the legislature attached Presidio County to El Paso County for judicial purposes.[5]

The state's official secession journal notes that the results from "2 unorganized counties [were] not heard from, viz: McCulloch and Presidio." The first county mentioned, McCulloch County, "was not organized in time to have a representative at the secession convention of 1861, and its involvement in the Civil War was limited." Perhaps the secession report meant Maverick County, not McCulloch County, as one of the unorganized counties "not heard from." In 1856, the Texas Legislature carved Maverick County out of Kinney County. Eagle Pass became the county seat. Eagle Pass had been growing steadily since the U.S. Army established Fort Duncan there seven years earlier, across the Rio Grande from Piedras Negras, Mexico. By 1860, Maverick County had almost 730 residents. Although not included in the state journal, Maverick County did hold a secession vote, and the tally was three votes for secession and eighty opposed.[6]

In Presidio County, officially represented as Precinct Six in El Paso County, there was some confusion over who was responsible for reporting the outcome. This confusion caused a delay in transmitting the results. On March 1, Presidio County election judge Daniel Murphy reported that no citizens had voted for secession, while 364 had voted against it. Murphy lamented that the results of "the vote did not get in in time, so it is all lost." Previous studies of Texas's secession referendum list eighteen counties as voting against disunion, but with the addition of Maverick and Presidio Counties, the correct total should now be twenty.[7]

At the time of the secession vote, the counties constituting the nucleus of historic West Texas—Maverick, Presidio, and El Paso—shared many common demographics. In Maverick County, less than 4 percent of residents were white Southerners. In Presidio County, the number was less than 5 percent. In El Paso County, only 2 percent of the population was from the South. In those three counties, there were only 21 slaves among the area's 5,300 residents, or less than 1 percent. In comparison, in East Texas's Harrison County, blacks accounted for more than 50 percent of the population. It should also be noted that west of the one-hundredth meridian in Texas, no Tejanos owned slaves, and excluding a few elites, the Mexican American community shared few cultural values with the South.[8]

El Paso historian W. H. Timmons says that "the issue of slavery locally was hardly the burning issue it had become nationally." He argues that a "southern transcontinental railroad route and its obvious implication for El Paso's strategic importance" more fully explains "the overwhelming pro-southern sentiment" among local Anglos. Timmons points out, "By early 1857 a transcontinental railroad at the thirty-second parallel had become the foremost demand of the El Paso leadership," including Simeon Hart and James Wiley Magoffin. The latter "was thoroughly convinced of the importance of the railroad in the El Paso area's future. Magoffin became actively involved in organizing community and state backing for a transcontinental railroad along the southern route through El Paso." By 1860, with Congress deadlocked over the course of the transcontinental railroad, local leaders realized that the prospect of a railroad along the thirty-second parallel appeared dim. Jefferson Davis and other Southerners, however, fully supported such a project. To Hart and Magoffin, then, joining the Confederacy seemed the best option for El Paso County's economic future and their own business prospects.[9]

When one tracks regional identity trends westward, the demographics typical of antebellum West Texas become even more pronounced in New Mexico Territory, El Paso County's immediate neighbor to the west. In 1860, New Mexico possessed a miniscule Southern presence. The territory had a total population of 93,516. Of these, 712 were Southerners from the Upper and Lower South, or less than 1 percent. There were 85 blacks and mulattoes in New Mexico, significantly less than 1 percent. In the county bordering El Paso County, Doña Ana County, there were no African American residents. While most of the 85 blacks in New Mexico were free persons of color, approximately 30 were slaves. The bulk of these were servants of army officers. Loomis Morton Ganaway, a leading authority on the territory's regional identity in 1861, says that Mexican Americans "were not interested in negro slavery. . . . Peonage, a system with which they had been familiar from the period of Spanish conquest, practically satisfied their need for unskilled labor." New Mexico did have a short-lived slave code (from 1859 to 1861), whose importance "should not be overstated" and which "local authorities were very lax in enforcing." New Mexico historian Mark Stegmaier notes that even slave code proponents acknowledged that "support for slavery in the territory was shallow, especially among the native Hispanic population." Stegmaier adds that "most New Mexicans had little interest in the Confederacy" and that once the Civil War started, "New Mexicans rallied to the Union cause." One can accurately state, then, that Southern identity and culture were of negligible concern to most New Mexico residents, who were Hispanic.[10]

Despite these facts, some have argued that El Paso's secession referendum was representative of a larger, regional mindset and that neighboring Mesilla, in Doña Ana County, New Mexico (fifty miles distant), was a hotbed of secessionist sentiment. Writing in the 1950s and 1960s, Martin Hardwick Hall claimed that in Mesilla, "a vigorous and aggressive Anglo minority were politically dominant," that these "American residents . . . were overwhelmingly pro-Southern in sentiment," and that they "completely controlled" the local Mexican population. Offering a more current perspective, Anthony Mora's work counters Hall's arguments: "To the dismay of many Euro-Americans, Mexicans in Mesilla controlled all of the municipal government institutions except the sheriff's office." By 1861, Hispanics also controlled the sheriff's office after Marcial Padilla assumed the position.[11]

W. Clement Eaton, in his study of the region, found that "[t]he American element in this town [Mesilla] was overwhelmed by the Mexicans." Eaton says, "There was a decided race feeling between the Mexicans and the American inhabitants." During one heated confrontation at a dance in 1859, the two groups exchanged gunfire. Federal officials quickly sent troops to restore order. In March 1860, more violence erupted, when an Anglo gambler in Mesilla pulled the hair of a Mexican. Shots rang out, and soon five Hispanics—including a woman—lay dead. More than three hundred Mexican residents quickly gathered in the town's plaza. The armed Mesilleros then "fulfilled some of [the] Euro-Americans' worst fears . . . [by] forcibly driving all Americans out of Mesilla . . . claiming that they were ridding the town of an 'unsavory element.'"[12]

Some of the Anglos eventually returned, although in the minds of local Hispanics, "Mesilla remained a Mexican town." In the summer of 1860, only 23 of Mesilla's 2,440 residents hailed from the South (Upper and Lower), or less than 1 percent. Federal superintendent of Indian affairs in New Mexico, James L. Collins, reported in June 1861, "The large majority of the population . . . are Mexicans who with few exceptions are loyal to the government. The disaffection is contained to a few Americans. . . . These Americans are Southerners, mostly from Texas."[13]

On March 16, 1861, a group of citizens from El Paso County, Texas, and New Mexico Territory met at Mesilla and issued a list of secession resolutions. The ringleader of the meeting was attorney Philemon Thomas Herbert, a resident of El Paso who practiced law in both El Paso and Mesilla. Herbert had recently returned to the region after representing El Paso County as a delegate to the Texas Secession Convention. Providing strong backing for Herbert and secession efforts in New Mexico were fellow El Pasoans Simeon Hart and James Wiley Magoffin. Interestingly, the Mesilla Resolutions never mentioned slavery. Primary grievances

included inadequate frontier protection and the rerouting of the Butterfield Overland Mail northward.[14]

At the March 16 gathering, attendees recommended splitting off southern New
Mexico and Arizona from the rest of the territory and joining the Confederacy.
The exact size of this group is unknown, and its legal standing is questionable, as
it clearly did not represent the vast majority of New Mexico residents. One should
also note that the northern half of New Mexico territory never voted for secession.
In any event, "despite the machinations of secession forces," such efforts "were
doomed to failure. Local institutions, an apathetic populace indifferent to contro-
versies alien to them, and nature itself were aligned with each other in determining
the political history of New Mexico."[15]

Ignoring local political realities, the Texans persisted in their efforts to make
New Mexico Territory part of the Confederacy. In July 1861, rebel units spear-
headed by Lieutenant Colonel John Robert Baylor's Second Texas Mounted Rifles
invaded New Mexico. Anthony Mora notes, "Mesilla became the unlikely capital
of the newly created 'Confederate Territory of Arizona' with the enthusiastic support of a small number of European-American Texans (whom Mexicans stilled
called 'diablo Texans')." By late March 1862, however, the Confederate offensive
in New Mexico had fizzled out. A postmortem on the military campaign by several Texan officers noted, "It had been erroneously supposed that the citizens of
New Mexico would greet us as benefactors and flock to our standard upon our
approach." The Texans instead discovered "that there was not a friend to our cause
in the [New Mexico] territory, with a few honorable exceptions."[16]

Forced to abandon New Mexico and the Texas Trans-Pecos, retreating Lone
Star troops encountered a local Hispanic populace that was not only hostile to
the Southern cause but also increasingly violent. Rebel soldiers were "committing
outrages upon the inhabitants," one report noted, and "the Mexican population are
much enraged against them on account of their rude treatment." Several bloody
and intense clashes in the Mesilla area claimed up to fifty lives. At Socorro, Texas,
violent firefights between the retreating soldiers and two hundred to three hundred
Tejanos and Pueblo Indians left another twenty to fifty dead. A Houston newspaper lamented, "Instead of fighting the Yankees . . . we have to fight the Mexicans."
When the last of the rebels finally straggled out of the Rio Grande valley toward
San Antonio, many Hispanics were glad to see them gone.[17]

In addition to demographics, another key indicator of regional identity was
the influence of the federal government. A major hallmark of the American West,
including West Texas and New Mexico, was the area's dependence on federal agencies, notably the U.S. Army and U.S. Postmaster General. West of the one-hundredth meridian, the State of Texas, both economically and militarily, was largely

absent. Significant Anglo-European settlement in western Texas did not occur until the government directly or indirectly provided the incentive.[18]

Numerous settlements in western Texas depended on federal military protection, supply contracts, and payrolls. As the Civil War approached, frontier residents worried that their livelihoods would disappear if the state seceded. In this part of the Lone Star State, the federal government and its agencies exerted far more influence over everyday life and the local economy than did Southern ideology and cotton slave culture.[19]

Given West Texas's and New Mexico's more western, unionist identity, why then did El Paso County buck regional demographics with its secession vote? The answer is that antebellum elections in El Paso County "were determined in advance by men who controlled the electorate either by prestige, bribery or violence." The leaders of the county's Democratic Party and its pro-Southern, secessionist agenda were Simeon Hart, James Magoffin, Josiah Crosby, and Archibald Hyde, who kept a tight grip on the political reins to ensure the outcome they desired.[20]

In his study of El Paso's legal history, J. Morgan Broaddus says, "[T]here is no doubt [that] a handful of . . . party bosses" controlled antebellum elections "by seeing to it that the laymen of the county formed ranks behind their candidates and endorsed their policies." El Paso has a long history of voter fraud. Both before and after the Civil War, Anglo political bosses frequently utilized the "Mexican vote" to win at the polls. While some Hispanics casting ballots were registered voters, others were temporarily imported from Mexico to help boost election results. An 1858 newspaper account of an El Paso election noted that the leaders of El Paso's Democratic Party "are waiting to ascertain how many votes will be necessary to elect Buckley, and when that is known they will furnish the requisite number. So you may keep cool and rest easy."[21]

Simeon Hart, the wealthiest and most powerful resident in the county, owned five slaves and became a rabid secessionist during his time in El Paso. For example, in March 1861, he wrote Jefferson Davis and offered a $150,000 personal loan on "moderate terms" in support of the Confederacy. By the fall of 1860, Texas's Democratic Party had appointed Hart as a presidential elector for El Paso County, and Hart used his position to exert influence at the ballot box. A newspaper account of the county's 1860 presidential vote reported more than one thousand ballots for John Breckenridge and noted that District Elector Hart had "contributed greatly towards this splendid result."[22]

James Wiley Magoffin, the second most powerful person in El Paso County, served as chairman of the county's Democratic Party in April 1857 and again in August 1860. Like Hart, Magoffin exerted much influence upon the county's economy and politics, thanks to his considerable wealth and numerous government contracts. Despite the prospective loss of federal dollars if Texas seceded, Hart and Magoffin welcomed disunion. Both men were certain they would secure commensurate army contracts and employment with the new Confederate government, which proved to be the case. Confident in their business prospects and in their beliefs, Hart and Magoffin resolutely steered the county's political machine toward secession. In an interview with an Austin newspaper, Magoffin offered "every assurance" that El Paso County "will cast her usual vote for the democracy [i.e., the South]." The same article noted, "[State District] Judge [Josiah] Crosby and [State] Senator [Archibald] Hyde . . . are doing all they can for the cause."[23]

Josiah Frazer Crosby of Charleston, South Carolina, was a third prominent member of this political ring. Crosby became a lawyer in 1848 and moved to El Paso in the early 1850s to cure his tuberculosis. Active in county politics, Crosby served as district attorney, district judge, and state senator before the Civil War. In 1858, he held the federal corn contract for Fort Bliss. Crosby was the first slaveholder in El Paso County, with two slaves in 1858. In October 1860, a group of friends honored the thirty-three-year-old attorney with a banquet in El Paso, thanking him for his "firm and devoted adherence to Southern rights." At the dinner, those present raised a toast to "[t]he memory of John C. Calhoun—the man is dead but 'his works live after him,' a tower light to shed the brightest truest rays upon the path of every confederacy of States, hereafter to be formed." A fourth member of this secession-minded group was state senator and former county judge Archibald C. Hyde. Hyde frequently sent in letters to Texas newspapers from El Paso promoting a strong southern agenda. "The South knows her course," he wrote in one 1860 letter, "and rest assured that El Paso county [sic] is ready to act and vote for the interest of the South, even if it becomes necessary to secede."[24]

El Paso's Democratic Party and local government were anything but democratic. Simeon Hart, James Magoffin, and their coterie controlled much of El Paso County's economic and political life. Rex Strickland wrote that in the antebellum period, "[a] few men, not more than a dozen or so, seized the leadership and by using their prestige and power imposed their will upon the great majority of poor or alien [Mexican] laborers." Strickland noted, "Violence was a political instrument which placed the dissident in danger of bodily harm." El Paso's frontier society was "autocratic" and "totalitarian," and those in power dominated through "sheer ruthlessness" and "predatory" exploitation.[25]

Several primary accounts reveal that in El Paso County, the Anglo secession ring employed physical intimidation and widespread voting fraud to influence the local referendum on February 18, 1861. A short time before the polling began, El Paso's Vigilance Committee ordered Anson Mills, a noted unionist, to appear before it. Mills declined, whereupon he was "notified by this same committee that the vote of the county must be unanimous for secession, and that I would imperil my life if I voted against it." Reported members of the Vigilance Committee included Simeon

Hart, saloon keeper and former postmaster Benjamin Dowell, county judge Henry Gillette, his brother John Gillette, a merchant, and hotel proprietor Braxton W. Gillock. Hart, however, denied membership in "any such committee, [claiming] that he has ever been opposed to them, and [has] conducted himself as a peaceful law abiding citizen."[26]

Despite Hart's denials, R. L. Robertson, a clerk who lived at Gillock's hotel, said that Hart was "the originator" of El Paso's Vigilance Committee. Regarding Hart, Robertson stated that "no Rebel in El Paso County was more cruel and oppressive towards Union men." Robertson said that members of the committee "sat in judgment upon the cases of Union men (myself among the number) and decided to hang us. These trials as they were called were in secret, without the persons charged being present."[27]

When Anson Mills cast his ballot on February 18 at Ben Dowell's saloon in El Paso, he encountered resistance from election judge Braxton Gillock, "a violent secessionist." When Mills submitted his vote, the election judge refused to take it. Only after another secessionist, Philemon T. Herbert, intervened on Mills's behalf did Gillock accept the ballot. Herbert interceded a second time when Anson's brother, W. W. Mills, tried to cast his vote. El Paso County district elector Simeon Hart spotted W.W. as he entered Dowell's Saloon with Herbert, and Hart shouted, "Champagne for a vote for secession and a halter [rope] for the Union men." Hart ordered Herbert to eject Mills "by force." Herbert replied that he was "as good a Southern man as any in the world but was no assassin, and Hart having made some insulting reply Herbert took a horse-whip and gave him a good horse whipping and then presented Mr. Mills with the whip." W. W. Mills then cast his vote.[28]

Another of El Paso County's polling stations was located at Smith's Ranch, the Butterfield station at Birchville, thirty-two miles upstream from Fort Quitman. During the county's secession referendum, William "Uncle Billy" Smith served as election judge at the stage stop. Captain Zenas Bliss, commander of the federal outpost at Fort Quitman, said that "Lying Billy Smith" reported hundreds of votes for disunion, notwithstanding the fact that "there were but two men at that place that had a shadow of a right to vote." In a third account, Noah Smithwick, who passed through El Paso shortly after the ballots had been cast, inquired how a county "so sparsely settled" could field such a large turnout. "'Oh, that was a light vote,' a local resident replied, 'we could have polled twice that number if the river [Rio Grande] hadn't taken a rise.'"[29]

Summing up the county's secession referendum, Anson Mills observed that some votes were "legal, but the majority cast by Mexican citizens from the other side of the river were not." Echoing these firsthand recollections, early El Paso chronicler Owen White noted that when the final results were tallied, "it was clearly apparent that not only practically all of El Paso, but also a large part of Paso del Norte, across the river, had expressed its desire to secede from the American Union."[30]

One cannot easily dismiss such period accounts, especially in light of the long-standing tradition of unlawful elections in El Paso. W. H. Timmons believes that the final secession tally included the fraudulent votes of several hundred Mexican nationals from across the river. In addition, without the Anglo secession ring's intimidation tactics, more of El Paso County's population, which was 90 percent Hispanic, would have voted as Tejanos in neighboring Presidio County did, against secession. Timmons notes, "The Mexican-American population of El Paso, which was far and away the majority, evinced little interest" in the Southern agenda. One should note, however, that some Mexican Americans in El Paso County did vote for secession. They did so for several reasons.[31]

After 1821 and Mexican independence from Spain, Hispanics in Texas experienced a fluid existence, facing ever-changing economic and political realities, adapting as best they could. Raúl Ramos notes that "[t]he political context" of the antebellum period "broadens the explanation of Tejano participation beyond Anglo-Texan manipulation to negotiation within a complex and dynamic set of choices." Many of these choices were difficult. In 1861, whites in El Paso County controlled local elections, the economy, and employment. "Politicians courted Tejano votes," Ramos says, "but participation in the core of the government eluded Tejanos. Their survival depended upon maintaining their ties to the Anglo-Texan power structure." While Mexican Americans in El Paso County had a range of options and responses available to them, Anglo political leaders ensured that those choices were limited.[32]

Texas's secession vote in February 1861 prompted Congress a few weeks later to move the overland mail service from the southern route to a central route through the country's midsection, far away from the Southern states. The Overland Mail Company agreed to switch operations to the central route, and on March 12, 1861, Postmaster General Montgomery Blair officially ordered the change. It took a few weeks for the news to filter down to all the stations along the line, but by early April, Butterfield was pulling out of Texas.[33]

In April and May 1861, the general superintendent for the mail line, Owen Tuller, traveled westward across Texas, closing out the company's business affairs. In mid-May, Tuller sold all of Butterfield's Trans-Pecos stations and equipment to San Antonio mail contractor George Giddings. Giddings continued mail service to El Paso and Mesilla until August 1862, when Texas and the Confederacy abandoned the Trans-Pecos to the Union Army, which occupied it for the duration of the war.[34]

Before selling Butterfield's Trans-Pecos properties to Giddings, Superintendent Tuller had to contend with a series of raids on his stage stops. Ironically, the marauders were not Comanches or Apaches but Texas Rangers. The principals involved included John Robert Baylor and his sidekick Harris A. Hamner, leaders of Texas's Indian reservation war in 1859 and the gang responsible for the assassination of federal Indian superintendent Robert Neighbors. Hamner, former editor of the *White Man* newspaper, was captain of an official Ranger detachment, part of a larger force commanded by Colonel William C. Dalrymple. Despite Hamner's checkered history, Dalrymple apparently had no qualms about him serving in his regiment.[35]

In February 1861, Tuller complained to Governor Sam Houston that Rangers were pillaging his company's mail stations at Belknap and Clear Fork of the Brazos. The superintendent said that a party of armed men commanded by Captain Hamner had stolen a load of grain from Belknap Station. When Tuller arrived at Clear Fork Station aboard a Butterfield coach on February 10, he discovered four hundred armed men camping around the stage stop. The Rangers had looted the overland building of all its grain and hay. As Tuller's coach pulled up to the station, Hamner came forward to converse with him. The superintendent confronted the Ranger captain about the thefts. Hamner claimed that he and his men had simply borrowed the forage at both mail stations and that the State of Texas would reimburse the mail company.[36]

Tuller asked Hamner "if it was his intention to stop the Overland Mail." Hamner replied "that it was not his desire to do so, but the line was very unpopular and there was no way knowing what they, the men might do." As the pair were talking, another Ranger captain named Johnson drew near and "was excessively abusive, approaching the stage and using the most profane language, calling us abolitionists, . . . and suggesting the propriety of breaking up the line at once." In a newspaper interview several weeks later, Hamner claimed that he had reimbursed Tuller in gold coin to cover the losses, a highly unlikely scenario.[37]

While Johnson and Hamner were threatening Tuller, other Texas Rangers were detaining overland stages and interfering with mail line operations. John Baylor's regiment rode into Fort Chadbourne during the latter part of February after a long scout in Comanche country. Baylor's command "was out of provisions and many of them almost destitute of clothes, and their horses nearly broken down." Around February 19, a Butterfield stage conductor and his passengers reported "outrages by secessionists" at Fort Chadbourne, including the seizure "of the coach, . . . its mail, . . . [and] the property of the company" at Chadbourne Station. Another Butterfield conductor told the St. Louis newspaper that while traveling through Texas with a "considerable amount of money" during this time when "Secession Rangers" were looting various mail stations, he pulled his coach off the road, deeming "it prudent to lie over till the Rangers had departed, lest the coin should be confiscated to the public benefit."[38]

A spokesman for Baylor's group refuted a report that "Col. Baylor's regiment robbed one of the Overland Stations of the provisions and provender it had in store." Hamner also denied any wrongdoing. Despite such denials, Colonel Henry McCulloch, state commander of the northwestern frontier, confirmed the Ranger depredations to his superiors in Austin and expressed contempt for the men's conduct. "I am unwilling to shield them from proper censure," he wrote; "[S]ome of them . . . acted very improperly." The colonel promised that when he learned the identity of the culprits he would expel them from the Texas Rangers. "The reputation of the service must and will be sustained by me or I will have no troops." The *Dallas Herald*, however, fully endorsed Hamner's pilfering of mail company property, saying, "Hit 'em again Hamner, they deserve it all."[39]

Despite McCulloch's letter, state officials took no action in the matter, and Texas Rangers at Fort Chadbourne continued harassing the overland mail. In early March 1861, troops stopped another coach containing Anson Mills of El Paso and seven others. After interrogating the occupants and enjoying a good laugh at their expense, the soldiers let the stagecoach continue eastward. By the end of March 1861, the wheels were coming off Butterfield's operations in Texas. On Friday, April 5, 1861, the postmaster at San Francisco announced, "The Overland Mail by the Butterfield route did not leave this city today for St. Louis as usual and will be discontinued hereafter." Effective June 1, Overland Mail Company stages would go from Missouri to California via the new Central Overland Route. In retrospect, it is not surprising that the nation's sectional issues eventually shuttered Butterfield's stations in Texas and elsewhere. The threat of secession had hung over the national mail line like a dark and menacing cloud throughout its entire existence.[40]

Although the Butterfield Overland Mail operated for just thirty months, from September 1858 until April 1861, during that time the mail line influenced and intersected much of Texas's frontier history. Since the Civil War, much of that legacy has been lost to time. Many of the old overland sites are now crumbling ruins. Some have disappeared. The names and stories of many of the people who lived and died at these remote settlements have faded from public memory. Over the past 150 years, significant chunks of this frontier heritage have receded into the past, seemingly lost forever.

The goal of this work has been to recover that legacy, first by identifying the relevant sites from the Red River to New Mexico and documenting them in person, then by discovering the human history that occurred at these places. Texas's frontier story, as told by the documents and artifacts unearthed in this study, is more complicated and nuanced than previous romanticized interpretations.

Although the action takes place within the Lone Star State, in many respects this is an American tale. The same secession concerns that challenged Texans confronted citizens across the country. Moreover, the federal government, through the U.S. Army and the Overland Mail Company, played a far greater role in spurring internal improvements and economic development in the American West (including West Texas) than did state legislatures. Along the nation's western frontier, from Texas to California, diverse cultures and differing worldviews collided with Anglo-American precepts of Manifest Destiny and racial superiority. Many of the historic locales encountered in this work, places such as Gainesville, Bridgeport, Belknap, Fort Stockton, and El Paso, serve as tangible touchstones, direct links to these antebellum issues, some of which still resonate today. With more of these pieces now in place, a richer and more intimate picture of the frontier comes into focus out of the blurred past, giving us a fuller understanding of Texas's role in this essential American story.

Notes

ABBREVIATIONS

AFT	author field trip
AGO	Adjutant General's Office
BIA	Bureau of Indian Affairs
BL	Baker Library
CJ	Conklings' Texas field trip journal
CM	Conklings' 1931 manuscript
DBC	Dolph Briscoe Center for American History
DCR	R. G. Dun and Co. Credit Report Volumes
DNM	Department of New Mexico
DP	District of the Pecos
FS	Fort Stockton
GLO	Texas General Land Office Archives
HL	Nita Stewart Haley Memorial Library and History Center
HRR	Governor Hardin Richard Runnels (Papers)
JA	with Joe Allen (author field trip)
JRW	J. R. Webb (Papers)
KFN	Kenneth Franklin Neighbours (Papers)
LR	letters received
LS	letters sent
LTS	letters and telegrams sent
M	microfilm series
MT	My Topo Terrain Navigator Pro Software, Version 10.3, topographic maps and aerial photographs
NA	National Archives
NACP	National Archives Cartographic and Architectural Section, College Park, Md.
OCE	Office of the Chief of Engineers
OR	*The War of the Rebellion: A Compilation of the Official Records of the Union and Confederate Armies*
PD	with Patrick Dearen (author field trip)

PGA	U.S. Postmaster General, Record of Appointment of Postmasters, 1832 to 1971
PGS	U.S. Postmaster General, Post Office Department Reports of Site Locations, 1837–1950
PHB	Governor Peter Hansbrough Bell (Papers)
R	roll
RPC	Roscoe P. Conkling (Papers)
RG	Record Group
RSN	Robert Simpson Neighbors (Papers)
S	series
SCL	Special Collections Library
SH	Governor Sam Houston (Papers)
SWC	Southwest Collection, Special Collections Library, Texas Tech University
THC	Texas Historical Commission
TIA	Texas Indian Agency
TRWD	Tarrant Regional Water District Archives
TSLAC	Texas State Library and Archives Commission
UT	University of Texas (Austin)
UTA	University of Texas–Arlington
UTEP	University of Texas–El Paso
VG	Virginia Garrett Cartographic History Library
WIA	Wichita Indian Agency
WTC	West Texas Collection
Atlas	Texas Historical Commission, *Online Atlas of Texas*
Giddings v. U.S.	*George Giddings v. The United States and the Kiowa, Comanche, and Apache Indians*, Indian Depredation Case No. 3873, NA, RG 123, U.S. Court of Claims
Handbook	Texas State Historical Association, *Handbook of Texas Online*

PREFACE

1. Roscoe "Rod" Platt Conkling, born on April 2, 1877, to Benjamin Franklin Conkling and Pauline Augusta Seymour Conkling, grew up in Catskill-on-Hudson, New York. One of the local heroes in the region was John Butterfield, who hailed from neighboring Utica, New York. As a youth, Conkling loved hearing tales about the American West, the open frontier, and Butterfield's legendary exploits in the staging business. It is no surprise, then, that he eventually migrated west, spending much of his life in the Texas Trans-Pecos and California. Conkling spent several decades as a mining engineer in Mexico and South America and worked fifteen years for American Smelting and Refining Company in El Paso. His active interest in the West spurred him to explore much of the West Texas–New Mexico region. In 1929, he discovered a prehistoric Indian cave (later named for him) in the White Sands of New Mexico. The Los Angeles County Museum of Natural History excavated Conkling Cave in 1930. In 1929, Roscoe Conkling met Margaret Badenoch Vear, a piano teacher from Chicago who had relocated to El Paso. Margaret Badenoch, born in Illinois on November 13, 1890, to Joseph and Elizabeth Badenoch, shared a passion with Roscoe for music and the outdoors. The two became inseparable, spending their dates out exploring old trails and historic sites in the El Paso region. Several trips during that year included visits to Hueco Tanks and Cornudas, both located on the Butterfield Overland Road. Christmas 1929 saw the two engaged, with their wedding set for the following year in Conkling Cave. It was the second marriage for both. After spending a year exploring the overland route in the El Paso area, in 1930 the couple decided to research the entire trail, from St. Louis to San Francisco, documenting all of the road's historic sites before they became lost to time. The years spent together exploring the Butterfield Overland Road became a wonderful and enduring love story. During the 1930s, while the Conklings con-

ducted their fieldwork over the route, they lived in El Paso. The pair became fond of California while researching the Butterfield Road in that state. When they moved to Inglewood, California, in 1943, Roscoe had already retired from the mining business and Margaret resumed teaching school at the nearby Inglewood School District. All told, Margaret taught a total of thirty-six years at various schools across the country. Wherever they lived, Roscoe and Margaret stayed active with local orchestras and symphonies. One notable musical event occurred on May 6, 1933, when Roscoe Conkling conducted a 130-person chorus and a 30-piece orchestra performing Haydn's *Creation* underground, inside Carlsbad Caverns, New Mexico. In June 1931, after only a year of fieldwork on the overland road, the Conklings sent an exploratory feeler for publication of their Butterfield study to the Arthur H. Clark Company of Glendale, California. Clark had previously published numerous books on western exploration and the American West, including LeRoy R. Hafen's *Overland Mail, 1849–1869.* Clark expressed a guarded enthusiasm and encouraged the Conklings to complete their research and submit a manuscript. He accepted their preliminary manuscript in 1933, although Roscoe and Margaret spent several more years revising it and conducting further field research. By May 1935, the couple had "worn out three cars in their journeys." On the eve of World War II, the Conklings turned in a completed Butterfield manuscript to Clark. Wartime shortages of zinc, copper, and brass made the book's publication costs prohibitive. Finally, in 1947, Clark issued Roscoe P. Conkling and Margaret B. Conkling's three-volume *Butterfield Overland Mail, 1857–1869.* After living twenty-eight years in California, Roscoe passed away at age ninety-four, on July 9, 1971. Margaret followed two years later, on December 30, 1973, at age eighty-three. Their ashes are interred in the Conkling family plot at Jefferson Rural Cemetery, Jefferson Heights, in Catskill, New York. Conkling biographical sketch compiled using the following sources: death records for Roscoe and Margaret Conkling, County Clerk, Los Angeles County, Calif.; undated Margaret Conkling speech to "The Antiquers," Roscoe Conkling burial instructions, Conkling family tree, Conkling family genealogy information, and July 1971 Roscoe Conkling obituary penned by Margaret Conkling, all in box 25, GC 1006, RPC Papers; letters from Arthur H. Clark to Roscoe Conkling dated June 26, 1931, Oct. 26, 1942, and Nov. 7, 1942, box 14, RPC Papers; *El Paso Herald-Post*, May 5, 1935 (endnote quotation).

Jesse Wallace Williams was born on June 3, 1891, in Cross Plains, Texas. He received his BA and MA from Hardin-Simmons University in Abilene, Texas. Williams taught mathematics in the Wichita Falls School District for much of his life. He also had a passion for southwestern trails, including the Butterfield Overland Mail Road. Williams's studies on the Butterfield include "The Marcy and Butterfield Trails across North Texas" (his master's thesis) and *Old Texas Trails.* Williams conducted much of his Butterfield research in Texas during the 1930s, at the same time the Conklings were doing their fieldwork in the Lone Star State. In 1952 and 1953, Williams served as president of the West Texas Historical Association. He also served on the Texas State Historical Association's Executive Council from 1961 to 1971. Williams died in Wichita Falls on February 22, 1977. For more on Williams's life, see Williams, *Old Texas Trails,* v–vi.

CHAPTER 1. THE TEXAS FRONTIER AND THE BUTTERFIELD OVERLAND MAIL

1. Lang, *First Overland Mail: . . . St. Louis to San Francisco,* 110; PGA, El Paso Co., Tex., NA, RG 28, M841, R123; Charles Hoppin and Simeon Hart to Peter Hansbrough Bell, Dec. 20, 1851, PHB Papers, folder 3, box 301-18, TSLAC; Hugh Stephenson, Simeon Hart, et al., to Millard Fillmore, Dec. 20, 1851, ibid.; Mills, *My Story,* 56–57; Anson Mills's Feb. 8, 1859, survey of Juan M. Ponce de Leon Survey 145 (El Paso County Abstract No. 52), El Paso County Surveyor Field Notes Book A, no. 1 (survey includes El Paso); 1860 U.S. Census, El Paso Co., Tex., RG 29, M653, R1293, pp. 7–17 (El Paso), 18–19 (Franklin). During its formative period, El Paso, Texas, had two names: El Paso and Franklin (after early pioneer Benjamin Franklin Coons). To simplify matters and to avoid confusion, this work uses "El Paso" when referencing this community. U.S. Postmaster General records for March 31, 1855, officially designate the name of the post office here as El Paso, Texas. There was no post office for Franklin in El Paso County. Additionally, in December 1851 letters to Texas governor Peter H. Bell and U.S. president Millard Fillmore, leading citizens of El Paso County addressed their correspondence as being from "El Paso, Texas." The first official plat of the community, drawn by Anson Mills and dated February 28, 1859, is titled "Town of El Paso." Lastly, the 1860 U.S. Census for El Paso County, Texas, includes listings for both El Paso (encompassing 11 pages) and Franklin (2 pages).

2. Lang, *First Overland Mail: . . . St. Louis to San Francisco,* 109–10.

3. Several studies in recent years have located the eastern boundary of the American West at the one-hundredth meridian. Two such works are Ely, *Where the West Begins,* 7–16; and Limerick, *Something in the Soil,* 23. John Wesley Powell was the first to demarcate this boundary line in his 1878 congressional report on aridity in the American West (*Arid Lands,* 11–13). See also "Cross Timbers and Prairies Ecological Region," Texas Parks and Wildlife, www.tpwd.state.tx.us/land-water/land/habitats/cross_timbers/ecoregions/cross_timbers.phtml (accessed Aug. 5, 2014). The Upper or Western Cross Timbers region in Texas is well illustrated in *S.A. Mitchell's No. 12 Map of the State of Texas, 1859;* and *A. R. Roessler's 1875 New Map of Texas Prepared and Published for the Bureau of Immigration of the State of Texas,* VG, SCL, UTA.

4. Ely, "Riding the Butterfield Frontier," 17.

5. Wooster, *Frontier Crossroads,* 29 (quotations); Wooster, *Military and . . . Indian Policy,* 215–16; Freeman, "History of Fort Chadbourne," 37. In October and November 1858, there were 50 and 40 men, respectively. In April 1860, there were 54 men at Fort Chadbourne. My "contested frontier" phrase was inspired by West, *Contested Plains.*

6. *Communication from the Commissioner of Indian Affairs and Other Documents in Relation to the Indians in Texas,* Senate Rep. Com. No. 171, 30th Cong., 1st Sess., 43 (quotations).

7. Newcomb, *Indians of Texas,* 337, 351 (quotation 1); La Vere, *Life among the Texas Indians,* 28, 33, 37 (quotation 2).

8. *Communication from the Commissioner,* Senate Rep. Com. No. 171, 30th Cong., 1st Sess., 20 (quotation 1), 48 (quotation 2).

9. Schilz and Schilz, *Buffalo Hump,* 32 (quotations 1–3), 38 (quotations 4–6).

10. Ely, "Riding the Western Frontier," 4.

11. Brown, *Strain of Violence,* 112 (quotation 1), 113 (quotation 2); Hollon, *Frontier Violence,* 53 (quotation 3).

12. Hämäläinen, *Comanche Empire,* 312 (quotation 1); Smith, *From Dominance to Disappearance,* 213 (quotation 2), 244; La Vere, *Texas Indians,* 201 (quotation 3). For more on Comanche groups in Texas's Llano Estacado and Canadian River regions, see Kavanagh, *Comanche Political History,* 82, 139, 145, 153–54, 179, 220, 237, 248, 325, 370, 373, 386, 389, 405, 407–8, 429, 431; Thomas W. Kavanagh e-mail to author, Feb. 23, 2010; Wallace and Hoebel, *Comanches,* 7, 12, 26–28; Kenner, *Comanchero Frontier,* 80n10, 126, 148, 163n31, 181, 191. Letters received by the U.S. Army's Adjutant General's Office during 1859–61, now housed at the National Archives in Record Group 94, document various bands of Comanches and Apaches in Texas, as do letters received by the Bureau of Indian Affairs in Record Group 75 at the National Archives.

13. Ray, *Ethnohistorical Analysis,* 7, 126–27, 129, 136–37, 150, 152, 164, 170–71; Opler, *Lipan and Mescalero Apache,* 226, 273–74, 368–69; Schilz, *Lipan Apaches in Texas,* 57–58; Hämäläinen, *Comanche Empire,* 79, 176,

222. Maps of Indian tribal territories are included in Ray's and Opler's works cited above.

14. 1860 U.S. Census, El Paso and Presidio Co., Tex., NA, M653, R1293; 1860 U.S. Census, Maverick Co., Tex., NA, M653, R1300; 1860 U.S. Census, Texas Slave Schedules, El Paso and Presidio Co., NA, M653, R1309, 289; 1860 U.S. Census, Texas Slave Schedules, Maverick Co., NA, M653, R1311, 146; Kennedy, *Population of the United States*, 566–73; Campbell, *Southern Community in Crisis*, 20.

15. Ely, "Riding the Butterfield Frontier," 28–32, 38–40; Ely, "Riding the Western Frontier," 9–10; Hafen, *Overland Mail*, 15 (quotation 1), 15–16 (quotation 2); White, *It's Your Misfortune* 57 (quotation 3), 58 (quotation 4), 59, 128.

16. Ely, "Riding the Western Frontier," 10; Haynes, *Soldiers of Misfortune*, 6–8, 211; Hogan, *Texas Republic*, 53, 55–56; Smith, *U.S. Army*, 12–13; Wooster, *Frontier Crossroads*, xi, 140–43.

17. Ely, "Riding the Western Frontier," 10; Ely, "Riding the Butterfield Frontier," 31–32; Smith, *U.S. Army*, 11–13; Wooster, "Fort Davis" (quotation).

18. Ely, *Where the West Begins*, 11–15.

19. Sonnichsen, *Mescalero Apaches*, 6 (quotation 1); Wallace and Hoebel, *Comanches*, 241 (quotations 2–3).

20. Cronon, *Changes in the Land*, 58 (quotations).

21. White, *Land Use*, 157 (quotation 1); Steinberg, *Down to Earth*, xi (quotation 2), xii (quotation 3).

22. Ely, "Riding the Butterfield Frontier," 282–85; Deutsch, *No Separate Refuge*, 14 (quotation); Bowden, *Spanish and Mexican Land Grants*, 140–64.

23. Bowden, *Spanish and Mexican Land Grants*, 140–64; Deutsch, *No Separate Refuge*, 16 (quotation 1); White, *It's Your Misfortune*, 213 (quotations 2–3).

24. Broaddus, *Legal Heritage of El Paso*, 57–58; Bowden, "Magoffin Salt War," 95–96, 106–10; Sonnichsen, *El Paso Salt War*, 7–8; Sonnichsen, *Pass of the North*, 181–82; Cool, *Salt Warriors*, 13.

25. *Report of the U.S. Postmaster General, March 3, 1859, Concerning the Contract with John Butterfield and his Associates*, Senate Exec. Doc. No. 48, 35th Cong., 2nd Sess., 1–11; Jackson, "New Look," 291–301; Wright, "Butterfield Overland Mail," 57 (quotation 1); Boggs, *My Playhouse*, 340 (quotation 2).

26. Hafen, *Overland Mail*, 91 (quotation 1), 92 (quotations 2–4); *Report of the U.S. Postmaster General, March 3, 1859*, 1–11; Billington and Ridge, *Westward Expansion*, 288 (quotation 5).

27. Wright, "Butterfield Overland Mail," 58 (quotation 1); Jackson, "New Look," 296 (quotation 2); "Since 1852," available at www.wellsfargo.com (accessed Apr. 5, 2014); "Becoming American Express: 150 Years of Reinvention and Customer Service," http://secure.cmax.americanexpress.com/ . . . /our_story_3.pdf (accessed Apr. 5, 2014).

28. Overland Mail Company Credit Reports, New York vol. 346, New York City 7, p. 693 (quotations), DCR, BL.

29. Ely, "Riding the Butterfield Frontier," 28–29. To date, researchers have found scant Butterfield corporate records for the antebellum period. One can glean much valuable information about the company's business dealings in Texas, New Mexico, and Arizona from recollections of former employees in *Giddings v. U.S.*

30. Ely, "Riding the Butterfield Frontier," 29. For more on Adam Rankin Johnson's life, see Johnson, *Partisan Rangers*, 6–36. For more detail regarding those working various jobs on the frontier, see Smith, *U.S. Army*, 206–8, 211–12. The Overland Mail Company operated on average 44 stations in Texas during its contract (40 stations in 1858–59 and 46 stations in 1859–61). There were 4 employees per station (more in the towns), or approximately 176 employees in Texas. In 1860, skilled workers such as blacksmiths, carpenters, and stonemasons earned $1.70 per day, whereas common laborers made $1.00 per day. Since most overland workers were laborers, a good average for all workers

might be $1.25 per day, or $456 per year, for a total annual Texas payroll of $80,256. For more on typical wages of the period, see Clarence D. Long's work for the National Bureau of Economic Research, *Wages and Earnings in the United States*, 94, 98–99.

31. Ely, "Riding the Butterfield Frontier," 30–31.

32. Ibid., 31. Economic specifics regarding mail line operations in Texas are in *Giddings v. U.S.* and the 1860 federal census for El Paso and Presidio Counties. See 1860 U.S. Census, El Paso Co., Tex., NA, M653, R1293; 1860 U.S. Census, Presidio Co., Tex., NA, M653, R1293 (this includes Fort Stockton, later in Pecos County). The 1860 census shows how many people worked at each station in these counties and their job descriptions. One report from October 1858 claimed that Butterfield had 20–25 men guarding each station, which is a noticeable exaggeration. See *Frank Leslie's Illustrated Newspaper*, Oct. 23, 1858.

33. Ely, "Riding the Butterfield Frontier," 31–32. For more on period stagecoaches and wagons, see Eggenhoffer, *Wagons, Mules, and Men*, 151–72. See also A. J. Fountain, David Koney, L. C. Adkins, William Buckley, Daniel Butterfield, John Butterfield, Jr., Nelson J. Davis, Parker Burnham, Josiah F. Crosby, Thomas Collins, and W. W. Mills depositions, *Giddings v. U.S.*

34. Ely, "Riding the Butterfield Frontier," 32.

35. Ibid., 32–33; Ormsby, *Butterfield Overland Mail*, 61 (coaches' rate of speed in Texas); Lang, *First Overland Mail: . . . St. Louis to San Francisco*, 127; Lang, *First Overland Mail: . . . San Francisco to Memphis*, 42 (quotation 2), 52, 85 (quotation 1).

36. Ely, "Riding the Butterfield Frontier," 33; J. A. Lucas, David Koney, L. C. Adkins, William Buckley, William M. Ford, John Butterfield, Jr., Nelson J. Davis, Parker Burnham, Anson Mills, Thomas Collins, and W. W. Mills depositions, *Giddings v. U.S.*

37. Ely, "Riding the Butterfield Frontier," 34; Parker Burnham and Josiah F. Crosby (quotation) depositions, *Giddings v. U.S.*

38. Ely, "Riding the Butterfield Frontier," 34–35; William Buckley and Thomas J. Bull depositions, *Giddings v. U.S.*

39. Ely, "Riding the Butterfield Frontier," 35; J. A. Lucas, David Koney, L. C. Adkins, William Buckley, William M. Ford, and Parker Burnham (quotations) depositions, *Giddings v. U.S.*

40. Ely, "Riding the Butterfield Frontier," 36; Smith, *U.S. Army*, 206, 211; 1860 U.S. Census, Mason Co., Tex., NA, M653, R1300, 482. For Martin family history, see National Ranching Heritage Center, "Hedwig's Hill Dogtrot House: 1855–1856," http://shaejae.com/ranch/4.html (accessed July 25, 2008).

41. Ely, "Riding the Butterfield Frontier," 35–36; Smith, *U.S. Army*, 207, 212; 1860 U.S. Census, Presidio Co., Tex., NA, M653, R1293, 87 (this includes Fort Stockton, later in Pecos County); El Paso County Surveyor Field Notes, Feb. 13, 1859, Sept. 28, 1859, and Apr. 24, 1860; Williams, *Texas' Last Frontier*, 64; J. A. Lucas, Albert Brackett, and G. H. Giddings depositions, *Giddings v. U.S.*

Chapter 2. From the Red River to Young County

1. Reynolds, "Texas Troubles," *Handbook* (quotations).

2. Reynolds, *Editors Make War*, 97–117; Reynolds, *Texas Terror*, 29–53, 83–85, 148–67; Reynolds, "Bewley, Anthony," *Handbook* (quotation 1); *White Man*, Sept. 13, 1860, Newspaper Collection, DBC, UT (quotation 2); Reynolds, "Texas Troubles," *Handbook*.

3. Reynolds, "Texas Troubles," *Handbook* (quotations).

4. Abel Rathbone Corbin to John B. Floyd, Washington, D.C., June 28, 1858, NA, RG 94, AGO, LR, M567, R577 (quotations).

5. Floyd to Corbin, Washington, D.C., July 12, 1858, ibid. (quotation).

6. Richardson, *Beyond the Mississippi*, 224; Lang, *First Overland Mail: . . . St. Louis to San Francisco*, 16–19.

7. Britton, "Preston, Texas," *Handbook* (quotation).

8. Overbeck, "Colbert's Ferry," 214, 215 (quotation); Britton, "Colbert's Ferry," *Handbook*; Wright, "Historic Places," 812–13.

9. Tallack, *California Overland Express*, 55 (quotations). After crossing the Red River, Tallack observed that the quality and character of the passengers in Indian Territory were a considerable improvement over those who had disembarked the overland coach at Sherman, Texas. When not riding Butterfield coaches across the United States, Tallack was a social activist working for penal reform in England.

10. Ormsby, *Butterfield Overland Mail*, ix–x, 34 (quotation 1), 35 (quotation 2); 1850 U.S. Census, Hudson County, N.J., M432, R452, 420B; 1860 U.S. Census, New York City, N.Y., M653, R795, 165; 1880 U.S. Census, Kings Co., N.Y., T9, R840, 28; *Rampant Colt* 34, no. 3 (Fall 2014): 30–34, 38–46; *New York Herald*, Apr. 30, 1908; *New York Tribune*, Apr. 12, 1914; "The Messler Line," http://trees.ancestry.com/tree/18719909/person/19935760249?ssrc= (accessed Mar. 12, 2015). Waterman Lilly Ormsby, Jr., was born in New York City on December 8, 1834. His father, Waterman Lilly Ormsby, Sr., an engraver renowned for his superb detail work on banknotes, lithographs, and firearms, was one of the founders of the Continental Bank Note Company and a close friend of Samuel Colt. Ormsby Jr. was a reporter for several New York newspapers, including the *Herald, World, Times*, and *Sun*. In October 1858, after his fatiguing twenty-four-day overland trip aboard a Butterfield stagecoach, Ormsby Jr. chose a different mode of travel for his return trip to New York, namely, a steamer. Around 1870, he took a job at the Continental Bank Note Company. After fourteen years there, in 1885 he started a new profession as stenographer for the city magistrates courts, where he worked for twenty-three years. Ormsby and his wife, Eliza, had four children. He died in New York City on April 28, 1908, and was interred at Greenwood Cemetery in Brooklyn, Kings County, New York. Two of his sons also became court stenographers; one of them, Waterman L. Ormsby III, worked for the state supreme court for twenty-eight years. After losing one of his typing fingers in a gardening accident, Ormsby III committed suicide in 1914.

11. Baker and Baker, *WPA Oklahoma Slave Narratives*, 258 (quotations); Roscoe Conkling unpublished sketch of Colbert's Station, RPC Papers.

12. Morrison, "Colbert Ferry," 311 (quotation).

13. Wright, "Historic Places," 800–801, 809, 812; Young, "Conflict Resolution," 13; Young, "Cherokee Nation," 506–7; Baker and Baker, *WPA Oklahoma Slave Narratives*, 257 (quotation 1), 258 (quotation 2), 257–58 (quotation 3). Colbert genealogy information is from K. M. Armstrong, "Descendants of James Logan Colbert," www.chickasawhistory.com/colbert/i0001287.htm-i1115b (Martin Colbert), www.chickasawhistory.com/colbert/i0001982.htm-i1982 (Benjamin Franklin "Frank" Colbert), www.chickasawhistory.com/colbert/i0001115.htm-i1115 (Henry Clay "Buck" Colbert) (accessed July 14, 2004). During his sixty-six years, Benjamin Franklin Colbert had four wives: Martha, who died in 1851; Malinda, who died in 1853; Georgia, who died in 1869; and Anna, who lived until 1927.

14. Baker and Baker, *WPA Oklahoma Slave Narratives*, 259 (quotations 1–2), 259–60 (quotation 3); *Dallas Herald*, July 1, 1858.

15. CM 1931, pp. 117–18, box 9, RPC Papers (quotations 1–2); CJ, Oct. 30, 1930, box 9, RPC Papers (quotation 3, quoting Mrs. W. H. Lucas of Sherman, Tex.). Holmes Colbert died in 1945; his family buried him in Lindsay, Oklahoma.

16. AFT, Colbert's Ferry, Okla., Oct. 24, 2001, and McBride Landing near Denison, Tex., Jan. 29, 2002 (JA, PD). Today underbrush chokes the route down the hillside to the Oklahoma crossing, but the old mail road and ford are still clearly visible. Over on the Lone Star shoreline, a fine broad trace of the Butterfield Road leads to a ledge overlooking the river channel. Here the trail makes a wide cut into the bank. The McBrides' store and home site were set back 200 yards from the river to avoid periodic flooding.

17. Foreman first unearthed this Red River feud in "California Overland Mail Route," 312n12. Overbeck developed considerably more primary research on this dispute in "Colbert's Ferry," 215–17, 220. See also 1860 U.S. Census, Grayson Co., Tex., NA, M653, R1295, 139; Grayson County Tax Rolls, reel 1, 1846–72, TSLAC; Landrum, *Grayson County*, 21. Regarding the McBride land in Texas, see Grayson County Deed Book L, 154. Although the sale date is July 28, 1855, Clinton Alexander did not officially file the document with the county clerk until March 29, 1859, almost four years later. In 1859, Martha and Michael McBride owned 960 acres and had a net worth of $6,115. By 1861, their assets had declined to $2,650.

18. B. F. Colbert to G. C. Whiting, Chickasaw Nation, Dec. 1, 1858, Office of Indian Affairs, LR, NA, RG 75, M234, R142; James W. Denver to B. F. Colbert, Washington, D.C., Dec. 18, 1858, NA, RG 75, Records of the Bureau of Indian Affairs, Entry 252, Indian Removal, Chickasaw Removal Records, LS, 1832–61, vol. 3; Douglas H. Cooper to Elias Rector, Choctaw and Chickasaw Agency, Office of Indian Affairs, Aug. 8, 1860, LR, NA, RG 75, M234, R142. According to Cooper's letter cited above, Colbert's legal reasoning in the ferry dispute was based on the following succession of treaties: Under the Treaty of 1819 between the United States and Spain, jurisdiction and ownership of the Red River was given to the United States and extended to the south bank. Subsequently, the United States ceded the same boundary to the Choctaw Tribe, who later ceded it to the Chickasaws.

19. John H. Reagan to Commissioner of Indian Affairs, Washington, D.C., Mar. 11, 1860, forwarding Nov. 28, 1859, letter from H. P. Teague of Kaufman, Tex., detailing the Chickasaws' burning of the store at the Texas Butterfield ferry landing, WIA, LR, NA, RG 75, M234, R928 (quotation 1); Morrison, "Colbert Ferry," 307 (quotation 2), 308 (quotation 3). Teague mentions that the proprietors of the store on the Texas side of Colbert's Ferry were a Mr. Hunter and S. H. McHenry, who either were managers of McBride's general store or were leasing the site. In his comments accompanying Teague's letter, Reagan mistakenly identifies the responsible Indians as Cherokees.

20. Douglas H. Cooper to Elias Rector, Choctaw and Chickasaw Agency, Aug. 8, 1860, Office of Indian Affairs, LR, NA, RG 75, M234, R142 (quotation 1); Douglas H. Cooper to B. F. Colbert and M. A. McBride, Aug. 6, 1860, ibid.; Charles Eli Mix to Jacob Thompson, Washington, D.C., Sept. 3, 1860, ibid. (quotation 2); Jeremiah Sullivan Black to Jacob Thompson, Washington, D.C., Sept. 25, 1860, ibid. (quotations 3–4); PGA, Grayson Co., Tex., NA, RG 28, M841, R123. James A. Maupin served as postmaster of Colbert's Ferry, Texas, from March 28, 1872, until July 11, 1873, when the U.S. Postmaster General discontinued said post office.

21. Donna Hunt, "Sherman's Jaco Building Had Long History," *Herald Democrat* (Sherman, Tex.), May 9, 2012; Landrum, *Grayson County*, 21–22; Morrison, "Colbert Ferry," 310–12; Overbeck, "Colbert's Ferry," 221–23. The financial history of the McBride property is a long and tangled thread. The couple originally purchased the 640-acre parcel from Clinton C. and Almarine M. Alexander in 1855 for $1,920 (Grayson County Deed Book L, 154). The Alexanders owned Alexander's Counting House in Bonham, Texas, which loaned money to individuals and businesses. In addition, A. M. Alexander had a general store in Sherman, Texas, while his brother, Clinton Alexander, ran a mercantile store in Bonham, Texas. In 1860, the McBrides secured a $719.53 loan from Clinton Alexander, using goods and merchandise from their store and home at the ferry landing as security (Grayson County Deed Book M, 356). In the same year, the McBrides took another loan for $1,200 from Alexander, using the bottom 440 acres of the land as collateral (Grayson County Deed Book N, 71). The husband and wife repaid the debt and in March 1861 took out a new loan for $1,691.76 from Alexander, using the same 440 acres as guarantee (Grayson County Deed Book M, 498–99). This time, however, the

McBrides defaulted on their note, and in 1866, the Grayson County District Court ordered the seizure and sale of the 440 acres to make restitution to Alexander (Grayson County Deed Book S, 248). In 1868, the land sold at public auction for $500. On January 5, 1871, John Blackburn paid the McBrides $3,088.23 for their remaining 200 acres, representing the upper end of the parcel and encompassing the ferry landing (Grayson County Deed Book V, 380–82), and four days later sold it to Colbert for exactly the same amount (Grayson County Deed Book V, 383–84). Combining both their 440-acre and 200-acre sales, the McBrides were paid roughly $4,700 for their $1,920 purchase in 1855. For his part, Colbert fared even better in the transaction. A year later, in 1872, he sold two parcels of land, including the McBride property, to the Missouri, Kansas, and Texas (MKT) Railroad for $21,000. The railroad built a bridge over the Red River adjacent to Colbert's Ferry; on Christmas Day in 1872, the first passenger train rolled down the tracks. With the arrival of the railroad, ferry traffic plummeted. Colbert adapted by building a toll bridge for nonrailroad traffic across the river in 1875, at a cost of $40,000. A major flood in August 1876 washed away the bridge and Colbert's investment, but the Chickasaw businessman persevered and started building a new span across the river. In the late 1880s, before completion of the second toll bridge, Colbert sold his interest to the Red River Bridge Company. The sale included both the toll bridge and the ferry.

22. Paddock, *Twentieth-Century History*, 1:116; 1860 U.S. Census, Grayson Co., Tex., NA, M653, R1295; AFT, Duck Creek and Munson Park, Denison, Tex., Jan. 29, 2002 (JA, PD); Minor, "Denison, Texas," *Handbook*. In 1858, county commissioners upgraded the old Red River Ferry–Sherman Road to a first-class overland road. Denison, Texas, did not exist in 1858. The community dates to 1872, when the MKT (Katy) Railroad came through the region. There has been considerable confusion among writers, who have mistakenly conflated the Butterfield Road with Marcy's 1849 California Emigrant Road. The Butterfield route through Grayson County did not follow the California Emigrant Road, laid out in 1849 by the army's Captain Randolph B. Marcy and Lieutenant Nathaniel Michler for gold rush travelers heading west to California. The California Emigrant Road stayed north of the Butterfield route all the way west to the Pecos River. Eventually the Butterfield Road and the California Emigrant Road intersected on the Pecos's east bank at Emigrant Crossing in H&TC RR (Houston and Texas Central Railway) Block 33, Section 15 in Ward County before continuing westward to California. For specifics on the California Emigrant Road, see Williams, *Old Texas Trails*, 219–44; GLO, Map #1985, *Resurvey of Portions of Young County, Peters Colony, Texan Emigration & Land Company, 1858*; GLO, Map #1986, *Map of the Surveyed Part of Young District, Young Land District, 1860*; GLO, Map #10110, Ward County Sketch File 22, *June 4, 1875 Map of Surveys along Pecos River from Horsehead Crossing to New Mexico State Line*; GLO, Map #10427, Ward County Sketch File 6, *Ward County Irrigation Company, Ward and Reeves Counties*; Senate Exec. Doc. No. 78, 33rd Cong., 2nd Sess., *Map and Profile No. 1, from the Red River to the Rio Grande, by Captain John Pope, 1854–1856: Explorations and Surveys for a Railroad Route from the Mississippi River to the Pacific Ocean*, War Department.

23. Sand Springs photos in box 7, RPC Papers; author interview with wife of Colbert's Ferry landowner, Oct. 24, 2001; *Denison Herald* article on Sand Springs, Sunday, Aug. 20, 1961; Grayson County Frontier Village, *History of Grayson County*, 1:23; Grayson County, "Historic Markers in Grayson County," Marker #072, Sand Springs, available at www.co.grayson.tx.us (accessed July 15, 2004) (quotation); AFT, Denison Armory on Loy Lake Road and railroad overpass, Oct. 24, 2001; AFT, Waterloo Lake Park in Denison, Jan. 29, 2002 (JA, PD); PGS, Grayson Co., Tex., NA, RG 28, M1126, R575. Three Grayson County post office maps, including one for Denison City dated September 16,

1872, show the stage road from Colbert's Ferry to Sherman heading south-southwest and passing to just to the west of Duck Creek and Denison City (as it was called then). Sand Springs apparently served as a crossroads for several trails running through the area. The site is at the intersection of the MKT railroad trestle and Loy Lake Road. The wife of the Colbert's Ferry landowner recalls her parents getting their household water from Sand Springs.

24. Grayson County Frontier Village, *History of Grayson County*, 1:22; Ormsby, *Butterfield Overland Mail*, 36 (quotation 1); Lang, *First Overland Mail: . . . San Francisco to Memphis*, 68 (quotation 2); Landrum, *Grayson County*, 21, 22 (quotation 3), 26 (endnote quotation); *Clarksville Northern Standard*, Apr. 16, 1859 (quotation 4); PGA, Grayson Co., Tex., NA, RG 28, M841, R123; Petersen, *Quantrill in Texas*, 134; CM 1931, p. 123, box 9, RPC Papers. City fathers named Sherman, founded in 1847, after noted early Texan Sidney Sherman. Benjamin W. Bradley was postmaster in Sherman during the Butterfield period (from 1858 to 1861). In their unpublished manuscript, the Conklings state that Ed Sacra ran the Butterfield livery stable in Sherman, but this is likely incorrect. Landrum says that Enoch M. Jones operated the Butterfield stable in Sherman and that Ed Sacra ran another livery stable "set somewhat apart" from the downtown square.

25. *Clarksville Northern Standard*, Jan. 29 (quotations 1–2) and Apr. 16, 1859 (endnote quotation); Tallack, *California Overland Express*, 54 (quotation 3). In April 1859, the county was constructing a new courthouse and Sherman residents were suffering through a drought. Local "wells were dry, and water for drink, was being hauled" to town.

26. 1860 U.S. Census, Grayson Co., Tex., NA, M653, R1295, 24, 25, 140; *Clarksville Northern Standard*, Jan. 29, 1859 (quotation); Petersen, *Quantrill in Texas*, 133; Grayson County Tax Rolls, reel 1, 1846–72, TSLAC. In 1860, Henry Bates owned a horse, four head of cattle, and Lot 16, Block 12 in Sherman, Texas, for a total net worth of $1,370. Bates and his family left Texas prior to Grayson County's July 1861 tax census. In contrast to the Grayson County tax assessor-collector's valuation, the 1860 federal census estimated Bates's assets at $3,000. Several other Overland Mail Company employees lived in Sherman at John Russell's hotel, including stage driver William Donoho and hostlers Daniel McVay and R. S. Butler. Ferry keeper William Cook lodged at Robert Condra's hotel.

27. *Clarksville Northern Standard*, Apr. 16, 1859 (quotation 1); Landrum, *Grayson County*, 26; Ormsby, *Butterfield Overland Mail*, 36 (quotation 2); AFT, Sherman, Tex., Sept. 21, 2008, and Jan. 19, 2013. See also GLO, Map #3600, *1859 Map of Grayson County*; GLO, Map #4961, *1885 Map of Grayson County*. According to Sanborn's map of Sherman, Texas, in 1885 the post office was at 100 Crockett Street, on the northwest corner of the town square at the intersection of Houston and Crockett Streets. Vintage Salon and Boutique is the present tenant of this building, which dates to 1856. There is a 1999 Texas Historical Commission marker commemorating the Butterfield route through Grayson County on the south side of the courthouse in Sherman. Just east of Highway 75 on Washington Street in Sherman is another Butterfield marker (featuring an old gristmill stone), placed by the Martha Jefferson Randolph Chapter of the DAR in 1936.

28. PGA, Grayson Co., Tex., NA, RG 28, M841, R123; Ormsby, *Butterfield Overland Mail*, 42 (quotation 1), 43 (quotation 2); Landrum, *Grayson County*, 31, 32 (quotation 3); Grayson County Frontier Village, *History of Grayson County*, 17, 263–65. The U.S. Postmaster General appointed Ambrose B. White postmaster of Whitesboro, Texas, on May 12, 1860. The U.S. Postmaster General discontinued the Whitesboro post office on Nov. 5, 1866, but reestablished it on May 26, 1874.

29. Ormsby, *Butterfield Overland Mail*, 43; 1860 U.S. Census, Grayson Co., Tex., NA, M653, R1295, 13, 18, 166; Tucker, *To the Golden Goal*, 181–82.

30. Tucker, *To the Golden Goal*, 183, 185 (quotations).

31. Ibid., 187 (quotations 1–2), 189 (quotation 3), 192 (quotation 4), 196. In *To the Golden Goal*, Tucker says that his Butterfield coach crossed the Red River and passed through Texarkana, but it would have been Sherman, Texas. Tucker also states that the coach stopped for dinner at the next station westward; the next station after Sherman is Diamond's. Tucker mentions traveling over a plain to the station, which description fits the terrain between Sherman and Whitesboro. The duel, therefore, likely took place at Diamond's. Tucker penned his reminiscences thirty-six years after the overland trip, so it is understandable that his recollection of Texas's geography and the Butterfield itinerary was a little fuzzy. A later writer recounting this same story, G. C. Tomkins, inexplicably placed the duel at Fort Chadbourne instead of near the Red River, as in Tucker's account. See Tompkins, *Compendium*, 148. Tucker never mentions Fort Chadbourne in his story. Why Tompkins located the gunplay at Fort Chadbourne is unclear, and he provides no documentation to support his erroneous claim.

32. Ormsby, *Butterfield Overland Mail*, 43; 1860 U.S. Census, Grayson Co., Tex., NA, M653, R1295, 13, 18, 166; AFT, Diamond's Station, Aug. 8 and Oct. 7, 2000, and June 10, 2003 (JA). At the ruins of the station, there is a scattering of sandstone blocks. The sides of the quarried sandstone bear the marks of the stonemason's tools. An old rock-lined well possibly dating from the Butterfield period is nearby. A sampling of artifacts at Diamond's Station shows occupation from the 1850s to the early 1900s. There appears to have been a blacksmith's shop here, as evidenced by the numerous remnants of metalwork. Today, a trace of the old overland route from Whitesboro to Diamond's Station is still visible, as is the segment of the road leading away from the stage stop, heading west-southwest across the pasture and down a line of trees toward Gainesville. A 1967 Texas Historical Commission marker, "Diamond Horse Ranch," at the site contains errors regarding family names and the occupants of the adjacent family cemetery. John R. Diamond and his wife, Emeline, are buried here, not "James R. Diamond," as the marker states. In 1859, John R. Diamond owned 320 acres, five horses, and a slave. He subsequently sold the slave and acquired forty-one cattle. In September 1860, he had a net worth of $3,700. In 1861, Diamond's worth declined to $2,370. In 1860, his brother W. W. Diamond owned seven acres and five slaves, for a net valuation of $4,000. See Grayson County Tax Rolls, reel 1, 1846–72, TSLAC.

33. *Dallas Herald*, Dec. 12, 1860, and Jan. 9, 1861 (quotations); Winkler, *Journal of the Secession Convention*, 65; Reynolds, "Texas Troubles," *Handbook*; Niemeyer and Derbes, "Diamond, William Winfield," *Handbook*; Acheson, "Diamond, George Washington," *Handbook*; Acheson and Allardice, "Diamond, James Jackson," *Handbook*; 1860 U.S. Census, Texas Slave Schedules, Grayson Co., NA, M653, R1310, 2–3.

34. Winkler, *Journal of the Secession Convention*, 89–90; Ely, *Where the West Begins*, 28, 139n43. The journal's secession referendum results omit Maverick and Presidio Counties, both of which voted against disunion, which increases the number of antisecession counties in Texas from eighteen to twenty.

35. McCaslin, *Tainted Breeze*, 14–16; Lang, *First Overland Mail: . . . St. Louis to San Francisco*, 109; 1860 U.S. Census, Cooke Co., Tex., NA, M653, R1291, 50; 1860 U.S. Census, Texas Slave Schedules, Cooke Co., NA, M653, R1309, 3; Cooke County Tax Rolls, reel 1, 1848–84, TSLAC; AFT, Bourland homestead site, Jan. 24, 2009, and June 29, 2012. County tax rolls show that in 1859 and 1860, South Carolina native James G. Bourland's assets varied from $29,407 to $37,005. This included 4,140 acres and his home and trading post/general store located at Bourland's Bend, now Delaware Bend, of Red River, north of present-day Dexter, Texas. In addition, Bourland owned twenty-three slaves (housed in four slave quarters on his property), 92 horses, 211 cattle, and a wagon and carriage. The federal 1860 census puts

Bourland's valuation significantly higher, at $56,260. The old Bourland home and slave quarters are long gone, but the visitor can still see the family cemetery (including James Bourland's grave) and the ruins of the old trading post.

36. Smith, *First 100 Years*, 12; Parker, *Through Unexplored Texas*, 84 (quotation 1); Williams, *Old Texas Trails*, 241, 318 (quotation 2); Ormsby, *Butterfield Overland Mail*, 43 (quotation 3); Lang, *First Overland Mail: . . . St. Louis to San Francisco*, 109; 1860 U.S. Census, Cooke Co., Tex., NA, M653, R1291, 40; W. R. Strong, "Reminiscences," *Gainesville Register*, June 16, 1914 (endnote quotation); Cooke County Abstract Office (R. M. Field's information); Michael Collins, *Cooke County, Texas*, 9; Conkling and Conkling, *Butterfield Overland Mail*, 1:294; Paddock, *Twentieth-Century History*, 1:116; PGA, Cooke Co., Tex., NA, RG 28, M841, R122. Residents founded Gainesville on August 15, 1850, naming it in honor of General Edmund Pendleton Gaines. Stephen D. Brown served as the first postmaster of Gainesville, starting on Halloween 1851. The town's Butterfield-era postmaster, Jeremiah E. Hughes, began his tenure on December 11, 1856. The Conklings, unable to definitively state the location of the Butterfield station in Gainesville, said the stage stop and stable was at a tavern somewhere on California Street. Pioneer resident W. R. Strong, however, clearly recalled the station being "where Field's store is now." Located at the northeast corner of the intersection of Rusk and California Streets, the R. M. Field's Store sold books and school supplies. City records show that in June 1913, Field purchased portions of Lots 4 and 5 in Block 17 at the corner of Rusk and California Streets. The site today is a drive-through bank and parking lot. According to J. W. Williams, in 1849, Marcy's California Emigrant Road passed 3 miles north of Gainesville. After Gainesville's founding the following year, a connecting road linked the settlement to the emigrant trail.

37. Cooke County Commissioners Court Minutes, vol. 1, 1857–77, Feb. 21, 1859, 28; Ormsby, *Butterfield Overland Mail*, 43, 44 (quotations). In February 1859, Cooke County commissioners ordered that the overland route be designated a first-class road throughout the county.

38. Diamond, *George Washington Diamond's Account*, 5 (quotations).

39. *Dallas Herald*, Oct. 26, 1859 (quotation).

40. Ibid. (quotations [original emphasis]); Reynolds, *Texas Terror*, 18; 1860 U.S. Census, Texas Slave Schedules, Cooke Co., NA, M653, R1309, 1; Paddock, *Twentieth-Century History*, 2:233; McCaslin, *Tainted Breeze*, 20, 64. Samuel C. Doss owned eight slaves.

41. Diamond, *George Washington Diamond's Account*, 6 (quotations).

42. "The Civil War Day by Day," Special Collections Library, UNC-Chapel Hill, www.lib.unc.edu/blogs/civilwar/index.php/2012/04/17/17-april-1862-it-is-beyond-question-the-most-important-measure-that-has-ever-passed-the-confederate-congress/ (accessed Feb. 18, 2013). See also Ely, "Gone from Texas," 160–84; McCaslin, *Tainted Breeze*, 55.

43. McCaslin, *Tainted Breeze*, 54, 55 (quotation), 58–59, 90–91 (endnote quotations), 94. Further illuminating Peace Party motives, McCaslin says that the majority of members were not involved in violent conspiracies but "simply sought a method by which they could protect themselves, their families, and their homes in a frontier environment beset with violence and chaos." He notes that most "had become convinced by wartime events that the Confederacy could not survive, and they trusted that the Peace Party could provide comparative security until the Federal government could restore order."

44. Clark, *Civil War Recollections*, 23 (quotations), 25; Diamond, *George Washington Diamond's Account*, 33; McCaslin, *Tainted Breeze*, 20, 70, 100 (endnote quotation), 101; GLO, Cooke County Abstract No. 143, Wiley Jones, 640 acres; Cooke County Commissioners Court Minutes, vol. 1, 1857–77, part A, July 4, 1859, p. 41 (Asbury Edminston); ibid., Feb. 17, 1862, p. 93 (Jonathan Edminston); ibid., Aug. 21, 1860, p. 61 (Wiley Jones—Clear Creek); ibid., Feb. 18, 1861, p. 62 (Wiley Jones—county commissioner). In October 1862, in the midst of the

hanging frenzy, military authorities picked up Asbury and Jonathan Edminston, two former Cooke County overseers for the Butterfield Road, and accused them of "duplicity in the Unionist conspiracy." Luckily for the Edminstons, Major John S. Randolph turned them over to the Confederate district court rather than to the Gainesville citizens court.

45. AFT, Great Hanging site in Gainesville on Pecan Creek, 1996–2012; Diamond, *George Washington Diamond's Account*, 52–53 (quotation 1), 53 (quotation 2); Clark, *Civil War Recollections*, 108.

46. Clark, *Civil War Recollections*, 108–9; Barrett and Diamond, *Great Hanging at Gainesville*, 174; AFT, Clark family cemetery near Gainesville, Texas, 1996–2012.

47. Barrett, *Great Hanging at Gainesville*, 7 (quotations).

48. Diamond, *George Washington Diamond's Account*, 17–18; McCaslin, *Tainted Breeze*, 61, 94, 131, 142–45; Acheson and Allardice, "Diamond, James Jackson," *Handbook* (endnote quotation). Sam Hanna Acheson and Bruce Allardice state that James Jackson Diamond "was [also] one of the organizers and managers of the 'citizens' court' formed in Gainesville in October 1862, which brought to trial and hanged . . . persons accused of participating in the supposed 'peace party conspiracy.'"

49. McCaslin, *Tainted Breeze*, 148; John R. Diamond headstone, Diamond Family Cemetery, Whitesboro, Tex.; Grayson County Deed Book S, 480, 601; Grayson County Deed Book T, 493–97; Grayson County Deed Book W, 52, 639; J. R. Diamond and Co., Whitesboro, Credit Report, Texas vol. 14, Grayson County, p. 182a (quotations), DCR, BL; Acheson and Allardice, "Diamond, James Jackson," *Handbook*; Acheson, "Diamond, George Washington," *Handbook*; Diamond, *George Washington Diamond's Account*, xvi, 1–3. George Washington Diamond died in Whitesboro in 1911. His account of the hangings remained unpublished until 1963.

50. Gogobot's online "Salem, Massachusetts, Travel Guide" makes several excellent points that are applicable to Gainesville, Texas: "Visitors to this historically infamous location are in for one of the most unique vacation experiences anywhere in the world. Where else carries [more] connotations of superstition and mystery than this Massachusetts town? The Salem Witch trials, which proceeded in the early 1660's, are now embraced by the local economy as a great way to generate tourist revenue." For more on this, see www.gogobot.com/salem-ma (accessed Feb. 20, 2013) (endnote quotation). For a full listing of tourist attractions in Salem, see "Official Salem MA Guide, Museums and Attractions," http://salem.org/advertisers/C8 (accessed Feb. 20, 2013). For more on the Samantha statue, see "Bewitched Statue, Salem, MA," www.yelp.com/biz/bewitched-statue-salem (accessed Feb. 20, 2013).

51. See Gainesville Chamber of Commerce website, www.gainesvillecofc.com/ (accessed Feb. 20, 2013). For more on the 2012 patriotic award, see "Gainesville, TX—The Most Patriotic Town in America," http://mostpatriotic.us/ (accessed Feb. 20, 2013). For more on Gainesville's Butterfield Stage Players, see www.butterfieldstage.org/#!/9/history/52 (accessed Feb. 20, 2013). See also Steve Campbell, "After 150 Years, a Dark Chapter of Gainesville's Past Still Stirs Passions," *Fort Worth Star-Telegram*, Oct. 7, 2012 (quotations).

52. Campbell, "After 150 Years" (quotations). The Clark family, descendants of hanging victim Nathanial Clark, took over sponsorship of the 150th anniversary event, which went off quietly.

53. Ely, *Where the West Begins*, 121–22, 167n1, 167–68n2; author discussions with former Gainesville mayor Margaret P. Hays in 1996 and 1999. Hays also served on the Cooke County Heritage Society.

54. Ormsby, *Butterfield Overland Mail*, 43, 44 (quotations 1–2), 45–46 (quotation 3); Francaviglia, *Cast Iron Forest*, 1–3, 38–39, 118–19; *S. A. Mitchell's No. 12 Map of the State of Texas, 1859*, VG, SCL, UTA; *A. R. Roessler's 1875 New Map of Texas Prepared and Published for the Bureau*

of Immigration of the State of Texas, ibid. Working its way from Gainesville to Clear Creek in the southwestern corner of Cooke County, the Butterfield Road crossed three drainages running together in close proximity, namely, Wheat, Williams, and Blocker Creeks. Williams Creek derived its name from Dr. Davidson's neighbor, John W. Williams, a thirty-three-year-old farmer from Tennessee, who owned acreage just above the physician's homestead.

55. Tallack, *California Overland Express*, 54 (quotation 1); Richardson, *Beyond the Mississippi*, 225 (quotation 2).

56. "Dr. John Davidson," www.sanjacintomuseum.org/Herzstein_Library/Veteran_Biographies/Browse_Biographies/ (accessed July 19, 2004); Mary Bonsal, "Davidson-Davison Family Resource 1850 Census—Texas," http://homepages.rootsweb.com/~genea/dtx1850.html (accessed July 19, 2004); Mary Bonsal, "Descendants of John Davidson and Ruth Clements," http://homepages.rootsweb.com/~genea/Dzjohnclements.html (accessed July 19, 2004); 1850 U.S. Census, Rusk Co., Tex., NA, M432, R914, 594; 1860 U.S. Census, Cooke Co., Tex., NA, M653, R1291, 65; Smith, *First 100 Years*, 25 (county polling place in 1857); GLO, John Davidson's Cooke County Land File; GLO, *1935 Map of Cooke County*; GLO, *1858 Map of Cooke County*; Cooke County Tax Rolls, reel 1, 1848–84, TSLAC; unpublished Conkling photo of Davidson's Station, box 7, RPC Papers. The 1850 federal census lists Davidson with a net worth of $5,000. By 1860, his net worth had almost quadrupled, to almost $19,000. The county tax rolls, however, provide differing valuations. From 1859 to 1861, his assets ranged from a low of $12,855 to a high of $13,679. This included 1,275 acres, 11 slaves, 22 horses, and 120 cattle, along with a buggy and wagon. Neighbor William Downing lived on nearby Blocker Creek.

57. "104 Year Old Inglish Home Rests on Historic Property," *Gainesville Daily Register*, Nov. 2, 1975; CM 1931, p. 133, box 9, RPC Papers; Smith, *First 100 Years*, 27; AFT, Davidson's Station and neighboring antebellum ruins, June 21 and July 22, 1999, and June 9, 2003 (JA).

58. Lang, *First Overland Mail: . . . San Francisco to Memphis*, 39 (quotation); AFT, route between Davidson's and Spring Station, 2005–13. The *San Francisco Daily Evening Bulletin* reporter listed the distance from Davidson's to Spring Station as 10 miles, but it is actually 13. See also 1860 U.S. Census, Montague Co., Tex., NA, M653, R1301, 70B, 71; copy of reading file for "Uz Community," Montague County historical marker, History Programs Division, Texas Historical Commission Library Archives. According to the July 1860 census, fifty-six-year-old Thomas Sales and his fifty-four-year-old wife Ann, both European immigrants, and their twenty-five-year-old stage driver–lodger, William Donoho of Tennessee, were neighbors of John and Henry Braden, whose namesake stream, Braden Branch, is next to the Spring Station site. Braden Branch is a tributary of Denton Creek, which runs southeasterly through Montague, Wise, and Denton Counties. Besides managing their Butterfield station, the Sales also farmed. William Donoho also bunked occasionally at John Russell's hotel in Sherman, Texas. Following the Overland Road today from Davidson's to Spring Station, one would take FM 922 to Rosston, Texas, then turn southwest onto County Road 362, then northwest to FM 455, and then west-southwest on Valentine Bluff Road (named after landowner W. H. Valentine). Valentine Bluff, which overlooks Spring Station, ranges in height from 1,100 to 1,134 feet. Nineteenth-century travelers through the area frequently commented on the impressive scenery, with its dramatic cliffs and sweeping panoramic views.

59. Texas Historical Commission, "Montague County: Butterfield Overland Stage Line Crossing," in *Atlas*; Montague County Historical Commission, *Story of Montague County*, 128 (quotation 1); "Addendum to Original Narrative History of Uz Community," 1990 research file for "Uz Community," Montague County historical marker, History Programs Division, Texas Historical Commission Library Archives

(quotation 2); Williams, "Marcy and Butterfield Trails," 69 (quotation 3); GLO, *May 1924 Montague County Land Map*; GLO, file notes for Montague County, John P. Braden (abstract no. 54), Henry Braden (abstract no. 55), Joseph S. Braden (file no. 55, certificate 10), W. R. Bean (abstract no. 105), W. H. Valentine (abstract no. 832); Montague County Abstract Office, plat for W. R. Bean survey (abstract no. 105); 1860 U.S. Census, Montague Co., Tex., NA, M653, R1301, 71; MT, New Harp; AFT, Spring Station site and Uz Community, 2005–13. After the Civil War, residents founded the now-vanished village of Uz near the Spring Station site.

60. W. R. Strong, "Reminiscences," *Gainesville Register*, June 16, 1914 (endnote quotations 1–2); AFT, Spring Station site and Uz Community, 2005–13. W. R. Strong of Gainesville mentions in his memoirs that "the next station [after Davidson's] was the town of Uz in Montague County." He recalls, "I helped to cut the stage line road through Cooke County, it went by Pleasant Mound and across the prairie to Uz." Strong's reminiscences as an elderly man place Pleasant Mound east of Uz, but the historic community of Pleasant Hill (not Mound) is actually located 4.5 miles southwest of Uz, on the Butterfield line. As previously mentioned, Braden Branch derives its name from Henry Braden and his son, John P. Braden. The father (in 1871) and son (in 1869) patented adjoining 160-acre parcels in the town of Uz. Braden Branch cuts through Henry Braden's Survey 3-3349. W. H. Valentine, namesake of Valentine Bluff, lived a mile east of the Bradens in Survey P-423. Today, several sections of the Upper or Western Cross Timbers in Wise and Montague Counties are part of the LBJ National Grasslands, which has its regional headquarters in Decatur, Texas.

61. *Dallas Herald*, Sept. 22, 1858 (quotations 1–2), Mar. 9, 1859 (quotations 3–5); Montague County Police Court (Commissioners Court) Minutes Book A, Aug. 10, 1874 (endnote quotation), and Oct. 18, 1875. Butterfield historians Margaret and Roscoe Conkling make no mention of Spring Station in their research. Spring Station is one of several previously unknown Texas Butterfield stations that are included in this study for the first time. In 1874, Montague County Commissioners requested that residents living along the Butterfield Trail "view and mark out alterations in the public road known as the Overland Stage Road from the eastern county line of Montague County [bordering Cooke County] at or near Mansfield Esters . . . to the Wise County line." Commissioners assigned Robert Bean, Ben Hodges, W. H. Valentine (who ran a post–Civil War store on the old road), A. Shelrum, and Joseph Gregg to carry out the work.

62. MT, New Harp, Smyrna; Ormsby, *Butterfield Overland Mail*, 44 (quotation 1), 44–45 (quotation 2); Ralph Roberts, "Relatives of Ralph and Pat Roberts, Joel Jackson Connely," http://worldconnect.rootsweb.com/cgi-bin/igm.cgi?op=GET&db=ralphroberts&id=I099819 (accessed July 20, 2004); Ralph Roberts, "Relatives of Ralph and Pat Roberts, Arberry Walker," http://worldconnect.rootsweb.com/cgi-bin/igm.cgi?op=GET&db=ralphroberts&id=I099894 (accessed July 20, 2004); Ralph Roberts. "Relatives of Ralph and Pat Roberts, Josiah Washington Connely," http://worldconnect.rootsweb.com/cgi-bin/igm.cgi?op=GET&db=ralphroberts&id=I100410 (accessed July 21, 2004); 1860 U.S. Census, Wise Co., Tex., NA, M653, R1308, 15; Wise County Tax Rolls, reel 1, 1856–86, TSLAC; Ball Knob Cemetery Information Table, "Joel Jackson Connely," http://homepages.rootsweb.com/~drycreek/ballknobinfo.htm (accessed July 21, 2004); GLO, *1862 Map of Wise County*; GLO, file notes for Wise County, J. J. Connelly [sic] (abstract nos. 228, 388, 903), S. E. Clement (abstract no. 217); GLO, file notes for Cooke County, S. E. Clement (abstract no. 273); Wise County Surveyor Records, Book A, 98, 294–95, Book B, 64; Wise County Deed Book F, 17. J. J. Connely was born March 12, 1818, and died July 11, 1878. In 1860, the federal census listed Joel Jackson Connely's net worth as $2,500. County tax rolls for 1861 show his assets as 160 acres, 3 horses, and 100 cattle, for a net worth of $800. In

1857, Joel Jackson's younger brother, Josiah Washington, lived in Wise County, but by the outbreak of the Civil War he had moved to Coles County, Illinois. Josiah likely helped his brother operate the mail station from 1858 to 1859. In 1860, J. W. Connely owned 640 acres and 75 cattle, for a net worth of $1,180. The county tax rolls misspell his name as "J. W. Conley." In 1860, Sam Meldred, a thirty-year-old Overland Mail Company stage driver from New York, was boarding with the Connelys at their stage stop. Joel Jackson Connely, his wife, Arbery, and their son, Joel Jackson, Jr., are buried at Ball Knob Cemetery in Wise County. The spelling "Connely" used in this text is what appears on the Connely headstones in Ball Knob Cemetery and in the 1860 census. Many authors misspell the name. The first Wise County land map, dating from 1862, shows J. J. Connely's name on Survey S-3468 near the stage stop. S. E. Clement later patented the survey near the station that Connely had originally filed on. Connely abandoned his preemption claim for this 160-acre parcel and filed for a new preemption elsewhere. Interestingly, Clement also patented another survey near another Butterfield station, Davidson's, in Cooke County.

63. Ormsby, *Butterfield Overland Mail*, 45 (quotations 1–2); Lang, *First Overland Mail: . . . St. Louis to San Francisco*, 125 (quotation 3); AFT, Connely's Station, July 18, 2000 (JA), and June 11, 2003 (JA); CJ, Oct. 27, 1930, and Aug. 17, 1932, box 9, RPC Papers; Sept. 24, 1945, letter from J. W. Edwards to Arthur H. Clark Co., box 14, RPC Papers (endnote quotation 1); Wise County Historical Survey Committee, *Wise County History*, 1:278, 279 (endnote quotation 2); Williams, "Marcy and Butterfield Trails," 67 (endnote quotation 3), 68 (endnote quotation 4). The Conklings left no pictures of Connely's, but they did say that landowner John Wesley Edwards assisted them in locating the stage stop situated near Sunset and the old community of Pella. Edwards died in May 1991, but in the years after the Conklings' visit, he conducted additional fieldwork here, determining the layout of the stage stop. In a 1945 letter to Arthur H. Clark, the publisher of the Conklings' book, Edwards discussed the extensive fieldwork he conducted at Connely's Station: "In a number of low mounds, excavations have yielded what appears to be fragments of human bone, some charred, mingled with charcoal, bits of dishes and crockery, square nails, charred acorns, very large teeth and the tusks of old boars. There are also a number of pointed instruments, of varying designs, some expertly carved, resembling toothbrush handles. Also a battered musket ball or two." Thirty years later, in 1975, Edwards wrote more about the layout of this Butterfield stage stop in an article for the new Wise County history book: "Connolly's [sic] Station site is about fifty or sixty yards wide. . . . The stage company barns were about a hundred yards west of the station site. The site of the blacksmith shop is about a hundred yards south of the station site." In a 1938 interview with J. W. Williams, L. K. Hunter recalled, "In the spring of 1882, I first saw the old stage stand. . . . The remains of the old chimney were still there; a few pickets were still there." Williams said, "Hunter remembered the name applied to the old stage depot as 'The Connelly [sic] Stage Stand.'" Today, the station ruins, located on a hill commanding a fine view of the western horizon, sit in a clearing ringed by a Cross Timbers forest of blackjack and post oak. Numerous large pieces of weathered, lichen-covered sandstone used for the log station's foundation lay on the edge of this clearing. A sampling of surface artifacts verified the location as Connely's, including period pistol balls, Henry and Spencer shell casings, a spoon, a barrel strap, harmonica ribs, square nails, pottery, glass, pieces of crockery, and hand-forged metal implements. Mr. Robert Lee Morris of Chico told the Conklings of a large sawmill located on Brushy Creek during the heyday of Connely's Station.

64. AFT, Connely's, July 18, 2000 (JA), and June 11, 2003 (JA).

65. See Paddock, *Twentieth-Century History*, 1:116, 2:497–98; Alton Cook, "The Decatur Cemetery and the Milhollon Family," http://freepages.genealogy.rootsweb.com/~drycreek/oaklawn.htm (accessed

July 20, 2004); Conley [*sic*] and Ball Credit Report, Texas vol. 33, Wise County, p. 340 (quotations 1–2), DCR, BL; Cates, *Pioneer History*, 172, 173 (quotation 3), 239–40; Wise County Surveyor Records, Book A, 294–95; Wise County Deed Book D, 107–108; Wise County Deed Book E, 63; Wise County Deed Book E-H-I-J, 72; Wise County Deed Book F, 151. Eventually Connely patented land in Wise County, 6.5 miles north of Decatur.

66. J. B. Earhart to Houston, Mar. 6, 1860, box 301-31, SH Papers, TSLAC (quotations). Information on Earhart comes from Britton, "Earhart, Joseph Bonaparte," *Handbook*; Cates, *Pioneer History*, 299–301; Conkling and Conkling, *Butterfield Overland Mail*, 1:300–303; 1860 U.S. Census, Jack Co., Tex., NA, M653, R1298, 77–78 (the census incorrectly lists his birthdate and birthplace); Thrapp, *Encyclopedia of Frontier Biography*, 44; Lang, *First Overland Mail: . . . St. Louis to San Francisco*, 109; Paddock, *Twentieth-Century History*, 1:122; McConnell, *West Texas Frontier*, 1:165.

67. 1860 U.S. Census, Wise Co., Tex., NA, M653, R1308, 17 (Elias Edens and James Doyle); MT, Smyrna, Sunset, Chico, Crafton; GLO, Map #63134, *1896 Map of Wise County, Texas* (Edens land parcels); GLO, file notes for Wise County, Elias Edens (abstract nos. 281, 282, 416, 417); GLO, Map #3701, *1868 Map of Jack County*; Cates, *Pioneer History*, 67; Wise County Commissioner Court Minutes, book 1, 15, 57–58, 78. When the Wise County Courthouse burned on November 25, 1881, most antebellum records were lost. References to the Butterfield Route through Wise County, however, appear in later commissioners' court minutes. On December 24, 1881, commissioners appointed J. T. Litchfield as county overseer of the portion of the Jacksboro-Gainesville Road between the crossing on Brushy Creek to Cumby Ranch. February 21, 1882, minutes reference the same road continuing northeast to the Pella community and Montague County line. From Connelly's to Earhart's, the Butterfield Road runs southwest to Venchoner Creek near its intersection with modern Wise County Road 1770 (where Elias Edens and his neighbor, Butterfield stage driver James Doyle of New York, lived in June 1860). Edens's four contiguous parcels are all in the Venchoner Creek vicinity. Farmer Elias Edens, of Tennessee, and his wife, Mary, of Arkansas, had a one-year-old daughter. Thirty-five year-old James Doyle and his thirty-six year-old wife, Julia (from Ireland), had four young children.

68. 1860 U.S. Census, Jack Co., Tex., NA, M653, R1298, 77–78; 1860 U.S. Census, Texas Slave Schedules, Jack Co., NA, M653, R1311, 3; Conkling and Conkling, *Butterfield Overland Mail*, 1:302 (quotation); CM 1931, p. 134, box 9, RPC Papers; Jack County Tax Rolls, reel 1, 1857–95, TSLAC. In 1860, the federal census listed J. B. Earhart's net worth as $9,500, whereas Jack County tax rolls from the same year put it at $6,660, which included 2 slaves, 4 horses, and 700 head of cattle.

69. Lang, *First Overland Mail: . . . San Francisco to Memphis*, 42 (quotations 2, 4, and 5), 45 (quotations 1 and 3).

70. Lang, *First Overland Mail: . . . St. Louis to San Francisco*, 125; CJ, Oct. 27, 1930, box 9, RPC Papers (quotation).

71. Conkling and Conkling, *Butterfield Overland Mail*, 1:302; CJ, Oct. 27 (quotation) and Oct. 28, 1930, box 9, RPC Papers; AFT, Earhart's Station, July 19, 2000 (JA). There are two versions of the Liff Earhart/Henry Bates story, one from the Conklings' book and the other from their unpublished Texas field trip journal. The original, unpublished version is used here. At Earhart's Station, much physical evidence remains. The stage stop sits on a high bluff overlooking Martin's Creek, with a panoramic view of the surrounding forest and pastures.

72. Brune, *Springs of Texas*, 477–78. Another local name for Earhart Springs is Reeder Springs.

73. 1860 U.S. Census, Jack Co., Tex., NA, M653, R1298, 78; Paddock, *Twentieth-Century History*, 2:387–88 (quotation); Feb. 22, 1882, Wise County Commissioner Court Minutes, book 1, 58; AFT, Earhart's Station and surrounding vicinity, July 19, 2000 (JA); Wise County Historical Survey Committee, *Wise County History*, 1:271; McConnell, *West Texas Frontier*, 1:159, 162, 165; Cates, *Pioneer History*, 321–22; Conkling and Conkling, *Butterfield Overland Mail*, 1:299–304, 306–308; McConnell, *West Texas Frontier*, 2:143–49; "Clark Cemetery, Grayson County" (RootsWeb.com); *Amarillo Daily News*, Mar. 13, 1931 (endnote quotation); Oversized Map and Sketch Box, RPC Papers; CJ, Oct. 27–28, 1930, box 9, RPC Papers. Getting the lay of the land at Earhart's is a daunting task because there are numerous historic sites of differing time periods commingling over many acres. At Hog-Eye there are several acres of ruins, evidenced by decaying notched cabin logs studded with old square nails, old rock-lined wells, a root cellar, quarried sandstone blocks, collapsed wood-framed barns, glass, china, and crockery. From the large amount of stone and lumber here, it is evident that in its prime Hog-Eye was an important and substantial settlement on the Wise-Jack County line. After the federal government withdrew its troops from the region in the spring of 1861, Indian attacks on Cross Timbers settlers increased markedly. Left on their own and without the support of the federal army, local Texas Ranger units proved unable to defend sections of the western frontier. At Hog-Eye Prairie, the severity of Comanche raids forced fifteen families to move their homes close together and "fort up" for communal protection. The Earhart family experienced three major attacks during the war, the third skirmish involving thirty-five Indians. By early 1865, the depredations had become so acute that Ranger captain J. B. Earhart abandoned Hog-Eye and moved his family eastward into Wise County, to son-in-law Joe Henry Martin's home, 15 miles from Decatur. Albert Gallatin McClure farmed and ranched on Hog-Eye Prairie until 1892. Not far from the Hog-Eye community is a nineteenth-century grave constructed in a large, stacked rock square, its occupants' identities unknown. Also nearby are the ruins of two other, and perhaps older, settlements. One of these sites is marked only by crudely quarried blocks of native sandstone that litter the ground, enough foundation stones for perhaps five or six log cabins. On the west side of Martin's Creek is the house Liff Earhart built in the 1870s or 1880s for his mother, Mary Earhart, widow of Joseph Bonaparte Earhart. After the Civil War, J. B. Earhart became one of the first cattleman in Clay County, Texas, and was active driving herds to Kansas during 1867 and 1868. He died on February 28, 1869, in Grayson County and is buried in Clark Cemetery in Denison. Wise County records reference an 1882 road from Chico to Hog-Eye. When the Conklings visited the Earhart's Station site in October 1930, they met the landowner, banker-rancher Robert Lee Morris of Chico and president of the Butterfield Trail Association. This association worked at improving cooperation between the federal government, states, and local counties in designating and promoting the Butterfield Road across the nation, an effort that never came to fruition. In Texas, legislation to designate the Butterfield Road as a Texas state highway in 1931 failed after "a fight between Sweetwater and Abilene over trade territories."

74. Huckabay, *Ninety-Four Years*, 20–21; Jack County Commissioners Court Minutes, vol. 1, Aug. 7 and 16, Sept. 9 (quotation), and Oct. 19, 1858. The 7 miles between Earhart's and West Fork of the Trinity is one of the shortest distances between stations on the Texas portion of the route.

75. GLO, Map #3701, *1868 Map of Jack County*; GLO, Map #3699, *February 1896 Map of Jack County, Texas*; CJ, Aug. 16, 1932, box 9, RPC Papers; Conkling and Conkling, *Butterfield Overland Mail*, 1:306–8; Richardson, *Beyond the Mississippi*, 226 (quotations 1–2).

76. 1860 U.S. Census, Jack Co., Tex., NA, M653, R1298, 99–100; 1860 U.S. Census, Texas Slave Schedules, Jack Co., NA, M653, R1311, 3; Winkler, *Journal of the Secession Convention*, 89; Huckabay, *Ninety-Four Years*, 76–77, 92 (quotation); Jack County Tax Rolls, reel 1, 1857–95. While the 1860 federal census for Jack County lists no station keeper

for West Fork, Bean managed the station there. At Earhart's and Connely's, the census taker also mentioned no station keeper, but primary sources indicate that both men ran their respective stage stops. In 1860, Bean owned 200 acres, 6 slaves, 3 horses, and 150 cattle, for a net worth of $7,795.

77. AFT, West Fork of the Trinity Station, July 18, 2000 (JA), and June 21, 2005.

78. Conkling and Conkling, *Butterfield Overland Mail*, 1:308.

79. GLO, Map #3701, *1868 Map of Jack County*; GLO, Map #3699, *February 1896 Map of Jack County, Texas*; MT, Jacksboro NE; Huckabay, *Ninety-Four Years*, 20; Kellogg, *M. K. Kellogg's Texas Journal*, 88 (quotation). Since the second half of the twentieth century, gas pipelines and power transmission lines have come dangerously close to obliterating both the West Fork stage stop and the river crossing. In 2005, I testified in Austin, before the Public Utility Commission of Texas, against a proposed utility transmission line through eastern Jack County. After determining that the utility construction might damage the historical integrity of the Butterfield line and, most notably, Earhart's and West Fork of the Trinity Stations, state officials ordered the line moved elsewhere.

80. Ormsby, *Butterfield Overland Mail*, 46; Richardson, *Beyond the Mississippi*, 226; AFT, Jacksboro, 1998–2014; Conkling and Conkling, *Butterfield Overland Mail*, 1:308–10; MT, Jacksboro; Huckabay, *Ninety-Four Years*, 27. The Jacksboro station is on the north bank of Lost Creek, across from present-day Fort Richardson. According to the Conklings, during the 1930s, this site was next to a set of Texaco storage tanks, just northeast of where a bridge once spanned Lost Creek. In 1860, county commissioners built the first Jack County jail next to the Jacksboro stage stop.

81. PGA, Jack Co., Tex., NA, RG 28, M841, R124; Postmaster General Order Journals, June 30, 1858, vol. 41, Jan. 18, 1858–June 30, 1858, NA, RG 28, entry 1; ibid., Jan. 15, 1859, vol. 43, Dec. 20, 1858–Mar. 12, 1859; Huckabay, *Ninety-Four Years*, 25; 1860 U.S. Census, Jack Co., Tex., NA, M653, R1298, 94; GLO, Jack County Abstract No. 449; 1859 Annual Report of the U.S. Commissioner of Indian Affairs, Nov. 26, 1859, p. 623, citing Dec. 25, 1858, resolutions passed by a gathering of Jack County citizens; Rochette, *Bourland in North Texas*, 1:269–71, A-313. Dr. John B. Baird and his wife, Agnes, both from Kentucky, had three children. Baird appears in the Jack County Commissioners Court Minutes for 1858 as a county school examiner and again in 1860 as a member of the Precinct Two Overland Road crew, which included William A. Nix.

82. Huckabay, *Ninety-Four Years*, 27; Richardson, *Beyond the Mississippi*, 226 (quotation).

83. Richardson, *Beyond the Mississippi*, 226 (quotations [original emphasis]).

84. B. L. Ham bail bond, Sept. 1, 1859, District Court Criminal Records, Jack Co., Tex. (quotation 1); Dorcas Ham divorce petition, Sept. 17, 1862, *Dorcas M. Ham v. Berry L. Ham*, Case No. 41, Divorce Records, District Clerk's Office, Jack Co., Tex.; Boggs, *My Playhouse*, 350 (quotation 2). The *San Francisco Bulletin* account in Boggs's book says that the Ham-Lowe shooting affray took place at Fort Chadbourne, but the newspaper is in error, as it occurred at Jacksboro Station. Jack County District Court records contain no subsequent reference to Lowe's murder, and authorities likely dropped the charges against Ham.

85. Jack County Commissioners Court Minutes, vol. 1, Aug. 19, 1857, Sept. 8, 1858; Horton, *History of Jack County*, 114 (endnote quotation 1); Huckabay, *Ninety-Four Years*, 19–21, 24–26, 31 (endnote quotation 2); McConnell, *West Texas Frontier*, 1:163; GLO, Map #3699, *February 1896 Map of Jack County, Texas*; 1860 U.S. Census, Jack Co., Tex., NA, M653, R1298, 98; MT, Jacksboro, Barton's Chapel; AFT, Burwick Road, Winn-Hill Cemetery, and Potato Valley, 2004–14; Williams,

"Marcy and Butterfield Trails," 73 (endnote quotation 3). In 1860, G. V. Alford, a Butterfield stage driver from North Carolina, was boarding with the Ham family. Jack County historian Thomas Horton wrote in 1933 that Berry L. Ham "lived six miles west from Jacksboro and kept the old Butterfield Stage Station." Another county chronicler, Ida Lasater Huckabay, wrote in 1947 that "Mr. Ham kept the stage stand at Ham Spring, a few miles west of town." A third regional historian, J. C. McConnell, also writing in 1933, said that Ham settled 12 miles west of Jacksboro. The conflicting mileages cited by these historians have confused people regarding Ham, his residence, and his duties for the Overland Mail Company. Ham lived at Ham Spring, 5 miles from Jacksboro. He managed two Butterfield stage stops: Jacksboro Station and Fishpond Station, 12 miles west of Jacksboro and southeast of Fishpond Mountain. Some locals insist that Ham Spring was a Butterfield station, but this is incorrect. Since Butterfield already had a stage stop in Jacksboro, the company would not locate another station only 5 miles away. Mules and horses do not need to be swapped out at 5 miles. The facts show that the average minimum mileage between Butterfield stations in Texas is 10 miles. It is possible that stage drivers briefly watered their livestock at Ham Spring before continuing on to Fishpond Station. Horton's and Huckabay's mileage figures correspond to Ham's homestead at Ham Spring, while McConnell cites the distance to Butterfield's Fishpond Station. The Conklings were unaware of Berry L. Ham, his ranch at Ham Spring, and the Butterfield station southeast of Fishpond Mountain. J. W. Williams says that the Butterfield Road went through "the H.B. Overby survey, [and] passed near Ham Spring near the northwest corner of the B.L. Ham survey, six miles west of Jacksboro." While Williams knew of Berry Ham, he was unaware of Fishpond Station.

86. Jack County Tax Rolls, reel 1, 1857–95, TSLAC; Texas Ranger Muster Roll index cards, 1838–1900, TSLAC; Dorcas Ham divorce petition, Sept. 17, 1862 (quotation 1), Berry Ham response, Sept. 18, 1863 (quotation 2), Berry and Dorcas Ham divorce agreement, Sept. 19, 1863, *Dorcas M. Ham v. Berry L. Ham*, Case No. 41, Divorce Records, District Clerk's Office, Jack Co., Tex.; *The State of Texas v. Henry Thompson, James Parrott, B. L. Ham*, Case No. 68, District Court Civil Records, Jack Co., Tex.; AFT, B. L. Ham grave, Myrtle Cemetery, Ennis, Tex., Mar. 28, 2015; AFT, Dorcas M. [Ham] Williams grave, Oakwood Cemetery, Jacksboro, Tex., Mar. 29, 2015. Berry Lewis Ham was born on October 16, 1812, in Tennessee and died in Ennis, Texas, on November 16, 1879. Dorcas Matilda Ham Williams was born on October 20, 1823, in Tennessee and died in Jacksboro, Texas, on July 4, 1914. Berry and Dorcas Ham married in June 1838 in Milam County, Texas. Their divorce was granted on September 19, 1863. Dorcas subsequently married Thomas W. Williams. In 1861, the Hams owned 2,338 acres in Jack County, a town lot in Jacksboro, 3 slaves, 5 horses, and 600 cattle. They also had property in Cass, Navarro, Ellis, and Milam Counties totaling 2,779 acres. In all, their net worth was $18,189. In September 1862, during the Hams' divorce proceedings, authorities arrested Berry Ham for illegal gambling (playing cards for money) in the Jack County district clerk's office. A jury subsequently found Ham guilty and fined him ten dollars. Berry Ham enrolled as a private in the Texas Rangers on three occasions: on April 11, 1841, on July 18, 1841, and on January 14, 1860.

87. Huckabay, *Ninety-Four Years*, 19–21, 24–26; Kellogg, *M. K. Kellogg's Texas Journal*, 151 (quotation).

88. Bourland to Runnels, Jan. 16, 1859, box 301-28, HRR Papers, TSLAC (quotation 1); *Dallas Herald*, Dec. 5 (quotation 2) and Dec. 12, 1860 (quotation 3). The December 12 issue also reported that a woman burned to death while camping with her father near Ham's Ranch on the overland road. Mr. Bragg and his daughter, concerned about numerous Indians in the area, had stopped for the evening rather than risk further travel. The daughter's clothing went up in flames while she

was tending the campfire. The Braggs were en route to a new home in neighboring Young County.

89. Kellogg, *M. K. Kellogg's Texas Journal*, 151; GLO, Map #76226, *Charles W. Pressler's 1867 Traveller's Map of the State of Texas*. Fishpond Mountain also appears on GLO, Map #3699, *February 1896 Map of Jack County, Texas*. Before splitting off from Burwick Road, the Butterfield Trail passed by Winn Hill Cemetery. Kellogg did not provide a name for this stage stop, so I have taken the liberty of naming it after the nearest prominent landmark, Fishpond Mountain, located in Jermyn, Texas. Period maps show the overland road from Jacksboro to Belknap passing to the south of Fishpond Mountain.

90. Kellogg, *M. K. Kellogg's Texas Journal*, 151 (quotations); AFT, Western Burwick Road, Dec. 2012, and Fishpond Station, Mar. 4–5, 2014 (JA, PD). During several field trips in December 2012, I tried unsuccessfully to locate exactly where the Butterfield Road split off from Burwick Road. During a subsequent outing in early March 2014 with Joe Allen and Patrick Dearen, Allen located this point. From here, Allen, Dearen, and I traced the overland road west across a mesquite and post-oak prairie to a prominent hill. Allen pinpointed the road going up the eastern side of this hill. On the west side, down in a flat next to the creek, we located the station site described by Kellogg. Here we found a wealth of artifacts, including pistol balls, Spencer and Henry cartridges, square nails, chain link, a harmonica rib, an old fork, a metal button, and period implements.

91. Copy of report from Capt. C. B. McLellan, 6th Cav., to Lt. S. H. Bodfish, Fort Richardson, Tex., July 16, 1870, in Carter, *From Yorktown to Santiago*, 141–46; Capps, *Warren Wagontrain Raid*, 32; Kellogg, *M. K. Kellogg's Texas Journal*, 149 (quotation 1), 150–51; Nye, *Carbine and Lance*, map between pp. 10 and 11, 123–30; Hamilton, *Sentinel of the Southern Plains*, 60–62, 70, 78–80; Wilbarger, *Indian Depredations in Texas*, 551–73, 579–82; MT, Bryson, Newcastle, Graham; McClellan, "Johnson, Britton," *Handbook*; King, "Salt Creek Prairie," *Handbook* (quotations 2–3); AFT, Turtle Hole Creek, Sept. 27, 2000 (JA); AFT, Loving Ranch Road, conical hill, and Warren Wagon Train site, 2000–2005 (JA). A short distance south of modern Loving Ranch Road and close to the Jack-Young County line lie the ruins of an old stage stop known as Rock Station. Over the years, some writers have incorrectly described Rock Station, a post–Civil War station on Ben Ficklin's Fort Concho–Fort Smith Mail Line, as a Butterfield stage stop. Ficklin's postbellum mail line ran over part of the same route that Butterfield had used a decade earlier. According to an 1870 report by Captain C. B. McLellan of the Sixth Cavalry, Rock Station was 16 miles from Jacksboro, which puts it 6 miles east of Butterfield's Murphy's Station. The antebellum Overland Mail Company would not have built stations only 6 miles apart, as this would be a wasteful duplication of service. Mules do not need to be changed out after only 6 miles. Moreover, the location of Rock Station does not fit the terrain Kellogg describes in his journal, nor does it match the mileage he provides. In sum, Rock Station is not Fishpond Station; these are two different sites from different periods. In July 1870, a raiding party led by the Kiowa chief Kicking Bird attacked the mail coach at Rock Station. In his report, McLellan calls the stage stop both Rock Station and Rocky Station. Benjamin Capps describes Rock Station as "abandoned," but Kicking Bird's braves attacked a stagecoach there in 1870, so apparently Ben Ficklin was still using the station. Just west of the county line, the Butterfield Road enters Salt Creek Prairie, which extends westward to Fort Belknap (Salt Creek, the namesake of the prairie, is 6 miles east of Fort Belknap and flows into present-day Lake Graham). On its way to Belknap, the overland road passes just to the north of 1,400-foot Cox Mountain, and almost 2 miles farther on, it approaches Flint Creek. As it crosses the creek, the overland trail passes under the shadow of a 1,300-foot conical sandstone hill a half mile to the northwest. The summit of this rocky outcrop provides a commanding view of the sur-

rounding grasslands. On May 18, 1871, a hundred Kiowa and Comanche raiders were hiding on the slope of this hill, waiting for suitable prey to pass below on the old Butterfield Road. At midafternoon, a train of ten wagons hauling corn to Fort Griffin approached from the east. Twelve teamsters guarded the wagons, owned by the freighting company Warren and Dubose. A bugle rang out from the sandstone knob, and a wave of warriors swept down into the Flint Creek watershed. The raiders decimated the wagon train, raining a hail of arrows and bullets upon the hapless teamsters. Seven of them died in the attack. Afterward, the Indians scalped, burned, and mutilated their corpses with axes. Continuing westward along the Butterfield Road, within 4 miles one comes to the site of another 1871 Indian massacre. On January 24 of that year, twenty-five Kiowa warriors forced Britt Johnson and three other black freighters to make a last stand along the overland road at Turtle Hole Creek, 2 miles south of Flat Top Mountain. The four African Americans, surrounded by Indians on Salt Creek Prairie with no chance of escape, killed their horses and used them as breastworks. The teamsters bravely kept up a withering rifle fire from behind their dead mounts until the Kiowas finally overran their position.

Chapter 3. Detour to Decatur and Bridgeport

1. Cates, *Pioneer History*, 109, 225–27, 310, 457–58, 460. Many writers have consulted Cliff D. Cates's 1907 book for information on early Wise County history. However, there are major deficiencies in Cates's work regarding Butterfield, which this chapter corrects.

2. Ibid.; Britton, "Hunt, William Hudson," *Handbook* (endnote quotation); Gammel, *Laws of Texas*, 5:238–40; Texas Surveyors Association, *Three Dollars Per Mile*, 429, 431. Hunt was born in Ithaca, New York, on May 1, 1815. In 1836, he relocated to Texas, where he became a surveyor and lieutenant colonel in the Republic of Texas army. Hunt was a member of the Santa Fe expedition and fought in the Mexican War. He and his wife, Catherine, had five children. Catherine died in April 1861. Three years later, Hunt was fatally injured in a wagon or buggy accident "involving a runaway team" near West Fork. He died on January 13, 1864, and was buried at Cactus Hill. During the construction of Lake Bridgeport, workers moved the Hunt family graves to Bridgeport's Eastside Cemetery. After Catherine and William Hunt's deaths, Sylvanus Reed, a family friend, a fellow director of the West Fork Bridge Company, and a lodger at Hunt's home, adopted the Hunt children and raised them.

3. 1860 U.S. Census, Wise Co., Tex., NA, M653, R1308, 21, 27, 67, 75; Cates, *Pioneer History*, 62 (quotation), 66–68, 97–98, 222–27; GLO, Wise County Abstract No. 7; Wise County Deed Book E, 248; Wise County Deed Book F, 38, 98, 129; State of Texas, *Journal of the House*, 490–91, 499, 598–99, 640, 659, 673–74; State of Texas, *Journal of the Senate*, 495, 510, 531–33; Gammel, *Laws of Texas*, 5:238–40; Daniel Howell and A. E. Allen, General Store, Taylorsville, 1859–60 Credit Reports, Texas vol. 33, Wise County, p. 31 (endnote quotations 1–5), DCR, BL; Absalom Bishop and Edward Blythe, Decatur, General Store and Retail Grocers Credit Reports, 1859–61, p. 318 (endnote quotations 6–8), in ibid.; PGA, Wise Co., Tex., NA, RG 28, M841, R127; 1860 U.S. Census, Texas Slave Schedules, Wise Co., NA, M653, R1286, 1–2; Wise County Tax Rolls, reel 1, 1856–86, TSLAC. Daniel Howell served as the postmaster of Decatur while it was still called Taylorsville (1857–58) from May 5, 1857, to September 23, 1857, and again from June 10, 1858, to March 13, 1861. Howell was one of the county's largest slaveholders, with seven slaves. In 1860, Howell's net worth was $23,000. He was reportedly "sober," "reliable," "honest," "energetic," and "of good business habits and business capacity." Howell's partner, thirty-year-old Alfred Elmore Allen of Tennessee, listed his net worth as $6,000. William Hudson Hunt was the postmaster of Cactus

Hill from June 30, 1858, until July 7, 1860, when the U.S. Postmaster General closed his post office. In 1860, the forty-five-year-old Hunt had a net worth of $19,000, including two slaves, 4,943 acres, a town lot in Decatur, 24 horses, 200 cattle, and 5,700 sheep. Hunt's business associate and neighbor, thirty-five-year-old Pearce Woodward of Pennsylvania, listed assets of $10,500, including two slaves, 1,908 acres, 12 horses, and 750 cattle. In 1864, residents elected Woodward a county commissioner. Thirty-six-year-old George Isbell, of Tennessee, had property valued at $5,000, including 160 acres, 75 horses, 12 cattle, and 1,200 sheep. Absalom Bishop owned 1,636 acres, a town lot in Decatur, and five slaves, for a total valuation of $15,183. Period credit reports state that Bishop was "[s]aid to get tipsy at times" and was "said to have failed once or twice before, once as a defaulter in Georgia." His "business capacity [was] poor . . . undoubtedly broke and unworthy of credit. Bishop is . . . undoubtedly a very unreliable man." In 1860, the sheriff seized the stock in Bishop's store, pending settlement of a debt.

4. "An Act to incorporate the Horse Head Crossing of the Pecos Bridge Company," Jan. 7, 1860, in Gammel, *Laws of Texas*, 5:59–60; "An Act to incorporate the Pecos Bridge Company," in ibid., 5:58–59; Cates, *Pioneer History*, 459. On the same day that A. C. Hyde received a state charter for his proposed Butterfield toll bridge at Horsehead Crossing, his close friend Jarvis Hubbell, also of El Paso County, received approval for a toll bridge downstream at the Pecos River crossing of the San Antonio–El Paso Mail Line, located in Indian Ford Canyon on the present-day Crockett-Pecos County line. One wonders whether W. H. Hunt got the idea for his West Fork venture from Hyde's and Hubbell's charters, which the state approved five weeks before Hunt's.

5. Map of Cactus Hill/Kate Hunt Craddock 40-Acre Parcel (part of Jabez Fitzgerald Survey, Wise County Abstract No. 295) and Old Jacksboro-Bridgeport Road across Lake Bridgeport, Lake Bridgeport Construction Files, 1929–31, TRWD; MT, Bridgeport West, Wizard Wells; GLO, Wise County Abstract No. 7; Wise County Deed Book E, 248; Wise County Deed Book F, 24, 38, 98, 129; Cates, *Pioneer History*, 67, 458.

6. Cooke County Commissioners Court Minutes, Aug. 21, 1860, vol. 1, 1857–77, part A, p. 61; 1860 U.S. Census, Montague Co., Tex., NA, M653, R1301, 70B, 71; 1860 U.S. Census, Wise Co., Tex., NA, M653, R1308, 15, 17; 1860 U.S. Census, Jack Co., Tex., NA, M653, R1298, 77–78; Conkling and Conkling, *Butterfield Overland Mail*, 1:305; Wise County Commissioners Court Minutes, book 1, 57–58; Ken Sprecher and Bridgeport Historical Society, *Images of America*, 12; PGS, Cooke Co., Tex., NA, RG 28, M1126, R590; PGA, Cooke Co., Tex., NA, RG 28, M841, R122; McDaniel, "Rosston, Texas," *Handbook*; Ross and Brothers Credit Report, Texas vol. 9, Denton County, p. 28, DCR, BL. The federal census taker visited Spring Station on July 8, 1860, Connely's on June 19, 1860, Venchoner Creek on June 20, 1860, and Earhart's on July 12, 1860. Unaware of this important census data, the Conklings incorrectly state that beginning in the spring of 1860, the new road ran from Gainesville to Davidson's, to present-day Rosston and Greenwood, and on to Decatur. They cite no evidence to support their statement. The Conklings base this part of their narrative on Cliff Cates's 1907 book and its flawed Butterfield history. Later studies that rely on the Conklings' account recycle the same errors. One recent publication, *Images of America: Bridgeport*, says that Butterfield's 1860 rerouting followed the Rosston-Decatur Road (including present-day FM 730) but provides no documentation for this claim. Cooke County Commissioners Court Minutes from August 21, 1860, disprove this statement. Moreover, local residents did not establish the Rosston-Decatur Road until after the Civil War. U.S. Postmaster General records show that Theodore A. Ross filed an application for a post office at Rosston in September 1874. The federal government received the application two months later, in November 1874. The U.S.

Postmaster General appointed Theodore Ross as Rosston's first postmaster on January 16, 1877. The Rosston-Decatur Road dates from the post office's establishment, and this route first appears on Texas maps during the 1870s. As further evidence, the Rosston-Decatur Road is not on GLO, Map #76226, *Charles W. Pressler's 1867 Traveller's Map of the State of Texas*, but it does appear on GLO, Map #76208, *Charles W. Pressler and A. B. Langermann's 1879 Pocket Map of the State of Texas*. The *Handbook of Texas* states that Rosston's founding occurred in 1870, when four brothers from the Ross family moved to Cooke County from Grayson County. This account dates Rosston's post office to 1872, two years earlier than U.S. Postmaster General records. Period credit reports note that the firm of Ross and Brothers started in business in Denton County in February 1868. By May 1876, they had a flour and gristmill, cotton gin, and horse ranch at Rosston in Cooke County. Road overseer reports in Wise County Commissioners Court Minutes from February 20 through 21, 1882, reference the Rosston-Decatur Road.

7. Cooke County Commissioners Court Minutes, Aug. 21, 1860, vol. 1, 1857–77, part A, 61, 79, 103, 107; GLO, Map #3439, *1868 Map of Cooke County*; GLO, Map #0766, *1871 Map of Wise County*; Dutton, "Greenwood, Texas," *Handbook*; MT, Era, Greenwood; Smith, *First 100 Years*, 8, 25, 236, 243; 1860 U.S. Census, Cooke Co., Tex., NA, M653, R1291, 68; U.S. Census, Texas Slave Schedules, Cooke Co., NA, M653, R1309, 4; Cooke County Tax Rolls, reel 1, 1848–84, TSLAC. One can trace the new 1860 route from Gainesville to Decatur using the following present-day landmarks. From Gainesville, the overland road went almost 11 miles southwest to Robert Wheelock's property on Spring Creek and continued on another 6 miles to William Downing's homestead on Blocker Creek. From Blocker Creek, Butterfield coaches steered southwest to the present-day Leo Community on Clear Creek. The Leo Road (Cooke County Road 398, then Wise County Road 379) runs from Clear Creek past Wiley Jones's homestead, which was 4 miles from Downing's. From Jones's to Decatur was 19 miles. After crossing the Cooke-Wise County line, the overland road approximates modern Prairie Road (Wise County Roads 2937 and 2740), which runs southwest to Greenwood (founded in the 1870s). From Greenwood to Decatur, Butterfield follows present-day Greenwood Road, also known as FM 1204. Robert Wheelock served as the first chief justice of Cooke County from 1848 to 1852. In 1861, Wheelock owned 1,120 acres, 24 horses, 100 head of cattle, and 25 sheep, for a net worth of $7,070. In 1857, William Downing officiated as Cooke County election judge at the precinct-voting site located a short distance upstream from his home on Blocker Creek. The precinct-polling place was at Dr. Davidson's home (a Butterfield station until August 1860) on Williams Creek. Williams Creek flows into Blocker Creek just above Downing's property. In 1858, Downing was on the committee overseeing construction of a new county courthouse. In 1859, Downing owned 320 acres, 3 horses, and 30 cattle, for a net worth of $2,230. Wiley Jones, a farmer originally from North Carolina, was a Cooke County commissioner from 1861 to 1864. In 1860, the fifty-seven-year-old Jones had ten slaves, who lived in three slave quarters on his property. Additionally, he owned 160 acres, 9 horses, and 30 head of cattle, for a net worth of $7,766. Jones's brother (also his neighbor), Josiah, was nine years younger.

8. Cooke County Commissioners Court Minutes, Aug. 21, 1860, vol. 1, 1857–77, part A, 61 (quotation); Cates, *Pioneer History*, 109; Wise County Deed Book C, 207 (Benjamin Sharp, Sept. 27, 1859, sale of 160 acres to J. B. Brandon for $400); GLO, Wise County Abstract File No. 773; 1860 U.S. Census, Wise Co., Tex., NA, M653, R1308, 1; 1860 U.S. Census, Texas Slave Schedules, Wise Co., NA, M653, R1286, 1; "Jerome B. Brandon," available at www.findagrave.com (accessed Mar. 20, 2013); Wise County, Aug. 5, 1867, voter list, 464; GLO, Denton County Abstract No. 102; GLO, Map #4161, *1878 Map of Wise County*;

Terrell, *The Terrells*, 29 (endnote quotation 1), 31 (endnote quotation 2). Cliff Cates states that the first station in Wise County on the new overland route was at Brandon's Station on Denton Creek, but he never specifies where on Denton Creek. Wise County native C. V. Terrell grew up on Denton Creek near Allison, Texas. Terrell recalled Brandon's Station being at "Brandon's Mound," which was "near Allison." He said that in the late 1860s, Brandon's was a stage stop on the Sherman–Pilot Point–Decatur–Jacksboro mail line. Tired of walking to their favorite swimming hole 2 miles from Decatur, Terrell and his friends would frequently steal a ride on passing stagecoaches. Jerome B. Brandon, a prosperous farmer and rancher, moved to Wise County in 1854. In November 1860, Brandon patented 160 acres in Wise County (abstract no. 773), 1 mile west of the Wise–Denton County line, on a hill overlooking Denton Creek, near present-day Allison. Locals called this hill Brandon's Mound. Allison, Texas, is 9 miles due east of Decatur. Because of Cates's book, subsequent writers continue to mistake Brandon's post–Civil War stage stop for an antebellum Butterfield station. One look at a map would be enough to quickly dispel this notion. Allison is far from the Butterfield Road. The Overland Mail Road does cross Denton Creek, but this crossing is almost 8 miles upstream from Allison, near present-day Greenwood, Texas. In sum, Brandon's Mound was not a Butterfield stage stop.

9. See Cooke County Commissioners Court Minutes, Aug. 21, 1860, vol. 1, 1857–77, part A, p. 61; MT, Gainesville South, Hood, Era, Greenwood, Slidell, Pecan Creek, Decatur; Kellogg, *M. K. Kellogg's Texas Journal*, 154–55 (quotation); Cates, *Pioneer History*, 47; PGA, Wise Co., Tex., NA, RG 28, M841, R127; CM 1931, p. 133, box 9, RPC Papers; CJ, Oct. 27, 1930, box 9, RPC Papers. Butterfield's August 1860 route change can be clearly seen in the following period maps of Texas, which show the road running from Gainesville to Wiley Jones's homestead, located near the eastern corner of the Cooke-Wise County line, and continuing on to Decatur on a straight line paralleling present-day Greenwood Road. See GLO, Map #79735, *Richardson's 1860 New Map of the State of Texas Including Part of Mexico*; GLO, Map #76226, *Charles W. Pressler's 1867 Traveller's Map of the State of Texas*; *Richardson's 1861 New Map of the State of Texas Including Part of Mexico*, and *A.J. Johnson's 1866 Map of Texas*, VG, SCL, UTA. It was 40 miles from Gainesville to Decatur over the new route. Given the distance, one new station may have been at Wheelock's in Cooke County, a second at Jones's, and a third on Denton Creek in Wise County, near present-day Greenwood. Ultimately, additional archival research combined with extensive fieldwork will be needed to conclusively pinpoint the new stations. The Conklings' unpublished manuscript and journal reveal that they received considerable conflicting information on this 1860 rerouting, hence the vagueness in their book concerning this matter.

10. Cates, *Pioneer History*, 47, 109; Brune, *Springs of Texas*, 477; Decatur Main Street Program, *Walk through Time*, 147, 170, 180, 251; AFT, Decatur, 2000–2015. In 1976, Gunnar Brune reported seeing a trickle of water flowing from historic Howell Springs, but within eighteen months, the flow had dried up. The Butterfield-era Daniel Howell and Alfred Elmore Allen General Store in Decatur was located on State Street, on the southwest side of the courthouse square. The McMurray-Gettys Building and Fuzzy's Tacos are now in this space. The 1859–79 Absalom Bishop and Edward Blythe Mercantile Store was on Walnut Street, on the northwest side of the square in a space now occupied by Swanky Shack, Sweetwater Baking, Embellish'd, and Sunshine Square.

11. Cates, *Pioneer History*, 47–48, 52–53, 76, 109, 130–31, 132 (endnote quotations 1–2), 132, 134, 135 (endnote quotation 3), 148, 149–53; McCaslin, *Tainted Breeze*, 94–95; Winkler, *Journal of the Secession Convention*, 90; Timmons, "Referendum in Texas," 16. Although Decatur is 40 miles from Gainesville, in 1862 the lethal paranoia associated with the Great Hanging quickly spread to Wise County. Several

of those arrested in the Gainesville roundup implicated residents of Prairie Point (present-day Rhome, Texas) of being members of the Peace Party and of holding unionist sympathies. Provost Marshall James Bourland and Adjutant J. J. Diamond of the Twenty-First Brigade of Texas State Troops (and former Butterfield employee), moved quickly to round up these new suspects. The pair ordered Twenty-First Brigade troops in Wise County under the command of John W. Hale to carry out the arrests: "Mysterious midnight searches, investigations and arrests . . . followed and the county was thrown into a fit of excitement." Over several days, Hale raided area homes and eventually brought several men to trial in Decatur. County officials established a courtroom upstairs in the Howell and Allen store, and a commission of twenty-four men chaired by Methodist minister James Bellamy heard testimony in the cases. Eventually, the tribunal found five of the accused guilty and sentenced them to hang. On October 18, 1862, Cliff Cates's uncle, Wise County sheriff Robert Cates, loaded the five men into wagons, seating them on top of their own coffins. The sheriff transported the condemned to the Swan property on the west side of Decatur. "Each of these men were conveyed to a tree . . . and hanged by the neck until dead . . . and it was from the wagons, pulled from under them that they fell to their death." The incident greatly distressed young pupils at a nearby school run by Miss Lutitia Wilson, the governess for Colonel William Hudson Hunt. The passing spectacle of armed guards, prisoners, and coffins terrified the students and "created much disturbance in the little institution." Winkler's *Secession Journal* mistakenly transposed Wise County's 1861 secession vote as 78 to 76 against secession. In fact, the final tally was 78 to 76 for secession.

12. Cates, *Pioneer History*, 458.

13. PGA, Wise Co., Tex., NA, RG 28, M841, R127; Daniel Howell 1857 postal route map and Bridgeport, Texas, post office application, Apr. 19, 1873, PGS, Wise Co., Tex., NA, RG 28, M1126, R593 (endnote quotation 1); Cates, *Pioneer History*, 458 (endnote quotation 2). The new post office at West Fork, Texas, created a duplication of postal services in western Wise County, and on July 7, 1860, the U.S. Postmaster General shuttered the post office in neighboring Cactus Hill. Applications filed with the U.S. Postmaster General show that local communities selected the names of their post offices. The official paperwork required applicants "to designate the [proposed] post offices by their true official names." Decatur postmaster Daniel Howell supplied the name of his town's proposed post office on an 1857 map of North Texas post offices that he sent in to the U.S. Postmaster General. Cliff Cates says that "Pierce [*sic*] Woodward . . . gave the place the name of Bridgeport." This is incorrect. Post office records indicate that local citizens, including Pearce Woodward, called their community West Fork from 1860 to 1867, when their post office closed. If West Fork settlers had changed the name to Bridgeport, post office records would have reflected this name change. Post office records detail other period name changes, such as Taylorsville to Decatur and Mesquiteville to Jacksboro.

14. Cates's father, Charles, and John W. Hale (Charles's father-in-law) secured a second state charter for a new $6,000 iron toll bridge, built in 1873 on the site of the previous antebellum bridge, which floods had washed away. "At one end of the [1873] bridge," Charles Cates "put up a store and built a saw and grist mill with cotton gin attachments." Whereas the first toll bridge failed, the second proved a success. See Bridgeport, Texas, postmasters and post office applications, PGA, Wise Co., Tex., NA, RG 28, M841, R127; PGS, Wise Co., Tex., NA, RG 28, M1126, R593; Cates, *Pioneer History*, 109, 225–27, 310 (endnote quotations), 457–58, 460; Wise County Historical Survey Committee, *Wise County History*, 1:118–19, 121–22. This latter book features a garbled and conflated account of West Fork's (1860–67) and Bridgeport's (1873–present) histories.

15. Map of Cactus Hill/Kate Hunt Craddock 40-Acre Parcel (part

of the Jabez Fitzgerald Survey [Wise County Abstract No. 295]) that includes Old Jacksboro-Bridgeport Road across Lake Bridgeport, map of landownership of parcels for Bridgeport and Lake Bridgeport, Kate Hunt Craddock June 1930 Hunt homestead/cemetery sale, Cactus Hill burial relocation letters and photos, Lake Bridgeport Construction Files, 1929–31, TRWD; copy of Feb. 25, 1860, Hunt-Alexander Deed Record, TRWD; MT, Bridgeport West, Wizard Wells. Toll bridge promoter W. H. Hunt owned a considerable amount of acreage in Wise County, including the Philip Nicholas Survey (Wise County Abstract No. 654) next to the toll bridge's William C. Anderson Survey. Hunt purchased some of his property from A. M. Alexander, who also conducted land deals with the McBrides at Colbert's Ferry in Grayson County. In February 1860, A. M. Alexander's brother, C. C. Alexander, purchased Hunt's share of the Jabez Fitzgerald Survey (almost 2,400 acres) for $4,207 (excluding 200 acres kept for the Hunt homestead at Cactus Hill). By 1930, the family's once-considerable acreage at Cactus Hill had dwindled to 40 acres, which included the Hunt home and family cemetery. In June of that year, Hunt's daughter, Kate, sold this remaining acreage to the water district for $1,200.

16. Conkling and Conkling, *Butterfield Overland Mail*, 1:305.

17. A close reading of Cates, *Pioneer History*, in relation to Butterfield operations reveals that Cates knew nothing about the original overland route through Wise County during 1858–60. In his book, Cates briefly mentions J. J. Connely and J. B. Earhart but seems unaware of their tenure as station managers for the Overland Mail Company. Cates likely had no knowledge of their connection to the mail line. His work is notably vague on Butterfield specifics and lacks supporting documentation. His understanding of Wise County's Butterfield history is limited to Decatur and West Fork/Bridgeport. Cates, who worked for the Decatur Chamber of Commerce, was obviously familiar with the town's history. He learned about the West Fork Bridge Company from his father, Charles, who was a leading figure in the Bridgeport community after the Civil War. Aside from his brief comments regarding these two communities, Cliff Cates has little to say about the Overland Mail Company. While his book has much information on early Wise County history, in matters pertaining to Butterfield, researchers should use Cates's work with considerable caution.

18. For more than fifty years, Wild West City in Stanhope, New Jersey, has been a popular summer tourist destination featuring stagecoach rides, panning for gold, and mountain men (see www.wildwestcity.com/home.htm, accessed Mar. 27, 2013). Frontier Town Theme Park in Ocean City, Maryland, offers visitors a chance to experience stagecoach rides, bank holdups, jailbreaks, the Shootout at the OK Corral, Indian dancing, and the Wild West Extravaganza Show (see www.frontiertown.com/western-theme-park/, accessed Mar. 27, 2013). Pioneer City in Florida featured saloons, shootouts, and stagecoach rides in its heyday (see www.flrcm.gov/attractions.cfm, accessed May 27, 2013). Other Florida attractions included Tombstone Territory, Petticoat Junction/Old Laredo, and Western Daze Putt Around (see www.florida-backroads-travel.com/lost-florida-tourist-attractions.html, accessed Mar. 27, 2013).

19. See 2001, 2005, and 2011 Official Texas Travel Maps, published by the Texas Department of Transportation. The 2005 map cover has the cowboy and his horse riding in a car, and the 2011 cover features a horseshoe. See also 2005 and 2011 Texas State Travel Guides, published by the same agency, which feature a cowboy boot (2011) and the cowboy, horse, and surfboard (2005) on the front cover. All of the maps and travel guides feature the Texas-branded leather patch on the front cover.

20. City billboard in Alpine, Texas, 2005; Abilene, Texas, Convention and Visitors Bureau, "The Friendly Frontier" tourist brochure, 2005; Frontier Texas tourist brochure, 2005; www.frontiertexas.com/

(accessed Mar. 24, 2005); 2002 Interstate 20 highway billboard for Frontier Texas; author visit to Frontier Texas, Mar. 12, 2005; Texas Senate, "Concurrent Resolution 11" (quotations).

21. Bridgeport Historical Society, "History Site," www.bridgeporttxhistorical.org (accessed Mar. 2, 2015); Bridgeport Chamber of Commerce website, esp. "Butterfield Stage Days," www.bridgeportchamber.org/sites/75844/pdf/bfsdvendorsboothapplication2013.pdf; AFT, Bridgeport and Butterfield Stage Days, 2000–15. For more on the National Park Service's potential designation of the Butterfield Overland Mail Route as a National Historic Trail, see National Park Service, "Butterfield Overland Trail Special Resource Study," http://parkplanning.nps.gov/projectHome.cfm?projectID=33568.

22. Texas Historical Commission, Marker #599, "Toll Bridge & Old Bridgeport," in *Atlas* (quotation).

23. Using St. Louis newspapers, Virginia Lillian Rebbing compiled an excellent list of all Butterfield departures from San Francisco and arrivals in St. Louis from September 15, 1858, through August 1, 1860. See Rebbing, "Southern Overland Mail," 156–60. See also Overland Mail Company, "Memorial," 4, available in Amon Carter Museum Microfilm Collection, Western Americana, Frontier History of the Trans-Mississippi West, 1500–1900, item 4076, R402.

24. Wise County Deed Book E, 248 (quotation).

25. 1860 U.S. Census, Wise Co., Tex., NA, M653, R1308, 20, 30, 67, 74, 75; Wise County Deed Book F, 38; Winkler, *Journal of the Secession Convention*, 91; Hafen, *Overland Mail*, 214.

26. Wise County Deed Book E, 248; Wise County Deed Book F, 38, 98.

27. Wise County Deed Book F, 129.

28. "An Act supplemental to an act entitled 'An Act to incorporate the West Fork Bridge Company,' passed February 11, 1860," in Gammel, *Laws of Texas*, 5:541.

29. Wise County Deed Book E, 88; Wise County Deed Book F, 218; PGA, Wise Co., Tex., NA, RG 28, M841, R127; Cates, *Pioneer History*, 310, 345–46, 458–60; Wise County Historical Survey Committee, *Wise County History*, 1:118; Hafen, *Overland Mail*, 209–14; 1930 U.S. Census, Wise Co., Tex., NA, T626, R2406, 16A (endnote quotation). Wise County historian Cliff Cates omits the West Fork Toll Bridge financial default and bankruptcy sale from his 1907 county history. He discusses Colonel William Hudson Hunt, Judge George Isbell, and Pearce Woodward in glowing terms. As secretary of the Decatur Chamber of Commerce and Wise County Old Settlers Association, Cates was by profession a booster and naturally put a positive spin on local history. Cates was also partial to Bridgeport and its heritage, since his father had played a major role in the town's post–Civil War development. Cates's Wise County history was by design part promotional and contained numerous advertisements for local businesses. The April 1930 census lists Cates's occupation as "Secretary, Chamber of Commerce." Interestingly, West Fork Bridge boosters were not the only people speculating on Butterfield's economic impact in Texas. Henry Bates, the Overland Mail Company's Division Six superintendent based in Sherman, conducted some insider trading in Wise County. Aware that Decatur's property values would rise when Butterfield rerouted its line through the county seat, Bates on June 15, 1860, purchased six lots in Decatur for $1,200. Bates sold his town lots on January 16, 1861, after South Carolina, Mississippi, Florida, and Alabama had voted to leave the Union. The superintendent had likely heard rumblings in Congress about moving the mail line to the Central Overland Route in response to Southern states seceding. LeRoy R. Hafen says that Congress's March 2, 1861, transfer of the transcontinental mail service to the Central Overland Route was inevitable. The new postmaster general preferred the Central to the Southern Overland Route (through Texas), which he viewed as an unnecessary

duplication and expense. Congress had been debating such a move for some months, and the secession of Texas and the other Southern states only accelerated their decision.

30. Limerick, *Legacy of Conquest*, 330 (quotation).

CHAPTER 4. BEDLAM AT BELKNAP

1. Young County Court Record, 1856 Book, Nov. 17, 1856; deposition of Dennis J. Murphy, Jr., Indian Depredation Claims nos. 8626, 10367, 10368, *Dennis J. Murphy v. The United States and the Kiowa and Comanche Indians*, U.S. Court of Claims, NA, RG 123; 1860 U.S. Census, Young Co., Tex., NA, M653, R1308, 2, 6. Dennis Murphy, Sr., Dennis Jr., and Margaret moved to Young County in June 1857. Dennis Sr. supplemented the family's income by keeping the books for several Belknap businesses.

2. AFT, Murphy's Station, Sept. 27, 2000 (JA), and May 29, 2007; 1860 U.S. Census, Young Co., Tex., NA, M653, R1308, 2, 6; Lang, *First Overland Mail: . . . St. Louis to San Francisco*, 125 (quotations); Young County Court Record, 1856 Book, Feb. 16, 1858, Feb. 23, 1859, Feb. 17, 1862; Young County Tax Rolls, reel 1, 1857–85, TSLAC; AFT, Oakwood Cemetery, Jacksboro, 2004–10; deed of Patrick Murphy to Anna Murphy, Dec. 9, 1859, Young County Deed Records, Book A-1. Dennis Murphy, Jr., provided lodging at his home for forty-two-year-old George Olford of Alabama, a Butterfield stage driver. Dennis also helped maintain the overland road in Young County. In 1862, Dennis Murphy had 1 horse and 500 cattle, for a net worth of $4,440. In 1860, Patrick Murphy had 320 acres and a town lot in Belknap. His wife, Anna, had 2 horses and 400 head of cattle. Their combined net worth was $3,410. Patrick and Anna left Young County prior to the start of the Civil War and do not appear in subsequent county tax rolls. They are not buried in the two Murphy plots in Jacksboro's Oakwood Cemetery. In 1859, Edward Cornett had no material assets. In 1860, twenty-four-year-old John Mosher, a Frenchman who was a Butterfield stage driver, boarded at Murphy's Station.

3. Frazer, *Forts of the West*, 142, 145, 156–57.

4. Young County Court Record, 1856 Book, Aug. 17, 1857, Oct. 6, 1857 (quotation 2), and Feb. 16, 1858 (quotation 1).

5. *Dallas Herald*, July 17, 1858 (quotation).

6. Ibid. (quotations [original emphasis]); Young County Court Record, 1856 Book, Oct. 6, 1857.

7. *Dallas Herald*, Sept. 1, 1858, Sept. 8, 1858 (quotation 1), Nov. 3, 1858 (quotations 2–3).

8. Ormsby, *Butterfield Overland Mail*, 47 (quotation 1); Ledbetter, *Fort Belknap*, 87 (quotation 2), 89, 99; Tallack, *California Overland Express*, 54 (quotation 3); Neighbours, *Robert Simpson Neighbors*, 273.

9. Neighbours, *Robert Simpson Neighbors*, 279, 317n34; Richardson, "Neighbors, Robert Simpson," *Handbook*. Neighbors, born in Virginia in November 1815, married Elizabeth "Lizzie" Ann Mays in 1851. Lizzie and the couple's two sons survived Neighbors's death.

10. *Seguin Union Democrat*, Oct. 8, 1859, RSN Papers, Collection No. 2E422/2R126, DBC, UT; William Burkett to Mrs. Lizzie A. Neighbors, Belknap, Tex., Sept. 14, 1859, ibid.; Col. Matthew Leeper to Commissioner of Indian Affairs A. B. Greenwood, Belknap, Tex., Sept. 15, 1859, WIA, NA, RG 75, M234, R928; PGA, Young Co., Tex., NA, RG 28, M841, R127; PGS, Young Co., Tex., NA, RG 28, M1126, R593. Alexander McRae Dechman (also the county judge in 1859) served as the first postmaster at Belknap, from August 14, 1856, to August 28, 1858, when William Burkett replaced him. George W. Fisher succeeded Burkett on December 10, 1860. Burkett also served as Young County clerk and district clerk. The Belknap Post Office continued to serve locals until its closure in 1908.

11. *Dallas Herald*, Sept. 21, 1859; *Seguin Union Democrat*, Oct. 8, 1859

(quotations 2 and 4) and Oct. 15, 1859 (quotation 1), RSN Papers, DBC, UT; *Texas State Gazette*, Nov. 5, 1859 (quotation 3); *Daily National Intelligencer* (Washington, D.C.), Sept. 30, 1859, box 39, KFN Papers, SCL, UTA. The Conklings put the distance between Murphy's and Jacksboro at 16 miles. In the fall of 1858, however, two passengers, Mr. Bailey and Mr. Farwell, recorded it as 19 miles, while a third passenger, Mr. Baer, listed it as 22 miles. I found it to be 22 miles.

12. Utley, *Indian Frontier*, 41 (quotations).

13. "An Act relating to the Indians of Texas," in Gammel, *Laws of Texas*, 3:1495–96; Neighbours, *Robert Simpson Neighbors*, 132.

14. Neighbours, *Robert Simpson Neighbors*, 121–22, 150, 158, 167, 212–13; Crouch, "Brazos Indian Reservation," *Handbook*; Dickerson, "Comanche Indian Reservation," *Handbook*; "Categories of Land Grants," Texas General Land Office, www.glo.texas.gov (accessed Oct. 30, 2013). I use the Texas General Land Office league to acre conversion ratio of 4,428.4 acres. Other accounts cite different acreage totals for the two four-league reservations.

15. "An Act supplementary to an Act relating to the Indians of Texas, approved Feb. 6, 1854," in Gammel, *Laws of Texas*, 4:258–59; "Indians in Texas: Joint Resolution of the Legislature of the State of Texas Relating to Indians West of the Pecos River," in House Misc. Doc. No. 76, 35th Cong., 2nd Sess. (quotation).

16. Neighbours, *Robert Simpson Neighbors*, 157, 159–64; Andrus, "Barnard, Charles E.," *Handbook*; Thompson, "Baylor, John Robert," *Handbook*; Kemp, "Ross, Shapley Prince," *Handbook*. Barnard hired John Shirley as assistant sutler on the Comanche Reserve. In 1858, Neighbors appointed Shirley as the interpreter for the Comanches and Zachariah Ellis Coombes as the schoolteacher for the Brazos Agency.

17. Neighbours, *Robert Simpson Neighbors*, 181 (quotation).

18. Thompson, "Baylor, John Robert," *Handbook*. Baylor married Emily Hanna in 1844, and the couple had ten children.

19. Kavanagh, *Comanche Political History*, 367; Richardson, *Comanche Barrier*, 112; Hämäläinen, *Comanche Empire*, 310.

20. Anderson, *Conquest of Texas*, 270 (quotation), 275; Richardson, *Comanche Barrier*, 109, 118.

21. *Texas State Gazette*, May 22, 1858, quoting the *Dallas Herald* (quotations).

22. MT, Sibley Creek and Reynolds Bend; Freeman, "History of Camp Cooper," 14–15; Frazer, *Forts of the West*, 142.

23. Sec. of Int. Jacob Thompson to Sec. of War John B. Floyd, Washington, D.C., Aug. 12, 1858, NA, RG 94, AGO, LR, M567, R581, 12–16; Anderson, *Conquest of Texas*, 296–99; Neighbours, *Robert Simpson Neighbors*, 204 (quotation). For more on Evans, Givens, Paul, and Stoneman, see Heitman, *Historical Register*, 410, 459, 776, 930; GLO, Throckmorton County Abstracts Nos. 21 and 185. Givens was working toward becoming a prominent rancher in Throckmorton County. As of July 1855, he had acquired almost 1,000 acres.

24. Neighbours, *Robert Simpson Neighbors*, 173, 175; Richardson, *Comanche Barrier*, 115–16; Anderson, *Conquest of Texas*, 297.

25. Frazer, *Forts of the West*, 124; Sec. of War John B. Floyd to Sec. of Int. Jacob Thompson, Washington, D.C., Nov. 12, 1857, NA, RG 94, AGO, LR, M567, R561; Runnels to Pres. of Texas Senate, Austin, Tex., Jan. 22, 1858, box 301-27, HRR Papers, TSLAC; Runnels to Sec. of War John B. Floyd, Austin, Tex., July 10, 1858, box 301-28, ibid.; Neighbors to Mix, San Antonio, Tex., Sept. 10, 1858, NA, RG 75, TIA, M234, R861. First called Camp Wichita, the new post had its name changed to Fort Sill in 1869.

26. Citizen petition to Col. Matthew Leeper, Clear Fork, Tex., Feb. 1, 1858 (quotation), NA, RG 75, TIA, M234, R861; Preston, McGhee, Stockton, Dawson, and Curtis to Capt. N.C. Givens, Feb. 1, 1858, ibid.; statement of Jo Chandler and David Seal, Comanche Agency, Tex., Mar. 27, 1858, ibid.

27. James H. Swindells to Neighbors, Belknap, Tex., June 10, 1858, ibid. (quotations). In addition to his duties as a physician, Swindells worked as a surveyor and delivered the mail on several mail routes in North Texas.

28. Matthew Leeper to *Dallas Herald*, Comanche Agency, Tex., July 26, 1858, ibid. (quotation 1); affidavit of W. G. Preston, Clear Fork of the Brazos, Tex., Aug. 9, 1858, ibid.; statement of Jo Chandler and David Seal, Comanche Agency, Tex., Mar. 27, 1858, ibid. (quotation 2).

29. Neighbors to Acting Commissioner of Indian Affairs Charles E. Mix, Brazos Agency, Tex., Apr. 2, 1858, ibid. (quotation 1); Matthew Leeper to *Dallas Herald*, Comanche Agency, Tex., July 26, 1858, ibid. (quotation 2).

30. J. R. Baylor to *Dallas Herald*, Buchanan Co., Tex., Aug. 30, 1858, ibid. (quotation 1); J. R. Baylor to *Dallas Herald*, Apr. 1, 1858, ibid. (quotation 2).

31. John Shirley to Charles E. Barnard, Comanche Agency, Tex., May 8, 1858 (quotation); Capt. Richard W. Johnson, 2nd Cav., Cmdr. Fort Belknap, to Ass't. Adj. Gen., Dept. of Texas, May 1, 1858, NA, RG 94, AGO, LR, M567, R591; Huckabay, *Ninety-Four Years*, 35–38; James B. Cambern entries for 1857 and 1858, Jack County Tax Rolls, reel 1, 1857–95, TSLAC; MT, Markley; Turner, "Lost Valley," *Handbook*. Several accounts spell the family's name as "Cameron" or "Cambren," but the correct spelling is "Cambern." Lost Valley is a short distance north of Butterfield's Fishpond Station, operated by Berry Lewis Ham. Prominent natural landmarks in Lost Valley include Spy Knob (used by both Indians and Texas Rangers for reconnoitering the surrounding terrain), Cameron Creek (really Cambern Creek, after the family involved in the massacre), and Stewart Creek.

32. O. S. Jordon to Runnels, Weatherford, Tex., May 2, 1858, box 301-27, HRR Papers, TSLAC; McConnell, *West Texas Frontier*, 1:295 (quotation); Huckabay, *Ninety-Four Years*, 38; Bernard to Neighbors, Waco, Tex., May 22, 1858, NA, RG 75, TIA, M234, R861 (endnote quotation 1); *Texas State Gazette*, June 5, 1858 (endnote quotation 2). Charles Bernard wrote to Neighbors informing him that "they have caught the white men that murdered the two frontier families in Jack County." A June newspaper report identified four of the white men involved in the murders as W. E. Willis, W. B. Morrison, Isaac Tipton, and Clairborne Jones, of Lampasas County, Texas. The article mentions, "The story was extensively circulated that these men were hung by Lynch law. The foregoing facts are from a reliable source."

33. John Shirley to Charles E. Barnard, Comanche Agency, Tex., May 8, 1858, NA, RG 75, TIA, M234, R861 (quotation).

34. Ford to Runnels, Brazos Agency, Tex., Apr. 7, 1858, box 301-27, HRR Papers, TSLAC (quotations).

35. Statement by John S. Ford, Austin, Tex., Nov. 22, 1858 (quotation 1), NA, RG 75, TIA, M234, R861; Neighbors to Mix, Washington, D.C., May 15, 1858, ibid. (quotations 4–5); J. M. Smith to Neighbors and Ross, n.d., NA, RG 75, WIA, M234, R928 (quotations 2–3).

36. Thompson to Floyd, Washington, D.C., Aug. 12, 1858, NA, RG 94, AGO, LR, M567, R581; Nelson to Buchanan, Waco, Tex., July 15, 1858, NA, RG 75, TIA, M234, R861 (quotation 1); T. C. Alexander to Buchanan, Meridian, Bosque County, July 22, 1858, ibid. (quotation 2); Barry, *Buck Barry*, 104 (quotation 3).

37. Hawkins to Mix, Camp Cooper, Tex., Oct. 30, 1858, NA, RG 75, TIA, M234, R861 (quotation).

38. Ibid. (quotation 1); Thomas Lambshead and J. M. Gibbins, Clear Fork Ranch (formerly Stem's Rancho), Tex., Oct. 1858 affidavit filed with Thomas Hawkins at Camp Cooper, Tex., NA, RG 75, TIA, M234, R861; statement by John S. Ford, Austin, Tex., Nov. 22, 1858, ibid. (quotations 2, 3, and 5); statement by Edward Buleson, Austin, Tex., Nov. 22, 1858, ibid. (quotation 4). Lambshead's ranch on the Clear Fork of the Brazos River was originally settled in 1853 by Jesse Stem, former Texas Indian agent.

39. Baylor, Nelson, Loving, et al., letter to Neighbors, Ross, and Leeper, Apr. 15, 1859, NA, RG 75, WIA, M234, R928 (quotations).

40. W. W. McNeill, et al., to Houston, Stephenville, Tex., Mar. 6, 1860, box 301-31, SH Papers, TSLAC; Neighbours, *Robert Simpson Neighbors*, 224–25. Peter Garland lived in Erath County, 15–16 miles north of Stephenville, Texas, on the road to Palo Pinto.

41. Haley, *Charles Goodnight*, 26 (quotation 1); Ford to Runnels, Camp Leon, Comanche Co., Tex., Dec. 28, 1858, box 301-28, HRR Papers, TSLAC (quotations 2–3); Erath to Runnels, Brazos Agency, Tex., Jan. 10, 1859, ibid.; Erath to Runnels, Stephenville, Tex., Jan. 13, 1859, ibid. (quotation 4).

42. Erath to Runnels, Stephenville, Tex., Jan. 13, 1859, ibid.; N. W. Battle to Runnels, Waco, Tex., Feb. 14, 1859, ibid. (quotation 1); Mar. 8, 1859, entry, Coombes, *Diary of a Frontiersman*, 55 (quotation 2); *Dallas Herald*, Feb. 2, 1859 (quotations 3–4).

43. *Dallas Herald*, Feb. 2, 1859; N. W. Battle to Runnels, Waco, Tex., Mar. 14, 1859, box 301-28, HRR Papers, TSLAC; N. W. Battle to Runnels, Waco, Tex., Feb. 14, 1859, ibid.; Runnels to Ford, Austin, Tex., Feb. 11, 1859, ibid. (quotations).

44. Runnels to Ford, Austin, Tex., Feb. 11, 1859, ibid.; Runnels to Ford, Austin, Tex., Mar. 3, 1859, ibid.; Runnels to Battle, Austin, Tex., Mar. 8, 1859, ibid. (quotation); Ford, *Rip Ford's Texas*, xxxiii–xxxiv, 249–50. The editor of Ford's memoirs, Stephen B. Oates, took his subject to task for his notable evasions of duty during the Choctaw Tom/Peter Garland crisis. For a more recent treatment of this matter, see McCaslin, *Fighting Stock*, 80–81.

45. McCaslin, *Fighting Stock*, 80–81; Runnels proclamation (printed broadside), Austin, Tex., Mar. 12, 1859, box 301-28, HRR Papers, TSLAC (quotations).

46. Runnels proclamation, Austin, Tex., Mar. 12, 1859, ibid.; Runnels to Twiggs, Austin, Tex., Mar. 18, 1859, ibid. (quotation 1); Withers to Runnels, San Antonio, Tex., Mar. 19, 1859, ibid. (quotation 2); Dept. of Texas Special Orders No. 3, Jan. 30, 1859, NA, RG 94, AGO, LR, M567, R614; Thomas to AGO, Camp Cooper, Tex., Dec. 15, 1859, NA, RG 94, AGO, LR, M567, R616; Hawkins to Thomas, Fort Belknap, Tex., Oct. 16, 1858, NA, RG 75, TIA, M234, R861 (endnote quotation). In October 1858, federal commissioner Thomas Hawkins wisely recommended that the army keep Fort Belknap open, since it provided needed military protection for the Brazos Reserve. Belknap commander Major George Thomas and Twiggs both wanted it shuttered, and in January 1859, Twiggs gave the order to abandon Fort Belknap. The closest army outpost for the Brazos Reserve would thenceforth be at Camp Cooper, 40 miles away, which effectively precluded a timely response in emergencies. Hawkins's warnings regarding Belknap's closure proved accurate. In a letter to Major Thomas explaining his reasoning, Hawkins said that Belknap's location served a four-fold purpose: "of inspiring settlers on this frontier with confidence[;] of protecting them and the Indians upon the reserve from the incursions of hostile tribes; of overawing and coercing the Reserve Indians to an orderly way of life[;] and finally [of] defending these latter from the violence of bad white men, many of whom lay at the door of the reclaimed red man the misdeeds not only of wild bands but also the exploits of professional horse thieves."

47. Twiggs to Thomas, San Antonio, Tex., Apr. 1, 1859, NA, RG 94, AGO, LR, M567, R614 (quotations). This letter includes the endorsement by Drinkard.

48. Neighbors to Runnels, Brazos Agency, Tex., Mar. 24, 1858, box 301-28, HRR Papers, TSLAC; Neighbors to Runnels, Mar. 28, 1859, ibid. (quotation).

49. Barnard to Runnels, Waco, Tex., May 4, 1859, box 301-29, HRR Papers, TSLAC (quotations).

50. Gurley to Neighbors, Waco, Tex., May 5, 1859, NA, RG 75, WIA, M234, R928 (quotations); *Dallas Herald*, Feb. 1, 1860; *White*

Man, Sept. 13, 1860, DBC, UT; Jack County Tax Rolls, reel 1, 1857–95; J. M. Smith to Neighbors and Ross, n.d., NA, RG 75, WIA, M234, R928. The *Dallas Herald* article specifically references receipt of the first issue of the *White Man* (January 21, 1860), initially published by Harris A. Hamner and Dr. Isaac Worrell. Harris Hamner had scant assets. In 1860, he owned 160 acres and a horse, for a net worth of $580. Harris Hamner, Patrick Murphy, and Berry Lewis Ham all filed complaints against the Reserve Indians and their agents in June 1859.

51. J. J. Sturm to S. P. Ross, Brazos Agency, Tex., May 8, 1859, NA, RG 75, WIA, M234, R928; Z. E. Coombes to Neighbors, Brazos Agency, Tex., May 8, 1859, ibid.

52. J. J. Sturm to S. P. Ross, Brazos Agency, Tex., May 8, 1859, ibid.; S. P. Ross to Neighbors, Brazos Agency, Tex., May 9, 1859, ibid. (quotation).

53. S. P. Ross to Neighbors, Brazos Agency, Tex., May 9, 1859, ibid.; J. J. Sturm to S. P. Ross, Brazos Agency, Tex., May 8, 1859, ibid.; extract of letter from 2nd Lt. William [Este] Burnet, 1st Infantry, to David [Gouverneur] Burnet, Camp at the Lower [Brazos] Reserve, Tex., May 9, 1859, published in the *Galveston Weekly News*, May 31, 1859.

54. Burnet to Burnet, Camp at the Lower [Brazos] Reserve, Tex., May 9, 1859, *Galveston Weekly News*, May 31, 1859 (quotation); Estep, "Two Last Letters," 193–94. In the Civil War, William Este Burnet served as a colonel in a Confederate artillery unit. He died on March 31, 1865, during the Battle of Spanish Fort in Alabama.

55. McConnell, *West Texas Frontier*, 1:329 (quotations 1–2); Leeper to Neighbors, Comanche Agency, Tex., May 12, 1859, NA, RG 75, WIA, M234, R928 (quotations 3–4).

56. Leeper to Neighbors, Comanche Agency, Tex., May 12, 1859, ibid.; Neighbors to Charles E. Mix, San Antonio, Tex., May 12, 1859, ibid. (quotations).

57. Capt. Joseph Bennett Plummer, 1st Inf., Camp on Brazos Agency, Tex., to AAG, Dept. of Texas, May 21, 1859, NA, RG 94, AGO, LR, M567, R614; Plummer to AAG, Dept. of Texas, Camp on Brazos Agency, Tex., May 23, 1859, ibid. (quotation); Ross to Neighbors, Brazos Agency, Tex., May 26, 1859, NA, RG 75, WIA, M234, R928.

58. Ross to Neighbors, Brazos Agency, Tex., May 26, 1859, ibid.; Neighbors to R. B. Hubbard and Thomas Duval, Comanche Agency, Tex., June 5, 1859, ibid. (quotations 3–5); Neighbors to Greenwood, Brazos Agency, Tex., June 10, 1859, ibid. (quotation 2); Thomas to Withers, Camp Cooper, Tex., May 26, 1859, NA, RG 94, AGO, LR, M567, R614 (quotation 1).

59. Thomas to Withers, Camp Cooper, Tex., May 26, 1859, ibid.; Twiggs to Runnels, San Antonio, Tex., June 2, 1859, ibid. (quotations 1–2); Neighbors to Greenwood, Brazos Agency, Tex., June 10, 1859, NA, RG 75, WIA, M234, R928 (quotation 3); Neighbors to Greenwood, Brazos Agency, Tex., June 28, 1859, ibid.; Fauntleroy to Buchanan, Palo Pinto, Tex., July 5, 1860, NA, RG 94, AGO, LR, M567, R623 (quotation 4).

60. Neighbors to Twiggs, Comanche Agency, Tex., Mar. 29, 1858, NA, RG 75, TIA, M234, R861; Runnels to Twiggs, Austin, Tex., June 8, 1859, box 301-29, HRR Papers, TSLAC (quotation 1); Twiggs to Runnels, San Antonio, Tex., June 11, 1859, ibid. (quotation 2).

61. Neighbors to Brown, Brazos Agency, Tex., July 17, 1859, box 301-29, HRR Papers, TSLAC (quotation 1); Brown to Runnels, Belton, Tex., Sept. 12, 1859, ibid. (quotation 2).

62. Brown to Runnels, Belton, Tex., Sept. 5, 1859, ibid. (quotation 1); Brown to Neighbors, Caddo Springs, Tex., July 31, 1859, ibid. (quotation 2); Neighbors to Brown, Brazos Agency, Tex., July 29, 1859, ibid. (quotation 3).

63. Murphy to Brown, Cotton[wood] Spring, Tex., Aug. 4, 1859, ibid. (quotation).

64. Nowlin to Brown, Aug. 1, 1859, ibid.; Neighbors to Greenwood, Camp on the False Wichita, Aug. 18, 1859, NA, RG 75, WIA, M234, R928; Neighbours, "Indian Exodus," 80 (quotation); Simpson, *Cry Comanche*, 132–34.

65. Leeper to Greenwood, Belknap, Tex., Sept. 15, 1859, NA, RG 75, WIA, M234, R928; *Dallas Herald*, Sept. 21, 1859; *Seguin Union Democrat*, Oct. 8 and 15, 1859, RSN Papers, DBC, UT; *Texas State Gazette*, Nov. 5, 1859; Neighbours, *Robert Simpson Neighbors*, 244; "Edward Cornett and Margaret Murphy," Texas Marriage Collection, 1814–1909, www.ancestry.com/ (accessed Feb. 24, 2014); 1860 Federal Mortality Census Schedule for Young County, Texas, NA, T1134, R55, 1. Edward Cornett, who originally hailed from Missouri, married Margaret Murphy on June 13, 1859.

66. Young County District Court Minutes, book 1, Murphy and Fisher bond for Cornett, May 24–25, 1860; *Seguin Union Democrat*, Oct. 8, 1859, RSN Papers, DBC, UT (endnote quotation); Estep, "Lieutenant William E. Burnet Letters," pt. 2, p. 384 (quotation 1); *Texas State Gazette*, Nov. 5, 1859 (quotation 2); Young County District Court Minutes, book 1, May 24–25, 1860. Young County treasurer George Fisher also provided money toward Cornett's $1,000 bond. Discussing Murphy's and Cornett's involvement in Neighbors's murder, Captain J. M. Smith of Waco wrote, "Murphy is thought to be clever. Cornet [*sic*] shot a man two years ago, and is a drinking, blustering, and boasting desperado—both Englishmen—keep stand [Murphy's Station] on Overland mail route between Belknap and Jacksboro. I myself know the men and fear the report is too true." In his letter to the *Texas State Gazette*, Patrick Murphy offers a dubious defense of his role in Neighbors's murder and reveals much of his true character.

67. Several reports mention the gang cooperating with Native American tribes living in Indian Territory, and foremost amongst these, Kickapoos. See S. A. Blain to Elias Rector, Wichita Agency, Indian Territory (hereafter I.T.), May 8, 1860, box 301-32, SH Papers, TSLAC; Lt. Col. J. M. Smith, commanding Mounted Regiment of Texas Rangers, to Houston, Wichita Agency, I.T., July 13, 1860, ibid.; Anderson, *Conquest of Texas*, 308, 309 (endnote quotation). Gary Clayton Anderson notes that it is "very unlikely" that Comanches were in league with the white outlaws.

68. *Dallas Herald*, Sept. 15, 1858, citing the *Texas State Gazette* (quotations 1–2); Huckabay, *Ninety-Four Years*, 51 (endnote quotation). Jack County historian Ida Lasater Huckabay noted that "citizens knew that white men preyed on their stock and that too often blame was laid to the Indians on the reservation."

69. Ford to Runnels, Camp Runnels, Tex., June 2, 1858, box 301-27, HRR Papers, TSLAC (quotations 1–2); Houston to Thompson, Austin, Tex., Feb. 17, 1860, box 301-31, SH Papers, TSLAC; Blain to Houston, Wichita Agency, I.T., Apr. 5, 1860, box 301-32, ibid. (quotation 3); Blain to Houston, Wichita Agency, I.T., May 29, 1860, ibid.; M. T. Johnson to Houston, Belknap, Tex., May 30, 1860, ibid.; National Park Service, "Bent's New Fort," www.nps.gov/safe/historyculture/bents-new-fort.htm (accessed Feb. 14, 2014); Houston to Thompson, Austin, Tex., May 4, 1860, Sam Houston Executive Order Letterpress Copybook, microfilm roll 5, TSLAC (endnote quotations); Anderson, *Conquest of Texas*, 309; Gary Clayton Anderson, Feb. 19, 2014, e-mail regarding Kansas jayhawkers and Kickapoos periodically cooperating on raids into Texas. Bent's New Fort (1853–60), situated at Big Timbers on the Arkansas River, was 12 miles from present-day Lamar, Colorado. Sam Houston told U.S. secretary of the interior Jacob Thompson that the raiders disposed of their stolen Texas livestock on the "waters of the Arkansas" and that from there the livestock were "driven as far as Lawrence in Kansas."

70. Col. Matthew Leeper to A. B. Greenwood, Fort Cobb, I.T., May 2, 1860, NA, WIA, M234, R928 (quotations). Captains Macintosh, Cabell, Huston, and Sturgis, along with Lieutenants Burnet,

Williams, and Lomax, from the First Cavalry and the First Infantry stationed at Fort Cobb, all endorsed Leeper's letter.

71. Samuel B. Watrous to *San Antonio Texan* and *Daily Ledger*, Fort Union, N.Mex., Dec. 18, 1859, NA, WIA, M234, R928 (quotations); W. T. Patterson to Houston, Canadian River, Apr. 20, 1860, box 301-32, SH Papers, TSLAC (endnote quotations). La Junta (now Watrous), New Mexico, is at the junction of the Mora and Sapello Rivers and was for many years a favorite rendezvous for Plains Indians and New Mexico traders. In April 1860, W. T. Patterson wrote to Governor Houston from the Canadian River informing him, "There is [*sic*] now white men stealing in this country. I am satisfied there is no connection with the whites and Indians [Comanches] in the way of stealing in this country." Patterson said that the Indians sold their stolen horses in New Mexico and that the comancheros "meet them this side of the settlements and trade with them."

72. Col. Thomas Turner Fauntleroy, 1st Dragoons, Cmdr. Dept. of New Mexico (hereafter DNM), to Lorenzo Thomas, Santa Fe, N.Mex., Mar. 3, 1861, NA, RG 94, AGO, LR, M619, R42; Bvt. Lt. Col. B. D. Roberts to Capt. Dabney Herndon Maury, Hatch's Ranch, N.Mex., Feb. 27, 1861, ibid.; Kenner, *History*, 82, 85, 173–74; Kenner, *Comanchero Frontier*, vi (endnote quotation). Merchants significantly expanded their business relationships with comancheros during and after the Civil War as a booming New Mexico market for stolen Texas livestock evolved. Charles Kenner says, "All accounts of the *comanchero* trade stress that the traders were in the pay of New Mexican businessmen."

73. Kenner, *History*, 181, 191 (endnote quotation 4); Haley, "Comanchero Trade," 160–62; M. T. Johnson to Houston, Belknap, Tex., May 30, 1860, box 301-32, SH Papers, TSLAC (endnote quotation 1); Garrett, *Authentic Life*, 89–93; deposition of James M. Reynolds, Indian Depredation Claim No. 5388, *John Chisum v. the United States and Comanche and Mescalero Apache Indians*, U.S. Court of Claims, NA, RG 123, 209 (endnote quotation 5); Map #575, *1864 Map of the Military Department of New Mexico, Drawn under the Direction of Brig. Gen. James H. Carleton by Capt. Allen Anderson*, NACP, RG 77, W83-2 (endnote quotation 3); Map #580, *1875 District of New Mexico Military Map by Lt. C.C. Morrison*, NACP, RG 77, W197-1; Map #1480a, *1878 Rand McNally Map of Texas*, TSLAC (endnote quotation 2); *1879 Rand McNally Map of New Mexico* and *1879 U.S. Department of the Interior General Land Office Map of the Territory of New Mexico*, both in David Rumsey Historical Map Collection, www.davidrumsey.com; MT, Muleshoe, Tex., Clovis, N.Mex., and Santa Rosa, N.Mex. In May 1860, Texas Ranger colonel M. T. Johnson reported, "All the trails and evidence as to where the stolen horses have been carried . . . point to the northwest, and large numbers have been taken, make no mistake about it. The horses are sold in . . . New Mexico." Period maps describe one of the main trails to New Mexico as a "Comanche Route said to be practicable for wagons" and as an "Overland route to the Texas settlements." This Comanche and comanchero trail led northwest from Cañon del Rescate (Yellow House Canyon in Lubbock, Texas) to Yellow House Lake (now Yellow Lake) to the headwaters of Yellow House Draw to El Coyote (Coyote Lake, 11 miles southwest of Muleshoe, Texas) to Laguna Salada (the 2,300-acre Salt Lake in Grulla National Wildlife Refuge, Roosevelt County, New Mexico), located a half mile west of the Texas state line. According to Charles Kenner, Laguna Salada was a meeting place where New Mexican livestock buyers traded with "the men who dealt directly with the Indians." From Laguna Salada, the trail continued on to Los Portales (Portales Springs, 6 miles southeast of Portales, New Mexico) to Tierra Blanca Lake (10 miles west of Portales) to Cañada del Tule (14 miles farther, at Tule Lake and Little Tule Lake, located 6 miles south-southwest of Melrose, New Mexico), then to Las Cañaditas (20 miles northeast of Bosque Redondo/Fort Sumner, near Lone Mesa

and Truchas Creek) before finally striking the Pecos River. Cattleman James M. Reynolds of Fort Worth testified in 1902 that Comanches often traded their stolen horses and mules "in the middle of the Staked Plains, at Portales [Springs], and Tulies [*sic*], and Tierro Blanco [*sic*] when they were not interrupted; when interrupted they went into the brakes [*sic*] of the Yellow House." Pat Garrett mentioned that Billy the Kid and his gang used this same road and the same water holes, notably, Los Portales and Las Cañaditas, in 1880 while moving stolen livestock. A second Comanche and comanchero route led from Mushaway or Mucha Que Peak in Borden County (near Gail, Texas) to Laguna Salada where it merged with the Yellow House Draw Trail and continued northwest to the Pecos. A third upper trail went from Quitaque, Texas, and the headwaters of the Pease River to Palo Duro Canyon and Trujillo Creek to the Canadian River, and then westward along the Fort Smith–Santa Fe Trail to Las Vegas, New Mexico. The foremost experts on the comanchero trade, Charles Kenner and J. Evetts Haley, largely agree on these main trade routes, although there are some minor variations between them.

74. Capt. Edmunds Balard Holloway, 8th Inf., to Capt. Dabney Herndon Maury, Hatch's Ranch, N.Mex., Oct. 5, 1860, NA, RG 94, AGO, LR, M619, R42; Col. Thomas Turner Fauntleroy, 1st Dragoons, Cmdr. DNM, to Lorenzo Thomas, Santa Fe, N.Mex., Mar. 3, 1861, NA, RG 94, AGO, LR, M619, R42 (quotations); Bvt. Lt. Col. B. D. Roberts to Capt. Dabney Herndon Maury, Hatch's Ranch, N.Mex., Feb. 27, 1861, ibid. (report includes signed trade passes for Pueblo Indians).

75. Col. Thomas Turner Fauntleroy, 1st Dragoons, Cmdr. DNM, to Lorenzo Thomas, Santa Fe, N.Mex., July 29, 1860, NA, RG 94, AGO, LR, M567, R628.

76. Ibid.; Capt. Edmunds Balard Holloway, 8th Inf., to Capt. Dabney Herndon Maury, Hatch's Ranch, N.Mex., Oct. 5, 1860, NA, RG 94, AGO, LR, M619, R42.

77. *Dallas Herald*, Sept. 15, 1858 (quotation 1), Oct. 20, 1858 (quotation 2); 1st Sgt. James Buckner Barry to Sam Houston, Flag Pond, Bosque Co., Tex., Aug. 14, 1860, box 301-33, SH Papers, TSLAC; Young County Court Record, 1856 Book, Oct. 6, 1857; Young County District Court Minutes, book 1, Nov. 27, 1858, and Nov. 24, 1859. According to the report, Edmonson was carrying a load of flour from Hugh Harper's store on the Clear Fork of the Trinity to the camp of one William Langford (likely Lankford) on the West Fork of the Trinity. At the time of his death, Edmonson was under indictment for murder. In November 1858, a grand jury indicted Young County commissioner Hugh Harper for selling liquor without a license and for permitting illegal gambling at his Clear Fork establishment.

78. *Dallas Herald*, Dec. 22, 1858 (quotations).

79. Ibid., Feb. 23, 1959 (quotation); Young County District Court Minutes, book 1, Nov. 27, 1858, and May 24, 1860; Young County Court Record, 1856 Book, Oct. 6, 1857, and Feb. 16, May 17, and July 6, 1858. One wonders whether this was the same William Langford (Lankford) mentioned in the previous endnote in relation to John Edmonson. Patrick Murphy was Edmonson's and Lankford's overseer on Young County's overland road maintenance crew from Belknap to Jacksboro.

80. *St. Louis Missouri Republican*, Mar. 14, 1859 (quotation 1); (*Austin*) *Southern Intelligencer*, Apr. 27, 1859; *Texas State Gazette*, May 7, 1859 (quotation 2); Neighbors to Greenwood, Brazos Agency, Tex., June 10, 1859, NA, RG 75, WIA, M234, R928 (quotation 3); *Dallas Herald*, Mar. 7 and 28, 1860 (Palo Pinto County and Camp Cooper thefts). A. A. Anderson and R. Anderson, who boarded a Butterfield coach at Belknap, provided details of the Belknap livestock theft to the St. Louis newspaper. The Andersons said the culprits were Comanches, but more likely they were members of the Old Law Mob.

81. Young County Deed Records, Book A-1, July 21, 1859; McCon-

nell, *West Texas Frontier*, 1:334; Patrick Murphy to Sec. of War John Floyd, Belknap, Tex., Nov. 15, 1859, NA, RG 94, AGO, LR, M567, R607; GLO, Map #76226, *Chas. W. Pressler's 1867 Traveller's Map of the State of Texas*; MT, Brad, Cove Creek; OLM; S. A. Blain to A. B. Greenwood, Comm. of Indian Affairs, Wichita Agency, I.T., Feb. 3, 1860, NA, WIA, M234, R928; endorsement by Capt. Charles Champion Gilbert, 1st Inf., Cmdr. Camp Cobb, I.T., Feb. 23, 1860, NA, RG 94, AGO, LR, M567, R607; A. B. Greenwood to Jacob Thompson, Washington, D.C., Apr. 4, 1860, ibid. Caddo Village was located in Palo Pinto County, between Cedar Creek and Caddo Creek and their junction with the Brazos River, now part of Possum Kingdom Lake. After her marriage to Edward Cornett, Patrick Murphy gave his sister a wedding present of ten head of cattle and one yoke of oxen. Several reports from Indian Territory in 1860 indicate that Indians did not kidnap Margaret Murphy Cornett but that she had left Texas voluntarily to live among friends north of Red River. These reports, based on hearsay, contain no actual sighting of Margaret or specific information as to who these friends were. The facts indicate that the Old Law Mob took her from Caddo Village, but beyond that her fate remains unknown.

82. *Texas State Gazette*, Mar. 3, 1860 (endnote quotation); George H. Sweet to Sam Houston, May 14, 1860, box 301-32, SH Papers, TSLAC; endorsement of W. W. Lowe, Camp Cooper, Tex., Apr. 28, 1860, and copy of O.L.M. letter, Texas Adjutant General's Department, Pre–Civil War Ranger Records, 1846–62, box 401-1135, folder 10, TSLAC (quotation 1); Holden, "Frontier Problems," 65 (quotation 2), 66–68; MT, Sibley Creek, Fort Griffin; 1860 U.S. Census, Throckmorton Co., Tex., NA, M653, R1308, 15. The *Gazette* published the full text of the O.L.M. letter in its March 3 edition. Holden's 1928 work was the first to take notice of this letter, one of the more important documents in Texas's antebellum frontier history. The boy who found the O.L.M. letter was either eleven-year-old Claiborne Self or seven-year-old Middleton Self. The boy's father, William Self, immediately turned the note over to Lieutenant William Warren Lowe of the Second Cavalry, the commanding officer at Camp Cooper. According to Lowe, the boy found the letter near his home on the Clear Fork of the Brazos at a point 15 miles below Camp Cooper. Lowe says the letter was discovered in "an old pocket book together with 50 cents in coin." Holden's dissertation states that the letter was found on Page's lifeless body. Thirty-six-year-old William B. Self of Georgia was a farmer. He and his wife, Mary, had six children and lived in Throckmorton County.

83. O.L.M. letter (quotation); James H. Swindells to Sam Houston, Belknap, Tex., Mar. 27, 1860, box 301-31, SH Papers, TSLAC.

84. O.L.M. letter (quotations); John R. Baylor to Dear Capt. [Allison Nelson], Weatherford, Texas, Dec. 15, 1859, box 301-30, SH Papers, TSLAC. Besides serving in the Texas House of Representatives, Allison Nelson was also in the Texas Rangers.

85. A. Nelson, House of Representatives, to Houston, Austin, Tex., Dec. 23, 1859, box 301-30, SH Papers, TSLAC; Hamner, Captain, Texas Rangers, to Houston, Jacksboro, Tex., Dec. 22, 1859, ibid.; *Dallas Herald*, Jan. 18 and Jan. 25, 1860 (quotation); Texas Ranger Muster Roll index cards, 1838–1900, TSLAC. Texas Ranger records show that Captain Hamner enrolled Cornett, Murphy, and Ham in his regiment in Jacksboro on January 14, 1860.

86. Houston to Chief Executive of Jack Co., Tex., Apr. 14, 1860, Sam Houston Executive Order Letterpress Copybook, microfilm roll 5, TSLAC; Hall to Faucett, Jacksboro, Tex., June 5, 1860, box 301-32, SH Papers, TSLAC (quotations).

87. Letter regarding Hamner and *White Man* printing presses dated Dec. 1, 1859, published in *Dallas Herald*, Dec. 14, 1859; *Texas State Gazette*, Mar. 3, Aug. 11 (quotations), and Sept. 29, 1860; Jack County Civil District Court Minutes, Book A, *State of Texas v. Hamner*. Dis-

trict Attorney W. H. Andrews later dismissed the intent to kill charge, and Hamner pled guilty to simple assault. A Jack County jury fined him $100.

88. O.L.M. letter (quotations); Twiggs to Cooper, San Antonio, Tex., Mar. 9, 1859, NA, RG 94, AGO, LR, M567, R614.

89. Ford to Runnels, Camp Cottonwood, Tex., Apr. 26, 1858, box 301-27, HRR Papers, TSLAC (quotation 1); Baylor to Gov. Edward Clark, Weatherford, Tex., Mar. 28, 1861, Governor Edward Clark Papers, box 301-35, TSLAC; Baylor to Allison, Weatherford, Tex., Dec. 15, 1860, box 301-30, SH Papers, TSLAC (quotation 2).

90. O.L.M. letter; Swindells to Houston, Belknap, Tex., Mar. 27, 1860, box 301-30, SH Papers, TSLAC (quotations 1–4); Scott to Houston, Cooke Co., Tex., Sept. 3, 1860, box 301-33, ibid. (quotation 5); Holden, "Frontier Problems," 67; Grant, "Early History," 87–90. While William Curry Holden was the first scholar to discover the O.L.M. letter, Ben Grant was the first to connect the initials "O.L.M." with the Old Law Mob. All of the period newspapers (*Texas State Gazette*, *San Antonio Herald*, *White Man*, and *Dallas Herald*) publishing or commenting on the O.L.M. letter use the initials "O.L.M." In addition, all primary documents in the Texas State Archives relating to the O.L.M. letter, including a copy of the original letter, feature the initials "O.L.M." Gary Clayton Anderson misread the initials and mistakenly concluded that "O.L.M." was "D.L.M." and that "D.L.M." stood for Dick McCarty, a rustler in the 1870s. Anderson does not discuss the Old Law Mob or its Texas frontier history. See Anderson, *Conquest of Texas*, 328–30.

91. Young County Deed Records, Book A-1, Dec. 9, 1859; Winfrey and Day, *Indian Papers*, 3:346 (endnote quotation). Anna Murphy, nine years younger than her husband, Patrick, was originally from Germany. In 1860, the couple had four young children: two boys and two girls. A December 10, 1859, letter to D. A. Bickel on the Clear Fork says, "Murphy's sister [Margaret] has not been heard of . . . and his stage stand was burned down and several animals stolen a few nights ago."

92. Ledbetter, *Fort Belknap*, 99 (quotation 1); *St. Louis Missouri Republican*, July 20, 1860 (quotation 2).

93. *Dallas Herald*, Apr. 18, 1860 (quotations 1–2); R. F. Luckett to Houston, Belknap, Tex., Apr. 15, 1860, box 301-31, SH Papers, TSLAC (quotation 3).

94. Houston to Jones, Austin, Tex., Aug. 6, 1860, Sam Houston Executive Order Letterpress Copybook, microfilm roll 5, TSLAC (quotations [original emphasis]); Williams and Barker, *Writings of Sam Houston*, 8:116.

95. Houston to Greer, Austin, Tex., Feb. 29, 1860, box 301-31, SH Papers, TSLAC (quotation 1); Drinkard to Houston, Washington, D.C., Mar. 14, 1860, ibid. (quotation 2).

96. Houston to Turner, May 31, 1860, Sam Houston Executive Order Letterpress Copybook, microfilm roll 5, TSLAC (quotations); Houston to Turner, Aug. 6, 1860, ibid.; Turner to Houston, Camp Cobb, I.T., July 10, 1860, Turner to Houston, Camp Radzminski, I.T., July 18, 1860, and Turner to Houston, Old Camp Colorado, Tex., July 29, 1860, box 301-32, SH Papers, TSLAC. Turner told Houston that he tried to hire Native American guides to take him to Bent's trading house on the Arkansas River but was unsuccessful because the Indians were afraid to go out onto the plains without a guard of fifty men.

97. James M. Cox to Houston, Coxville, Hill Co., Tex., Aug. 2, 1860, box 301-33, SH Papers, TSLAC; 1st Sgt. James Buckner Barry, Flag Pond, Bosque Co., Tex., Aug. 14, 1860, ibid.; James M. Cox to Houston, Coxville, Hill Co., Tex., Aug. 25, 1860, ibid. (quotation).

98. James M. Cox to Houston, Coxville, Hill Co., Tex., Aug. 2, 1860, box 301-33, SH Papers, TSLAC (quotation 3); 1st Sgt. James Buckner Barry, Flag Pond, Bosque Co., Tex., Aug. 14, 1860, ibid. (quotations 1–2); James M. Cox to Houston, Coxville, Hill Co., Tex., Aug. 25, 1860, ibid.

99. Young County District Court Minutes, book 1, May 24–26, 1860; *Texas State Gazette*, June 23, 1860.

100. *Dallas Herald*, June 6, 1860; *Texas State Gazette*, June 9 and 23, 1860; "Edward Wolfforth," http://genforum.genealogy.com/germany/messages/59821.html; Young County District Court Minutes, book 1, Oct. 22, 1858. Ironically, in 1858, Young County District Court officials selected Ed Wolfforth and Edward Cornett to serve on the same grand jury. Numerous authors misspell Wolfforth's name, likely because the listing of his last name is incorrect in both the 1860 U.S. Census for Young County and the 1870 U.S. Census for Jack County. Young County Commissioners Court and District Court records also misspell his name and use several variations.

101. *Texas State Gazette*, June 9 and 23, 1860; *Dallas Herald*, June 6, 1860; Strong, *My Frontier Days*, 17 (quotation); 1860 U.S. Census, Young Co., Tex., NA, M653, R1308, 1. In 1860, twenty-six-year-old Wolfforth and his twenty-one-year-old wife, Charity, had two children.

102. *Texas State Gazette*, June 9 and 23 (quotation), 1860; *Dallas Herald*, June 6, 1860; Crouch, *History of Young County*, 112 (endnote quotation 1); see "Edward Cornett," available at www.findagrave.com (endnote quotation 2) (accessed Feb. 20, 2014); McConnell, *West Texas Frontier*, 1:334; Neighbours, *Robert Simpson Neighbors*, 289–90, 319n88, 319n91; Ledbetter, *Fort Belknap*, 83n27, 91–92n4; MT, Newcastle. Over the past 150 years, writers have presented a number of widely divergent stories regarding Cornett's demise. Most of these authors provide no documentation in support of their accounts, and all but one fail to cite period newspaper reports on the May 25, 1860, killing. It is therefore necessary and important to set the record straight. Carrie Crouch's 1937 work garbles many of the facts and the timeline. Subsequent authors have only compounded the problem by recycling Crouch's erroneous account. Crouch claims that on the opening day of Cornett's trial for Neighbors's murder, some people burst into the courtroom with the news that Indians had kidnapped Margaret Murphy Cornett. In fact, officials did not indict Cornett until May 24, 1860, almost six months after Margaret's disappearance from Caddo Village on November 7, 1859. What is more, court officials had yet to set a date for Cornett's trial when the posse killed him on May 25, 1860. Crouch next claims that Cornett "was found dead in the Belknap Hills" but again provides no documentation. Some residents of Young County have often retold Crouch's tale about Cornett expiring in the Belknap Hills. Locals have even erected a headstone for what they claim is Cornett's grave on private property in the Belknap Mountains (Hills). The *Find a Grave* text says that some citizens "located the grave from the correspondence of Young County Sheriff Woolfarth [*sic*]." The text, however, provides no actual citations or quotations from the alleged Wolfforth communication. J. C. McConnell's earlier (1933) work echoes Crouch's in its narrative. He also garbles the timeline, confuses the facts, and provides no detailed sources. Referring to the Belknap Hills story, Kenneth Neighbours's work also cites Crouch's narrative. Neighbours is the only author to consult the June 6, 1860, report in the *Dallas Herald*. The *Herald* account, however, never mentions where the posse killed Cornett. In addition, Neighbours missed the two, far more detailed *Texas State Gazette* accounts of June 9 and 23, 1860, as did the other authors. Barbara Ledbetter twice cites the Belknap Hills story but provides no documentation. The June 9 issue of the *Gazette* reports that the sheriff's posse caught Cornett 9 miles from Belknap on Salt Creek, which places the location on the overland road heading northeast across the Salt Creek Prairie toward Murphy's Station and the Jack County line. The June 23 issue of the *Gazette* says that Cornett was fleeing toward Kansas, which is due north. The Belknap Mountains (Hills) are 4 miles southeast of Fort Belknap, near Miller Bend of the Brazos River, which is the opposite direction from Salt Creek Prairie and Kansas. None of the period newspaper reports on Cornett's death references the Belknap Hills. In sum, Crouch's story of Cornett and the Belknap Hills is suspect.

103. Young County Probate Book 1, Mar. 25, 1861; *Texas State Gazette*, June 23, 1860; deposition of Dennis J. Murphy, Jr., Indian Depredation Claims Nos. 8626, 10367, 10368, *Dennis J. Murphy v. The United States and the Kiowa and Comanche Indians*, U.S. Court of Claims, NA, RG 123; 1860 U.S. Census, Young Co., Tex., NA, M653, R1308, 6; 1880 U.S. Census, Jack Co., Tex., NA, T9, R1313, 58B; Young County Tax Rolls, reel 1, 1857–85, TSLAC; AFT, Oakwood Cemetery, Jacksboro, 2004–10; Judge N. B. Battle, et al., to Sam Houston, Hamilton, Tex., Nov. 13, 1860, NA, RG 94, AGO, LR, M567, R634. Edward Cornett left few personal effects behind. When the county probated his estate ten months after his death, his assets (horse, saddle, gun, and Colt Navy revolver) totaled $253. *White Man* publisher Harris Hamner reported on July 30, 1860, that incendiaries had burned Patrick Murphy's home. This was the second fire at Murphy's in seven months. See *Texas State Gazette*, Aug. 11, 1860. Patrick Murphy likely left Texas for St. Louis sometime between July and December 1860. Murphy appears in the June 27, 1860, federal census for Young County. A November 1860 report references "Murphy's old stage stand on the Fort Belknap Road," which leads one to suspect that it may have been abandoned after the second fire. Many years passed before Murphy returned to North Texas. His brother Dennis Jr. said that he went to St. Louis in 1860, but his whereabouts during the Civil War is unknown. Patrick and his son, Patrick Jr., appear in the 1880 Jack County Census. This census lists Patrick Sr. as suffering from malarial fever. Patrick Murphy, Jr., was born in St. Louis in 1862. What happened to Patrick Murphy and his son after 1880 is unclear. Dennis J. Murphy, Jr., was also living in Jack County in 1880. The Irish-born Dennis became an American citizen in 1854. After the war, he worked as a rancher and government contractor, supplying wood and beef (as a subcontractor) to Fort Richardson, as well as corn to Fort Griffin. His father, Dennis Murphy, Sr., died in 1876. Both Dennis Sr. and Dennis Jr. are buried in Jacksboro's Oakwood Cemetery, in two separate plots. The connections among various Butterfield people persisted for many years. James M. Frans, manager of Frans's and Clear Fork stations, had numerous business dealings with Dennis J. Murphy after the Civil War.

104. Young County Court Record, 1856 Book, Apr. 10, 1865 (quotation); Neighbours, *Robert Simpson Neighbors*, 284; AFT, Fort Belknap and Belknap Cemetery, 1991–2014; Gournay, *Texas Boundaries*, 72. For a detailed analysis of this depopulation and the Confederacy's failed defense of the Texas frontier during the Civil War, see Ely, "Gone from Texas," 160–84.

105. Richardson, *Frontier of Northwest Texas*, 205; Hunter, *Bloody Trail in Texas*, 57 (quotation).

106. Randolph to Magruder, Richmond, Va., Nov. 7, 1862, in Scott et al., *War of the Rebellion*, 15:857; Jefferson Davis endorsement to J. A. Seddon, Mar. 29, 1863, 15:919 (quotation).

107. Baylor to Magruder, Houston, Tex., Dec. 29, 1862, ibid., 15:914, 915 (quotation 1), 916, 917 (quotation 2), 918; Magruder endorsement on same Baylor letter, Houston, Tex., Feb. 6, 1863, ibid., 15:918 (quotation 3).

108. Ely, "Riding the Western Frontier," 117–19.

109. Thompson, "Baylor, John Robert," *Handbook*; Cutrer, "Nelson, Allison," *Handbook*; Hamilton, "Hamner, Harris A.," *Handbook*; Wilkins, "Peter Garland, 1805–1873: Hero or Villain?" Hood County Texas Genealogical Society, www.granburydepot.org/z/bio92/GarlandPeter.htm (originally published in *Granbury! Magazine* in the fall of 1986).

CHAPTER 5. FROM THE BRAZOS TO VALLEY CREEK

1. For the exact route of the Butterfield Road (also the U.S. military road) from Belknap to the Throckmorton County line, see GLO, Map #4174, *1880 Map of Young County, Texas*; GLO, Map #87374, *1860 Map of the Surveyed Part of Young District*; GLO, Map #4173, *1859 Map of Young County*; MT, Newcastle, Proffitt, Proffitt Crossing. Although the Texas Legislature created Throckmorton County in January 1858, locals did not officially organize the county until 1879. During the two-decade interval, the state legislature ordered Throckmorton County attached to Young County for judicial purposes. See Gournay, *Texas Boundaries*, 82; Young County Court Record, 1856 Book, Aug. 17 and Sept. 23, 1857, June 22, July 2, and August 20, 1860, and May 20, 1861. In December 1937, J. W. Williams interviewed Mrs. Mac Gaither, the granddaughter of James Madison Frans, who said that her grandfather "tended at least two of the [Butterfield] stations." See Williams, "Marcy and Butterfield Trails," 85 (endnote quotation). In the 1930s, two pioneer area ranchers, Phin Reynolds and J. C. Irwin, gave interviews placing Frans at the Clear Fork Station in 1860–61. See Webb, "Recollections and Experiences of the Frontier Life of Phin W. Reynolds, May 1936 and April 1938," 86–87, and "Frontier Life of John Chadbourne Irwin, Fall and Winter 1934," 36, both in JRW Papers. See also Elizabeth Frans Tharp (Frans's daughter) interview, CJ, Aug. 13, 1932, box 9, RPC Papers. The Conklings spell his name as "Franz," but his 1905 headstone reads "Frans." From 1857 to 1861, Young County Commissioners Court Minutes consistently record his name as Frans. His April 1850 Peters Colony application for a land grant in Montague County lists his name as Frans, and he signed his name on the back of the document as such. See GLO, Montague County Abstract No. 265; GLO, Map #3888, *1868 Map of Montague County, Texas*. Frans was born in Virginia on October 30, 1814. See "James Madison Frans," available at www.findagrave.com (accessed Feb. 28, 2015).

2. "Dutchman," *Merriam-Webster Online Dictionary*; Pearsall and Trumble, *Oxford English Reference Dictionary*, 439; AFT, Ben Krebs grave, Newport Cemetery, Lone Grove, Okla., Jan. 16, 2013; Young County Tax Rolls, reel 1, 1857–85, TSLAC; 1867 Texas voter registration lists, Montague County, microfilm reel VR-9, p. 408, entry 148, TSLAC.

3. MT, Proffitt, Proffitt Crossing; 1860 U.S. Census, Young Co., Tex., NA, M653, R1308, 6; Young County Tax Rolls, reel 1, 1857–85, TSLAC; AFT, Krebs's Station and Cribb Station Creek water hole, Jan. 21 and Apr. 16, 2005 (JA). In October 1853, the Texas Emigration and Land Company (TELC) surveyed the 320-acre parcel that later became the site of Krebs's Station. Both the 1861 Young County tax roll and the 1865 Montague County tax roll show Krebs owning a 320-acre TELC parcel. Ben Krebs's name appears as "Cribbs" in both the 1860 and the 1870 federal census. The 1857–62 Young County tax rolls and 1865–67 Montague County tax rolls list him as "Kribbs," as do Ranger muster rolls. Although several historians wrote about Krebs's Station during the 1930s, none of them located the site. For almost a century and a half, the ruins of the old Butterfield stage stop lay hidden among the rolling Cross Timbers country of Young County. After a previously unsuccessful attempt to find the station in 2004, the landowner and I finally found the long-lost station in January 2005. The ruins of Krebs's Station lie on the east side of Cribb Station Creek. A thick growth of mesquite trees rings an extensive scattering of cut sandstone slabs. Pieces of stagecoach trace chain, military uniform buttons, broken crockery, bullets, and glass litter the ground. At the intersection of the overland route and the creek, the deep ruts of the old road are clearly discernable where they cross the streambed. Near the crossing, the stage stop's water hole sits three-quarters full.

4. 1860 U.S. Census, Young Co., Tex., NA, M653, R1308, 6; Crouch,

History of Young County, 91 (quotation); CJ, Oct. 26, 1930 (endnote quotation 1), Aug. 13, 1932 (endnote quotations 2 and 3), box 9, RPC Papers; Conkling and Conkling, *Butterfield Overland Mail*, 1:321 (endnote quotation 4). In October 1930, G. W. Newcomb of Fort Griffin, Texas, told Butterfield historians Roscoe and Margaret Conkling about a livestock relay station "called Crib [*sic*] Station." In their August 1932 interviews with John Chadbourne Irwin, who as a young boy saw the Butterfield line in operation, the Conklings learned that "Crib [*sic*] Station was a log station." In August 1932, the Conklings also met eighty-six-year-old Elizabeth Frans Tharp, daughter of Butterfield overseer James Madison Frans. Tharp, of Throckmorton, Texas, was thirteen when Butterfield was operating its stage line and recalled a log cabin stage stop on Cribb Station Creek. During this interview, Mrs. Tharp's son told the Conklings that "there was an old log crib at the site and he always supposed it was the old log house of the Crib Station days." The Conklings, however, never used Newcomb's, Irwin's, or Tharp and son's information in their published Butterfield study. Likely they were uncertain about this story line and unable to verify the facts or locate the station ruins. Eventually, the Conklings ended up conflating Krebs's Station with Frans's Station, the next stop, 12 miles to the west on Middle Kings Creek. The couple mistakenly assumed that their four interviewees were discussing only one station, Frans's Station. In their 1947 published work, the Conklings erroneously state that "later in the sixties, the station [Frans's] was operated by a man named Cribb and was known as Cribb's station." This statement exemplifies their conflating of the two stations. By later in the 1860s, Ben Krebs had already moved on to marriage and farming in Montague County.

5. Lang, *First Overland Mail: . . . San Francisco to Memphis*, 39; *Dallas Herald*, Feb. 8, 1860. William Powell, born in North Carolina in 1837, was a laborer who lived near Fort Belknap.

6. *Dallas Herald*, Feb. 8, 1860 (quotations).

7. 1870 U.S. Census, Montague Co., Tex., NA, M593, R1599, 5; Young County Tax Rolls, reel 1, 1857–85, TSLAC; Montague County Tax Rolls, reel 1, 1858–89, TSLAC; Rochette, *Bourland in North Texas*, vol. 1 appx., A-318. Ben Krebs died in Lone Grove, Oklahoma (near Ardmore) on February 21, 1901. Oliver Loving died from his wounds at Fort Sumner, New Mexico, on September 25, 1867. For more on the 1867 Goodnight-Loving cattle drive to Fort Sumner, see Haley, *Charles Goodnight*, 162, 170–83.

8. MT, Proffitt Crossing, Murray, Woodson; 1860 U.S. Census, Throckmorton Co., Tex., NA, M653, R1308, 14; Tharp interview, CJ, Aug. 13, 1932, box 9, RPC Papers; CJ, Aug. 14, 1932, box 9, RPC Papers (endnote quotations); Conkling and Conkling, *Butterfield Overland Mail*, 1:321; AFT, Frans's Station, Sept. 21 (JA) and Oct. 18, 1999 (JA), and Jan. 28, 2002 (JA, PD). During the Conklings' trip to Frans's Station in August 1932, local old-timer Ben Fry took them to an "old well hole, foundation rocks of [an] old barn . . . and the place in a post oak grove where Mr. Fry said there were some log houses with rock foundations." When a later landowner built a dam above the stage stop, all the "rocks were carried off and used in the dam. The lumber was carried off a long time ago. Mr. Fry [saw] as many as eight wagons carrying off the lumber." Several field trips I took to Frans's Station revealed a large amount of historic material on the west side of Middle Kings Creek, where the Butterfield Road crossed the stream. At the northwest corner of this intersection are numerous quarried brown sandstone blocks used in the foundations for the station house and outlying buildings. Fieldwork at the site uncovered period bullets and square nails in a trace of the old road leading into the stage stop from the Clear Fork to the west. Directly across from the station, on the east bank of Middle Kings Creek, there is a large, exposed rock face bearing several sets of hand-carved graffiti dating from both 1868

and April 1869. Continuing east, back toward Krebs's Station and the Brazos River, a line of artifacts clearly marked the Butterfield Road for over half a mile. Artifacts found at Frans's include pre–Civil War pistol balls, Henry and Spencer cartridges, unstamped internal-primed center-fire cartridges, mule shoes, green and brown pieces of early bottles, white china, large square nails, hand-forged hooks and screws, buckles, cinch rings, wagon/coach axles, pieces of a cast-iron stove, wagon or coach metal bracing, metal buttons, a coffee grinder, and wagon/coach trace chain. Frans's and other North Texas Butterfield stations also saw service in 1869–72 for Ben Ficklin's Fort Concho, Texas, to Fort Smith, Arkansas, stagecoach line.

9. Tharp interview, CJ, Aug. 13, 1932, box 9, RPC Papers; Conkling and Conkling, *Butterfield Overland Mail*, 1:321; Greene, *900 Miles*, 151 (endnote quotation), 152; AFT, A. C. Greene location north of Woodson near old railroad grade and FM 1710, Oct. 18, 1999 (JA). In 1994, A. C. Greene and his friend J. R. "Bob" Green of Albany, Texas, erroneously placed Frans's Station north of Woodson, Texas, near an abandoned railroad grade just east of FM 1710. Greene says, "Franz (or France or Frans) Station is today a pile of stone along the bank of Middle Kings Creek, near the right of way for the long abandoned Cisco & Northwestern Railroad. . . . The pilings for a former railroad trestle remain nearby. The station site can be viewed from Highway 1710 a short distance north of Woodson." First, this pile of stone, railroad trestle, and abandoned track near FM 1710 are not on the bank of Middle Kings Creek, which lies almost 2 miles to the east. Second, it is physically impossible for one to see the station site from FM 1710, as it is too far away and is obscured by 1,300-foot ridges and hundreds of trees. Greene's published opinion as to the station site necessitates a response. Walking along the old railroad grade north of Woodson, adjacent to FM 1710, one can see the pile of stone that Greene identified near the abandoned track. Fieldwork I conducted here with Joe Allen (using a metal detector) showed that this mound of rock ballast originated during construction of the railroad bed. A thorough examination of the surrounding area with a metal detector revealed not one artifact dating from 1850–70. The few pieces of metal found were from a later period, and all were railroad related. Because Greene and Green had no metal detector to positively pinpoint Frans's Station, they could only speculate as to its location. Their conjecture erred by almost 2 miles, as the Conklings' research and my field trips show.

10. Ormsby, *Butterfield Overland Mail*, 47 (quotation); 1860 U.S. Census, Throckmorton Co., Tex., NA, M653, R1308, 14 (endnote quotation 1); Young County Court Record, 1856 Book, Aug. 2, 1860 (endnote quotation 2); Young County Tax Rolls, reel 1, 1857–85, TSLAC. On July 10, 1860, the Throckmorton County U.S. Census listed Virginia natives "J. M. France [*sic*]," his wife, Frances, and their six children living at the Clear Fork Station. In July 1860, the forty-five-year-old Frans's net worth was $600. In August 1860, county commissioners ordered that "an election precinct be established on Clear Fork of the Brazos, and that elections be held at the house of James M. Frans." The county election notice and 1860 census date make clear that Frans relocated from his station on Middle Kings Creek (near present-day Woodson, Texas) to Clear Fork of the Brazos prior to July 10, 1860. By 1861, Frans's assets had declined to $407 in value and included 1 horse and 65 cattle. For the exact route of the Butterfield Road through Throckmorton County, see GLO, Map #4079, *March 1880 Map of Throckmorton County, Texas*.

11. 1853 TELC Survey 480 and Connecting Line Survey (includes Surveys 1642 and 774), Peters Colony Surveys, County Clerk's Office, Throckmorton Co., Tex.; GLO, Throckmorton County Abstracts Nos. 223, 225, 236, 259, 263; MT, Sibley Creek, Reynolds Bend; GLO, Map #4079, *March 1880 Map of Throckmorton County, Texas; January 18, 1855 R.B. Marcy–R.S. Neighbors Comanche Indian Reserve Map*, County Clerk's Office, Throckmorton Co., Tex.; GLO, Map #76284,

Capt. R.B. Marcy's 1854 Map of the Country upon the Brazos and Big Wichita Rivers; Ormsby, *Butterfield Overland Mail*, 48 (quotations 1–2); Lang, *First Overland Mail: . . . San Francisco to Memphis*, 39 (quotation 3); 1860 U.S. Census, Throckmorton Co., Tex., NA, M653, R1308, 16; 1860 U.S. Census, Shackelford Co., Tex., NA, M653, R1302, 42–43; T. E. Jackson and Co., Fort Griffin and Albany, Credit Report, Texas vol. 27, Shackelford County, DCR, BL; "Margaret Boyles Jackson," available at www.findagrave.com (accessed June 10, 2013); 1850 U.S. Census, Navarro Co., Tex., NA, M432, R913, 109A; Young County Tax Rolls, reel 1, 1857–85, TSLAC. The Overland Mail Road struck the Clear Fork of the Brazos River near Stagestand Branch. Two TELC land surveys from August 1853 show the military's "Phantom Hill–Belknap Road" coming into this Clear Fork of the Brazos crossing, located in a 320-acre parcel located on the east bank of the river. Both the U.S. Army and the Overland Mail Company used the Clear Fork crossing. The old Cornelius K. Stribling homestead near the crossing is the site of Butterfield's Clear Fork Station. Two miles upstream from this ford, in the C. W. Marquess Survey, were Robert Neighbors's Comanche Indian Agency buildings and an old Tonkawa Indian village. Another 5 miles upstream, in the J. M. Larn Survey, is the site of Camp Cooper, where the U.S. Army stationed troops for the Comanche Indian Reserve. Marcy's 1849 California Emigrant Road, always staying well north of the Butterfield, entered Throckmorton County in Survey 774, crossing the northwest corner of the Comanche Reserve and continuing into the Thomas Lambshead Survey. Lambshead, like Frans, received a Peters Colony grant and patented his Throckmorton County land in May 1859. The Reynolds-Matthews family later took his name for their large landholdings, today the well-known Lambshead Ranch. Tryal Evan Jackson was born in Indiana in 1820. In 1839, he wed Margaret Boyles in Missouri. In 1850, the Jacksons were living in Navarro County, Texas, but they had moved to the Clear Fork by 1858, when Butterfield commenced operations. By 1860, Tryal and Margaret had eight children. In 1861, Jackson's net worth was $1,042, which included 10 cattle, store merchandise, and a wagon. After the Civil War, Tryal Jackson was a rancher and merchant in the Albany and Fort Griffin area. Jackson enjoyed a good reputation in business until 1877, when his son-in-law Julius Wallach absconded with most of the firm's cash. The theft crippled Jackson financially, forcing him to close his Fort Griffin store and saddling him with considerable debts. He died on April 8, 1891, and is buried next to Margaret in Jester Cemetery, Plainview, Oklahoma. The February 1859 Dixson and Kasson map of the nation's overland mail routes identifies the Clear Fork station simply as "Jackson." See Tallack, *California Overland Express* (map reproduction).

12. *Contracts with the War Department*, House Exec. Doc. No. 47, 36th Cong., 2nd Sess., vol. 8, ser. 1099, p. 48; 1860 U.S. Census, Throckmorton Co., Tex., NA, M653, R1308, 14; Webb, "Frontier Life of John Chadbourne Irwin," 34, 35 (quotations 1–2), 36, and "Frontier Life of Phin W. Reynolds," 86 (endnote quotation), both in JRW Papers; Minatra, "Life near the Heart," Richardson Library, Hardin-Simmons University (quotations 3–4); Samuel P. Newcomb and Susan E. Reynolds Newcomb diaries, 1865–73, Anne Watts Baker Collection, SWC; Young County Tax Rolls, reel 1, 1857–85, TSLAC; affidavits of James M. Frans, J. L. Thorp, Elizabeth Frans Thorp, Thomas J. Shaw, Sarah Akin, and Cornelius K. Stribling, *James M. Frans v. The United States and the Comanche Tribe of Indians*, Indian Depredation Claim No. 5507, U.S. Court of Claims, NA, RG 123; 1880 U.S. Census, Hemphill Co., Tex., NA, T9, R1310, ED198, 100D; 1900 U.S. Census, Throckmorton Co., Tex., NA, T623, R1672, ED154, 2A. See "Jothorp's Frans Family Tree," http://trees.ancestry.com/tree/44575446/person/6222621315?ssrc= (accessed June 9, 2013); "James Madison Frans," available at www.findagrave.com (accessed June 10, 2013). John G. Irwin's Camp Cooper beef contract ran from October 1, 1860, to September 30, 1861. The

Irwin and Frans families were close neighbors in Stephens County during the Civil War and periodically saw each other during the 1870s, when both ranched near Fort Griffin, Texas. In 1861, John G. Irwin's net worth was $2,107, including 2 horses, 284 cattle, and 26 sheep. Another local resident who remembered Frans on the Clear Fork was Phineas Reynolds. Reynolds, born in 1857, said that Frans "was the station agent at the Butterfield Stage Line stand on the Clear Fork of the Brazos until the abandonment of the stage line at the outbreak of the war." During the Civil War, the Frans family forted up with other area residents at Fort Davis, located 15 miles downstream on the Clear Fork in neighboring Stephens County. Besides the Frans family, others living at Fort Davis included the Irwins, Newcombs, Reynolds, and Selmans (including John Selman, killer of John Wesley Hardin). In May 1870, James M. Frans was ranching on Hubbard's Creek in Stephens County. By May 1872, Frans had moved to Fort Griffin on the Clear Fork. In 1880, Frans was living in Hemphill County in the Texas Panhandle. Frans later moved back to Throckmorton County, where he operated a fruit and candy company at the county seat. The 1900 Throckmorton County census lists him as a widower. By 1905, Frans had moved yet again, back to the Texas Panhandle. He died in Dimmitt, Texas, on June 8, 1905.

13. AFT, Clear Fork Station/Stribling homestead, Oct. 20, 1999 (JA); Webb, "Frontier Life of John Chadbourne Irwin," 35, JRW Papers; AFT, Larn Grave and Camp Cooper, Oct. 20, 1999 (JA); CJ, Aug. 13, 1932 (quotation), and Aug. 14, 1932, box 9, RPC Papers; DeArment, *Bravo of the Brazos*, 65–66, 136, 143; Holden, *Lambshead before Interwoven*, 153–54, 157 (endnote quotation). Cornelius K. Stribling and his wife, Nancy, are buried in the city cemetery in Throckmorton, Texas. At the Stribling homestead, additional pieces of old limestone and yellow sandstone from the stage stop lie scattered in the backyard and along the fence line. When Butterfield historians Roscoe and Margaret Conkling investigated the history of the mail company's Clear Fork operations, they relied heavily on the combined knowledge of Shackelford County judge John Alexander Matthews and his wife, Sallie Reynolds Matthews, for much of their information. The Matthews and Reynolds families intermarried and settled in the Clear Fork country, establishing the historic Lambshead Ranch near Albany, Texas. While conducting their research in the area in August 1932, the Conklings were guests for several days at Lambshead, and Judge Matthews served as their local guide. Matthews introduced them to Frans's daughter, Elizabeth Frans Thorp, in Throckmorton, Texas. Next came an outing to the Clear Fork Butterfield station. The judge and his wife also took the couple to a scenic Clear Fork vista overlooking Camp Cooper. On this hill is the grave of noted area outlaw John Larn. During the 1870s, Larn was a disreputable, Dr. Jekyll and Mr. Hyde character; he was both the Shackelford County sheriff and a livestock rustler. Many local ranchers, including John Chadbourne Irwin, suspected Larn of stealing their cattle. Many were also unenthusiastic about his choice in deputies, notably, John Selman, who later achieved notoriety for gunning down John Wesley Hardin in El Paso in 1895. In June 1878, officials arrested Larn, but a gang of masked vigilantes murdered him in the Albany jail on June 24 before his case went to trial. The assassins were members of the Vigilance Committee or Tin Hat-Band Brigade, which was active in the Clear Fork area during Reconstruction (For more on this vigilante group, see text and endnotes below concerning Cornelius Stribling and Tryal Jackson). Speaking of Larn, Lambshead rancher Watt Matthews said, "He was a charmer with many attributes of a gentleman, but he was an outlaw, a cow thief, and a killer." Across the Clear Fork from Larn's grave, on the north bank of the river, is his first homestead, the Honeymoon Cottage, built in the early 1870s utilizing rock from the ruins of neighboring Camp Cooper. Today, the old building sits isolated out on the forlorn prairie, and its empty shell retains a lonely and desolate feel.

14. For more on Stribling, see "C. K. Stribling," available at www.terrystexasrangers.org (accessed Aug. 1, 2004); Robinson, *Frontier World*, 139; DeArment, *Bravo of the Brazos*, 124, 142, 188n81 (listing Stribling and Jackson as members of the Vigilance Committee); 1880 U.S. Census, Shackelford Co., Tex., NA, MT9, R1326, ED119, 6; 1930 U.S. Census, Throckmorton Co., Tex., NA, MT626, R2400, ED224, 4B. For more on the Old Law Mob and the Vigilance Committee, see Grant, "Early History," 88 (quotations 1–2), 89 (endnote quotation). Commenting further on the Vigilance Committee/Tin Hat-Band Brigade, Grant says that in the beginning, "its members were *bona fide* cattlemen working for the advancement of law and order and their own preservation. It is alleged that certain lawless and criminally disposed men came into the organization. The subject still provokes controversy in Shackelford County and men are divided in their opinions of the merits of the organization. At any rate, it was effective in reducing cattle theft."

15. Davis, "Camp Cooper," *Handbook*; MT, Reynolds Bend. The only in-depth history of Camp Cooper to date is Freeman's unpublished manuscript "A History of Camp Cooper, Throckmorton County, Texas."

16. 1860 U.S. Census, Throckmorton Co., Tex., NA, M653, R1308, 14; Paul to AAG, Dept. of Texas, Fort Belknap, Oct. 1, 1857, NA, RG 94, AGO, LR, M567, R566. In 1860, the fifty-year-old Harper, originally from Tennessee, listed a net worth of $7,000.

17. 1860 U.S. Census, Throckmorton Co., Tex., NA, M653, R1308, 16; U.S. Census, Shackelford Co., Tex., NA, M653, R1302, 42–43; Charles E. Mix, Acting Comm. of Indian Affairs, to Sec. of Int. Jacob Thompson, Washington, D.C., June 4, 1857, NA, RG 94, AGO, LR, M567, R561; Capt. James Nelson Caldwell, 1st Inf., to AAG, Dept. of Texas, Camp Cooper, July 14, 1857, ibid. The Maxwells immigrated to Texas from Ireland. Besides the 1860 Throckmorton County census, Margaret and John Maxwell also appear in the 1860 Shackelford County census, where their last name is erroneously recorded as "Maxfield" and their ages differ.

18. *White Man*, Sept. 13, 1860, DBC, UT; Webb, "Frontier Life of John Chadbourne Irwin," 38, JRW Papers; Young County District Court Minutes, book 1, Nov. 27, 1858, and Nov. 24, 1859. In November 1858, a Young County grand jury indicted M. B. King for aggravated assault and battery. When the case finally went to trial in November 1859, the prosecutor, K. P. Record, said he was dropping the charges against King. King does not appear in 1860 census records for either Young or Throckmorton County. Birdville, Texas, his former residence, is in Tarrant County. According to National Archives records, census takers lost the 1860 records for Tarrant County.

19. Webb, "Frontier Life of John Chadbourne Irwin," 37, 38 (quotation 1), JRW Papers; *White Man*, Sept. 13, 1860, DBC, UT (quotations 2–3); MT, Fort Griffin; Grant, "Early History," 87. Grant erroneously says that this story is about a man named Fisch, but his details are exactly the same as those that J. C. Irwin relates in his memoirs. Indeed, Grant cites a January 4, 1935, interview with J. C. Irwin as his lone source, so this must be the story of M. B. King. Irwin told Grant that he saw King's bones still lying in Maxwell Creek a year after the lynching. Mill Creek, formerly Maxwell Creek, flows into the Clear Fork of the Brazos just east of present-day Fort Griffin State Park, half a mile downstream from the Highway 283 Bridge.

20. John G. Previn to Charles Neuhaus, May 27, 1860, Clear Fork Brazos, Texas, Neuhaus Family Papers, KFN, SCL, UTA (quotation 1); *Texas State Gazette*, June 23, 1860; *White Man*, Sept. 13, 1860, DBC, UT (quotations 2–3); Webb, "Frontier Life of John Chadbourne Irwin," 38, JRW Papers. Most historians have not consulted these issues of the *Gazette* and *White Man*, leading to a flawed recounting of the Maxwell and Collins stories, erroneously discussing them in the

context of the Clear Fork's post–Civil War period instead of the antebellum period. The lone exception is Cashion, *Texas Frontier*, 48–49. There is no reference to L. F. Collins in the 1860 census for Buchanan, Young, Throckmorton, or Shackelford County. His murder may have preceded the taking of the census during the summer of 1860. The *White Man* article makes a fleeting reference to Collins's alleged membership in the Old Law Mob. Collins Creek merges with the Clear Fork just north of present-day Fort Griffin State Park. The Collins homestead, located near what was later the Fort Griffin crossing of the Clear Fork (a post–Civil War crossing), is a mile upstream from the current Highway 283 Bridge over the Clear Fork. L. F. Collins's home was 1.5 miles north-northwest of M. B. King's lynching site on Maxwell Creek. Maxwell Creek was, in turn, 3.5 miles west-northwest of where Mr. Self's son found the Old Law Mob letter and the murdered courier, Page. All three of these murders took place close to or on the Clear Fork of the Brazos and all within a 7-mile radius of the Butterfield stage stop run by Tryal Jackson and J. M. Frans.

21. 1860 U.S. Census, Throckmorton Co., Tex., NA, M653, R1308, 14 (quotation); Ledbetter, *Fort Belknap*, 101 (endnote quotation); Young County Tax Rolls, reel 1, 1857–85, TSLAC. Local historian Barbara Ledbetter claims some people suspect that MacKay "helped set up Major Robert S. Neighbors for easy assassination on the streets of Belknap." One should note that Ledbetter provides no documentation to substantiate her incriminating statement about MacKay. In 1861, A. J. MacKay had 1 slave, 8 horses, 434 head of cattle, and miscellaneous property, for a total net worth of $6,280 on county tax rolls.

22. *Contracts with the War Department*, House Exec. Doc. No. 22, 36th Cong., 1st Sess., vol. 5, ser. 1047, pp. 13–14, 25; *Contracts with the War Department*, House Exec. Doc. No. 47, 36th Cong., 2nd Sess., vol. 8, ser. 1099, pp. 24, 30, 48; 1860 U.S. Census, Throckmorton Co., Tex., NA, M653, R1308, 14. The MacKay and Gooch partnership did not limit its operations to Texas. During 1860, John C. Gooch was also the federal beef contractor for Fort Cobb, Indian Territory.

23. AFT, Lambshead Creek and Clear Fork Crossing, June 15, 1999, and Aug. 21 (JA) and Sept. 25 (JA), 2004.

24. Holden, *Lambshead before Interwoven*, 26 (quotation); Ormsby, *Butterfield Overland Mail*, 58. Butterfield passenger Waterman Ormsby relates that the Overland Mail Company considered installing a ferry on the Brazos River near Fort Belknap, but there is no record of such a ferry ever operating. Company employees did set up ferries at Pope's Crossing and Horsehead Crossing on the Pecos River. Regardless of ferry operations, all Butterfield river crossings in Texas had only one mail station in the vicinity. For examples, see Colbert's Ferry/Station on the Red River, West Fork Station on the West Fork of the Trinity, Belknap Station near the Brazos River, Clear Fork Station on the Clear Fork of the Brazos, Colorado Station on the Colorado River, North Concho Station on the North Concho River, and Horsehead Crossing Station on the Pecos River.

25. The historical cachet of having a Butterfield stage stop on their property is a source of pride among landowners in Texas.

26. GLO, Throckmorton County, Joseph N. Dalton Surveys (abstracts 189 and 190) (endnote quotation); GLO, Throckmorton County, Thomas Mounts Surveys (abstracts 228 and 229); 1853 TELC Survey 480 and Connecting Line Survey (includes Surveys 1642 and 774), Peters Colony Surveys, County Clerk's Office, Throckmorton Co., Tex.; GLO, Throckmorton County Abstract No. 259; *January 18, 1855 R.B. Marcy–R.S. Neighbors Comanche Indian Reserve Map*, County Clerk's Office, Throckmorton Co., Tex.; GLO, Map #76284, *Capt. R.B. Marcy's 1854 Map of the Country upon the Brazos and Big Wichita Rivers*; GLO, Map #1867, *1854 Map of the Surveyed Part of Peters Colony, Texas*; Parker, *Through Unexplored Texas*, 184–86; Holden, *Lambshead before Interwoven*, 11, 19; Smith, *U.S. Army*, 204. Texas land records from August 1853 show that Stem owned 640 acres in the Joseph Dalton

and Thomas Mounts Surveys. The field notes for the Dalton Survey mention the location as "at the crossing of the road from Belknap to Phantom Hill." Two Peters Colony survey maps reveal the ford's exact position. When Major Robert S. Neighbors and Captain Randolph B. Marcy surveyed the region in 1854, they drew two maps. Close-up details from these maps show "Stem's Farm" on the west side of the Clear Fork Crossing.

27. Pope, *Report of Exploration*, entry for Apr. 24, 1854, 86 (quotations); Marcy, *Thirty Years*, 209; Parker, *Through Unexplored Texas*, 186–208; AFT, Marcy-Neighbors August 1854 campsite and spring, Sept. 25, 2004 (JA).

28. Parker, *Through Unexplored Texas*, 184 (quotation 1); Marcy, *Thirty Years*, 208 (quotation 2).

29. Richardson, *Frontier of Northwest Texas*, 75–85; Holden, *Lambshead before Interwoven*, 9–17; Parker, *Through Unexplored Texas*, 184–85 (quotation); Mayhall, "Stem, Jesse," *Handbook*.

30. Mayhall, *Indian Wars of Texas*, 94; Holden, *Lambshead before Interwoven*, 18–19; Neighbours, *Robert Simpson Neighbors*, 284.

31. Young County Court Record, 1856 Book, Dec. 3, 1856; Holden, *Lambshead before Interwoven*, 22–23; *January 18, 1855 R.B. Marcy–R.S. Neighbors Comanche Indian Reserve Map*, County Clerk's Office, Throckmorton Co., Tex.; GLO, Map #76284, *Capt. R.B. Marcy's 1854 Map of the Country upon the Brazos and Big Wichita Rivers*; GLO, Map #1867, *1854 Map of the Surveyed Part of Peters Colony, Texas*.

32. 1841 England Census, Class H0107, piece 253, book 23, Ilsington, Devon Enumeration District 3, folio 5, p. 5, l. 15, GSU Roll 241324, www.ancestry.com/ (accessed Mar. 11, 2008); Connor, *Peters Colony of Texas*, 307; GLO, Map #4079, *1880 Map of Throckmorton County, Texas*; GLO, Throckmorton County, Abstracts 210 and 223; Throckmorton County Deed Records, vol. M, 73–76; Thomas Lambshead, Mexican War Compiled Service Records, Organizations from the State of Texas, NA, RG 94, AGO, M278, R11. A "William Hammock" appears in the same 1858 Young County tax roll that lists Thomas Lambshead's assets. Whether this is Samuel Hammick listed under his middle or first name (or Hammick's brother) is unknown. In the 1858 tax roll, William Hammock had one horse, twenty cattle, and a net worth of $175. Information about Samuel Hammick after his arrival in Texas (prior to July 1848) is scant. Records reveal that Hammick was in Texas at least until May 14, 1859, when he patented title to his Paint Creek property. Hammick witnessed Thomas Lambshead's Peters Colony May 11, 1850, application for 640 acres of land, and Lambshead returned the favor for Hammick's application of the same date for 320 acres next to Lambshead. Lambshead and Hammick had their parcels surveyed on the same date, August 14, 1853. In May 1859, Lambshead and Hammick patented title to their lands. Samuel's sister, Eliza Elizabeth Lambshead, born in 1825, was also from Devon, England. There is a Mexican War service record for a Thomas Lambshead dated August 8, 1848, from Kaufman Station, Texas, for service with Bell's Regiment, Texas Mounted Volunteers. This may well be the same Thomas Lambshead, as he and his wife were already in Texas before July 1848.

33. For exact details on Marcy's 1849 California Emigrant Trail through Texas, see Williams, *Old Texas Trails*, 219–44; GLO, Maps #1985, *Resurvey of Portions of Young County, Peters Colony, Texan Emigration & Land Company, 1858*; #1986, *Map of the Surveyed Part of Young District, Young Land District, 1860*; #10110, *Ward County Sketch File 22, June 4, 1875 Map of Surveys along Pecos River from Horsehead Crossing to New Mexico State Line*; #10427, Ward County Sketch File 6, *Ward County Irrigation Company, Ward and Reeves Counties*; Senate Exec. Doc. No. 78, 33rd Cong., 2nd Sess., *Map and Profile No. 1, from the Red River to the Rio Grande, by Captain John Pope, 1854–1856: Explorations and Surveys for a Railroad Route from the Mississippi River to the Pacific Ocean*, War Department. See also Young County Tax Rolls,

reel 1, 1857–85, TSLAC; Throckmorton County Deed Records, vol. M, 73–76.

34. 1850 U.S. Census, Navarro Co., Tex., NA, M432, R913, 114; Navarro County Tax Rolls, reel 1, 1846–79, TSLAC.

35. Ormsby, *Butterfield Overland Mail*, 52; Holden, *Lambshead before Interwoven*, 20, 22, 24–25, 27; Young County Tax Rolls, reel 1, 1857–85, TSLAC; *Contracts with the War Department*, House Exec. Doc. No. 50, 35th Cong., 2nd Sess., vol. 7, ser. 1006, p. 29. Lambshead's beef contract at Camp Cooper ran from April 1, 1858, to March 31, 1859. John G. Irwin succeeded Lambshead as beef contractor in October 1860. Army records list no beef contractor for Camp Cooper from April 1, 1859, to September 30, 1860. Perhaps Camp Cooper informally renewed Lambshead's contract for an additional year.

36. Ormsby, *Butterfield Overland Mail*, 52; *Dallas Herald*, May 2, 1860; R. T. Luckett to Sam Houston, Apr. 16, 1860, SH Papers, box 301-32, TSLAC; contract between Conrad Neuhaus and Thomas Lambshead, Aug. 25, 1858, Belknap, Tex., Neuhaus Family Papers, KFN, SCL, UTA (quotations). Conrad's brother, Charles Neuhaus, and M. B. King (whom the Old Law Mob would later lynch in May 1860) witnessed the Lambshead-Neuhaus contract. Period tax rolls and government quartermaster records indicate that Lambshead kept his lease on the Stem homestead during his tenure with the Overland Mail Company. Dr. Birch, a Butterfield employee, helped establish the stations in this section during the summer and fall of 1858, but Lambshead was the overseer of the stations' day-to-day operations.

37. Ormsby, *Butterfield Overland Mail*, 52; *Dallas Herald*, May 2, 1860; R. T. Luckett to Sam Houston, Apr. 16, 1860, SH Papers, box 301-32, TSLAC. Comanche Springs is at Fort Stockton, Texas. On some maps, Mountain Pass (near Merkel, Texas) is shown as Comanche Pass. The Great Comanche War Trail crossed the Pecos River at Horsehead Crossing and continued through Comanche Springs on its way to Mexico.

38. Ormsby, *Butterfield Overland Mail*, 49 (quotations).

39. For more on Texas's environmental and cultural transition zone, see Ely, *Where the West Begins*, 7–18; MT, Merkel East. The Butterfield Road crossed the one-hundredth meridian 16 miles southwest of modern Abilene, Texas, in Taylor County, 1.5 miles north of Castle Peak, where County Road 283 doglegs south to intersect County Road 353.

40. Ormsby, *Butterfield Overland Mail*, 49 (quotation 1); Williams, *Old Texas Trails*, 330 (quotation 2); Lang, *First Overland Mail: . . . St. Louis to San Francisco*, 125; *San Francisco Daily Evening Bulletin*, Nov. 25, 1858; MT, Reynolds Bend, Collins Creek, Antelope Hills, Collins Creek SW, Acampo, Smoky Draw. From Stem's Farm on Lambshead Creek, the overland road followed the north bank of Lambshead Creek, passing by present-day Lambshead Ranch headquarters, then to the Throckmorton-Shackelford County line, then southwesterly along the eastern flank of the 1,700-foot-high Antelope Hills, then southward, to a water hole two-thirds of a mile below the mouth of Bluff Creek Canyon, 15.5 miles east of Phantom Hill, a site called Comanche Springs in the Leach Wagon Train Journal of 1857. This landmark is not to be confused with the more famous Comanche Springs, far to the west at Fort Stockton, Texas. From Bluff Creek, the overland road continued southwest to Chimney Creek, site of Smith's Station.

41. Ormsby, *Butterfield Overland Mail*, 48 (quotation 2); AFT, Smith's Station, July 13, 1999 (JA, PD), and Jan. 26, 2002 (JA, PD); MT, Acampo; GLO, Map #2251, *1879 Map of Shackelford County, Texas*; CJ, Aug. 14, 1932, box 9, RPC Papers (quotation 1); PGA, Shackelford County, NA, RG 28, M841, R126; PGS, Shackelford and Taylor Counties, NA, RG 28, M1126, R580 and 588. Chimney Creek and Phantom Hill appear on post office mail route maps until October 1884. In January 1880, Jesse Canter Roberts filed an application for a post office at Chimney Creek, located on the Fort Griffin to Fort Concho mail route. Roberts served as postmaster from January to May 1880, when the post office closed.

42. GLO, Map #2251, *1879 Map of Shackelford County, Texas*; GLO, Map #4574, *May 1879 Map of Jones County, Texas*; GLO, Map #76232, Charles W. Pressler, *Pressler's 1858 Map of the State of Texas*; GLO, Map #4327, Charles W. Pressler, *1867 Traveller's Map of the State of Texas*; GLO, Map, #2133, Charles W. Pressler, *1879 Map of the State of Texas*; GLO, Map #76254, *A.R. Roessler's 1874 Latest Map of the State of Texas*; "History of Abilene and Territory," *Abilene Reporter-News*, May 20, 1928 (quotations 1–2), SWC; Conkling and Conkling, *Butterfield Overland Mail*, 1:328 (quotation 3); MT, Smokey Draw, Nugent, Hamby. En route to Phantom Hill, the overland road crossed Deadman Creek in Block 14, Survey 13, and then the Jones County line in Block 14, Survey 14. Next, it crossed Surveys 21 and 22 in Block 14, modern County Road 313, and then Elm Creek, and finally arrived at Phantom Hill, located in Block 14 on the William T. Evans Survey, 12 miles north-northeast of present-day Abilene, Texas.

43. Anderson, *Fort Phantom Hill*, 17, 19; Freeman, "History of Fort Phantom Hill," 5, 62; Frazer, *Forts of the West*, 156–57; AFT, Fort Phantom Hill, 1991–2004.

44. Marks, *Turn Your Eyes*, 178 (quotation). During his lifetime, Samuel A. Maverick of San Antonio amassed a considerable portfolio of West Texas real estate.

45. Anderson, *Fort Phantom Hill*, 19; Freeman, "History of Fort Phantom Hill," 62 (quotations). Sometimes the problems with land titles and federal contracts were the result of federal incompetence. In other cases, land speculators and post sutlers had close friends in the army who provided valuable insider information concerning site selection and potential business opportunities.

46. Elkins, *Indian Fighting*, 93, 94 (quotation), 95–96; Richardson, *Frontier of Northwest Texas*, 93. Some historians say that 250 is a more accurate number for the number of Comanches with Buffalo Hump during this visit to Fort Phantom Hill.

47. Anderson, *Fort Phantom Hill*, 17, 21 (quotation); Freeman, "History of Fort Phantom Hill," 65–67.

48. Anderson, *Fort Phantom Hill*, 25, 26 (quotations); Freeman, "History of Fort Phantom Hill," 65–67, 85–86.

49. Anderson, *Fort Phantom Hill*, 16 (quotations 2–3), 17, 20, 21 (quotation 1), 33; Freeman, "History of Fort Phantom Hill," 65 (quotation 4), 66.

50. Anderson, *Fort Phantom Hill*, 36, 42–44; Freeman, "History of Fort Phantom Hill," 86 (quotations 1–2), 91; Williams, *Old Texas Trails*, 331 (quotation 3).

51. Anderson, *Fort Phantom Hill*, 36, 42–44; Freeman, "History of Fort Phantom Hill," 89 (quotation 1); Williams, *Old Texas Trails*, 332 (quotation 2); Richardson, *Frontier of Northwest Texas*, 95–96. While traveling through in November 1854, army paymaster Colonel Albert Sidney Johnson observed the charred ruins at Phantom Hill.

52. *Texas State Gazette*, Aug. 5, 1854; Strickland, *El Paso in 1854*, 25; Bliss, *Reminiscences*, 142–43.

53. *Texas State Gazette*, Aug. 5, 1854; Strickland, *El Paso in 1854*, 25; Bliss, *Reminiscences*, 142–43; *Price Cooper v. The United States*, Indian Depredation Case No. 1561, U.S. Court of Claims, NA, RG 123. Oxen cost $40 per yoke, cows about the same, and horses were $80 to $100 each. Freighter Price Cooper, a former mail line employee, detailed the value of livestock in his depredations claim against Comanches and Apaches. Comanches attacked Cooper's wagon train at the old Butterfield Head of Concho Station in 1866.

54. GLO, Map #K-&-11, Film No. 22, *1852 Sketch of the Route from the Camp on the Concho River to Phantom Hill, Texas*; Anderson, *Fort Phantom Hill*, 20, 26; Freeman, "History of Fort Phantom Hill," 5 (quotation), 76; Freeman, "History of Fort Chadbourne," 10–11, 29. The origins of this military road date to the fall of 1851, when Captain

Joseph Eggleston Johnston scouted the region between Belknap and the North Concho and laid out a trail. During 1852, Corporal I. Cotterell of the Fifth Infantry sketched a detailed color map of the new route.

55. Ormsby, *Butterfield Overland Mail*, 48, 50 (quotation); Conkling and Conkling, *Butterfield Overland Mail*, 1:330; contract between Conrad Neuhaus and Thomas Lambshead, Aug. 25, 1858, Belknap, Tex., Neuhaus Family Papers, KFN, SCL, UTA; Lang, *First Overland Mail: . . . San Francisco to Memphis*, 67–68. At the Clear Fork Station and again at Phantom Hill, Ormsby mentions Butterfield agent Dr. Birch, who helped establish operations along this section. Thomas Lambshead, however, was the day-to-day overseer of this portion of the route, as evidenced by his long-term contract with Conrad Neuhaus. This contract, made on behalf of the Overland Mail Company, was for supplies to multiple stations, to be paid on a quarterly basis.

56. Ormsby, *Butterfield Overland Mail*, 50 (quotations 1–3); Lang, *First Overland Mail: . . . San Francisco to Memphis*, 67–68; *St. Louis Missouri Republican*, Feb. 1, 1859 (quotation 4), Feb. 7, 1859.

57. Lang, *First Overland Mail: . . . San Francisco to Memphis*, 67, 68 (quotations 2–3); Richardson, *Beyond the Mississippi*, 228 (quotation 1).

58. For specifics regarding the route of the Butterfield Road through Jones and Taylor Counties, see GLO, Map #4574, *May 1879 Map of Jones County, Texas*; GLO, Map #4073, *February 1879 Map of Taylor County*; W. A. Riney, *November 1927 Map of the Butterfield Trail through Taylor County, Texas*, Richardson Library, Hardin-Simmons University; MT, Hamby, Hawley, Abilene West, Merkel East, View, Mountain Pass; AFT, Sept. 26, 1999, John Davis Chapter, D.A.R., 1929 "Butterfield Trail" stone marker on north frontage road of Interstate 20 in Tye, Tex.; AFT, Sept. 26, 1999, "Butterfield Mail and Stage Line" 1969 THC marker on north frontage road of Interstate 20 in Tye, Tex. See also Ormsby, *Butterfield Overland Mail*, 51 (quotation); Lang, *First Overland Mail: . . . St. Louis to San Francisco*, 109, 124–25; Lang, *First Overland Mail: . . . San Francisco to Memphis*, 39; Pate and Fort Chadbourne Foundation, *Fort Chadbourne*, 141–42; Freeman and Pate, "Fort Chadbourne Chronology," 172, 173 (endnote quotation). On August 22, 1867, near East Peak on the overland road, fifty Native American warriors (likely Comanches) ambushed nine troopers from the Fourth Cavalry. Sergeant Benjamin Jenkins and his men quickly dismounted, taking up a defensive position on a neighboring hill. During the intense firefight that followed, the well-armed raiding party utilized rifles and revolvers, along with bows and arrows, against Jenkins's party. The soldiers finally repulsed their attackers, but not before the Indians killed Privates John Maroney and Daniel Wurm. A detail sent back to find the two slain men reported that their almost unrecognizable bodies were "pierced with arrow[s] and bullet wounds, scalped and otherwise horribly mutilated." The soldiers buried the hapless privates alongside the Butterfield Road. The attack took place on the Overland Mail Route 6 miles east of Mountain Pass, which is where the road passes under the north side of East Peak in the Guadalupe County School Land Survey.

59. CJ, May 9, 1931, box 9, RPC Papers (quotation 4); CM 1931, p. 147, box 9, RPC Papers (endnote quotation); Sam Butman, Sr., to Roscoe Conkling (quotations 1–3), Oct. 22, 1936, box 14, RPC Papers; "Mountain Pass Station" 1968 THC marker near station site; AFT, Mountain Pass Station, Sept. 26, 1999 (JA), and Aug. 10, 2000 (JA). A short distance north of the spring, a settler in the early twentieth century built a wood frame house with stone chimney. Nothing remains of this clapboard house today. Margaret Conkling speculated, "The old settler's home . . . is probably constructed of some of the stones from the old station." Barry Scott, a local resident, spent much time hiking and exploring the area as a youth forty years ago and collected many items from the Butterfield station, including bullets, mule shoes, crockery, military buttons, and even a Confederate officer's cufflinks.

60. *Dallas Herald*, May 2, 1860; Ormsby, *Butterfield Overland Mail*, 51–52.

61. *Dallas Herald*, May 2, 1860; Ormsby, *Butterfield Overland Mail*, 51 (quotation 1), 52 (quotations 2–3); Lang, *First Overland Mail: . . . St. Louis to San Francisco*, 124 (quotation 4).

62. Lang, *First Overland Mail: . . . St. Louis to San Francisco*, 124 (quotation 1); *St. Louis Missouri Republican*, Oct. 6, 1859 (quotations 2–5).

63. Lang, *First Overland Mail: . . . St. Louis to San Francisco*, 124 (quotation 1); *New York Times*, July 23 and 24 (quotations 2–3) and Aug. 18, 1860. The deceased cattle drover named MacKay is not to be confused with Andrew J. MacKay.

64. GLO, Map #4073, *February 1879 Map of Taylor County* (quotation 1); *1867 Sketch of Comanche Pass, Texas*, NACP (quotation 2); R. T. Luckett to Sam Houston, Apr. 16, 1860, SH Papers, box 301-32, TSLAC; Williams, *Old Texas Trails*, 333 (quotations 3–4); Lang, *First Overland Mail: . . . St. Louis to San Francisco*, 124 (Comanche Springs).

65. *St. Louis Missouri Republican*, Feb. 1, Mar. 10 (quotation 1), and Mar. 14 (quotation 2), 1859.

66. *Dallas Herald*, May 2, 1860 (quotations); 1841 England Census, Class H0107, piece 253, book 23, Islington County, Devon Enumeration District 3, fol. 5, p. 5, l. 15, GSU Roll 241324, www.ancestry.com/ (accessed Mar. 11, 2008).

67. Austerman, *Sharps Rifles*, 231; May 27, 1871, Department of Texas Headquarters, NA, RG 393, MF 145, LS, M1114, R1; Texas Historical Commission, Marker #3565, "Near Site of Indian Battle," Taylor Co., Tex., in *Atlas*.

68. Texas Historical Commission, Marker #5646, "Vicinity of Indian Fight," Taylor Co., Tex., in *Atlas*; Aug. 15, 1871, Fort Concho, Records of Headquarters, NA, RG 393, MF 68, LS, Group A, R2.

69. AFT, Elm Creek Rock House site, Jan. 27, 2007 (JA); GLO, Map #4073, *February 1879 Map of Taylor County*; GLO, Map #3916, *Map of Nolan County*, no date; W. A. Riney, *November 1927 Map of the Butterfield Trail through Taylor County, Texas*, Richardson Library, Hardin-Simmons University; Ormsby, *Butterfield Overland Mail*, 51–52; Lang, *First Overland Mail: . . . St. Louis to San Francisco*, 109, 124; Lang, *First Overland Mail: . . . San Francisco to Memphis*, 39; MT, Mountain Pass, Hylton; *Taylor County: An Early History of Pioneer Settlers*, Taylor County Old Settlers Association, 1923, SWC. The present county road exits via the gap's eastern channel, heading straight south to Ranch Road 89. The Butterfield, however, departed via the pass's western channel toward Elm Creek. Before reaching this stream, however, the road passed by the ruins of a 10- by 30-foot rock house. Local history holds that in 1858, a man named Smith erected this two-room structure, complete with wood-shingled roof. The building allegedly served as a Butterfield "run house" or safe house where passengers took shelter in case of Indian attack. Smith supposedly served as a veterinarian for the Overland Mail Company, caring for worn-out or sick livestock at his ranch. Locals called the rock structure the "Smith House Ranch" in 1928, when the current owner's family purchased the property. A visit to the site in early 2007 confirmed that the old ruin is indeed located on the Butterfield Road. Joe Allen (with metal detector) located period artifacts in the trail leading to and away from the rock house. It bears noting, however, that at no other point on the line in Texas did the mail company operate a safe house for stagecoach travelers. In addition, there are no references to Smith's Ranch House or a stage station on Elm Creek in any period itinerary, newspaper, journal, or book. Finally, a thorough search with a metal detector around the rock ruin found no pre–Civil War artifacts, which makes it likely that this structure dates from the 1870s, when ranchers first moved into the Elm Creek drainage.

70. Ormsby, *Butterfield Overland Mail*, 51–52; Lang, *First Overland Mail: . . . St. Louis to San Francisco*, 109, 124; Lang, *First Overland Mail:*

. . . *San Francisco to Memphis*, 39; Tate, *Frontier Army*, 119 (quotation).

71. AFT, Valley Creek, Sept. 26, 1999 (JA), Sept. 13, 2000 (JA), and Feb. 9, 2008; Williams, *Old Texas Trails*, 335 (quotation); MT, Hylton. According to the 1857 Leach journal, where the road crossed Valley Creek, the clear, shallow water was only several feet wide. At the falls, a short distance below the ford, the creek dropped almost a foot in elevation. Below the falls, there was a large pool 40–50 yards deep and 200–300 yards wide.

72. In August 1864, authorities called Lambshead as a witness in a court of inquiry investigating the conduct of Captain George C. Rives, post quartermaster, Second Congressional District. See Thomas Lambshead, Confederate Citizens File, NA, RG 109, M346. For a detailed discussion concerning the collapse of Texas's frontier line during the Civil War, see Ely, *Where the West Begins*, 35–61.

73. Young County Tax Rolls, reel 1, 1857–85, TSLAC; Holden, *Lambshead before Interwoven*, 20, 24–25, 27; Ormsby, *Butterfield Overland Mail*, 52; Connor, *Peters Colony of Texas*, 307; Throckmorton County Deed Records, vol. M, 73–76; GLO, Brazos County Abstract 223; Brazos County Tax Rolls, reel 1, 1842–88, TSLAC; Thomas Lambshead, June 18, 1869, probate, pp. 14–15, England and Wales, National Probate Calendar (Index of Wills and Administrations), 1858–1966, Principal Probate Registry, www.ancestry.com/ (accessed June 27, 2013). Thomas Lambshead's probated will listed assets of less than £200. Information regarding Samuel Hammick and his death is scant. For records concerning Eliza Lambshead and her remaining years in Devon, England, see 1871 England Census, Class RG10, piece 2082, fol. 107, p. 15, GSU Roll 831780; 1881 England Census, Class RG11, piece 2172, fol. 94, p. 50, GSU Roll 1341523; and 1901 England Census, Class RG13, piece 2066, fol. 146, p. 24 (all at www.ancestry.com); England and Wales, Free BMD Death Index, 1837–1983, General Registrar Office, England and Wales Civil Registration Indexes, Year 1906, vol. 5b, p. 106, www.ancestry.com.

CHAPTER 6. FROM FORT CHADBOURNE TO THE NORTH CONCHO

1. GLO, Map #4073, *February 1879 Map of Taylor County, Texas*; GLO, Map #3916, *Map of Nolan County, Texas*, no date; GLO, Map #4912, *November 1904 Map of Coke County, Texas*; GLO, Map #4004, *November 1858 Map of Runnels County, Texas*; GLO, Map #4003, *May 1867 Map of Runnels County, Texas*; W. A. Riney, *November 1927 Map of the Butterfield Trail through Taylor County, Texas*, Richardson Library, Hardin-Simmons University; MT, Hylton, Church Peak; AFT, Valley Creek to Fort Chadbourne, Feb. 9, 2008; Gournay, *Texas Boundaries*, 81, 113; PGA, Runnels Co., Tex., NA, RG 28, M841, R126; Freeman and Pate, "Fort Chadbourne Chronology," 147, 187; Frazer, *Forts of the West*, 145–46. The state legislature carved Coke County out of Tom Green County in March 1889. U.S. Postmaster General records list the first post office for Fort Chadbourne as being in Runnels County. Although the legislature created Runnels County in February 1858, area residents did not organize the county until February 1880. Federal troops abandoned Fort Chadbourne on March 23, 1861. The government regarrisoned Chadbourne on May 25, 1867, only to deactivate it in 1868. George Leigh assumed his postmaster duties at the fort on January 28, 1859.

2. Tallack, *California Overland Express*, 51 (quotation 1), 51–52 (quotation 2), 52 (quotation 3).

3. Freeman, "History of Fort Chadbourne," 28–32; Conkling and Conkling, *Butterfield Overland Mail*, 1:353; AFT, Camp J. E. Johnston, June 20, 2004 (JA, PD), and Feb. 9, 2008 (with Garland and Lana Richards). Freeman, like many other writers over the past century, conflates the army's 1852 Camp J. E. Johnston (named after Captain Joseph Eggleston Johnston and located on the south bank

of the North Concho River near Carlsbad, Texas) with Butterfield's Camp Johnson (namesake of Adam Rankin Johnson and located on the north bank of the Middle Concho River near Arden, Texas). The error originates with Butterfield historians Margaret and Roscoe Conkling, who were not aware that they were dealing with two different sites. Garland Richards, owner of Fort Chadbourne and an expert on nineteenth-century military artifacts, thoroughly examined all of the artifacts found at Camp J. E. Johnston and dated them to 1852.

4. Freeman, "History of Fort Chadbourne," 29 (quotation), 32.

5. Ibid., 30, 34–35, 38.

6. Ibid., 34–35, 38; Ormsby, *Butterfield Overland Mail*, 54; Capt. J. N. Caldwell, 1st Inf., Cmdr. Camp Cooper, Tex., to AGO, Mar. 13, 1857, NA, RG 94, AGO, LR, M567, R560; Post Sutler Review Board to AGO, Fort Chadbourne, Tex., Apr. 30, 1860, NA, RG 94, AGO, LR, M567, R624; Evans and Howard Credit Reports, Texas vol. 3, Bexar County, p. 92, DCR, BL; R. A. Howard Credit Reports, p. 94, DCR, BL (endnote quotations); Richard Howard and Flint, Fort Mason, Credit Reports, Texas vol. 11, Gillespie County, p. 150, DCR, BL; Downing and Swift, "Howard, Richard Austin," *Handbook*; Jerry Ponder, *Fort Mason, Texas*, 108. During 1849, Richard Howard served as a scout for the U.S. Army. His brother was in Congress, which may have aided him in securing military sutlerships in Texas. Howard originally worked at Wallace and Co. and later partnered with Onesimus Evans from 1852 to 1854. The firm served as sutlers for five companies of the Eighth Infantry. Howard married Evans's daughter. In 1854, he went into business for himself. He subsequently partnered with George Leigh, an association that ended by May 1858. From 1859 to 1861, Howard had a store at Fort Mason. He also leased the land for Fort Mason to the government. Regarding his business character, credit reports state that Howard was "a very honest young man, good habits" and "a man of family, good for his contracts, owns good landed estate," and that he was "good for all he will buy."

7. 1860 U.S. Census, Throckmorton Co., Tex., NA, M653, R1308, 14; GLO, Abstract 440, Runnels Co., Texas; 1850 U.S. Census, Milam and Williamson Co., Tex., NA, M432, R916, 338; Freeman and Pate, "Fort Chadbourne Chronology," 112; GLO, Map #4004, *November 1858 Map of Runnels County, Texas*; GLO, Map #4003, *May 1867 Map of Runnels County, Texas*; MT, Hylton, Church Peak; Freeman, "History of Fort Phantom Hill," 76; A. J. MacKay, Georgetown, Credit Report, Texas vol. 33, Williamson County, p. 300 (endnote quotations), DCR, BL. Before Fort Phantom Hill's closing, William Dalrymple held the federal hay contract for the post. Reports noted that in 1852, prior to purchasing the Fish Creek acreage, A. J. MacKay was living at Fort Gates, "the military station on the Leon," and that "since the break up of that station [MacKay] has gone far up the country."

8. GLO, Abstract 527, Menard Co., Texas; 1860 U.S. Census, San Saba Co., Tex., NA, M653, R1304, 382; 1850 U.S. Census, Milam and Williamson Co., Tex., NA, M432, R916, 153, 337, 339, 340; Smith, *U.S. Army*, 203–204; *Texas State Gazette*, July 29, 1854. In 1854, MacKay purchased a second parcel of land, a 347-acre ranch on the San Saba River, 11 miles southeast of present-day Menard, near another federal outpost, Fort McKavett. Rancher Thomas Gooch, another brother of John C. Gooch's, lived upriver from MacKay's Fort McKavett property, in San Saba, Texas.

9. Smith, *U.S. Army*, 205–208, 210, 212; 1860 U.S. Census, Throckmorton Co., Tex., NA, M653, R1308, 14; *Southern Intelligencer*, Nov. 24, 1858 (quotations).

10. Minnesota Territorial and State Censuses: 1849–1905, www.ancestry.com/ (accessed Mar. 11, 2008); 1870 U.S. Census, Mason Co., Tex., M593, R1597, 463; Deposition of Ben F. Gooch, *Joel D. Hoy v. The United States and the Apache Indians*, Indian Depredation Case No. 2626, U.S. Court of Claims, NA, RG 123; Freeman and Pate, "Fort Chadbourne Chronology," 15. After the Civil War, a man with the same

name and approximating MacKay's general description was living in Goodhue County in Minnesota Territory. In 1875, this forty-five-year-old New Yorker was living with Annie, his twenty-four-year-old wife. Ben F. Gooch served for a number of years as the Mason County clerk in Mason, Texas, dabbling in real estate and raising cattle.

11. Freeman and Pate, "Fort Chadbourne Chronology," 15, 51 (quotation); Boyd, *Archeological Investigations*, ii, 12–19; Heitman, *Historical Register*, 1:795.

12. Freeman and Pate, "Fort Chadbourne Chronology," 49 (quotation); *Texas State Gazette*, Oct. 7, 1854; Heitman, *Historical Register*, 1:274.

13. *New York Daily News*, Oct. 18, 1854; *Texas State Gazette*, Oct. 7, 1854 (quotations 1–3); Ormsby, *Butterfield Overland Mail*, 53 (quotation 4); Richardson, *Beyond the Mississippi*, 228 (quotation 5).

14. AFT, Fort Chadbourne, 1991–2014; *Dallas Herald*, July 17 and Aug. 14, 1858.

15. *Dallas Herald*, July 17, Aug. 14, Sept. 1, Sept. 8, Sept. 22, and Nov. 24, 1858; *St. Louis Missouri Republican*, Jan. 28 (quotation) and Oct. 6, 1859.

16. *St. Louis Missouri Republican*, Feb. 4, 1859 (quotation 1); *New York Times*, Feb. 7, 1859 (quotations 2–4); Hollon, *Frontier Violence*, 203 (endnote quotations). Eugene Hollon said that Butterfield stages were "never stopped by highwaymen" and "did not carry shipments of gold," but period accounts show otherwise.

17. *St. Louis Missouri Republican*, Jan. 12, 1859 (quotation); *New York Times*, Mar. 14, 1860.

18. Field notes for Alfred Dorsey Survey, GLO, Coke County Abstract 85, located a short distance southwest of Fort Chadbourne, referencing the Butterfield Road ("road leading to head of the Concho River"); field notes for Survey 474, Coke County Clerk's Office, Field Notes Book 2; AFT, Oak Creek Butterfield crossing southwest of Fort Chadbourne, Feb. 10, 2008; J. E. Johnston, *1853 Map of the Frontier of the Eighth Military Department*, NACP, RG 77, Records of the Office of the Chief of Engineers (hereafter OCE), Map No. Q50; J. E. Johnston, *Fort Belknap to North Concho 1851 Reconnaissance*, NACP, RG 77, OCE, Map No. Q52; Lt. Col. E. J. Strang, *Topographical Sketch of the Road from Fort Stockton to Fort Chadbourne, October and November 1867*, NACP, RG 77, OCE, Q135 Roll, H374, Texas; Hunt, "Hayrick, Texas," *Handbook*; "Hayrick Mountain," *Handbook*; phone interview with Garland Richards, Fort Chadbourne, Tex., Dec. 28, 2007; AFT, Nipple Peak and West Kickapoo Creek, Jan. 27, 2002 (JA, PD); Ormsby, *Butterfield Overland Mail*, 53–56; Lang, *First Overland Mail: . . . St. Louis to San Francisco*, 109, 124; Lang, *First Overland Mail: . . . San Francisco to Memphis*, 39. The overland trail exited Fort Chadbourne's parade ground and crossed Oak Creek a short distance beyond. Today, the Butterfield crossing is still evident by the deep, wide channels on both sides of the creek, carved by countless coaches and wagons over the years. Local residents and travelers continued to use portions of the trail into the twentieth century, in yet another example of the Butterfield Road's enduring historical significance. After crossing Oak Creek, the Butterfield passed east of Nipple Peak and the 2,440-foot Kickapoo Mountain. Along this section, the old trail is still clearly visible, and one can see many grooves cut into the exposed sandstone bedrock by countless wagon wheels. Next, the overland road forded West Kickapoo Creek southeast of the towering 2,400-foot regional landmark, Hayrick Mountain. In the 1880s, a small group of settlers founded the town of Hayrick just south of the mountain. When local residents organized Coke County in 1889, Hayrick became the first county seat. However, several of its courthouses burned quickly in succession over the next two years, and many people suspected arson. It seems that some county residents did not want Hayrick as the county seat, preferring the town of Robert Lee, 7 miles to the southwest. After Hayrick's destruction, Robert Lee won a new county seat election in

1891 by forty-eight votes. Following the election, Hayrick rapidly faded into obscurity and is now a long-forgotten Texas ghost town.

19. Richardson, *Beyond the Mississippi*, 228 (quotations 1–2), 230, 231 (quotations 3–4).

20. Ibid., 228 (quotation); "Southern Overland Mail, 1858–1861," 1966 Texas Historical Commission marker at Cow Creek and Highway 158, 5.75 miles east of Robert Lee, Texas, where Butterfield Road crosses the highway; MT, Robert Lee, Cement Mountain; AFT, Highway 158, Cow Creek, and Butterfield crossing of the Colorado River, Sept. 28, 1999 (JA). The Butterfield crossing on the north bank of the Colorado is downstream from the mouth of Machae Creek and upstream of where Cow Creek empties into the watershed. At the ford, the river bottom is solid, with gentle, sloping banks and sandbars on both sides. The crossing on the south bank of the Colorado is below Jack Miles Creek near Buffalo Creek.

21. J. E. Johnston, *Fort Belknap to North Concho 1851 Reconnaissance*, NACP, RG 77, OCE, Map No. Q52; J. E. Johnston, *1853 Map of the Frontier of the Eighth Military Department*, NACP, RG 77, OCE, Map No. Q50; Conkling and Conkling, *Butterfield Overland Mail*, 1:345 (endnote quotation); Ormsby, *Butterfield Overland Mail*, 55 (quotations), 57; MT, Cement Mountain; AFT, Buffalo Creek and Cement Creek, Sept. 20, 1999 (JA). For much of the next 15-mile section from the Colorado to the stage station on Grape Creek, the Overland Mail Road paralleled the Buffalo Creek drainage to its headwaters. See GLO, Map #66757, *November 1904 Map of Coke County, Texas*, Tom Green County Field Notes, Book C, 188, WTC. The D&SE Railroad Co. Survey 1 (Coke County Abstract No. 126) shows Buffalo Creek and the "Butterfield trail" less than 200 feet apart. The overland road first crosses through Caldwell County School Land Survey (Coke County Abstract No. 46), immediately to the north, before entering Survey 1. In their study of the Butterfield route between the Colorado and the Concho Rivers, Roscoe and Margaret Conkling confuse the layout and dates of the U.S. Army's military roads in West Texas. The Conklings mistakenly state that 4 miles from the Colorado River crossing, the Butterfield Road left the "old Military road which followed on southwest by way of Pecan spring [*sic*], while the Butterfield road from this junction to the Middle Concho River, was a newly opened Company-built section of the road." This is incorrect. The military road to Pecan Spring the Conklings describe is a post–Civil War trail the U.S. Army blazed between Fort Chadbourne and Fort Concho in 1867. In fact, from the Colorado to the North Concho, the Butterfield Road continued following Captain J. E. Johnston's 1851 military road. At the North Concho, the Butterfield route finally left Johnston's road, which continued southeast to Fort Mason. From the North Concho to the Middle Concho, overland stagecoaches utilized a new segment laid out by the mail company in 1858.

22. Tom Green County Field Notes, Book C, 188, WTC; Henderson and Overton Railroad, R. H. Harris Survey No. 10 (Coke County Abstract No. 1617), June 3, 1879, Coke County Field Notes Book 2; GLO, Map #66757, *November 1904 Map of Coke County, Texas*; AFT, Butterfield Peak, Buffalo Creek, Cement Creek, and Butterfield Canyon, Sept. 20, 1999 (JA); MT, Cement Mountain, Pecan Motte; Coke County Commissioners Court Minutes, book 1, 17–19; Survey 11, Block Z, Tom Green County Field Notes Book 15, 105, WTC; Williams, *Old Texas Trails*, 340 (quotation). From the west bank of the Colorado, the trail approximated present-day Valley View Road for roughly 4 miles. Then, in the Caldwell County School Land Survey, the Butterfield Road crossed one prong of Buffalo Creek, and the route intersects modern Highway 208 half a mile below the old community of Valley View. Early Coke County Commissioners Court minutes record the Butterfield crossing of the Robert Lee and San Angelo Road at 9 miles south of Robert Lee.

23. Ormsby, *Butterfield Overland Mail*, 56 (quotation); AFT, But-

terfield Peak, Buffalo Creek, Cement Creek, and Butterfield Canyon, Sept. 20, 1999 (JA); MT, Cement Mountain, Pecan Motte; GLO, Map #66757, *November 1904 Map of Coke County, Texas*; AFT, Highway 208 south of Robert Lee, Tex., Mar. 30, 2007, for Butterfield Peak Ranch and Butterfield Canyon Ranch signage. A GLO Scrap File Sketch for Coke Co., Texas, cites Butterfield Canyon in the southwest corner of H&OB RR Co. Survey 9.

24. MT, Pecan Motte; AFT, Butterfield Draw and Grape Creek, Aug. 21, 1999 (JA, PD, Jock March), June 19 (JA, PD) and Aug. 15 (JA), 2004, July 30–31, 2007, and May 7–8, 2008; CJ, July 27, 1933, box 9, RPC Papers. Jock March (now deceased) is the only person I encountered throughout my twenty-five years of Butterfield research who actually met Roscoe and Margaret Conkling. Jock appears as a young boy with his father, John Abe March, and Roscoe Conkling in a photograph from the Conklings' field trip to Coke County.

25. Williams, *Old Texas Trails*, 341 (quotations).

26. Ormsby, *Butterfield Overland Mail*, 56 (quotation); Lang, *First Overland Mail: . . . St. Louis to San Francisco*, 109, 124; Lang, *First Overland Mail: . . . San Francisco to Memphis*, 39.

27. Lang, *First Overland Mail: . . . St. Louis to San Francisco*, 109, 124; Lang, *First Overland Mail: . . . San Francisco to Memphis*, 77 (quotations).

28. Elkins, *Indian Fighting*, 103–105; Johnson, *Partisan Rangers*, 8.

29. Elkins, *Indian Fighting*, 103, 104 (quotation 1), 105 (quotation 4); Johnson, *Partisan Rangers*, 8 (quotations 2–3); 1860 U.S. Census, Mason Co., Tex., NA, M653, R1300, 486–87; 1860 U.S. Census, Burnet Co., Tex., NA, M653, R1289, 161. Elkins and Johnson spell the station keeper's name as "Pennington," while the 1860 federal census for Mason County spells it as "Penington." When not managing stage stops for Butterfield, Pennington, a forty-five-year-old Tennessean, raised cattle. His twenty-eight-year-old wife, Harriet, was from Missouri. Charles Cox, Pennington's neighbor at Fort Mason and a fellow Tennessean, worked as a laborer. Cox lived with his mother and his brother Thomas, the sheriff of Mason County. In addition to his job for the mail company, thirty-six-year-old Elijah Helms of Kentucky ran a blacksmith shop in Burnet, Texas. Helms lived with his twenty-seven-year-old wife, Jerusia, and his brother, John. Over the past 150 years, Grape Creek Station has eluded detection. Butterfield historians Roscoe and Margaret Conkling never found it, despite three trips to the area over a three-year period. Finally, after a nine-year search in which Joe Allen and Patrick Dearen participated, in May 2008, the landowner and I found the elusive Overland Mail Company station in Butterfield Draw.

30. Freeman, "History of Fort Chadbourne," 37. In October and November 1858, troop strength at Fort Chadbourne was 50 and 40 men, respectively. In April 1860, it was 54.

31. AFT, military and civilian campsite near Ruby Point, Aug. 21, 1999 (JA, PD), and June 19, 2004 (JA, PD); Williams, *Old Texas Trails*, 341; MT, Pecan Motte, Murph Draw, Mt. Nebo, Carlsbad, Tex.; "Message from the President of the United States, Dec. 4, 1860," in Senate Exec. Doc. No. 1, 36th Cong., 2nd Sess., 24; Ely, *Where the West Begins*, 54, 149; Maj. George Henry Thomas, 2nd Cav., Cmdr. Camp Cooper, to AAG, Dept. of Texas, Aug. 31, 1860, NA, RG 94, AGO, LR, M567, R634 (endnote quotation). The site near Ruby Point may be where the Leach Wagon Train camped for several days in September 1857. In August 1860, Major George Thomas (later called the "Rock of Chickamauga" at the 1863 Civil War battle of same name) and troopers from Company D, Second Cavalry camped at the same Grape Creek site as the Leach Wagon Train or very close to it. Thomas's description of his camp's location between the Grape Creek mail station and the Butterfield crossing on the North Concho is a perfect match to Leach's. Thomas noted that on a high bank of Grape Creek "is a beautiful position for a small cavalry post, on a gravelly hill, overlooking

the creek and shaded with fine large live oak trees." Joe Allen found a cavalry spur and numerous period artifacts at this military and civilian campsite on Grape Creek near Ruby Point.

32. AFT, current D.A.R. marker site in picnic area on Highway 87, July 30, 2007; Richardson, *Beyond the Mississippi*, 231 (quotations). In 1928, the San Angelo Pocahontas D.A.R. Chapter placed a monument where the Butterfield Trail struck the San Angelo to Carlsbad highway, not far from the North Concho crossing. During a recent widening of this thoroughfare, the Texas Highway Department moved the marker several miles eastward toward San Angelo, placing it in a picnic area next to the Texas A&M Agrilife Research and Extension Center on Highway 87. Unfortunately, the monument's present location serves only to mislead visitors stopping to read it. The picnic area is nowhere near the old Butterfield crossing of the North Concho.

33. Richardson, *Beyond the Mississippi*, 231 (quotations).

34. *Mesilla Times*, Apr. 13, 1861, SCL, UTEP; Conkling and Conkling, *Butterfield Overland Mail*, 1:351; AFT, site of old Blocker Ranch, Apr. 3, 2004 (JA); AFT, Butterfield station and crossing on North Concho River, Mar. 1, 2004 (JA, PD); Tom Green County Commissioner's Court Minutes, July 1877 term (endnote quotation 2) and Sept. 1877 term (endnote quotation 1), WTC; Lt. Col. E. J. Strang, *Topographical Sketch of the Road from Fort Stockton to Fort Chadbourne, October and November 1867*, NACP, RG 77, Q135 Roll, H374, Texas; Capt. Joseph Rendlebrock, 4th Cav., Apr. 17, 1872, report and Apr. 20, 1872, scouting map of Grape Creek, North Concho, and Middle Concho Rivers, NA, RG 393, vol. 54, Reports of Scouts, Jan. 15, 1872, to Oct. 25, 1878, Fort Concho, Texas; Heitman, *Historical Register*, 1:823; Haley, *Fort Concho*, 90–95. The mail company may have discontinued the North Concho stage stop by early 1861, as the last published Butterfield itinerary for Texas does not list it. The Conklings mistakenly placed the Butterfield crossing of the North Concho on the old Blocker Ranch near Carlsbad, Texas. The couple also claimed that the Blocker Ranch site was a Ben Ficklin stage stop after the Civil War. This is incorrect. The Blockers, prominent West Texas cattlemen after the Civil War, conducted far-ranging cattle operations across Texas and the western United States. A thorough survey of the old Blocker Ranch by Joe Allen and me conducted in March 2004 with metal detectors revealed no antebellum artifacts, only items from the 1880s and later. The actual site of Butterfield's North Concho Station was upriver, west of the Blocker Ranch, and adjacent to Butterfield's crossing of the North Concho. Albert Richardson describes the North Concho Station as a log cabin, but at some point, there was a station house built of stone at the North Concho site, perhaps after the Comanche attacks of 1859. Tom Green County records from 1877 mention "the old Butterfield Station known as the Rock House," and "the Rock House on the north side of the North Concho River." In addition, Captain Joseph Rendlebrock's April 1872 army scouting map shows the Stone House at the Overland Mail route's crossing of the North Concho. In the late 1870s, county commissioners used the old Butterfield station on the North Concho as a demarcation point between county precincts. County commissioners also reference this same rock house in later court minutes dating from 1879 to 1882. Joseph Rendlebrock, originally from Prussia, retired from the army in 1879 and died ten years later. J. Evetts Haley is the only writer who mentions the overland mail station on the North Concho. Although the Conklings and A. C. Greene cite Albert D. Richardson's book throughout their respective studies, they omit Richardson's reference to Butterfield's North Concho Station. Neither the Conklings nor Greene knew of this Overland Mail Company station or its location and were likely confused by Richardson's narrative. Additionally, keeping track of different Butterfield place-names can be tricky. Careful attention is required to avoid conflating events and mail stations, which even Haley did along this section of the route. Butterfield often named its stage stops after the

initial station keepers. These managers subsequently moved around a lot, managing various stations along the line.

CHAPTER 7. FROM THE NORTH CONCHO TO HORSEHEAD CROSSING

1. MT, Carlsbad, Knickerbocker NW, Arden, Mertzon SW; Neighbours, "Expedition," 56. For more information on Lieutenant Francis Theodore Bryan's exploration of the Upper Emigrant Road from San Antonio to El Paso during the summer of 1849, see Senate Exec. Doc. No. 64, 31st Cong., 1st Sess., 14–25. For more background on Bryan, see Heitman, *Historical Register*, 257. For additional details on the average speed of coaches on the route, see Ormsby, *Butterfield Overland Mail*, 61. Ormsby's mileage chart for Texas, including from Fort Chadbourne to El Paso, appears on page 60. The Concho River, which empties into the Colorado River near Paint Rock, Texas, is fed by three separate strands, namely, the South Concho, the Middle Concho, and the North Concho. As it approached the Middle Concho watershed from the southeast, the 1849 Upper Emigrant Road from San Antonio and Fredericksburg passed by the 2,600-foot Green Mounds (now called Lopez Peaks, 5.5 miles northwest of Sherwood, Texas), eventually striking the watershed near the intersection of present-day Irion County Road 412 and the Middle Concho. Pages 17 and 18 of Lieutenant Bryan's report specifically detail the section of the Upper Emigrant Road from Kickapoo Spring to Lipan Spring to the South Concho to Dove Creek to Good Spring Creek to the Green Mounds and on to the Middle Concho.

2. MT, Arden; CJ, Aug. 6, 1932, box 9, RPC Papers; 1861 Quartermaster Returns for Camp Concha [*sic*], box 401-835, Texas State Troop Records, Civil War Records, Texas Adjutant General's Department, TSLAC; Ely, *Where the West Begins*, 54, 149n48; Ashmore, *Archaeological Investigations*; Conkling and Conkling, *Butterfield Overland Mail*, 1:352–53; Dry Creek pictures, box 6, Texas Stage Photos, RPC Papers; Ormsby, *Butterfield Overland Mail*, 57; Lang, *First Overland Mail: . . . St. Louis to San Francisco*, 109, 124; Lang, *First Overland Mail: . . . San Francisco to Memphis*, 39; *Mesilla Times*, Apr. 13, 1861, SCL, UTEP; Tom Green County 1879 Probate Records, 62, 68–69, 80; Tom Green County 1880 Probate Records, 143, 171; Irion County Deed Records, vol. B, 35–37. While some period timetables and accounts list the name of this Butterfield stage stop as Johnson's Station, others call it Camp Johnson. Although the Conklings did not find the ruins of Johnson's Station near West Rocky Creek, they camped very close to the site on August 5, 1932. A year later, on June 4, 1933, the couple visited a second time. During the Civil War, a small force of Texas Rangers garrisoned Johnson's Station. Wartime records list the Middle Concho site as "Camp Concho." The outpost's location near the junction of the Butterfield Road and Upper Emigrant Road from San Antonio and Fredericksburg allowed Rangers to keep a watchful eye on overland traffic through the region. The Concho Valley Archaeological Society conducted extensive fieldwork at Johnson's Station near West Rocky Creek during 2009–2010. The numerous artifacts they unearthed detail occupation here from the antebellum period to the early twentieth century. The report's archaeological section is well done, but its historical narrative contains numerous errors, such as dating construction and occupation of the stage stop to March 1857. Butterfield did not choose its final route, let alone construct its stations, until the summer of 1858. For more than seventy years, there has been considerable confusion concerning Johnson's Station, because there are three different locations for this mail station along the Middle Concho watershed. The Southern Pacific Railroad owned the land in Block 10 encompassing all three of these sites, which the company surveyed in July and August 1857 and subsequently patented title to in 1860. The first is near West Rocky Creek, the second is several miles to the west near

Dry Creek, and the third is almost 2 miles west of the Dry Creek site. Butterfield historians Roscoe and Margaret Conkling believed that the Overland Mail Company moved Johnson's Station in the fall of 1858 from West Rocky Creek to Dry Creek but provide no documentation to support their claim. In August 1932, the couple visited the site near Dry Creek. Roscoe Conkling took photographs of and sketched the outline of a sizeable ruin. Unfortunately, there is no way to corroborate the Conklings' hypothesis regarding the station's relocation to the Dry Creek area. Despite several requests over two decades, the landowner refused me access to this site. Without a thorough survey of the ruins and its artifacts, this structure cannot be accurately dated. Period accounts provide varying mileages for Camp Johnson. Several fit the Rocky Creek site, while others match Dry Creek. Writing in September 1858, *New York Herald* correspondent Waterman Ormsby noted that the station was 25 miles from Grape Creek. In October 1858, U.S. Postmaster General special agent G. Bailey put the distance at 22 miles. In November 1858, *Daily Alta California* reporter J. M. Farwell estimated it at 22 miles, while the *San Francisco Daily Evening Bulletin*'s Mr. Baer said it was 20. None of the overland passengers in 1858 provides a name for this Middle Concho stage stop. The last known Texas Butterfield itinerary from 1861 says that "Camp Johnson" was 25 miles from Grape Creek. Regarding the third reported location for Johnson's Station, this site, just under 2 miles west of the ruins near Dry Creek, dates from the post–Civil War period. The mileage to this location from Grape Creek does not fit the period accounts listed above, as it is too far west. In 1867, Ben Ficklin received the government contract for the San Antonio–El Paso mail line, and in March 1868 he rerouted operations along the Middle Concho. Some time after, employees constructed a new stage stop on the north bank of the river above a large water hole. Because this location was near Butterfield's antebellum station, the company kept the old name, calling this new location Johnson's Station. After Ficklin's death in 1871, F. C. Taylor and his partner, Charles Bain, assumed the mail contract. Taylor and Bain took title to the Johnston's Station property in December 1878 after purchasing it from C. D. Foote for $200. Bain became the sole operator of the San Antonio–El Paso stage line after Taylor died in 1879. In November 1880, C. H. Merritt, the administrator for F. C. Taylor's estate, sold Taylor's half interest in Johnson's Station to Bain for $200. Charles Bain and Co. operated the San Antonio–El Paso mail line until 1881, when Bain began liquidating his assets. In August 1882, Bain sold the Johnson's Station 640-acre parcel to H. M. Comer for $640. A good period map detailing this third Johnson's Station site is in the August 20, 1869, entry in "Journal Showing the Route Taken by the Government Train from Austin, Texas to Ft. Craig, New Mexico," by Brevet Lieutenant Colonel Thomas B. Hunt, NACP, RG 77, Q154 (hereafter cited as Hunt, "Journal"). The landowner declined several of my requests to visit this site.

3. Johnson, *Partisan Rangers*, 16 (quotation), 18, 26–28; 1860 U.S. Census, Burnet Co., Tex., NA, M653, R1289, 169, 175. See numerous surveys at GLO, for Bexar, Irion, and Reagan Counties along the Middle Concho and Centralia Draw conducted by Johnson's posse during 1858 and 1859. Both Oscar Call and Neil Helm shared lodging with Johnson in Burnet, Texas, as did a third member of their outfit, John Barnet of Tennessee. In 1859, while managing his Butterfield stations, Johnson accepted a job surveying Texas school lands on Grape Creek. Johnson and his surveying crew camped along the stream for several days, between Grape Creek Station and the North Concho.

4. El Paso County Field Notes, May 24 and June 15, 1860; Leatherwood, "Llano Estacado," *Handbook* (quotation); Bancroft, *History of . . . Texas*, 569 (endnote quotation). Hubert H. Bancroft erroneously stated that Johnson purchased the Staked Plains or Llano Estacado Station in 1855. The Overland Mail Company did not commence operations in Texas until September 1858 and did not build that station until 1859.

In addition, Bancroft wrote that Johnson "acquired other stations [on the route], but was compelled to give them up on account of the difficulty he experienced in obtaining men, owing to the hostility of the Indians." This is also incorrect. Johnson, by his own account, stated that he managed his stations until the start of the Civil War, when Congress ordered Butterfield to move its operations northward to the Central Overland Route.

5. Johnson, *Partisan Rangers*, 5, 6 (quotations 1–2); *St. Louis Missouri Republican*, Jan. 5, 1859, copied in *New York Times*, Jan. 8, 1859 (quotation 3). From Johnson's Station westward to Head of Concho Station, the Butterfield Road ran along the Middle Concho watershed.

6. *Sacramento Weekly Union*, Sept. 28, 1859 (quotations); Boggs, *My Playhouse*, 350; Conkling and Conkling, *Butterfield Overland Mail*, 1:353; *Mesilla Times*, Apr. 13, 1861, SCL, UTEP. The Conklings' conflating of the U.S. Army's 1852 Camp J. E. Johnston, located on the south bank of the North Concho, with Butterfield's Johnson's Station, located on the north bank of the Middle Concho, explains why their narrative repeatedly misspells the name of the Butterfield stage stop as "Johnston" (after Joseph Eggleston Johnston) instead of the correct spelling, "Johnson" (after Adam Rankin Johnson), as discussed previously. Subsequent writers have relied on the Conklings' account, only to compound the error. Additionally, readers of Johnson's autobiography, *The Partisan Rangers*, must be very careful interpreting his use of some place-names, particularly Johnson's Station. Johnson wrote his memoirs in 1904 when he was seventy, more than four decades after he worked for Butterfield. In several instances in his book, he mistakenly conflates Llano Estacado Station (also known as Staked Plains Station), located on Centralia Draw, with Johnson's Station on the Middle Concho. The vast majority of primary records from the period refer to this antebellum Butterfield station in Centralia Draw as Llano Estacado Station or Staked Plains Station. The last published Butterfield itinerary from 1861 lists the Butterfield stations eastward from the Pecos to the Middle Concho as follows: Horsehead Crossing, Castle Gap Station, Llano Estacado Station, Head of Concho Station, Camp Mather, and Camp Johnson.

7. *Sacramento Weekly Union*, Sept. 28, 1859 (quotation). On pages 84–86 of Wilbarger's *Indian Depredations in Texas*, there is a garbled account of a Comanche raid at Johnson's Station on the Middle Concho. The first problem with the story is the date of the alleged attack: March 27, 1857. Butterfield coaches did not start running until September 1858. In addition, Wilbarger's narrative is clearly a conflating of the Grape Creek raid in March 1861, during which Comanches shot Joel Pennington in the face (see chapter 6), and the above *Sacramento Weekly Union* report of the September 1859 raid on Johnson's Station. Wilbarger says that Indians shot a Butterfield employee named Evaness in the face. Evaness is the wrong name. On page 7 of his autobiography *(Partisan Rangers)*, Adam Rankin Johnson mentions that Bob Cavaness managed Johnson's Station. Therefore, Wilbarger is discussing Cavaness, not Evaness. The autobiography's account of the Grape Creek raid and Pennington's shooting follow immediately after a discussion of Cavaness and the Johnson's Station raid. In sum, Wilbarger erroneously conflated the two different raids. Subsequent scholars recycling Wilbarger have further muddied the waters. Brad Agnew cites Wilbarger in his "War against the Comanches" article. Without telling his readers that he is doing so, Agnew changes the date of the raid in Wilbarger's book from March 1857 to March 1858, which is still six months prior to Butterfield's inaugural run in Texas. There was no Johnson's Station in March 1858, as the mail company did not build many of its stations until late August or early September 1858. Agnew then says that the Comanche chief Iron Jacket led the attack on Johnson's Station. Both Rip Ford and Rupert Richardson say that a force comprising federal troops, Texas Rangers, and Texas reservation Indians killed Iron Jacket in the May 12, 1858, battle of Little

Robe Creek on the Canadian River. See Ford, *Rip Ford's Texas*, 233; Richardson, *Comanche Barrier*, 119. This battle was four months before Butterfield commenced operations. If Ford is correct, Iron Jacket was already dead when the Overland Mail Company built Johnson's Station. Writing eighteen years after Agnew, Jodye and Thomas Schilz cite Agnew's article and repeat the same story of Iron Jacket's raid on Johnson's Station in *Buffalo Hump and the Peneteka Comanches*, 44. Finally, Comanche expert Thomas Kavanagh says that the record is unclear as to whether Ford and his men killed Iron Jacket or another Indian wearing an iron mail shirt. Kavanagh points out that a Comanche named Iron Shirt was present during several negotiations with various Indian agents after 1858, specifically, in 1861, 1865, and 1868. He also acknowledges, however, that this later Iron Shirt could be a completely different Comanche with a similar name. See Kavanagh, *Comanche Political History*, 365–67, 388, 400, 420.

8. *New York Times*, Jan. 6, 1859 (quotation); MT, Bradford Draw, Causey Draw.

9. Ormsby, *Butterfield Overland Mail*, 54 (quotation 1), 55 (quotation 2); *Mesilla Times*, Apr. 13, 1861, SCL, UTEP; Capt. Joseph Rendlebrock, 4th Cav., Apr. 17, 1872, report and Apr. 20, 1872, scouting map of Grape Creek, North Concho, and Middle Concho Rivers, NA, RG 393, vol. 54, Reports of Scouts, Jan. 15, 1872–Oct. 25, 1878, Fort Concho, Texas; Lt. Col. E. J. Strang, *Topographical Sketch of the Road from Fort Stockton to Fort Chadbourne, October and November 1867*, NACP, RG 77, Q135 Roll, H374, Texas. Both maps show Johnson's Station, Camp Mather, and Head of Concho. Strang's map calls each of these an "old stage station." It is important to remember that at the time of this map's creation, the only buildings along this part of the Middle Concho were old Butterfield stage stops. The San Antonio–El Paso Mail Line under Ben Ficklin did not operate along the Middle Concho until March 1868. Prior to that date, it ran along the Lower Emigrant Road, from San Antonio to Uvalde, Brackettville, Fort Lancaster, Fort Stockton, and beyond. Therefore, Strang's map provides an accurate look at the region as it was on the eve of the Civil War. Regarding Camp Mather, this Butterfield station on the Middle Concho near North Liveoak Draw and Bradford Draw should not be confused with the post–Civil War military outpost called Camp Charlotte, which is located some miles upstream on the Middle Concho at Kiowa Creek. The 469-acre Camp Mather parcel in Irion County was surveyed in 1857, title to the land was issued on February 27, 1860, and a patent was issued by the General Land office on October 22, 1861.

10. Johnson, *Partisan Rangers*, 9; MT, Bradford Draw, Causey Draw; Hunt, "Journal," Aug. 22, 1869 (quotations 1–3); Lang, *First Overland Mail: . . . San Francisco to Memphis*, 39 (quotation 4).

11. *New York Times*, Jan. 8, 1859 (quotations); *Mesilla Times*, Apr. 13, 1861, SCL, UTEP; AFT, Head of Concho Station, Oct. 1998 (PD, Hal Joyce), June 16, 2000 (JA), and June 23, 2004.

12. *St. Louis Missouri Republican*, Jan. 14, 1859; *St. Louis Democrat*, July 6, 1860, copied in *New York Times*, July 9, 1860; *St. Louis Missouri Republican*, July 7, 1860, copied in *New York Times*, July 11, 1860; *Texas State Gazette*, Aug. 4, 1860 (quotation).

13. *St. Louis Democrat*, July 6, 1860, copied in *New York Times*, July 9, 1860; *St. Louis Missouri Republican*, July 7, 1860, copied in *New York Times*, July 11, 1860; *Texas State Gazette*, Aug. 4, 1860 (quotation 1); Johnson, *Partisan Rangers*, 7 (quotations 2–3).

14. *St. Louis Democrat*, July 6, 1860, copied in *New York Times*, July 9, 1860; *St. Louis Missouri Republican*, July 7, 1860, copied in *New York Times*, July 11, 1860; Tallack, *California Overland Express*, 51 (quotation 1, endnote quotation 1); *Texas State Gazette*, Aug. 4, 1860 (endnote quotation 2). Tallack mentioned that his coach had passed "a small party of Texas Rangers" searching for the Head of Concho raiders. Period records indicate that during the antebellum period, the presence of Texas Rangers on the frontier beyond Fort Chadbourne was infre-

quent. Among the personal effects of the station manager, Shephard, was "a check in his pocket for some considerable amount."

15. *St. Louis Missouri Republican*, July 7, 1860, copied in *New York Times*, July 11, 1860 (quotations 1–2); *Texas State Gazette*, Aug. 4, 1860 (quotation 3). The *Gazette* gives the date for the Shellenberger shooting as July 23, 1860, while the other reports cite July 24, 1860. On February 28, 1855, Adam Rankin Johnson and John Connor purchased 640 acres, constituting two surveys, for $50 in the Fisher-Miller/German Colony Grant. Connor and Johnson sold off 160 acres to Shellenberger in October 1859 for $160, making a profit of $110, plus retaining all 480 acres in the second parcel. Shellenberger, originally from Ohio, filed a patent with the General Land Office for his 160-acre Head of Concho parcel on December 18, 1860. Johnson also purchased acreage above and adjacent to Head of Concho, giving him control over the last permanent water source westward along the Middle Concho and Centralia Draw. The watershed that feeds Head of Concho's water holes was called Correll Creek and Coryell Creek in the late nineteenth century.

16. Hunt, "Journal," Aug. 21, 1869 (quotations); 1870 U.S. Census, Menard Co., Tex., NA, M593, R1594, 155. The 1870 census shows Shellenberger living at Fort McKavett, Texas. Shellenberger's name is also spelled "Shellenburger," "Shallenberger," and "Schellenbarger" in period documents and accounts.

17. Ormsby, *Butterfield Overland Mail*, 63 (quotations 1–2), 64 (quotations 3–4). As mentioned previously, in nineteenth-century Texas, people often used the term "Dutchmen" when talking of Germans. Ormsby's cook at Head of Concho may well have been Louis Shellenberger.

18. Ibid., 64 (quotations 5–6), 65 (quotations 1 and 4), 66 (quotations 2–3), 67.

19. Ibid., 65.

20. *New York Times*, Jan. 8, 1859; *Mesilla Times*, Apr. 13, 1861, SCL, UTEP; MT, Garrison Draw. Llano Estacado Station is located on the north side of Centralia Draw near its intersection with Garrison Draw. Llano Estacado, built in 1859, is on the last-known Butterfield itinerary, published in the spring of 1861.

21. Tallack, *The California Overland Express*, 49 (quotation 1), 50 (quotations 2–4); Lang, *First Overland Mail: . . . St. Louis to San Francisco*, 123 (quotations 5–6); Richardson, *Beyond the Mississippi*, 232 (quotation 7).

22. Richardson, *Beyond the Mississippi*, 231–32 (quotations 1–2); *St. Louis Missouri Republican*, Jan. 28, 1859 (quotations 3–4).

23. Bartlett, *Personal Narrative*, 1:89 (quotations); Justice, "Stiles, Texas," *Handbook*; CJ, July 25, 1933, box 9, RPC Papers, and the Conklings' unpublished photographs of Stiles and Centralia Draw, boxes 6 and 7, RPC Papers; Hunt, "Journal," Aug. 23 (endnote quotation) and Aug. 24, 1869; AFT, Flat Rock Waterholes/Ponds near Best Lane, Reagan County, Dec. 21, 2000 (JA). Flat Rock Waterholes/Ponds in Centralia Draw, just east of present-day Best Lane in Reagan County, should not be confused with Flat Rock Waterholes near Rankin, Texas, on Ben Ficklin's postbellum stage line. The Conklings incorrectly identified Flat Rock Ponds during their visit in July 1933 to Stiles, Texas, and Centralia Draw. They placed the ponds a half mile west of Stiles on some limestone ledges on the north side of the draw overlooking several windmills and deserted homesteads dating from the 1890s to the World War I period. Patrick Dearen and I investigated the Conklings' site near Stiles in October 1998. Stiles served as the Reagan County seat from 1903 until 1925, when the county seat was moved to Big Lake, after the development of the Santa Rita Oil Field nearby. Stiles later became a ghost town, and shortly after my 1998 visit there, an arsonist burned the picturesque abandoned courthouse. Today only a rock shell remains. As is true of several West Texas towns, Stiles sits astride the old Butterfield Road, sections of which

served as a major transportation artery for the region well into the 1920s. The correct location for Flat Rock Waterholes/Ponds is some miles to the west of Stiles, exactly where Hunt's journal places it. The ponds (actually more of a wide water hole) are situated in the bottom of the draw, underneath a long rock shelf on the draw's south bank. When Hunt's wagon train came through in August 1869, he found water here, noting, "Water only temporary, there was enough though for . . . 356 men and about 450 mules, quite good for drinking. No wood, grazing fair."

24. Johnson, *Partisan Rangers*, 9; *St. Louis Missouri Republican*, Oct. 6, 1859; MT, Garrison Draw; letter from F. C. Taylor, agent-in-charge, El Paso Mail Line, Nov. 8, 1871, Fort Stockton, NA, RG 393, LTS, R1189 (construction date for Centralia Station); Notson, *Fort Concho Medical History*, 50 (reporting construction of Centralia Station); CJ, Oct. 20–21, 1930, and July 25–26, 1933, box 9, RPC Papers, and Conklings' unpublished photographs and sketches of Centralia and Llano Estacado Stations, boxes 6 and 7, RPC Papers; AFT, Belcher homestead and Centralia Draw, 1998–2007 (JA, PD, Hal Joyce); GLO, Map #11206, *Crane County Sketch File 3B*; GLO, Map #75551, *Tom Green County Sketch*. Some writers have confused Butterfield's Llano Estacado Station, built in 1859, with Centralia Station, a post–Civil War stage stop several miles to the east, near Best Lane in Reagan County. F. C. Taylor, manager of the San Antonio–El Paso Mail Line, constructed Centralia Station on the north bank of Centralia Draw near Garrison Draw during the latter half of November 1871. When the Conklings visited Centralia Station twice in the early 1930s, rocks from the station walls lay scattered across the site. Sometime after the couple's two trips here, the Belcher family, who owned land on the south side of the draw, loaded up most of the limestone from the stage stop and moved it across the draw. The Belchers then built an impressive rock corral adjacent to the family homestead. The home later burned, but the stone chimney still stands. Nearby are the graves of two early cowboys. Mrs. James Belcher told the Conklings that she had first moved to Centralia Draw in 1888. Over the years, many people have mistaken the Belchers' rock corral for Centralia Station. Several nineteenth-century survey maps, however, clearly pinpoint the stage stop's location on the north side of the draw. A field survey that I conducted on August 1, 2007, identified the station site on the north side, marked by numerous pieces of dressed (i.e., cut and shaped) limestone and period artifacts. A. R. Johnson and his posse (chain carriers Thomas Johnson and James Nored, field notes signed by Oscar Call) surveyed the future Centralia parcel on March 22, 1859. The General Land Office issued a patent for the land on February 16, 1861.

25. MT, South Mustang Draw NE, Moore Hill, Garrison Draw; AFT, ledge overlooks and mortar holes along Centralia Draw, June 23, 2004; AFT, eastern end of Centralia Draw, Oct. 1998 (PD, Hal Joyce), and June 16, 2000 (JA); Conklings' unpublished photographs of Centralia Draw, boxes 6 and 7, RPC Papers; CJ, Oct. 21, 1930, box 9, RPC Papers. Most of the old mileage signposts along Centralia Draw dating from the 1920s have long since disappeared, likely taken as souvenirs of a bygone era. During the 2000 trip, I found one remaining signpost lying hidden in some brush along the old road in Centralia Draw, east of present-day Best Lane in Reagan County. The Conklings took pictures of the overlooks, mortar holes, and mileage signposts during their visit here in October 1930.

26. MT, South Mustang Draw NE, Moore Hill; Senate Exec. Doc. No. 64, 31st Cong., 1st Sess., 19 (quotations 1–3); Bartlett, *Personal Narrative*, 1:87 (quotation 5), 88 (quotation 4); Martin, "From Texas to California," May 28, 1849 entry (quotation 6).

27. *St. Louis Missouri Republican*, Jan. 2, 1859 (quotation 1); Johnson, *Partisan Rangers*, 9 (quotation 2). Johnson purchased Mustang Waterholes from W. B. Coffee in Burnet, Texas, on March 1, 1859. Johnson and Call surveyed the 153-acre parcel, located in the Fisher-Miller

Grant, on March 22, 1859. Johnson patented his land on December 18, 1860.

28. Hunt, "Journal," Aug. 22–23, 1869; *St. Louis Missouri Republican*, Nov. 10, 1859; *Dallas Herald*, Nov. 9, 1859 (both reports, quotations); Johnson, *Partisan Rangers*, 14; MT, South Mustang Draw NE, Moore Hill; AFT, Mustang Waterholes, June 16, 2000 (JA), and June 23, 2004. Local historian and archaeologist Hal Joyce of Big Lake, Texas, offered much help on this section of the overland road and generously shared his research. Joyce's knowledge of the Middle Concho country and its history is considerable. There is one unresolved mystery regarding this part of the route. Hunt's journal entry for August 23, 1869, shows the location for an "Old Mail Station" between Head of Concho Station and Mustang Waterholes. On June 16, 2000, Joe Allen, the ranch foreman, and I located this old ruin precisely where Hunt marked it. Nineteenth-century artifacts and pieces of quarried limestone litter the earth around the outline of the building's foundation. The structure is a short distance from a large pond that holds water for much of the year. The building's origins are unclear. Hunt called this an old abandoned mail station, but this does not make sense, as it is so close to an existing stage stop, Head of Concho, used by both Butterfield and Ben Ficklin.

29. Johnson, *Partisan Rangers*, 9 (quotation).

30. Ibid., 10 (quotations).

31. Ibid., 10 (quotation); AFT, Mustang Waterholes, June 16, 2000 (with Joe Allen and ranch foreman), and June 23, 2004 (with ranch foreman); MT, South Mustang Draw NE, Moore Hill.

32. *Texas State Gazette*, Nov. 3, 1860 (quotation). The story line for this article is slugged "The Overland Passengers for Breckenridge and Lane, Llano Estacado, Oct. 16, 1860."

33. Ibid. (quotations).

34. Johnson, *Partisan Rangers*, 6 (quotation 1), 13 (quotation 2).

35. Ibid., 13 (quotations).

36. It was 31 miles from Head of Concho to Llano Estacado Station. See Hunt, "Journal," Aug. 22–23, 1869; MT, Garrison Draw; AFT, Centralia Draw, Llano Estacado Station, and road fork to Pontoon Bridge, Oct. 10, 2000 (JA, Hal Joyce).

37. MT, Garrison Draw; AFT, Llano Estacado Station, 1998–2004 (JA, PD); CJ, July 25–26, 1933, box 9, RPC Papers; interview with landowner, Nov. 29, 2003; Ely, *Where the West Begins*, 60. The Conklings could barely read Mary Alice Foreman's headstone in 1933. Seventy years later, it is impossible to discern more than a few letters and a number or two etched into the rock. Some accounts have the spelling as "Forsman" and "Foseman." In May 1864, a large caravan of more than five hundred disaffected Texans bound for New Mexico and California left from Butterfield's Head of Concho Station. Mary Alice Foreman's parents were part of this group. Some years after settling in California, the Foremans wrote to Llano Estacado landowner Viola Belcher asking whether she knew about a child's grave near the old station.

38. Hunt, "Journal," Aug. 23–25, 1869; MT, Garrison Draw, Sevenmile Corner SE, Sevenmile Corner, Marlboro Canyon SE, Marlboro Canyon, Castle Gap, Crane SW, Girvin NW; Senate Exec. Doc. No. 64, 31st Cong., 1st Sess., 19 (quotation 1); Bartlett, *Personal Narrative*, 1:90 (quotations 2–3).

39. Martin, "From Texas to California," June 3, 1849 entry (quotation 1); Bartlett, *Personal Narrative*, 1:90 (quotations 2–3); Hunt, "Journal," Aug. 24, 1869; Ormsby, *Butterfield Overland Mail*, 91; GLO, Map #8065, *Sketch of Road from Wild China Ponds to Horsehead Crossing*; GLO, Map #63086, *1887 Map of Upton County with Castle Gap and Wild China Ponds*; GLO, Map #5043, *Wild China Ponds and Horsehead Crossing*; GLO, Map #82060, *Early Tom Green County Map with Wild China Ponds*; CJ, Oct. 19, 1930, box 9, RPC Papers (endnote quotation); Conkling and Conkling, *Butterfield Overland Mail*, 1:370;

Dearen, *Halff of Texas*, 128; Eagleton, *On the Last Frontier*, 9, 13, 55, 82. The George Washington Elliott family (Eliza Elliott) patented the 677-acre parcel containing Wild China Ponds located in Upton County on March 24, 1883. During their visit to Wild China Ponds, the Conklings found "a large pond of fresh, sweet water, many large mesquite trees and the ruts of the old road plainly visible. No wild china trees—were told they had long since died off." Five miles to the east of this water hole is the old homestead of Dr. George Washington Elliott. The Conklings initially mistook this rock house, built in 1883, for a Butterfield stage stop. Locals told them that limestone blocks from the old stage stand had been used in constructing the Elliott home. Elliott's 1883 home later served as the site for the first organizational meeting for Upton County. It is the second-oldest European American building in the county, the oldest being the Butterfield's Castle Gap Station at Castle Gap, 15 miles distant, near the county's western boundary. When I visited the Elliott homestead in the fall of 1998 with Patrick Dearen and Joe Allen, several goats were living in the old rock house. In her book, Ethie Eagleton makes several references to an old Butterfield station across from and near Dr. Elliott's house, but she is mistaken, for Butterfield had no such station here. The overland road did run through Elliott's property and passed by his home. The Butterfield route through Upton County, including Wild China Ponds and Castle Gap, can be traced on the GLO map drawn by Roy Buckholts: *Feb. 11, 1969 Upton County Map*.

40. John Theophil Strentzel, "Autobiography," hand-written manuscript, BANC MSS C-D 778, Bancroft Library, University of California–Berkeley (quotations).

41. Ormsby, *Butterfield Overland Mail*, 107 (quotation), 108.

42. Ibid., 66 (quotations 1 and 3), 91, 107, 108 (quotation 2).

43. *Texas State Gazette*, May 27 and Aug. 5, 1854; Haley, *Diary of Michael Erskine*, 17 (quotations), 18–19.

44. Haley, *Diary of Michael Erskine*, 18–19; Dearen, *Cowboy of the Pecos*, 23, 27n54. Agreeing with Haley, Patrick Dearen says that an oversupply of beef in California and a drop in prices during 1855 dampened the antebellum Texas-California cattle trade. During and after the Civil War, Texas cattlemen continued using the overland road along the Middle Concho, out to Castle Gap and the Pecos River, en route to sell their herds to the U.S. Army at Fort Sumner, New Mexico. Even after the Overland Mail Company left Texas in April 1861, the Butterfield Trail served for many years as a major thoroughfare for emigrants, cattle drovers, soldiers, and Native Americans. For more on the Texas cattle trade to Fort Sumner, see Ely, *Where the West Begins*, 61–72.

45. MT, Castle Gap, Crane SW; Bartlett, *Personal Narrative*, 1:91 (quotation 1); Powers, *Afoot and Alone*, 132 (quotation 2); Hunt, "Journal," Aug. 25, 1869; AFT, Castle Gap, 1990–2006 (JA, PD); Lang, *First Overland Mail: . . . San Francisco to Memphis*, 39 (endnote quotation); *Mesilla Times*, Apr. 13, 1861, SCL, UTEP; Castle Gap segment in the Forest Glen Productions documentary video *Graveyard of the West*. Butterfield's Castle Gap Station at Castle Gap is not on the mail company's original 1858 schedule but does appear on the final itinerary published in 1861. One should be careful in using distances provided in period reports without cross-checking them against other accounts. Mr. Baer, the reporter for the *San Francisco Daily Evening Bulletin* traveling east on the Butterfield in November 1858, discussed this issue when providing a mileage table for his readers. Baer noted, "These, and all my other estimates of distance, are not from the printed schedule, but are stated as given to me by the drivers, corrected by my own calculations. Many of the drivers vary from one another as to the length of distances, and I found it a difficult task to arrive at any given result."

46. Myres, *Ho for California*, 269 (quotations 1–3); June 30, 1868 entry, Ruth Shackelford, "To California by the Mormon Trail, 1865," in Holmes, *Covered Wagon Women*, 9:192 (quotations 4–5), 193. Maria

Shrode recorded her observations while traveling west from Hopkins County, Texas, to California in 1870. Ruth Shackelford went to California from Missouri in 1865, became disillusioned with the land of gold, and took the southern route back through Texas in the summer of 1868.

47. Williams, *Old Texas Trails*, 353 (quotations).

48. Haley, *Fort Concho*, 1–13; Bieber, *Exploring Southwestern Trails*, 265 (quotation 1); Hooper, "To California in '49," 320–21 (quotation 2).

49. Dearen, *Castle Gap*, 10, 44; Headquarters, Fort Stockton to AAG, Dept. of Texas, June 28, 1878, LTS, Headquarters Records, Fort Stockton, Texas, 1867–1886 (hereafter FS), NA, RG 393, M1189, R1; Dennis J. Murphy, Feb. 24, 1894, petition, and Matlock to DeWitt, Fort Worth, Tex., Apr. 2, 1897, Indian Depredation Claim No. 10369, *Dennis J. Murphy v. The United States and Apache Indians*, U.S. Court of Claims, NA, RG 123; Lang, *First Overland Mail: . . . San Francisco to Memphis*, 38 (quotations). Native American warriors decimated numerous cattle drives and wagon trains passing through the ravine. In 1865, Comanches struck a large caravan of 123 families camped for the night at Castle Gap, driving off more than 1,050 cattle. In 1867, Indians ambushed Lew Soyer and his cowboys, making off with all their beeves. In June 15, 1868, raiders stole 2,500 head of cattle, 92 horses, and 4 mules in the canyon from wranglers en route from Fort Griffin, Texas, to Denver, Colorado. Cattleman Dennis Murphy, Jr. (brother of Patrick Murphy) estimated his losses in this 1868 raid at $112,300.

50. Senate Exec. Doc. No. 64, 31st Cong., 1st Sess., 19 (quotation 1); Hunt, "Journal," Aug. 25, 1869 (quotation 2); Headquarters, Fort Stockton to AAG, District of Pecos, Fort Concho, Aug. 6, 1878, NA, RG 393, FS, LTS, M1189, R1 (quotation 3); CJ, Oct. 18, 1930, box 9, RPC Papers (endnote quotation 1); unpublished Conkling photos of Castle Gap and Castle Gap Station sketch, boxes 6 and 7, RPC Papers (endnote quotation 2). Roscoe and Margaret Conkling visited Castle Gap in October 1930. The day was a cool 46 degrees when the couple climbed over the fence leading to the gorge. They "walked over to the ruins of an old stage station on the south side of the Butterfield Road near the entrance of the gap" and took pictures of the ruin. Roscoe Conkling also made a rough sketch of the station, which shows a corral attached to a two-room rock station house, with one room measuring 12 feet by 12 feet and the second, 12 feet by 16 feet. Conkling's sketch notes state, "Up to four years ago the walls of the station were standing. They were demolished and used for building and road work." Although the Conklings visited Butterfield's Castle Gap Station in 1930, they made no mention of it in their published 1947 work.

51. Hunt, "Journal," Aug. 24, 1869; MT, Garrison Draw; AFT, Centralia Draw, Llano Estacado Station, and road fork to Pontoon Bridge, Oct. 10, 2000 (JA, Hal Joyce); Uglow, *Standing in the Gap*, 38–39, 48, 144. GLO, Map #76208, *Charles Pressler's 1879 Pocket Map of the State of Texas* shows the U.S. Army's "Castle Gap Mil[itar]y Sub Post," as does *Rand, McNally & Co.'s 1882 Railroad and County Map of Texas*, VG, SCL, UTA. In the summer of 1868, San Antonio–El Paso mail contractor Ben Ficklin modified a section of the overland road so that instead of heading to Castle Gap and Horsehead Crossing as Butterfield had, Ficklin's new road branched off from Centralia Draw, headed southwest toward modern Rankin, Texas, continued on to Five Mile Draw, and then crossed the Pecos River at Pontoon Bridge, adjacent to Camp Melvin. The location where the new road branched off from Centralia Draw was west of its intersection with Garrison Draw and just east of Llano Estacado Station. Lieutenant Colonel Thomas Hunt called the building at Castle Gap an "old mail station" in the August 25, 1869, entry in his "Journal Showing the Route." In June 1868, the commander of Fort Stockton ordered Brevet Lieutenant Colonel Lewis "to withdraw [his] detachment at Castle Mountain and place one sergeant and fifteen men at China Ponds." Lack of dependable water at Castle Gap prompted the relocation. Cognizant of the

historic water shortages that also plagued those relying on Wild China Ponds, Fort Stockton's commander ordered Lewis to haul water from the Pecos to Wild China Ponds if necessary, a distance of 62 miles. See Fort Stockton to Lewis, June 4, 1868, NA, RG 393, FS, LTS, M1189, R1. On same microfilm roll, see also July 31, 1874, letter from Captain E. G. Burk to Fort Stockton's commander detailing a futile search for water in Castle Gap.

52. Dearen, *Castle Gap*, 11 (quotation 1); GLO, 1884 Upton County field notes for survey of Castle Gap (quotation 2).

53. Dearen, *Castle Gap*, 16–20.

54. Ibid., 16–20, 33; AFT, Castle Gap and Castle Gap Station, 1990–2006 (JA, PD).

55. Hunt, "Journal," Aug. 25, 1869 (quotations 1–2); Hooper, "To California in '49," 321 (quotation 3); June 25, 1849, entry in William P. Huff Journal, 1849–50, 2-vol. typescript, Accession No. 2001-174, DBC, UT (hereafter cited as Huff, "Journal").

56. June 14, 1849, entry in Demarest, "Diary, March 8, 1849–May 1850, of a Trip in a Bark Norumbega to Galveston, Texas, then Overland to California," BANC MSS C-F 15, Bancroft Library, University of California–Berkeley (hereafter cited as Demarest, "Diary").

57. Powers, *Afoot and Alone*, 135 (quotation).

58. Dearen, *Castle Gap*, 44, 48, 55, 57; Shackelford, June 30, 1868, entry, in Holmes, *Covered Wagon Women*, 9:192 (quotation).

59. Hunt, "Journal," Aug. 25, 1869 (quotations); Demarest, "Diary," June 18, 1849.

60. Powers, *Afoot and Alone*, 135 (quotation 1); Huff, "Journal," June 28, 1849 (quotation 2), June 29, 1848 (quotations 3–4); Lewis B. Harris letter to brother, in Martin, "From Texas to California," 216 (quotations 5–7); May 29, 1849, entry, John Murchison writing in "John B. Cameron Journal of the La Grange Company," M0082, Department of Special Collections, Stanford University Libraries (quotations 8–9); June 14, 1849, entry, Robert Beeching, "Journal of a Trip from New York on the Bark Norumbega to Galveston and thence Overland through Texas, Mexico, Arizona, and Southern California to San Diego, 1849, March 8–October 20," MS HM 1730, Huntington Library, San Marino, Calif. (quotation 10).

61. Shackelford, June 28, 1868, entry, in Holmes, *Covered Wagon Women*, 9:191 (quotation 1); Powers, *Afoot and Alone*, 135 (quotations 2–4).

62. Bieber, *Exploring Southwestern Trails*, 264–65 (quotation 1); Senate Exec. Doc. No. 64, 31st Cong., 1st Sess., 46 (quotation 2).

63. Senate Exec. Doc. No. 64, 31st Cong., 1st Sess., 19 (quotation 1); Powers, *Afoot and Alone*, 135 (quotation 2); Browne, "Out on the Plains," 505 (quotation 3), 506.

64. Horsehead Crossing segment in the Forest Glen Productions documentary video *Graveyard of the West*; Johnson, *Partisan Rangers*, 30; Senate Exec. Doc. No. 64, 31st Cong., 1st Sess., 45 (quotation 1); Huff, "Journal," June 28, 1849 (quotation 2); Demarest, "Diary," June 20, 1849 (quotation 3); Baldridge, *Reminiscence*, 21 (quotation 4); Hunt, "Journal," Aug. 26, 1869 (endnote quotation 1); AFT, east and west banks of Horsehead Crossing, 1990–2007 (JA, PD). Horsehead actually consists of several crossings. In 1936, the Texas Historical Commission placed a granite sign at a ferry crossing used during the 1850s and 1860s. A short distance above the marker, one can see a major ford (and several lesser crossings) used by travelers on horseback and by cowboys driving their cattle. Colonel Hunt's map shows an "old station" upriver from these crossings, which field research corroborated. On the Crane County side of the river, Horsehead Crossing is in GLO, Crane County Abstract 103 (endnote quotations 2–3). In the abstract's files are Horsehead land surveys from September 1872 and July 1888 that reference "the old station," several road intersections, and "a grave." On the Pecos County side, Horsehead is in GLO, Pecos County Abstract 274.

65. Richardson, *Beyond the Mississippi*, 233 (endnote quotation). Albert Richardson mentions halting at a "station of adobe" at the Pecos in October 1859. Ormsby, *Butterfield Overland Mail*, 68 (quotations); 1860 U.S. Census, El Paso Co., Tex., M653, R1293, 52, 53, 58, 90, 92.

66. Johnson, *Partisan Rangers*, 30, 31 (quotations 1–2), 32 (quotation 3).

67. Ibid., 14 (quotations 1–3), 15 (quotations 4–6).

68. *Texas State Gazette*, Aug. 21, 1858 (quotation 1); *Dallas Herald*, Sept. 8, 1858; *St. Louis Missouri Republican*, Jan. 7, 1859; *Texas State Gazette*, June 4, 1859 (quotation 2); *New York Times*, Sept. 29, 1860 (quotation 4); *Sacramento Weekly Union*, Oct. 5, 1859 (quotation 3).

69. Johnson, *Partisan Rangers*, 473, 475.

CHAPTER 8. THE UPPER ROAD TO EL PASO

1. Ely, "Riding the Butterfield Frontier," 180; MT, Red Bluff, Orla NE; *Report of the Secretary of War*, Senate Exec. Doc. No. 1, 34th Cong., 1st Sess., appendix, ser. 811, p. 96; *Report of the Secretary of War*, Senate Exec. Doc. No. 1, 35th Cong., 2nd Sess., vol. 2, ser. 975, pp. 590–608; Myers, "Pope's Wells," 283. One variation of the Upper Road used by emigrants and forty-niners heading to California crossed the Pecos at Horsehead Crossing and traveled up the west bank of the river to Delaware Creek, near the thirty-second parallel, before turning westward to El Paso.

2. Ely, "Riding the Butterfield Frontier," 180–81; Myers, "Pope's Wells," 273–99; *Report of the Secretary of War*, Senate Exec. Doc. No. 1, 35th Cong., 2nd Sess., ser. 975, pp. 590–608; Pope, *Report of Exploration*, 35, 37.

3. Ely, "Riding the Butterfield Frontier," 181; Pope, *Report of Exploration*, 35, 37. In reading Pope's railroad survey report, one can say that the army captain was overly optimistic and put a little spin on his findings: the route was certainly not as rosy as portrayed. One could also say the same about his entire artesian well project, as revealed in his embellished reports and projections to the secretary of war and Congress.

4. "Artesian Well Experiment," in *Report of the Secretary of War*, Senate Exec. Doc. No. 2, 36th Cong., 1st Sess., ser. 1024, pp. 540–44, 545 (quotations), 546–49 (hereafter cited as "Artesian Well Experiment"); Myers, "Pope's Wells," 296; "Artesian Wells on the Plains," *New York Times*, Apr. 30, 1858; "Artesian Well Expedition," *Texas State Gazette*, May 22, 1858.

5. Ely, "Riding the Butterfield Frontier," 181–82; Pope's Wells segment in the Forest Glen Productions documentary video *Graveyard of the West*; "Artesian Well Experiment," 540–49; Myers, "Pope's Wells," 296; "Artesian Wells on the Plains," *New York Times*, Apr. 30, 1858; "Artesian Well Expedition," *Texas State Gazette*, May 22, 1858; MT, Orla NE; AFT, Pope's artesian well site, 1991 and Sept. 11, 2000 (JA).

6. Ely, "Riding the Butterfield Frontier," 182; "Artesian Well Experiment," 540–49; Myers, "Pope's Wells," 296 (quotation 1); Limerick, *Legacy of Conquest*, 28–29 (quotation 2), 29 (quotation 3).

7. Ely, "Riding the Butterfield Frontier," 185. For additional insight on the legacy of irrigated agriculture in West Texas, see Ely, *Where the West Begins*, 99–119.

8. Pope, *Report of Exploration of a Route for the Pacific Railroad*, 60 (quotation 1), 66 (quotation 2), 67 (quotation 3).

9. "Artesian Well Experiment," 545 (quotation 3), 546 (quotation 1), 547 (quotation 2).

10. Ely, "Riding the Butterfield Frontier," 186; Pisani, *Water*, 272 (quotation 1); Skeet Lee Jones interview, Mentone, Tex., Mar. 12, 2006 (quotation 2); Jim Ed Miller, Pecos, Tex., phone interview, Oct. 20, 2007 (quotation 3).

11. Ely, "Riding the Butterfield Frontier," 186–87; *Texas State Gazette*,

Mar. 27, 1858 (quotation); *New York Times*, Mar. 4, 1858.

12. Ely, "Riding the Butterfield Frontier," 187; *New York Times*, Apr. 19, 1858; Pope, *Report of Exploration*, 35, 37; White, *It's Your Misfortune*, 125–26. Congress finally approved the route for the transcontinental railroad during the Civil War.

13. *New York Times*, Apr. 30, 1858; Ormsby, *Butterfield Overland Mail*, 72. The Overland Mail Company's advance expedition laid out this section of the route in March and April 1858. The team spent the night at Pope's Camp on April 10, 1858, before heading westward.

14. Ormsby, *Butterfield Overland Mail*, 68; *Contracts with the War Department*, House Exec. Doc. No. 59, 35th Cong., 2nd Sess., ser. 1006, p. 30; Hammond and Howes, eds., *Overland to California*, 104–105; Bieber, *Exploring Southwestern Trails*, 311–12. Besides being the most famous Butterfield stage driver in Texas, Skillman was arguably the most renowned frontiersman in West Texas. During the Mexican War, he served as a scout, guide, and interpreter for Colonel Doniphan and Lieutenant Colonel Lane. In 1847, the men of Company B elected him captain. Following the Mexican War, the U.S. Army hired Skillman as a scout and courier in West Texas. In 1851, Skillman started the first mail service between San Antonio, Texas, and Santa Fe. From 1854 to 1857, he worked for George Giddings's mail line. In 1858, he became a stage driver and route overseer for the Overland Mail Company. After Butterfield ceased operations in Texas in 1861, Skillman operated a spy network in West Texas for the Confederacy. Union troops led by Captain A. H. French attacked Skillman's group at Spencer's Ranch (modern Presidio, Texas) on April 15, 1864, killing Skillman and three others. For more on Henry Skillman's wartime spying activities in the Big Bend and Chihuahua, see Ely, "Skullduggery at Spencer's Ranch." For more on Skillman's Civil War intelligence operations in the El Paso area, see Ely, "What to Do about Texas."

15. Ormsby, *Butterfield Overland Mail*, 68 (quotations).

16. Ibid., 69 (quotation); Myers, "Pope's Wells," 283.

17. See the Salt Crossing/Juan Cordona Lake segment in the Forest Glen Productions documentary video *Graveyard of the West*; MT, Girvin NW, Crane SW, Juan Cordona Lake; AFT, Salt Crossing and Juan Cordona Lake, 1991–2004 (JA, PD). Salt Crossing on the Pecos is almost 6 miles east of present-day Imperial, Texas, and almost 2 miles north of FM 11, where the Old Crane Road dead-ends at the river. On the Crane County side, Juan Cordona Road leads directly from Salt Crossing to Juan Cordona Lake, 5 miles to the northeast.

18. Holt, "Story of Salt," 345 (quotation); GLO, Crane County Abstract No. 1. In January 1867, Annie James, wife of San Antonio entrepreneur John James, purchased the 3,700-acre Juan Cordona Lake parcel for $1,000. Peter Gallagher, John James's business associate, subsequently mined Juan Cordona's salt for commercial purposes.

19. Santleban, *Texas Pioneer*, 141 (quotations 1–2), 142–44, 189 (quotations 3–4). For Camp J. E. Johnston subsistence items and prices paid, see Green, "Forgotten Fort," 24. For more information on prices Butterfield paid for its supplies, see William Buckley and Thomas J. Bull depositions, *Giddings v. U.S.*

20. MT, Juan Cordona Lake, Imperial, Grandfalls, Grandfalls SW; Ormsby, *Butterfield Overland Mail*, 69; GLO, Ward County Abstract 141; AFT, near Langston's Station on Pecos River, May 23, 1999 (JA), and Langston's Station on Pecos River, July 30, 2001 (JA, PD). In 2001, a resident of Grandfalls, Texas, directed Joe Allen to several ruins astride a trace of the old mail road. The site consisted of several adobe buildings that have long since disappeared; it was likely first used by the mail company as a stage stop from early November 1858 to May 1859 and then again by farmers in the late 1880s. If one consults the following surveys from Ward County Field Notes Book 1 and cross-references them with GLO, Map #63110, *August 1902 Map of Ward County, Texas*, the Butterfield Road can be found running west from the Crane-Ward County line, located in H&TC RR Block 1, Survey

32. After leaving the east side of Dagger Bend in Block 1, Surveys 32–33, the road runs west, across the top of Dagger Bend, in H&TC RR Block 4, Survey 35 and H&TC RR Block 5, Survey 10, and continues west to Block 32, Surveys 4–5, heading west-northwest of Grand Falls of the Pecos. In Survey 6, the road is on the west side of Dagger Bend, a mile north of Grand Falls of the Pecos and a mile south of the present-day town of Grandfalls, Texas. The Butterfield route continues upriver in Surveys 8–9, 13–14, and 19.

21. Lang, *First Overland Mail: . . . St. Louis to San Francisco*, 123; Lang, *First Overland Mail: . . . San Francisco to Memphis*, 38 (quotations 1–2); W. R. Owen interviews with J. Evetts Haley, Jan. 12, 1927, and Mar. 2, 1933 (quotation 3), HL. Although the Conklings discuss Langston's Station in their work, their field journals reveal that they never visited the site. See Conkling and Conkling, *Butterfield Overland Mail*, 1:377; CJ, box 9, RPC Papers.

22. On the Ward County side of the river, Grand Falls of the Pecos is in GLO, Ward County Abstract 136. On the Pecos County side, it is in GLO, Pecos County Abstract 243. See also GLO, Map #63110, *August 1902 Map of Ward County, Texas*; GLO, Map #76038, *June 1896 Map of Pecos County, Texas*; "Report of Bvt. 1st Lt. Francis Theodore Bryan," in Senate Exec. Doc. No. 64, 31st Cong., 1st Sess., 20 (quotations 1 and 2), 25; Myres, *Ho for California*, 270 (quotation 3); Monahans Junior Chamber of Commerce, *Water, Oil, Sand and Sky*, 13, 15, 25. *Water, Oil, Sand and Sky* confuses the details regarding Grand Falls of the Pecos and Great Falls of the Pecos, incorrectly calling Grand Falls the upper falls and Great Falls the lower one, when their arrangement is exactly opposite. The monograph erroneously states that Great Falls was just above the Highway 18 bridge. In fact, this is the location for Grand Falls. Great Falls, also known as Pecos Falls, was 10 miles upstream, just above the FM 1776 bridge. It is important to restore the correct historical and geographical narrative concerning these two waterfalls, which were significant regional resources and landmarks during the nineteenth century.

23. E. W. Sweatt, "Early Memories of Things and Places in Ward County, Dec. 5, 1959" (hereafter cited as "Early Memories"), Jim Ed Miller Papers, Pecos, Texas, 3–4 (quotation 1), 4 (quotation 2 and endnote quotations); GLO, Ward County Abstracts 141, 439, and 419; GLO, Map #63110, *August 1902 Map of Ward County, Texas*. In 1891, E. W. Sweatt's family settled on Pecos riverfront acreage near the ruins of Butterfield's Langston's Station, 3.5 miles upstream from Grand Falls. Decades after the mail company ceased operations here, travelers continued to rely on the overland road as a major transportation artery through West Texas. "During the early 1890s there were many people in covered wagons going west," Sweatt recalled. "I would say in two years as many as 2,000 wagons went west, some to California, some Arizona, New Mexico. . . . [T]hey followed the old California trail up the river." The Sweatt homestead was on a hill 100 yards above the Butterfield Road, and it was from here that the family observed the caravans heading west for a fresh start in distant lands. Preferring not to drink the marginal river water, emigrants would stop at the Sweatt home to refresh themselves with a cool, clean drink of water from the adjacent well.

24. Ormsby, *Butterfield Overland Mail*, 71 (quotation); Senate Exec. Doc. No. 64, 31st Cong., 1st Sess., 20; Hamilton, "Frazer, George Milton," *Handbook*; Daggett, *Pecos County History*, 1:108–10; Hughes, *Pecos*, 1:75; Brune, *Springs of Texas*, 359–60; GLO, Map #76038, *June 1896 Map of Pecos County, Texas*; GLO, Pecos County Abstracts 228, 3924, and 4495; Pecos County School Land File No. 10545; Mar. 16, 1874, sketch and report of scout to Pecos River by 2nd Lt. Thomas Corbin Davenport, Co. M, 9th Cav., Fort Stockton, Tex., Journal of Marches, Scouts, and Expeditions, Sept. 1873–Dec. 1879, NA, RG 393, 20–21 (endnote quotation); Ward County Historical Commission, *Ward County*, 182. In his reconnaissance of the region in July 1849, Lieutenant Bryan

observed several major Indian trails crossing the river at Grand Falls. One trail ran southwest to Santa Rosa Spring, Monument Springs, and Comanche Springs (at Fort Stockton), important regional water holes for Native Americans, Hispanics, and Anglos. Santa Rosa Spring was located near George Milton Frazer's ranch. Frazer's Pecos County ranch was an important crossroads, where four trails converged. Frazer, a merchant, miner, and U.S. marshal before the Civil War, later got into ranching. He served as Pecos County judge from 1872 until 1884 and as Reeves County judge from 1889 until 1895. Frazer's ranch was in H&GN RR Block 8, Survey 68 and was watered by "a small stream of fresh clear water." The stream's headwater was Santa Rosa Spring, located in neighboring Survey 69. Gunnar Brune says that the spring, dry since the 1950s because of irrigation pumping, was once a desert oasis. Jumanos and Apache Indians visited the water hole regularly and left numerous artifacts. From Santa Rosa Spring, the trail to Fort Stockton passed by Monument Springs, 7 miles below Frazer's Ranch and 20 miles north of Fort Stockton. At Monument Springs, two streams ran over the surface for a short distance before disappearing underground.

25. Lang, *First Overland Mail: . . . St. Louis to San Francisco*, 122 (quotations).

26. GLO, Map #63110, *August 1902 Map of Ward County, Texas*; GLO, Map #76038, *June 1896 Map of Pecos County, Texas*; Browne, "Out on the Plains," 495 (quotations). In Ward County, Great Falls of the Pecos is in GLO, Ward County Abstract 129. In Pecos County, it is in GLO, Pecos County Abstract 196. Author's copy of J. M. Browne's account is courtesy of Patrick Dearen.

27. Browne, "Out on the Plains," 495 (quotations).

28. Mar. 16, 1874, sketch and report of scout to Pecos River by 2nd Lt. Thomas Corbin Davenport, Co. M, 9th Cav., Fort Stockton, Tex., Journal of Marches, Scouts, and Expeditions, Sept. 1873–Dec. 1879, NA, RG 393, 20–21; Browne, "Out on the Plains," 495 (quotation).

29. Sweatt, "Early Memories," 3 (quotations); MT, Rio Pecos Ranch, Grandfalls SW; AFT, adobe townsite and Great Falls of the Pecos, Oct. 18, 2003 (JA); GLO, Map #63110, *August 1902 Map of Ward County, Texas*; GLO, Ward County Abstract 129; Ward County Field Notes Book 1, Block 34, Surveys 18–19, and Block 33, Survey 1. All three of these 1888 Ward County surveys specifically mention the adobe town. At the townsite, numerous period artifacts—including square nails, colored glass, crockery, and lead-lined tin cans—litter the ground. The artifacts date the site from the late 1870s to the early 1880s. The survey for Block 33, Survey 5 from August 1888 mentions an irrigation ditch, so this was likely an irrigated farming community at that time. Apparently, Indian Crossing on the Pecos was not very practical for a wagon and team, so locals carved out a new ford, called Frazer's Crossing (after George Milton Frazer), 3.5 miles downstream. This new crossing was 3–4 feet deep with a hard bottom and steep riverbanks on both sides. Frazer's Crossing was 6.5 miles due north of Frazer's Ranch.

30. Sweatt, "Early Memories," 3 (quotation 1), 4 (quotations 2–3); Browne, "Out on the Plains," 495 (quotation 4).

31. Nye, *Carbine and Lance*, 235; Anderson, "Comancheros," *Handbook*. The Butterfield Road in the Great Falls area can be found by consulting the following surveys from Ward County Field Notes Book 1 and cross-referencing them with GLO, Map #63110, *August 1902 Map of Ward County, Texas*. A short distance downstream, southeast of the falls, the overland road is in Block 32, Section 19, a mile and a half off the river. In Block 33, Survey 1, it is a mile north of the river, and in Survey 4, it is very close to the river as it rounds the Great Falls bend heading upstream.

32. Capt. Alexander Scammel Brooks Keyes, 10th Cav., June 8, 1878, to Post Adj., Fort Concho, Tex., Fort Concho Reports of Scouts, 1872–81, Frank Temple Compilation of U.S. Army Scouts in West Texas,

Microfilm Roll 1, Fort Davis National Historic Site, Fort Davis, Texas (quotations). For more on Keyes, who retired from the army as a major in 1896, see Heitman, *Historical Register*, 595.

33. "Report of Bvt. 2nd Lt. Nathaniel Michler, Jan. 28, 1850," in Senate Exec. Doc. No. 64, 31st Cong., 1st Sess., 38 (quotations); MT, Ligon Ranch.

34. Pope, *Report of Exploration*, 69 (quotations).

35. Author and Mike Cox interview with Barney Hubbs, Oct. 21, 1991, Pecos, Tex. (quotation 1), in the Forest Glen Productions documentary video *Graveyard of the West*; Dearen, *Crossing Rio Pecos*, 39 (quotation 2—this quotation is a composite of two Hubbs interviews, one by me and Cox in 1991, and the second by Dearen in 1992). In 1991, Dearen and I went to the mass gravesite and filmed it for the documentary.

36. Ward County judge T. B. Anderson interview, CJ, Oct. 3, 1931, box 9, RPC Papers (quotation 1); Dearen, *Crossing Rio Pecos*, 37, 38 (quotations 2–4); MT, Ligon Ranch; AFT, Emigrant Crossing on the Pecos, to Reeves County side, 1991 (PD), and to Ward County side, Oct. 17, 2003 (JA, PD, Jim Ed Miller, Sid Sullenger, and Doug Fernandes). Over the years, numerous writers have given conflicting and inaccurate information as to the exact location of this important and historic West Texas landmark. This endnote corrects the misinformation. On the Ward County side of the river, Emigrant Crossing is in Block 33, Survey 15. See GLO, Map #10110, *June 4, 1873 Ward County Rolled Sketch #22*. This map specifically pinpoints "Emigrant Crossing" in Survey 15. See also GLO, Ward County Abstract 152; GLO, Map #63110, *August 1902 Map of Ward County, Texas*. On the Reeves County side, the ford is in the Bryan Callahan Surveys. See GLO, Reeves County Abstracts 3533 and 1030; GLO, Map #7476, *1891 Map of Blocks 5, 6, & 7, Houston and Great Northern Rail Road Surveys in Reeves County, Texas Owned by William Walter Phelps*. Block 33, Survey 15 in Ward County is 40 miles upstream from Horsehead Crossing. The Callahan surveys are 39 miles above Horsehead Crossing. Lieutenant Michler put the distance between Emigrant Crossing and Horsehead Crossing at "about forty miles," which makes these surveys a perfect fit. See Michler report in Senate Exec. Doc. No. 64, 31st Cong., 1st Sess., 38; Emigrant Crossing segment in Forest Glen Productions documentary video *Graveyard of the West*; Conkling and Conkling, *Butterfield Overland Mail*, 1:378; CJ, Oct. 3, 1931, box 9, RPC Papers. The Conklings' field journals reveal that they never visited Emigrant Crossing. In their 1947 book, the couple states that the distance from Emigrant Crossing to Emigrant Crossing Station upriver at the Narrows is 13 miles. This is incorrect. On October 3, 1931, while they were in the Pecos/Barstow area, former Ward County judge T. B. Anderson of Barstow (county judge, 1897–98) told the Conklings that it was 6 miles, which is close to the actual distance. How and why the couple then erred in publishing this as 13 miles is unclear.

37. Browne, "Out on the Plains," 496–97 (quotation 1), 497 (quotations 2–3); MT, Ligon Ranch, Quito Draw; AFT, Emigrant Crossing Station, 1999–2008 (JA, PD). For a detailed look at the overland road as it heads upstream from Great Falls, see Sketch No. 3, *1883–1884 Surveys of Western Texas by Captain W. R. Livermore*, NACP.

38. Browne, "Out on the Plains," 496 (quotations).

39. Ormsby, *Butterfield Overland Mail*, 70 (quotations).

40. *Report of the Secretary of War*, Senate Exec. Doc. No. 2, 36th Cong., 1st Sess., ser. 1024, pp. 604, 606; *Report of the Secretary of War*, Senate Exec. Doc. No. 1, 36th Cong., 2nd Sess., ser. 1079, pp. 218, 222; *Report of the Secretary of War*, House Exec. Doc. No. 2, 35th Cong., 2nd Sess., ser. 999, pp. 776–77; *Protection of the Frontier of Texas*, House Exec. Doc. No. 27, 35th Cong., 2nd Sess., ser. 1004, p. 12 (quotations).

41. Sketch No. 3, *1883–1884 Surveys of Western Texas by Captain W. R. Livermore*, NACP; Dearen, *Cowboy of the Pecos*, 111; J. Evetts Haley interview with Mrs. J. W. Carter, Oct. 31, 1927, Dimmit, Tex., HL

(endnote quotations 1–2); Patrick Dearen e-mail, Sept. 20, 2004 (endnote quotations 3–4). The Carter ranch house is shown on Livermore's map. Cowhands built several dugouts for shelter on the hills above, overlooking the river. Mrs. J. W. Carter recalled that there were five dugouts "built back in the hill, walled with rock and covered with dirt and mesquite bushes." She said, "We had fireplaces in these [and] a place for a door, but no doors. Each was about fourteen feet square." Cowboy Jim Witt, who lived at this ranch for a time during the 1920s, told Patrick Dearen in a July 17, 1993, interview that he recalled seeing "an old Ranger fort" at the Narrows, which was, as Dearen says, "undoubtedly the stage stand." Joe Allen, Dearen, and I located the dugouts during field trips to the Narrows. The Emigrant Crossing Station/Adobe Walls ruins at the Narrows should not be confused with a different Adobe Walls settlement downstream near Bakersfield, Texas, adjacent to Pecos Station, a San Antonio–San Diego Mail Company stage stop operated by George Giddings. Raiding Comanches decimated Pecos Station in early January 1862. After the Civil War, Pecos County commissioner Cesario Torres established the Adobe Walls irrigated farming community next to the ruins of Pecos Station. Joe Allen, Patrick Dearen, Mary Williams, and I were the first to locate the ruins of the long-lost Pecos Station, on January 10, 1999. See the Pecos Station and stagecoach segment in the City of Fort Stockton documentary video *Gateway to the West*.

42. Haley, *Charles Goodnight*, 170–73, 174 (quotation 1), 175 (quotation 2), 176–83.

43. Ely, *Where the West Begins*, 103, 108–110; Monahans Junior Chamber of Commerce, *Water, Oil, Sand and Sky*, 10, 15, 21; GLO, Map #63110, *August 1902 Map of Ward County, Texas*. The Big Valley Irrigation Company erected its dam at the Narrows in 1906. The company used red sandstone from the nearby Barstow quarry in the construction. By consulting the following surveys from Ward County Field Notes Book 1 and cross-referencing them with the 1902 Ward County Map, one can identify the Butterfield Road running along the river 1–3 miles below the Big Valley Irrigation Canal in H&TC RR Block 32, Surveys 4–5, 8–9, 13–14, and 19, and in H&TC RR Block 33, Surveys 1–2, 4–5, 10–11, 14–15, and 18–19. In Survey 19, the road comes very close to the canal, and the two almost merge as they run upstream to the Narrows. Field notes show the overland route close to the Narrows in Block 33, Surveys 23–24. W. R. Owen recalled that the old trail left the river just above Great Falls of the Pecos and then rejoined the Pecos at the Narrows. See W. R. Owen interviews with J. Evetts Haley, Jan. 12, 1927, and Mar. 2, 1933, HL. Ward County Field Notes Book 1 shows the Butterfield Road heading northwest from the river upstream from the Narrows, through the Quito Hills in Block 33, Survey 27, and then on to Soda Lake, located in H&TC RR Block 34, Surveys 198, 207, and 208.

44. Monahans Junior Chamber of Commerce, *Water, Oil, Sand and Sky*, 10 (quotation 1), 21; Ely, *Where the West Begins*, 108–109; Ward County Historical Commission, *Ward County*, 63 (quotation 2).

45. Myres, *Ho for California*, 270–71 (quotation); MT, Quito Draw, Soda Lake. Surveys from Ward County Field Notes Book 1 show the Butterfield Road close to Soda Lake in H&TC RR Block 34, Survey 187; these surveyor notes specifically mention the "old stage road." The overland route then passed immediately to the north of Soda Lake (located in Surveys 198, 207, and 208) before striking the lower right corner of Survey 225 in Block 34; once again, these field notes mention the "old stage road." Continuing on, the Butterfield trail crossed the survey line between Surveys 13 and 225 in Block 34, with yet another reference to the "old stage road." From here the road turned back northwest toward the river, running through W&NW RR Block 1, Surveys 4 and 17, 26 and 29, and 29 and 71, then crossing into H&TC RR Block 33, Surveys 64–65, located a mile and a half off the river. By taking this detour above modern Barstow, Texas,

the Overland Mail Company saved considerable mileage on its route, bypassing an enormous bend in the Pecos before finally returning to the river 4 miles below the Ward-Loving County line. The last overland road citation (heading west) in Ward County Field Notes Book 1 occurs in H&TC RR Block 33, Surveys 70–71, located close to the county line. In W&NW RR Block 1, Survey 17, a feeder road connected with the Butterfield. Heading south to the river, this feeder road led to what is identified as an "old emigrant ford" on the Pecos in H&TC RR Block 33, Surveys 56 and 57. This road then crossed the river, entering Reeves County in H&GN RR Block 4, Survey 15, near the floodgate for the Pioneer Canal Company. This crossing was at the "Little Falls" of the Pecos, near which there were several sets of riffles, two above and one below the falls. This old emigrant ford is located on modern Ward County Road 175, at Barstow Dam. See GLO, Ward County Abstract 327, W&NW RR Block 1, Survey 15, dated Nov. 9, 1888; GLO, Ward County Sketch 2 and Ward County Sketch 6, Maps #10426 and #10427 respectively, *1888 Ward County Irrigation Company Map*, *Ward and Reeves Counties, Texas* (these are two similar but different maps). On September 21, 1849, Captain Randolph Barnes Marcy crossed at or near the Little Falls Ford on his return trip from Doña Ana, New Mexico, to Fort Smith, Arkansas. Grant Foreman says that Marcy forded the Pecos somewhere near present-day Barstow, Texas. The Little Falls Ford is at Barstow Dam, not far from Barstow. See Foreman, *Marcy and the Gold Seekers*, 358.

46. Ward County Historical Commission, *Ward County*, 88 (quotation), 89; Hentz, "Geology," *Handbook*; Myres, *Ho for California*, 270–71; GLO, Map #7476, *1891 Map of Blocks 5,6, & 7, Houston and Great Northern Rail Road Surveys in Reeves County, Texas Owned by William Walter Phelps*; TSLAC, Map #76219, *Map of the Country between the Frontiers of Arkansas and New Mexico by Capt. R.B. Marcy, 1849–1852*; *1849 Topographical Map of the Road from Fort Smith, Arkansas to Santa Fe, N.M. and from Dona Ana, N.M. to Fort Smith by Capt. R.B. Marcy*, VG, SCL, UTA; "Report of Captain R. B. Marcy, November 20, 1849," Senate Exec. Doc. No. 64, 31st Cong., 1st Sess., 205, 221; MT, Sand Lake, Pecos West, Worsham, Verhalen North, Soda Lake, Soda Lake NE. Marcy's map and journal note that after crossing to the east side of the Pecos, he traveled 9 miles to a large salt lake about 2 miles in length. This was Soda Lake in Ward County, which is the only salt lake of this size in the immediate area. Soda Lake is the crescent-shaped "laguna" shown in Marcy's 1849–52 map (TSLAC #1025). After camping at Soda Lake the nights of September 22 and 23, on September 24, Marcy marched northeast into the range of sand hills above modern Monahans, Texas. Continuing on to Big Spring, then to Preston, Texas, on the Red River, Marcy reached Fort Smith on November 20, 1849. On his return trip to Fort Smith, Marcy used a viameter, attached to a wagon wheel, to measure distance. The captain remarked on page 172 of his report that this instrument was less accurate than measuring with a chain and that he had to recalculate his viameter readings to approximate chain measurements. The point here is that some of his stated mileage may be slightly off. Maria Shrode's party stopped at Soda Lake on August 9, 1870. After the Civil War, residents of both Reeves and Ward Counties used the Little Falls Crossing. Ward County Sketch 2 (GLO Map #10426) shows a "wagon trail" heading south-southeast from the ford to Pecos City in Reeves County and on to Hackberry Spring near Toyah Lake. On the Ward County side of the crossing, a trail led northeast to the W Ranch headquarters (present-day Willow Wells Ranch in Winkler County), located 8.5 miles north-northeast of the intersection of Ward, Loving, and Winkler Counties. In 1887, the Johnson brothers of Pecos, Texas, started the W Ranch, one of the largest in the region, encompassing 768,000 acres. See Fannin Woodyard Johnson biography in Paddock, *Twentieth-Century History*, 1:392–93; Skeet Lee Jones phone interview, Aug. 13, 2013. Marcy's and Shrode's Soda Lake in Ward County is not

be confused with the Soda Lake downstream in Crane County, 9.5 miles west-northwest of McCamey, Texas.

47. Dunn, "History of Loving County" (thesis), 63, 65; AFT, Porterville, Texas, 1998 (JA, PD). MT, Mentone. Dr. Phil Porter was one of the first residents of Porterville and the town's namesake. At its peak, Porterville had one hundred residents, a school, a post office, and two stores. The ruins of the old townsite are located near present-day Goodrich Ranch on Ranch Road 867.

48. Loving County, Texas, *Quickfacts*, U.S. Census Bureau Online, U.S. Department of Commerce, http://quickfacts.census.gov/qfd/states/48/48301.html (accessed Aug. 12, 2013); Cathy Newman, "ZipUSA 79754," September 2000, *National Geographic Online*, http://ngm.nationalgeographic.com/ngm/0009/fulltext7.html (quotation); MT, Soda Lake, Mentone, Anderson Ranch. The Ward-Loving County line hits the Pecos River in H&TC RR Block 33, Survey 76. See Loving County Clerk's Office, Land Survey Field Notes; GLO, Map #77358, *December 1932 Map of Loving County, Texas*. Continuing upstream in Loving County, one can see the Butterfield Road in Block 33, Surveys 82, 89, 90, 94, and 95. On State Highway 302, a half mile south of Mentone, is a roadside park with two state historical markers, commemorating the Butterfield Overland Mail and the Goodnight-Loving Cattle Trail. (The county is named after Loving.) Directly behind these two markers, one can see an excellent trace of the overland road heading northwest toward the 2,800-foot Narboe Point and the river. On May 22, 1999, Joe Allen, Patrick Dearen, and I followed this trace from the roadside park to the Pecos. In some sections of this trace, the overland trail parallels Private Road 1001.

49. Lang, *First Overland Mail: . . . St. Louis to San Francisco*, 123; Lang, *First Overland Mail: . . . San Francisco to Memphis*, 38; MT, Mentone, Anderson Ranch, Lindley Ranch, Orla SE; AFT, Mentone, Old Mentone, and Skillman's Station, 1998–2014 (JA, PD); *1859 United States and Texas Boundary Commission Maps #1, 2, 3, and 15*, Senate Exec. Doc. No. 70, 47th Cong., 1st Sess., ser. 1987; *Map No. 4, Boundary 68 Roll, 1859 Map of Texas Boundary Line Surveyed under the Direction of the U.S. Department of the Interior*, RG 49, NACP; Connor, *Peters Colony of Texas*, 350; "Passenger Lists of Vessels Arriving at New York, 1820–1897," NA, M237, R16, line 1, list 123; GLO, Dallas County Abstracts 1077, 1078, 1079, and 1080; 1850 U.S. Census, Dallas Co., Tex., NA, M432, R910, 82A; 1860 U.S. Census, Tulare Co., Calif., NA, M653, R71, 44; AFT, Hueco Tanks, 1989–2004; 1867 Texas Voter Registration Lists, Parker County, R9, 418, TSLAC; 1870 U.S. Census, Kern Co., Calif., NA, M593, R73, 325B; Haley, *Charles Goodnight*, 130; Dearen, *Cowboy of the Pecos*, 111. The site of Skillman's Station at Narboe Bend is on a sandy bluff just above the river, a short distance upriver from Narboe Crossing. The adobe stage building has long since disappeared. At Skillman's, Joe Allen and Skeet Lee Jones found an 1854 Seated Liberty half dollar, along with a fork and other artifacts. Maps from the 1859 boundary survey of Texas show the location of Skillman's Station to be precisely at the point where Allen and Jones found the 1854 half dollar. Skillman's Station proved one of the more elusive stage stops to locate, requiring numerous field trips over sixteen years. In a 1998 interview with me, the landowner said that when they purchased the property in the 1930s, the seller told them that an old dugout above the river near Narboe Point had previously been an old stage station. This is incorrect. The actual station site is a mile below this dugout, at Narboe Bend on the Pecos. A handful of early settlers lived in the immediate vicinity of Skillman's Station, starting in the late nineteenth century. One can see several dugouts littered with turn-of-the-century artifacts (circa 1890–1900) in drainages below the 2,800-foot ridge that heads north-northwest from Narboe Point. John P., John Jr., Peter, and Paul Narboe immigrated to America on March 12, 1832, landing at the Port of New York. As Peters Colony residents, all four Narboes received adjacent land parcels in Dallas County in the

1840s. The John and Elizabeth Narboe family left Texas during the 1850s, and by 1860 they were living in Tulare County, California. In July 1856, J. Narboe wrote his name on the rocks at Hueco Tanks, in El Paso County, Texas. Hueco Tanks is on the Upper Emigrant Road (also the Butterfield Road) to California. An August 28, 1867, Parker County voter registration list shows Peter Narboe as having been in Texas for twenty-five years but in the county for only one year. By 1870, Peter Narboe had left Texas and joined brother John and his wife in Kern County, California. After the Civil War, some of the Narboe descendants moved westward to take part in the booming cattle business. Charles Goodnight recalled riding herd along the Pecos after the Civil War with Peter Narboe, a Palo Pinto County rancher. John Gibson had a partner named Narboe in his Hookity-Hook ranch operations, established in the late 1870s and located on the east bank of the Pecos, 40 miles north of Fort Stockton. Goodnight and others spell the name as "Narbo," but numerous period documents show the correct spelling as "Narboe." Besides Narboe Point, Narboe Crossing, and Narboe Bend, there is also Narrow Bow (Narboe) Draw, which empties into the Pecos upstream of Skillman's.

50. Lang, *First Overland Mail: . . . St. Louis to San Francisco*, 123; Sketch No. 3, *1883–1884 Surveys of Western Texas by Captain W. R. Livermore*, NACP. An important observation concerning Roscoe and Margaret Conkling's 1947 Butterfield publication is that if the couple did not provide an actual "on the ground" account of a site, this indicates that they never visited it. In this case, the Conklings omit a firsthand, detailed description of Skillman's Station. This is because they never found it.

51. *United States and Texas Boundary Commission*, Maps #1, 2, 3, and 15, Senate Exec. Doc. No. 70, 47th Sess., 1st Sess., ser. 1987 (hereafter cited as *U.S. and Texas Boundary Commission*); *Map No. 4, Boundary 68 Roll, 1859 Map of Texas Boundary Line surveyed under the direction of the U.S. Department of the Interior*, RG 49, NACP; U.S. General Land Office, *Annual Report*, 1890, 57; Brock, "Perhaps the Most Incorrect," 431–62; Baker, "Northwest Boundary of Texas," 12, 14–21, 44–50; Roeder, "Texas–New Mexico Boundary"; *St. Louis Missouri Republican*, Jan. 19, 1859 (endnote quotation). A newspaper in January 1859 noted, "Mr. Clark, the U.S. Boundary Commissioner, had recovered his papers, which had been stolen from him at Franklin [now El Paso, Texas]. They had been buried in the outskirts of town." Congress neglected to publish reports and maps concerning the 1859 Texas boundary survey until 1882.

52. Mills, *My Story*, 54–55.

53. Ibid., 54 (quotations 1–2); *U.S. and Texas Boundary Commission*, 271 (quotation 3), 271–72 (quotation 4). In printing the correspondence between Clark and Scurry, the U.S. Government Printing Office spelled the latter's name as "Scurvy."

54. *U.S. and Texas Boundary Commission*, 271 (quotation 1), 275 (quotation 2).

55. U.S. House of Representatives, *Boundary Line*, 8–9; Baker, "Northwest Boundary of Texas," 38, 48–49; Brock, "Perhaps the Most Incorrect," 456–59; MT, Mentone, Anderson Ranch, Lindley Ranch, Orla SE. Despite Clark's significant error, Congress and Texas ratified his survey in 1891. When New Mexico applied for statehood in 1910, one of Congress's conditions for approval was that New Mexico accept the erroneous boundary line, an error that ultimately shortchanged New Mexico of more than 603,000 acres.

56. Dunn, "History of Loving County," (thesis), 99–104.

57. Ibid., 102 (quotation). The author and Skeet Lee Jones also found evidence of a few dwellings at the base of this bluff, on an August 2004 field trip to Old Mentone.

58. Ibid., 104, 114–19; AFT, Old Mentone, 1998–2008 (JA, PD, Skeet Lee Jones).

59. Dunn, "History of Loving County" (thesis), 75–77.

60. AFT, Mentone, 1998–2008; Dunn, "History of Loving County," (thesis), 82–84, 119; 2006 Loving County census figures from U.S. Census Bureau, http://quickfacts.census.gov (accessed Sept. 24, 2008); MT, Mentone.

61. From Tunstill Bend on the Pecos, located in T&P RR Township 1, Block 56, Survey 47, the mail road left the river and ran along the foothills overlooking the Pecos all the way to Pope's Camp upstream. MT, Red Bluff; Pope's Wells segment in the Forest Glen Productions documentary video *Graveyard of the West*; AFT, Pope's Camp and Pope's Crossing, Sept. 11, 2000 (JA, Skeet Lee Jones, Harvey Hicks); AFT, Pope's artesian well site, 1991, and Sept. 11, 2000 (JA, Skeet Lee Jones, Harvey Hicks); *Report of the Secretary of War*, Senate Exec. Doc. No. 1, 35th Cong., 2nd Sess., ser. 975, pp. 592–607; "Artesian Well Experiment," 545–48; *1859 United States and Texas Boundary Commission Maps #3 and 15*, Senate Exec. Doc. No. 70, 47th Cong., 1st Sess., ser. 1987; *Map #4, Boundary 68 Roll, 1859 Map of Texas Boundary Line surveyed under the direction of the U.S. Department of the Interior*, RG 49, NACP. These two maps show Pope's 1855–58 military road heading northeast to the thirty-second parallel and the well site 8 miles east of the Pecos.

62. Ormsby, *Butterfield Overland Mail*, 72 (quotation 1); Myers, "Pope's Wells," 282 (quotation 2), 283, 287. The construction of nearby Red Bluff Dam in the mid-1930s submerged Pope's Camp, the oldest European American structures in Loving County, which were under water for decades. A recent drought lowered water levels and exposed the long-lost site to view once again.

63. Ormsby, *Butterfield Overland Mail*, 72 (quotation 1); *St. Louis Missouri Republican*, Jan. 7, 1859 (quotations 2–3); MT, Red Bluff. GLO, Map #10110, *June 4, 1873 Ward County Rolled Sketch #22* shows "Pope's Camp" in H&TC RR Survey 127, File #S-3321 (later changed by GLO to T&P RR, Block 57, Township 1, Survey 24, Loving County Abstract No. 1318), and the later GLO Map #2303, *Sectional Map No. 3 of the Lands and of the Line of the Texas & Pacific R'Y. Co. in Reeves and Parts of Tom Green, Pecos, Presidio & El Paso Counties* shows "Capt. Pope Camp" in T&P RR Block 57, Township 1, Survey 24 (Loving County Abstract No. 1318). Several citations of Pope's 1855–58 wagon road (also the overland road) heading upstream appear in Loving County survey field notes. See GLO, H&TC RR Block 33, Surveys 82, 89, 90, and 95.

64. Pope's Crossing is in T&P RR Block 57, Township 1, Survey 10 (Loving County Abstract No. 225). See GLO, Map #2303, *Sectional Map No. 3 of the Lands and of the Line of the Texas & Pacific R'Y. Co. in Reeves and Parts of Tom Green, Pecos, Presidio & El Paso Counties*; Dearen, *Crossing Rio Pecos*, 27. A lithograph and accompanying text in a November 1858 newspaper article indicates that the Overland Mail Company was operating a ferry on the Pecos River. The report says that the ferry was at 31 degrees, 45 minutes latitude, the location of Old Mentone. Pope's Crossing is at 31 degrees, 59 minutes, while Horsehead Crossing is at 31 degrees, 14 minutes. The report was likely referring to Pope's Crossing, since this is where the mail road crossed the Pecos from September 1858 to May 1859. See *Frank Leslie's Illustrated Newspaper*, Nov. 27, 1858. Because of Red Bluff Lake, Pope's Crossing was under water for many years. During the 2000 drought, both Clay Allison's homestead and the upper channel of this well-worn crossing were visible. In the early 1900s, John Haley bought the Allison property and used the sandstone building as his ranch headquarters. Allison's grave is located at West of the Pecos Museum in Pecos, Texas. For more on Clay Allison, see Parsons, *Clay Allison*. Roscoe Conkling drew a detailed sketch of the Allison homestead during his visit to the crossing. See CJ, Oct. 16, 1931, box 9, RPC Papers. From April through August 1879, there was a post office at Pope's Crossing on the west side of the Pecos in Reeves County, Texas, situated on the Fort Stanton, New Mexico, to Fort Stockton, Texas, mail road. James Raynor served

as postmaster. See Feb. 10, 1879, Pope's Crossing post office application, PGS, Reeves Co., Tex., NA, RG 28, M1126, R587; PGA, Reeves Co., Tex., NA RG 28, M841, R126.

65. Senate Exec. Doc. No. 64, 31st Cong., 1st Sess., 203 (quotations). The route of the overland road from the Pecos to Delaware Springs is in GLO, Paul McCombs, *1884 Map of the T&P Railroad Surveys in El Paso County, Texas*; GLO, Paul McCombs, *September 17, 1883 Map of the Texas & Pacific R-Y Reserve*; GLO, Map #2304, *Sectional Map No. 4 of the Lands and of the Line of the Texas & Pacific R'Y. Co. in El Paso and Part of Presidio Counties*. Two spur roads from the Pecos River merge in Block 60, Township 59, Survey 11. Westward from Delaware Springs Station to the Guadalupe Mountains, the Butterfield Trail passed through Blocks 60–64.

66. Ormsby, *Butterfield Overland Mail*, 72 (quotations); AFT, Delaware Springs Station, 1989 and Nov. 3, 2002 (JA, PD). See also the Delaware Springs and Butterfield segment in the Forest Glen Productions documentary video *History of the Guadalupe Mountains.*

67. Lang, *First Overland Mail: . . . St. Louis to San Francisco*, 122; Lang, *First Overland Mail: . . . San Francisco to Memphis*, 38.

68. Conkling and Conkling, *Butterfield Overland Mail*, 1:387–88; *St. Louis Missouri Republican*, Feb. 7, 1859 (quotation); AFT, Delaware Springs Station, 1989 and Nov. 3, 2002 (JA, PD); Delaware Springs/ Butterfield segment in the Forest Glen Productions documentary video *History of the Guadalupe Mountains.* Today, much of the company's stone fortress at Delaware Springs is in ruins, and quarried pieces of stone litter the ground. Only a small remnant of the original station wall remains intact. The springs at the site still flow and are fascinating to observe.

69. Ray, *Ethnohistorical Analysis*, 159; Opler, *Lipan and Mescalero Apache*, 203, 205, 208 (quotation), 209–211. I base my discussion of Mescalero Apaches on research by Morris Opler, Averam Bender, Verne F. Ray, and Harry Basehart. Ray provides a detailed, well-researched map of traditional tribal territories. Lipan Apaches also ranged west of the Pecos River. Most Lipan lands, however, were in central and South Texas. The reader should keep in mind that these Native American zones are fluid, general demarcations and are neither rigid nor static.

70. Opler, *Lipan and Mescalero Apache*, 208 (quotations 1–3), 209–11.

71. Bender, *Study of Mescalero Apache*, 79, 82; Ray, *Ethnohistorical Analysis*, 19–22, 179–85; Opler, *Lipan and Mescalero Apache*, 215 (quotations 1–2); 253 (quotations 3–5).

72. Basehart, *Mescalero Apache Subsistence*, 119 (quotation 2), 121 (quotation 1); Martin, "From Texas to California," entry for Sunday, June 10, 1849 (quotation 3).

73. Basehart, *Mescalero Apache Subsistence*, 10–78, 104–10, 130 (quotations).

74. Ibid., 80 (quotation 1), 88 (quotation 2), 89 (quotations 3–6). See also Mescalero Apache history segment in the Forest Glen Productions documentary video *History of the Guadalupe Mountains*; AFT, Shumard Canyon Trail and Salt Overlook Trail, west side of Guadalupe Mountains, 1989, with Mark Owen Rosacker. Basehart does not mention the natural staircase, which I learned of in 1989 from Mark Owen Rosacker, Living Desert State Park ranger, Carlsbad, New Mexico. For many years, Rosacker organized an annual Mescalero Apache ceremony at the park during which Mescaleros harvested native mescal from the Guadalupes and then cooked it in an underground oven at the park. In the evening, Mountain Spirit Dancers performed a dance ceremony and blessed the mescal before eating it. Over a twenty-year period, Rosacker became close to several Mescalero elders, who told him of the natural staircase leading to the supernatural cave on the west side.

75. Martin, "From Texas to California," entry for June 13, 1849 (quotations 1–2); Ormsby, *Butterfield Overland Mail*, 73–74 (quotation 3).

Both C. C. Cox and Waterman Ormsby fully appreciated the Guadalupe Mountains' outstanding natural and scenic assets. Not surprisingly, in 1971 the southern half of this mountain range became a national park. As such, these lands are not to be owned by any one person but instead have been set aside for public benefit so that all may enjoy them. America's national park concept resembles early Spanish and Mexican attitudes regarding communal ownership of natural resources.

76. Ormsby, *Butterfield Overland Mail*, 73–74; Basehart, *Mescalero Apache Subsistence*, 89 (quotations); AFT, the Pinery and Guadalupe Pass, 1988–2008; Conkling and Conkling, *Butterfield Overland Mail*, 1:390–92; Pinery/Butterfield segment in the Forest Glen Productions documentary video *History of the Guadalupe Mountains*; Presidio County Field Notes, Apr. 17, 1874; El Paso County Field Notes, Dec. 27, 1884. On January 25, 1858, Samuel Maverick was the first to file a claim on Pine Springs, located in Survey 303. This 80-acre parcel later included Butterfield's Pinery Station. Today, Pinery Station is in Guadalupe Mountains National Park and is accessible to the public from the El Paso–Carlsbad highway, one of the few Butterfield stage stops in Texas located on public lands. In August 2014, the National Park Service added the section of the Butterfield Overland Mail Road in Guadalupe Mountains National Park to the National Register of Historic Places. See National Park Service, National Register of Historic Places, Case No. 14000524, "Butterfield Overland Mail Route Corridor, Guadalupe Mountains National Park," http://www.nps.gov/ nr/research/.

77. Lang, *First Overland Mail: . . . St. Louis to San Francisco*, 122; Lang, *First Overland Mail: . . . San Francisco to Memphis*, 37 (quotation 1), 38 (quotation 2).

78. Ormsby, *Butterfield Overland Mail*, 74 (quotations).

79. AFT, Guadalupe Pass and Polancio's grave, 1989–2008, including a trip on June 29, 1999, with Larry Henderson following traces of the Butterfield Road through Guadalupe Mountains National Park. Henderson was formerly park superintendent at Guadalupe Mountains in the 1990s. See also Ormsby, *Butterfield Overland Mail*, 75–76; Lang, *First Overland Mail: . . . St. Louis to San Francisco*, 122; Guadalupe Pass/Polancio segment in the Forest Glen Productions documentary video *History of the Guadalupe Mountains.* J. M. Farwell of the *Daily Alta California* said that Longstreet sent Polancio ahead to scout for water. In Guadalupe Pass today, many of the mail road's original retaining walls are still intact. Down below, in Guadalupe Canyon, one can see Polancio's grave, several examples of historic graffiti, and excellent traces of the overland road.

80. Ormsby, *Butterfield Overland Mail*, 75–76; Conkling and Conkling, *Butterfield Overland Mail*, 1:395 (quotations); AFT, Guadalupe Sand Dunes and Salt Lakes on the park's west side, 1989–2008 (JA).

81. The overland road exited present-day Culberson County in Survey 45, Block 66, Township 1 and entered Hudspeth County in Survey 41 (same block and township). See U.S. Dept. of the Interior, *Map NP-GM-7000*, Map Cabinet, County Clerk's Office, Hudspeth Co., Tex.; Conkling and Conkling, *Butterfield Overland Mail*, 1:395–96 (quotation 1), 396 (quotations 2–3). Today, one can trace the old Butterfield Trail along the national park's west side. Some portions of the overland road here have very deep ruts. The walk in fall, winter, or spring is a memorable one. In summer, the heat is brutal.

82. Bieber, *Exploring Southwestern Trails*, 315 (quotation 1); Senate Exec. Doc. No. 64, 31st Cong., 1st Sess., 202 (quotation 2); Basehart, *Mescalero Apache Subsistence*, 72 (quotation 3).

83. Senate Exec. Doc. No. 64, 31st Cong., 1st Sess., 202 (quotations); Bieber, *Exploring Southwestern Trails*, 315; GLO, Maverick Lake Files, Hudspeth County Abstracts Nos. 1310 and 1311; GLO, Hudspeth County Abstract No. 672, 320 acres; GLO, Zimpleman Lake Files, Hudspeth County Abstract Nos. 2042, 2043, and 2044; Hudspeth

County Clerk's Office, Texas & Pacific and Private Surveys book 6, pp. 494, 517–23; GLO, Map #5683, Culberson County Sketch File S.L., *Map of Salt Lakes*, drawn on Oct. 23, 1930, by Paul McCombs; AFT, Guadalupe Salt Lakes, 1989–2008; Holt, "Story of Salt," 347; Dearen, *Castle Gap*, 66. For more on the Salt War, see Broaddus, *Legal Heritage of El Paso*, 126–28; Bowden, "Magoffin Salt War," 108–13; Sonnichsen, *El Paso Salt War*, 7–61; Sonnichsen, *Pass of the North*, 192–210; Cool, *Salt Warriors*, 81.

84. Crow Spring is located close to the line separating Blocks 67 and 68 in Texas and Pacific Railway Lands, Township 1. The best maps for tracing the exact route of the Butterfield from Delaware Springs west to Crow Spring on the thirty-second parallel (via historic Independence Springs) are GLO, Map #2304, *Sectional Map No. 4 of the Lands and of the Line of the Texas & Pacific R'Y. Co. in El Paso and Part of Presidio Counties* and GLO, Map #8743, Culberson County Rolled Sketch 14, *1902 Sketch of Black Mountain Cattle Company Ranch.* The latter map also shows the Maverick and Zimpleman Salt Lakes. The exact location of the Crow Spring stage stop has been a riddle to historians for almost 150 years, because the station was built with gypsum blocks. Gypsum is not durable, and the structure had long melted by the 1930s. However, on December 16, 2002, Joe Allen, the landowner, and I finally confirmed the location of the long-lost station. We found the site a short distance south of the springs, adjacent to the mail road. Several test holes dug in a gypsum mound produced pieces of an old cast-iron stove, square nails, glass, crockery, pistol balls from the antebellum period, and quarried rock used for the station's foundation. Rock, let alone quarried rock, is nonexistent in the sandy gypsum soil, so clearly Butterfield employees had hauled in these pieces. In January 1880, twelve Apaches besieged two miners named Andrews and Wiswall in the old Crow Spring station house and stole their horses. Leaving stuffed dummies in their stead and their faithful watchdog, Shep, on guard inside the station, the two men slipped out of the building unobserved and made their way on foot to Ysleta, Texas. Nine Texas Rangers sent to investigate the incident found, upon their arrival at Crow Spring, the loyal canine Shep still alive and guarding the two dummies. For more on this story see Baylor, *Into the Far, Wild Country*, 292–98.

85. Ormsby, *Butterfield Overland Mail*, 76; Lang, *First Overland Mail: . . . San Francisco to Memphis*, 36 (quotations 1–2); Texas Surveyors Association, *One League to Each Wind*, 196 (quotation 3); AFT, Orange, N.Mex., 1989, and Butterfield Road trace on rocky hill north of Dell City, June 29, 1999, with Larry Henderson; Conkling and Conkling, *Butterfield Overland Mail*, 1:397 (endnote quotation 1); Senate Exec. Doc. No. 64, 31st Cong., 1st Sess., 22 (endnote quotations 2–3). *Daily Evening Bulletin* reporter Baer reported that Crow Spring and the lake spanned nearly an acre. The Conklings mention that the stage company put in a well fifty yards northwest of the spring. "This well[,] it is said, provided a supply of water less tainted than the spring." This may be the same well that Lieutenant Francis Bryan first located in July 1849. Bryan, describing Crow Spring as "brackish," searched the site for a better source of water. He proved fortunate in his quest: "We found a hole, dug under the bushes by some California party, which furnished us tolerable water." Joe Allen, the landowner, and I found Bryan's hand-dug well on December 16, 2002, close to the old mail road. From Crow Spring, the trail crossed the New Mexico state line and en route passed by the rock ruins of a pioneer homestead near the ghost town of Orange. Next, one can discern a visibly distinct cut the road made across a rocky hill north of Dell City, Texas, and the state line. From the summit of this ridge, one can see the Cornudas (horns) of the Wind and San Antonio Mountains (part of the Cornudas Mountains), looming on the western horizon.

86. Ely, *Where the West Begins*, 15–16. In the Trans-Pecos desert today, disparate interests are vying for control over the region's valuable natural resources. At Dell City, near Guadalupe Mountains National Park, farmers currently use the Bone Spring–Victorio Peak Aquifer to irrigate their crops. Regional municipalities are also interested in this aquifer to help sustain their populations. Water studies by the State of Texas since the 1960s show that irrigated agriculture consumes 75 percent of the available water, a figure that is rapidly proving unsustainable in the arid regions of West Texas. Most experts agree that by 2100, a radical shift in regional water usage will occur, cutting allocations to irrigation and shifting these to urban areas.

87. GLO, Map #2300, Paul McCombs, *Oct. 20, 1885 Map of the Texas and Pacific R'y Company's Surveys in the 80-Mile Reserve* (quotations 2–3); Smith, *Grazing Problems*, 28 (quotation 1); Bentley, *Cattle Ranges*, 8 (quotations 4–5). For detailed documentation and discussion of overgrazing and rangeland degradation in West Texas, see Ely, *Where the West Begins*, 110–17.

88. Dale, *Range Cattle Industry*, 130 (quotation 1); Smith, *Grazing Problems*, 10 (quotation 2), 14 (quotation 3); Marks, *Three-Mile and Sulfur Draw*, 30, 33; Box, "Range Deterioration," 37, 45 (endnote quotation). Thadis Box's 1967 study of West Texas grasslands found that chronic overgrazing after 1880 "raped the range in thirty years."

89. At Cornudas, the landowner has done an excellent job of clearing the creosotebush and other brush surrounding the station that obscured Roscoe and Margaret Conkling's view during their visit here in the 1930s. According to the Conklings, the mail company built the station of rock and adobe. Measuring 75 by 75 feet, the station had two rooms with fireplaces and a corral. Ormsby noted, "There is quite a large station here." Butterfield passengers stopped here for a meal, while a fresh set of mules were put in harness. The exact route of the Butterfield Trail and the stage stations in this section appear on several excellent maps. See *1859 United States and Texas Boundary Commission Maps #2 and 15*, Senate Exec. Doc. No. 70, 47th Cong., 1st Sess., ser. 1987; *Map #2, Boundary 68 Roll, 1859 Map of Texas Boundary Line Surveyed under the Direction of the U.S. Department of the Interior*, RG 49, NACP. The latter is a larger-scale map. See also Conkling and Conkling, *Butterfield Overland Mail*, 1:398–99; Ormsby, *Butterfield Overland Mail*, 76 (endnote quotation); Cornudas/Butterfield segment in the Forest Glen Productions documentary video *History of the Guadalupe Mountains*; AFT, Cornudas, 1989–2006 (JA, PD); May 25, 1880 entry from M. M. Maxon field book, Fort Davis National Historic Site Archives, Fort Davis, Texas; Captain French, Commanding Fort Davis, Texas, to Assistant Adjutant General, Aug. 20, 1878, NA, RG 393, DP, LR, M1381, R2; Baylor, *Into the Far, Wild Country*, 295. After attacking the Rangers, the Apache warriors rode west on the overland road in the direction of Alamo Spring at Alamo Mountain.

90. Heitman, *Historical Register*, 958; Herman Thorn biographical essay, Carl T. Hayden Pioneer Biographies Collection, Arizona State University Library, Tempe, 1–4; Huff, "Journal," July 9, 1849 (quotation); June 24 and June 26, 1849, entries in Martin, "From Texas to California." C.C. Cox, part of another California emigrant train, stopped at Cornudas/Thorn's Well on June 24, 1849, and ran into Lieutenant Thorn's wagon train two days later, at Hueco Tanks, 36 miles to the west. First Lieutenant Herman Thorn, Second Infantry, was from New York. He drowned near the junction of the Colorado and Gila Rivers on October 16, 1849, while providing escort for a wagon train.

91. Senate Exec. Doc. No. 64, 31st Cong., 1st Sess., 22 (quotations 1–2), 200 (quotation 3); Bartlett, *Personal Narrative*, 1:130; Lang, *First Overland Mail: . . . St. Louis to San Francisco*, 122; *Frank Leslie's Illustrated Newspaper*, Oct. 23, 1858 (endnote quotations). An article from October 1858 said that Butterfield was handling the water shortages along the Upper Road with a water delivery service. The company had installed large tin boilers on several wagons, "capable of holding as much water as a team of six mules can draw." The report says that the company's water trains were "conveying water to the different stations."

92. Lang, *First Overland Mail: . . . San Francisco to Memphis*, 36; Senate Exec. Doc. No. 64, 31st Cong., 1st Sess., 23 (quotation 1), 199, 200 (quotation 2); Bartlett, *Personal Narrative*, 1:130; AFT, Alamo Spring Station, 1989–2006 (JA, PD). Butterfield conductor Roberts and passenger Baer in November 1858 unexpectedly found a spring 10 miles west of Cornudas, which must have been Alamo Spring (also known as Cottonwood Spring). Why this was unexpected is unclear, since federal expeditions in 1849 and 1850 had already located this spring.

93. Senate Exec. Doc. No. 64, 31st Cong., 1st Sess., 200 (quotation); Conkling and Conkling, *Butterfield Overland Mail*, 1:402–406. Several interviews over a decade with an area landowner provided background information on the history of human occupation at Alamo Spring. At the base of Alamo Mountain, the stage company constructed one of the largest stations on the Upper Road. The structure was approximately 57 feet by 69 feet and had three rooms, the outlines of which can be identified because they are the only walls that were chinked with mud. A large corral within the enclosure encircles the rooms on three sides. A blacksmith shop was located in the corral, as evidenced by many period square nails and horseshoe nails. The walls were 11 feet high. The Conklings state that the building's water was supplied by an acequia or aqueduct that drained runoff water into a tank in the corral. There are several graves at Alamo Spring, including that of a person named Gentry, who died June 24, sometime in the 1850s. One wonders if this is the same Frank Gentry who carved his name on the entranceway to Thorn's Well at Cornudas in 1852. Perhaps some of the people buried here were members of pioneer ranching families that later used the station for their home, beginning with Charlie Rhodius in the early 1880s. These early ranchers built additional structures, including extensive stacked-rock corrals. A large concrete tank was added nearby with a feeder pipe to the springs. Improvements were also made to the spring itself, and the aqueduct was enlarged to increase water flow to the tank. Period lead-lined cans, crockery, glass, nails, and iron are found only at the stage station and nowhere else, helping to effectively date the various buildings at Alamo Spring. The Conklings noted that the spring was still seeping in 1931 and remarked on the beauty of three to four large, healthy cottonwoods at the site. Today, the spring is dry and the trees are dead.

94. GLO, Map #2300, Paul McCombs, *Oct. 20, 1885 Map of the Texas and Pacific R'y Company's Surveys in the 80-Mile Reserve*; GLO, Map #11804, *Nov. 1918, Hudspeth County Sketch File 29, Helms Ranch Survey* (endnote quotation); Bartlett, *Personal Narrative*, 1:131; AFT, Cerro Alto, Nov. 1, 2002 (with Roland Ely). The best historic maps of this section that clearly identify the mail road and the Butterfield stations are *1859 United States and Texas Boundary Commission Maps #1*, Senate Exec. Doc. No. 70, 47th Cong., 1st Sess., ser. 1987; *Map #1, Boundary 68 Roll, 1859 Map of Texas Boundary Line Surveyed under the Direction of the U.S. Department of the Interior*, RG 49, NACP. The latter is a larger-scale map. These maps show the mail road going around the north side of Cerro Alto. A mile west of Alamo Mountain and Alamo Spring Station, a local landowner pointed out to me a well-defined trace of the overland trail heading to Cerro Alto across a level plain. The landowner and I followed this excellent Butterfield trace westward for some distance. En route to Cerro Alto, the mail road reentered the Lone Star State in Texas University Lands, Block B, Survey 5. In November 1918, the Butterfield Road was still in use in New Mexico and Texas as an "auto road." From the New Mexico–Texas state line, the overland road ran to the base of Cerro Alto, where it forked. Bartlett said he was advised to take the left, or southern, route around Cerro Alto, which was shorter. However, as noted above, the stage company took the northern route, which was better suited for wagons. Dry-stacked rock retaining walls were built on the steep hillsides to help guide Butterfield coaches at night. Today, one can still

see these retaining walls and traces of the old road along Cerro Alto's northern passage.

95. Lang, *First Overland Mail: . . . St. Louis to San Francisco*, 121 (quotations).

96. Ormsby, *Butterfield Overland Mail*, 77 (quotations); GLO, El Paso County Abstract No. 44. Friedrich Hausmann was the first to file a claim on Hueco Tanks, located in Survey 275. In July 1854, Hausmann sold the 640-acre parcel to Adolph Meyer for $35. Meyer then sold it to Samuel Maverick the following month for $160. In October 1872, William E. Sweet purchased Hueco Tanks from Samuel Maverick, Jr., for 320 gold dollars.

97. *1859 United States and Texas Boundary Commission Maps #1*, Senate Exec. Doc. No. 70, 47th Cong., 1st Sess., ser. 1987; *Map #1, Boundary 68 Roll, 1859 Map of Texas Boundary Line Surveyed under the Direction of the U.S. Department of the Interior*, RG 49, NACP; AFT, Hueco Tanks, 1989–2004 (JA); Ormsby, *Butterfield Overland Mail*, 77 (quotation 1); Lang, *First Overland Mail: . . . St. Louis to San Francisco*, 122; Lang, *First Overland Mail: . . . San Francisco to Memphis*, 35–36; *St. Louis Missouri Republican*, Feb. 7, 1859 (quotation 2). Aerial photographs of Hueco Tanks show two well-defined parallel ruts of the mail road passing by a present-day gun club, heading to the northeast side of the tanks. Today both ruts are easily traceable into Hueco Tanks State Park. The traces come together at the site of the old mail station, in the middle of the tanks, on the east side of the amphitheater. The mail road ran through the middle of the tanks, where it exited on the west side, heading on to El Paso. Unfortunately, nineteenth-century landowners destroyed the historical integrity of Hueco Tanks when they plowed under the ruins of the old stage stop. I noticed a few pieces of period glass, pottery, and some quarried rock at the site.

98. Lang, *First Overland Mail: . . . San Francisco to Memphis*, 35, 36 (quotation). Today, one can trace the route of the Butterfield Road from Hueco Tanks to El Paso, Texas, using the following present-day signposts: The old overland route runs through the middle of the tanks, exiting on the west side. It then parallels Hueco Tanks Road, passes by Ramons Tank, then runs along a pipeline to Araceli Avenue, past Ryan Wesley Street, to south of (underneath) the mesa, crossing Tamara Drive, Cruz Tierra Street, and Jim Browning Street, past Krag Street, just south of the Wagon Trail Dr./Hunton intersection. Next, it joins Wagon Trail Road, just before its intersection with Flager Street. Then heading west, Wagon Trail Road appears on current maps and aerial photographs as "Old Butterfield Trail/Old Richardson Trail." Next, the route of the overland road runs southwest onto Fort Bliss Military Reservation, passing north of Nations South Well, north of Square Dance Road, crossing Hwy 375, and crosses Global RCH. It then enters El Paso Airport and crosses George Perry Blvd., before intersecting the airport runway. Next, it heads onto Concordia Cemetery (see Butterfield Street in the cemetery). Then the course of the old road runs through downtown on Overland Street to its intersection with El Paso Street, the location of Block 34 and the Overland Mail Company's regional operations hub.

99. Numerous authors, beginning with the Conklings, have incorrectly stated that Postmaster General Joseph Holt ordered Butterfield to move its operations to the Lower Road by August 1, 1859. As proof of Holt's order, the Conklings cite an 1862 mail contract between a subsequent postmaster general, Montgomery Blair, and mail contractor Benjamin Holladay, found in Senate Exec. Doc. No. 211, 46th Cong., 2nd Sess., ser. 1886, pp. 3–4. See Conkling and Conkling, *Butterfield Overland Mail*, 2:13. This post office document, likely cited in error, has nothing to do with Butterfield or with antebellum overland mail service in Texas. In addition, a close reading of the original handwritten Postmaster General Order Journals at the National Archives in Washington, D.C., reveals that Postmaster General Joseph Holt

issued no such directive to the Overland Mail Company regarding its service in Texas. See Postmaster General Order Journals, vols. 42–48 (July 1, 1858–May 29, 1861), NA, RG 28, entry 1. Finally, a thorough perusal of published House and Senate documents from 1858 to 1861, including annual U.S. Postmaster General reports, shows no such order from Holt. In fact, the government's unique contract with the Overland Mail Company gave the mail contractor considerable latitude: the company could change its route at its own discretion, and the government could not curtail or discontinue service on Butterfield's Route No. 12578, from St. Louis to San Francisco. Most mail contracts contained a clause allowing the postmaster the authority to curtail or amend service on a route, such as from weekly to twice a month. The Butterfield contract, however, deliberately omitted such language, much to Holt's consternation. U.S. attorney general Jeremiah Sullivan Black strongly urged the postmaster general to abide by the terms of the Overland Mail Company contract signed by Holt's predecessor, Aaron Brown, on September 16, 1857. See J. S. Black to Joseph Holt, May 28, 1859, in Senate Exec. Doc. No. 26, 36th Cong., 1st Sess., ser. 1031, pp. 1–5. In sum, the postmaster general did not order Butterfield's 1859 route change. This alteration was voluntary and was initiated by the mail company. Next, regarding the exact timing of the route change, in a May 12, 1859, letter written near Skillman's Station on the Pecos, the head of the U.S. Boundary Survey Commission, John H. Clark, informed his superior that he would try to send his next report via Butterfield coach "if the 'overland route' is not changed along this portion of it [i.e., the Upper Road], which is contemplated," before his return on June 3, 1859." In fact, Clark sent his June 3 report from the Pecos to El Paso not by overland coach but via Lieutenant Henry Martyn Lazelle, Eighth Infantry, who commanded the Boundary Commission's military escort. See *United States and Texas Boundary*, Senate Exec. Doc. No. 70, 47th Cong., 1st Sess., ser. 1987, pp. 270–71 (endnote quotation 1), 276. When Lieutenant Wesley Owens and his men made a reconnaissance of the Guadalupe Mountains region in July 1859, they found the mail route deserted. Owens's report noted, "On the evening of the same day [July 19, 1859] I camped at the foot of the [Guadalupe] mountains near a deserted mail station [the Pinery]." See 2nd Lt. Wesley Owens, 2nd Cav., Camp Van Camp, Tex., to Capt. George Stoneman, 2nd Cav., Cmdr. Pecos Expedition, Aug. 3, 1859, NA, RG 94, AGO, LR, M567, R613 (endnote quotation 2). Ironically, the Upper Road proved no better than the route originally selected by Butterfield, i.e., Marcy's California Emigrant Trail. The Upper Road possessed many of the same shortcomings as Marcy's, namely, lack of military protection and a shortage of water.

100. Frazer, *Forts of the West*, 143, 148, 157, 162; 2nd Lt. John P. Sherburne, 1st Inf., Camp Stockton, Tex., to Col. Samuel Cooper, Apr. 20, 1859, NA, RG 94, AGO, LR, M567, R612. The army named Fort Bliss after Captain William Wallace Smith Bliss, Fort Davis in honor of U.S. secretary of war Jefferson Davis, Fort Quitman for Major General John Anthony Quitman, and Camp (later Fort) Stockton after First Lieutenant Edward Dorsey Stockton, Company A, First Infantry.

CHAPTER 9. THE LOWER ROAD TO EL PASO

1. See various depositions of mail line employees, superintendents, contractors, and passengers in *Giddings v. U.S.* for an overview of Overland Mail Company operational expenses. These depositions detail the cost of adobe and stone station houses, forage, livestock, freighting, and labor.

2. Mar. 30, 1860, Overland Mail Company Credit Reports, New York vol. 346, New York City 7, p. 693 (quotation 1), DCR, BL; Overland Mail Company, *Memorial*, 2 (quotation 2), available at Amon Carter Museum Research Library, Document 4076, microfilm R402,

Western Americana, Frontier History of the Trans-Mississippi West, 1550–1900.

3. Jackson, "New Look," 296, 297 (quotation 1), 298 (quotation 2).

4. Ibid., 298, 300 (quotation), 301, 303.

5. *St. Louis Missouri Republican*, Oct. 6, 1859; Dallas *Herald*, Apr. 3, 1861; Boggs, *My Playhouse*, 386 (endnote quotation 2); Postmaster General Order Journals, May 21, 1861, vol. 48, Mar. 7, 1861–May 29, 1861, NA, RG 28, entry 1; Richardson, *Beyond the Mississippi*, 233 (quotation 1); Tallack, *California Overland Express*, 48 (quotation 2); deposition of William Buckley, *Giddings v. U.S.* (endnote quotation 1); Powers, *Afoot and Alone*, 136 (endnote quotation 3); Smith, *Old Army in Texas*, 87, 101. For many years, there has been some debate as to exactly when the Overland Mail Company terminated its service in Texas. The *Monitor* (of Sherman, Texas) reported that Butterfield coaches from both the East and the West passed through the city on March 27, 1861. Butterfield's Division Four (El Paso to Tucson) superintendent, William Buckley, said that he pulled all the stock and coaches off the line starting "about April 1, 1861." On April 5, 1861, the postmaster at San Francisco announced, "The Overland Mail by the Butterfield route did not leave this city today for St. Louis as usual and will be discontinued hereafter." On May 21, 1861, Postmaster General Montgomery Blair authorized payment to the Overland Mail Company for carrying the mails to El Paso via Fort Stockton through March 31, 1861. Regarding Horsehead Crossing, Second Lieutenant Henry Clay Wood and one company of the First Infantry maintained a temporary outpost there from April to August 1859. After the Civil War, Ben Ficklin's San Antonio–El Paso Mail Line operated a ferry at Horsehead Crossing for several months during 1868, until the company rerouted the mail road to cross downstream at Camp Melvin's Pontoon Bridge. Stephen Powers crossed the Pecos at Horsehead in 1868 and recalled, "The women and children were ferried over in a Government yawl at Horsehead Crossing, and the dainty belles of the South, as well as the more robust maidens, accepted the hand of a negro corporal, who assisted them into and out of the boat."

6. On the east side of the Pecos, Horsehead Crossing is located in present-day Crane County. On the river's west side, the crossing is in Pecos County. See GLO, Crane County Abstract No. 103; GLO, Pecos County Abstract No. 274; GLO, Map #3955, *1891 Map of Blocks Number 8, 9, and 10 Houston and Great Northern Railroad Company Surveys in Pecos County, Texas Owned by William Walter Phelps*; "An Act to incorporate the Pecos Bridge Company" and "An Act to incorporate the Horse Head crossing of the Pecos Bridge Company," Jan. 7, 1860, in Gammel, *Laws of Texas*, 5:18–20; Hunt, "Journal," Aug. 26, 1869 (endnote quotation); AFT, Horsehead Crossing, 1989–2006 (JA, PD); Horsehead Crossing segment in the Forest Glen Productions documentary video *Graveyard of the West*. Lieutenant Colonel Thomas B. Hunt arrived here in August 1869 and sketched two crossings at Horsehead: one upstream, where livestock and those on horseback forded the river, and the other downstream, which served as the ferry crossing. Hunt said, "The crossing at the [upstream] ford is rather risky," likely because of the river's swift currents and quicksand bottom. Joe Allen, Patrick Dearen, and I conducted in-depth examinations of the site and concluded that the old ferry crossing is near a large V-shaped notch in the riverbank where the State of Texas erected a marker in 1936 on the Pecos County riverbank (west side of the river). The more dangerous ford was a short distance upstream, in between the ferry crossing and the stage station, at a point marked at one time by several wooden stakes in the Crane County riverbank (east side of the river). Here, deep, wide cuts are evident on both sides.

7. Richardson, *Beyond the Mississippi*, 233 (quotation 1); Powers, *Afoot and Alone*, 136 (quotations 2–4); *Mesilla Times*, Apr. 13, 1861, SCL, UTEP. The last-published Butterfield itinerary for West Texas lists

the name of the station at Antelope Spring as Camp Pleasant. One should note that Butterfield historians Roscoe and Margaret Conkling were unaware of the overland station at Antelope Spring and never visited the site.

8. Holmes, *Covered Wagon Women*, 9:191 (quotations 1–5); Hunt, "Journal," Aug. 27, 1869 (quotation 6); El Paso County Field Notes for Agua Bonita (Antelope Spring), May 20, 1874; GLO, Pecos County Land File for Agua Bonita; Brune, *Springs of Texas*, 361. Antelope Spring and "old stage station" are shown in Bvt. Lt. Col. E. J. Strang, *Topographical Sketch of the Road from Fort Stockton to Fort Chadbourne, October and November 1867*, RG 77, Q135, NACP. One can trace the first part of the overland road from Horsehead Crossing to Antelope Spring in GLO, Map #3955, *1891 Map of Blocks Number 8, 9, and 10 Houston and Great Northern Railroad Company Surveys in Pecos County, Texas Owned by William Walter Phelps*. The remainder of the overland trail (labeled as "Road from Fort Stockton to Horsehead Crossing") is in GLO, Map #76038, *June 1896 Map of Pecos County, Texas*, running through Blocks 2 and 10. AFT, Antelope Spring, July 18, 1999 (JA, PD, and Mary Williams). In 1943, before intensive irrigation pumping of the local water table, Agua Bonita/Antelope Spring flowed at a rate of 14 liters per second (222 gallons per minute). Adjacent to the now-dry spring are the stone foundations and outline of what was obviously a sizeable stage station during the Butterfield period. In 1874, a settler filed a homestead preemption claim for 160 acres here that included Agua Bonita. Upon leaving Antelope Spring, the overland road steered southwest toward Seven Mile Mesa and Comanche Creek.

9. Capt. Charles Jarvis Whiting, 2nd Cav., Camp Radziminski, to Col. Samuel Cooper, Dec. 6, 1858, NA, RG 94, AGO, LR, M567, R594; El Paso County Field Notes for Camp Van Camp/Casa Blanca, Jan. 16, 1868 (endnote quotation); GLO, Pecos County Land File for Camp Van Camp/Casa Blanca; Brune, *Springs of Texas*, 361; AFT, Camp Van Camp, July 18, 1999 (JA, PD); Capt. Albert Gallatin Brackett, 2nd Cav., to 2nd Lt. Henry Clay Wood, Fort Davis, Tex., May 16, 1859, NA, RG 94, AGO, LR, M567, R597; 2nd Lt. Wesley Owens, 2nd Cav., to Capt. George Stoneman, Camp Van Camp, Tex., Aug. 3, 1859, NA, RG 94, AGO, LR, M567, R613; Price, *Across the Continent*, 77–79, 82, 630, 641; Williams, *Never Again*, 3:194–95. The U.S. Army named Camp Van Camp after Second Lieutenant Cornelius Van Camp, Second Cavalry, killed during an engagement with Comanche Indians near Wichita Village in Indian Territory on October 1, 1858. Peter Gallagher filed for the title on this 137-acre parcel in 1868. The survey field notes for Gallagher's acreage note that it "includes the abandoned military camp known as Camp 'Van Camp' and a sulphur spring." El Paso County surveyor Jarvis Hubbell conducted the survey for Gallagher, and Tom Rife, Hubbell's friend and fellow compatriot in Henry Skillman's Confederate Spy Company, was one of the chain carriers. Local Tejanos called the old army outpost Casas Blancas (white houses) and the adjacent spring, Casa Blanca. Anglos knew it as Travertine Springs. In 1924, the spring flowed at a rate of 2.8 liters per second (44.38 gallons per minute). The rock ruins here are considerable. Clayton Williams, Sr., said that the army had built stone breastworks around the camp to protect against Indian attack. Williams also noted numerous small rock outlines here, apparently for the soldiers' tents.

10. Williams, *Never Again*, 3:191 (quotations).

11. 2nd Lt. John P. Sherburne, 1st Inf., Camp Stockton, Tex., to Col. Samuel Cooper, Apr. 20, 1859, NA, RG 94, AGO, LR, M567, R612; Williams, *Never Again*, 3:201; Fort Stockton Post Returns, Apr. and Aug. 1859, May 1860, Jan. and Feb. 1861, NA, M617, R1229. Many books, including Frazer's *Forts of the West*, 162, erroneously state that the military named Fort Stockton after Commodore Robert Stockton of the U.S. Navy. Lieutenant Sherburne, who founded the post, makes

clear in his report that he named it in honor of Lieutenant Stockton. The acting secretary of war, William R. Drinkard, subsequently approved Sherburne's action on July 16, 1859.

12. Williams, *Never Again*, 3:199 (quotation); Postmaster General Order Journals, May 10, 1859, vol. 44, Mar. 14, 1859–Aug. 10, 1859, NA, RG 28, entry 1.

13. Gournay, *Texas Boundaries*, 59–61; Postmaster General Order Journals, July 21, 1859, vol. 44, Mar. 14, 1859–Aug. 10, 1859, NA, RG 28, entry 1; ibid., August 29, 1859, and Jan. 19, 1860, vol. 45, Aug. 11, 1859–Mar. 16, 1860. The postmaster journals use several different spellings on Greene's and Holliday's names.

14. *New York Times*, July 11, 1860 (quotation 1); Postmaster General Order Journals, Oct. 22, 1858, vol. 42, July 1–Dec. 18, 1858, NA, RG 28, entry 1 (quotation 2); ibid., Mar. 12, 1860, vol. 45, Aug. 11, 1859–Mar. 16, 1860; ibid., July 13, 1860, vol. 46, Mar. 17–Sept. 20, 1860 (quotation 3); U.S. Atty. Gen. Jeremiah Sullivan Black to Postmaster Gen. Joseph Holt, May 28, 1859, in Senate Exec. Doc. No. 26, 36th Cong., 1st Sess., ser. 1031, pp. 1–5. For more on Holt's antipathy toward expensive overland routes that generated insufficient revenues, see "Report of the Postmaster General, Dec. 3, 1859," in Senate Exec. Doc. No. 2, 36th Cong., 1st Sess., ser. 1025, pp. 1410–12; and "Report of the Postmaster General, Dec. 1, 1860," in Senate Exec. Doc. No. 1, 36th Cong., 2nd Sess., ser. 1080, pp. 435–38.

15. Postmaster General Order Journals, Apr. 14, 1859, vol. 44, Mar. 14, 1859–Aug. 10, 1859, NA, RG 28, entry 1; ibid., Feb. 1 and Mar. 12, 1860, vol. 45, Aug. 11, 1859–Mar. 16, 1860; ibid., July 12 and 14, 1860, vol. 46, Mar. 17, 1860–Sept. 20, 1860; ibid., Mar. 13, 1861, vol. 48, Mar. 7, 1861–May 29, 1861; "Memorial of George H. Giddings," in Senate Misc. Doc. No. 15, 36th Cong., 2nd Sess., ser. 1089 (hereafter cited as "Memorial of . . . Giddings," pp. 1–9; George H. Giddings Credit Reports, Texas vol. 3, Bexar County, p. 100 (endnote quotations 1–3), DCR, BL; Giddings and Doyle, San Antonio San Diego Mail Contractors, Credit Reports, ibid., p. 114 (endnote quotation 4). George H. Giddings, a merchant and mail contractor based in San Antonio, had a mixed reputation in his business dealings. Credit reports for 1854 noted that his "finances [were] not of the most promising character, suits [were] being instituted against him," and he was "not noted for honesty of purpose." Subsequent reports stated, "As to his character, there exist many doubts in regard to his honesty, but nobody can give positive proof of his being dishonest. He is considered a smart man and will take advantage wherever he can even at the cost of other people." The postmaster general's cutbacks in 1859 and 1860 affected Giddings's financial standing. Credit reports for 1860 advised, "Very difficult to report, to be credited with caution. Contract said to be uncertain."

16. Postmaster General Order Journals, Oct. 22, 1858, vol. 42, July 1–Dec. 18, 1858, NA, RG 28, entry 1; ibid., July 13, 1860, vol. 46, Mar. 17–Sept. 20, 1860; ibid., Mar. 13, 1861, vol. 48, Mar. 7–May 29, 1861; "Memorial of . . . Giddings," 1–9.

17. Overland Mail route itinerary, *Mesilla Times*, Apr. 13, 1861, SCL, UTEP; deed records for May 18, 1861, Doña Ana Co., N.Mex. (endnote quotation), and May 15, 1861, El Paso Co., Tex. The stations between Fort Stockton and El Paso were Comanche Springs–Fort Stockton, Leon Holes, Barilla Spring, Cottonwood, Fort Davis, Barrel Spring, El Muerto, Van Horn's Wells, Eagle Spring, Camp Fargo, Camp Rice, Camp Hawkins, Smith's Ranch, San Elizario, and El Paso. Exactly which ten stations were Butterfield's and which five were Giddings's is unknown. One can deduce the ownership details on several of these stations, but the complete picture remains murky. On May 18, 1861, in Mesilla, New Mexico, Giddings purchased "nine stage stations formerly occupied by the Overland Mail Company on the mail road between Fort Stockton and El Paso" from OMC super-

intendent Owen Tuller. This sale did not include the tenth Butterfield station, in El Paso, which Giddings had purchased separately from Tuller in El Paso three days earlier, on May 15, 1861.

18. "Memorial of . . . Giddings," 1; Postmaster General Order Journals, Mar. 11, 1858, vol. 41, Jan. 18–June 30, 1858, NA, RG 28, entry 1. Holliday's role as agent for Giddings's San Antonio–San Diego Mail Line is in J. A. Lucas, Albert Brackett, and George H. Giddings depositions, *Giddings v. U.S.* See also Feb. 13, 1859, Eagle Spring and Comanche Springs survey request by Holliday and subsequent Sept. 28, 1859, surveys of Eagle Spring, Section 1, Survey 150 (Comanche Springs), and Survey 151 for J. D. Holliday, as well as Apr. 24, 1860, survey of Survey 160 for J. D. Holliday, El Paso County Field Notes.

19. *Giddings v. U.S.*, Aug. 12, 1891, petition recapitulation, 11–12; Williams, *Never Again*, 3:212 (quotations). In addition to his San Antonio–San Diego mail contract, during the antebellum period Giddings also operated the San Antonio to Santa Fe, New Mexico, mail route. See Austerman, *Sharps Rifles.*

20. Williams, *Never Again*, 3:212, 224; El Paso County Field Notes, Sept. 28, 1859, Survey 151 done for J. D. Holliday, and Apr. 24, 1860, Survey 160 done for J. D. Holliday; Thompson, *Texas and New Mexico*, 116; *Contracts with the War Department*, House Exec. Doc. No. 22, 36th Cong., 1st Sess., ser. 1047, p. 25; *Contracts with the War Department*, House Exec. Doc. No. 47, 36th Cong., 2nd Sess., ser. 1099, pp. 2–3, 18; 1860 U.S. Census, Presidio Co., Tex., M653, R1293, 87 (this includes the civilian hamlet of "Comanche" next to Fort Stockton); Conkling and Conkling, *Butterfield Overland Mail*, 2:15 (endnote quotation); Williams, *Texas' Last Frontier*, 64; Bexar County Tax Rolls, reel 1, 1837–73, TSLAC; El Paso County Deed Records, May 3, 1868; Pecos County Deed Records, Mar. 13, 1874. In volume 2 of *Butterfield Overland Mail*, the Conklings placed Fort Stockton's Butterfield station in a vacant lot "directly west" of the present county courthouse, at James and Nelson Streets. In the Conklings' *Butterfield Overland Mail*, volume 3, plate 45 map of Fort Stockton (which is inaccurate and should not be relied upon), they marked the stage stop at the corner of James and Nelson (incorrectly shown as Main Street). In contrast, Clayton Williams, Sr., believed that the overland station was likely where the old jail building now stands at the corner of Gallagher and Main Streets. Down the hill from the jail a short distance to the northeast is Comanche Springs. Williams also says that J. D. Holliday's sutler store was probably located in an old adobe building at the corner of Sherer and Nelson Streets, a block southwest of the mail station. Known today as "The Oldest House," this crumbling ruin from 1859 is the only structure that survives from antebellum Fort Stockton. Period documents appear to corroborate Williams's statements. See Sept. 22, 1871, Bexar County deed record referencing survey plat of St. Gall (now Fort Stockton), Tex., by El Paso County deputy surveyor Thomas C. Nelson, copied in Pecos County Deed Records, vol. 1, 70–71; copy of Thomas C. Nelson's survey plat of St. Gall, Pecos County Plat Book, 100–107; copy of Colonel J. K. F. Mansfield's Nov. 1860 sketch of Fort Stockton, Tex., NA, CP, courtesy of Jerry Thompson. The 1859 and 1860 Bexar County tax rolls show that John D. Holliday owned two town lots in San Antonio, for a net worth of $2,200. The majority of Holliday's assets lay in still-unorganized Presidio County and thus escaped the tax appraisers and valuation taxes. When Holliday sold Surveys 150 and 151 to Giddings on August 2, 1862, for $3,175.45, he made another prescient transaction. Within three weeks of the sale, Confederate troops abandoned Fort Stockton, Giddings's mail line ceased operations, and Union forces moved into the Trans-Pecos region for the remainder of the war. Giddings's financial dealings often seem star-crossed. Strapped for cash following the Civil War, he sold these same surveys, 150 and 151, to John James and Peter Gallagher in 1868 for $500, far less than his purchase price. On March 13, 1874, Holliday's widow, Annette, sold the adjoining Survey 160, also on Comanche Creek and downstream of 151, for 50 gold dollars to John James and Peter Gallagher, who were buying up acreage along Comanche Creek for a large irrigated farming venture.

21. Hammond and Howes, *Overland to California*, 100 (quotations 1–2), 101 (quotations 3–5); AFT, Comanche Springs and Fort Stockton, 1976–2008.

22. Bieber, *Exploring Southwestern Trails*, 266 (quotations), 267.

23. Froebel, *Seven Years' Travel*, 415 (quotation 1), 455 (quotation 2); Williams, *Old Texas Trails*, 358 (quotation 3). In a 2008 discussion with me, western historian Todd M. Kerstetter remarked that natural resources attract both prey and predators.

24. Brune, *Springs of Texas*, 356–58; Bill Moody interview, Fort Stockton, Tex., May 6, 2002 (endnote quotation). I converted Brune's liters per second into gallons per minute. Bill Moody told me that when his family and his neighbors finally gave up farming and sold their lands along Comanche Creek, it was "heart-breaking."

25. Brune, *Springs of Texas*, 356 (quotation 1), 357 (quotation 3), 358 (quotation 2); Ronald Kaiser, "Who Owns the Water?" *Texas Parks and Wildlife Magazine* (July 2005), www.tpwmagazine.com/archive/2005/jul/ed2/ (endnote quotation 1); Texas Board of Water Engineers, *Geology*, 43–49, 58–61, 70–72; Ely, *Where the West Begins*, 15, 135; Lyxan Toledanes, "Fort Stockton Holdings Calls Court Decision a 'Huge Victory,'" *Odessa American Online*, Mar. 3, 2012, www.oaoa.com/article_5024 dea5-9c6b-5a30-b3e2-05d81b4c606a.html (endnote quotations 2–5); Sarah Mueller, "Fort Stockton Considers Settlement in Water Dispute," *Odessa American Online*, Aug. 27, 2012, www.oaoa.com/news/government/article _6077fd42-9e83-5833-96cc-d48326691bc1.html?mode=jqm (endnote quotations 6–7); Juilián Aguilar, "Clayton Williams Explains His Company's New Permit," *Texas Tribune*, Apr. 22, 2012, www.texastribune.org/2010/04/22/clayton-williams-explains-his-companys-new-permit/; minutes for May 4, 2011, and June 10, 2011, Middle Pecos Groundwater Conservation District, Fort Stockton, Tex.; phone conversation with Middle Pecos Groundwater District general manager Paul Weatherby, Sept. 9, 2013. Once contested between Native Americans and European Americans, Comanche Springs is today a flashpoint between citizens of Pecos County and business interests. Many Fort Stockton residents, both Anglo and Hispanic, favor the time-honored Tejano concept of communal natural resources, that is, the water belongs to the community, to be used by all. Under Texas's Rule of Capture Law, however, water beneath the ground belongs to the landowner. Rule of Capture did not exist when this region was part of Spain and Mexico; it is a Texas creation. In 1954, a local water control board sued the landowners at Leon-Belding to limit irrigation pumping. The 1954 lawsuit, *Pecos County Water Control and Improvement District No. 1 v. Clayton Williams, et al.*, ended in victory for the landowners. Upholding the Rule of Capture, "The Texas Court of Civil Appeals ruled that the groundwater contributing to the flow in Comanche Springs belonged to Clayton Williams while it was under his land." The debate over who controls the region's water resources and who determines their best use is far from finished. One aspect of this debate concerns attempts to market and export water from underground aquifers in West Texas. Clayton Williams's son, Clayton Williams, Jr., wants to sell water from the Pecos County Edwards-Trinity Aquifer and export it to regional cities and industries. Williams's plan has ignited a firestorm among Pecos County citizens, many of who are still bitter over the 1954 lawsuit that his father won. While a Texas Supreme Court decision affirmed Williams's and other landowners' pumping rights under the state's Rule of Capture Law, local groundwater districts "still have the ability to control groundwater use." To date, Williams has not received permission to export the water. The Middle Pecos Groundwater Con-

servation District in Fort Stockton denied his application to pump water and export it out of the county. Williams in turn sued the district, and the case remains in litigation. District general manager Paul Weatherby believes that for those who live in an arid environment like the Chihuahuan Desert, "there has to be a balance for present day and future generations." Weatherby asks people to consider what they would do if they were out in the desert sharing a glass of water with several thirsty people. They "might let them take a gulp," he says, "but not the whole glass." Ernest Woodward, whose family has ranched in the Trans-Pecos for generations, believes that Pecos County's aquifers are like the arteries of the heart, "delivering blood to areas that need to be replenished by this natural, God-given resource." Woodward says that Williams "wants to stick a straw into the heart of it and suck it dry."

26. Williams, *Old Texas Trails*, 358 (quotation 1); Senate Exec. Doc. No. 64, 31st Cong., 1st Sess., 47 (quotation 2). An excellent map of the Leon Holes area is in Pecos County Plat Book, *February 15, 1917 Map of Land Subdivisions of Leon Springs Irrigation Company near Fort Stockton, Pecos County, Texas*. Surveyor O. W. William's 1885 field notes for a 640-acre parcel mention the "old stage stand on Leon," near the Fort Stockton to Fort Davis Road. See Pecos County Field Notes, Book E, Oct. 1, 1885 (endnote quotation).

27. Bieber, *Exploring Southwestern Trails*, 267 (quotation 1); Senate Exec. Doc. No. 64, 31st Cong., 1st Sess., 47 (quotation 2); Froebel, *Seven Years' Travel*, 415 (quotation 3); Williams, *Old Texas Trails*, 358 (quotation 4); Wallace and Hevly, *From Texas to San Diego*, 42 (quotation 5); Hunt, "Journal," Sept. 2, 1869 (quotation 6); Holmes, *Covered Wagon Women*, 9:190 (quotations 7–8). From Fort Stockton, the Butterfield Road passed through Block 28 and then entered Block OW (named after Clayton Williams, Jr.'s grandfather, O. W. Williams), the location of Leon Holes. See GLO, Map #76038, *June 1896 Map of Pecos County, Texas*; GLO, Map #2303, *Sectional Map No. 3 of the Lands and of the Line of the Texas & Pacific R'Y. Co. in Reeves and Parts of Tom Green, Pecos, Presidio & El Paso Counties*; AFT, Belding and Leon Holes, 1996, 1999 (JA, PD), Nov. 7, 2000 (JA, PD). The adobe Butterfield station near the water holes has since melted, but Joe Allen, Patrick Dearen, and I found numerous quarried foundation rocks at the station site, along with many period artifacts, including square nails, pistol balls, glass, crockery, and lead-lined cans. During my first visit, in 1999, there was water in Leon Holes, but the holes were bone dry on subsequent visits. After the Civil War, Ben Ficklin's San Antonio–El Paso Mail Line built a new mail station several miles east of the Butterfield station, on the other side of the hill, next to a long, narrow water hole in a draw. Why Ficklin located his stage stop here is unclear, as the original antebellum site provides superior water. In 2000, Allen, Dearen, and I found the foundation rocks of this later station, which was also made of adobe, plus several graves and numerous artifacts. The muddy water hole did not look inviting to drink from. All told, the post–Civil War location seems a miserable spot for a station.

28. 1860 U.S. Census, Presidio Co., Tex., M653, R1293, 87 (this includes Leon Holes Station); Tallack, *California Overland Express*, 48 (quotations).

29. *Texas State Gazette*, Sept. 4, 1858; Bliss, *Reminiscences*, 85; *Report of the Secretary of War*, Senate Exec. Doc. No. 1, 35th Cong., 2nd Sess., ser. 975, p. 262 (quotation).

30. Johnson, *Partisan Rangers*, 15 (quotations); El Paso County Field Notes, May 24, 1860; entry for July 3, 1859, by Bvt. 2nd Lt. William Holding Echols, Topographical Engineers, Journal of Camel Expedition & Reconnaissance in Trans-Pecos and Big Bend, Texas (dated Aug. 22, 1859), NA, RG 94, AGO, LR, M567, R601 (endnote quotation). An army expedition stopped at Leon Holes in the summer of 1859 and reported, "The overland mail has a station here, where it was reported to us that Indians passed in their vicinity every week, and

only about two weeks since a party camped within two hundred yards of the station in the bushes, but without their knowledge till leaving."

31. *New York Times*, Sept. 17, 1860 (quotation); recapitulation statement of losses incurred, 1854–61, *Giddings v. U.S.*; *San Antonio Weekly Alamo Express*, Mar. 30 and May 4, 1861. The family massacred by Indians 6 miles west of Leon Holes in late March 1861 had recently shuttered their general store in Fort Stockton and were heading west in two wagons containing all of their belongings and merchandise.

32. Ely, *Where the West Begins*, 99–119; Brune, *Springs of Texas*, 358 (quotations 2–3 [original emphasis]), 359 (quotation 1).

33. The overland road through southwestern Pecos County and eastern Jeff Davis County is shown in GLO, Map #76038, *June 1896 Map of Pecos County, Texas*; GLO, Map #9262, *May 3, 1890 Jeff Davis County, Texas, Rolled Sketch File No. 5*; GLO, Map #4991, *June 1887 Map of Jeff Davis County, Texas*; GLO, Map #11857, *Jeff Davis County Sketch File No. 8, June 27, 1889 Block 11 G.H.&S.A.Ry.Co*. See also Conkling and Conkling, *Butterfield Overland Mail*, 2:23–24; AFT, Coyanosa Holes and Hackberry Holes, May 19, 2001 (JA, PD); AFT, Barilla Spring Station, Mar. 9, 2000 (with Ike and Sue Roberts), and Feb. 7, 2001 (JA, PD, Mary Williams); Hunt, "Journal," Sept. 3–4, 1869. The Conklings thought they had found Hackberry Holes, but they were in error. The couple located several water holes behind an old house at Kennedy Ranch and assumed that these were Hackberry Holes. This building is several miles south of the overland road. Hackberry Holes are some distance from the building at Kennedy Ranch. Lieutenant Colonel Hunt's map also shows Coyanosa Holes, which are on the mail route, 10.5 miles east of Hackberry Holes. After the Civil War, the U.S. Army ran a telegraph line over this section of the overland route. Today, pieces of old green telegraph insulators litter the ground west of Hackberry Holes. Just west of Barilla Spring Station, the mail road crossed Limpia Creek and followed the south side of the creek before crossing over to the north side several miles to the west, in Survey 70. There are two station sites at Barilla Spring: first, the post–Civil War Ben Ficklin adobe building near the windmill and twentieth-century ranch house, and second, the Butterfield station, built out of stone, located near Barilla Spring. The Conklings, unaware of the Butterfield location, mistook the Ben Ficklin adobe station site for it.

34. Johnson, *Partisan Rangers*, 16 (quotations), 29.

35. Froebel, *Seven Years' Travel*, 461 (quotation 1), 462 (quotations 2–4).

36. Ibid., 462 (quotation 1), 463 (quotations 2–3).

37. 1860 U.S. Census, Presidio Co., Tex., M653, R1293, 88; recapitulation statement of losses incurred, 1854–61, *Giddings v. U.S.*; *San Antonio Herald*, Oct. 29, 1859; El Paso County Field Notes, May 24, 1860. From Barilla Spring to Fort Davis, there are several old ruins in Limpia Canyon. Some of these are old stage stops, while others are early homesteads. Some of the stage stops (Giddings and Butterfield) are from the antebellum period, while others date from after the Civil War, operated at various times by Ben Ficklin, Frederick Sawyer, F. C. Taylor, and Charles Bain. The notes that follow for each site serve to clarify this confusion. Known Butterfield stations in this section were Barilla Spring, Cottonwood Station, and Fort Davis. Known Giddings stations were Barilla Spring, Cottonwood Station, and Painted Comanche Camp/La Limpia. The Conklings made several errors in this section that need correction. On pages 23–24 of volume 2 of their *Butterfield Overland Mail*, they mention a station 10 miles from Barilla Spring called Limpia Station. George Giddings/Ben Ficklin expert Wayne Austerman identified this location as "probably a Butterfield station." See Austerman, "Identifying a 'Lost' Stage Station," 6 (endnote quotation 1). This site is not a mail station. The ruins here are old rock pens for livestock dating from the post–Civil War ranching period. Joe Allen, using a metal detector, found no pre–Civil War artifacts at this location. AFT, rock pens, Mar. 9, 2000 (JA, Ike and Sue

Roberts). On page 24 of volume 2 of *Butterfield Overland Mail*, the Conklings discuss another ruin near these rock pens, a short distance upstream on Limpia Creek. This building appears as "old stage station" on an October 1867 army map. The post–Civil War mail contractor Ben Ficklin was still getting his San Antonio–El Paso Mail Line up and running in the fall and winter of 1867 and had not yet reestablished stage stops along the route, so this ruin must date from the antebellum period. See Bvt. Lt. Col. Edward Jenner Strang, *October 1867 Topographical Sketch of the Route from Fort Stockton to Fort Davis*, NACP, RG 77, Q135-3 (endnote quotation 2); Austerman, *Sharps Rifles*, 210–14. Austerman knew of this site but could not locate it. See Austerman, "Identifying a 'Lost' Stage Station," 6. This ruin was likely a pre–Civil War homestead and/or stage stop. Artifacts found here by me and Joe Allen range from the 1860s to the 1880s. I have found no reference to a station here in period records or in the Giddings and Butterfield itineraries. This site on Limpia Creek is located near the early twentieth-century settlement of Limpia (not to be confused with La Limpia upstream at Painted Comanche Camp). The U.S. Postmaster General established a post office here on October 15, 1912, after local residents filed an application. William McKutcheon served as the first postmaster. See Limpia Post Office Application, PGS, Jeff Davis Co., Tex., NA, RG 28, M1126, R580; AFT, Limpia Creek station and ruins of Limpia Post Office settlement, 2000 (JA, Bill and Betty Hargus).

38. Bieber, *Exploring Southwestern Trails*, 279 (quotation); MT, Barilla Mountains East, Barilla Mountains West, Big Agua Mountain, Swayback Mountain, Fort Davis SE, Fort Davis. Once again, as in the case of the Guadalupe Mountains, all of the early travelers highlighted Wild Rose Pass and Limpia Creek's outstanding scenery. Throughout time, Limpia Canyon has enchanted the visitor. The federal government and the State of Texas confirmed the value of this unique landscape and its history with the establishment of Fort Davis National Historic Site and the adjacent Davis Mountains State Park in Fort Davis, Texas.

39. Froebel, *Seven Years' Travel*, 460 (quotations 1–2); Smith, *Life and Times*, 390 (quotations 3–4). At the eastern (or northern) end of Wild Rose Pass there is an old antebellum ruin, of which little is known. Lieutenant Colonel Hunt described this site as an "old mail station" when he camped here in September 1869. His sketch shows a spring next to the old station. I found this ruin and the spring exactly where Hunt placed it. See Hunt, "Journal," Sept. 5, 1869. This site is not referenced in any documents or itineraries, and it is likely an antebellum stage stop or homestead. AFT, station at eastern end of Wild Rose Pass, May 20, 2001 (JA, PD, Mary Williams). There are also two rock ruins in the heart of Wild Rose Pass, which may also be old stage stops or homesteads. Artifacts found at these structures range from the 1860s to the 1880s. The July 23, 1860, census for Wild Rose Pass shows seven station keepers and their fellow station employees all living here. For the record, there were not seven stations in this 1.5-mile-long canyon. Census enumerator Henry L. Dexter lumped all the mail stations between Fort Davis and Camp Fargo into this one listing at Wild Rose Pass. None of the period itineraries lists a station at Wild Rose Pass. AFT, Wild Rose Pass, Nov. 21, 1999 (JA, Mildred Nored, Jim Ed Miller, Mary Williams). The Conklings were not aware of these three Wild Rose Pass structures (one at the east end and two in the interior). Some locals believe that these three ruins are stations, but there is no primary documentation to support this. See Austerman, "Identifying a 'Lost' Stage Station," 6 (Scannell and Weatherby interviews).

40. Richardson, *Beyond the Mississippi*, 234 (quotations).

41. AFT, Cottonwood Station, Nov. 21, 1999 (JA, Jim Ed Miller, Mary Williams, Mildred Nored); *Mesilla Times*, Apr. 13, 1861, SCL, UTEP; 1860 U.S. Census, Presidio Co., Tex., M653, R1293, 88; Austerman, *Sharps Rifles*, 136; Jacobson and Nored, *Jeff Davis County*, 371–72; *San Antonio Herald*, July 1, 1859; *Weekly Alamo Express* (San Antonio),

May 4, 1861, reporting on events from late March 1861 (quotation); Parker Burnham deposition, *Giddings v. U.S.*; AFT, May 20, 2001, Webster homestead (JA, Mary Williams). Parker Burnham, agent and stage driver for George Giddings, called this stage stop Cottonwood Springs. Both Giddings and Butterfield used Cottonwood Station, and the stage stop appears on the final Butterfield itinerary from 1861. The July 1, 1859, *San Antonio Herald* article says that Indians raided the Butterfield station here, providing additional confirmation that the Overland Mail Company was operating over its new Lower Road route in June 1859. One should not confuse Cottonwood Station in Jeff Davis County with Cottonwoods Ranch near present-day Anthony, Texas, in El Paso County. E. P. Webster surveyed this property in 1881 and patented title to it the following year. From the 1880s to the early 1900s, Webster (1842–1916), who served as county judge and a county commissioner, systematically acquired several thousand acres along the old overland road in Limpia Canyon. Continuing south along Limpia Canyon, there is another stage stop ruin directly astride the old overland road, close to Limpia Creek. This station, operated by the San Antonio–El Paso Mail Line after the Civil War, is a few miles above Fort Davis and appears on the September 7, 1869, entry and sketch in Hunt, "Journal." Hunt describes this site as a "mail station" (i.e., active), as opposed to an "old mail station," a description he always uses for abandoned stage stops throughout his journal. This property was Edward P. Webster's homestead. Webster drove stagecoaches for the mail line after the Civil War. The Conklings and Austerman make no mention of this building and were likely unaware of it. For many years, there has been some debate as to the exact passage of the overland road through Limpia Canyon from Barilla Spring to Fort Davis. GLO, Map #9262, *May 3, 1890 Jeff Davis County, Texas, Rolled Sketch File #5*, clears up this question and definitively details the route, survey by survey, heading up the canyon to Fort Davis. Today, State Highway 17 parallels Limpia Creek and the overland road in the canyon.

42. Hunt, "Journal," Sept. 5, 1869 (quotation 1); *Report of the Secretary of War*, House Exec. Doc. No. 2, 35th Cong., 1st Sess., ser. 943, pp. 74–77; *Report of the Secretary of War*, House Exec. Doc. No. 2, 35th Cong., 2nd Sess., ser. 999, pp. 776–79; *Report of the Secretary of War*, Senate Exec. Doc. No. 2, 36th Cong., 1st Sess., ser. 1024, pp. 604–7; *Report of the Secretary of War*, Senate Exec. Doc. No. 1, 36th Cong., 2nd Sess., ser. 1079, pp. 218–23; Wooster, *Frontier Crossroads*, 29, 57 (quotation 2).

43. Wooster, *Frontier Crossroads*, x (quotations 3–4), 141 (quotations 1–2).

44. GLO, Map #76433, *El Paso Rolled Sketch No. 2, November 9, 1855 Map of the District Composed of the Counties of El Paso and Presidio by Frederick A. Percy*; Jeff Davis County Abstract No. 771, A. S. Lewis Survey No. 6, field notes containing Henry Skillman's personally signed survey request (a rare Skillman signature), field notes for the original survey and subsequent resurvey for Skillman, and John James's patent for said parcel. Several studies have incorrectly cited this as the "A. L. Lewis Survey." Wooster, *Frontier Crossroads*, 39, 42; 1860 U.S. Census, Presidio Co., Tex., M653, R1293, 67; Strong, "James, John [1819–77]," *Handbook*; *Contracts with the War Department*, House Exec. Doc. No. 58, 35th Cong., 1st Sess., ser. 955, p. 2; *Contracts with the War Department*, House Exec. Doc. No. 22, 36th Cong., 1st Sess., ser. 1047, p. 10; James and Sweet, San Antonio, Credit Reports, Texas vol. 3, Bexar County, p. 93 (quotation 1), DCR, BL; *Contracts with the War Department*, House Exec. Doc. No. 47, 36th Cong., 2nd Sess., ser. 1099, p. 2; Alexander Young, Fort Davis country store, Credit Reports, Texas vol. 3, Bexar County, p. 110 (quotations 2–5), DC, BL; U.S. Postmaster General, Record of Appointment of Postmasters, 1832–1971, Bexar Co., Tex., NA, RG 28, M841, R121. Alexander Young became postmaster at Fort Davis on March 25, 1857. John James's partner on many of his post–Civil War Fort Stockton real estate ventures was Peter Gallagher

of San Antonio. In addition, James also held title to the army's Camp Hudson acreage on the Devil's River, located on the San Antonio–El Paso Lower Road. James charged the army $50 per month, or $600 per year, rent on Camp Hudson.

45. Bieber, *Exploring Southwestern Trails*, 279 (quotations); 1860 U.S. Census, Presidio Co., Tex., M653, R1293, 65–67; Thompson, *Texas and New Mexico*, 102; Duffen, "Overland via 'Jackass Mail,'" pt. 1, 43, 50 (endnote quotation); Austerman, "Identifying a 'Lost' Stage Station," 5, 8–10; Austerman, *Sharps Rifles*, 74; Scobee, *Fort Davis*, 40; AFT, Fort Davis, 1986–2006; AFT, Painted Comanche Camp/La Limpia Station site, Nov. 21, 1999 (JA, Mildred Nored, Jim Ed Miller, Mary Williams); Edward Webster, 1890 Veterans Schedules, Fort Davis, Tex., NA, M1123, R102; Edward P. Webster, 1900 U.S. Census, Jeff Davis Co., Tex., NA, T623, R1648. Colonel J. K. F. Mansfield's October 29, 1860, sketch of Fort Davis shows the location of the Butterfield mail station a short distance southwest of the soldiers' barracks. In the 1860 census, census enumerator Henry Dexter of El Paso County called the civilian community north of the fort Las Lympias. Giddings stagecoach passenger Phocion Way stopped at La Limpia Station in June 1858 and was disparaging in his remarks about the station's accommodations. Way wrote, "We had our suppers here in a hotel about 6 feet high and 12 feet long made out of mud. We then spread out our blankets on the ground and slept soundly." A 1999 field trip to Painted Comanche Camp corroborated Wayne Austerman's research identifying the site as the location of Giddings's La Limpia Station. In his "Identifying a 'Lost' Stage Station" article, Austerman states that Edward P. Webster established La Limpia Station in the early 1850s. He also says that Webster was guarding stagecoaches for Henry Skillman's mail line in 1851 and 1852. Austerman cites earlier writers Carlysle G. Raht and Barry Scobee as his sources. These statements are incorrect. Webster, born in Illinois in December 1842, would not have been guarding the mail line at age nine, nor would he have been running a stage stop. In sum, it was Henry Skillman or George Giddings that established La Limpia Station, not Webster. Regarding Patrick Murphy, the merchant at Fort Davis and Las Lympias of that name was not the same Patrick Murphy from Young County who waylaid Robert Neighbors.

46. Bliss, *Reminiscences*, 80 (quotation). The percentages cited are from my in-depth study of the 1860 U.S. Census, Presidio Co., Tex., NA, M653, Roll 1293, pp. 66–76 and 85–88. Fort Davis was originally part of Presidio County but is now the county seat of Jeff Davis County.

47. AFT, Point of Rocks, Feb. 18, 2002; MT, Blue Mountain, Paradise Mountain; GLO, Jeff Davis County Abstract No. 776; El Paso County Deed Records, Dec. 1, 1874 (sale to Hague); GLO, Map #27920, *Presidio County Sketch File 2*; Bliss, *Reminiscences*, 110, 111 (quotation). At the base of the 5,700-foot Point of Rocks is a spring and a bronze plaque commemorating "Ed Waldy, John M. Dean, and August Frensell, and all other stage drivers who traveled this route, fearless heroes of frontier days, by their courage the West was made." Former Texas Ranger James B. Gillett installed the plaque in 1935. Simeon Hart of El Paso owned Skillman's Grove until his death in January 1874. Hart acquired the property on February 18, 1854, from H. Clay Davis and patented his claim to Survey 22 (Skillman's Grove) on May 28, 1858. Butterfield station manager Henry Ramstein (the Pinery and El Muerto) was a chain carrier on the April 10, 1856, survey for the 640-acre Skillman's Grove parcel. After Hart's death, estate administrator Archibald Hyde sold it on December 1, 1874, to James P. Hague. Since 1890, Skillman's Grove has been the site of Bloys Camp Meeting, an annual religious encampment.

48. AFT, Barrel Spring, 1996 (with Neil Mangum); Presidio County Field Notes, Oct. 3, 1881, Barrel Spring Survey; 1860 U.S. Census, Presidio Co., Tex., M653, R1293, 88; Conkling and Conkling,

Butterfield Overland Mail, 2:30–31; Conkling's Barrel Spring Station sketch, box 22, RPC Papers; Hunt, "Journal," Sept. 8, 1869 (quotation 1); Holmes, *Covered Wagon Women*, 9:226 (quotation 2); GLO, Map #27893, *1889 Map of Block 1 GH&S.A. Ry. Co.* This excellent detailed map shows the route of the stage road from Skillman's Grove to Barrel Spring. David Merrill secured title to the 640-acre Barrel Spring parcel in November 1882. James B. Gillett owned the property after Merrill. Roscoe Conkling's April 21, 1935, sketch of the layout here shows the station a quarter mile from the spring, a two-room stockade with a gated entrance. At one time, two small adobe rooms adjoined the station's south wall.

49. Tallack, *California Overland Express*, 45 (quotations 1–2), 46 (quotations 3–4). This nineteenth-century story perfectly illustrates the enduring Lone Star ethos, "Don't mess with Texas."

50. MT, Paradise Mountain, San Antonio Pass, El Muerto Peak; 1860 U.S. Census, Presidio Co., Tex., M653, R1293, 88; AFT, El Muerto/Dead Man's Hole, 1996 (with Neil Mangum); Hunt, "Journal," Sept. 9, 1869; Conkling and Conkling, *Butterfield Overland Mail*, 2:31–33; Reid, *Reid's Tramp*, 124–25 (quotation 1); Smith, *Life and Times*, 391 (quotation 2); Presidio County Field Notes, June 4, 1877; El Paso County Clerk Archives, El Paso County Deed Records, Settlement of Louis Cardis Estate, July 22, 1878. From Barrel Spring, the mail road headed for the 5,900-foot Muerto Peak and El Muerto Spring. After the Civil War, San Antonio–El Paso Mail Line contractor F. C. Taylor owned El Muerto Station and the adjacent spring. See El Paso County Field Notes, Apr. 20, 1873. Four years later, in 1877, James C. Kimzey acquired the 640-acre parcel and had a survey made. Louis Cardis, a stage contractor and a prominent figure in the 1877 Salt War, also owned an interest in El Muerto in 1877.

51. *Texas State Gazette*, Jan. 5, 1855 (quotation); Austerman, *Sharps Rifles*, 60–61; recapitulation statement of losses incurred, 1854–61, *Giddings v. U.S.*

52. Lt. Col. Washington Seawell, 8th Inf., Cmdr. Ft. Davis, to AAG, Dept. of Texas, Aug. 30, 1859, NA, RG 94, AGO, LR, M567, R612; Bliss, *Reminiscences*, 150 (quotation); *St. Louis Missouri Republican*, Oct. 6, 1859.

53. Bliss, *Reminiscences*, 109, 110 (quotation); *San Antonio Express*, Aug. 22, 1877; Williams, *Pioneer Surveyor—Frontier Lawyer*, 103 (endnote quotation). In August 1877, Mescalero Indians killed stage driver Hank Dill at El Muerto. Dill was tending to the station's livestock, ten mules and a horse, when the Apaches caught him out in the open a short distance from the stage stop. In 1880, the stagecoach carrying O. W. Williams (later chief justice of Pecos County) stopped at El Muerto. Williams recalled, "At 7:00 A.M. we were in El Muerto, a name that was enough to raise the hair on a traveler's head in Indian times. The stock tender here assured us that another week would see him out of the damned country; a helper at the station was not going to wait even that long."

54. Haley, *Diary of Michael Erskine*, 55–56 (endnote quotation); Williams, *Old Texas Trails*, 361–62; Heitman, *Historical Register*, 982–83; Kohout, "Van Horn, James Judson," *Handbook*; Kohout, "Van Horne, Jefferson," *Handbook*; Bliss, *Reminiscences*, 89; Thompson, *From Desert to Bayou*, 19 (quotation 1); Froebel, *Seven Years' Travel*, 466 (quotations 2–3); Hunt, "Journal," Sept. 11, 1869; AFT, Van Horn's Wells, 1996 (with Neil Mangum), and June 27, 1999 (JA, PD, James Irby). For a detailed map of the overland road from El Muerto to Van Horn's Wells, see GLO, Map #10506, *Jan. 23, 1875 Jeff Davis County Sketch No. 6*. In July 1854, Michael Erskine, part of a cattle drive from Texas to California, stopped at "Van Horns [sic] Wells, got water for [the] Horses & Mules, and a little for the oxen, none for the herd. Have to lift it out in buckets." Three years later, members of the Leach Wagon Train, a federal road-building crew, paused here to replenish their water casks and water their animals.

55. A good map detailing the route of the Butterfield Road from Van Horn's Wells to Eagle Spring is GLO, Map #2304, *Sectional Map No. 4 of the Lands and of the Line of the Texas & Pacific R'Y. Co. in El Paso and Part of Presidio Counties.* See also Froebel, *Seven Years' Travel,* 466 (quotation). Many of the forty-niner journals cited in this volume contain similar accounts of wagon trains arriving at West Texas water holes only to find them exhausted by previous visitors. The degree of anguish and suffering in some of these narratives is profound.

56. Recapitulation statement of losses incurred, 1854–61, James Cloud deposition, William Ford deposition, *Giddings v. U.S.*; 1860 U.S. Census, Presidio Co., Tex., M653, R1293, 88; El Paso County Deed Records, Feb. 13, 1859 (Holliday), and Apr. 25, 1873 (F. P. Sawyer). The route of the Butterfield Road from Van Horn's Wells to the Rio Grande is well documented in the following excellent maps: GLO, Map #65333, *1879 Texas & Pacific Railroad Surveys, West of the Pecos*; and GLO, Maps #83559–561, *1883 Map of the Texas & Pacific Reserve, by Paul McCombs* (in two parts).

57. Johnson, *Partisan Rangers,* 15–16; Thompson, *Civil War,* 127 (endnote quotations); Noel, *Autobiography,* 64–65. In July 1862, Confederate soldiers retreating from New Mexico reached Van Horn's Wells. Famished and desperate for water, the men discovered that Indians had "filled the well with dead wolves." The troops had no choice but to trudge on to El Muerto. William Davidson recalled, "Tired and weary we limped along, the road lined with broken down wagons and carcasses of dead horses, and oxen that had starved for water." A fellow soldier said that the Indians had stuffed the well with dead sheep, not wolves.

CHAPTER 10. FROM VAN HORN'S WELLS TO EL PASO

1. Brune, *Springs of Texas,* 240; MT, Van Horn Wells, Bass Canyon; *San Antonio Herald,* Jan. 16, 1869; *San Antonio Daily Express,* Jan. 22, 1869 (quotation); Maj. Napoleon Bonaparte McLauglen, 10th Cav., to Asst. Adj. Gen., May 17, 1880, NA, DP, LR, M1381, R4; Humphries, *Apache Land,* 20–21; AFT, Bass Canyon and Van Horn's Wells, June 27, 1999 (JA, PD, James Irby). In GLO, Map #83558, Paul McCombs, *1885 Map of Texas and Pacific Railway Company's Surveys in the 80 Mile Reserve,* Bass Canyon runs through Surveys 7 and 12 in Township 9, T&P RR Blocks 66 and 67. In GLO, Map #65333, *1879 Texas & Pacific Railroad Surveys, West of the Pecos,* however, Bass Canyon is in Township 9, Surveys 48, 37, 38, and 39. In May 1880, eleven years after the Bass-Hubbell ambush, a band of Apaches under Victorio waylaid an emigrant wagon train in Bass Canyon, killing Harry Grant and Maggie Graham. Employees for the mail contractor buried the pair next to the adobe station house at Van Horn's Wells.

2. Smith, *Life and Times,* 392 (quotations 1–2); *St. Louis Missouri Republican,* Oct. 6, 1859 (quotation 3); El Paso County Deed Records, Feb. 13, 1859, and Apr. 25, 1873. John D. Holliday made a 160-acre claim in 1859 for Eagle Spring at the same time he filed on the Van Horn's Wells property. In 1873, mail contractor F. P. Sawyer (of the San Antonio–El Paso Mail Line) filed deeds for both Eagle Spring and Van Horn's Wells.

3. *Texas State Gazette,* July 29, 1854; recapitulation statement of losses incurred, 1854–61, *Giddings v. U.S.*; Reid, *Reid's Tramp,* 125–30.

4. *Texas State Gazette,* Feb. 11, 1860; 1860 U.S. Census, Presidio Co., Tex., M653, R1293, 88; recapitulation statement of losses incurred, 1854–61, George Giddings deposition, David Koney deposition, *Giddings v. U.S.*; Hunt, "Journal," Sept. 12, 1869; Austerman, *Sharps Rifles,* 172–73; GLO, Map #65333, *1879 Texas & Pacific Railroad Surveys, West of the Pecos*; MT, Devil Ridge. Wayne Austerman garbles the facts concerning this late 1860/early 1861 Apache raid at the Butterfield-Giddings Eagle Spring Station. Austerman says the attack occurred in June 1861, but this is incorrect. David Koney said it was in late fall

1860 or early 1861. Koney drove stagecoaches for Butterfield from 1858 until April 1861, when the overland mail route moved north. Koney was at Eagle Spring 24–36 hours after the raid. George Giddings said that the depredation was in March 1861 and that he visited the station three months later, in June 1861, on his way to San Antonio in the company of Major James Longstreet and Second Lieutenant William Hicks Jackson.

5. Senate Exec. Doc. No. 64, 31st Cong., 1st Sess., 48 (quotations); AFT, Eagle Spring, 1996 (with Neil Mangum, James Irby) and Mar. 9, 2003 (JA, James Irby, Gary Williams, Mary Williams); Brune, *Springs of Texas,* 241; El Paso County Field Notes, Sept. 27, 1886 (endnote quotations). In 1976, Gunnar Brune measured Eagle Spring's flow at 0.15 liters per second, or 2.37 gallons per minute. An 1886 survey of Eagle Spring references an "old adobe stage stand" and "Eagle Spring Rock House."

6. AFT, Tinaja de las Palmas, 1996 (with Neil Mangum) and Mar. 15, 1999 (JA, Jerry Thompson, James Irby). See GLO, Map #65333, *1879 Texas & Pacific Railroad Surveys, West of the Pecos*; MT, Devil Ridge; Eagle Mountain Sheet and Sierra Blanca Sheet, *Progressive Military Map of the United States, Southern Department, Topography, March 1916,* El Paso County Historical Society Archives; McChristian, "Grierson's Fight," 53–54; Gott, *In Search,* 34–37. West of Eagle Spring, the old mail road passed by Stage Road Tank on its way to Love's/McAdoo Tank, situated in between Devil Ridge and Love Hogback. After rounding the lower end of Devil Ridge, the trail crossed the southern end of another ridge to the west. Along this second, more western ridge (Rocky Ridge) are several sets of stone redoubts where Grierson's detachment defended against Victorio's party. Tinaja de las Palmas, located 12 miles west of Eagle Spring, is an intermittent, seasonal water hole located in a gravel wash at the southern tip of Rocky Ridge. Seven drainages from surrounding hillsides flow into this tinaja. Grierson's defensive tactics successfully blocked Victorio's forces from replenishing their water supplies at the water hole, forcing the Apaches to withdraw.

7. For the exact route through Quitman Canyon in Block 3, Surveys 34, 33, 40, and 41, see GLO, Map #00713, *July 14, 1879 Plat of Surveys in El Paso Co. Made for Maddox Bro's & Anderson and Gunter & Munson.* See also Froebel, *Seven Years' Travel,* 467 (quotation 1), 468 (quotations 2–3); MT, Devil Ridge, Sierra Blanca SW; AFT, Quitman Canyon, 1991–2008 (JA, PD); El Paso County Surveyor Field Notes, Nov. 11, 1884, Block 4, Survey 43 (Calamity Pass); GLO, Map #65333, *1879 Texas & Pacific Railroad Surveys, West of the Pecos* (Sierra de los Lamentos/Quitman Mountains and Puerto de los Lamentos/Quitman Pass). After passing Tinaja de las Palmas, the Butterfield Road ran north of the Old Patterson Place in Red Light Draw and south of Henshaw Well before entering Quitman Canyon. Apache or Indian Post Office, located in the middle of Quitman Canyon, is 25 miles from Eagle Spring.

8. Powers, *Afoot and Alone,* 150 (quotations 1–2); Smith, *Dose of Frontier Soldiering,* 185 (quotation 3); *San Antonio Herald,* July 25, 1868; Baylor, *Into the Far, Wild Country,* 304–305; Gillette, *Six Years,* 258–59, 288–91; Byrne/Walde and Crenshaw/Morgan army depredation reports, Aug. 13 and 19, 1880, and Jan. 10, 23, and 29, 1881, NA, DP, LS, M1381, R1. In July 1868, ten Apaches armed with lances ambushed the mail coach and its one-soldier escort in Quitman Canyon. Both the stage driver and the escort suffered lance wounds but made a run for their lives. After a desperate eighty-minute race with the pursuing Native Americans, the stage party reached the safety of Fort Quitman, with both men still bleeding from the attack. In August 1880, Apaches waylaid a stagecoach carrying General J. J. Byrne of Fort Worth. In the Indians' opening volley, one bullet struck Byrne in the chest, and a second entered his thigh. With Byrne's body hanging out of the coach, driver Ed Walde quickly turned the vehicle around and made a

dash for Fort Quitman, with the warriors racing after him in a frantic 6-mile dash. The Indians literally shot the coach to pieces during the chase, but Walde escaped unharmed. Finally, in January 1881, raiders struck a stagecoach at Apache or Indian Post Office in the middle of Quitman Canyon. The lone passenger in the Celerity wagon was gambler Red Crenshaw, and the driver was a man named Morgan. After the Indians killed a mule with their rifle fire, Crenshaw and Morgan sprinted toward cover, but neither made it. Texas Rangers later found their skeletons near the road, along with the coach and mailbags.

9. The October 6, 1859, issue of the *St. Louis Missouri Republican* specifically mentions Camp Fargo. Several army scout maps from Record Group 77, NACP, show the stage stop's name as Fargo. A good example of this is the *1878 Military Map of Western Texas by Capt. W. R. Livermore*. Some post–Civil War military scout maps also refer to the old stage station as Fargo. These scout maps are on Frank Temple's microfilm compilation of various West Texas military scouts at Fort Davis National Historic Site. In addition, post-Civil War army post returns reference Camp Fargo. See Fort Quitman Post Returns, Oct. 3, 1868, NA, M617, R985. See also MT, Indian Hot Springs, Tex., and Los Fraires, Mex., 1:100,000 scale map; AFT, Camp Fargo, 2000–2008 (JA, PD, James Irby, Mary Williams, Gary Williams). The site name "First Camp on the Rio Grande" appears in GLO, Map #79735, *Richardson's New Map of the State of Texas, 1860*. Over the years, I have had many discussions with local landowners about the history of the region, including Quitman Pass and Smuggler's Gap (eight miles to the southeast).

10. Richardson, *Beyond the Mississippi*, 236 (quotation); 1860 U.S. Census, Presidio Co., Tex., M653, R1293, 88; Hunt, "Journal," Sept. 14, 1869; *Mesilla Times*, Apr. 13, 1861, SCL, UTEP; Bliss, *Reminiscences*, 220; Thompson, *Texas and New Mexico*, 107. During the Mexican Revolution, the U.S. Army and National Guard maintained a subpost near the old stage stop. Many artifacts from this period litter the ground here. Nothing is left of the old adobe station at Camp Fargo, which was a small building located at the bottom of Quitman Canyon near the Rio Grande. Some good traces of the old mail road lead from Camp Fargo to Fort Quitman 6 miles upstream, including some excellent examples of rock retaining walls along the overland trail. Zenas Bliss mentioned one or two houses a mile from Fort Quitman that had formerly been mail stations. The buildings Bliss described could have belonged to George Giddings. From June 1859 to 1861, however, the Butterfield mail station was at Camp Fargo. Both Bliss's *Reminiscences* and J. K. F. Mansfield confirm this, as does the last published Butterfield itinerary.

11. Recapitulation statement of losses incurred, 1854–61, Joseph Hettler deposition (quotation), *Giddings v. U.S.*

12. Apr. 20, 1858, survey request from A. C. Hyde, Jarvis Hubbell, and William M. Ford for Six Mile Waterhole Survey (future Fort Quitman site), El Paso County Private Surveys Book A (endnote quotation); Richardson, *Beyond the Mississippi*, 236; Frazer, *Forts of the West*, 157; Thompson, *Texas and New Mexico*, 107. The army established Fort Quitman on September 28, 1858. Locals also called the Fort Quitman site "Six-Mile Camp or Waterhole." The distance from where the overland road first struck the river to Fort Quitman was almost 6 miles. The U.S. Army abandoned Fort Quitman at the beginning of the Civil War and reoccupied it after the conflict, before finally shutting it down on July 5, 1882, when the men stationed here moved upriver to Second Camp Rice, later the site of Fort Hancock.

13. Thompson, *Texas and New Mexico*, 107 (quotations).

14. *Contracts with the War Department*, House Exec. Doc. No. 22, 36th Cong., 1st Sess., ser. 1047, p. 24; *Contracts with the War Department*, House Exec. Doc. No. 47, 36th Cong., 2nd Sess., ser. 1099, p. 27; *Report of the Secretary of War*, Senate Exec. Doc. No. 2, 36th Cong., 1st Sess., ser. 1024, pp. 604–605; *Report of the Secretary of War*, Senate Exec. Doc. No. 1, 36th Cong., 2nd Sess., ser. 1079, pp. 218–19.

15. Bliss, *Reminiscences*, 220 (quotations 1–2); Hunt, "Journal," Sept. 14, 1869 (quotation 3); Smith, *Life and Times*, 393 (quotations 4–5). The outpost's location is truly abysmal. I visited Fort Quitman several times from 1991 to 2004. On a few occasions, clouds of mosquitoes descended on me and my companions, rendering fieldwork a most unpleasant experience. Rattlesnakes are common. The ground is barren with loose, blowing sand, and in midsummer, the heat is searing and stifling. There is often no breeze here because the fort is down in a depression. The soldiers likely cursed the person who approved the site's location.

16. Ruhlen, "Quitman's Owners"; Smith and Hubble [*sic*] Credit Reports, Texas vol. 10, El Paso County, p. 36 (endnote quotations), DCR, BL; *Contracts with the War Department*, House Exec. Doc. No. 58, 35th Cong., 1st Sess., ser. 955, p. 39; 1860 U.S. Census, El Paso Co., Tex., M653, R1293, 108; *San Antonio Herald*, Jan. 16, 1869 (Hubbell's death); Apr. 20, 1858, survey request from A. C. Hyde, Jarvis Hubbell, and William M. Ford for John Doran Survey and Six Mile Waterhole Survey (future Fort Quitman site), in El Paso County Private Surveys Book A; Dec. 20, 1858, survey request from A. C. Hyde, Jarvis Hubbell, and William M. Ford for Survey 127 (Fort Quitman), El Paso County Field Note Records, Book A-1; GLO, William C. Stanley Survey, El Paso County Abstracts 170 and 171; GLO, Clark L. Owen Survey (Fort Quitman parcel), El Paso County Abstract 164; GLO, John Doran Survey (immediately adjacent to Fort Quitman), El Paso County Abstracts 32 and 33; Ely, "Skullduggery at Spencer's Ranch," 16–21; Ely, "What to Do about Texas," 385–92; Jim Wheat, "Postmasters and Post Offices of Texas, 1846–1930," microfilm reel 1, TSLAC. Wheat's postmaster compilation has Hubbell as El Paso's first postmaster, starting on July 26, 1852, but the U.S. Postmaster General, Record of Appointment of Postmasters, 1832–1971, El Paso Co., Tex., NA, RG 28, lists Archibald Hyde (March 31, 1855) as the first. Previous works have provided scant information regarding Jarvis Hubbell, who was born in Connecticut in 1822. Hubbell operated a business in El Paso in 1853 and 1854 with a partner named Smith. Credit reports say that the firm's "capacity/capabilities [are] doubtful & [its] standing not altogether free from embarrassment." By 1859, the firm was "out of business and credit not above par." In 1857, Jarvis Hubbell secured the federal beef contracts for Forts Fillmore and Thorn in New Mexico. Hubbell and Hyde were business partners in two Pecos River toll bridge projects for the Butterfield and the San Antonio–San Diego mail roads, and in several real estate ventures, including Fort Quitman and land adjacent to the post. New Yorker William Ford, their neighbor in San Elizario, was a partner with them in the Fort Quitman real estate speculation. In 1860, Jarvis Hubbell was 38 years old, Archibald Hyde, 50, and William Ford, 31. In 1860, Jarvis Hubbell listed his occupation as a miller. Besides working as a miller, from 1859 to 1862, Hubbell served as district surveyor for El Paso and Presidio Counties. During the Civil War, both Hubbell and Ford were part of Henry Skillman's Confederate spy company operating in West Texas.

17. Sept. 27 and Nov. 8, 1858, orders, Postmaster General Order Journals, vol. 42, July 1–Dec. 18, 1858, NA, RG 28, entry 1; ibid., June 8, 1860, order, vol. 46, Mar. 17–Sept. 20, 1860; ibid., Dec. 13, 1860, and Jan. 31, 1861, orders, vol. 47, Sept. 21, 1860–Mar. 6, 1861; 1860 U.S. Census, El Paso Co., Tex., M653, R1293, 78.

18. The overland road upriver from Fort Quitman to Ysleta is specifically detailed, survey by survey, in GLO, Map #8852, El Paso County Oversize Rolled Sketch 8, *December 1882 Map Accompanying Field Notes of Surveys in Blocks Nos. L, M, N, O, & P Situated in El Paso County*. See also *June 24, 1914, Sketch of Rio Grande Surveys 53 to 90 in the El Paso County Valley Made by J. Tivy*, Map Cabinet, County

Clerk's Office, Hudspeth Co., Tex.; *Mesilla Times*, Apr. 13, 1861, SCL, UTEP; Hunt, "Journal," Sept. 16, 1869; AFT, Camp Rice Station and Fort Hancock site, Oct. 1, 1999 (JA, James Irby); Nathanial Bedford drowning report, Aug. 29, 1880, NA, DP, LR, M1381, R2; 1860 U.S. Census, El Paso Co., Tex., M653, R1293, 78; Baylor, *Into the Far, Wild Country*, 305; Thomas Rife deposition, *Giddings v. U.S.*; Ely, "Skull-duggery at Spencer's Ranch," 16–19; Ely, "What to Do about Texas," 389–92; "Capt. Thomas C. 'Tom' Rife," available at www.findagrave.com (accessed Mar. 11, 2015); "Tom Rife Marriage Record" and "A Tree Grows in Texas Family Tree," both available at www.ancestry.com; 1850 U.S. Census, Bexar Co., Tex., M432, R908; Austerman, *Sharps Rifles*, 28, 34, 45, 117, 142. Some historians confuse the original Camp Rice, a Butterfield stage stop near modern McNary, Texas, with the second Camp Rice, a post–Civil War army camp located on the railroad near present-day Fort Hancock, Texas. An 1861 published itinerary for the Butterfield Overland Mail lists the original Camp Rice as a company stage stop. After the Civil War, from 1867 to 1881, mail contractors Ben Ficklin, F. C. Taylor, and Charles Bain all used this same Camp Rice stage stop on their San Antonio–El Paso Mail Line. The old station site, like most El Paso County stage stops, has been badly mauled by agricultural improvements over the years. However, today one can still see traces of the old mail road running to and from the first Camp Rice site. Artifacts found at the location date from the period. After the Civil War, the army occasionally detailed a picket here to guard the mail line from Apache raids. One tragic mishap occurred at Camp Rice in August 1880, when Private Nathanial Bedford drowned while bathing next to the stage stop. On June 9, 1882, the army founded the second Camp Rice and on May 14, 1886, renamed it Fort Hancock.

19. Williams, *Old Texas Trails*, 363 (quotation); Mar. 11, 1858, order, Postmaster General Order Journals, vol. 41, Jan. 18–June 30, 1858, NA, RG 28, entry 1.

20. Duffen, "Overland via 'Jackass Mail,'" pt. 1, 53 (quotations); Duffen, "Overland via 'Jackass Mail,'" pt. 2, 148; PGA, El Paso Co., Tex., NA, RG 28, M841, R123; Butterfield Overland Mail Itinerary, *Mesilla Times*, Apr. 13, 1861, SCL, UTEP; AFT, Smith's Ranch, Jan. 21, 2000 (JA, James Irby); Hunt, "Journal," Sept. 17, 1869 (endnote quotation); GLO, *September 1883 Paul McCombs Map of the Texas & Pacific R-Y Reserve*; GLO, Map #1586, U.S. House of Representatives Exhibit 93, *1877 El Paso Troubles in Texas, Map of Salt Lakes to Accompany Statement of W. B. Blanchard in Appendix F, No. 3*; Hudspeth County Plat No. 8, *March 1906 Survey of Jesse Burdett Survey No. 52*, and *June 24, 1914, Sketch of Rio Grande Surveys 53 to 90 in the El Paso County Valley Made by J. Tivy*, Map Cabinet, County Clerk's Office, Hudspeth Co., Tex. These last two maps show the old stage road, a house with cottonwood trees, a water tank, and water wells. The adobe buildings are long gone, but a fine trace of the mail road runs through the site. After the Civil War, Fred L. Pierpont ran the mail station at the old Smith's Ranch location. McCombs's 1883 map shows Pierpont's mail station across the river from San Ignacio, Mexico. Hunt's journal shows that it was 2 miles upriver from Pierpont's Station to the ford across the Rio Grande to San Ignacio, Mexico. Hunt says that the Mexican village was "a small place" with adobe houses.

21. Giddings and Koney depositions, *Giddings v. U.S.*; Smith, *U.S. Army*, 184–85, 204, 206, 208, 211; Bliss, *Reminiscences*, 223; Mills, *My Story*, 52 (quotation); *Contracts with the War Department*, House Exec. Doc. No. 58, 35th Cong., 1st Sess., ser. 955, p. 8; El Paso County Deed Records, Mar. 29, 1860 (endnote quotations). George Giddings recalled that he leased facilities at Smith's Ranch. Butterfield stage driver David Koney confirmed this. On March 29, 1860, George B. F. Lyles and his associate John G. Bryant purchased 320 acres in the William Stanley Survey 51, "about 50 miles below the town of El Paso," from Richard S. Robertson for $3,500. The parcel included the site

known as "Birchville or Smith Ranch" and all the improvements upon it. Robertson had purchased this acreage the previous month from Middleton J. Johnson for $500.

22. *Contracts with the War Department*, House Exec. Doc. No. 58, 35th Cong., 1st Sess., ser. 955, pp. 2, 32; *Contracts with the War Department*, House Exec. Doc. No. 50, 35th Cong., 2nd Sess., ser. 1006, pp. 11, 17; *Contracts with the War Department*, House Exec. Doc. No. 22, 36th Cong., 1st Sess., ser. 1047, p. 25; 1860 U.S. Census, El Paso Co., Tex., M653, R1293, 79; Hunt, "Journal," Sept. 17, 1869 (quotation). George Lyles's wife, Basilia, was a Mexican American, and the couple had five children.

23. AFT, Camp Hawkins, Oct. 1, 1999 (JA, James Irby), and Jan. 3, 2001 (with Gary Williams); *Mesilla Times*, Apr. 13, 1861, SCL, UTEP; Mar. 22, 1880, F. C. Taylor estate valuation (re Bain), C. H. Merritt, estate administrator, Tom Green County Probate Records, San Angelo, Tex.; 1860 U.S. Census, El Paso Co., Tex., M653, R1293, 80; Baylor, *Into the Far, Wild Country*, 276; Hunt, "Journal," Sept. 18, 1869, sketch and entry. For those interested in following the mail road upstream from Fargo to El Paso, Lieutenant Colonel Hunt's journal provides an accurate itinerary. Hunt's sketch of Camp Hawkins shows that in wet weather travelers had to detour up and around a bog to higher ground at the edge of the foothills. The wet-weather loop road made a big arc around the bog. One can still see the foothill loop today, bordering the boggy section, which is now under cultivation. Hawkins Stage Station also appears in a 1909 post office route map for Fabens and Tornillo, Texas. See PGS, El Paso County, Tex., NA RG 28, M1126, R572.

24. AFT, San Elizario, Jan. 22 and June 30, 2000 (both with Gary Williams); 1860 U.S. Census, El Paso Co., Tex., M653, R1293, 108, 115; El Paso County Deed Records, Apr. 30, 1862; Koney, Collins, and Giddings depositions, *Giddings v. U.S.*; Strickland, *Six Who Came*, 30; Hunt, "Journal," Sept. 18, 1869 (quotation); Hendricks and Timmons, *San Elizario*, ix, xiii, xv, 15; Kohout, "San Elizario, Texas," *Handbook*. In 1860, Fred Pierpont, a thirty-three-year-old Pennsylvania native, was living in San Elizario with his seventeen-year-old wife, Juana María, of New Mexico, and their three-month-old son. In 1867, Pierpont served as San Elizario's postmaster for six months. By 1869, he had moved downriver to the old Smith's Ranch site, where he was managing the San Antonio–El Paso stage stop. Exactly who owned and operated the Butterfield station in San Elizario remains a tangled story, a case of too much and often-conflicting information. George Giddings stated that he owned the station, but records show that he did not purchase it from Pierpont until April 1862. Giddings operated and/or leased a station here as early as 1855. Thomas Collins of New York, who was also the town's miller, claimed that he ran the San Elizario station for Giddings for about eight or nine months in 1859. Thomas Brown and William Thompson helped him. Local tradition states that the stage station in San Elizario was located in Lalo's and Ralph's Grocery, northwest of the old presidio. In addition, one San Elizario landowner believes their house was a stage station. To date, there is no documentation to support these last two scenarios.

25. PGA, El Paso Co., Tex., NA, RG 28, M841, R123; Jim Wheat, "Postmasters and Post Offices of Texas, 1846–1930," microfilm reel 1, TSLAC; 1860 U.S. Census, El Paso Co., Tex., M653, R1293, 108, 115; Hyde and Ford depositions, *Giddings v. U.S.*; Strickland, *Six Who Came*, 30; Mills, *Forty Years*, 183; Broaddus, *Legal Heritage*, 60–61.

26. 1860 U.S. Census, El Paso Co., Tex., M653, R1293, 90–116; 2nd Lt. Henry Martyn Lazelle, 8th Inf., to 2nd Lt. William Hicks Jackson, R.M.R., Post Adj., Ft. Bliss, Tex., Feb. 18, 1859, NA, RG 94, AGO, LR, M567, R607. In his report, Lazelle mentions heading toward the Cornudas Mountains and stopping at Cottonwood Spring, also known as Alamo Spring. The Spanish word for cottonwood is *álamo*.

27. Lazelle to Jackson, Feb. 18, 1859 (quotations).

28. Aug. 12, 1891, petition recapitulation, p. 12, and Hyde deposition, *Giddings v. U.S.*; PGA, El Paso Co., Tex., NA, RG 28, M841, R123.

29. "Socorro, Texas," *Handbook*; Hamilton, "Ysleta, Texas," *Handbook*; PGA, El Paso Co., Tex., NA, RG 28, M841, R123; 1860 U.S. Census, El Paso Co., Tex., M653, R1293, 27–46 (Ysleta), 47–65 (Socorro).

30. Sonnichsen, *Pass of the North*, 105 (quotations); 1860 U.S. Census, El Paso Co., Tex., M653, R1293, 3; El Paso County Tax Rolls, reel 1, 1852–94, TSLAC; Strickland, *Six Who Came*, 34–36; Mills, *Forty Years*, 191; *1859 United States and Texas Boundary Commission Map #1*, Senate Exec. Doc. No. 70, 47th Cong., 1st Sess., ser. 1987; Ely, "What to Do about Texas," 385–92; Ely, "Skullduggery at Spencer's Ranch," 12–21; Thompson, "Drama in the Desert," 107–26; 1860 U.S. Census, El Paso Co., Tex., M653, R1293, 3; *Contracts with the War Department*, House Exec. Doc. No. 50, 35th Cong., 2nd Sess., ser. 1006, p. 30; Hugh Stephenson Credit Report, Texas vol. 10, El Paso County, p. 37 (endnote quotations), DCR, BL. Period credit reports noted that Stephenson's store had a "large stock," that he was "considered eminently" in the community, and that he was worth $100,000. Besides his mercantile business, Stephenson's commercial interests included a silver mine in the Organ Mountains north of El Paso and the site for Fort Fillmore, New Mexico, which he leased to the federal government. El Paso County tax rolls for 1860 show him with a net worth of $14,314, less than the $40,000 listed in the federal census. In 1860, Stephenson owned 740 acres, 5 horses, 220 cattle, and 777 sheep. During the Civil War, Stephenson was an ardent supporter of the Confederacy. In 1861 and 1862, he rented Fort Fillmore to rebel forces and furnished supplies to General H. H. Sibley at Fort Bliss for the ill-fated Confederate campaign in New Mexico. El Paso County tax rolls for 1860 list Henry Skillman's total assets as $1,200. Today, the last vestige of the old Concordia settlement is at Concordia Cemetery in El Paso, at the corner of North Stevens Street and East Yandell Drive.

31. Hunt, "Journal," Sept. 22, 1869; Mills, *My Story*, 50–56; Timmons, *El Paso*, 111; *Sanborn Maps of Texas*, Perry-Castañeda Map Collection, University of Texas Library Online, www.lib.utexas.edu/maps/sanborn/d-f/txu-sanborn-el_paso-1883-1.jpg (accessed Sept. 17, 2013); El Paso County Tax Rolls, reel 1, 1852–94, TSLAC; Jim Wheat, "Postmasters and Post Offices of Texas, 1846–1930," microfilm reel 1, TSLAC; PGA, El Paso Co., Tex., NA, RG 28, M841, R123; 1860 U.S. Census, El Paso Co., Tex., M653, R1293, 11–12; AFT, El Paso Station, 1998–2004; El Paso County Deed Records, May 15, 1861, and May 20, 1867. These deed transactions explain the land donation by the citizens of El Paso to Butterfield for Block 34 and the Frontier Hotel. Sheet 1 of the October 1883 map of El Paso published by Sanborn Map and Publishing Company provides a detailed look at the layout of Block 34. County tax rolls for 1860 placed a $25,000 valuation on the Overland Mail Company building in Block 34. Postmasters for El Paso during this period were Jarvis Hubbell (July 26, 1852–March 31, 1855), A. C. Hyde (March 31, 1855–March 6, 1857), Benjamin Dowell (March 6, 1857–September 15, 1860), and Vincent St. Vrain (September 15, 1860, to the spring of 1861).

32. Anson Mills deposition, *Giddings v. U.S.* (quotations 1–2); Frontier Hotel ad in *Mesilla Times*, Apr. 13, 1861, SCL, UTEP (quotations 3–4).

33. 1860 U.S. Census, El Paso Co., Tex., M653, R1293, 12.

34. Frontier Hotel ad in *Mesilla Times*, Nov. 1, 1860, SCL, UTEP (quotations 1, 2, and 4); Timmons, *El Paso*, 143 (quotation 3).

35. Timmons, *El Paso*, xi, xviii–xix, 137, 141.

36. Ibid., 141 (quotation), 170.

37. Hendricks and Timmons, *San Elizario*, 76 (quotation).

38. Reid, *Reid's Tramp*, 154 (quotation), 155.

39. Ibid., 158, 159 (quotation 1); Hendricks and Timmons, *San Elizario*, 78 (quotations 2–3).

40. 1860 U.S. Census, Texas Slave Schedules, El Paso Co., M653, R1309; Timmons, *James Wiley Magoffin*, 75; Timmons, *El Paso*, 109 (quotation); Strickland, *Six Who Came*, 37; Mills, *Forty Years*, 182; El Paso County Tax Rolls, reel 1, 1852–94, TSLAC; Bowden, *Ascarate Grant*, 68–69. Simeon Hart was born March 28, 1816, at Highland (Ulster County), New York. While still a young man, he moved to St. Louis. During the Civil War, Major Simeon Hart served as a quartermaster and a purchasing agent for the Confederacy. He died at Hart's Mill (Molino) on January 19, 1874.

41. Ramos, *Beyond the Alamo*, 195 (quotation).

42. Timmons, *El Paso*, 109; Strickland, *Six Who Came*, 37, 38 (quotation 1), 39 (quotation 2); Mills, *Forty Years*, 182; 1860 U.S. Census, El Paso Co., Tex., M653, R1293, 6; El Paso County Tax Rolls, reel 1, 1852–94, TSLAC. There is a significant difference between El Paso County's tax valuations of Hart's assets for 1860 and those listed in the federal census. The census shows Hart's net worth as $350,000, while the county has it as $48,090. In 1860, besides the mill, Hart owned 5 slaves, 100 horses, 20 cattle, and 40 sheep.

43. Hendricks, "Marriages," 75–76; Magoffin Home State Historic Site, "James Wiley Magoffin," 2, 4–5, 8; Magoffin Home State Historic Site, "Amondarain/Valdés Family," 10–12.

44. Strickland, *Six Who Came*, 26–29, 32–33; Mills, *Forty Years*, 184; Timmons, *James Wiley Magoffin*, 20; 1860 U.S. Census, El Paso Co., Tex., M653, R1293, 19; Col. J. W. Magoffin Credit Reports, Texas vol. 10, El Paso County, p. 38 (endnote quotations), DCR, BL; El Paso County Tax Rolls, reel 1, 1852–94, TSLAC; Bowden *Ascarate Grant*, 62. Credit reports note that Magoffin's overland freighting business had a "large stake and [was] considered eminently." He was "said to be wealthy, owns a large train of wagons, makes a great deal of money, spends liberally, a perfect gentleman, honest, his credit here is A No. 1." As in Simeon Hart's case, there is a disparity between federal and county records regarding the value of James Magoffin's assets. The 1860 federal census lists his net worth as $100,000, but El Paso County tax rolls show it as $27,815. Tax rolls reveal that Magoffin owned 1,000 acres, 1 cow, and 62 horses. Magoffin died in San Antonio on September 28, 1868.

45. Gilderhus, *Second Century*, 22 (quotation).

46. Reséndez, *Changing National Identities*, 1–11.

47. Ibid.; 1860 U.S. Census, El Paso Co., Tex., M653, R1293; 1860 U.S. Census, Texas Slave Schedules, El Paso Co., M653, R1309; Mora, *Border Dilemmas*, 22 (quotation).

48. Strickland, *Turner Thesis*, 14 (quotation 1); Garcia, *Desert Immigrants*, 7 (quotation 2); Ely, "What to Do about Texas," 381. During their occupation of El Paso County from 1862 to 1867, federal officials from the Department (later District) of New Mexico also relied on Tejano elites.

49. El Paso County District Court grand jury petition to Peter Hansbrough Bell, Oct. 4, 1851, PHB Papers, folder 26, box 301-20, TSLAC (quotations). Such attitudes were typical of the Anglo-American mindset in the nineteenth century. For more on this, see Horsman, *Race and Manifest Destiny*, 234–35.

50. Bowden, "Magoffin Salt War," 95 (quotations); Strickland, *Six Who Came*, 30–31; Timmons, *James Wiley Magoffin*, 53–54.

51. *Texas State Gazette*, Jan. 24, 1854; Strickland, *Six Who Came*, 30–32. William "Clown" Garner later served in Henry Skillman's Confederate spy company.

52. Martinez, *Chicanos of El Paso*, 7 (quotations).

53. Arneson, "Early Irrigation in Texas," 121–22, 127–28; Hutchins, "Community Acequia," 261, 264, 268, 269.

54. Arneson, "Early Irrigation in Texas," 121–22, 127–28; Hutchins,

"Community Acequia," 261, 264, 268, 269 (quotation 2 and endnote quotation); El Paso County District Court grand jury petition to Peter Hansbrough Bell, Oct. 4, 1851, PHB Papers, folder 26, box 301-20, TSLAC (quotation 1); White, *Out of the Desert*, 54–55; Bowden, *Spanish and Mexican Land Grants*, 95; Bartlett, *Personal Narrative*, 1:199; Timmons, *El Paso*, 41–42. Wells A. Hutchins notes that a later irrigation code passed by Texas in 1913 ignored the 1852 regulations and did "not provide for the government of community *acequias*."

55. AFT, Frontera site, 2005–2008; Strickland, *Six Who Came*, 4–5; Capt. Allen Anderson, *1864 Map of the Military Department of New Mexico: Drawn under the Direction of Brig. Gen. James H. Carleton*, www.davidrumsey.com. This map shows the road split at Doña Ana, New Mexico. The *1859 United States and Texas Boundary Commission Map #1*, in John H. Clark's 1859 boundary report, shows the exact route of the overland road upriver from El Paso to Frontera and the New Mexico line. See Senate Exec. Doc. No. 70, 47th Cong., 1st Sess., ser. 1987. The map shows several places between El Paso and Frontera where alternative loop roads, used during times of wet weather and flooding, led up and around the river road. The lithograph also includes excellent detail of the Franklin Mountains. In addition, this map reveals that Clark's boundary commission established an astronomical observatory a short distance below the New Mexico line near Butterfield's Cottonwoods Ranch. The March 2, 1884, survey sketch for GLO, El Paso County Abstract No. 2716 places Frontera's astronomical observatory midway on the southern boundary line of T. F. White Survey No. 3, directly on the railroad tracks that parallel modern Highway 20. I spent many years researching and locating this historic site. Robert Seipel of the Texas Society of Professional Surveyors, El Paso chapter, corroborated my findings.

56. MT, Smeltertown; *1852 U.S.-Mexico Boundary Map, Sheet No. 29*, showing Frontera, Molino, Franklin, Magoffinsville, and Paso del Norte, Mexico, in *U.S.-Mexico Boundary Commission Report*, El Paso, *Texas*, published March 1, 1899, El Paso County Historical Society Archives; Bieber, *Exploring Southwestern Trails*, 313 (quotation 1), 314 (quotations 2–3); Anson Mills's Feb. 8, 1859, plat of Juan M. Ponce de Leon Survey 145, El Paso County Abstract No. 52, El Paso County Field Notes Book A-1. Fort Bliss at Magoffinsville was in N.W. Burdett Survey 1, GLO, El Paso County Abstract No. 12.

57. Timmons, *El Paso*, 131; *Contracts with the War Department*, House Exec. Doc. No. 50, 35th Cong., 2nd Sess., ser. 1006, pp. 5, 28–29; Mills, *Forty Years*, 177–78; Gammel, *Laws of Texas*, 3:1261–63; Strickland, *Six Who Came*, 12 (quotation); Bowden, *Ascarate Grant*, 70–71; CJ, Dec. 7, 1930, box 9, RPC Papers. For correspondence referencing regional boundary surveys and Frontera in 1851, see *Report of the Secretary of War, Communicating in Compliance with a Resolution of the Senate the Report of Lieutenant Colonel Graham on the Subject of the Boundary Line between the United States and Mexico*, Senate Exec. Doc. No. 121, 32nd Cong., 1st Sess., pp. 2–250. The sketch for the September 22, 1869, entry in Hunt, "Journal," shows Frontera as a "ranche [*sic*]" and "mail station." Henry L. Dexter's purchase of Frontera from White is in El Paso County Deed Records, April 3, 1855. Dexter married María Soledad Luján in 1859 but deserted her in 1862. In 1871, María Soledad Luján Dexter sold the 320-acre Frontera parcel to William B. Rohman for $200. Three years after selling his Frontera property, T. F. White worked as a contractor for the U.S. Army. In 1858, he held the federal contracts to supply beans to Fort Bliss in Texas and Forts Fillmore and Thorn in New Mexico. Additionally, from November 1857 to September 1858, White was the corn contractor for Fort Fillmore. Butterfield historians Roscoe and Margaret Conkling visited the Frontera site on December 7, 1930. During the early 1930s, when the Conklings were conducting much of their field research for their book, they lived at 4507 Pershing Drive in El Paso, Texas.

58. Bowden, *Spanish and Mexican Land Grants*, 94 (quotation 1), 95 (quotations 2–3); Bartlett, *Personal Narrative*, 199 (quotation 4); MT, El Paso, Smeltertown, Canutillo; James Wiley Magoffin to Committee of El Paso Co., Aug. 5, 1852, PHB Papers, folder 36, box 301-21, TSLAC; GLO, El Paso County Abstract No. 2439, Anson Mills's Aug. 9, 1860, Survey and Plats of El Canutillo (6,642-acre grant to J. Sanchez, G. Miranda, and R. Barelo); GLO, Map #8858, E. L. De Shazo, *May 1908 Map of Santa Teresa Grant*. Researchers should corroborate stated mileages in Bartlett and other period accounts. Cited distances from My Topo software are more precise than mid-nineteenth-century instruments of measurement. In an August 1852 letter, Magoffin mentions the distance from El Paso to El Canutillo as 15 miles. I found it to be 13 miles from the Butterfield station in downtown El Paso, Texas, located at Overland and El Paso Streets. From Magoffin's home in Magoffinsville, east of El Paso, the mileage would be closer to 15. Anson Mills executed a beautiful color plat of his 1860 Upper Valley surveys, including El Canutillo. Mills's detailed plats (both black and white and color) and De Shazo's map show Canutillo Lake, the old 1824 ranch (a short distance north-northeast of the lake), and a later ranch farther north in the foothills near present-day Canutillo, Texas.

59. James Wiley Magoffin to Committee of El Paso Co., Aug. 5, 1852, PHB Papers, folder 36, box 301-21, TSLAC (quotation); Timmons, *El Paso*, 131; AFT, El Canutillo, 2005–2008; Bowden, *Spanish and Mexican Land Grants*, 97.

60. Bowden, *Spanish and Mexican Land Grants*, 94–101; *Mesilla Times*, Apr. 13, 1861, SCL, UTEP; Anson Mills deposition, *Giddings v. U.S.* (quotations); Conkling and Conkling, *Butterfield Overland Mail*, 2:94; Richardson, *Beyond the Mississippi*, 245; Mills, *My Story*, 55 (endnote quotation). Bowden fully details the legal proceedings for the Canutillo land dispute and its final resolution in September 1886. The Conklings mistakenly state that stagecoach passenger Albert Richardson stopped at Los Tres Hermanos in October 1859 on his way to Santa Fe. Richardson says that he stopped at an adobe station for dinner 20 miles after entering New Mexico. Los Tres Hermanos, in Texas, was 26 miles to the south, near El Canutillo, and did not exist in October 1859. The Mills brothers built their ranch just before the Civil War. Canutillo is listed as a stage stop on the last overland itinerary, published in the April 13, 1861, *Mesilla Times*. In 1918, twenty-four years after his May 7, 1894, deposition for George Giddings's depredation claim, Anson Mills stated that his brother Emmett "occupied this ranch, which was made into a Santa Fe Mail station." Exactly when this building served as a station on the El Paso–Santa Fe route is unknown.

61. MT, El Paso, Smeltertown, Canutillo; Duffen, "Overland via 'Jackass Mail,'" pt. 2, 147–48; Ormsby, *Butterfield Overland Mail*, 76; Lang, *First Overland Mail: . . . St. Louis to San Francisco*, 108. Waterman Ormsby put the distance to Cottonwoods Ranch from El Paso at 21 miles, while Special Agent G. Bailey of the U.S. Post Office listed it as 22 miles. My Topo software shows that the distance is actually 20 miles.

62. Duffen, "Overland via 'Jackass Mail,'" pt. 2, 149 (quotation 1); J. A. Lucas deposition, *Giddings v. U.S.* (quotation 2); GLO, Map #8865, R. J. Owen, *August 1919 Map of the Valley Lands in Texas Lying South of the 32nd Parallel and North of the Canutillo Grant in El Paso County, Texas*; GLO, El Paso County Abstract No. 2439, Anson Mills 1860 color plat of the Upper Valley lands. The October 4, 1849, field notes for GLO, Maria Rodriguez Survey 35, El Paso County Abstract No. 167, reference being a half mile below "the Alamitas." Longtime West Texas frontiersman Thomas Rife was a chain carrier on this 1849 survey. The location of Cottonwoods Ranch, just below the New Mexico line, is correct in *R. P. Kelley's 1860 Map of the Territory of Arizona*, by Arthur Witzleben, SCL, UTEP.

63. Initial AFT locating Cottonwoods Ranch site, Oct. 23, 2001; subsequent AFT, Cottonwoods Ranch, July 23, 2007, and Sept. 6, 2008.

CHAPTER 11. THE END OF THE LINE

1. Over the past 150 years, there has been much dissembling regarding the reason for Texas's and the South's secession from the Union. Many claim that protection of states' rights was the foundational issue. In considering this claim, to what rights are they referring? According to Confederate vice president Alexander Stephens, it was the right to own slaves. Stephens made this clear on March 21, 1861, when identifying slavery as the fundamental motivation for secession. The vice president noted that the new Confederate Constitution "has put at rest, forever, all the agitating questions relating to our peculiar institution—African slavery as it exists amongst us—the proper status of the negro in our form of civilization. *This was the immediate cause of the late rupture and present revolution*" (my emphasis). Despite these facts, Texas's State Board of Education appears to be borrowing a page from George Orwell's *1984* in its persistent attempts to dilute the state's Civil War and civil rights history in social studies textbooks. See Winkler, *Journal of the Secession Convention*, 62 (quotation); Alexander Stephens, "Cornerstone Speech, Savannah, Georgia, March 21, 1861," www.ucs.louisiana.edu/~ras2777/amgov/stephens.html (accessed July 7, 2015) (endnote quotation); Emma Brown, "Texas Officials: Schools Should Teach That Slavery Was 'Side Issue' to Civil War," *Washington Post*, July 5, 2015, www.washingtonpost.com/local/education/150-years-later-schools-are-still-a-battlefield-for-interpreting-civil-war/2015/07/05/e8fbd57e-2001-11e5-bf41-c23f5d3face1_story.html; "How Texas Is Whitewashing Civil War History," *Washington Post*, July 6, 2015, www.washingtonpost.com/opinions/whitewashing-civil-war-history-for-young-minds/2015/07/06/1168226c-2415-11e5-b77f-eb13a215f593_story.html?hpid=z3. For more on western identity in Texas and the state's environmental and cultural transition zone, see Ely, *Where the West Begins*, 7–34.

2. Winkler, *Journal of the Secession Convention*, 89–90.

3. Ibid.; Buenger, *Secession*, 18 (quotation 1); Sonnichsen, *Pass of the North*, 151 (quotations 2–3), 154 (quotation 4).

4. Texas Secretary of State, El Paso County, Feb. 18, 1861, Election Returns, box 2-12/532, TSLAC; Winkler, *Journal of the Secession Convention*, 58–59 (see sections 1, 6, 7, and 9). For more on El Paso County during the Civil War, see Ely, "What to Do about Texas."

5. El Paso County Judge H. S. Gillett to Secretary of [Secession] Convention, El Paso County, Feb. 20, 1861, Election Returns, box 2-12/532, TSLAC (quotation); Gournay, *Texas Boundaries*, 60–61. For more on Presidio County and the Big Bend region during the Civil War, see Ely, "Skullduggery at Spencer's Ranch."

6. Winkler, *Journal of the Secession Convention*, 89 (the journal omits returns for Presidio and Maverick Counties), 90 (quotation 1); Smyrl, "McCulloch County," *Handbook* (quotation 2); Gournay, *Texas Boundaries*, 71; Ochoa, "Maverick County," *Handbook*. The Maverick County secession vote (3 votes for secession, 80 against) can be found in Sumpter, *Paso Del Águila*, 83–85, 86 (endnote quotation). Maverick County's election results apparently did not sit well with rabid secessionists in the area. Jesse Sumpter says that Confederate captain Harris A. Hamner (see chapter 4), stationed at Fort Clark, came to Eagle Pass to murder four local Unionists, including Sumpter. Sumpter and two others managed to escape, but Hamner gunned down the fourth, Aleck Oswald. Sumpter says, "Hamner was never arrested or accused for the killing."

7. One previous study states that Presidio County voted for secession. Another source (likely based on Winkler's *Journal*) says the county never reported its referendum results. Both of these are mistaken. Presidio County's final tally, which was 364 to 0 against secession, appears in both the March 25, 1861, edition of the *San Antonio Alamo Express* and in two letters from Fort Davis merchant, post sutler, and county election judge Daniel Murphy to former Texas governor Elisha M. Pease. Daniel Murphy worried that his county's stance in the referendum would invite pro-secession retaliation. Murphy feared that "there is [now] a poor chance for us getting any [frontier] protection in this section of county." See Timmons, "Referendum in Texas," 15–16; Campbell, *Gone to Texas*, 245; map of Texas's 1861 referendum on secession, "Secession and the Civil War," Texas State Historical Association, *Texas Almanac*, http://texasalmanac.com/topics/history/timeline/secession-and-civil-war; Daniel Murphy to Elisha M. Pease, Feb. 25, 1861, and Daniel Murphy to Pease, Mar. 1, 1861 (quotation and endnote quotation), Elisha M. Pease Papers, Austin History Center.

8. Ely, "Riding the Butterfield Frontier," 191–92; 1860 U.S. Census, El Paso and Presidio Co., Tex., NA, M653, R1293; 1860 U.S. Census, Maverick Co., Tex., NA, M653, R1300; 1860 U.S. Census, Texas Slave Schedules, El Paso and Presidio Co., NA, M653, R1309, 289; 1860 U.S. Census, Texas Slave Schedules, Maverick Co., NA, M653, R1311, 146; Timmons, *James Wiley Magoffin*, 75; Campbell, *Southern Community in Crisis*, 20; El Paso County Tax Rolls, reel 1, 1852–94, TSLAC. I conducted a detailed study of the 1860 census and slave schedules for El Paso, Presidio, and Maverick Counties. Two of the three slaves listed for Maverick County in 1860 were actually in Frio County, on the Frio River. The 1860 federal census lists fifteen slaves for El Paso County, but the county tax rolls for 1860 show only eight. In addition, there are no slaves listed on El Paso County tax rolls from 1852 to 1857. The first documented slaveholder in the county was Josiah F. Crosby in 1858, with two slaves.

9. Timmons, *El Paso*, 147 (quotations 1–3); Timmons, *James Wiley Magoffin*, 68 (quotation 5), 72 (quotation 4); 1860 U.S. Census, El Paso and Presidio Co., Tex., M653, R1293; 1860 U.S. Census, Texas Slave Schedules, El Paso and Presidio Co., M653, R1309; Hendricks and Timmons, *San Elizario*, 79–80 (endnote quotation). Regarding El Paso's secession vote, El Paso historians Rick Hendricks and W. H. Timmons note that a "more significant explanation for the overwhelming pro-South sentiment was the identification of Jefferson Davis, president of the Confederate States, with the southern transcontinental railroad and its obvious implications for El Paso's future."

10. Kennedy, *Population of the United States*, 566–73 (New Mexico Territory data); 1860 U.S. Census, Doña Ana Co., N. Mex. Terr., NA, M653, R712; Ganaway, *New Mexico and the Sectional Controversy*, 123–24 (quotation 1); Stegmaier, "Law That Would Make Caligula Blush," 57, 58 (quotation 3), 62, 72 (quotation 4), 74 (quotation 5), 75 (quotations 2 and 6). The 1860 federal census contains no slave schedules for New Mexico Territory. Kennedy's *Population of the United States in 1860* compilation lists eighty-five free persons of color in the territory.

11. Hall, "*Mesilla Times*," 338 (quotation 1), 343 (quotation 2); Hall, "Formation of Sibley's Brigade," 388 (quotation 3); Finch, *Confederate Pathway*, 39; Mora, *Border Dilemmas*, 87 (quotation 4); *Chicago Tribune*, Mar. 22 and 27, 1860; Owen, *Las Cruces*, appx. 1 ("List of County Sheriffs, 1835–1998"); Price, *Pioneers of the Mesilla Valley*, 65–68; public officials Pablo Melendres, Gregorio Meadonado, and Blas Sedillo payment vouchers, 1852–55, New Mexico State Records Center and Archives, Doña Ana County Clerk Accounts, 1852–1867. During his time in public office, Melendres served as justice of the peace, alcalde, and county probate judge (the chief executive of Doña Ana County in the antebellum period).

12. Eaton, "Frontier Life," 174 (quotation 1), 189 (quotation 2); *Chicago Tribune*, Mar. 22 and 27, 1860; Mora, *Border Dilemmas*, 87 (quotation 3).

13. 1860 U.S. Census, Doña Ana Co., N. Mex. Terr., NA, M653, R712; Mora, *Border Dilemmas*, 88 (quotation 1); Wilson, *When the Texans Came*, 25 (quotation 2).

14. *Mesilla Times*, Feb. 23, Mar. 16 (endnote quotation 2), Mar. 23, and Mar. 30, 1861; *Texas State Gazette*, Feb. 23, 1861; Broaddus, *Legal Heritage*, 66; Newspaper clipping "Proceedings of a Convention of the People of Arizona, Held in the City of Mesilla, March 16, 1861," Folder 1, Box 301-35, Governor Edward Clark Papers, TSLAC; Ganaway, *New Mexico*, 108–109, 111 (endnote quotation 1); Hall, "The *Mesilla Times*," 343; *Texas State Gazette*, Mar. 30, 1861 (endnote quotation 3); Wilson, *When the Texans Came*, 36. Hall places much emphasis on the March 16, 1861, secession meeting in Mesilla, less than a month before Fort Sumter (April 12) and the start of the Civil War. This gathering included residents from El Paso County, Texas, Doña Ana County, New Mexico, and a handful from Tucson, Arizona. Sixty-six people originally promoted the event in the February 23 edition of the Mesilla newspaper, but the newspaper's coverage of the March 16 proceedings mentions fewer than fifteen people by name, which leaves considerable uncertainty as to the exact size of the crowd. Citing the March 30, 1861, *Mesilla Times*, Loomis Morton Ganaway says that "several hundred" attended the Mesilla meeting. Ganaway is in error. The March 30 edition never specifies the number of people in attendance. The March 16 edition of the *Mesilla Times* says only that there was "a handsome turnout." Another account estimated the number of secessionists residing in Mesilla at around twenty. Regarding the perspective of the *Mesilla Times*'s Anglo owners, the *Texas State Gazette* noted that the newspaper "is proslavery in politics and advocates a Southern Confederacy with great force." Southern New Mexico demographics paint a different picture: only four of Las Cruces's 767 residents were from the South, in Doña Ana, one of 651, and in La Mesa, two of 617.

15. *Mesilla Times*, Mar. 16, 1861; New Mexico state historian Dennis Trujillo e-mail to author, Mar. 7, 2011; Ganaway, *New Mexico*, 125 (quotations).

16. Mora, *Border Dilemmas*, 89 (quotation 1); Wilson, *When the Texans Came*, 305 (quotations 2–3); Ely, *Where the West Begins*, 29; Thompson, *New Mexico Territory*, 2–6.

17. Enclosure in Canby to Chivington, June 18, 1862, NA, RG 94, AGO, LR, M619, R122 (quotations 1–2); Wilson, *When the Texans Came*, 288–91, 311–14; *Houston Tri-Weekly Telegraph*, Aug. 18, 1862 (quotation 3); *San Antonio Semi-Weekly News*, July 21, 1862; Howe to Chapin, July 15, 1862, NA, RG 393, Southern Dept. of New Mexico, entry 734, LS, vol. 118/300.

18. Ely, *Where the West Begins*, 26–28; Lamar, *Dakota Territory*, xxv; Lamar, *Far Southwest*, 6, 7, 13, 19.

19. Ely, *Where the West Begins*, 26–28.

20. Ely, "Riding the Butterfield Frontier," 429–30; Strickland, *Turner Thesis*, 12 (quotation), 13; Broaddus, *Legal Heritage*, 69 (endnote quotation 1); Timmons, *James Wiley Magoffin*, 76 (endnote quotation 2). J. Morgan Broaddus mentions "the secessionist leaders of El Paso, mainly Magoffin, Hart, and Crosby," and W. H. Timmons notes that their significant influence ultimately "carried the day."

21. Broaddus, *Legal Heritage*, 65 (quotations 1–2); *Austin Southern Intelligencer*, Sept. 22, 1858 (quotation 3); Timmons, *El Paso*, 175, 191–92; Garcia, *Desert Immigrants*, 6–7, 155–69; Ramirez, "El Pasoans," 218–24; *El Paso Times*, Apr. 10 and 11, 1889, and July 24, 1892.

22. *Texas State Gazette*, Mar. 30, 1861 (quotation 1); Strickland, *Six Who Came*, 39; *Texas State Gazette*, Dec. 1, 1860 (quotation 2).

23. Strickland, *Six Who Came*, 26–33; *Texas State Gazette*, July 23, 1859 (quotations), Aug. 25, 1860, Sept. 22, 1860; James W. Magoffin to U.S. president Andrew Johnson, Washington, D.C., Sept. 3, 1867 (endnote quotations), James W. Magoffin Amnesty Application File, Applications from Former Confederates for Presidential Pardons,

1865–67, NA, RG 94, M1003, R54; *Daily Alta California* clipping, no date but likely from Sept. 1862, Bancroft Scraps, vol. 96, 21–22, Bancroft Library; James Magoffin Confederate Citizens Files and Simeon Hart Confederate Citizens Files, NA, RG 109, M346. In Magoffin's 1867 amnesty application, the secessionist leader and die-hard supporter of the Confederacy exhibited a bold mendaciousness, spuriously claiming that "in the year 1861, he was a loyal citizen of the United States." When El Paso County and Texas joined the Confederacy, "he was compelled by a superior rebel force, . . . to yield involuntary submission to their authority and take the oath of loyalty to the Confederate Government." President Johnson pardoned Magoffin on September 7, 1867.

24. Broaddus, *Legal Heritage*, 51–53, 61, 64–67, 76; Mills, *Forty Years*, 176, 183; 1860 U.S. Census, El Paso Co., Tex., M653, R1293, 12, 108; *Texas State Gazette*, Oct. 6 (quotations 1–2) and Dec. 8, 1860 (quotations 3–4); El Paso County Tax Rolls, reel 1, 1852–94, TSLAC; Judge Hyde Credit Reports, Texas vol. 10, El Paso County, p. 38 (endnote quotations), DCR, BL; Bowden, *Ascarate Grant*, 75, 150–51. In 1860, thirty-three-year-old Josiah F. Crosby reported a net worth of $6,000. Early in the Civil War, Crosby was Confederate general H. H. Sibley's acting quartermaster general during the New Mexico campaign. Later in the conflict, he served Texas governor Pendleton Murrah and Confederate general Edmund Kirby Smith, as Kirby Smith's munitions agent in Europe. Crosby died in El Paso on January 3, 1904. Archibald C. Hyde, born near Norwich, Connecticut, in 1813, moved to Texas in 1836, where he became postmaster general of the republic. He served as El Paso County judge (1850–52 and 1854–56), tax assessor-collector (1852–54), district attorney (1856–57), and Texas state senator (1857–61). In 1860, Hyde listed a net worth of $50. Credit reports state that he was also involved in the freighting business, transporting goods overland to El Paso from the Texas Gulf. While Hyde was said to be "clever" and "doing a general business" in 1859, by the following year he was "insolvent." County tax rolls show that during the 1850s, Hyde had little money. During the antebellum period, his financial apex was in 1860, with $464 in assets. Hyde died in January 1894 near Elmendorf, Texas.

25. Unpublished manuscript, Rex Strickland Papers, box 5, vol. 2, SCL, UTEP (quotations); Strickland, *Turner Thesis*, 12, 14.

26. Mills, *My Story*, 61 (quotation 1); R. L. Robertson to U.S. Atty. Gen. James M. Speed, Mobile, Ala., Oct. 4, 1865, and Simeon Hart affidavit, Oct. 20, 1865 (quotation 2), Simeon Hart Amnesty Application File, Applications from Former Confederates for Presidential Pardons, 1865–67, NA, RG 94, M1003, R53.

27. Robertson to Speed, Oct. 4, 1865 (quotations), Simeon Hart Amnesty Application File, Applications from Former Confederates for Presidential Pardons, 1865–67, NA, RG 94, M1003, R53.

28. Mills, *My Story*, 62 (quotation 1); John S. Watts to U.S. Atty. Gen. James Speed, Santa Fe, N.Mex., Oct. 21, 1865 (quotations 2, 4, and endnote quotation), Simeon Hart Amnesty Application File, Applications from Former Confederates for Presidential Pardons, 1865–67, NA, RG 94, M1003, R53; Strickland, *Six Who Came*, 39 (quotation 3). Strickland cites an eyewitness account of the Hart-Herbert altercation in the August 24, 1861, issue of the *Mesilla Times*. From 1851 to 1854, John S. Watts was an associate justice on the New Mexico Supreme Court, and after the war, he served as chief justice. Watts strongly urged Attorney General Speed not to grant Hart amnesty, commenting that if Hart "be pardoned, then the President might just as well shut his eyes and sign everything presented in the shape of a pardon from Jeff Davis down." Despite Watts's concerns, President Johnson pardoned Hart on November 3, 1865.

29. Bliss, *Reminiscences*, 223 (quotations 1–2); Smithwick, *Evolution of a State*, 256 (quotations 3–4). More on El Paso County's secession

vote can be found in Mills, *Forty Years*, 37; Hamilton, *Ben Dowell*, 29; Sonnichsen, *Pass of the North*, 202–204.

30. Mills, *My Story*, 62 (quotation 1); White, *Out of the Desert*, 61 (quotation 2). The primary sources presented here document the secession ring's importation of illegal Mexican votes from across the Rio Grande, its coercion of citizens (both physical and verbal), and other illegal activities that occurred at county polling stations.

31. Timmons, *James Wiley Magoffin*, 75 (quotation), 76; Broaddus, *Legal Heritage*, 67.

32. Ramos, *Beyond the Alamo*, 216 (quotations 1–2), 228 (quotations 3–4). While Ramos is discussing Tejano identity in antebellum Bexar County, many of his observations are applicable to El Paso County.

33. Mar. 12, 1861, Postmaster General Order Journals, vol. 48, Mar. 7–May 29, 1861, NA, RG 28, entry 1; *Report of the Postmaster General*, Senate Exec. Doc. No. 1, 37th Cong., 2nd Sess., ser. 1119, p. 560.

34. May 18, 1861, deed record, County Clerk's Office, Doña Ana Co., N.Mex.; El Paso County Deed Records, May 15, 1861, and May 20, 1867; recapitulation statement of losses incurred, 1854–61, *Giddings v. U.S.*; *Mesilla Times*, May 17, 1861 (endnote quotations). By May 1861, Butterfield was pulling out of Texas. One report noted that "a large train of men, stock, and coaches of the Fort Davis [Texas] and Mesilla [New Mexico] Division of the Overland [Mail] Company passed through" Mesilla on May 17, en route for California. "The whole outfit presented quite an imposing cortège," featuring one hundred men, hundreds of animals, and twenty-one coaches. For more on Union occupation and the Texas Trans-Pecos during the Civil War, see Ely,

"Gone from Texas," 165–66; Ely, "What to Do about Texas"; Ely, "Skullduggery at Spencer's Ranch."

35. McCulloch to Robertson, Mar. 9, 1861, *OR*, S1, vol. 53, 643–45. Although Governor Houston had strenuous objections to Hamner serving in the Texas Rangers, Colonel Dalrymple enrolled Hamner's company. By that time, Houston's political influence was on the wane. The Texas Secession Convention removed him from office on March 16, 1861.

36. Owen Tuller to Sam Houston, Fort Chadbourne, Tex., Feb. 19, 1861, box 301-34, SH Papers, TSLAC (endnote quotation). The commander at Fort Chadbourne, Lieutenant Colonel Gouverneur Morris, First Infantry, endorsed Tuller's letter to Houston, attesting that "the foregoing statements to his excellency are true."

37. Ibid. (quotations); *New York Times*, Mar. 26, 1861.

38. McCulloch to Robertson, Fort Chadbourne, Tex., Mar. 1, 1861, in Winkler, *Journal of the Secession Convention*, 375 (quotation 1); *New York Times*, Feb. 21 (quotations 2–3) and Feb. 22, 1861; *St. Louis Missouri Republican*, Mar. 22, 1861 (quotations 4–6). In the February 22 *New York Times* report, postal officials confirmed the Ranger depredations at Chadbourne.

39. *Dallas Herald*, Mar. 13, 1861 (quotations 1 and 5); McCulloch to Robertson, Camp Cooper, Tex., Mar. 9, 1861, *OR*, S1, vol. 53, 643, 644 (quotations 2–3), 645 (quotation 4).

40. Mills, *My Story*, 64; Boggs, *My Playhouse*, 386 (quotation); Ely, "Riding the Western Frontier," 23–25, 34.

Bibliography

ARCHIVES

Amon Carter Museum Library Research Room (Fort Worth, Tex.)
    Historic Newspaper and Western Americana Microfilm Collection

Austin History Center, Austin Public Library (Austin, Tex.)
    Elisha M. Pease Papers

Baker Library, Harvard Business School (Cambridge, Mass.)
    R. G. Dun and Co. Credit Report Volumes

Bancroft Library, University of California–Berkeley (Berkeley, Calif.)
    Bancroft Scraps
    Demarest, David Durie. "Diary, March 8, 1849–May 1850, of a Trip in a Bark *Norumbega* to Galveston, Texas, Then Overland to California."
    Strentzel, John Theophil. "Autobiography."

Coke County Archives (Robert Lee, Tex.)
    Coke County Commissioners Court Minutes
    Coke County Road Minutes
    Coke County Surveyor Field Notes

Cooke County Abstract Office (Gainesville, Tex.)

Cooke County Appraisal District (Gainesville, Tex.)

Cooke County Archives (Gainesville, Tex.)
    Cooke County Commissioners Court Minutes
    Cooke County Deed Records
    Cooke County District Court Records, Criminal Cases

Culberson County Appraisal District (Van Horn, Tex.)

Department of Special Collections, Stanford University Libraries (Stanford, Calif.)
    Collection M0082: The LaGrange Company Journal

Dolph Briscoe Center for American History, University of Texas (Austin, Tex.)
    William P. Huff Journal, 1849–50
    Robert Simpson Neighbors Papers, 1852–59
    Texas Newspaper Collection

Doña Ana County Archives (Las Cruces, N.Mex.)
    Doña Ana County Deed Records

El Paso County Abstract Office (El Paso, Tex.)

El Paso County Appraisal District (El Paso, Tex.)

El Paso County Archives (El Paso, Tex.)
    El Paso County Deed Records
    El Paso County Probate Records
    El Paso County Surveyor Field Notes

El Paso County Historical Society Archives (El Paso, Tex.)
    U.S.-Mexico Boundary Commission Report (1899)

Fort Belknap Archives (Newcastle, Tex.)
    Jesse Wallace Williams Papers

Fort Davis National Historic Site (Fort Davis, Tex.)
    Frank Temple Microfilm Rolls, Reports of Scouts, 1867–81
    M. M. Maxon Field Book
    Map Collection

Grayson County Appraisal District (Sherman, Tex.)

Grayson County Archives (Sherman, Tex.)

Grayson County Deed Records

Hudspeth County Appraisal District (Sierra Blanca, Tex.)

Hudspeth County Archives (Sierra Blanca, Tex.)
    Hudspeth County Clerk Map Cabinet
    Hudspeth County Deed Records
    Hudspeth County Surveyor Field Notes

Huntington Library (San Marino, Calif.)
    Beeching, Robert. "Journal of a Trip from New York on the Bark *Norumbega* to Galveston and thence Overland through Texas, Mexico, Arizona, and Southern California to San Diego 1849, March 8–October 20."

Irion County Appraisal District (Mertzon, Tex.)

Irion County Archives (Mertzon, Tex.)
    Irion County Deed Records
    Irion County Surveyor Field Notes

Jack County Appraisal District (Jacksboro, Tex.)

Jack County Archives (Jacksboro, Tex.)
    Jack County Civil District Court Minutes
    Jack County Commissioners Court Minutes
    Jack County Deed Records
    Jack County District Court Records
    Jack County Divorce Records
    Jack County Surveyor Field Notes

Jeff Davis County Appraisal District (Fort Davis, Tex.)

Hal Joyce Collection (Big Lake, Tex.)

Loving County Archives (Mentone, Tex.)
    Loving County Deed Records
    Loving County Surveyor Field Notes

Jim Ed Miller Papers (Pecos, Tex.)

Montague County Appraisal District (Montague, Tex.)

Montague County Archives (Montague, Tex.)
    Montague County Commissioners Court Minutes
    Montague County Court Records
    Montague County Criminal Court Minutes
    Montague County Deed Records
    Montague County District Court Records
    Montague County Police Court Minutes

National Archives and Records Administration (Washington, D.C., and College Park, Md.)
    Record Group 28: Records of the Post Office Department
    Postmaster General, Post Office Department Reports of Site Locations
    Postmaster General, Record of Appointment of Postmasters
    Postmaster General Order Journals
    Record Group 29: Records of the Bureau of the Census
    1850 Federal Census
    1860 Federal Census
    1860 Federal Census, Slave Schedules
    1870 Federal Census
    1880 Federal Census
    1900 Federal Census
    1910 Federal Census

1920 Federal Census
1930 Federal Census
Record Group 49: Records of the Bureau of Land Management
    Maps
Record Group 75: Records of the Bureau of Indian Affairs
Chickasaw Removal Records
Office of Indian Affairs, Letters Received
    Records of the Choctaw and Chickasaw Agency
    Records of the Comanche Indian Agency
    Records of the Texas Indian Agency
    Records of the Wichita Indian Agency
Record Group 77: Records of the Office of the Chief of Engineers
    Maps
Record Group 94: Records of the Adjutant General's Office,
    1780s–1917
Applications from Former Confederates for Presidential Pardons
    Letters Received
Mexican War Compiled Service Records, Organizations from the
    State of Texas
Record Group 109: War Department Collection of Confederate
    Records
    Confederate Citizens Files
Record Group 123: Records of the United States Court of Claims
    Indian Depredation Claims
Record Group 393: Records of United States Army Continental
    Commands, 1821–1920
    Letters and Telegrams Sent
Records of the Department of New Mexico
Records of the District of Texas and the 5th Military District
Records of Fort Concho, Texas
Records of Fort Davis, Texas
Records of Fort Stockton, Texas
Records of the Southern Department of New Mexico
Reports of Marches, Scouts, and Expeditions, Fort Stockton, Fort
    Concho, Fort McKavett, Fort Griffin, and Fort Richardson,
    Texas
New Mexico State Records Center and Archives (Santa Fe, N.Mex.)
    Doña Ana County Clerk Accounts, 1852–67
Nita Stewart Haley Memorial Library and History Center (Midland,
    Tex.)
    J. Evetts Haley Collection
    Clayton Wheat Williams Collection
Pecos County Archives (Fort Stockton, Tex.)
    Pecos County Clerk Map Cabinet
    Pecos County Deed Records
    Pecos County Surveyor Field Notes
Presidio County Appraisal District (Marfa, Tex.)
Presidio County Archives (Marfa, Tex.)
    Presidio County Deed Records
    Presidio County Surveyor Field Notes
Rupert N. Richardson Library, Hardin-Simmons University (Abilene,
    Tex.)
    Minatra, Odie. "A Life near the Heart of Texas History: J. C. Irwin
        Recalls First Hand Many Memorable Events of Pioneer Days,
        September 1935."
    Riney, W. A. *November 1927 Map of the Butterfield Trail through*
        Taylor County, Texas.
    Jesse Wallace Williams Map Collection
    J. R. Webb Papers
Seaver Center for Western History Research, Natural History Museum
    (Los Angeles, Calif.)
    Roscoe P. Conkling Papers, 1904–71
Southwest Collection, Special Collections Library, Texas Tech University

(Lubbock, Tex.)
    Anne Watts Baker Collection
Special Collections Library, University of Texas–Arlington (Arlington,
    Tex.)
    Kenneth Franklin Neighbours Papers
    Virginia Garrett Cartographic History Library
Special Collections Library, University of Texas at El Paso (El Paso, Tex.)
    Rex Strickland Papers
Tarrant Regional Water District Administration Archives (Fort Worth,
    Tex.)
    Lake Bridgeport Construction Files, 1929–31
Taylor County Appraisal District (Abilene, Tex.)
Taylor County Archives (Abilene, Tex.)
    Taylor County Deed Records
    Taylor County Surveyor Field Notes
Texas General Land Office Archives (Austin, Tex.)
    Brazos County Abstracts
    Coke County Abstracts
    Coke County Map Drawer
    Coke County Scrap Files
    Coke County Sketch Files
    Cooke County Abstracts
    Cooke County Map Drawer
    Crane County Abstracts
    Crane County Map Drawer
    Crane County Sketch Files
    Culberson County Map Drawer
    Culberson County Sketch Files
    Dallas County Abstracts
    Denton County Abstracts
    Denton County Map Drawer
    El Paso County Abstracts
    El Paso County Map Drawer
    El Paso County Sketch Files
    Grayson County Abstracts
    Grayson County Map Drawer
    Hudspeth County Abstracts
    Hudspeth County Map Drawer
    Hudspeth County Sketch Files
    Irion County Abstracts
    Irion County Map Drawer
    Jeff Davis County Abstracts
    Jeff Davis County Map Drawer
    Jeff Davis County Sketch Files
    Jones County Abstracts
    Jones County Map Drawer
    Loving County Abstracts
    Loving County Map Drawer
    Paul McCombs Survey Books
    Montague County Abstracts
    Montague County Map Drawer
    Pecos County Abstracts
    Pecos County Map Drawer
    Peters Colony Survey Map Files
    Presidio County Abstracts
    Presidio County Map Drawer
    Presidio County Sketch Files
    Charles W. Pressler's Maps of Texas
    Reagan County Abstracts
    Reagan County Map Drawer
    Reeves County Abstracts
    Reeves County Map Drawer
    Reeves County Sketch Files

Willard Richardson's Maps of Texas
Shackelford County Abstracts
Shackelford County Map Drawer
Taylor County Abstracts
Taylor County Map Drawer
Texas and Pacific Railroad Survey Map Files
Throckmorton County Abstracts
Throckmorton County Map Drawer
Tom Green County Abstracts
Tom Green County Map Drawer
Tom Green County Sketch Files
Upton County Abstracts
Upton County Map Drawer
Ward County Abstracts
Ward County Map Drawer
Ward County Sketch Files
Wise County Abstracts
Wise County Map Drawer
Young County Abstracts
Young County Map Drawer
Texas Historical Commission Library Archives, History Programs Division (Austin, Tex.)
    Old Bridgeport and Toll Bridge, Wise County Historical Marker File
    Uz Community, Montague County Historical Marker File
Texas State Library and Archives Commission (Austin, Tex.)
    1861 Election Returns
    1867 Texas Voter Registrations Lists
    Adjutant General's Department, Pre–Civil War Ranger Records, 1846–61
    Bexar County Tax Rolls
    Brazos County Tax Rolls
    Cooke County Tax Rolls
    El Paso County Tax Rolls
    Executive Order Letterpress Copybooks
    Governor Edward Clark Papers
    Governor Hardin Richard Runnels Papers
    Governor Peter Hansbrough Bell Papers
    Governor Sam Houston Papers
    Grayson County Tax Rolls
    Jack County Tax Rolls
    Map Collection
    Montague County Tax Rolls
    Navarro County Tax Rolls
    Ranger Muster Roll Index Cards, 1838–1900
    Texas Index Card Collections, 1800–1900
    Wise County Tax Rolls
    Young County Tax Rolls
Throckmorton County Appraisal District (Throckmorton, Tex.)
Throckmorton County Archives (Throckmorton, Tex.)
    Throckmorton County Deed Records
    Throckmorton County Surveyor Field Notes
Tom Green County Appraisal District (San Angelo, Tex.)
Tom Green County Archives (San Angelo, Tex.)
    Tom Green County Deed Records
    Tom Green County Probate Records
West Texas Collection, Angelo State University (San Angelo, Tex.)
    Tom Green County Surveyor Field Notes
Wise County Appraisal District (Decatur, Tex.)
Wise County Archives (Decatur, Tex.)
    Wise County Commissioners Court Minutes
    Wise County Deed Records
    Wise County Road Minutes

Wise County Surveyor Field Notes
Young County Archives (Graham, Tex.)
    Young County Commissioners Court Minutes
    Young County Court Records
    Young County Deed Records
    Young County District Court Records
    Young County Land District Records
    Young County Probate Records
    Young County Surveyor Field Notes

NEWSPAPERS

Abilene Reporter-News
Austin Southern Intelligencer
Chicago Tribune
Clarksville Northern Standard
Daily Alta California
Daily National Intelligencer
Dallas Herald
Dallas Morning News
Denison Herald
El Paso Herald-Post
El Paso Times
Fort Worth Star-Telegram
Gainesville Register
Galveston News
Galveston Weekly News
Houston Tri-Weekly Telegraph
Mesilla Times
New York Daily Times
New York Times
Sacramento Weekly Union
San Antonio Alamo Express
San Antonio Daily Express
San Antonio Herald
San Antonio Semi-Weekly News
San Francisco Daily Evening Bulletin
Seguin Union Democrat
St. Louis Democrat
St. Louis Missouri Republican
Texas State Gazette
Washington Post
White Man

PUBLISHED WORKS

Acheson, Sam Hanna. "Diamond, George Washington" (2010). In *Handbook of Texas Online*, www.tshaonline.org/ . . . /fdi02.

Acheson, Sam Hanna, and Bruce Allardice. "Diamond, James Jackson" (2010, mod. 2011). In *Handbook of Texas Online*, www.tshaonline.org/ . . . /fdi03.

Agnew, Brad. "War against the Comanches." *Chronicles of Oklahoma* 49, no. 2 (Summer 1971): 211–29.

Anderson, Gary Clayton. *The Conquest of Texas: Ethnic Cleansing in the Promised Land, 1820–1875*. Norman: University of Oklahoma Press, 2005.

Anderson, H. Allen. "Comancheros" (2010). In *Handbook of Texas Online*, www.tshaonline.org/ . . . /dfc2.

———. *Fort Phantom Hill: Outpost on the Clear Fork of the Brazos*. Lubbock: West Texas Museum Association, Texas Tech University, 1976.

Andrus, Pearl. "Barnard, Charles E" (2010). In *Handbook of Texas Online*, www.tshaonline.org/ . . ./fbabf.

Arneson, Edwin P. "Early Irrigation in Texas." *Southwestern Historical Quarterly* 25, no. 2 (October 1921): 121–30.

Ashmore, Tom. *Archaeological Investigations, Johnson's Station (41IR123), Irion County, Texas*. San Angelo, Tex.: Concho Valley Archaeological Society, 2010.

Austerman, Wayne R. "Identifying a 'Lost' Stage Station in Jeff Davis County." *Password* 25 (Spring 1980): 3–10.

———. *Sharps Rifles and Spanish Mules: The San Antonio–El Paso Mail, 1851–1881*. College Station: Texas A&M University Press, 1985.

Baker, Marcus. "The Northwest Boundary of Texas." *Bulletin of the United States Geological Survey 194*. Washington, D.C.: Government Printing Office, 1902.

Baker, T. Lindsay, and Julie Baker. *The WPA Oklahoma Slave Narratives*. Norman: University of Oklahoma Press, 1996.

Baldridge, M. *A Reminiscence of the Parker H. French Expedition through Texas and Mexico to California in the Spring of 1850*. Los Angeles: privately printed, 1959.

Bancroft, Hubert Howe. *History of the North Mexican States and Texas*. Vol. 16 of *The Works of Hubert Howe Bancroft*. San Francisco: History Company, 1889.

Barrett, Thomas. *The Great Hanging at Gainesville, Cooke County, Texas, October A.D. 1862*. Austin: Texas State Historical Association, 1961.

Barrett, Thomas, and George Washington Diamond. *The Great Hanging at Gainesville, 1862: The Accounts of Thomas Barrett and George Washington Diamond*. Denton: Texas State Historical Association, 2012.

Barry, Buck. *Buck Barry: Texas Ranger and Frontiersman*. Edited by James K. Greer. Lincoln: University of Nebraska Press, 1984.

Bartlett, John Russell. *Personal Narrative of Explorations and Incidents in Texas, New Mexico, California, Sonora, and Chihuahua, 1850–1853*. 2 vols. Chicago: Rio Grande Press, 1965.

Basehart, Harry W. *Mescalero Apache Subsistence Patterns and Socioeconomical Organization*. New York: Garland Publishing, 1974.

Baum, Dale. *The Shattering of Texas Unionism: Politics in the Lone Star State during the Civil War Era*. Baton Rouge: Louisiana State University Press, 1998.

Baylor, George Wythe. *Into the Far, Wild Country: True Tales of the Old Southwest*. Edited by Jerry D. Thompson. El Paso: Texas Western Press, 1996.

Bender, Averam B. *A Study of Mescalero Apache Indians, 1846–1880*. New York: Garland Publishing, 1974.

Bentley, H. L. *Cattle Ranges of the Southwest: A History of the Exhaustion of the Pasturage and Suggestions for Its Restoration*. Washington, D.C.: Government Printing Office, 1898.

Bieber, Ralph P., ed. *Exploring Southwestern Trails, 1846–1854*. Glendale, Calif.: Arthur H. Clark, 1938.

Billington, Ray Allen, and Martin Ridge. *Westward Expansion: A History of the American Frontier*. 6th ed. Albuquerque: University of New Mexico Press, 2001.

Bliss, Zenas R. *The Reminiscences of Major General Zenas R. Bliss, 1854–1876: From the Texas Frontier to the Civil War and Back Again*. Edited by Thomas T. Smith, Jerry D. Thompson, Robert Wooster, and Ben Pingenot. Austin: Texas State Historical Association, 2007.

Bogener, Stephen. *Ditches in the Desert: Irrigation in the Lower Pecos Valley*. Lubbock: Texas Tech University Press, 2003.

Boggs, Mae Hélène Bacon. *My Playhouse Was a Concord Coach*. Oakland, Calif.: Howell-North Press, 1942.

Bowden, Jocelyn Jean. *The Ascarate Grant*. New York: Garland Publishing, 1974.

———. "The Magoffin Salt War." *Password* 7, no. 3 (Summer 1962): 95–121.

———. *Spanish and Mexican Land Grants in the Chihuahuan Acquisition*. El Paso: Texas Western Press, 1971.

Box, Thadis W. "Range Deterioration in West Texas." *Southwestern Historical Quarterly* 71, no. 1 (July 1967): 37–45.

Boyd, Douglas K. *Archaeological Investigations at Fort Chadbourne and the Flat on Oak Creek*. Unknown: Texas Archaeological Society, 2004.

Britton, Morris L. "Colbert's Ferry" (2010). In *Handbook of Texas Online*, www.tshaonline.org/ . . ./rtc01.

———. "Earhart, Joseph Bonaparte" (2010). In *Handbook of Texas Online*, www.tshaonline.org/ . . ./fea13.

———. "Hunt, William Hudson" (2010). In *Handbook of Texas Online*, www.tshaonline.org/ . . ./fhu66.

———. "Preston, Texas" (2010). In *Handbook of Texas Online*, www.tshaonline.org/ . . ./hlp52.

Broaddus, J. Morgan, Jr. *The Legal Heritage of El Paso*. Edited by Samuel D. Myres. El Paso: Texas Western Press, 1963.

Brock, Ralph R. "'Perhaps the Most Incorrect of Any Land Line in the United States': Establishing the Texas–New Mexico Boundary along the 103rd Meridian." *Southwestern Historical Quarterly* 109, no. 4 (April 2006): 431–62.

Brown, Richard Maxwell. *Strain of Violence: Historical Studies of American Violence and Vigilantism*. New York: Oxford University Press, 1975.

Browne, J. M. "Out on the Plains." *Overland Monthly* 16, no. 95 (November 1890): 495–508.

Brune, Gunnar. *The Springs of Texas*. Vol. 1. Fort Worth: Branch-Smith, 1981.

Buenger, Walter L. *Secession and the Union in Texas*. Austin: University of Texas Press, 1984.

Campbell, Randolph B. *Gone to Texas: A History of the Lone Star State*. New York: Oxford University Press, 2003.

———. *A Southern Community in Crisis: Harrison County, Texas, 1850–1880*. Austin: Texas State Historical Association, 1983.

Capps, Benjamin. *The Warren Wagontrain Raid*. New York: Dial Press, 1974.

Carter, William Harding. *From Yorktown to Santiago with the Sixth U.S. Cavalry*. Baltimore, Md.: Lord Baltimore Press, 1900.

Cashion, Ty. *A Texas Frontier: The Clear Fork Country and Fort Griffin, 1849–1887*. Norman: University of Oklahoma Press, 1996.

Cates, Cliff D. *Pioneer History of Wise County*. Decatur, Tex.: Wise County Historical Society, 1971.

City of Fort Stockton, Texas, and Pecos County Historical Commission. *Gateway to the West: A History of Pecos County, Texas*. Documentary video directed and produced by Glen Sample Ely. Fort Stockton: Pecos County Historical Commission, 2002.

Clark, James Lemuel. *Civil War Recollections of James Lemuel Clark*. Edited by L. D. Clark. College Station: Texas A&M University Press, 1984.

Collins, Michael. *Cooke County, Texas: Where the South and the West Meet*. Marceline, Mo.: Walsworth Publishing, 1988.

Condra, Gary D., Ronald D. Lacewell, Daniel C. Hardin, Kenneth Lindsey, and Robert E. Whitson. *An Economic Feasibility Study of Irrigated Crop Production in the Pecos Valley of Texas*. College Station: Texas A&M University, 1979.

Conkling, Roscoe P., and Margaret B. Conkling. *The Butterfield Overland Mail, 1857–1869*. 3 vols. Glendale, Calif.: Arthur H. Clark, 1947.

Connor, Seymour V. *The Peters Colony of Texas: A History and Bio-

graphical Sketches of the Early Settlers. Austin: Texas State Historical Association, 1959.

Cool, Paul. *Salt Warriors: Insurgency on the Rio Grande*. College Station: Texas A&M University Press, 2008.

Coombes, Z. E. *Diary of a Frontiersman, 1858–1859*. Edited by Barbara Neal Ledbetter. Newcastle, Tex.: privately printed, 1962.

Cronon, William. *Changes in the Land: Indians, Colonists, and the Ecology of New England*. New York: Hill and Wang, 1983.

Crouch, Carrie J. "Brazos Indian Reservation" (2010, mod. 2011). In *Handbook of Texas Online*. www.tshaonline.org/ . . . /bpb03.

———. *A History of Young County*. 2nd ed. Austin: Texas State Historical Association, 1956.

Cutrer, Thomas W. "Nelson, Allison" (2010, mod. 2014). In *Handbook of Texas Online*, www.tshaonline.org/ . . . /fne13.

Daggett, Marsha Lea, ed. *Pecos County History*. 2 vols. Canyon, Tex.: Staked Plains Press, 1984.

Dale, Edward Everett. *The Range Cattle Industry*. Norman: University of Oklahoma Press, 1930.

Davis, Charles G. "Camp Cooper" (2010, mod. 2011). In *Handbook of Texas Online*, www.tshaonline.org/ . . . /qbc09.

Dearen, Patrick. *Castle Gap and the Pecos Frontier*. Fort Worth: Texas Christian University Press, 1988.

———. *Cowboy of the Pecos*. Plano: Republic of Texas Press, 1997.

———. *Crossing Rio Pecos*. Fort Worth: Texas Christian University Press, 1996.

———. *Halff of Texas: Merchant Rancher of the Old West*. Austin: Eakin Press, 2000.

DeArment, Robert K. *Bravo of the Brazos: John Larn of Fort Griffin, Texas*. Norman: University of Oklahoma Press, 2002.

Decatur Main Street Program. *A Walk through Time: The Decatur Square, Wise County, Texas*. Austin: Nortex Press, 2009.

Deutsch, Sarah. *No Separate Refuge: Culture, Class, and Gender on an Anglo-Hispanic Frontier in the American Southwest, 1880–1940*. New York: Oxford University Press, 1987.

Diamond, George Washington. *George Washington Diamond's Account of the Great Hanging at Gainesville, 1862*. Edited by Sam Acheson and Julie Ann Hudson O'Connell. Austin: Texas State Historical Association, 1963.

Dickerson, W. E. S. "Comanche Indian Reservation" (2010). In *Handbook of Texas Online*, www.tshaonline.org/ . . . /bpc10.

Downing, Charles G., and Roy Swift. "Howard, Richard Austin." In *Handbook of Texas Online*, www.tshaonline.org/ . . . /fho90.

Duffen, William A., ed. "Overland via 'Jackass Mail' in 1858: The Diary of Phocian Way, Part One." *Arizona and the West* 2, no. 1 (Spring 1960): 35–53.

———, ed. "Overland via 'Jackass Mail' in 1858: The Diary of Phocian Way, Part Two." *Arizona and the West* 2, no. 2 (Summer 1960): 147–64.

Dunn, Robert Walker. "The History of Loving County, Texas." MA thesis, University of Texas, 1948.

———. "The History of Loving County, Texas." *West Texas Historical Association Year Book* 24 (October 1948): 93–119.

Dutton, Robin. "Greenwood, Texas" (2010). In *Handbook of Texas Online*, www.tshaonline.org/ . . . /hng33.

Eaton, W. Clement. "Frontier Life in Southern Arizona, 1858–1861." *Southwestern Historical Quarterly* 36, no. 3 (January 1933): 173–92.

Eagleton, N. Ethie. *On the Last Frontier: A History of Upton County, Texas*. Edited by S. D. Myres. El Paso: Texas Western Press, 1971.

Eggenhoffer, Nick. *Wagons, Mules, and Men: How the Frontier Moved West*. New York: Hastings House Publishers, 1961.

Elkins, John M. *Indian Fighting on the Texas Frontier*. Waco: Texian Press, 2000.

Ely, Glen Sample. "Gone from Texas and Trading with the Enemy: New Perspectives on Civil War West Texas." In *Lone Star Blue and Gray: Essays on Texas and the Civil War*, edited by Ralph A. Wooster and Robert Wooster, 160–84. 2nd ed. Denton: Texas State Historical Association, 2015.

———. "Riding the Butterfield Frontier: Life and Death aboard the Butterfield Overland Mail in Texas, 1858–1861." Ph.D. diss., Texas Christian University, 2008.

———. "Riding the Western Frontier: Antebellum Encounters aboard the Butterfield Overland Mail." Master's thesis, Texas Christian University, 2005.

———. "Skullduggery at Spencer's Ranch: Civil War Intrigue in West Texas." *Journal of Big Bend Studies* 21 (2009): 9–29.

———. "What to Do about Texas? Texas and the Department of New Mexico in the Civil War." *New Mexico Historical Review* 85, no. 4 (Fall 2010): 375–408.

———. *Where the West Begins: Debating Texas Identity*. Lubbock: Texas Tech University Press, 2011.

Estep, Raymond, ed. "Lieutenant William E. Burnet: Notes on Removal of Indians from Texas to Indian Territory." Part 1. *Chronicles of Oklahoma* 38, no. 3 (Autumn 1960): 274–309.

———. "Lieutenant William E. Burnet Letters: Removal of the Texas Indians and the Founding of Fort Cobb." Part 2. *Chronicles of Oklahoma* 38, no. 4 (Winter 1960): 369–96.

———. "Lieutenant William E. Burnet Letters: Removal of the Texas Indians and the Founding of Fort Cobb." Part 3. *Chronicles of Oklahoma* 39, no. 1 (Spring 1961): 15–41.

———. "Two Last Letters on the Life of William E. Burnet." *Chronicles of Oklahoma* 39, no. 2 (Summer 1961): 193–96.

Finch, L. Boyd. *Confederate Pathway to the Pacific: Major Sherod Hunter and Arizona Territory, C.S.A.* Tucson: Arizona Historical Society, 1996.

Ford, John Salmon. *Rip Ford's Texas*. Edited by Stephen B. Oates. Austin: University of Texas Press, 1963.

Foreman, Grant. "The California Overland Mail Route through Oklahoma." *Chronicles of Oklahoma* 9, no. 3 (September 1931): 300–317.

———. *Marcy and the Gold Seekers: The Journal of Capt. R. B. Marcy with an Account of the Gold Rush over the Southern Route*. Norman: University of Oklahoma Press, 1939.

Forest Glen Productions. *Graveyard of the West: The Pecos River of Texas, Where Myth Meets History*. Documentary video produced by Patrick Dearen, Glen Sample Ely, and Mike Cox. Fort Worth: www.TexasHistory.com, 1993.

———. *A History of the Guadalupe Mountains and Carlsbad Caverns, 1848–1948*. Documentary video directed and produced by Glen Sample Ely. Fort Worth: www.TexasHistory.com, 1989.

Foster, Morris W. *Being Comanche: A Social History of an American Indian Community*. Tucson: University of Arizona Press, 1991.

Francaviglia, Richard A. *The Cast Iron Forest: A Natural and Cultural History of the North American Cross Timbers*. Austin: University of Texas Press, 2000.

Frazer, Robert W. *Forts of the West: Military Forts and Presidios and Posts Commonly Called Forts West of the Mississippi River to 1898*. Norman: University of Oklahoma Press, 1988.

Freeman, Martha Doty. "A History of Camp Cooper, Throckmorton County, Texas." Unpublished ms., Feb. 1997, prepared for Aztec of Albany Foundation, Albany, Tex.

———. "A History of Fort Chadbourne, Coke County, Texas." Unpublished ms., Sept. 2001, prepared for Fort Chadbourne Foundation, Bronte, Tex., and Summerlee Foundation, Dallas, Tex.

———. "A History of Fort Phantom Hill: The Post on the Clear Fork of the Brazos River, Jones County, Texas." Unpublished ms., May

1999, prepared for Fort Phantom Foundation, Abilene, Tex.

Freeman, Martha Doty, and Ann Pate. "Fort Chadbourne Chronology." Unpublished ms., Dec. 2007, prepared for Fort Chadbourne Foundation, Bronte, Tex.

Froebel, Julius. *Seven Years' Travel in Central America, Northern Mexico, and the Far West of the United States.* London: Richard Bentley, 1859.

Gammel, Hans Peter Mareus Neilsen. *The Laws of Texas: 1822–1897.* 10 vols. Austin: Gammel Book Company, 1898.

Ganaway, Loomis Morton. *New Mexico and the Sectional Controversy, 1848–1861.* Philadelphia: Porcupine Press, 1976.

Garcia, Mario T. *Desert Immigrants: The Mexicans of El Paso, 1880–1920.* New Haven, Conn.: Yale University Press, 1981.

Garrett, Pat F. *The Authentic Life of Billy the Kid.* Santa Fe: New Mexican Printing and Publishing, 1882.

Gilderhus, Mark T. *The Second Century: U.S.–Latin American Relations since 1889.* Wilmington, Del.: Scholarly Resources, 2000.

Gillette, James B. *Six Years with the Texas Rangers.* Chicago: Lakeside Press, 1943.

Gott, Kendall D. *In Search of an Elusive Enemy: The Victorio Campaign.* Fort Leavenworth, Kans.: Combat Studies Institute Press, 2004.

Gournay, Luke. *Texas Boundaries: Evolution of the State's Counties.* College Station: Texas A&M University Press, 1995.

Grant, Ben O. "The Early History of Shackelford County." MA thesis, Hardin-Simmons University, 1936.

Grayson County Frontier Village. *The History of Grayson County, Texas.* 2 vols. Winston-Salem, N.C.: Hunter Publishing, 1979.

Green, Billy. "Forgotten Fort." *Junior Historian* 22, no. 5 (March 1962): 21–29.

Greene, A. C. *900 Miles on the Butterfield Trail.* Denton: University of North Texas Press, 1994.

Hafen, LeRoy R. *The Overland Mail, 1849–1869: Promoter of Settlement, Precursor of Railroads.* Cleveland, Ohio: Arthur H. Clark, 1926.

Haley, J. Evetts. *Charles Goodnight: Cowman and Plainsman.* Norman: University of Oklahoma Press, 1989.

———. "The Comanchero Trade." *Southwestern Historical Quarterly* 38, no. 3 (January 1935): 157–76.

———, ed. *The Diary of Michael Erskine: Describing His Cattle Drive to California Together with Correspondence from the Gold Fields, 1854–1859.* Midland, Tex.: Nita Stewart Haley Memorial Library, 1979.

———. *Fort Concho and the Texas Frontier: 50 Years of Western History in Its Most Dramatic Era.* El Paso: Carl Hertzog, 1952.

Hall, Martin Hardwick. "The Formation of Sibley's Brigade and the March to New Mexico." *Southwestern Historical Quarterly* 61, no. 3 (January 1958): 383–405.

———. "The *Mesilla Times*: A Journal of Confederate Arizona." *Arizona and the West* 5, no. 4 (Winter 1963): 337–51.

Hämäläinen, Pekka. *The Comanche Empire.* New Haven, Conn.: Yale University Press, 2008.

Hamilton, Allen Lee. *Sentinel of the Southern Plains: Fort Richardson and the Northwest Texas Frontier, 1866–1878.* Fort Worth: Texas Christian University Press, 1988.

———. "Warren Wagontrain Raid" (2010). In *Handbook of Texas Online,* www.tshaonline.org/handbook/online/articles/btw03.

Hamilton, Matthew K. "Frazer, George Milton" (2012, mod. 2013). In *Handbook of Texas Online,* www.tshaonline.org/ . . ./ffr47.

———. "Hamner, Harris A." (2011). In *Handbook of Texas Online,* www.tshaonline.org/. . ./fhaka.

Hamilton, Nancy. *Ben Dowell: El Paso's First Mayor.* El Paso: Texas Western Press, 1976.

———. "Ysleta, Texas" (2010). In *Handbook of Texas Online,* www. tshaonline.org/ . . ./hny06.

Hammond, George P., and Edward H. Howes, ed. *Overland to California on the Southwestern Trail, 1849: Diary of Robert Eccleston.*

Berkeley: University of California Press, 1950.

Handbook of Texas Online. Austin: Texas State Historical Association, 1999. www.tshaonline.org/handbook.

Harrington, H. H. *A Preliminary Report on the Soils and Waters of the Upper Rio Grande and Pecos Valleys in Texas.* Bulletin No. 2. Austin: State of Texas, Department of Agriculture, Insurance, Statistics, and History, 1890.

Hart, Charlie, Ric Jensen, Will Hatler, and Mike Mecke. *Water Issues Facing the Pecos Basin of Texas.* Report 3.6.07. San Marcos: Texas Water Resources Institute, 2007.

Haynes, Sam W. *Soldiers of Misfortune: The Somervell and Mier Expeditions.* Austin: University of Texas Press, 1997.

Hayter, Delmar J. "Red Bluff Dam and Reservoir" (2010). In *Handbook of Texas Online,* www.tshaonline.org/handbook/online/articles/ ruro2.

Heitman, Francis B. *Historical Register and Dictionary of the United States Army, from Its Organization, September 29, 1789, to March 2, 1903.* Vol. 1. Washington, D.C.: Government Printing Office, 1903.

Hendricks, Rick. "The Marriages of James Wiley Magoffin." *Password* 50, no. 3 (Summer 2005): 64–79.

Hendricks, Rick, and W. H. Timmons. *San Elizario: Spanish Presidio to Texas County Seat.* El Paso: Texas Western Press, 1998.

Hentz, Tucker F. "Geology" (2010). In *Handbook of Texas Online,* www. tshaonline.org/ . . ./swgqz.

Hogan, William Ransom. *The Texas Republic: A Social and Economic History.* Austin: Texas State Historical Association, 2006.

Holden, Frances Mayhugh. *Lambshead before Interwoven: A Texas Range Chronicle, 1848–1878.* College Station: Texas A&M University Press, 1982.

Holden, William Curry. "Frontier Problems and Movements in West Texas, 1846–1900." Ph.D. diss., University of Texas at Austin, 1928.

Hollon, W. Eugene. *Frontier Violence: Another Look.* New York: Oxford University Press, 1974.

Holmes, Kenneth L., ed. *Covered Wagon Women: Diaries and Letters from the Western Trails, 1840–1849.* Vol. 1. Spokane, Wash.: Arthur H. Clark, 1983.

———. *Covered Wagon Women: Diaries and Letters from the Western Trails, 1864–1868.* Vol. 9. Lincoln: University of Nebraska Press, 1990.

Holt, R. D. "The Story of Salt in Texas." *Frontier Times* 19, no. 10 (July 1942): 345–48.

Hooper, H. O. "To California in '49." *Overland Monthly* 22, no. 129 (1893): 318–29.

Horsman, Reginald. *Race and Manifest Destiny: The Origins of American Racial Anglo-Saxonism.* Cambridge, Mass.: Harvard University Press, 1981.

Horton, Thomas F. *History of Jack County.* Centennial Edition. Jacksboro, Tex.: W. W. Bill Dennis, 1975.

Huckabay, Ida Lasater. *Ninety-Four Years in Jack County: 1854–1948.* Waco: Texian Press, 1979.

Hughes, Alton. *Pecos: A History of the Pioneer West.* Vol. 1. Seagraves, Tex.: Pioneer Book Publishers, 1978.

Humphries, Keith J. *Apache Land: From Those Who Lived It.* El Paso: Printing Corner, 1988.

Hunt, Michael H. "American Ideology: Visions of Greatness and Racism." In *Imperial Surge: The United States Abroad, the 1890s–Early 1900s,* edited by Thomas G. Patterson and Stephen G. Rabe, 14–31. Lexington, Mass.: D. C. Heath, 1992.

Hunt, William R. "Hayrick, Texas" (2010). In *Handbook of Texas Online,* www.tshaonline.org/ . . ./hvh38.

Hunter, J. Marvin, ed. *The Bloody Trail in Texas: Sketches and Narratives of Indian Raids and Atrocities on Our Frontier.* Bandera, Tex.: privately printed, 1931.

Hutchins, Wells A. "The Community Acequia: Its Origin and Development." *Southwestern Historical Quarterly* 31, no. 3 (January 1928): 261–84.

Jackson, W. Turrentine. "A New Look at Wells Fargo, Stagecoaches and the Pony Express." *California Historical Society Quarterly* 45, no. 4 (December 1966): 291–324.

Jacobson, Lucy Miller, and Mildred Bloys Nored. *Jeff Davis County, Texas*. Fort Davis, Tex.: Fort Davis Historical Society, 1993.

Jensen, Ric, Will Hatler, Mike Mecke, and Charles Hart. *The Influence of Human Activities on the Waters of the Pecos Basin of Texas*. #SR-2006-03. San Marcos: Texas Water Resources Institute, 2007.

Johnson, Adam Rankin. *The Partisan Rangers of the Confederate States Army*. Edited by William J. Davis. Austin: State House Press, 1995.

Justice, Glenn. "Stiles, Texas" (2010). In *Handbook of Texas Online*, www.tshaonline.org/ . . . /hns86.

Kavanagh, Thomas W. *Comanche Political History: An Ethnohistorical Perspective, 1706–1875*. Lincoln: University of Nebraska Press, 1996.

Kellogg, M. K. *M. K. Kellogg's Texas Journal, 1872*. Edited by Llerena Friend. Austin: University of Texas Press, 1967.

Kemp, L. W. "Ross, Shapley Prince" (2010). In *Handbook of Texas Online*, www.tshaonline.org/ . . . /fro86.

Kennedy, Joseph C. G. *Population of the United States in 1860: Compiled from the Original Returns of the Eighth Census*. Washington, D.C.: Government Printing Office, 1864.

Kenner, Charles L. *The Comanchero Frontier: A History of New Mexican–Plains Indian Relations*. Norman: University of Oklahoma Press, 1994.

———. *A History of New Mexican–Plains Indian Relations*. Norman: University of Oklahoma Press, 1969.

King, Steve M. "Salt Creek Prairie" (2010). In *Handbook of Texas Online*, www.tshaonline.org/handbook/online/articles/ryseu.

Kohout, Martin Donell. "San Elizario, Texas" (2010). In *Handbook of Texas Online*, www.tshaonline.org/ . . . /hjs05.

———. "Van Horn, James Judson" (2010). In *Handbook of Texas Online*, www.tshaonline.org/ . . . /fva07.

———. "Van Horne, Jefferson" (2010). In *Handbook of Texas Online*, www.tshaonline.org/ . . . /fva08.

Lamar, Howard Roberts. *Dakota Territory, 1861–1889: A Study of Frontier Politics*. Fargo: Institute for Regional Studies, North Dakota State University, 1997.

———. *The Far Southwest, 1846–1912: A Territorial History*. New Haven, Conn.: Yale University Press, 1966.

Landrum, Graham. *Grayson County: An Illustrated History of Grayson County, Texas*. Fort Worth: University Supply and Equipment, 1960.

Lang, Walter B. *The First Overland Mail: Butterfield Trail, St. Louis to San Francisco, 1858–1861*. Washington, D.C.: privately printed, 1940.

———. *The First Overland Mail: Butterfield Trail, San Francisco to Memphis, 1858–1861*. Washington, D.C.: privately published, 1945.

La Vere, David. *Life among the Texas Indians: The WPA Narratives*. College Station: Texas A&M University Press, 1998.

———. *The Texas Indians*. College Station: Texas A&M University Press, 2004.

Leatherwood, Art. "Llano Estacado" (2010). In *Handbook of Texas Online*, www.tshaonline.org/ . . . /rylo2.

Ledbetter, Barbara A. Neal. *Fort Belknap: Frontier Saga, Indians, Negroes and Anglo-Americans on the Texas Border*. 2nd ed. Newcastle, Tex.: Lavender Books, 1990.

———. *Indian Raids on Wagon Trains in Texas, 1871*. Newcastle, Tex.: Lavender Books, 1991.

Limerick, Patricia Nelson. *The Legacy of Conquest: The Unbroken Past of the American West*. New York: W. W. Norton, 1987.

———. *Something in the Soil: Legacies and Reckonings in the New West*. New York: W. W. Norton, 2000.

Long, Clarence D. *Wages and Earnings in the United States, 1860–1890*. Princeton: Princeton University Press, 1960.

Magoffin Home State Historic Site. "Amondarain/Valdés Family Paper." El Paso, 2011.

———. "James Wiley Magoffin Family Paper." El Paso, 2009.

Marcy, Randolph B. *Thirty Years of Army Life on the Border*. New York: Harper and Brothers, 1866.

Marks, George C. *Three-Mile and Sulfur Draw Watershed Project, Hudspeth and Culberson Counties, Texas: Final Environmental Impact Statement*. Temple, Tex.: U.S. Department of Agriculture, Soil Conservation Service, 1975.

Marks, Paula Mitchell. *Turn Your Eyes toward Texas: Pioneers Sam and Mary Maverick*. College Station: Texas A&M University Press, 1989.

Martin, Mabelle Eppard. "From Texas to California in 1849: Diary of C. C. Cox." *Southwestern Historical Quarterly* 29, no. 1 (July 1925): 36–50.

Martinez, Oscar J. *The Chicanos of El Paso: An Assessment of Progress*. El Paso: Texas Western Press, 1980.

Massey, Sara R., ed. *Black Cowboys of Texas*. College Station: Texas A&M University Press, 2000.

Mayhall, Mildred P. *Indian Wars of Texas*. Waco: Texian Press, 1965.

———. "Stem, Jesse" (2010). In *Handbook of Texas Online*, www.tshaonline.org/ . . . /fst34.

McCaslin, Richard B. *Fighting Stock: John S. "Rip" Ford of Texas*. Fort Worth: TCU Press, 2011.

———. *Tainted Breeze: The Great Hanging at Gainesville, Texas, 1862*. Baton Rouge: Louisiana State University, 1994.

McChristian, Douglas C. "Grierson's Fight at Tinaja de las Palmas: An Episode in the Victorio Campaign." *Red River Valley Historical Review* 7 (Winter 1982): 45–63.

McClellan, Michael E. "Johnson, Britton" (2010). In *Handbook of Texas Online*, www.tshaonline.org/ . . . /fjo07.

McConnell, Joseph Carroll. *The West Texas Frontier*. Vol. 1. Jacksboro, Tex.: Gazette Print, 1933.

———. *The West Texas Frontier*. Vol. 2. Palo Pinto: Texas Legal Bank and Book, 1939.

McDaniel, Robert Wayne. "Rosston, Texas" (2010). In *Handbook of Texas Online*, www.tshaonline.org/ . . . /hlr46.

Mills, Anson. *My Story*. Washington, D.C.: Byron S. Adams, 1918.

Mills, W. W. *Forty Years at El Paso, 1858–1898*. Edited by Rex Strickland. El Paso: Carl Hertzog, 1962.

Minor, David. "Denison, Texas" (2010). In *Handbook of Texas Online*, www.tshaonline.org/ . . . /hed04.

———. "White Man" (2010). In *Handbook of Texas Online*, www.tshaonline.org/ . . . /eew11.

Monahans Junior Chamber of Commerce. *Water, Oil, Sand and Sky: A History of Ward County, Texas*. Monahans, Tex., 1962.

Montague County Historical Commission. *The Story of Montague County, Texas: Its Past and Present*. Edited by Melvin E. Fenoglio. Dallas: Curtis Media, 1989.

Morrison, W. B. "Colbert Ferry on Red River, Chickasaw Nation, Indian Territory." *Chronicles of Oklahoma* 16, no. 3 (September 1938): 302–14.

Mora, Anthony. *Border Dilemmas: Racial and National Uncertainties in New Mexico, 1848–1912*. Durham, N.C.: Duke University Press, 2011.

Myers, Lee. "Pope's Wells." *New Mexico Historical Review* 38, no. 4 (October 1963): 273–99.

Myres, Sandra L., ed. *Ho for California: Women's Overland Diaries from the Huntington Library.* San Marino, Calif.: Huntington Library, 1980.

National Park Service. "Butterfield Overland Trail Special Resource Study." http://parkplanning.nps.gov/projectHome.cfm?project ID=33568.

———. "Butterfield Overland Mail Route Corridor, Guadalupe Mountains National Park." *National Register of Historic Places.* www.nps.gov/nr/research/.

Neighbours, Kenneth Franklin. "The Expedition of Major Robert S. Neighbors to El Paso in 1849." *Southwestern Historical Quarterly* 58, no. 1 (July 1954): 36–59.

———. "Elm Creek Raid" (2010). In *Handbook of Texas Online,* www.tshaonline.org/ . . . /bte01.

———. "Fort Belknap" (2010). In *Handbook of Texas Online,* www.tshaonline.org/handbook/online/articles/qbf02.

———. "Indian Exodus out of Texas." *West Texas Historical Association Yearbook* 36 (Oct. 1960): 80–97.

———. *Robert Simpson Neighbors and the Texas Frontier, 1836–1859.* Waco: Texian Press, 1975.

Newcomb, W. W. *The Indians of Texas: From Prehistoric to Modern Times.* Austin: University of Texas Press, 1961.

Niemeyer, Stephanie Piefer, and Brett Derbes. "Diamond, William Winfield" (2011). In *Handbook of Texas Online,* www.tshaonline. org/ . . . /fdi50.

Noel, Theophilus. *Autobiography and Reminiscences of Theophilus Noel.* Chicago: Theo. Noel Company, 1904.

Notson, William M. *Fort Concho Medical History.* San Angelo, Tex.: Fort Concho Preservation and Museum, 1974.

Nye, W. S. *Carbine and Lance: The Story of Old Fort Sill.* Norman: University of Oklahoma Press, 1974.

Ochoa, Ruben E. "Maverick County" (2010). In *Handbook of Texas Online,* www.tshaonline.org/ . . . /hcm06.

Opler, Morris E. *The Lipan and Mescalero Apache in Texas.* New York: Garland Publishing, 1974.

Ormsby, Waterman L. *The Butterfield Overland Mail.* Edited by Lyle H. Wright and Josephine M. Bynum. San Marino, Calif.: Huntington Library, 1942.

Overbeck, Ruth Ann. "Colbert's Ferry." *Chronicles of Oklahoma* 57, no. 2 (Summer 1979): 212–23.

Overland Mail Company. *Memorial of the Overland Mail Company, Butterfield & Co., to the Honorable Senate and House of Representatives of the United States.* Washington, D.C.: Gideon Printer, 1860.

Owen, Gordon. *Las Cruces, New Mexico, 1849–1999: Multicultural Crossroads.* Las Cruces, N.Mex.: Red Sky Publishing, 1999.

Paddock, B. B., ed. *A History of Central and Western Texas.* Vol. 1. Chicago: Lewis Publishing, 1911.

———. *A Twentieth-Century History and Biographical Record of North and West Texas.* 2 vols. Chicago: Lewis Publishing, 1906.

Parker, W. B. *Through Unexplored Texas.* Austin: Texas State Historical Association, 1990.

Parsons, Chuck. *Clay Allison: Portrait of a Shootist.* Seagraves, Tex.: Pioneer Book Publishers, 1983.

Pate, Ann, and Fort Chadbourne Foundation. *Fort Chadbourne: A Military Post, a Family Tradition.* Abilene, Tex.: H. V. Chapman and Sons, 2010.

Pearsall, Judy, and Bill Trumble, eds. *Oxford English Reference Dictionary.* New York: Oxford University Press, 2003.

Petersen, Paul R. *Quantrill in Texas: The Forgotten Campaign.* Nashville, Tenn.: Cumberland House Publishing, 2007.

Pisani, Donald J. *Water and American Government: The Reclamation Bureau, National Water Policy, and the West, 1902–1935.* Berkeley: University of California Press, 2002.

Ponder, Jerry. *Fort Mason, Texas: Training Ground for Generals.* Mason, Tex.: Ponder Books, 1997.

Pope, John. *Report of Exploration of a Route for the Pacific Railroad, near the Thirty-Second Parallel of North Latitude, from the Red River to the Rio Grande.* Washington, D.C.: Government Printing Office, 1854.

Powell, John Wesley. *The Arid Lands.* Edited by Wallace Stegner. Lincoln: University of Nebraska Press, 2004.

Powers, Stephen. *Afoot and Alone: A Walk from Sea to Sea by the Southern Route, Adventures and Observations in Southern California, New Mexico, Arizona, Texas, Etc.* Edited by Harwood P. Hinton. Austin: Book Club of Texas, 1995.

Price, George Frederick. *Across the Continent with the Fifth Cavalry.* New York: D. Van Nostrand, 1883.

Price, Paxton P. *Pioneers of the Mesilla Valley, 1823–1912.* Las Cruces, N.Mex.: Yucca Tree Press, 1995.

Ramirez, Manuel Bernardo. "El Pasoans: Life and Society in Mexican El Paso, 1920–1945." Ph.D. diss., University of Mississippi, 2000.

Ramos, Raúl A. *Beyond the Alamo: Forging Mexican Ethnicity in San Antonio, 1821–1861.* Chapel Hill: University of North Carolina Press, 2008.

Ray, Verne F. *Ethnohistorical Analysis of Documents Relating to the Apache Indians of Texas.* New York: Garland Publishing, 1974.

Rebbing, Virginia Lillian. "The Southern Overland Mail, 1857–1861." MA thesis, Washington University, 1943.

Reid, John C. *Reid's Tramp, or a Journal of the Incidents of Ten Months of Travel through Texas, New Mexico, Arizona, Sonora, and California.* Austin: Steck Company, 1935.

Reséndez, Andrés. *Changing National Identities at the Frontier: Texas and New Mexico, 1800–1850.* New York: Cambridge University Press, 2004.

———. *A Texas Patriot on Trial in Mexico: José Antonio Navarro and the Texan Santa Fe Expedition.* Dallas: William P. Clements Center for Southwest Studies, 2005.

Reynolds, Donald E. "Bewley, Anthony" (2010). In *Handbook of Texas Online,* www.tshaonline.org/ . . . /fbe71.

———. *Editors Make War: Southern Newspapers in the Secession Crisis.* Nashville, Tenn.: Vanderbilt University Press, 1970.

———. *Texas Terror: The Slave Insurrection Panic of 1860 and the Secession of the Lower South.* Baton Rouge: Louisiana State University Press, 2007.

———. "Texas Troubles" (2010). In *Handbook of Texas Online,* www.tshaonline.org/ . . . /vetbr.

Richardson, Albert D. *Beyond the Mississippi.* Hartford, Conn.: American Publishing, 1867.

Richardson, Rupert N. *The Comanche Barrier to South Plains Settlement.* Abilene, Tex.: Hardin-Simmons University Press, 1991.

———. *The Frontier of Northwest Texas, 1846–1876.* Glendale, Calif.: Arthur H. Clark, 1963.

———. "Neighbors, Robert Simpson" (2010, mod. 2014). In *Handbook of Texas Online,* www.tshaonline.org/ . . . /fne08.

Robinson, Charles, III. *The Frontier World of Fort Griffin: The Life and Death of a Western Town.* Spokane, Wash.: Arthur H. Clark, 1992.

Rochette, Patricia Adkins. *Bourland in North Texas and Indian Territory during the Civil War: Fort Cobb, Fort Arbuckle and the Wichita Mountains.* 2 vols. Broken Arrow, Okla.: BourlandCivilWar.com, 2005.

Roeder, Fred. "Texas–New Mexico Boundary." *American Surveyor* (Winter 2007). Available at www.amerisurv.com.

Ruhlen, George. "Quitman's Owners: A Sidelight on Frontier Realty." *Password* 5, no. 2 (April 1960): 54–64.

Santleban, August. *A Texas Pioneer.* Edited by I. D. Affleck. New York: Neale Publishing, 1910.

Scannel, Jack C. "A Survey of the Stagecoach Mail in the Trans-Pecos, 1850–1861." *West Texas Historical Association Yearbook* 47 (1971): 115–26.

Schilz, Jodye Lynn Dickson, and Thomas F. Schilz. *Buffalo Hump and the Penateka Comanches*. El Paso: Texas Western Press, 1989.

Schilz, Thomas F. *Lipan Apaches in Texas*. El Paso: Texas Western Press, 1987.

Scobee, Barry. *Fort Davis, Texas, 1583–1960*. El Paso: Hill Printing, 1963.

Scott, Robert N., H. M. Lazelle, George B. Davis, Leslie J. Perry, Joseph W. Kirkley, Fred C. Ainsworth, John S. Moodey, and Calvin D. Cowles. *The War of the Rebellion: A Compilation of the Official Records of the Union and Confederate Armies*. 70 vols. Washington, D.C.: Government Printing Office, 1880–1901. (Cited as *OR* in notes.)

Simpson, Harold B. *Cry Comanche: The 2nd U.S. Cavalry in Texas, 1855–1861*. Hillsboro, Tex.: Hill College Press, 1979.

Smith, A. Morton. *The First 100 Years in Cooke County*. San Antonio: Naylor, 1955.

Smith, F. Todd. *From Dominance to Disappearance: The Indians of Texas and the Near Southwest, 1786–1859*. Lincoln: University of Nebraska Press, 2005.

Smith, George G. *The Life and Times of George Foster Pierce*. Sparta, Ga.: Hancock Publishing, 1888.

Smith, Jared G. *Grazing Problems in the Southwest and How to Meet Them*. Washington, D.C.: Government Printing Office, 1899.

Smith, Thomas T., ed. *A Dose of Frontier Soldiering: The Memoirs of Corporal E. A. Bode, Frontier Regular Infantry, 1877–1882*. Lincoln: University of Nebraska Press, 1994.

———. *The Old Army in Texas: A Research Guide to the U.S. Army in Nineteenth-Century Texas*. Austin: Texas State Historical Association, 2000.

———. *The U.S. Army and the Texas Frontier Economy, 1845–1900*. College Station: Texas A&M University Press, 1999.

Smithwick, Noah. *The Evolution of a State, or Recollections of Old Texas Days*. Austin: University of Texas Press, 1983.

Smyrl, Vivian Elizabeth. "McCulloch County" (2010). In *Handbook of Texas Online*, www.tshaonline.org/ . . . /hcm07.

Smythe, William E. *The Conquest of Arid America*. Norwood, Mass.: Norwood Press, 1905.

"Socorro, Texas." (2010). *Handbook of Texas Online*. https://tshaonline.org/ . . . /hls62.

Sonnichsen, C. L. *The El Paso Salt War of 1877*. El Paso: Texas Western Press, 1967.

———. *The Mescalero Apaches*. Norman: University of Oklahoma Press, 1958.

———. *Pass of the North: Four Centuries on the Rio Grande, 1529–1917*. Vol. 1. El Paso: Texas Western Press, 1968.

Sprecher, Ken, and the Bridgeport Historical Society. *Images of America: Bridgeport*. Mount Pleasant, S.C.: Arcadia Publishing, 2010.

State of Texas. *Journal of the House of Representatives, Eighth Legislature*. Austin: John Marshall, 1860.

———. *Journal of the Senate, Eighth Legislature*. Austin: John Marshall, 1860.

Stegmaier, Mark J. "A Law That Would Make Caligula Blush? New Mexico Territory's Unique Slave Code, 1859–1861." In *African American History in New Mexico: Portraits from Five Hundred Years*, edited by Bruce A. Glasrud, 56–84. Albuquerque: University of New Mexico Press, 2013.

Steinberg, Ted. *Down to Earth: Nature's Role in American History*. New York: Oxford University Press, 2002.

Strickland, Rex W. *El Paso in 1854*. El Paso: Texas Western Press, 1969.

———. *Six Who Came to El Paso: Pioneers of the 1840s*. El Paso: Texas Western Press, 1963.

———. *The Turner Thesis and the Dry World*. El Paso: Texas Western Press, 1960.

Strong, Bernice. "John James [1819–1877]" (2010). In *Handbook of Texas Online*, www.tshaonline.org/ . . . /fja17.

Strong, H. R. *My Frontier Days and Indian Fights on the Plains of Texas*. Unknown: privately printed, no date.

Sumpter, Jesse. *Paso Del Águila: A Chronicle of Frontier Days on the Texas Border*. Edited by Ben E. Pingenot. Austin: Encino Press, 1969.

Tallack, William. *The California Overland Express: The Longest Stage Ride in the World*. Los Angeles: Historical Society of Southern California, 1935.

Tate, Michael L. *The Frontier Army in the Settlement of the West*. Norman: University of Oklahoma Press, 1999.

Terrell, C. V. *The Terrells: 85 Years Texas from Indians to Atomic Bomb*. Austin: privately printed, 1948.

Texas Board of Water Engineers. *Geology and Ground-Water Resources of Pecos County, Texas*. Vol. 1. Bulletin 6106. Austin: State of Texas, 1961.

Texas Historical Commission. *Online Atlas of Texas*. n.d. http://atlas.thc.state.tx.us/.

Texas Senate. "Senate Concurrent Resolution 11, 81st Regular Session, March 27, 2009." Legislative Reference Library of Texas. www.legis.state.tx.us/BillLookup/History.aspx?LegSess=81R&Bill=SCR11.

Texas State Soil and Water Conservation Board. *A Watershed Protection Plan for the Pecos River in Texas, TSSWCB Project #04-11 Draft Report*. Austin: Texas State Soil and Water Conservation Board, 2007.

Texas Surveyors Association. *One League to Each Wind*. Edited by Sue Watkins. Austin, Tex.: Von-Boeckmann-Jones Printers, 1973.

———. *Three Dollars Per Mile*. Edited by Marilyn J. Good. Burnet, Tex.: Eakin Publications, 1981.

Thomas, W. Stephen. *Fort Davis and the Texas Frontier: Paintings by Captain Arthur T. Lee, Eighth U.S. Infantry*. College Station: Texas A&M University Press, 1976.

Thompson, Jerry Don. "Baylor, John Robert" (2010). In *Handbook of Texas Online*, www.tshaonline.org/ . . . /fbaat.

———, ed. *Civil War in the Southwest: Recollections of the Sibley Brigade*. College Station: Texas A&M University Press, 2001.

———. *Colonel John Robert Baylor: Texas Indian Fighter and Confederate Soldier*. Hillsboro, Tex.: Hill Junior College Press, 1971.

———. "Drama in the Desert: The Hunt for Henry Skillman in the Trans-Pecos, 1862–1864." *Password* 37 (Fall 1992): 107–26.

———. *From Desert to Bayou: The Civil War Journal and Sketches of Morgan Wolfe Merrick*. El Paso: Texas Western Press, 1991.

———. *New Mexico Territory during the Civil War: Wallen and Evans Inspection Reports, 1862–1863*. Albuquerque: University of New Mexico Press, 2008.

———. *Texas and New Mexico on the Eve of the Civil War: The Mansfield and Johnston Inspections, 1859–1861*. Albuquerque: University of New Mexico Press, 2001.

Thrapp, Dan L., ed. *Encyclopedia of Frontier Biography*. Vol. 1. Lincoln: University of Nebraska Press, 1991.

Timmons, Joe T. "The Referendum in Texas on the Ordinance of Secession, February 23, 1861: The Vote." *East Texas Historical Journal* 11, no. 2 (October 1973): 12–22.

Timmons, W. H. *El Paso: A Borderlands History*. El Paso: Texas Western Press, 1990.

———. *James Wiley Magoffin: Don Santiago—El Paso Pioneer*. El Paso: Texas Western Press, 1999.

Tompkins, G. C. *A Compendium of the Overland Mail Company of the*

South Route, 1858–1861, and the Period Surrounding It. El Paso: G. T. Co., 1985.

Tucker, J. C. *To the Golden Goal and Other Sketches.* San Francisco: William Doxey, 1895.

Turner, Mary Carter. "Lost Valley" (2010). In *Handbook of Texas Online,* www.tshaonline.org/ . . . /rklo7.

Uglow, Loyd M. *Standing in the Gap: Army Outposts, Picket Stations, and the Pacification of the Texas Frontier, 1866–1886.* Fort Worth: Texas Christian University Press, 2001.

U.S. Congress. House of Representatives.
    Exec. Doc. No. 2, 35th Cong., 1st Sess.
    Exec. Doc. No. 58, 35th Cong., 1st Sess.
    Exec. Doc. No. 2, 35th Cong., 2nd Sess.
    Exec. Doc. No. 27, 35th Cong., 2nd Sess.
    Exec. Doc. No. 50, 35th Cong., 2nd Sess.
    Exec. Doc. No. 59, 35th Cong., 2nd Sess.
    Misc. Doc. No. 76, 35th Cong., 2nd Sess.
    Exec. Doc. No. 22, 36th Cong., 1st Sess.
    Exec. Doc. No. 47, 36th Cong., 2nd Sess.
    Exec. Doc. No. 73, 36th Cong., 2nd Sess.
    Report No. 1883, 61st Cong., 3rd Sess.

U.S. Congress. Senate.
    Rep. Com. No. 171, 30th Cong., 1st Sess.
    Exec. Doc. No. 64, 31st Cong., 1st Sess.
    Exec. Doc. No. 121, 32nd Cong., 1st Sess.
    Exec. Doc. No. 78, 33rd Cong., 2nd Sess.
    Exec. Doc. No. 1, 34th Cong., 1st Sess.
    Exec. Doc. No. 1, 35th Cong., 2nd Sess.
    Exec. Doc. No. 48, 35th Cong., 2nd Sess.
    Exec. Doc. No. 2, 36th Cong., 1st Sess.
    Exec. Doc. No. 26, 36th Cong., 1st Sess.
    Exec. Doc. No. 1, 36th Cong., 2nd Sess.
    Exec. Doc. No. 2, 36th Cong., 2nd Sess.
    Misc. Doc. No. 15, 36th Cong., 2nd Sess.
    Exec. Doc. No. 1, 37th Cong., 2nd Sess.
    Exec. Doc. No. 211, 46th Cong., 2nd Sess.
    Exec. Doc. No. 70, 47th Cong., 1st Sess.

U.S. General Land Office. *Annual Report of the Commissioner of the U.S. General Land Office, September 13, 1890.* Washington, D.C.: Government Printing Office, 1890.

U.S. House of Representatives. *Boundary Line between Texas and New Mexico.* Report 1883. House Reports, vol. 1. 61st Cong., 3rd Sess. Washington, D.C.: Government Printing Office, 1911.

Utley, Robert M. *The Indian Frontier, 1846–1890.* Rev. ed. Albuquerque: University of New Mexico Press, 2003.

Wallace, Andrew, and Richard H. Hevly. *From Texas to San Diego in 1851: The Overland Journal of Dr. S. W. Woodhouse, Surgeon-Naturalist of the Sitgreaves Expedition.* Lubbock: Texas Tech University Press, 2007.

Wallace, Ernest. *Ranald S. Mackenzie on the Texas Frontier.* College Station: Texas A&M University Press, 1993.

Wallace, Ernest, and E. Adamson Hoebel. *The Comanches: Lords of the South Plains.* Norman: University of Oklahoma Press, 1952.

Ward County Historical Commission. *Ward County, 1887–1977.* Dallas: Taylor Publishing, 1978.

West, Elliott. *The Contested Plains: Indians, Goldseekers, and the Rush to Colorado.* Lawrence: University Press of Kansas, 1998.

White, Owen. *Out of the Desert: The Historical Romance of El Paso.* El Paso: McMath, 1923.

White, Richard. *It's Your Misfortune and None of My Own: A New History of the American West.* Norman: University of Oklahoma Press, 1991.

———. *Land Use, Environment, and Social Change: The Shaping of Island County, Washington.* Seattle: University of Washington Press, 1980.

Wilbarger, J. W. *Indian Depredations in Texas: Reliable Accounts of Battles, Wars, Adventures, Forays, Murders, Massacres, Etc., Etc., Together with Biographical Sketches of Many of the Most Noted Indian Fighters and Frontiersmen of Texas.* Austin: Hutchings Printing House, 1889.

Williams, Amelia W., and Eugene C. Barker, eds. *The Writings of Sam Houston.* 8 vols. Austin: University of Texas Press, 1938–43.

Williams, Clayton. *Never Again.* 3 vols. San Antonio: Naylor, 1969.

———. *Texas' Last Frontier: Fort Stockton and the Trans-Pecos, 1861–1895.* Edited by Ernest Wallace. College Station: Texas A&M University Press, 1982.

Williams, J. W. "The Marcy and Butterfield Trails across North Texas." Master's thesis, Hardin-Simmons University, 1938.

———. *Old Texas Trails.* Edited by Kenneth F. Neighbours. Austin: Eakin Press, 1979.

Williams, O. W. *Pioneer Surveyor—Frontier Lawyer: The Personal Narratives of O. W. Williams, 1877–1902.* Edited by S. D. Myres. El Paso: Texas Western Press, 1966.

Wilson, John P. *When the Texans Came: Missing Records from the Civil War in the Southwest, 1861–1862.* Albuquerque: University of New Mexico Press, 2001.

Winfrey, Dorman H., and James M. Day, eds. *The Indian Papers of Texas and the Southwest, 1825–1916.* 5 vols. Austin: Texas State Historical Association, 1995.

Winkler, Ernest William, ed. *Journal of the Secession Convention of Texas, 1861.* Austin: Austin Printing, 1912.

Wise County Historical Survey Committee. *Wise County History: A Link with the Past.* 2 vols. Edited by Rosalie Gregg. Decatur, Tex.: Nortex Press, 1975.

Wooster, Robert. "Fort Davis and the Close of the Military Frontier." Presidential address at the annual meeting of the Texas State Historical Association, Austin, Mar. 3, 2006.

———. *Frontier Crossroads: Fort Davis and the West.* College Station: Texas A&M University Press, 2006.

———. *The Military and United States Indian Policy, 1865–1903.* New Haven, Conn.: Yale University Press, 1988.

Wright, Muriel H. "The Butterfield Overland Mail One Hundred Years Ago." *Chronicles of Oklahoma* 35, no. 1 (Spring 1957): 55–71.

———. "Historic Places on the Old Stage Line from Fort Smith to Red River." *Chronicles of Oklahoma* 11, no. 2 (June 1933): 798–822.

Young, Mary E. "The Cherokee Nation: Mirror of the Republic." *American Quarterly* 33, no. 5 (Winter 1981): 502–24.

———. "Conflict Resolution on the Indian Frontier." *Journal of the Early Republic* 16, no. 1 (Spring 1996): 1–19.

Index